A Treatise on the Science of War and Fortification
by Simon François Gay de Vernon (baron)

Address:
HardPress
8345 NW 66TH ST #2561
MIAMI FL 33166-2626
USA
Email: info@hardpress.net

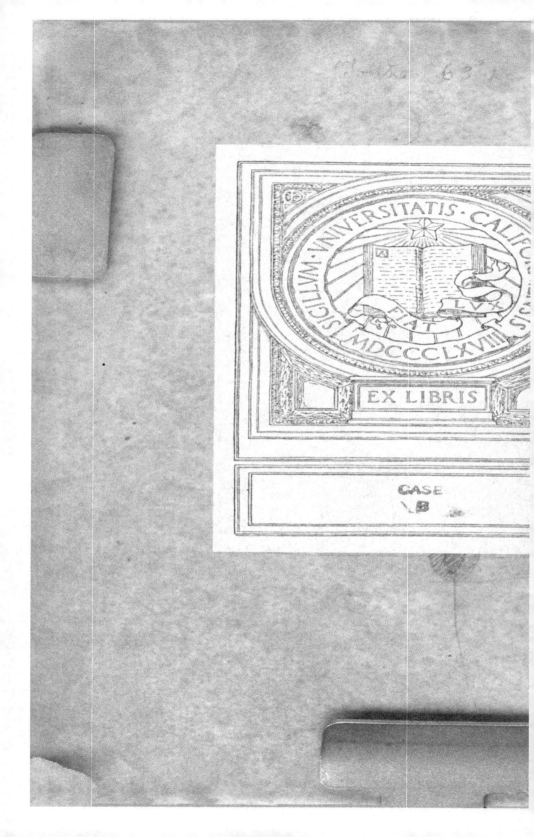

A

TREATISE

ON THE

SCIENCE OF WAR

AND

FORTIFICATION:

COMPOSED FOR THE USE OF THE

IMPERIAL POLYTECHNICK SCHOOL, AND MILITARY SCHOOLS;

AND

TRANSLATED FOR THE WAR DEPARTMENT,

FOR THE USE OF THE

MILITARY ACADEMY OF THE UNITED STATES:

TO WHICH IS ADDED A

SUMMARY OF THE PRINCIPLES AND MAXIMS

OF

GRAND TACTICS AND OPERATIONS.

BY JOHN MICHAEL O'CONNOR,

CAPTAIN OF ARTILLERY, AND LATE MAJOR AND ASSISTANT ADJUTANT-
GENERAL IN THE NORTHERN ARMY.

" Without the rivalship of Nations, and *the practice of war*, civil society
" itself could scarcely have found an object or a form."

Ferguson on Civil Society.

IN TWO VOLUMES,

With a Volume of Plates and Maps.

VOL. II.

NEW-YORK:

PRINTED BY J. SEYMOUR, NO. 49 JOHN-STREET.

1817.

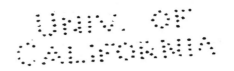
A

TREATISE

ON THE

SCIENCE OF WAR AND FORTIFICATION.

PART III.

ON PERMANENT FORTIFICATION,

OR

THE FORTIFICATION OF FORTRESSES.

CHAPTER I.

*Circumstances that give rise to Permanent Fortification; its
Use; Definition of a Fortress; the Constructions suitable for
Permanent Fortification; Properties of Fortresses; Exam-
ples, &c.; the Organization of Frontiers by Fortresses, &c.*

107. IN describing, in the Second Part, the operations of an offensive or defensive war, and the execution of a plan of campaign, we constantly pointed out the necessity of frontiers being organized for the two-fold object of repulsing the enemy, and carrying the war into his own territory. We even carried our thoughts further forward, and described the progress of an offensive and defensive war. We have shown that the resources of fortification should be unceasingly employed, and in a thousand modes, according to ground and circumstances. We proved; 1st, That particular points and positions should be occupied by intrenched camps or small forts (*fortins*), &c., in which a small body of men would be able to defend themselves against an enemy superior in numbers and in weapons of attack: 2d, That magazines must be formed upon the frontiers; and that the lines of operations must be supported and protected by intrenched positions, &c.: 3d, That the several parts of a

107. Examination of the causes that give rise to the importance of fortification, and which in all ages have shown its necessity and utility.

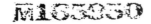

frontier must be united and connected together, and the different frontiers placed in immediate relation with each other. Exclusive of these general considerations, it may frequently happen that an army on the defensive is reduced by the fortune of war to such a state of weakness, as to be unable to face the enemy, who now being five to ten times stronger, would compel the former to lay down their arms, if they had not intrenched camps upon the frontier into which to retire and give battle.

To the preceding reasons, which are the province of the military, may be added others which all polished nations who have had to sustain wars, have ever attended to. The various nations in the present state of their political relations, have their territories covered and defended by maritime or inland frontiers. On these frontiers there are populous and commercial cities of great wealth, national depôts whose safety deserves the greatest attention and precautions. These cities must protect and gather in the harvests and productions of the country, and shield them from the enemy.

Among the ancients, whose states were of small extent, their defence was not as complex as those of the moderns. And these defences, instead of being upon the extremes of their territory, were established in the heart of the country. When the enemy appeared in such force as could not be repulsed, the people of the country sought refuge in some large city for themselves and property.

In this manner and by the same motives, the ancients, like the moderns, were led to the use of permanent fortification ; and in proportion as the boundaries of states increased, and military science improved, these reasons acquired much greater force.

Purpose of permanent fortification; a fortified city or fortress; its garrison. The object of permanent fortification, is to intrench a given point in such a manner, that a *weak army* may shut itself up in it and there fight, notwithstanding the disproportion of its forces and weapons: the defences must be such, as to preclude the possibility of storming them. A field of battle thus prepared, will secure results that will excite the astonishment of the soldier who is unacquainted with fortification.

Definition of a fortress. A fortress or fortified city ("*place forte ou ville de guerre*"), is an intrenched and enclosed field battle, in which a small army called a *garrison* is safe from assault, and may long resist step by step an army very superior in numbers and in means of attack.

We may form some idea of a fortress by imagining a small field fort to be greatly increased in dimensions, or that an intrenched camp, enclosed on all sides, were contracted to a moderate capacity; equally supposing in each case, that the relief is greatly increased, and that the scarp and counterscarp are vertical.

Idea of a fortress, taken from field works.

The works and constructions used in temporary fortification, are entirely inadequate for permanent fortification. Their degree of resistance cannot transcend the force of an assault, and they do not afford the defendants the advantage of making head against the assailants in spite of their numbers.

The constructions used in field fortifications, are not proper for permanent fortification.

We must therefore for permanent fortification, use constructions in masonry, iron, wood and earth, that it may possess all the qualities required by its nature, and be exempt from the defects of field fortification. In this kind of fortification, the *time* and *expense* are taken into account. And exclusive of the various branches of the physico-mathematical sciences, upon which the theory of fortification is founded, it requires the most immediate application of descriptive geometry, and presupposes a knowledge of the subjects treated in the courses of mineralogy, of civil works, and of architecture.

The constructions required in fortresses: the time & expense.

Descriptive geometry applied to fortification.

108. Before the improvements that have taken place within 200 years in military science, fortresses were not considered as possessing any other property than that of enabling a small body of troops to resist seven or eight times their numbers. They were considered as entirely isolated points, without exterior relations, and forming no system with the other parts of the frontier.

108. Properties of fortresses, under the relation of the organization of frontiers, and of their relations with the grand movements of armies. (See the works of Maigrin, and Foissac, and the Military Reflections of General D'Arçon.)

An ephemeral and truly mischievous opinion became current about 25 years ago among many French Generals, who thought that war should entirely consist in the tactics of the troops, and that all fortified cities ought to be razed, after the example of the Emperor Joseph II of Germany, who about this time caused several to be dismantled. A long peace seemed to have obliterated the true principles of war, and to have effaced the memory of the important advantages obtained by the fortresses that Vauban had constructed on all the frontiers of France.

The time however was not far distant, when the utility of fortresses and of all the branches of permanent fortification, was to be proved by events so striking and numerous, that officers would disdain to discuss so idle a question, which never would have obtained currency if the study of that part of war which is the province of fortification, had been more general among officers of all arms.

It is demonstrated by theory, and confirmed by experience, that fortresses should be considered under an aspect totally different from the preceding. They should be used in the organization of frontiers, to render the conquest of them almost impossible, and to facilitate and protect the execution of an offensive or defensive plan of campaign. They must be properly disposed, and in their reciprocal relations preserve the advantages of a continuous system, without the defects which render such a system impracticable. They are preparatory and protecting means that guarantee success, repair disasters, and increase the power or momentum of the active forces, if these be guided by profound tactics and their manœuvres be in relation with the fortresses.

Operations of an army upon a frontier destitute of fortresses.

To make these truths still plainer to the student who has just begun to devote his mind to military subjects, we will describe in a few words the operations of two armies on two frontiers differently organized : one, destitute of any secure points ; and the other, properly fortified.

The army in the first case, must drag after it all its equipage, baggage and provisions. These must be placed in the rear, and covered by detachments sufficiently strong to protect them from the enterprises of the enemy. If now we suppose this army to be upon the offensive, and marching forward upon a line of operations continually prolonged ; this line must be protected by formidable corps posted at intervals, in order that the army may preserve its relations with its depôts, and have its flanks secured against the attempts of the enemy. Without these indispensable precautions, the army could enjoy no security, would be continually harassed in its operations, and compelled after five or six day's march, if the enemy were strong enough to act, to retrograde for the purpose of re-establishing its communications with its own frontier. But if this army advanced methodically and made successively the necessary detachments, it would soon be so reduced, that the enemy would be able to contend with advantage against this disposeable corps. Accordingly, on this supposition all the operations of a campaign would be reduced to mere incursions, without the possibility of undertaking great sieges or fighting battles that would secure possession of the enemy's country.

If we now suppose the army to be on the defensive, it must be evident that without fortresses it will have no means of covering its provisions and maintaining itself in front of the enemy, the freedom of whose movements will not be checked or restrained by any obstacles; and it will be compelled to disperse, unless the nature and topography of the country enable it to carry on a war of positions, by affording those advantages that are derived from fortresses when operating in a plain country.

Let us now take a view of the operations of an army acting upon a frontier organized with fortresses. If the army be on the offensive, the fortresses from which it takes its departure to penetrate into the enemy's country, will contain all the equipages and magazines. From these the convoys will daily move, escorted by the garrisons that guard the flanks and rear. The army will be secure of its depôts and communications, and can never sustain any checks of great importance. On the slightest reverse, it can quietly fall back under the cannon of the nearest fortress, and arrest the triumphs of the enemy. If the various detachments on the flanks and on the most important points of the line of operations, be attacked, they will be able to defend themselves, to rally and form in a body, and retire under the nearest fortress and threaten the enemy's corps in their turn.

Operations of an army acting upon a frontier provided with fortresses.

Finally, if this army be necessarily upon the defensive, the influence of the fortresses upon its operations will be such, that it will be able to keep the field and maintain itself against a powerful enemy whose plan is to conquer the frontier and penetrate into the bosom of the country. Fortresses placed with skill upon the part of the frontier threatened by the enemy, will contain all the provisions, munitions of war and equipages; they cover the flanks and rear of the covering position that the army has taken to observe the movements of the enemy; and their garrisons serve as flank and van guards. The army thus disencumbered of every thing that could alarm and restrain its motions, must acquire a lightness, activity and mobility that will render it formidable, if the General understand the art of choosing positions covered by fortresses, and of occupying them by bold and able manœuvres. Defensive war, like the war of sieges, must be conducted on a system of combinations, but at the same time with great daring. The defending army must constantly keep the enemy in awe, and by unwearied activity conceal from him the science of calculations. If the hostile army warmly press, it must fall back without exposing itself, and throwing itself *en potence* upon one of the enemy's flanks give him his option to advance ; if he advance, the army will fall upon his rear and cut his line of operation, and by a bold attack re-establish an equality and assume the offensive. It is not probable however that the enemy would behave in this manner ; he would doubtless determine upon the siege of some fortress, to make it a place of arms ; and would remain in observation during the siege. In this case, the defending army would be able to act against the *lines*, or against the army in observation, and might hope to obtain some success from the state of weakness in which the enemy is placed by circumstances. And even if these successes were not realized, those of the hostile army would be reduced to taking at most two fortresses during the course of a whole campaign. Accordingly, fortresses upon frontiers render a defensive war practicable even with feeble means. They afford an able general the means of reducing a war to a very small number of general and decisive actions, of greatly contracting the theatre of the war, and of lengthening it out. They serve as points of retreat and support to an unfortunate army, by protecting its wrecks and saving its fame ; and they cover all the operations of an offensive war, exempting nations from those enormous losses that followed the wars of ancient people, and whose consequences were national destruction.

We might perhaps be inclined to think, that so many fortresses distributed upon a frontier must, from the numbers of their several garrisons, greatly weaken an army. But this opinion, which has been so frequently advanced, can neither stand the test of reason nor of experience ; the last war completely demonstrated its falsehood. Indeed an officer who has any knowledge of war and its conduct, knows that the enemy, however numerous his army, can only act upon a front occupied by 4 or 5 fortresses, with which the defending army puts itself in relation ; and that their garrisons serve in place of the strong detachments with which the army would be obliged to cover itself, if it were independent and isolated.

It is further urged, that the expense of constructing and maintaining fortresses is a great burthen upon the state. Here let us consider, that exclusive of the great active forces for which they are a substitute, they preserve during the war great wealth which would otherwise become the spoils of the enemy; that they secure cities from contributions, protect agriculture and the harvests, and receive within their walls all those productions of the country that the enemy's detachments would not fail to seize: lastly, that a frontier occupied in a military manner by fortresses, does not become a frightful desert by the flight of its inhabitants and the miseries inseparable from war; the population on it remains tranquil and orderly, and even commerce is prosecuted to a certain extent. So many and such great advantages, fully compensate for the expenses of permanent fortifications.

All these truths relating to the principal advantages of fortresses, have been developed and illustrated by many writers who enjoy merited reputation. Our young readers will peruse them with interest when they have formed of fortification the idea that we propose to give them; and at every step in ancient or modern military annals, they will become more convinced of these truths. The ancients attached great importance to fortification and the attack and defence of towns; for their liberties, and political and individual existence, depended upon it. Accordingly, their Generals regarded it as a great honour to be intrusted with the siege or defence of a city; and the glory that they hoped thus to acquire, was considered by them as far greater than that of winning a battle. They were skilled in all the methods of industry and ingenuity (*procédés d'industrie*), and in all the details of attack and defence; in time of peace they were careful to exescise their troops in these particulars. The moderns have greatly extended the use of fortification; but they have neglected the military education of their officers, and the exercises of their troops with respect to the construction of works and their attack and defence. In antiquity, all works were executed by the troops under the direction of their officers. In modern times, the leisure of peace is entirely devoted to the exercises belonging to battles and combats; every thing relating to the construction of works, to the attack and defence of towns and intrenchments, is completely forgotten. Hence, when the war breaks forth afresh, the troops are unaccustomed

General reflections.

to labour, the officer doubts the utility of fortifications, and he is obliged to serve as it were an apprenticeship in attack and defence; and a thousand errors are daily committed for want of a proper military education.

109. Instances to prove the use of fortresses.

109. Ancient and modern history abound in numberless instances of the utility of fortresses; and the age of Louis XIV, especially, was productive of military events in which fortification held a distinguished influence. We will however restrict ourselves to quoting a few events of the last war.

Instance of the army of the North in 1792 and 1793.

At the opening of the campaign of 1792, the French forces debouched from Lille to penetrate into Belgium. They were repulsed and overthrown; and the enemy taking advantage of their panic, pursued them under the cannon of Lille. If this fortress had not protected the army, the measure of its disasters must have been completed. Soon after, the army having been accustomed to discipline under the immediate protection of the fortresses, re-entered Belgium and quickly conquered the country, because it was destitute of fortresses. But indiscipline, the want of forecast, and treason, again involve the army in the most perilous dangers. It is attacked in all its positions, and regains the frontier by scattered divisions. Under the protection of the fortresses, it is re-organized; and though destitute of cavalry, and inferior to the enemy by one half, still keeps the field. Had this army been commanded by Generals of more comprehensive genius, it might have resumed the offensive against the combined army which had undertaken at the same time to blockade Condè and besiege Valenciennes. These recent facts prove, that had the northern frontier been without fortresses, the loss of these two battles would have been followed up by the entire destruction of the French army, and the threatening of the capital itself by the enemy. But let us continue the narration of a few of the operations of the French armies. Dunkirk, Quesnoy, and Maubeuge, resist the efforts of the combined army, and give time to the army of the North to receive reinforcements and discipline itself under cover of the fortresses. As soon as it is in a situation to act, it fights the battles of Hondscoote, Menin, and Vattignies, defeats and forces the hostile armies to retreat; and this campaign, which promised to be so disastrous, is concluded with the loss of only Quesnoy and Valenciennes.

Example of the army in the Eastern Pyrenees.

On the Pyrenees, the army is furiously attacked in its co-

vering positions ; the fortress of Perpignan receives and pro-
tects it, and the enemy are checked, and soon after repulsed
beyond the frontier.

In Italy, the single fortress of Mantua had the most remarkable influence on the operations of the war.   The necessity of
possessing it arrests the rapid current of events ; and this city
becomes the object of all the combinations of the belligerent
Generals.   Its importance induces them to risk every means,
and to exhaust every resource for its succour.   But the genius
of the French General derives even from the efforts of the enemy new and brilliant triumphs.   Mantua surrenders, and its
loss strikes fear and terror into the very capital of Austria.
The premature reduction of this fortress, is in the following
campaigns the cause of great reverses to the French army,
which are only repaired by the victory at Marengo.

Example of the army of Italy.

We think that we have now sufficiently proved by reason,
and by the brief sketches that we have drawn, the utility of
permanent fortification, and the relations that should exist between fortresses and the manœuvres of armies.

110. The organization of a frontier in fortresses, consists in
the choice of positions to be fortified, and in the degree of
strength that each separate fortress should possess.   This combination depends upon the nature of the country and its variations and resources ; likewise upon the relations that exist between the two opposite frontiers.   A flat country whose passages
are free, must be occupied in a different manner from a rugged,
broken and mountain country, covered with woods and intersected by streams.   Between these two extreme cases, there
are countries of a medium aspect, which require an organization modified according to ground.

110. General idea of the organization of a fron tier by fortresses.

To treat with the hand of a master this sublime part of war,
requires both the talents of an able engineer and of a consummate
General ; an union of the genius of Luxembourg with that of
Vauban.

We will first discuss the simplest case ; that of a frontier in
a plain country with its avenues perfectly open.   If this frontier have not upon its front any hostile fortresses, and it be designed to preserve the power of rapidly assuming the offensive,
the first fortresses should evidently be constructed as near as
possible to the enemy's border.   But if on the contrary the
enemy have fortresses, and it be only intended to organize the

Fortresses upon a level frontier, perfectly accessible.
First Princi-ple.

frontier and give it respectable defences ; in this case, it is proper to retire the boundary and first fortresses 15 to 20 leagues into the interior, in order to lengthen the enemy's line of operations and render his communications more difficult.

Second Princi-
ple. respecting
the distances be-
tween the for-
tresses.

As the fortresses must be in immediate relation, the garrison of each must be able to unite with those of the collateral fortresses, in order that they may act together, retire within their walls each night to repose, and then resume the course of their daily operations. The enemy must also find great difficulty to circumvallate any one of the fortresses, in consequence of the protection afforded to it by the collaterals. These two conditions are fulfilled by not eloigning the fortresses further from each other than 4 myriamètres (7 to 8 leagues).

Front of the
First Line com-
posed of fortres-
ses of the second
order.

These principles being established, we may make upon the defensive front, drawn in consequence of the first, a disposition of fortresses of the first line, distant from each other about $3\frac{1}{2}$ myriamètres (nearly 22 miles). Their capacity and strength must be such, that the enemy to lay siege to them must be obliged to display the whole power of his artillery. Each fortress should have a diameter of 7 to 800 mètres (780 to 890 yards), and should be able to contain a garrison of 5 to 6,000 men, and sustain a siege of about two months. The object of this first line of fortresses, is to check the enemy and resist his first efforts : they must be disencumbered of all kinds of establishments and supplies foreign to their defence.

Front of the
Second Line
composed of for-
tresses of the
first order.

Upon a front drawn about 3 myriamètres (nearly 19 miles) in rear of the first and facing the centres of the intervals, will be established in second line the places of arms and depôts ("*les places d'armes et de dépôts*"), destined to contain all the equipages and supplies requisite for the army. These fortresses of the first order may have a diameter of 12 to 1500 mètres (1350 to 1670 yards), and should be able to contain a garrison of 10,000 men : they must be strong enough to stand a siege of at least three months. It is under the cannon of these fortresses of the second line, that the army takes post on the defensive, to observe the enemy and act against him according to circumstances and the errors that he may commit.

Front of the
Third Line com-
posed of fortres-
ses of the third
order.

Lastly ; upon a third front drawn 3 myriamètres (19 miles) in rear of the second, may be established a third line of fortresses of the second or third order ; their diameter will be 500 mètres (560 yards), and they should be capable of containing a garrison of 3 or 4,000 men, and must be able to endure a siege of about a month.

These fortresses of the third line, which are the last resource, must be connected by intrenched camps established in rear, in which will be assembled and daily exercised the new and extraordinary levies that have been raised to oppose the progress of a powerful enemy whom two or three victorious campaigns have enabled to penetrate the frontier, and who by the conquest of several fortresses has secured his line of operations. *Intrenched camps connecting the fortresses of the Third Line.*

It is calculated that an open frontier thus organized, is an effectual barrier to the enterprises of an enemy to whose side the fortune of war may have inclined. If this supposed frontier were 15 myriamètres (30 leagues) in length, there would be on the first line, five fortresses of the second order ; on the second line, four fortresses of the first order ; and on the third line, five fortresses of the third order. With such a system, an army of 50,000 men commanded by an able General and with officers skilled in defensive war, could without risk face an army of 120,000, and prevent it from undertaking any great or bold strokes. *Application.*

In examining the other extreme case, where we supposed a frontier covered with natural obstacles and bounded by chains of high and steep mountains ; we see at once that in such a case, a disposition of three lines of fortresses would be absurd. The difficulties that the enemy must experience in bringing up his supplies, equipages and besieging train, the fewness of the roads and their known directions, and the facility of making head against the enemy under favour of the natural obstacles ; all these are circumstances which favour the operations of defensive war, and whose consideration leads to greatly simplifying the defensive system. *Disposition of fortresses upon a rugged frontier, or upon a frontier bounded by high and steep mountains.*

All the commanding heights that overlook the dividing slopes ("*versans*") on the side of the enemy, must be intrenched and prepared in such a manner that all the movements of the enemy will be closely observed. These posts should have easy communications with the interior, that they may be supplied with cannon of small calibers, and their garrisons be supported or easily withdrawn. This first line of posts of observation, is substituted in this case for the first line of fortresses of the second order.

In rear of these and upon the secondary mountains, will be established the fortresses, occupying the most favourable points, especially those at which several debouchès or valleys unite. These fortresses must be of the first order ; a single line will be sufficient.   They will be connected by easy communications with the posts of the first line.

In rear of these fortresses there will be established in time of war, intrenched camps which will complete the defences.

Disposition of fortresses upon a frontier bounded by a river. When a frontier is bounded by a river or a stream, the object of the defences is to watch the enemy and prevent his passing the river.   In this particular case, a single line of fortresses distant 4 myriamètres, (25 miles) apart, constitutes a complete defence ; but each fortress must be sufficiently distant from the enemy's shore, to be under no fear of bombardment ; this distance should be about 3,000 mètres (3350 yards).

Defences of frontiers that are low and covered with water. Frontiers that are low and marshy, require defences of a particular kind.   The resources afforded by nature, must be taken advantage of ;   all the practicable defiles must be destroyed, and defended by redoubts surrounded by waters ; whole quarters of the frontier must be covered and made inaccessible by inundations ; the fortresses must be few in number, but should oppose to the enemy all the obstacles that art can create by a proper use of waters.   In this case the defences do not bend to the daily offensive manœuvres that are executed under the protection of fortification ; but the loss of these advantages is compensated for by the strength acquired by the proper use of waters.

The defences of maritime frontiers. The defences of maritime frontiers or coasts should consist of ;—1st, A single line of fortresses enclosing the harbours, defending the roads, and preventing disembarkations : 2d, Forts or batteries established in the intervals, to defend the approaches of points favourable for disembarkations, and to watch the motions of the enemy.   In the tracé and construction of maritime fortresses, it must be considered that they enclose depôts, magazines and arsenals, whose preservation is an object of the greatest importance ; and consequently that they should be sheltered and secured from the bombardments and conflagrations that the enemy may attempt by water or by temporary debarkations.

The salient point at which a maritime frontier unites with an inland frontier, must receive the particular attention of the engineer.   It is indispensable that the defences of this important point should be so arranged as to repulse the combined attacks by land and water.

In general the topography of frontiers is not of those extreme cases that we have examined.   They embrace in their display, plains, heights, woods, marshes, rivers, brooks, &c. ; these natural varieties are diversified and combined in a thousand modes, and vary the natural strength of a frontier at all its points.   The defences of these mixed frontiers must vary like their topographical organization ; their plan on the ground must be determined by the coup-d'œil of the General and the talents of an able engineer.   In one part, the disposition of three lines of fortresses will be necessary ; in another, two lines will suffice ; here, an inundation will render the approaches inaccessible ; there, a great fortress will support connected intrenched camps, to which it will serve as a kind of redoubt.   The fortresses will occupy the rivers, debouchès, &c.   All these fortifying elements, whose degrees of strength must be exactly calculated, will preserve between each other the most intimate relations, and permit the armies to display their offensive and defensive manœuvres.

It belongs only to a warrior consummate in the theory and practice of war, to treat under all their relations the defences of frontiers, upon which depends the safety of states.

Defences of mixed frontiers.

CHAPTER II.

Calculation of the Strength of a Fortress ; Regular Fortification, its Trace, and Primitive Profile ; the Origin and Progress of Fortification ; Fortification at the Epoch of the Use of Cannon ; Invention of the Bastioned Enceinte and its Trace ; the Bastioned Front with Razant Lines of Defence.

HAVING taken a rapid survey of the utility of fortresses, and of the preponderating influence that they must possess upon the theatre of war, we will now begin the immediate study of permanent fortification, of which we have already given a general idea and definition (107).

111. Mode of expressing the value or strength of a fortified town.

111. As a fortress is an intrenched position in which a garrison is secure from assault, and in which they are able to defend themselves during a more or less extended period against the repeated and constant attacks of an army eight to ten times stronger than themselves ; it follows, that the value or strength of a fortified town is in proportion to the length of the siege, and as the ratio of the garrison to the besieging army, and the expense of constructing the fortress, are small. The expense should only be taken into consideration to a certain limit ; it is not so essential as the two first. Accordingly, the strength of a fortress may be defined to be in a direct proportion to the probable length of the siege, and in an inverse ratio to the garrison and expense.

The principles of fortification, deduced from the experience of sieges.

As the theory of tactics and of temporary fortification is founded upon truths confirmed by observation and experience ; so likewise is the theory of the fortification of fortresses built upon facts collected from the practice of sieges. This exhibits the progress of the attack, and the necessary dispositions that the besieger is obliged to make to approach the besieged. It is from a knowledge of these, confirmed by enlightened experience, that those rules and principles are deduced for disposing and constructing the fittest defences to retard the progressive steps of the attack.

Regular fortification upon an horizontal site ; plane of site ; the horizontal plane of projection, and primitive profile.

Let us first suppose the simplest case ; that the fortification is established upon horizontal and perfectly uniform ground. The dispositions made upon this hypothesis, will constitute a kind of formula, susceptible of modification in its application to irregular ground; the application depends upon the coup d'œil of the engineer.

What we shall lay down on fortification in the Third Part of this Treatise, will only include the preliminary knowledge which should precede the study of the application or practice of this art.

The *plane of site*, is the plane upon which the fortification is established; in the simple case new under consideration, this plane is horizontal. It is undistinguishable from the surface of the ground, and we shall consider it as the *horizontal plane of projection*. As in the theory of temporary fortification, we will determine the vertical projection of the different intrenchments by constructing the *primitive profiles* upon vertical planes perpendicular to the directions of the horizontal projection. We shall see in the sequel, how the plane of site and general profiles are varied in irregular fortification, and what ingenious methods are substituted for the multiplication of the latter.

According to the general idea that we have given of a forti- *General figure of the horizontal projection of the directrix, determines the configuration of a fortified town.* fied town, it is obvious that its defences should present a front on all sides; because the occupied position is assailable on every side. Consequently the horizontal projection of the directrix that configurates the enclosed ground and serves as a basis for the dispositions, must be a curve, or rather a re-entering polygonal figure.

In all the defensive dispositions treated in the Second Part, *Constitution of the primitive profile.* there are employed only slight constructions, whose ease and rapidity of execution constitute their chief merit. But these feeble means are insufficient in permanent fortification, in which the *primitive profiles* must be constituted according to its nature and the end for which it is established. It should be composed of solid permanent works, capable of resisting attacks of a novel kind, and of standing for centuries against the injuries of time. Accordingly, besides those arts of building in which earth, wood, and iron are used, we avail ourselves chiefly of masonry; in order to obtain stronger, more durable, and more multiform works. Hence, if we construct the generating profiles in such a manner that the scarps in masonry shall be vertical and about 80 decimètres (27 feet) high, the principal defects and weaknesses of temporary fortification will vanish; as will likewise the possibility of storm or escalade.

Having laid down these preliminary general ideas, it would

seem proper to take a brief survey of the origin of fortification, and its progress from various epochs to its present state.

112. Origin of fortification, and the epoch during which it made the greatest progress.

112. Fortification is indebted for its existence to civilization, with the progress of which it has ever kept pace. When the scattered tribes united together to form nations, they at first knew no other relations among themselves, than the law of the strongest. Each people organized a force with which they harassed their neighbours or their rivals, carried off their property, invaded their territory, or reduced them to slavery. In consequence of this state of action and reaction, nations found themselves necessitated to seek out the means of defending themselves from the violence of rapacity and ambition ; and of enabling them to repulse or check a powerful enemy by obstacles that would prevent their coming in contact, would increase the strength of the assailed, and re-establish an equilibrium between the two forces.

These interposed obstacles, whatever may be their nature, are called *intrenchments :* and the art of constructing and disposing them, constitutes the *science of fortification.* Fortification consequently originated with societies, and has followed step by step the advances of civilization and the arts. The first people who had to defend themselves from the incursions of their neighbours, surrounded themselves with slight ditches, stakes, hedges, and other defences analogous to the offensive weapons of those early ages. These weapons were, maces, clubs, stones, &c. When the small towns became great cities, and the asylums to which a people threatened, by enemies brought their wealth and property for shelter ; these cities were then enveloped by strong high walls called *ramparts,* which covered their defenders and enabled them at the same time to repulse the enemy.

First era of fortification when walls crowned with ma. hicoulis were u-ed The prin.itive profile (PLATE I, fig. 1.)

The era in which fortification assumed a character really defensive, is that in which each people, in consequence of their knowledge in the arts, surrounded their cities with walls of sufficient thickness to post troops upon them. Originally these walls were crowned with another wall breast high and of little thickness, and established on the exterior side of the summit of the rampart. This slight wall served as a parapet, and was furnished with battlements or loop-holes. It was soon observed that it was impossible to see the foot of the wall, at which the enemy might easily operate ; it therefore became necessary to invent a disposition that would enable the assailed to discover the foot of the ramparts, and that would secure the besieged from the missiles of the assailants. These inestimable advantages were obtained by the ingenious invention of *machicoulis*. Machicoulis consist of a parapet wall projecting 5 to 6 decimètres (20 to 24 inches) beyond the exterior side of the rampart, and supported by corbels of free-stone 10 decimètres (3¼ feet) apart. We yet find machicoulis in all the ancient castles, and among the ruins of old fortified towns. This method, combined with battlements, greatly improved fortification. The ascent to the ramparts was by interior stairs of cut stone. The first towns of the Egyptians, Greeks, and Romans, of France, under the kings of the first race, and of other modern nations, were all fortified according to this primitive profile ; they were without ditches, and the figure of the directrix was that of a simple polygon without any defensive modifications.

During this first era of fortification, towns were attacked either by escalade, by means of ladders and the tortoise formation ; or by mines. The formation in tortoise, was thus : Part of the assailants, armed with bows and slings, drove off the defendants from the top of the rampart ; whilst another party formed the tortoise with their bucklers ; and a third party, consisting of the most valiant soldiers, mounted the tortoise and pushed on to the escalade. As this operation was very difficult and seldom succeeded, the attack by mines was invented. Covered by a small moving gallery called the *musculus*, which the besiegers pushed forward against the wall, their miners demolished part of the foot of it, and excavated inside a great chamber furnished with props to support the wall. When the mine was ready, it was filled with very combustible materials, which being fired, was followed by the burning of the props and the subversion of a great portion of the wall. As soon as the mine had produced a practicable breach, the troops marched to the assault.

The capture of towns by mining and escalade, was rare ; and at this period the defence was so superior to the attack, that sieges frequently lasted many years*, and were only

* The siege of Veii by the Romans, lasted 10 years ; and the siege of Numantia by Scipio, lasted many years. The protracted duration of the siege of Troy, shows how superior the defence was at that time to the attack.

Mode of attacking towns during the first era ; formation in tortoise ; mines to subvert walls.

(See the description of the musculus in *La Milice Française*)

New methods invented for attacking towns ; the tortoise. the battering ram.the moving towers, the balista, and the catapulta. (See Daniel, Folard. and the Encyclopedia.)

brought to a conclusion by stratagem and treason.   This naturally led to the improvement of the attack by skill and industry (*l'attaque industrielle*); and perhaps to this cause is owing
the rapid progress of carpentry and masonry.   Covered galleries leading from the camp to the foot of the walls, were invented ; and likewise the tortoise or battering tower, to receive
the battering ram, whose effects are so well known.   The famous moving towers, made of timbers, were also invented ;
they were several stories high, and were provided with bridges
to let fall upon the walls and make a passage to them ; whilst
the upper part, which overlooked the ramparts, was filled with
soldiers who by their missiles drove off the besieged that opposed the assault.   Lastly, the balista and catapulta, together
with the battering ram, formed a complete system.

The catapulta launched heavy javelins against the besieged ;
and in the end, some were made to throw heavy beams.

The balista threw stones exceeding 50 pounds weight.

Modes of at-tack.   All writers agree that the range of these weapons was about
600 mètres (670 yards).   In using them in a siege, high ter-
races were constructed as near the wall as possible, and on
these the machines were established ; under their protection
the galleries of approach, the battering and moving towers, &c.
were directed and constructed.

The Methods of defence.   After the invention of all these powerful means of attack,
the art of the defence consisted in making frequent sorties to
burn the works of the besiegers, in opposing balista to balista,
and catapulta to catapulta, and in rendering unavailing all the
efforts of the battering ram.

Second era of the progress of fortification. In-troduction of ditches and flank-ing towers.   When the various engines used in attack were improved to a
certain degree, the defence lost its superiority ; and it became
necessary to improve fortification, and increase the strength of
the material obstacles opposed to the besiegers.   Two dispo-
tions in fortification restored the ascendancy of the defence,

Mines were used also against the besiegers.   At the siege of Rhodes,
an engineer made a mine out under the wall ; and next day when the
enemy advanced their high moving tower to storm the wall, " the
" ground immediately sunk beneath the prodigious weight, and they
" found it impossible either to recover it, or get it nearer the wall."—
Vegetius, Book IV.

TRANSLATOR.

which it preserved until the invention of powder and fire arms.

The enlightened men who directed the defence of towns, were not long in perceiving that the disposition of machicoulis was inadequate to guard the foot of the walls, and that it would be very advantageous to uncover the flanks of the besiegers' attacks. To effect this, square towers were erected against the enceinte, and separated apart by intervals equal to the range of the arrows most used in defence. The height of these towers even exceeded that of the enceinte, that they might command it, and render the use of the wooden towers more difficult and dangerous. By means of these towers, the battering towers were attacked in flank, the operation of mining became more slow and perilous, and escalade almost impossible. In the course of time, semi-circular towers were substituted for the quadrangular.

They did not stop at the disposition of towers reciprocally flanking each other; the enceinte was covered with a revested ditch of considerable width and depth. The great advantages of the ditch so much increased the difficulties of the attack, that the defence immediately resumed that complete ascendancy which it had for a short time lost. The necessary operation of filling up a wide and deep ditch, in order to be able to advance and establish the battering ram, &c., required such a length of time, that the besiegers often became disheartened. The Generals of antiquity accordingly considered the siege of a town as an operation, which if successful, must cover them with glory.

All the people of antiquity, whose towns contained their families and individual and national wealth, paid great attention to permanent fortification and to the methods of attack and defence. Their towns were fortified with walls crowned with machicoulis and flanked by towers, and surrounded by a great ditch.

The Romans who were conquerors from their political system, particularly studied the modes of attacking towns*. Their

* The Romans under and after their kings, were ignorant of the engines for besieging towns; they did not even know the use of galleries, to cover themselves from the weapons of the besieged. Accordingly they always endeavoured to take towns by escalade. *Montesquieu, Grandeur et Decadence.*

TRANSLATOR.

knowledge and methods in these branches, were in some measure borrowed by the Gauls, who transmitted them down to the Franks and other northern nations*.   At the siege of Paris by the Normans or Norwegians in 886, they chiefly used in the defence a great number of balistæ and catapultæ, of various forms and dimensions.

Use of powder and fire arms for attack and defence.

Such was the general form and constitution of fortification, down to the use of powder and fire arms for attack and defence.

We showed in the First Part.(9) that the use of fire arms was as remote as 1330 ; but it was not 'till under Charles VIII, about 1500, that artillery began to be used against fortified towns.   At the beginning of the sixteenth century, great quantities of artillery were used in sieges.

Invention of modern mines towards the close of the 15th century.

The idea of using gunpowder in mines, was not long unperceived.   The first experiment was made in 1487 by an engineer at the siege of Serezanella, a Florentine town, besieged by the Genoëse.   The engineer caused the chamber of a mine to be made in the rampart of the castle ; it was loaded with powder, and set on fire ; but in consequence of some peculiar causes, the effect did not correspond with his dreadful design.   Pierre de Navarre, a Spanish engineer, who had been a spectator of this attempt, thought that it must succeed ; and in 1495 he repeated the experiment at Naples against the castle of *Oeuf*, which was defended by the French with great obstinacy.   The castle having been surrounded towards the sea, this engineer caused himself and some miners to be let down into a chasm in the rocks, and thence pushed the gallery of a mine to beneath the ramparts of the castle, and there made a chamber which he filled with a great quantity of powder.   Having closed up the mine with caution, he sprung it.   The effect was tremendous ; part of the ramparts was blown into the sea ; and the French were unable to sustain the assault, which was made at the same instant.

* We have the authority of *Ephorus* for believing that an engineer named Artemon, was the inventor of the battering ram, the testudo, and of many great improvements in the war of sieges ; and *Plutarch* says that they were first used by Pericles at the siege of Samos.   Pericles had this engineer with him.   *See Plutarch in Pericles, Dionysius of Halicarnassus, and Montesquieu.*

TRANSLATOR.

The effects of artillery upon uncovered walls and machicoulis, the difficulty of establishing cannon upon narrow ramparts and in round or square towers whose gorge and salient did not each exceed 20 mètres (22 yards), and the necessity of defending fortresses by the same weapons with which they were attacked, rendered great changes in the primitive profiles indispensable. It became necessary to lay aside the use of machicoulis, and to substitute in their place covering masses (*massifs couvrans*) ; to terrace the rampart, in order to enlarge the terra-plain and be able to manœuvre upon it the new arms ; and to increase the size of the flanking towers, and post them at proper distances. It was towards the year 1500 that this revolution in fortification took place, which constitutes the third era of its progress.

So long as artillery continued to be of small dimensions, and its service difficult and badly executed, it was more favourable for the defence than for the attack. Accordingly in the first ages after the use of artillery, fortification preserved the ascendant and strength that it had acquired by the ancient weapons ; and the relations of attack and defence remained nearly the same. This is proved by the sieges that took place at this period ; the sieges of Rhodes, Malta, and Candia, &c. may be compared with the most famous sieges of antiquity, as for instance of Tyre, Carthage, and Lillybaume. But in proportion as artillery improved and pieces were made of large dimensions, capable of acting with accuracy at great distances and with immense force, and when bombs were invented ; artillery then became more favourable to the attack than to the defence, and the strength or value of fortification began to decrease. That which, exclusive of moral causes, most tended to protract the sieges of antiquity to such a length of time as to defy all probable calculations, and to secure to ancient fortification defences of long duration, was the impracticability of the besiegers destroying any thing within the walls, or of annoying the besieged in the interior of the works; inside of which they were in perfect security from stones, darts, &c. The use of artillery has deprived the defence of this great advantage ; and the besieged are now so constantly and terribly harassed by bombs in the very interior of their works, that they are compelled to have recourse to all kinds of precaution to shield themselves from their destructive ravages.

Changes that the use of artillery has necessarily produced in fortification.

Third era of fortification. at the use of artillery towards 1500.

Reflections upon the value of modern fortifications.

In proportion as the situation of the besieged has become perilous, that of the besiegers is ameliorated. The latter act from a distance, and converge all their fires upon the defences; they occupy a large space, upon which they display without constraint all their dispositions; and they advance upon that ground which is fittest for their operations. Finally, their depôts of ammunition are sheltered from danger or enterprises, and their subsistence is secured.

These new relations between the attack and the defence, have made fortification still more complicated and difficult; and though several persons of the greatest talents and experienced in great numbers of sieges, have devoted their efforts to restore to fortification its primitive ascendancy, yet it has always been far below that strength or value which its importance and utility indicate to belong to it.

Description of the primitive profile of the enceinte of a fortress, at the epoch of the use of cannon in sieges; nomenclature of the profile. (PLATE I. fig. 2.)

In the primitive profile of the enceinte of a fortified town, at the epoch of which we now speak, there are distinguished; 1st, the counterscarp; 2d, the revested scarp; 3d, the rampart and its terra-plain; 4th, the parapet.

The *revested counterscarp*, is the depth of the ditch on the side next to the enemy.

The *revested scarp*, is the height of the wall of the enceinte up to the level of the rampart; the wall is crowned by a thick plinth or cordon of cut stone.

The *rampart*, is the bank of earth erected against the revêtement, and is raised to a certain height above the ground line; the superior surface, upon which the cannon are established and the defensive dispositions are made, is called the *terra-plain* of the rampart.

The *parapet*, is the covering bank revested exteriorly, and is established upon the exterior side of the rampart to cover its terra-plain and shelter the cannon and troops from the fire of the besiegers.

The magistral line.

The *magistral line* is the summit of the revetement of the scarp, or the intersection of the scarp line with the line of the terra-plain. The magistral line serves as the directrix in the horizontal projection of the different parts of a system.

Interior crest of the parapet, or covering line.

The *interior crest* of the parapet may be called the *covering line*; it is also called the *line of musketry fire*. It is by this line that the relief of the fortification is judged and determined; and by its display or extent, is calculated the quantity of fires that the intrenchments can furnish.   Its consideration is of the greatest importance, even in arranging the horizontal projection.

The plunge or superior slope (*la plongée*) of the parapet, is the same in permanent, as in temporary fortification ;   and it is regulated in such a manner, that the edge of the counterscarp is scoured by the musketry fires.   Thus, if we draw a right line from the crest of the parapet through a point 10 decimètres ($3\frac{1}{4}$ feet) above the counterscarp, this line will be the superior boundary of the plunge or slope.   The inclination of this line below the horizontal, must not exceed 15 degrees (old measure) ; because, 1st, the angle at the summit would be too weak and easily ruined ; 2d, beyond this limit lines of fire are not effective.

Superior slope or plunge of the parapet.

113. Until about the year 1500, the old tracé of the enceinte was constantly adhered to ;   they had contented themselves with enlarging the towers, &c., and adopting the primitive profile that we have just described.   The relief was greater or less, according to the plans of the engineers, and was always at least 60 decimètres (20 feet) above the natural ground.   This tracé however had a radical defect that experience pointed out in every siege, and which engineers endeavoured to remedy. The towers being established at distances equal to the range of the small arms (*armes de main*) most commonly used, that is, about 250 mètres (280 yards) apart ; the curtain *xx* included between two towers, was defended by the flanks of these towers ; provided that the relief and superior slope of the parapets were so regulated that the line *mn* drawn on the bottom of the ditch perpendicular to the centre of the curtain, was the intersection of the planes of the plunge of the flanks, or that these planes cut each other only below the bottom of the ditch, and that their directions were like *m'n'* or *m''n''*.   If we draw the extreme lines of fire *ik*, *lo*, *ep*, *gh*, &c., we find that there must necessarily be a space *abc* at the foot of each tower, whether square or circular, that is not seen from any point, and where the enemy may attack by mining and quickly make a breach.

113. Fourth era of fortification, and its most remarkable changes Discovery and use of bastions, towards 1500.

(PLATE I, fig. 2.)

Fortifications of this tracé, had consequently a striking defect from which the ancient fortification anterior to the suppression of the machicoulis, was exempt.   It therefore became necessary to invent a tracé that would restore to fortification the property of discovering the foot of the walls around the whole ambit of the enceinte.

Many engineers devoted their attention to this subject, and investigated the question under a more general aspect. They proposed to discover what figure should be given to any polygonal enceinte, in order that its most exposed parts might be flanked and defended by other parts less exposed to the weapons of the besiegers ; which flanking parts, must be themselves flanked.

The original inventor of the bastion is unknown.

Perhaps the great simplicity of the question, is the reason that we are ignorant of the name of the man who first solved it. The solution evidently consisted in including in the enceinte, the small space *abc*, and in bounding the heads of the towers by the lines of fire ; and in order that each flank might entirely defend the new line *ab* or *bc*, the lines of fire from the extremities *x* of the opposite flanks, were taken as the extreme lines of fire. By this tracé the front of each tower became a redan whose faces were directed upon the extremes of the flanks ; the form of each tower was that of a quadrilateral figure *defgk*.

PLATE 1 (Figure 4)

The bastion.

The towers thus modified, were called *bastions ;* and an enceinte thus disposed, was styled a *bastioned enceinte.* We see that in this bastioned figure, each flank defends the face and flank of the opposite bastion, and likewise its contiguous half curtain ; provided however that the plunge of its parapet cut the bottom of the ditch at the line perpendicular to the centre of the curtain.

The bastioned front.

If we examine the portion of a bastioned enceinte corresponding to the distance *AB* separating two bastions, which is called the interior side of the polygon ; and if we draw the two bastion capitals *Vu, Vu,* passing through the points *A* and *a,* and *B* and *f ;* we perceive at once that this portion of the enceinte will be symmetrically repeated upon each interior side, that it is composed of two half bastions connected together by a curtain, and that these elements are in the most intimate relations of defence, and are independent of the other parts of the enceinte. The system of two half bastions connected together by a curtain, is what is called a fortified front (*front de fortification*) ; accordingly an enceinte consists of several bastioned fronts.

The bastioned enceinte used by Errard of Bar-le-Duc, in 1554.

Errard of Bar-le-Duc was the first engineer who seized with the grasp of genius the happy idea of a bastioned enceinte, and made use of it in France.

By *systems of fortification*, we understand the various methods of forming the tracé of a bastioned enceinte ; this is the same as the construction of a front upon one side of the polygon enclosing the space that is to be fortified.   We know that if a front *AB* be given, there are an infinite variety of modes of disposing the lines or elements which form the front *abcdef*: we will show in the sequel the various systems that were invented and used. *The systems of fortification.

We have seen that from the second era of permanent fortification, the ditches became, as in temporary fortification, an essential outwork to the enceinte ; they increase the strength of the obstacles, and furnish the earth necessary for constructing the intrenchments. . 'Tis with the earth taken from the ditches, that the ramparts and parapets are constructed.   And under these relations, the dimensions of the ditches should be properly determined ; this is a subject that we will investigate hereafter. For the present we will suppose that the width of the ditches of the enceinte is established at about 25 to 30 mètres (28 to 33 yards). The ditches a fortified town; their dimensions.

To form an idea of the tracé of the enceinte of a regular fortress, we must enclose the space that it occupies with a circle, and inscribe within it a regular polygon with sides equal to the distance that the bastions are to be separated apart.   This distance is regulated according to the range of small arms, and varies from 250 to 350 mètres (280 to 390 yards).   This being done, then upon each side of the polygon construct a fortified front (*front de fortification*) according to the system that has been adopted, and draw the tracé of the ditch on each front ; the assemblage of all these fronts, forms the first bastioned enceinte that appeared after the suppression of the towers. General tracé of the enceinte of a fortress. regular and irregular.

When the fortification is irregular, the tracé is made in the same manner.   After establishing, according to the ground, the irregular polygon that is to enclose the site, we construct upon each side of the polygon a fortified front.   But we must observe ; 1st, That each side of the irregular polygon should have the length laid down for a fortified front by the rules of defence, or a length double or triple this extent : 2d, That the angles of the polygon must be sufficiently open, so that the salient angles of the tracé will never be less than 60 degrees (old measure).

The parts composing a bastioned front, and the several lines whose consideration is very important, have denominations with which it is necessary that we be acquainted. Nomenclature of the elements of the bastioned front.

(PLATE I, fig. 4.) The line *AB* is the *interior side* of the, polygon ; and the line *af* is its *exterior side ;* one or other of them serves as a base for the tracé of the front of each system.

The salient angles *a* and *f*, are called the *flanked angles* of the bastions *A* and *B*.

The right lines *ef, fg*, that form the flanked angle of a bastion, are called its *faces*.   The faces *ab* and *ef* are connected with the *curtain cd*, by the *flanks cb* and *de*.

The salient angles *b* and *e*, are called the *shoulder angles*, and are formed by the meeting of the faces and flanks.

The re-entering angles *bcd* and *edc* are the *angles of the flank*, and are formed by the intersection of the flanks and curtain.

The lines *ad* and *fc*, from the flanked angle to the angle of the flank, are called the *lines of defence ;* and the angle *bcf*, formed by the flank and the line of defence, is called the *angle of defence*.   The angle *fad*, formed by the exterior side and the line of defence, is called the *diminished angle (l'angle diminué)*.

The line *mn*, drawn perpendicularly upon the centre of the interior or exterior side, is called the *perpendicular*.

Lastly ; The lines *Vu, Vu*, which bisect the flanked angles into two equal portions, are the *capitals of the bastions A* and *B*.

The lines of defence are razant or plunging. The lines of defence may be either *razant* or plunging (*fichantes*) ; they are razant when they terminate at the angle of the flank ; and they are plunging when they have an interior direction, such as *at, fs*, and cut the curtain ; a portion of which, *tx* or *ys*, may then flank the face of the opposite bastion in a very oblique manner.

The interior angles formed by the covering line. All the angles that we have just described, have their summits upon the magistral line ; their equal interior angles have their summits upon the covering line.

The relations between the linear and angular quantities that must be considered in the bastioned front with razant lines of defence. In a bastioned front with lines of defence razant, there are six quantities to be considered whose relations are expressed by two equations ; so that when four of these quantities are given, it is always practicable to draw the front by a geometral or graphical construction.   ·

The six quantities whose relations may be found, are :

(Figure 5.) The exterior side $AB = a$; the curtain $CD = b$; the line of defence $AD = c$; the flank $CE = f$; the face $AE = d$; the angle of defence $ADF = k$.   Moreover let $EF = m$; and $AF = n$.

These being established, the triangle EDF gives the equation $m^2 = f^2 + (c-d)^2 - 2f(c-d) \cos. k. \ldots \ldots \ldots \ldots (1)$.

The quadrilateral $CDEF$, by making the product of the diagonals equal to the sum of the products of the opposite sides, gives, $(c-d)^2 = f^2 + bm \ldots \ldots \ldots \ldots \ldots \ldots \ldots (2)$.

By comparing the three like triangles CKD, EKF, and AKB, we find $ac - mc - ad - bd = 0. \ldots \ldots \ldots \ldots \ldots \ldots \ldots (3)$.

If between these three equations we rejected m, we would have two equations between the six elements of the bastioned front : but it is easier to retain the three equations, and from them to deduce a fourth that is but the consequence of the three preceding.

The triangle ADF gives, $n^2 = c^2 + f^2 - 2 cf \cos. k.$

The quadrilateral $AEFB$ gives, $n^2 = am + d^2$; from which we obtain $am + d^2 - c^2 - f^2 + 2 cf \cos. k = 0. \ldots \ldots \ldots \ldots (4)$.

With these four equations, and four quantities being given, we can find or construct the two others. This leads to the consideration of fifteen different cases, six of which are solvible by the rule and compass, seven by the construction of conic sections, and the two others by curves that must be constructed by points.

The first case, in which a and b are the unknown quantities ; the equation (1) gives m, the equation (2) will give b, and the equation (3) will give a. This case is constructed by the right line and circle.

First case, when a and b are unknown, resolvable by the right line and circle.

Second case, in which a and f are the unknown ; the equations (1) and (2) will give m and f by the intersection of a circle and parabola ; a will be found by the equation (3).

Second case, when a and f are the unknown ; solvible by the circle and parabola.

The equation (2) will give m, and then the equations (1) and (3) will make known a and $\cos. k.$

Third case, when a and k are the unknown ; resolvable by the right line and circle.

These two cases are the same as the second.

Fourth case, when a and d are the unknown : Fifth case, a and c are unknown ; resolvable like the second case, by the circle and parabola.

The equations (1) and (4) will give the values of m and of f by the intersection of a circle and parabola ; and the equation (3) will give the value of b.

Sixth case, b and f are the unknown ; resolvable by the circle and parabola

Seventh case, *b* and *k* are the unknown, solvible by the right line and circle.

Eighth case *b*, and *d* are unknown.

Ninth case, *b* and *c* are unknown: solvible by the circle and parabola

Tenth case. *f* and *k* are the unknown : solvible by the right line and circle

Eleventh case, *f* and *d* are unknown : resolvable by the circle and right line.

Twelfth case, *f*, & *c* are unknown: cannot be solved by conic sections.

Thirteenth case, *k* and *d* are unknown : solvible by the right line and circle

Fourteenth case, *k* and *c* are unknown : resolvable by the hyperbola and parabola.

Fifteenth case, *d* and *c* are unknown : cannot be solved by conic sections.

The equations (2) and (3) will give by the right line and circle the values of *b* and *m ;* and we then find the *cos. k* by the equation (1).

The equations (1) and (4) will give *m* and *d* or *e* by the intersection of a circle and parabola ; and from the equation (1) is deduced the value of *b.*

The equation (3) will give *m ;* the equation (2) will give *f ;* and the equation (1) will show the value of *cos. k.*

By taking away the equation (2) from the equation (4), we will have a linear equation between *m*, *f* and *d ;* which being combined with the equations (2) and (3), will give the values of *m*, *f* and *d* by the rule and compass.

By rejecting *m* between the equations (2), (3) and (4), we find the equations of the most simple curves, which must be constructed by points.

The equations (2) and (3) will give *m* and *d* by the rule and compass ; then the equation (1) will give *cos. k.*

The equations (2) and (3) will give *m* and *c* by the intersection of a parabola and hyperbola ; *cos. k* is deduced from the equation (1).

This case is of the same nature as the Twelfth, which cannot be solved by conic sections.

In this manner the 1st, 3d, 7th, 10th, 11th and 13th cases are resolvable by the straight line and circle.

The students will solve some particular cases, in which they will suppose the angle of defence to be a right angle. This supposition is a necesary data dependent on the rules of defence.

CHAPTER III.

The Theory of Fortification; the modern Bastioned Front; thickness of Revêtements, and their Profiles; description of the Horizontal Projection upon the Plane of Site of all the elements of the Bastioned Front; Communications of all kinds, &c.; Description of the relief of all the elements of the Bastioned Front; the Commandment that all Works should possess; Planes of Defilement; Depth of Ditches, &c.; the Buildings used in Fortification; Construction of a Fortress, &c.

HAVING exhibited the principal changes and modifications that the fortification of fortresses has undergone in proportion as the means of attack were improved and extended, and in what manner fortification was constituted in modern times in order to resist the powerful effects of artillery ; we must now follow a different course to establish its theory, and to give our young readers in the most simple, methodical, and brief manner, general and accurate ideas on this grand branch of military science.   From the beginning of this elementary treatise, we have constantly shown that the art of defence first establishes the general and necessary measures of the attack, in order to dispose in consequence its defensive means.   This principle is general ; it is applied to the orders of battle taken by an army on the defensive, to temporary fortification, and to the fortification of fortresses, in which it becomes of still greater importance.   All enlightened minds concur on this important point— that the study of permanent fortification can only be pursued rationally and to advantage, by establishing from experience the facts resulting from the measures of the attack, and the effects produced by the means within its power.   Hence it is that the investigation of the numerous sieges in the time of Vauban and subsequent to his days, is a labour necessary to verify the principal facts upon which repose the theories of the attack and of the defence ; and that the experience acquired in sieges, is so useful to the soldier whose genius leads him to improve fortification.

We have said that the chief element of the value of a fortress, is *the probable duration of the siege.*   The art of fortification,

General reflections on the principles of the theory of fortification. and on the mode of studying them.

therefore consists in so constituting and disposing the works, that this probable duration of the siege will (all other things being equal) be the longest possible. This method of studying fortification, points out the route that should be followed to teach young officers the elements of this grand art. We each day congratulate ourselves on having introduced it in the courses that we have taught in the polytechnick school during seven years.

The order of this study consists, 1st, in adopting a system of modern fortification and describing and laying out a regular fortress constituted agreeably to this system, and preparing and providing it with a garrison and with all the other means for a complete defence ; 2d, in displaying before the fortification, the figure of which is known and drawn, the works of a regular attack ; such as were invented and followed by Vauban and his successors ; 3d, in calculating by approximation and according to the experience acquired, the time necessary to succeed in approaching the works, to ruin and seize them, and for the besiegers to find themselves opposed man to man to the besieged. By this method we arrive at the knowledge of the probable duration of the siege, and of the garrison required to defend the fortress. And as its description exhibits the expense, we thus obtain the three elements which establish the value of a system of fortification.

By following the same course with any other system, we can compare their respective values, and class them according to the order of their merit in war. By this method we obtain a second very important advantage ; that of estimating the advantages and defects of each defensive disposition, and how to increase the first and correct the latter. But this method, though the only one by which to discern the good from the bad, requires in its application an enlightened judgment, and a previous profound study of attack and defence. Many engineers of the first merit, have successfully made use of it to determine the comparative value of the several parts of a fortress ; and have deposited in the archives of the directions of engineering, works that attest the excellence of the principles upon which the theory of modern fortification is founded.

Of all the different systems, we think proper to adopt as a term of comparison and as an unit of force, the first system of Vauban, enlarged and corrected by Cormontaigne. Of all the engineers who succeeded Vauban, this General most devoted his attention to the improvement of fortification. **He has written** most extensive works upon the art of mining, which are fruitful sources of instruction for officers of artillery and engineers. By taking this system as a basis, we will have the advantage of rendering the students familiar with the form of the greater number of fortresses that have been constructed within 150 years. For with the exception of a few planned by Coehorn, and of the two fortresses of Landau and New-Brisach, which were constructed by Vauban after his system of bastioned towers ; all the others were laid out according to the system of Pagan, modified first by Vauban and afterwards by Cormontaigne, who made considerable additions to it.

114. In temporary fortification, a simple primitive profile and the horizontal projection of the directrix suffice to form a complete idea of that kind of fortification. But in permanent fortification, the object, though simple, is nevertheless more complicated. Each front of the enceinte is composed of, 1st, *a body of the place (un corps de place)*, with a ditch ; 2d, several exterior works, also covered by ditches ; 3d, a species of field intrenchment called the *covert-way (chemin couvert)*, which envelops and surrounds all the other works. It follows that a knowledge of the general forms can only be deduced from the system of the *primitive profiles* of the elements of the front. These profiles must have a certain relation dependent on the theory of the *relief;* that is, the height that the magistral and covering lines should be above the plane of site. We cannot therefore at present form the system of primitive profiles ; because we have not yet described the elements or exterior works that form part of the bastioned front. But we can describe the composition of each profile, without alluding to the elevation of the covering and magistral lines above the plane of site.

114. Description of the modern bastioned front adopted as a limit of comparison.

The modern profile of a permanent fortification is, as we have already seen, composed of a revested counterscarp, and of a scarp likewise revested*; this is a thick wall of masonry capable of great resistance, and terraced in rear with earth which forms the terra-plain of the rampart. The large cordon of cut

Description of the primitive modern permanent fortification. (PLATE I, fig. 6.)

---

* In permanent fortification, revêtement generally signifies the wall of brick or stone that supports the earth embankments or forms the declivities of the ditches : and hence to revest, or revesting.

TRANSLATOR.

stone which used to crown the scarp, has been suppressed and replaced by a simple coping (*tablette*) 25 centimètres (10 inches) thick, and salient 10 centimètres (4 inches) beyond the face of the wall.   The small wall that supported on the outside the mass of the parapet, is suppressed ; its exterior slope is made with falling earth or sods.

Construction of the primitive profile of a permanent fortification. (Fig. 6)   To construct the profile of a permanent fortification, take for the directrix the ground line VV' ; draw the indefinite vertical oPO representing the scarp ; lay off the height RP of the scarp above the direction of the plane of site ; and we have the position P of the magistral line.   Draw the horizontal XY elevated above the plane of site by the quantity mr, given by the relief ; and make om equal to oP added to the thickness

Thickness of the parapet. nm that the parapet must have at the summit.   This quantity mn is fixed by experience at 60 decimètres (20 feet) for the strongest works ; and may vary from 60 to 40 decimètres (20 to 13 feet), according as the parapets are more or less exposed. We will suppose the distance om of the magistral line to the interior crest of the parapet, to be 80 to 85 decimètres (26¾ to 28½ feet).

Height of the parapet : the breast heigh.; the banquette an its slope.   The height of the parapet above the terra-plain of the rampart, is fixed as in field fortification at 25 decimètres (8¼ feet) ; in certain circumstances however, it is reduced to its minimum 20 decimètres (6¾ feet).   The breast height (*hauteur d'appui*) and the banquette and its slope, are profiled as in temporary fortification, and occupy a width of 40 decimètres (13¼ feet).

The terra-plain of the rampart, and its width.   The width of the terra-plain of the rampart varies from 120 to 145 decimètres (40 to 48¼ feet), measuring from the covering line ; a breadth less than 120 decimètres would not be sufficient to manœuvre the cannon, &c. ; and if it exceeded 145 decimétres, it would require a superfluous quantity of earth, which may be scarce, or better employed elsewhere.

The terra-plain of the rampart is sloped towards the place about 20 centimètres (8 inches), to drain off the waters.   And towards the interior, the rampart is allowed the natural slope of falling earth ; a sufficient number of ramps are made in its slope, to ascend to the terra-plain and bring up artillery and ammunition.   These ramps must be 6 or 7 mètres (20 to 23 feet) wide ; their slope is so regulated, that their base contains seven or eight times their height.

115. The question of what thickness should be given to the revêtement walls of scarps and counterscarps and gorges of works, has greatly engaged the attention of engineers in all ages. It is a question in mechanics, the solution of which depends upon the hypothesis that is established respecting the manner in which the earth presses against the wall with a constant tendency to overthrow it, and indeed destroying the wall when its thickness is not properly calculated. The difficulty is to succeed in calculating this force, which varies with each kind of earth according as it is more or less tenacious and of greater or less specific gravity. Hitherto all authors who have treated this subject, have determined the pressure by imagining from the interior foot M of the wall, a plane MN to be drawn and inclined 45 degrees (old measure) for common and made earth, $25°$ for quick-sand whose particles are almost destitute of tenacity, $30°$ for fresh and tenacious earth; in fine, they give to this plane the inclination that the earths would assume when totally unsupported. They then suppose that the masses of earth situated above this inclined plane MN, have a tendency to descend upon this plane and act against the wall with their weight, tending to force it over its exterior foot O. Prony, in his course of mechanicks in the Polytechnick School, has investigated the problem of the pressure of earths under another point of view. He considers the earths as more or less imperfect fluids, and thus reduces it to a question in hydrostatics. From this theory he deduces a very ingenious practical method of determining the thicknesses of terraced walls in each particular case.

As soon as engineers devoted their attention to this question, (and of all of them, Vauban appears to have given it the most serious consideration), they perceived at once that of two walls of equal height and the same cubic contents, that which had an *exterior slope* would be stronger than the other; because the arm of the lever of resistance, which is measured by the distance from the fulcrum O to the vertical cutting the centre of gravity, becomes greater in proportion as the slope is increased. Accordingly of two walls having the same base and height, but one of which is vertical and the other triangular, the arm of the lever of resistance in the first case would be only expressed by 1, whilst in the second it would be by $\frac{4}{3}$. If we seek the ratio of two cubic contents affording the same

115. Thickness of the Revêtements of the scarp and counter-carp (See Belidor, the Encyclopedia and the Memoirs of Coulomb Burda, and Prony.) (PLATE I, fig. 6.)

(See the Memoir of Prony on the Pressure of Earths, &c.)

Revêtements constructed with sides of considerable slope; their advantages and defects.

resistance, we will find that the two generating sections are to each other as 1:0.6125 ; that is, to possess the same resistance, more than one third less materials are required for a triangular, than for a vertical construction.   Experience however does not exactly confirm this theory ; 1st, because revêtements not being bodies perfectly solid, especially when the masonry is still fresh, the pressure acts before the mortar has acquired its consistence ; accordingly it frequently happens that the action of the pressure of the earth against walls, produces bulgings out and breaks above the foot of the wall ; 2d, because the nature of the pressure is often changed by local causes ; if the ground of the terrace-work easily imbibe water. and heavy rains fall immediately after the construction, the wall may be overthrown although its thickness was accurately calculated ; the effect of a severe frost may also occasion accidents of this kind, by the swelling of the sheet of water lying between the wall and the earth.: Lastly, a revêtement wall may slip from its foundations in spite of its thickness, if the precautions required by certain grounds have not been observed*.

It follows from these general considerations, that experience is the safest guide in this nice question ; and that this the engineer should unceasingly consult by studying works of art constructed by men consummate in practice.

The advantages of slopes are obvious as respects economy ; but the rules of building require that all walls, whether surmounted or not with parapets, have a certain thickness at the summit ; and that the slope do not exceed $\frac{1}{5}$ of the height. Therefore triangular walls cannot be used, since their slopes are very great, especially in small heights, where they are from $\frac{1}{4}$ to $\frac{1}{3}$ of the height.

But though slopes are so very economical for the present, they are in the course of time subject to such evils, that modern engineers are unanimous in exploding them.   It has been observed that seeds of grass and shrubs are deposited upon the slopes of courses of stones and take root in their interstices ; so that after a few years, the materials of these courses are severed

* The precautions are, piling the ground with long and heavy piles driven very deep, and their heads cut smooth and a ground frame or timber grating established upon them.   These measures are very often necessary. The earth must be bored to ascertain its substrata.

TRANSLATOR.

and disjointed by the mere power of vegetation. The wall then bulges out in every quarter; and soon crumbles to the earth It is very costly to repair these dilapidations: and it can only be done by excoriations or cutting away a little of the thickness of the wall, and covering it with a kind of facing (*chemise*) which does not unite with the old masonry. This vicious mode of building is very palpable in countries where they build of brick. There are very few engineers who have not like ourselves lamented to expend large sums in repairing old ruined walls, and to be obliged to do it by excoriations of the wall (*par les écorchemens*), which necessarily destroy a portion of the strength of the old revêtement. All the fortresses constructed by Vauban, present this melancholy spectacle; whilst ancient perpendicular towers, with the same exposure, have preserved their walls in all their strength and solidity.

Several engineers have proposed to build revêtements almost vertical; and to make the side against which the earth rests, consist of successive retreats of 2 decimètres (8 inches) in 10 decimètres (3½ feet) height. This more advantageous method, produces upon the retreats vertical pressures which increase the stability of the wall; besides, this method is economical. 'Tis true indeed that the arm of the lever of resistance is not so great as when the slope is exterior; but it is proved by calculation, that this construction is very little more expensive.

Revêtements with retreats in rear and slight slopes. (Fig. 6.)

Marshal Vauban, guided by his great experience, endeavoured to obtain in constructions of masonry a resistance equal to their expense. For this purpose he adopted two rules: 1st, the exterior talus or slope to be one fifth of the height; 2d, the use of counterforts behind the revêtements, distant 18 feet (19¾ feet) from centre to centre, and sometimes only 15 feet (16 feet). The idea of counterforts was suggested to Vauban, by the ease with which breaches were made in simple revêtements; which in their fall brought down with them not only the mass of the parapet, but part of the terra-plain of the rampart also. Vauban fixed in a manner unalterable the thickness of the summit of the scarp and counterscarp. He took for the summit of the scarp, the cordon, supposed to be on a level with the terra-plain of the rampart. When the position of this cordon was lower, he measured from the first point to find the thickness at the summit. This thickness was equal to the first added to the fifth of the difference of height between the cordon and terra-plain.

Description of marshal Vauban's profiles; interior counterforts. (Fig 2)

This famous engineer established the constant thickness of the summit of the scarp at 5 feet ($5\frac{1}{3}$ feet), and of the summit of the counterscarp at 3 feet ($3\frac{1}{3}$ feet). The thickness of the base and of the retreats, varied according the height; it was equal to the constant quantity of the summit added to $\frac{1}{5}$ of the height.

(Fig. 2.) He made his counterforts of the trapezoïdal form, having its rear side *mn* equal to $\frac{2}{3}$ of the root *rs*; these two dimensions, as well as the length, varied with the height. For the least height, 10 feet ($10\frac{2}{3}$ feet), he made the length of the counterfort 4 feet ($4\frac{1}{4}$ feet), and the root 3 feet ($3\frac{1}{5}$ feet); and when the height was increased 5 feet ($5\frac{1}{3}$ feet), he increased the length 1 foot (13 inches) and the root 6 inches ($6\frac{1}{2}$ inches).

Remarks on Vauban's profile. In fixing the dimensions of his general profile, Vauban certainly intended to balance the pressure of the earth by the single strength of the revêtement; and to obtain by the counterforts an excess of strength to overcome this pressure, and resist the concussion of the artillery and the attempts to effect a breach.

Although the experience of a great many years has proved the excellence of Vauban's profile, nevertheless it is obvious, that in considering the thickness of the summit as constant, it is not calculated in a proper manner; that the excess of strength is too great for small heights; that it is sufficiently accurate for mean heights; and that it is too little for great heights. It follows that the thickness of a summit 10 feet high ($10\frac{2}{3}$ feet), should be fixed at $3\frac{1}{2}$ feet ($3\frac{3}{4}$ feet), and should vary proportionally as far as 5 feet ($5\frac{1}{3}$ feet), the thickness adopted for a height of 40 feet (43 feet): and for all heights between 40 and 100 feet (43 and 107 feet), the thickness should increase from 5 to 7 feet ($5\frac{1}{3}$ to $7\frac{1}{2}$). With respect to the counter-forts, we cannot discover the reason for making them trapezoïdal; it would be better to make them of the opposite form; but to facilitate their building, it is preferable to make them rectangular.

TABLE

Of the Dimensions of Vauban's General Profile.

Height of the revêtements.		Thickness at the summit.		Thickness of the retreat.		Distance between the central lines of the counterforts.		Length of the counterforts.		Thickness at the root.		Thickness at the rear.	
French feet	English feet.	French feet.	English feet.	French feet.	English feet.	French feet.	English feet.	French feet.	English feet.	French feet.	English feet	French ft. ins.	English feet. inches.
10	$10\frac{5}{7}$	5	$5\frac{5}{14}$	7	$7\frac{1}{2}$	18 or 15	$19\frac{1}{3}$ or 16	4	$4\frac{2}{7}$	3	$3\frac{3}{14}$	2 0	2 2
20	$21\frac{3}{7}$	5	do	9	$9\frac{3}{5}$	do	do	6	$6\frac{3}{7}$	4	$4\frac{2}{7}$	2 8	2 $10\frac{1}{2}$
30	$32\frac{1}{7}$	5	do	11	$11\frac{11}{14}$	do	do	8	$8\frac{4}{7}$	5	$5\frac{1}{3}$	3 4	3 7
40	$42\frac{6}{7}$	5	do	13	14	do	do	10	$10\frac{5}{7}$	6	$6\frac{3}{7}$	4 0	4 $3\frac{1}{2}$
50	$53\frac{4}{7}$	5	do	15	16	do	do	12	$12\frac{6}{7}$	7	$7\frac{1}{2}$	4 8	5 0
60	$64\frac{2}{7}$	5	do	17	$18\frac{1}{5}$	do	do	14	15	8	$8\frac{4}{7}$	5 4	5 $8\frac{1}{2}$
70	75	5	do	19	$20\frac{1}{3}$	do	do	16	$17\frac{1}{7}$	9	$9\frac{9}{14}$	6 0	6 5
80	$85\frac{5}{7}$	5	do	21	$22\frac{1}{2}$	do	do	18	$19\frac{2}{7}$	10	$10\frac{5}{7}$	6 8	7 2

The modern profiles of scarps & counterscarps. The general profile of the scarp should be so calculated, that the revêtements shall fulfil three essential conditions ; 1st, Their outside faces must sustain themselves for the longest possible time against the powerful action of the atmosphere and vegetation : 2d, They must resist the pressure of the earth and of the weight that they are to support, and the concussion of the artillery : 3d, They must oppose a resistance to the enemy's artillery that will render the effecting of a breach very difficult. Hence it follows that their sides must be vertical or nearly so ; that the thickness of the revêtements must be adequate to resist the pressure of the earth ; and that interior counterforts should be used to increase the resistance and render breaches more difficult.

(PLATE I, 6g. 6) Agreeably to these general considerations, we will make the slope of the general profiles only $\frac{1}{20}$; the thickness at the summit of the scarp shall vary proportionally from 13 decimètres (4½ feet) to 20 (6¾ feet) for heights of from 40 decimètres to 150 (13½ to 50 feet), and from 20 decimètres to 26.5 (6⅔ to 3¾ feet) for heights of 150 to 300 decimètres (50 to 100 feet). When the thickness of the summit is established, a step or interior retreat of 53 centimètres (21 inches) for every height of 10 decimètres (3½ feet), will be made : the sum of the retreats, added to the slope of one twentieth and to the thickness of the summit, will give the thickness of the wall at its foundation.

The central lines of the counterforts shall be only 5 mètres (16⅔ feet) apart ; they will be rectangular, and will be 15 decimètres (5 feet) thick for heights of 40 to 150 decimètres (13½ to 50 feet) ; 20 decimètres (6⅔ feet) for 150 to 200 decimètres (50 to 67 feet) height ; and 25 decimètres (8¼ feet) for heights of from 200 to 300 decimètres (67 to 100 feet). The length of (Figure 6.) the counterforts will be about equal to the thickness of the revêtement at the foundation ; and a retreat of 5 decimètres (20 inches) will be made for every height of 20 decimètres (6⅔ feet). In applying these principles to a scarp profile for a revêtement 100 decimètres high (33½ feet), 17 decimètres (5¾ feet) will be allowed for the thickness of the summit, and 34 decimètres .5 (11½ feet) for the base. The counterfort will be 30 decimètres (10 feet) long at the base, and 28 (9½ feet) at the summit.

As to the profiles of counterscarps, of gorges of works, and of terrace walls, it is expedient to suppress in these cases th-counterforts, whose construction is difficult and troublesome. The slope of these will be $\frac{1}{16}$ of the height, and the thickness at the summit 12 decimètres (4 feet); taking care to make interior steps as in the profiles of scarps.

It is acknowledged that revêtements exposed to be battered in breach, should be built in a particular manner; this is an important subject, and has in recent times engaged the attention of engineers. In these parts, counterforts may be multiplied, and joined together by arches of free-stone; and even relieving revêtements (*revêlemens en décharge*) may be constructed. Experience has proved, especially at the siege of Dillembourg, that these arches, incased in the body of the rampart, oppose a great resistance to cannon; and that breaches are made in them with the greatest difficulty. This species of construction possesses also the great advantage of almost entirely removing the pressure of the earth, and has inestimable advantages under other relations. Coehorn built his Great Orillon after this method of construction.

Remarks upon the revêtements of scarps exposed to be battered in breach relieving revêtements.

All engineers agree as to the utility of relieving revêtements (*revêlemens en décharge*), even for counterscarps; but there have not yet been any profiles definitively adopted according to this plan.

We may form a general idea of it by imagining rectangular counterforts serving as piers to relieving vaults (*voutes en décharges*) established one above another, from the bottom of the ditch to the coping (*tablette*). A wall of moderate thickness forms the face of the scarp, and conceals from the besieger.the art of the construction. In counterscarps there is no facing wall, and the vaults form coverts of great importance in the daily operations of the defence and for carrying on a subterranean war; but in the scarps, the vaults are filled with earth heavily rammed.

To better illustrate this ingenious and easily executed plan, let us suppose the case of a scarp-wall of common height, and secure from escalade. If we suppose the height of the counterscarp to be 60 decimètres (20 feet), that of the masonry of the scarp may be fixed at 80 decimètres ($26\frac{2}{3}$ feet) to be well covered by the covert way. The scarp wall E will be 13 decimètres ($4\frac{1}{3}$ feet) thick, and built vertically; the counterforts or piers P, P, P will be 12 to 13 decimètres (4 to $4\frac{1}{3}$ feet) thick, and 60 (20 feet) in length: consequently they will not

(PLATE I, fig. 8.)

extend beyond the body of the rampart, which will entirely
cover them. The centre lines of the piers will be 63 decimètres (21 feet) apart, that the relieving vaults may be 50 decimètres (16¾ feet) wide ; their height beneath the key-stone
must be 30 decimètres (10 feet), and their thickness beneath
the key-stone 10 decimètres (3⅓ feet). According to these data,
there will be two stories of relieving vaults. In order to conceal from the besiegers the art of the construction, the heads of
the vaults will be inserted 3 decimètres (1 foot) in the scarp-
wall. These heads of vaults, as likewise the piers, must be
independent of the facing wall ; so that they will be perfectly
solid after the battering artillery has crumbled down this
facing (*chemise*).

Listening galleries V, V, &c. pass under the rampart, and
cross through the earth of the lower vaults ; their object is to
watch the enemy's miners. In the upper story, casemates G
may be constructed of timber with three embrasures for musketry or light artillery pieces. These embrasures have the disadvantage of enabling the enemy to discover the construction of
the revêtement ; but they on the other hand have the great advantage of defending the terra-plain of the covert-way with
most effective fires which render an assault impossible, and the
attack by gradual approaches much more perilous and long.
The communication with these casemates is by frame galleries
from the foot of the interior slope of the rampart ; these galleries are made at the moment of the siege.

The advanta-
ges of relieving
revêtements.

The advantages of relieving revêtements over the common
constructions of scarps and counterscarps, are very numerous ;
1st, the expense of building them is not one-fourth greater : 2d,
breaches are more difficult to make either with cannon or by
mining. By using the former method, the besiegers will first
batter down the facing (*chémise*), the ruins of which will form
but a very small slope at the foot of the scarp ; all the rest of
the revêtement will be vertical and supported by the vaults,
which can only be ruined slowly and by small portions, because they are incased in well rammed earth. It will consequently be very difficult to form a slope inclined even 45°. If
the besiegers, to hasten the work, undertake to mine, the difficulty will be not less great. When the enemy attempt to effect a lodgement in the flanks of the piers of the vaults, they
will be anticipated by the miners of the besieged, who being

always in the listening galleries, can at any moment suffocate the hostile miners by the smoke of combustibles or " *camouflets*," or by other weapons of subterraneous war.

Finally, counterscarps thus constructed, will procure advantages whose great importance will be exhibited by the Theory of Attack and Defence.

116. The general profile being described, and all its elements known, we will now follow the course that we did in the Second Part, and describe the trace of the modern bastioned front on the plane of site, considered as the plane of projection.

The composition of the general profile exhibits that the forms of the object are very simple ; and that it is sufficient to know the horizontal projection of the *magistral line*, to find that of all the lines which bound the several planes composing a fortification ; for this fortification is generated by the general profile moving square along the directrix. The figure of this directrix on the horizontal plane, is deduced, as in temporary fortification, from the rules of attack and defence.

The primitive figure of the enceinte is a polygon, the length of whose sides is determined according to the rules of defence, of which we will treat hereafter. This length is included between the two limits of 260 to 360 mètres (290 to 400 yards). As this latter dimension affords the most advantageous trace, we will adopt it for the exterior side of the polygon that is to be fortified after a bastioned system with razant lines of defence. The trace is effected by a simple method, applicable to all practical cases.

The extremities of the exterior side of the polygon, are the summits of the flanked angles. At the centre of this side a *perpendicular* is raised, upon which is laid off interiorly ⅙ of the side = 60 mètres (67 yards); this point is then joined by two lines with the summits of the flanked angles, and these lines are the *lines of defence*.

On the lines of defence, and measuring from the flanked angles, lay off a quantity equal to ⅓ of the side = 120 mètres (133 yards) ; this gives the shoulder angles and faces of the bastions.

From the flanked angles as centres, with a radius equal to the distance of the opposite flanked from the shoulder angle, describe arcs of circles cutting the lines of defence in two points ; the three right lines that connect these two points to-

116. Description of the graphical delineation of all the elements of the modern bastioned front, consisting of the enceinte and of several exterior works. (PLATE II, fig. 1.)

Exterior side of the polygon of the enceinte.

Drawing the bastioned front by the *perpendicular;* length of the perpendicular.

Length of the faces of the bastions, and drawing the flanks and the curtains.

Remarks upon drawing the flanks. gether and with the shoulders, will give the curtain and the two flanks. The flanks and curtain may be drawn by letting fall perpendiculars from the shoulder angles upon the lines of defence : in the first tracé, the angle of defence is a little less than a right angle.

Drawing the covering line. As the covering line is parallel to the magistral, and by the general profile is 9 mètres .5 (31¾ feet) distant, the projection of this line will be drawn.

Remarks upon drawing the curtain. It must be observed that by protracting the line of defence, it will cut the covering line of the flank ; so that the interior part of this line will not uncover the face of the bastion. Therefore, if it be thought expedient, this part of the flank may be suppressed, and the magistral of the curtain advanced 8 mètres .5 (28¼ feet). This new tracé will diminish the expense and increase the interior capacity of the fortress. But on the other hand, it diminishes the space of the ditch included between the flanks and curtain ; and takes from the flank a part, which although it does not uncover the face of the bastion, discovers advantageously the opposite covert-way. These considerations seem to us, to render the first tracé preferable to the second.

Modifications that the tracé sustains, when the side of the polygon is less than 360 mètres (400 yards), and when the angle of the polygon is less than that of a hexagon. When the side of the polygon is smaller and decreases to 320 metres (356 yards), the perpendicular and the length of the faces of the bastions must be so diminished, that the tracé will give constantly flanks of 30 metres (33 yards), measured on the covering line. Attention must also be paid to the measure of the angle of the polygon, and to draw the tracé in such a manner that the flanked angles will never be less than 60 degrees : this is the smallest salient angle that can be admitted into fortification, as we will show more fully.

Projection of all the parts of the parapet and rampart. By drawing parallels to the magistral at the distances determined by the general profile, we find the projection of all the parts of the parapets and ramparts. The only line that remains undetermined, is the foot of the interior slope of the rampart ; and consequently the ramps also. This projection can only be made when the relief above the plane of site is known. Let us then suppose for the moment, that the height of the terra-plain is 35 decimetres (11¾ feet) ; and that its base is 145 (48¼ feet) ; in order that the students may complete the projection of the two fronts that are the object of their study. The ramps will be 6 mètres (20 feet) wide, and their base will be seven times their height. By repeating this construction upon each side of the polygon, we have the projection of the body of the place (*corps de place*) or principal enceinte upon the plane of site.

Modern, like ancient fortification, considers the ditches that envelope the enceinte as the most effectual means of arresting the impetuosity of the assailants and compelling them to advance step by step, and to use the method of attack by art and industry, the progress of which is ever slow.

The obstacles or works exterior to the enceinte, called outworks : the ditch, its advantages and dimensions : drawing the counterscarp.

In the early ages of modern fortification, the ditches were almost always dry ; they served as places of rendezvous for the troops of the garrison, from which to make sorties upon the works of the besiegers, and repulse an assault. But since the invention of covert-ways, which are better adapted to the manœuvres of the besieged, the ditches may be inundated by flowing or stagnant waters without losing the advantages of an active defence.

The dimensions of the ditches were formerly established almost arbitrarily, and merely with a view of obtaining the earth necessary for forming the embankments of the relief ; but the theory of attack and defence now prescribes rules for determining these dimensions. The width of the ditch must be at least double the relief of the work in those parts where a breach is practicable. Its depth is deduced from many considerations ; from that of the excavated earth supplying the quantity required for the embankments (*du deblai et du remblai*) ; from the rule which requires that the bottom of the ditch be defended effectually throughout its whole extent ; and from the position of the breaching batteries, &c.

For a common relief of 110 decimètres (37 feet), the width of the ditches in front of the faces of the bastions, should be 30 mètres (33⅓ yards). We will see hereafter, that it will be more advantageous to reduce this width to 20 mètres (22¼ yards) ; provided always, that the plunge of the parapet affords effectual fires on the edge of the counterscarp.

The width of the ditch in front of the faces of the bastions, is about 30 mètres (33 1-3 yards.)

To draw the counterscarp, describe from the flanked angles, as centres, with a radius of 25 mètres (28 yards nearly), arcs of circles; then from the opposite interior shoulder angles draw tangents to these arcs, and these will be the horizontal projection of the counterscarp.

In order to easily communicate between the body of the place and the ditches, *posterns* are built under the centre of the curtains : these are descending vaults built according to the

Great vaulted posterns, made under the centres of curtains to communicate with the ditches : their advantages and dimensions.

rules of stone cutting, and leading from the foot of the slope of the rampart down under the terra-plain and into the ditch 20 decimètres (6¾ feet) above its bottom, or at the level of the waters if the ditch be inundated.

All the posterns of existing fortresses have been constructed on too small dimensions ; they are so narrow that artillery cannot be passed through them without dismounting all the guns from the carriages, &c., and the troops defile through them slowly and with difficulty. To obviate these important defects, we will make the width of the postern 32 decimètres (10¾ feet), and the height beneath the key-stone 25 (8⅓ feet).

Posterns are so constructed as to be shut outside by iron doors, and inside by oaken doors. Every thing relating to the opening (*mouvement*) of these doors, must be attended to with the greatest care.

The tenaille :
its utility : its
trace, & postern. The necessity of covering the outlets of posterns in the ditches, led Vauban to conceive the plan of establishing a work between the flanks and before the curtain, and to which he gave the name of *tenaille*. This work masks not only the postern, but likewise the flanks and almost the whole curtain. Suitably planned and organized, the tenaille possesses many important advantages which we will hereafter display. Nevertheless it is proper to observe, that the tenaille, in whatever manner it be disposed, will ever mask the fires of the flanks, and occasion in the ditches in front of it a space destitute of fires, and which the enceinte cannot scour.

The primitive tracé that Vauban adopted for the tenaille after inventing it, was to draw it like a small front placed parallel to the curtain, and with its two small flanks parallel to those of the enceinte. But he abandoned this plan, and substituted for it the re-entering angle formed upon the perpendicular by the lines of defence. His tenaille is eloigned 8 to 10 mètres (9 to 11 yards) from the flanks and from the curtain opposite the re-entering angle.

The modern tracé of the tenaille, is that of Vauban ; to which has been added a straight face (*un pan coupé*) parallel to the curtain. The position of its magistral is found by laying off 24 to 25 mètres (26⅔ to 28 yards) upon the perpendicular, measuring from the magistral of the curtain ; and 10 mètres (11 yards) to find its gorge-line. By this plan there is formed in rear of the tenaille a kind of place of arms, of great advantage for debouching into the ditch: the parapet of the tenaille is made 50 decimètres (16¾ feet) thick. The profiles parallel to the flanks of the enceinte, may be rounded ; and the extremities of the covering line for a length of 3 or 4 mètres (10 13⅓ feet), may be broken inwards. The tenaille is crossed along its centre by a great postern leading under its terra-plain ; and when the ditch is filled with water, this vaulted passage serves as a harbour for boats.

The postern of the tenaille.

The experience of sieges soon taught engineers that the body of a fortress surrounded by a ditch and counterscarp, was not secure from the attacks by storm or surprise of a skilful, vigilant, and daring enemy. Parties of the enemy glided into the ditches and gained the gates to affix the petard ; and afforded to the corps d'armée the means of carrying the place by surprise or escalade.

The covert-way: its use : its advantages, and tracé.

In a regular attack, the rendezvous of troops to act outside, could be no where but in the ditches ; unless they debouched over a bridge, under the galling fire of the besiegers who knew its position. The troops could not form without great difficulty upon the counterscarp, and then in view of the enemy ; and when a sortie was made, the retreat or return into the fortress was a matter of great difficulty, and often accompanied by the loss of the town. Accordingly there was neither tranquillity within, nor close guarding without the enceinte ; and it was almost impossible to execute the movements of an active defence. Finally, the enceinte did not afford musketry fires sufficiently well supported and scouring.

'Twas these considerations that led to the invention of *covert-ways*, originally called *corridors*. This defensive disposition consists in surrounding the whole circumference of the counterscarp with a continuous field intrenchment, formed of a simple parapet whose figure is that of a *glacis* cutting the natural ground at a certain distance from its covering line, and affording no cover to the besiegers. Behind the parapet of the covert-way, a banquette is made ; and upon this a *strong palisading* is planted. The covering line of the covert-way, is called the *crest of the glacis.*

Covert-ways have numerous and striking advantages ; 1st, by means of the small posts established upon them, and the rounds that patrole them, we are apprized of every thing that takes place without ; 2d, they make the defence more free and obstinate ; 3d, they afford the most effectual musketry fires ; 4th, they are assembling places at any moment for troops destined to act outside ; 5th, they protect and collect these troops when they retreat ; 6th, finally ; they cover by their relief the scarp of the enceinte.

Covert-ways are always drawn parallel to the counterscarp ; their terra-plain is 10 to 12 mètres (11 to 13½ yards) wide, including the banquette and its slope.   The crest of the glacis is raised 22 to 28 decimètres (7½ to 9¼ feet) above the plane of site ; and such a slope is given to the glacis, that its prolongation will pass beneath the plane of fire from the parapet of the enceinte, in order that its surface may be grazed (*rasée*) or scoured by the fires of the body of the place.   This description will be more easily understood when we describe the relief.

It was soon perceived that the long branches of the covert-way make in front of the centre of the curtain a very obtuse angle ; and that these branches and the capitals of the two bastions, were badly defended by musketry.   But it was also perceived, that this re-entering part afforded a valuable space for the rendezvous of troops to sustain with vigour the salient parts, which are the first attacked.   To effect this object, a redan was established in this re-entering part with faces of 20 mètres (22 yards), and making an angle of 90° to 100° with the branches of the covert-way.   This part of the covert-way is called the *re-entering place of arms ;* and the salient part included between the rounding of the counterscarp and the prolongations of the faces of the bastion, is called the *salient place of arms.*

In the old method of conducting the attacks against a fortress, they began by seizing the salients, in order to afterwards carry the re-entering places of arms.   This method of attack gave rise to the division of the branches of the covert-way by defensive traverses, which divide them into portions capable of being successively defended.   Two defensive traverses were established on the prolongations of the parapets of bastion faces, to close the salient place of arms ; and two more traverses were established on the prolongations of the faces of the re-entering place of arms, in order to enclose it : the profiles of these traverses are in the plane of the counterscarp.   Lastly, two or three interior traverses are constructed along that portion of the branch comprised between the places of arms.

Marginal notes:

Slope of the glacis.

Salient and re-entering places of arms.   (See the front, in Figure 2, PLATE II.)

Traverses of the covert way : their use, and situation.

These latter traverses, and that of the salient place of arms, have a passage of 2 mètres (7 feet) between them and the counterscarp.

The traverses of re-entering places of arms are 50 decimètres thick (16¾ feet) at the summit ; the others are only 30 (10 feet) at most, so that we may easily batter them down with cannon when the enemy would cover himself by them.

In order that we may be able to freely communicate with the whole ambit of the covert-way and move from the re-entering to the salient place of arms, a passage of 2 to 3 mètres (7 to 10 feet) is left between the glacis and the traverses, and is called a *defile*. Each defile is covered by a crotchet of 2 to 3 mètres made in the crest of the glacis. In the space occupied by this passage, the banquette is suppressed : the second and sixth figures show this disposition.

Defiles of the traverses, and the crotchets made in the crest of the glacis, to cover them. (Fig. 2, and 6.)

The relations of a fortified town with the exterior, have always been established by means of great gates constructed in the ramparts of certain fronts, and by draw-bridges and fixed bridges (*ponts-levis et ponts-dormans*) crossing the great ditch. These constructions were always on the strongest and best defended parts, and consequently upon the perpendicular of the front. In this position the bridge and gate were covered by the re-entering place of arms, in which a guard house (*corps de garde*) was constructed. But notwithstanding these precautions, it frequently occurred that fortresses were carried by surprise by their gates. Several successful attempts of this kind, induced engineers to propose surrounding the guard house with a redan, revested, and furnished with small flanks ; to this work they gave the name of *ravelin*.

The half moon, its origin and advantages : its tracé in the front of the system described. (PLATE II, fig. 1)

This work outside the enceinte, though originally of very small capacity, acquired a great influence in regular attacks directed against the side of the gate. In consequence, its dimensions were increased, and ravelins were constructed upon all the fronts ; and thenceforward the ravelin or *half-moon* (*demilune*) became a constituent element of the bastioned front.

The advantages of *half-moons*, which we will hereafter more fully detail, are apparent at first sight. They furnish cross and commanding fires upon the capitals of the bastions that were destitute of them ; they support the covert-ways of the body of the place, and render the attack upon them slower and more difficult and perilous ; they form two re-enterings furnished with re-entering places of arms nearer the capitals of the bastions, the approaches of which are thus defended in a more effectual manner ; they cover the debouchè of the postern of the tenaille, or of the body of the place when there is no tenaille ; they cover the flanks and curtain of the body of the place ; finally, the half-moon has become in the hands of modern engineers, one of the best and strongest means of defence.　We will exhibit the great effects of it.

Tracé of the ravelin or half-moon. (Fig. 1.) The tracé of the half-moon, in the system that we are describing, is executed on the principle that its salient should advance towards the country as far as possible ; and that it should cover the shoulders of the bastions.　Accordingly, from the shoulder angles formed by the covering line, 30 mètres ($33\frac{1}{2}$ yards) are laid off ; and these two points are connected together by a right line, upon which an equilateral triangle is constructed, whose two sides are the magistral of the ravelin　It is evident from this simple construction, that it will be as salient as possible, because its flanked angle will be 60° ; its interior capacity will likewise be as great as possible.

The ditch of the half moon, and its tracé The ditch of the half-moon is not so wide as that of the body of the place ; its counterscarp is parallel to the magistral.　Its width is established at 18 to 20 mètres (20 to 22 yards) ; and the salient is rounded like that of the counterscarp of the enceinte.

The redoubt of the half-moon : its use and plan No sooner had Vauban and the engineers who succeeded him adopted the half-moon of great dimensions, and recognized its advantages, than they perceived the necessity of forming in it an *interior intrenchment ;* in order that it might be defended with obstinacy, without risk of its being carried by storm. This intrenchment is called *the redoubt of the half-moon* (*reduit de la demi-lune*).　It is drawn in the following manner : From the interior shoulder angle of each bastion, lines are drawn parallel to the faces of the ravelin ; these lines give the projection of the magistral of the redoubt-faces : its ditch will be 10 mètres ($11\frac{1}{4}$ yards) wide ; this will reduce the total width of the half-moon, from the scarp to the counterscarp, to about 18 mètres (20 yards).

Plan of the gorges of the ravelin and of the redoubt : flanks of the redoubt The half-moon and gorge of the redoubt are commonly terminated at the prolongation of the counterscarp of the body of the place ; but considerations, of which we shall speak when we analyze the system described, induce a suppression

of part of the terra-plain of the ravelin and redoubt, and to terminate them at the line of fire *mnp* which passes through the
flanked angle of the bastion and through the projection of the
extreme of the breast-height of the parapet of the half-moon.
The redoubt is made with flanks of at least 15 mètres ($16\frac{1}{4}$
yards), and they are thus drawn : through the point *r* where
the prolonged scarp of the half-moon meets the face of
the bastion, and through the point *o* of the gorge of the redoubt, draw the right line *rox*, on which take *ox* of 13 mètres ($14\frac{1}{2}$ yards); and to the point *x* draw the right line *ty*,
making with *rx* an angle of 100 degrees ; this right line will be
the magistral of the flank of the redoubt.

The counterscarp of the half-moon is surrounded by a covert-
way uniting and connected with that of the fortress by two
great re-entering places of arms, whose faces are at least 40
mètres ($44\frac{1}{2}$ yards). The width of the ravelin covert-way is
equal to that of the covert-way of the body of the place ; and
it is drawn in the same way, parallel to the counterscarp.

The ravelin co-
vert way, and the
two re-entering
places of arms :
tracé of these
elements.

To draw the re-entering place of arms, first describe the
projection of the face next to the bastion, with a view to make
this place of arms as spacious as possible. To this end take
upon the covering line of the bastion 10 to 12 mètres (11 to
$13\frac{1}{4}$ yards), and through the point *v* draw the line *vhg* making
with the counterscarp or branch of the covert-way an angle of
100 degrees ; this line will give the undefined left face of the
place of arms : make *sK = sh*, and draw *Kg* making an angle
of 100 degrees with the counterscarp or branch of the ravelin
covert way. This construction will make the faces, measured
on the counterscarp, about 54 mètres (60 yards). Draw afterwards the great traverses *T* closing the re-entering places of
arms *X*, *X*, and separating them from the bastion salient places
of arms *P*, *P*. The salient ravelin places of arms *S*, *S*, &c.,
must be enclosed as we have already said by traverses 30 decimètres (10 feet) thick, and placed on the prolongations of the
ravelin parapets. Finally, two intermediate traverses of small
thickness will be placed upon the branches of the covert-way
of each half-moon. All the crotchets to cover the defiles, will
be drawn as shown in Plate II, fig. 6.

(PLATE II.
fig 6.)

The re-entering place of arms in the modern system, exercises such a distinguished influence in the defence of the covert-
way, that it is reinforced with a redoubt which greatly in-

Redoubt of the
re entering place
of arms : its use
and plan.

creases its advantages. The tracé of this redoubt cannot be understood until we have described the stages of the attack : it is laid out by taking the covering line for its directrix. From the intersection of each face with the counterscarp, lay off 22 mètres (24¼ yards) from *a* to *b*, and 15 mètres (16⅔ yards) from *c* to *d* on the collateral branch of the covert-way, and draw the right lines *bd*, *bd*, which are the covering lines of the redoubt : these serve as directrices for drawing the scarp and counterscarp. By making the ditch 6 mètres (20 feet) wide, there will remain 5 to 6 mètres between the traverse and the counterscarp. The extreme of the covering line of the redoubt-face next to the half-moon, is broken to form a small flank *F* of 7 or 8 mètres (8 or 9 yards), which sees in reverse a part of the ravelin face. Lastly, the gorge of the redoubt next the ravelin, is bounded by the line of fire *efi* passing through the flanked angle of the half-moon and the extremity of the small flank *F*.

Observations upon the defiles of the traverses, and upon the figure of the re-entering places of arms.

We see that the common manner of planning the defiles of traverses with small crotchets made in the crest of the glacis, necessarily interrupts the banquettes, and consequently deprives this portion of the covert-way of its fires. To remedy this inconvenience, we may make the defiles and the crotchets that cover them, 32 decimètres (nearly 11 feet) wide ; and then make with fascines two steps and a banquette of 50 centimètres (20 inches) to fire from : there will then be between the traverse and last step, a breadth of 13 decimètres (4⅓ feet) to establish the barrier of the passage upon ; and this will be enough.

F Reflections upon the covert-ways.

When the places of arms are made about rectangular, they are very much exposed to the ricochets of the enemy's batteries. In order to correct this defect, St. Paul wisely proposed to make them in the circular form *a'b'c'*; which is much more advantageous. A covert-way, well constituted and properly organized, affords a fortress the means of making a long and glorious defence ; compels the enemy to act with great caution ; to approach step by step, and by the tardy and perilous methods of ingenuity and industry. Notwithstanding that fortification has in this respect made great advances since the time of Vauban, it is still, in comparison with the vigour of the attack, in a real state of weakness.

Intrenchments constructed in the interior of bastions : advantages of these works, and their plan.

For the same reasons that we arm a ravelin with an interior redoubt, to make it as strong as possible ; we must construct on the inside of the terra-plain of bastions an interior intrenchment, that will increase the strength of the bastions, secure to the besieged the use of all their means, enable them to stand one or even several assaults, and compel the enemy to carry on his attacks with great caution and by slow degrees.

This intrenchment in the bastion may be drawn in several ways. If the bastion be very open, we may construct a front upon the line VV' which joins the intersections of the ravelin covering lines with the scarp of the bastions ; this line will be about 150 mètres (166 yards), &c. We may also draw a redan in the interior of the terra-plain, as shown in G ; the gorge of this redan is enveloped by a parapet which joins that of the hinder part of the bastion, and serves as a second intrenchment. The descent from the terra-plain of the bastion into the ditch of the gorge of the intrenchment, is by a postern. The portion ee of the face of the bastion, must be at least 18 mètres (20 yards), in order to flank the ravelin terra-plain and the ditch of the redoubt. Bridges P, P, will be constructed of timbers to freely communicate with the terra-plain of the bastion ; they will be preserved as long as possible. Finally ; a last intrenchment K, made of timbers and earth, will be raised upon the gorge of the bastion during the siege, to sustain the assault on the permanent intrenchment G.

When we intend to have great command over the adjacent country, to overlook low grounds, hollow ways, gorges, and valleys, *cavaliers* of greater or less height are erected upon the terra-plains of the bastions and serve instead of interior intrenchments. These cavaliers are small interior bastions, having their faces and flanks parallel to those of the bastion : they are drawn like that in the bastion of Plate II. In order to detach that portion of the bastion which is not covered by the ravelin, a cut (*coupure*) is made at the extremity of the face of the cavalier and parallel to the face of the ravelin. To lay it out, its covering line must be drawn 18 mètres (20 yards) from the interior shoulder angle of the bastion, and then the scarp and counterscarp are drawn ; this latter line will be in a converging direction from the counterscarp of the cavalier to the extreme of the covering line of the ravelin face. The ditch of this cut (*coupure*) debouches into the great ditch of the enceinte. As there would be a dead angle at M, at the bottom of the ditch of the cut and cavalier, a *retirade* R is made, which removes it. The figure exhibits the details of its plan.

Cavaliers raised in bastions ; their cuts (*coupures*;) their advantages and tracé (PLATE II. fig. 2.)

We shall more fully show the advantages of cavaliers and interior intrenchments; for the present it will suffice to observe, that independently of the strength which they add to the bastions, and the commanding fires that they afford over the country, they serve as excellent traverses to defend the curtain from ricochets, and as paradoses to defend the flanks; finally, great souterrains may be made under their terra-plain, and be of the greatest advantage.

The communications of all kinds that should be in all the parts of a bastioned front. consisting of posterns. ramps, etairs, & defensive caponniers, and of the gates and debouches of the covert ways

All the elements of which the bastioned front is composed, should have communications of different kinds; in order that the defending troops may at pleasure move to all the separate fields of battle, and that all the manœuvres of the defence may be executed. The art of disposing a system of communications, is a very important branch of fortification; and in this respect the science is yet susceptible of great improvements.

The six posterns of the bastioned front and their situation.

The first kind of communications, consists of *posterns;* we have already said that there must be one under each curtain, and under each tenaille; and that it is requisite to make them of proper dimensions.

Two other posterns are constructed in the interior of the redoubt of each ravelin; they pass under the flanks, and debouche into the ditch near the shoulder angle. Two more posterns are similarly constructed in the redoubts of the re-entering places of arms, to descend from their terra-plains into the ditch. These four posterns are not wider than 12 to 15 decimètres (4 to 5 feet); nor higher than 20 (6¾ feet). Consequently there are six posterns on each front. The debouchès of the posterns in the ditches, must not be seen from any point on the crest of the glacis; because the enemy might thence annoy the defendants.

The ramps.

We have already said that wide ramps of a gentle slope are made to ascend the ramparts of the body of the place; they should be 40 to 50 decimètres (13⅓ to 16⅔ feet) wide, and so constructed as not to diminish the width of the terra-plain. These ramps are made on the extremities and centres of curtains; on the faces of bastions, when they are empty (*vide*); and on the gorges of cavaliers, to ascend from the terra-plain of the bastion to their particular terra-plain, &c.

The other ramps that are made in other parts of the front, are only 35 decimètres (12 feet) wide; and their slope is regulated according to the ground, by making their base three or four times their height.

Of all the methods used for communicating between the ditches and the terra-plains, ramps are the most advantageous ; and they should be used on all occasions that local circumstances permit. Even when their slope is only three times their height, they are preferable to stairs of free-stone, which are broken and splintered by falling bombs and howitzes, and ultimately rendered impracticable. At the last siege of Fort St. Phillip by the French and Spaniards, not a single stone stairs was practicable at the end of the siege ; they had been entirely ruined by shells.

The means most commonly used for communicating from the ditches to the terra-plains of the works and covert-ways, are stairs (*pas de souris*) of free-stone 10 decimètres wide ($3\frac{1}{3}$ feet). These stairs are *single* and *double;* the first consist of a single flight (*rampe*) from a landing-place (*palier*); the latter consist of two flights, one leading to the right and the other to the left from the same landing-place.

These stairs are made at the points where they are indispensable : 1st, in the centre of the gorge of the tenaille to ascend into its terra-plain, there is a double stairs having the same landing-place as the postern ; when the ditch is filled with water, each stairs has its landing-place on a level with the water : a *blindage* may be made to cover the debouchè of the postern and stairs : 2d, in the gorge of the ravelin redoubt a recess is made, in which a double stairs is constructed to ascend to the plane of site, and thence the ascent is by *ramps* to the ravelin redoubt rampart : 3d, at the extreme of the flanks of the ravelin redoubt, single stairs are constructed to ascend into the first part of the ditch, and small ramps to ascend into the ditch of the face of the redoubt : 4th, in the extremes of the ravelin faces, single stairs are constructed to ascend from the ditch of the flank of the redoubt into the ravelin terra-plain ; and in the *rounding* of the counterscarp, a double stairs is built : 5th, in the re-enterings of the redoubts of the re-entering places of arms, single or double stairs are constructed : 6th, in the roundings of the counterscarp, double stairs are built to ascend into the salient places of arms : 7th, in the extremities of the counterscarp of the re-entering places of arms, single stairs or small ramps are made to ascend into their terra-plains. Ac-

Observations upon these ramps.

The stairs to ascend from the ditches into the works : their situation, &c.

cordingly there are sixteen stairs (*pas de souris*) upon each front.

The defects of these stairs consist, 1st, in their little width, which must be at least 14 decimètres (4⅔ feet) ; 2d, in their construction, for when their steps (*marches*) are broken by falling shells the communication becomes difficult for armed men ; especially in a rather precipitate retreat before an enterprising enemy skilled in the war of sieges ; 3d, in the great expense that they cost, particularly in countries where free-stone is scarce. All those officers of engineers and artillery who have had experience in the wars of sieges, are unanimously of opinion that stairs and landing-places of free-stone are vicious and defective ; and that ramps should be substituted in their place, with sufficient width to pass cannon over them, &c.

Defensive cap-
onnières : their
use. & situation.

Caponnières are defensive dispositions made across certain parts of the ditch to communicate in safety with the stairs (*pas de souris*) and ramps. Their second object is to furnish scouring fires of musketry when the besiegers are approaching through the ditches. They are simple epaulments of earth with banquettes inside, and whose parapet is a glacis uniting with the ditch towards the approaches of the enemy. Accordingly, caponnières connect the communications from the body of the place with those of the out-works ; and in this respect fulfil a most important object, and deserve the serious attention of the engineer : they are only proper for dry ditches, and for ditches inundated at pleasure.

(PLATE II,
fig. 3)

Figure 3d, represents the profile of a double caponnière, covered on the two flanks. The chief use of caponnières, indicates their position in each system. In the system that we are describing, it is easily perceived that it is necessary to establish several caponnières on each front : 1st, a double caponnière C, of 5 mètres .8 (19¼ feet) between the two covering lines, must secure the communication from the postern of the tenaille to the stairs or ramps made in the recess of the gorge of the ravelin redoubt: 2d, two single caponnières c' must cover the passage from the debouchés of the tenaille to the stairs or ramps in the ditches of the flanks of the ravelin redoubt ; 3d, two other single caponnières c'' must cross the great ditch perpendicularly to the face of the bastion, to cover the stairs or ramps of the redoubt of the re-entering places of arms : 4th, two single caponnières c''' will cross the ravelin ditch, to cover on that side the stairs or ramps of the redoubts of the re-entering places of arms ; 5th, two single caponnières c^{iv} will cross the ditch of the ravelin redoubt, to cover the debouchès of that portion of the ditch corresponding to the flanks.

When the ditches of a place are wet, the communications with the out-works are difficult to establish and preserve. For this purpose wooden bridges are constructed and established upon trestles or boats, and lead from the communications of the enceinte to those of the out-works. But these bridges are continually getting damaged, and cannot exist after the enemy sees into the ditches. Accordingly, dry ditches are the most favourable for a defence not purely passive ; they afford to the besieged the means of striking offensively at any moment when the strength and activity of the garrison place them in this fortunate position. Wet ditches are adapted for fortresses whose garrisons are not strong, and whose defence depends chiefly upon the fires of artillery and musketry.

Communications when the ditches are filled with water, or wet.

In dry ditches or those that are inundated at pleasure, a small ditch or trench called a *cunette* is made in the middle, for drawing off the rain-waters, &c. In those parts where caponnières are to be made, aqueducts or drains are constructed of masonry under the caponnières and form a passage for the waters.

The trench called *cunette*, in the middle of the ditch.

In certain parts of the covert-way, openings and gentle and convenient ramps are made, to move out in force from the covert-way upon the glacis or into the country. The cavalry and artillery should be able to easily pass through these kinds of gates. These outlets (*passages de sortie*) are 40 decimètres ($13\frac{1}{3}$ feet) wide, and are closed by strong barriers established upon the direction of the crest of the glacis : we described this kind of barrier in the Second Part (Art. 90). These openings and their barriers, are covered and defiled from the view of the enemy by the profiles of the glacis, to which a circular and re-entering direction is given towards the covert-way of the collateral parts. The exterior gates of the covert-ways are established upon the faces of the re-entering places of arms, and upon the branches of the ravelin covert-ways between the second and third traverses. By these means, the retreat of sorties is effectually protected by the salients of the ravelin and bastion covert-ways.

The gates and barriers of the covert way, to positions, and plan. pass out: their

Caponnières made of earth, like those that we have just described, as communications, are not sufficiently secure for the

Reflections upon caponnières.

besieged when the enemy has established himself upon the crest of the glacis. He has then a plunging fire into the ditches, and sees in reverse the great double caponnière C, and even the single caponnières c', because of the suppression of a portion of the gorge of the ravelin redoubt; this gorge defiles by its relief that portion of the ditch when it terminates on the prolongation of the counterscarp of the body of the place. It is thought, and with reason, that the double caponnière C should be considered as a permanent work; that its dimensions should be

(PLATE II. fig. 4.)

enlarged; and that the vaulted gallery G, sunk about 15 decimètres (5 feet) below the ditch and covered with earth and bomb proof, should be added to it. The extrados of this gallery, thus covered over with earth, will project above the bottom of the ditch about 20 decimètres (6½ feet), and will serve as a parados to the half caponnières C constructed open to the heavens (à ciel ouvert), and which it would be easy to blind, if judged necessary or proper.

(Figure 5.)

As wood is not scarce in fortified towns threatened with siege, we may construct the double caponnière of a gallery of timbers, blinded with head-pieces (chapeaux) surmounted with string pieces (longerons), and covered over with planks and earth. The walls P, P of this gallery, are made of two rows of thick timbers planted vertically in the ground, and pierced with loopholes m, m: the small glacises r, r are on a level with the loopholes. This mass does not project beyond the surface of the glacis more than 16 decimètres (5¼ feet); so that if the enemy's batteries established upon the crest of the covert-way, threaten it with destruction, the flanks P, P may be fortified with gabionnades. These gabionnades will mask the loopholes m, m, which then can be no longer of any service; but they may be easily unmasked if their utility becomes apparent.

The great communications or outlets, called the city gates.

Besides the communications belonging to fortifications that we have just described, gates, bridges, and barriers, are established on several fronts of a fortress to maintain the relations with the country without. As these openings diminish the strength of works, they must be made in the strongest parts of the fronts least exposed. We will treat this subject in the sequel.

General reflections on the communications established in all the parts of the bastioned front.

The complete system of communications that we have just described, shows that all the materials of defence may be transported from the interior of the fortress to the outworks;

that the troops can freely move towards any quarter, assemble in the covert-way, and thence make a sortie in force against the enemy ; and that these same troops may retire on the co-vert-ways without danger of being too closely pressed by a daring enemy.   Hence it follows, that in this respect modern bastioned fortification is favourable to an interior and exterior active defence.

In examining the direction of the lines of fire in the horizon-tal projection of the bastioned front that is the subject of our contemplations, it is easy to discover the laws of flanking and the reciprocal defence of all its component elements : 1st, All parts of the covert-way flank each other by rectangular lines of fire, which effectively cross each other upon the capitals. 2d, The covert-ways are directly swept and flanked by almost rectangular lines of fire from the principal works.   3d, The ditches of the re-entering places of arms, are defended by the faces of the ravelin and bastion ; and those of the ravelin and its redoubt, are flanked by the faces of the bastions.   4th, The ditches of the enceinte, are flanked by the flanks of the bastions. There is only one part of the ditch, that in front of the scarp *efgh* of the tenaille, which is sheltered from the fires of the en-ceinte by the relief of this tenaille ; but the besieged are in such strength in this re-entering part, that the enemy cannot hope to make any serious impression upon it.

Examination of the reciprocal de-fence of all parts of the bastioned front.

117. Having described the horizontal projection of the bas-tioned front, and shown on the horizontal plane the arrange-ment and relation of all its elements ; we will now proceed to describe their *relief*.   This part is no less essential than the first ; and it is from their re-union that a perfect knowledge of a system is derived.   However well disposed the horizontal projection of the parts of a system may be, its strength or value is undetermined so long as the relief is not fixed.   And if this relief be not established agreeably to the rules of the theory, the system will not fulfil the conditions prescribed by defence, and will not obtain the results for which fortifications are con-structed.

117. Descrip-tion of the relief of all the ele-ments of the bas-tioned front, whose horizontal projection is known.

It is by drawing and constructing a suitable number of gene-ral profiles that we establish the relief of a system whose hori-zontal projection is known.   The plan and proportions of these profiles, are equally deduced from the rules of defence and from the rules of building (*construction matérielle*).   We have seen

The general profiles to deter-mine the relief, and the princi-ples from which their proportions are deduced.

(114) in what manner the primitive profile of a work is drawn ; and that to effect this graphical construction, we must, 1st, draw the ground line or direction of the plane of site ; 2d, know the height of the covering line above the plane of site ; 3d, know the depth of the ditch below the plane of site.

It now remains to determine the relation that should exist between the covering lines of all the elements. This relation should be such, that all the works constituting the system shall effectually overlook the adjacent country and have a proper power over each other. Consequently the outmost works should not mask the fires of the works in rear ; the works should therefore be disposed in amphitheatre, and it is only by making them commanding that we arrive at this result.

The commandment of works; its definition; planes of defilement, &c.

Commandment assumes in fortification a peculiar character (104) ; but to understand the definition, we must know what is meant by the *plane of defilement* of a work. The plane of defilement of a work, is the horizontal plane that passes through its covering line. In regular fortification, this plane is parallel to the plane of site ; so that its direction upon the vertical plane of projection, is parallel to the ground line. The commandment of a work over the plane of site, is expressed by the numerical height or reference (*cote numerique*) of the vertical included between the planes of site and defilement ; and the command of one work over another, is also the numerical height of the vertical included between their planes of defilement. Hence, commandment in a fortified front is represented by the system of the numerical heights of command of the constituent works above the plane of site ; and the relief is represented by the system of the numerical heights from the bottom of the ditches, below the plane of site, added to the system of the heights of commandment. Accordingly, to find the total relief of a work, we must find the numerical height that expresses its commandment, and add it to that which represents the depth of the ditch.

Description of the relief and commandment of the bastioned front (PLATE II, Second Part.)

We will now describe the relief and commandment of all the elements of the bastioned front, agreeably to the general idea that we have given of them ; and we will afterwards construct the general profiles necessary to perfect our understanding of its arrangement.

General principle of defining the relations of the planes of defilement.

As all the fires of the works should be unmasked, and should batter the works of the besiegers ; of course the commandment of the outmost works should be the smallest possible. But in proportion as the works retire towards the interior of the field of battle, their commandment should increase according to a certain law, which varies in each system and in each particular case of irregular fortification.   We will examine this relation in the fifth chapter, in which we will analyze the system. Pursuant to these general views, we shall regulate as follows, and in an approximating manner, the commandment of all the elements of the bastioned front.

The terra-plain of the ravelin covert-way is established in the very plane of site, above which its plane of defilement is elevated 22 to 25 decimètres (7⅓ to 8⅓ feet) at most.

Commandment of the covert-way of the ravelin.

Decimètres.

The *reference (la cote)* expressing the commandment of this outmost work will be ....22 to 25

The covert-way of the body of the place has commonly the same plane of defilement, and consequently the same commandment as the preceding work ; but as it is less advanced, it is proper to slightly increase its command and to fix its reference or height at (10 feet) 30

Commandment of the covert-way of the body of the place.

The redoubt of the re-entering place of arms should command its covert-way by about 10 decimétres (3⅓ feet) ; accordingly the reference of its plane of defilement will be expressed by (13⅓ feet) 40

Commandment of the redoubt of the re-entering place of arms.

The commandment of the ravelin will be expressed by the reference of (15 feet); 45

Commandment of the ravelin, and its redoubt.

And the reference of command of its redoubt, will be expressed by (18⅓ feet) 55

The commandment of the body of the place will be the greatest, and its reference shall be (21⅔ feet)...... 65

Commandment of the body of the place.

Lastly ; the commandment of the intrenchment of the bastion may be (28⅓ feet) 85

When the intrenchment of the bastion is a cavalier, its command will be in relation to the particular position of the exterior points that are to be discovered and battèred.

Commandment of the intrenchment of the bastion, and of the cavalier.

The plane or planes of defilement of the tenaille, are determined according to particular data dependent on the attack and defence.   Whilst waiting until these circumstances can be detailed, we must content ourselves with knowing in general, that the tenaille should not mask the fires of the flanks which defend the ditches of the bastion faces.

Commandment of the tenaille, and its plane of defilement.

The glacises, and their slope or declivity.

The parapets of the covert-ways are constructed in glacis. These glacises are inclined planes which pass through the crest and cut the plane of site at a distance greater or less, in proportion to their declivity. It is obvious that all glacises should be under the fire of the works that they cover; and that consequently the prolongation of their plane should pass through the line of fire of these works, or be below it a certain quantity, as will be shown subsequently. Accordingly, the plan and slope of glacises are determined by the commandment. Indeed if we were to imagine that the plane of the glacis of the face of a work turned upon its crest, it should pass through the line of fire, if these two lines be parallel; or through the most distant point of this line, if these two lines be not situated in the same plane.

The depth of the ditches, or their excavation below the plane of site.

The depth or excavation of ditches below the plane of site, is determined; 1st, by the consideration that the counterscarps of the ravelin and body of the place, should not be less than 45 to 50 decimètres high (15 to 16⅔ feet); this rule is deduced from the theory of attack and defence: 2d, by the solution of the question of the excavation and embankment (*du deblai et du remblai*) for the construction of all the works: in this important question, the depth of the ditches of the enceinte and ravelin is considered as an unknown quantity, the value of which is

Question of the equalization of the excavation and embankment.

found (as we will show hereafter) by the equation expressing the equalization of the excavation and embankment. The depth of all the other ditches is, fixed as follows:

The depth of the ditch of the re-entering place of arms, will be 30 to 35 decimètres (10 to 11½ feet).

That of the redoubt of the ravelin, will be 40 to 45 decimètres (13½ to 15 feet).

That of the intrenchment of the bastion, will be 40 to 45 decimètres.

We will suppose that the equalization of the excavation and embankment gives for the depth of the ditch of the enceinte and of the ravelin, below the plane of site, 50 decimètres (16⅔ feet).

Remark upon the portion of the ditch of the ravelin redoubt corresponding to the flanks. (PLATE II, fig. 1.)

It must be remarked, that as the depth of the ditch of the ravelin redoubt is less than that of the great ditch by 20 to 25 decimètres (6⅔ to 8⅓ feet), this elevation or *ressault* (*ressaut*) will be divided into two portions, as indicated in the plan; but in such a manner that the part *A* of the ditch corresponding to the flanks, will be raised about 15 decimètres (5 feet) above the great ditch.

Three general profiles are sufficient to show the relief of all the elements of the front. The first profile will be taken upon ABC perpendicular to the face of the intrenched bastion; the second, upon DEF perpendicular to the face of the ravelin: the third, upon OH perpendicular to the face of the redoubt of the re-entering place of arms. Construction of the general profiles of all the elements of the bastioned front. (PLATES II, & II, Second Part.)

We have seen (114) that to construct the profile of a work, we must know; 1st, the height of the covering line above the plane of site; 2d, the height of the magistral line above the same plane; 3d, the thickness of the summit of the parapets; 4th, the depth of the ditch below the plane of site.

The height of the scarp above the plane of site in each element of the front, is established in pursuance of the principle, that all masonry-work must be concealed from the views of the besiegers. This proves that the summit of scarps must not be elevated above the plane of defilement of the covert-way. Accordingly, the magistral will be in this plane. Height of the magistral line or summit of the scarp, above the plane of site.

The distance from the magistral to the covering line, is, as in the horizontal projection, equal to the thickness of the summit of the parapet added to the difference between the heights of the covering line and magistral. According to this principle and that preceding, and the thickness of parapets being fixed at 60 decimètres (20 feet) for the body of the place, at 55 (18¼ feet) for the ravelin, at 50 (16¾ feet) for its redoubt, and at 46 (15⅓ feet) for the redoubt of the re-entering place of arms; we have for the distances from the magistrals to the covering lines of these several works, viz: 9 mètres .5 (31¾ feet) for the body of the place, and 8 mètres (26¾ feet) for the intrenchment of the bastion; 8 mètres for the ravelin and 7 (23⅓ feet) for its redoubt; and 6 mètres (20 feet) for the redoubt of the re-entering place of arms. Distance from the magistral to the covering line; the thickness of parapets.

The superior slope or plunge (*plongée*) of parapets is so regulated, that its prolongation cuts the foot of the banquette of the covert-way, or at least the middle of its slope. The relation of the planes of defilement of all the works with respect to the plane of site, being known; and the horizontal dimensions being given upon the horizontal projection; we have all the elements requisite to construct all the general profiles, and any section, or elevation whatever in a vertical plane whose direc- The superior slope or plunge of parapets.

tion on the horizontal plane is determined. To scarps and counterscarps will be applied the principles that we have laid down respecting the thicknesses of revêtements, and the figure of their profiles (114).

Conclusion

It follows from the preceding descriptions, that the subject of our studies is now completely described, its figure perfectly determined, and likewise the connexion and relations of all the component parts.

118. The essential additions to fortification, consisting of buildings and coverings of all kinds, constructed within a fortified town.

118. Having described the intrenched enclosure of a fortified town, we must now say a few words about the additions or *accessaries* that should be included within it. These appendages have become, in the present state of the attack, of the greatest importance ; and their good or bad disposition and construction influence the defence so powerfully, that they deserve to be established with the greatest care. Upon the preservation during the siege of the troops and materials of the defence, evidently depends the certainty with which we can calculate the probable length of the siege, estimated agreeably to the strength of the fortifications. This class of buildings necessary in fortresses, comprehends the following : 1st, *great gates*, of which we have already spoken and on which we shall enlarge hereafter, and guard houses (*corps de garde*); 2d, *souterrains* constructed under the terra-plains of bastions, curtains, &c. ; 3d, military buildings, barracks or caserns, provision magazines, bake-houses, and store-houses or sheds ; 4th, powder magazines ; 5th, *blindages*, and other temporary coverings constructed only at the moment of siege.

Nature of the buildings used in the defences of a town

The great use that is made of bombs and howitzes in the attack, requires that buildings exposed to their effect should be solidly built and covered with bomb-proof vaults Without this precaution, they would be ruined and rendered uninhabitable from the very beginning of the siege ; and would spread terror and consternation among the troops and citizens. But when these buildings resist and render nugatory the power of shells, they are no longer dreaded. A vault to be bomb-proof, must be 10 decimètres ($3\frac{1}{3}$ feet) thick on its back ; and its extrados is made like a cope or very flat roof. As soon as the siege is declared, all the wood-work of buildings is removed, and the vaults are covered with 10 decimètres ($3\frac{1}{3}$ feet) of earth or dung. It is desirable that the extrados of vaults should be co-

vered over with a mortar on which frost and wet will have no
effect.

When the buildings are not vaulted, the first floor is supported with thick stancheons and covered over with a bed of earth
15 to 18 decimètres (5 to 6 feet) thick.   But buildings thus
arranged, are unhealthy ; the rains penetrate through them, and
they soon become uninhabitable.

Caserns are large buildings destined in time of peace to lodge
the garrison ; they commonly consist of a vaulted ground floor
and two common stories.   All the caserns of a fortress should
be constructed and disposed in relation to the defence.   Consequently ; 1st, they should be in situations most distant from attacks, and least exposed ; 2d, they should consist of only a
ground floor, vaulted bomb-proof ; 3d, they should be sufficiently spacious to contain one third of the garrison.   By this
general arrangement of the caserns, one third of the garrison
can always repose in security.   When there are situations in
the fortress that are healthy and sheltered from the fires of the
enemy, the troops should be encamped upon them, in preference
to unhealthy and wet grounds destitute of a free circulation
of air.

The most proper situation for caserns, is along the curtains ;
but a wide street must be left between them and the ramparts.

We perceive at once how important it is to establish the
provision magazines, the store-houses, and the baking-ovens,
in the most secure and least exposed places.   Their capacity is calculated according to the strength of the garrison
and probable duration of the siege.   It is indispensable that
they be vaulted bomb-proof, and consist of only a ground
floor (*rez de chaussée*).

Powder magazines must be constructed in a peculiar manner ;
the barrels of powder must be arranged in them in the most
convenient and safest manner ; and they must be defended from
any dampness, and vaulted perfectly bomb-proof.   The great
magazines should be concealed from the view of the enemy ;
but upon each front there should be a small vaulted magazine,
to contain the ammunition necessary for daily service.

Too many *souterrains* cannot be constructed in a fortress ;
they may be established beneath full bastions and curtains.
These souterrains should not be considered as quarters for the

The caserns;
their use and si-
tuation.

Provision stores
& baking ovens.

The powder-
magazines.

The souter-
rains.

troops, but as of great use in other respects. Souterrains must always be made under the rampart on the right and left of the posterns ; these serve as magazines of deposit for ammunition destined for the out-works.

Blindages. *Blindages* are shelters or coverts prepared at the moment of siege, to cover the troops from shells. They are made of long heavy timbers laid with a slope against each other ; so that the superior extremities rest against a solid wall, whilst the others are sunk into the ground. These coverts are of no value as quarters ; but established along the fronts of attack, they are there very useful to assemble in the daily guards and additional troops that are frequently required.

The military hospital. The military hospital is likewise an indispensable edifice in a besieged fortress : it should be in the most retired situation, vaulted and perfectly aired.

The distribution and construction of military buildings. The art of distributing and constructing the buildings and edifices belonging to fortification, constitutes a branch of military architecture that the students will study with advantage in the school of practice (*école d'application*) ; the general principles of this branch are acquired by them at the polytechnick school. The characteristics and fitness of this branch of architecture, should be very distinguishable ; the only objects to be attended to, are, solidity, strength, and salubrity : the forms of the buildings are prescribed by the destination of each kind.

119. General idea of the building of the parts of a fortress. 119. The construction of a fortress depends upon that branch of military architecture which is the province of public works ; it is however distinguished into the following parts : 1st, The removal of the earths or excavation of the ditches, with which all the embankments are formed. 2d, The foundations of all the scarps and counterscarps, which must be established upon a solid bottom, or upon piles, gratings of timber, &c., according to the nature of the ground ; all parts of the ground below the bottom of the ditches, must be sounded before the project of the foundations is established and taken into the general estimates of the expense. 3d, The construction of the posterns, souterrains, stair cases and stairs (*escaliers et pas de souris*), ramps, and trenches or cuvettes, &c. All these constructions require drawings in detail made upon a great scale, agreeably to the rules taught in the preliminaries of descriptive geometry and in stone cutting. 4th, The construction of sluice bridges (*ponts éclusés*), dikes or *batardeaux*, overfalls (*déversoirs*), refluent dikes

(*reversoirs*), &c. ; that is, of all works relating to the use of waters, if there are to be any.   These works require very detailed drawings, accurately exhibiting the section and the re-union of all the parts.   5th, The laying out and constructing all the subterranean galleries that compose the system of mines, if the place is to have any.   6th, The formation of the parapets, banquettes, barbettes, &c.

From this brief exposition it will be seen, what extensive knowledge and experience a young officer of engineers must previously acquire, to be able to direct the immense labours that the establishment of a fortress requires.

The equalization of the earth of the excavation and embankment, is, in the construction of a fortified front and fortress, the data according to which the depth of the ditches of the enceinte, and ravelin is estimated.   For this purpose, the centre of gravity of the part situated above the plane of site of the generating profile of each element of the front, is determined ; the horizontal projection of the path described by this centre of gravity, is made ; each generating surface of the embankment is multiplied by the path described by its centre of gravity ; and all these cubic quantities are added together to find the total cubic quantity of the embankment.   From this cubic quantity is deducted the cubic quantities of the ditches that are determined ; and the remainder, divided by the surface of the ditch of the enceinte and ravelin, gives for quotient the depth that the ditches of the body of the place and ravelin should have, in order that the quantity of earth excavated may equal the quantity required for the embankments.   If the calculation give a height of counterscarp less than 45 to 50 decimètres, the width of the ditches must be a little diminished, or the dimensions of the profile of the body of the place must be a little augmented.   Again, if the nature of the ground do not permit sinking sufficiently deep, other means must be used to obtain the earth necessary for forming the embankments ; for instance, we may make protracted glacises (*glacis coupés*), that is, the planes of the glacis are protracted beyond their foot ; this will furnish earth with which the embankment of the glacis may be formed.   There will in this case be a ressault or rise at the foot of the glacis, and which will be favourable for the defence.

Attention must be paid in calculating the earth for the em-

The equalization of the excavation and embankment; the removal of the earths and their mean carriage.

bankments, to the space occupied by the revêtements of the scarps and counterscarps.

Although the equation relative to the equalization of the excavation and embankment contains many terms, it is nevertheless very easy to establish by means of a plan and by profiles correctly drawn according to scales suitably chosen.

The question of the general removal of the excavated earths and their transportation to the embankment, is not so easily solved. It is effected by establishing the project of the *mean carriage* (*portée moyenne*) of the earths ; that is, forming a plan upon which shall be inscribed or numbered the several cubic quantities of the excavation, and the paths that they must pass over to corresponding parts of the embankment. This simple method shows that there are numerous modes of forming the embankments ; but as the expense should be taken into consideration, the officer must seek amidst all these solutions that which gives a *minimum* of labour, and consequently of expense. This labour is called the *mean carriage* (*portée moyenne*) of the earths.

(See the Memoir *Sur le Déblai et le Remblai* by G. Monge : Memoirs of the Academy, 1782.)

It is requisite to have recourse to analysis, to find guides in this complicated labour. The students will read with attention the Memoir of G. Monge on this interesting subject. The analysis shows, that the excavation must be divided into a great number of cubic quantities, and that the embankment should be imagined to be divided into an equal and respectively corresponding number of quantities ; and it must be supposed that each of these cubic quantities is concentrated upon its centre of gravity, whose position is known. It also shows, that the correspondence of the cubic quantities of the excavation to those of the embankment, must be so established, that the path which the centre of gravity of each partial excavation must follow to arrive at the centre of gravity of the embankment, must never cross another path ; and that when the whole removal is effected, the sum of the products of the cubic quantities into the paths described by their centres of gravity, shall be a minimum. By these general principles we may form the plan representing the project of the *mean carriage of the earths*, and determine the expense of it in an approximating manner.

This general view of the manner in which the excavation should be conducted, shows that the embankment of the rem-

parts and parapets should respectively be formed of the excavated earth from the parts of the ditch next to the scarp and
foundations. Its width will consequently be marked out ; and
the excavation of this latter part will be the first executed, to
uncover and lay the foundations. It is thought that we should
gain the bottom of the foundation by steps or very gentle slopes.
As fast as the revêtements are raised, the embankment behind
them is formed and the terracing carried up. It is perhaps
proper to deposit the earth for the parapets upon the interior
side of the rampart, in order not to load the scarp before the
masonry has settled and indurated (*pris leurs tassement*). The
residue of the earth from the great ditch, will be divided into
portions for embanking the ravelin redoubt, the traverses of the
covert-way, and the glacises. The made terra-plains, and likewise the parapets, must be raised 20 centimètres (8 inches)
higher than is indicated in the profiles ; because of the settling
(*tassement*) of the earths, which takes a good while before it is
completed.

The construction of banquettes, breast heights, ramps, barbettes, &c. is too simple to make it necessary for us to enter
into any details ; besides, these subjects were fully treated in
the Second Part. We will only remark, that formerly it was
the custom to make the breast heights of parapets and covert-
ways in masonry ; but it is preferable to make them of sods or
fascines, to avoid the destructive splinters occasioned by cannon balls ricochèing on all sides.

Neither are barbettes any longer made in the salients of
works ; this disposition is useless since the invention of the new
garrison gun carriage (*l'affut de place*), which enables us to fire
over the parapets with less danger to the cannoniers.

The building of masonry works, requires on the part of the
engineer a knowledge of all the kinds of materials used in
each country for public works. He must attend to their properties as respects solidity, resistance to the variations and
power of the atmosphere or seasons, and to the effects of artillery. He should carefully study the composition, preparation,
properties, and various uses of all kinds of mortars and cements
for uniting the materials into one single mass ; the method of
jointing the layers of stones to prevent the filtration of waters,
and of covering over the extrados of vaults, terraces, &c. so
that the waters will not penetrate through them.

The building of the masonry works or revêtements, and other parts of fortification.

The materials of which fortifications are constructed, consist of siliceous, calcareous, and aluminous substances, and their compounds ; these are taken from quarries, and are suitably prepared and cut before they are used. They are divided into the following classes : rough rag-stones (*moellons bruts*), rough hewn rag-stones, or chipped for regular courses (*moellons essemillés, ou piqués d'assise règlées*), free-stones for regular courses (*pierres de taille d'assise règlées*), &c. To these must be added bricks of all patterns, the use of which is very frequent in districts where stone is scarce ; the proper use of them in fortification greatly strengthens walls against the power of artillery.

The foundations of large rag-stones. The foundations of revêtements and counterforts are laid out by making a retreat outside, varying from 30 to 100 centimètres (12 to 40 inches), and one inside of about 20 centimètres (8 inches). They are sunk to the solid bottom, and made of large unhewn stones laid with the greatest care upon a bed of mortar.

When the foundation is 30 centimètres (1 foot) below the bottom of the ditch, and is well levelled, the retreats are formed, and the foot of the facing of the revêtement is laid out. The retreats of the counterforts are also formed ; and the whole work is raised at the same time, so as to form one single mass of masonry.

Revêtements of rag-stones, and facings of free stones. Most commonly the exterior courses or facings (*paremens*), and especially those of the scarp, are built of free-stones (*pierre de taille*) laid in regular layers lengthways and athwart. The salient angles are formed with great care, and constructed with free-stones of the largest and most perfect size. It would be proper to round the summit of the salient angles ; the laying of the stones would in this case be a little more troublesome, but the solidity of the work would be increased. When the facing courses are sloped, the stones of the salient and re-entering angles are cut according to the bevel determined by the common methods of stone cutting.

Facings in regular layers of rag-stones. Exterior courses of rag-stones in regular layers, are not suitable for scarps ; this kind of stone has too little tail to form a strong union and connexion, and forms only a kind of covering (*chemise*) that is soon overthrown, and which the smallest cannon shot disunites from the rest of the masonry. Rag-stones may however be sometimes used in regular courses with cut joints, in the revêtements of counterscarps of little height.

Whenever a revêtement has not its facing or exterior courses made of free-stone (*pierres de taille*), a basement (*soubassement*) of free-stone is added to it of about 20 decimètres high (6¾ feet) in dry ditches, and rising about 3 decimètres (12 inches) above the waters in wet ditches. This basement has a projection of only 10 centimètres (4 inches), cut in chamfer. In counter-scarps built of rag-stones, the basement (*soubassement*) in wet ditches is as high as that of the scarp ; but in dry ditches it is only as high as two regular courses. The basement.

The free-stone (*pierre de taille*) used for the facings of revêtements, should be cut merely with regard to solidity. The edges of the joints and layers should be square ; and the planes of both should be perfectly squared on the greatest thickness that the size of each stone will allow : the remainder of the exterior surface should only be chipped with the pointed chissel. Remark upon cutting the stones used in facing revêtements.

When the scarcity of free-stone and rag-stones compel us to build the revêtements and their facings with bricks, the walls are not the worse for it in most respects. The property that bricks possess of perfectly consolidating with the mortar, makes the building very solid, and the more advantageous in fortification, as it is more difficult for artillery to ruin such constructions ; for the balls penetrate and lodge in the walls. Hence the shaking caused by discharges or salvoes of cannon, is less ; and breaches are more difficult to make. But walls of brick have this defect ; their facings or exterior courses cannot long resist the influence of the atmosphere, and are soon overthrown ; and whenever excoriations (*écorchemens*) are made, it is almost impossible to repair them solidly, because of the difficulty of uniting old and new mortar work. Facings and revêtements made of bricks ; bands of free-stone, and stones laid end-ways.

Before raising a brick revêtement, a basement rising out of the foundation is made and revested with free-stone as described above ; and upon this basement the brick facing is raised. To support this facing, there is if possible made at intervals horizontal and even vertical bands (*chaines*) of free-stone, laid end-ways. If the scarcity of stone does not allow this arrangement, we must content ourselves with interlarding the facing with long stones or headers, laid end-ways and in quincunx. But in any case, it is indispensable that all the salient angles should be of free-stone, as well as the re-entering angles if possible. The parts made of free-stone in brick revêtements.

The most advantageous construction for scarps that are exposed to be battered in breach.

We must distinguish with great care the parts of a fortification that are exposed to be battered in breach ; for their construction must be attended to with great care, and executed in a peculiar mode.   In conformity with the preceding observations we may lay it down as a rule, that these scarps should have their exterior courses or facings of free-stone, in regular layers laid lengthways and across ; that behind this facing there should be an excellent masonry of brick 12 decimètres (4 feet) thick, and well united to the facing; finally, that the interior facing and counterforts should be constructed of common unhewn rag-stones, with fragments of bricks : the whole laid and filled in with excellent mortar.   When the facing of a wall is to be washed by waters, cement will be substituted in it for mortar.

Crowning copings substituted for the large cordon formerly used.

Instead of the large cordon that formerly crowned the scarps, a plain coping (*tablette*) has been substituted, projecting about 12 centimètres (5 inches) beyond the face or side of the scarp. The foot of the exterior slope of the parapet rests upon this coping at about 30 centimètres (12 inches) from its edge.   The counterscarps are also crowned with a coping.

The drawings for buildings.

The construction of each part of the fortification requires drawings on a sufficiently large scale to guide the *appareilleurs**, stone-cutters, carpenters, and directors of the works or master-workmen.   All details which in their construction require the aid of descriptive geometry, should be separately executed, and by the graphical methods most applicable to practice.

We will extend no farther these general views on the art of building, which constitutes the greatest part of the science of engineering ; we should have restrained ourselves to a few hints, showing the immediate relation of the course of fortification with the courses of civil works and architecture.   In these two courses, the fundamental knowledge of the art of using the materials for buildings of all kinds, is illustrated in a manner that leaves nothing more to be desired on this interesting and useful part of practical descriptive geometry.   Those young officers and other students who are not of the Polytechnick School, may study Belidor and other authors on this subject.

* Those who show how the stones designed for a building, are to be cut, matched, and placed.

TRANSLATOR.

CHAPTER IV.

General Reflections on the Attack and Defence of a Fortress ; the Armament of a Fortress ; Description of its Attack and Defence, distinguished into their three Principal Periods, &c. -

120. ALTHOUGH our readers are as yet little advanced in the study of fortification, nevertheless the precepts that we have laid before them on attack and defence in general, must have convinced them of the necessity of being acquainted with the general theory of the attack, in order to make progress in the study of the defence. Accordingly, after describing the general forms and material strength of the works which compose the defensive system of a fortress, we should, to follow the most natural course of instruction, describe the operations of a siege ; that is, all the labours and measures that constitute *offensive fortification*, by placing an army in a position to carry or gain possession of a fortress.

120. General reflections upon the theory of the attack and defence of fortresses.

In this branch of military science, as in all others, there is an immediate relation between the attack and the defence ; and upon this relation is founded the art which guides the officers of engineers and artillery in practice. Indeed it is easily conceived, that the defence whose single object is to procure for the *active arms* the means of *destroying, slackening*, and constantly *counteracting* the labours of the attack, cannot dispose its *resisting means* but according to the necessary progress of a regular attack, displayed conformably to a theory which reason, grand tactics, and numerous facts have confirmed.

The relation between the attack and the defence.

We will in consequence suppose that a garrison shut up in a fortress, constituted as we have described in the preceding chapter, is to be vanquished ; and we will then describe all the procedures of this grand operation : that is, we will show the mode of determining that chief element of the value of a fortress, called the *probable duration of the siege*. This method has been considered for many years by enlightened minds, as the best that young officers can pursue to study fortification and all the other branches of war to advantage.

In the regular attack of the modern bastioned front, we will abstract from our consideration subterranean war, and the defences to be obtained by ditches capable of being inundated with waters. We will also throw out of the question those moral causes that might retard or advance the progress of the attacks ; such as the unskilfulness of the besiegers, the extraordinary sacrifices which the assailants are determined to make in consequence of circumstances, and the daring activity of the besieged, &c. We will suppose a garrison of ordinary courage, always restrained within their defences by offensive dispositions which they cannot prevent, and which the history of sieges proves may be-made by numerous besiegers provided with ample means of attack ; and who, to accomplish their purpose, are determined to make the sacrifices of men and time that the undertaking requires.

At the same time that we describe the labours of the attack, we will concisely state the measures of the defence ; that is, the manner in which the besieged should make use of fortification, to compel the besiegers to advance slowly and cautiously.

The attack and defence divided into three principal periods. The attack and the defence in the war of sieges, consist of three principal periods. During these periods the operations and means of the besiegers and besieged are diversified, and assume a character depending upon their respective positions.

The first period of attack comprehends the preparatory operations of the siege and investment, to the opening of the trenches.

The first period of the defence comprehends the conduct of the besieged from the moment of expecting to be besieged, to the opening of the trenches.

The *second period* embraces the operations that take place from the opening of the trenches, to the establishment of the besiegers at the foot of the glacis.

The *second period* includes the conduct of the besieged from the moment of the opening of the trenches, to the establishment of the besiegers at the foot of the glacis.

The *third period* comprehends the operations that take place from the third parallel, to the reduction of the place.

The *third period* exhibits the conduct of the besieged from the third parallel, to the capitulation.

121 The arming of a fortress, and its state of siege. 121. By the *armament* of a fortress, is understood the dispositions which place it in *a state of siege*. This armament is a part of the duties of artillery and engineer officers, and is as difficult as it is important.   It consists in calculating and forming estimates (*etats de situation*) that exhibit for each fortress, 1st, the strength of its garrison at the maximum and minimum; 2d, the quantity of cannon, muskets, rampart guns, blunderbusses (*espingoles*), grenades, caltrops or crows-feet, sithes, and pikes, &c., requisite for sustaining the longest siege that the place is capable of standing; 3d, the munitions of war with which it should be provided; 4th, the provisions, calculated for the garrison and the inhabitants who are to remain in the town; 5th, the supplies of timber or wood of all kinds, to palisade the covert-ways and other works, to make blindages, frame tambours, batteries, small powder magazines, galleries, &c.   All these estimates require on the part of the officers of both arms, great experience and knowledge in attack and defence.   The two most difficult points to establish, are, the strength of the garrison, and the quantity of cannon : these are subordinate to the estimated probable duration of the siege, and the nature of the fortifications of the site.   These general relations of material fortification with the other arms, and all the other essential accessaries to defence, can only be deduced from the relation that exists between the attack and the defence.   In consequence, we will suppose that all these supplies are in the fortress; and that it has been placed in a state of siege.   All parts of the works will be repaired, the banquettes of the parapets will be formed, the superior slopes will be levelled or made smooth, the barbettes constructed, heavy pieces of artillery will be placed in battery upon the cavaliers and salients of the bastions, the covert-ways will be palisaded and the barriers mounted on all the outlets, the souterrains will be aired, the powder and other munitions of war will be properly distributed in the several magazines, the supplies of provisions will be carefully and wisely arranged, the hospital department will be established, and several separate hospitals organized.

A company of artificers will be formed, consisting chiefly of carpenters, blacksmiths, and locksmiths, who will unceasingly work upon the palisadings and barriers of the covert-ways, and at the blindages and out-houses or sheds.   These artificers will prepare the timbers requisite for frame tambours, galleries, small powder magazines, batteries, &c.   Lastly, the garrison must be instructed by its commander in all the branches of ser-

vice, and will be daily exercised within and outside the works,
to render them skilful in the tactics of sieges and familiar with
all the kinds of combats and stratagems that take place in the
defence of fortresses. By these means the activity of the soldiers is maintained, and they are inspired with confidence and
accustomed to fatigues which preserve their health and stimu-
late their courage.

Arming the co-
vert-ways with
palisades & bar-
riers.
A covert-way, such as we have described, is not a disposition secure from an attack by storm ; it does not sufficiently
protect the retreat of the besieged from the outside into the works,
and from the covert-way into the re-entering places of arms
and ditches. We obtain for it these advantages to a certain
degree, by arming it with a strong palisading that extends along
the display of the crest of the glacis and along the line of fire
of all the banquettes ; and by closing all the great outlets with
double barriers, and the defiles of the traverses with single
barriers. The single palisadings are planted vertically upon
the banquettes 3 decimètres (1 foot) from the foot of the slope
of the breast height ; their heads rise about 4 decimetres (16
inches) above the crest of the glacis. By these dispositions, the
besiegers cannot penetrate into the covert-way ; the besieged
can freely move to any part of it ; and their retreat through the
defiles is protected ; but it is far from being effectually protected. It is proved by experience, that the barriers of the defiles of intermediate traverses tend only to impede the circulation of the troops, without being of any utility : it is therefore
sufficient to close with barriers the defiles of the salient and re-
entering places of arms. A covert-way thus prepared, and under the immediate effect of the fire of the principal works, has
long been considered as the fittest invention to produce an active and obstinate defence suitable to the character of good
troops. But in this respect, as in many others, fortification appears to the soldier in a state of weakness, which the improvements of the art will doubtless at a future day remove.
We will divide this chapter into three sections.

FIRST SECTION.

The attack and the defence during the first period of the siege.

THE FIRST PERIOD OF THE ATTACK.

The Conduct of the General who prepares to undertake a Siege ; the Investment ; Reconnaissances ; the Means of Attack ; general Description of all the Works ; Opening of the Trenches.

122. We will not discuss the political and military reasons which induce the General of an army to besiege a fortress whose reduction is of importance to him ; we will suppose that his intentions are against a fortress immediately upon the theatre of war.

122. Conduct of a general who intends to besiege a fortress ; the preparatory means, &c.

As soon as his plans are matured, they should be enveloped in the most profound secrecy ; he should execute marches and countermarches to divert the attention of the enemy who is watching him, and to induce them to strip the fortress of troops and ammunitions, or to neglect to provide it with those supplies necessary for its defence ; for independent of the material strength of fortifications, a place will make a bad and weak defence in proportion as it is unprovided with all the supplies that concur to procure a good defence.

By *means of attack*, is understood the re-union and organization of all the means necessary for undertaking a siege. These means are active and executive bodies, and inert and prepared materials. The first are men and horses ; the second are warlike machines, cannon, shot, bombs and other projectiles, fascines, pickets, saucissons, gabions, shovels, and mattocks, &c. All these materials are used by the soldiers according to the orders of the General ; and he should provide a sufficient quantity of these absolute essentials. Lists of them are drawn up by the chiefs of services, and they are collected in the depôts in rear of the army ; and the transport is arranged.

The means of attack in general.

All the articles that compose the material of the attack, constitute the grand park of artillery and the engineer park. They are both organized, as we will show hereafter, on points properly chosen within reach of the attack, and out of gun shot.

The parks of artillery and engineers.

The strength of the garrison of the place, the nature and

The strength of the besieging army.

extent of its fortifications, the fear that the enemy's army may arrive to the succour of the place, serve as a basis for calculating the effective numbers of the besieging army. We will suppose that the General has formed his army suitably in all respects ; and that the depôts situated in rear upon the line of operations, contain all the objects of which the artillery and engineer parks are composed.

The companies of artillery, and of artificers, and those of sappers and miners which are to follow the park, will be assembled. The sappers and miners will follow the engineer park, under the orders of the officers charged with the organization of the park. The other brigades of engineers will be at the head-quarters of the grand army, ready to march at the first order. They will have two wagons (*fourgons*) drawn by stout horses, and escorted by 20 mounted sappers. These wagons will contain ; 1st, all the instruments used for reconnoitring, drawing plans, and laying out works ; 2d, the maps, plans, &c. ; 3d, shovels, pick-axes, and axes, &c.

123. The first preparatory operation, called the investment ; the manoeuvres for this operation.

123. The first operation and the first offensive measure that the besieging army should undertake against the place, is its *investment ;* this should be effected with the greatest secrecy and despatch. To *invest a fortress*, is to march upon the position that it occupies with a corps of 5 to 6000 men, almost entirely dragoons and light cavalry. This corps envelops the fortress, occupies all the avenues to it, and cuts off all its communications with the exterior. By this operation the place is reduced to dependence on its own strength, and deprived of all the advantages that it might possess from its exterior relations.

The composition, movements and manoeuvres of the investing corps.

The General charged with the investment of a fortress, should know the extent of its fortifications, the strength of its garrison, and especially the nature of the country around it : he obtains these particulars from the engineers, who should accompany and aid him with their talents. The investing corps will always include two companies of horse artillery and more or less light infantry, according as the country is more or less broken and covered with hedges, woods, &c. The brigades of engineers, and the mounted sappers, will follow the investing corps.

As soon as the General of division charged with the investment of the place has arrived with the greatest expedition within about $1\frac{1}{2}$ myriamètre (3 leagues) of the fortress, he will divide his corps into several detachments which will move round the place and seize all the avenues.   On a given signal of several discharges of cannon, all the detachments will move forward towards the fortress and carry off all that they can find of men, cattle, provisions, &c. : they will seize all the advantageous posts, the villages, castles, parks, &c.

The investment has two chief objects : 1st, to shut and mask all the passages or roads, so that no succours can arrive in the place, and no person pass out of it : 2d, to facilitate the reconnaissance by the engineers of the fortifications and their environs.   To fulfil this double object, the General must establish around the place a chain of posts at a distance of about 2400 mètres (about 1½ miles)* from the town, and which by means of patroles form the *daily cordon*.   When there are villages or important posts within about 1800 mètres (2000 yards) of the place, they are seized and intrenched and occupied with infantry or dragoons ; in order to prevent the garrison from making excursions, and to preclude them from carrying off any posts, collecting provisions and forage, or facilitating the arrival of succours in the place.

The daily and nightly cordons, & the reconnaissance of the fortress.

The posts established during the day out of reach of the cannon of the place, are inadequate during the night to intercept the succours that attempt to penetrate into the fortress, and to enable the engineers to closely reconnoitre the immediate approaches of the place.   Therefore towards night-fall all the detachments quit the posts that they occupied during the day, and advance to within about 1200 mètres (1340 yards) of the works and form the *nightly cordon*, which is almost continuous ; they sieze every thing attempting to penetrate into the place, repulsing at the same time all the enterprises of the garrison to favour the introduction of succours and give intelligence of their situation to the hostile army.

The formation of the nightly cordon requires great ability and activity in the general ; it depends upon the nature of the site, the strength of the garrison, and the force of the detachments that the enemy's army may be able to make to impede the operation.   Accordingly, it is necessary that the army

* In the original, this is erroneously stated at 24,000 mètres (about 15 miles).   The typographical errors in the original work, are not fewer than about 200 : we have endeavoured as much as possible to discover and correct all of them.

TRANSLATOR.

which is about undertaking the siege, take such a position as will prevent the enemy from making any movements threatening the investing corps. When day begins to break, the engineers will commence reconnoitring and making notes ; and the whole will gradually retire upon the posts assigned for the day. These daily and nightly manœuvres will be repeated until the arrival of the army, which commonly takes place after three or four day's march.

124. Reconnaissance of the environs of the fortress, in relation to the lines of circumvallation and countervallation ; the use of the air-balloon, &c.

124. During the three or four days that the investment lasts, the engineers are constantly engaged in reconnoitring the environs of the place and the nature of the fortifications.

Protected by the troops, they will daily and nightly approach as near as possible, to discover the form of the ground, ascertain its first stratum, and judge of the state of the works. They will endeavour to make some prisoners, to interrogate them ; and they will gather from the country people all the particulars to form a clear idea of what they cannot see. Unquestionably a few ærial stations (*stations aérostatiques*) in balloons raised over several points and at a distance of 1500 mètres (1670 yards), will obtain for the engineers the most valuable knowledge of the nature of the works and of their figure and relations with the exterior ground ; they will thus be able to discover the exact position of all the magazines and other buildings, the communications established in the ditches, the armament of the place, and all the additions that the besieged attempt to make to the fortifications.

The general plan for establishing the plan of the lines : its scale.

From the first moment, the brigades of engineers will distribute among themselves the labour of a reconnaissance around the whole extent ; in order to form a general plan representing the environs within a distance of at least 3000 mètres (3350 yards). This plan will be on a scale of 1 millimètre to 10 mètres ($\frac{1}{25}$ of an inch to $33\frac{1}{3}$ feet). It must exhibit all the accidents of ground with the greatest exactness ; such as water courses, marshes, inundations, slopes, woods, quarries, &c. The nature of the soil will be carefully observed, to ascertain what difficulties it will oppose to cutting the trenches and constructing the works of earth. It must be ascertained whether the woods are within reach, and can furnish fascines, gabions and palisades, of which great quantities will be required. Finally, the state of the roads and paths that lead to the places of depôt, will be reconnoitred ; and such parts of them as are in bad order or broken up, will be repaired.   Ten or twelve thousand pioneers will be collected to work on the lines, and kept within sight in the villages.

All these reconnoitring and topographical labours should be completed within the four days that the investment lasts ; and the project for the lines of circumvallation and countervallation, will be submitted to the General in Chief by the commandant of engineers as soon as the army arrives to pitch its' camps around the place.

125. The *circumvallation* is an exterior defensive line surrounding the place, and substituted for the daily cordon composed of moving forces.   Its use is to cover the several camps established around the place, to prevent any enemy's troops by a bold stroke from getting into the town, and to preclude succours and spies from passing in during the night.   Its use is often of still greater importance—to repulse a succouring army which has arrived to raise the siege.   In this case, its characteristics are peculiar, and analogous to its important destination.

125. The circumvallation ; its use, and distance from the place.

In order that a besieging army may shut itself up within lines and push the siege with great vigour, two conditions are essentially necessary ; 1st, from the configuration of the ground, natural obstacles, and from the plan and arrangement of the lines, their points of attack must be few in number ; that is, the succouring army must only hope to be able to force them at two or three points : 2d, the besieging army must maintain its communications, to obtain supplies of provisions and ammunition.

The circumvallation is circularly established at a distance of about 3000 mètres (3340 yards) from the place, so that the camps may be beyond the range of random firing.

When the garrison is numerous, and can operate far from the fortifications and against the several camps, another defensive enclosure is established against them ; this is called the *countervallation,* and its defences face towards the place.   Its use is to secure the camps against the enterprises of the garrison ; and to facilitate and protect the operations of opening the trenches. The line of countervallation is established at a distance of about 2400 mètres (2670 yards) from the works ; the space of 600 mètres (670 yards) being required for the sites of the camps.

The line of countervallation.

It is rarely necessary that the countervallation should be a continuous line ; it should most generally consist of a few advantageous points, fortified to cover those camps that are too much exposed, and especially the artillery and engineer parks. It must however include the villages and posts advanced towards the place ; these it is important should be occupied, to establish in them *bivouacs*, &c.

The general project of the lines, is drawn upon the general plan of the environs of the fortress : and the military memoir upon the nature and strength, &c., of the fortifications, the convenience and advantages of the exterior ground, and the ease and conveniency of transport, &c., will also express the opinion of the *council of engineers* relative to what part of the works it is proper to attack.

This important document is presented to the General before the arrival of the columns and park of artillery ; and he will decide upon the manner in which the circumvallation is to be established, and what side of the fortress shall be attacked. The general project of the lines will then be modified agreeably to these two decisions ; and the position of the parks of artillery and engineers will be determined in the general plan, of which a copy will be given to the General commanding the artillery.

The distribution of the camps around the place, and the posting of the parks of artillery and engineers. The chief engineer, and the chief of the staff of the army, will lay down upon the general plan the separate camps of the different corps of the army : the disposition of these camps will be in relation to the nature of the ground and operations of the siege   The camp of each species of *arm*, is established on the ground adapted for it, and 200 mètres (225 yards) in rear of the circumvallation.   In each separate camp there will be stationed enough of infantry to flank the cavalry and line the intrenchments.   When infantry is deficient, dragoons will be used for this purpose.

The parks of artillery and engineers will be placed within reach of the points of attack designated by the General ; they must be concealed from the knowledge and view of the besieged.   Those parts of the circumvallation and countervallation that cover the parks, must be capable of a good defence; their flanks will be covered by some detached works.   The parks will be defended by infantry of the line and dragoons ; and the villages situated in advance of the circumvallation, will be occupied by light infantry and cavalry.   All the communications leading to the parks, will be free, and in good order.

The different positions that the corps of the besieging army occupy around the place, to intercept all succours from without, and to defend the lines that cover these positions, are called their *quarters.* It is obviously of the greatest importance to establish easy communications between all the quarters, in order to be able to carry from one quarter to another, and from the park to any quarter, the bodies of troops and the artillery and ammunition that circumstances may require. Accordingly if a river or brook separate quarters, bridges on trestles, boats or pontons, will be thrown across it ; each point will require three or four bridges, situated about 100 mètres (111 yards) apart ; and each bridge should be covered by a palisaded redan, provided with an interior redoubt. If the quarters be separated by inundations or marshes, two dikes must be constructed of fascines, sufficiently elevated not to be washed over by the highest waters. Lastly : if the quarters be separated by slopes and steep declivities, roads must be laid out and constructed with gentle and convenient slopes. And in general the different quarters must be considered as a circular system of defences, all whose parts should be connected and mutually support and protect each other, and must receive reinforcements from the corps of reserve.

The communications between the different quarters.

The lines composing a circumvallation, are drawn according to the principles that we have laid down in the Second Part. The topographical features of the ground, and the manner in which the General proposes to cover the siege, decide what system should be displayed upon each particular position ; it will be of continuous lines, or detached works, or abattis, or inundations whose dikes will be defended by works ; and all these defensive and separate positions will be connected by the communications that we have just described. But the principle to which the General of Engineers should most adhere, is to profit of the natural obstacles, to render several portions of the extent of the lines unassailable. This great end is obtained by taking advantage of water-courses, rendering marshes impassable, forming inundations, making woods impervious, and profiting of slopes, &c. ; and by making use of some artillery, and disposing it in fixed batteries to the best advantage. The circumvallating system being thus reduced by the art of fortification to a small number of assailable points ; these fronts will be fortified with their wings resting upon the inaccessible parts.

The principles upon which the circumvallation or lines are drawn. (PLATE III, fig 2)

which will project out beyond and flank them. These several partial fronts will be displayed either on right lines, flanked at intervals by salient works strongly constituted, or on lines concave to the exterior. All that has been said in the theory of field fortification, here directly applies ; both in respect to the general and auxiliary tracés, the details of the construction, and the armament and manner of defending the lines.

Drawing the lines, and the time required for their construction. The military memoirs and reconnaissances, enable the General of Engineers to determine upon the general plan the project of the lines at the very moment that he receives the last orders of the General in Chief. He immediately charges several officers with the laying out and construction of all the parts of the lines ; their total display or extent will be about 25 to 30,000 mètres (16 to 19 miles), exclusive of the countervallation. As fast as the different works are laid out, the sappers dispose the workmen drawn from the infantry of the line, and cause the earth to be removed agreeably to the profiles determined by the engineers. To relieve the troops and expedite the work, the 12 or 15,000 pioneers who were collected and guarded from the investment, are united to them. Whilst the works in earth are modelling under the direction of the soldiers of engineers, detachments of peasants and soldiers, conducted by the most intelligent sappers, will go into the woods and prepare the palisades, barriers, and abattis, &c. : all these materials will be brought into the lines as fast as they are ready.

We may with 20,000 labourers, either fatigue men from the line or people of the country, in 8 or 10 days construct the lines and make them as strong as their nature requires. They will be armed with barriers or chevaux de frise, palisades, &c., and provided with barbettes and embrasure epaulments, as has been already explained (art. 84).

Formation of the park of artillery, the supplies and collections of materials that should precede the opening of the trenches. Even if 8 or 10 days are not consumed in constructing the lines, this time is nevertheless necessary to complete the following measures : 1st, to make the reconnaissances and plans for opening the trenches : 2d, to collect and place in order in the grand park of artillery, the cannon of all kinds and calibers, shot, shells, powder, and other articles belonging to the artillery service : 3d, to form the engineers' park opposite the fronts of attack, and at a distance of 1500 mètres (1670 yards) from the place ; this park will contain the intrenching implements, the instruments for laying out the trenches, pickets, measuring lines, head-pieces (*pots en tête*) and cuirasses for the sappers and officers of engineers, &c. : 4th, to collect in the little park of artillery supplies of fascines for making the saucissons requisite for constructing the batteries ; and collecting likewise a certain quantity of gabions : 5th, to form in the neighbourhood of the engineers' park, two or three large collections of fascines, gabions, pickets, and sap fagots (*fagots de sape*). These various materials, of which an enormous quantity is used during a siege, are prepared in the woods by the country people and by the cavalry, who in a few hours learn to make fascines and gabions and carry them to the depôts. The sappers teach the soldiers to make gabions, fascines, and pickets ; they direct this work, and receive the articles as fast as they are completed. Every day these articles are paid for at the rate of 3 to 4 centimes (from ¾ to 1 cent) for each fascine, together with a picket ; and 10 centimes (1¾ cent) for each gabion. This is a judicious expenditure, as it is a stimulus to the workmen.

The trenches should not be opened until the materials necessary for constructing them and the batteries, are collected ; thus avoiding any languor in the works that the besieged might take advantage of, and which would very uselessly cost many lives. It is easily perceived, and confirmed by experience, that ten days are required to make all these preliminary and indispensable preparations.

The detailed description of the operations of a siege, shows how useful it is to have a well instructed and numerous body of sappers, to direct and superintend the labours, and at the same time to teach the soldiers of the line those simple constructions in which they are employed in war. *Reflections upon the duties of the soldiers of engineers.*

The circumvallation being at least 20,000 mètres (22,300 yards or 12¾ miles) in extent, will require 40,000 men to defend it ; and at least 10,000 men are necessary to guard the countervallation, and serve as a reserve to the circumvallation. Accordingly, an army of 50,000 men is requisite to guard the exterior during the operations of the siege. There are particular cases where the circumvallation of a fortress requires only a small extent of works, and consequently much fewer men to defend the lines. Besides the army that watches the enemy without, there is required another and special corps, consisting almost entirely of infantry, to carry on the operation of the siege. The first, is called the *army of observation* ; and the lat- *The number of troops necessary for defending the lines.*

The army of observation.

The besieging army. ter, the *besieging army*. These two corps d'armée united, commonly constitute a body of 60 to 70,000 men.

In 1793 the combined armies, upwards of 100,000 strong, under the command of the King of Prussia, laid siege to Mentz. In the same year, the combined armies of England and Austria invested Valenciennes with 120,000 men. The Prince of Cobourg besieged Quesnoy with 60,000 men ; and the Duke of York could not invest Dunkirk and Bergues with 50,000 men.

In 1794 the fortresses of Valenciennes and Quesnoy were enveloped and besieged by a detachment of the French army about 20,000 strong ; but in this case, the besieging army had only to contend with the garrison.

During the same year, the French laid siege to Charleroi with an army 80,000 strong.

In 1796 Napoleon invested Mantua with 20,000 men ; but the siege was undertaken by only 9 to 10,000 men. The blockade of this same fortress was effected by 15 to 18,000 men.

This variation in the strength of besieging armies, depends upon the topographical situation of the place, the strength and energy of the garrison, and the circumstances in which the belligerent armies are placed.

126. The conduct of the general during the siege.

126. Many military writers have attempted to determine the great and important question—What course of conduct ought to be pursued by the General who undertakes to besiege a place ? Each one has his peculiar opinion upon this subject, supported by authorities equally weighty, and by the conduct of renowned Generals who have sometimes acted in one manner, and sometimes in another.

They have proposed to examine, whether lines of circumvallation were necessary and useful ; whether the army should enclose itself within them in mass, to resist a succouring army ; or whether it should keep the field in an attitude of observation, and march to meet and fight the army of succour.

The first part of the question is resolved by what we have precedingly said. Lines are useful and even necessary to intercept all succours, and to enable the besieging army to repulse detachments of greater or less strength that attempt to make their way into the town ; and they are indispensable in cases where the army is too weak to be separated into two parts, and may expect to repulse the succouring army by defending

well constituted lines which expose few assailable fronts to the
enemy, and upon which formidable obstacles have been raised.
Finally ; lines may collect an army of observation that has been
beaten, and afford it the means of recovering from the check
that it has sustained, and of continuing the siege ; but here it is
supposed that the subsistence of the army is secured, and that
the enemy cannot cut off all its communications.

Before we lay down the general precepts, it will be well to
examine a few great events recorded in military annals.   This
examination may guide us in the solution of the second part of
this interesting question.

The method of erecting lines and enclosing an army within
them, is derived from the ancients, who constantly used them,
and devoted to their construction the time and labour necessary
to render them almost impregnable.   The use of them was neglected and forgotten until the sixteenth century, when the
Princes of Nassau, and the ablest Generals of those times, re-
vived the use of them with energy and the greatest success.
After the example of the ancients, they constructed their lines
with all the care of which the art was susceptible. By degrees
lines were constructed with less care, and they were attacked
with more skill and boldness ; and as they were frequently
forced, they gradually lost their pristine reputation, and in our
days have fallen under a kind of proscription.

eneral consi-
derations   on
lines.

In 1654 Arras was invested by the great Condé, and by the
Archduke Leopold ; their army, consisting of Lorrains, Spaniards and Italians, was enclosed within lines constructed with
great care and covered with obstacles. Turenne marched to
succour the place ; but finding that it would be very difficult to
force the lines, he formed the plan of investing the enemy in
their own lines, and depriving them of subsistence by cutting off all their exterior communications.   Notwithstanding
the admirable enveloping dispositions that this illustrious General made with his army, the enemy still succeeded in procur-
ing provisions ; and they pushed the siege so warmly, that Turenne, after keeping his station a month, determined to fight
and force the lines.   If all the quarters had been guarded like
those in which Condé commanded, it is probable that the attack would not have been attempted ; but Turenne knew how
to take advantage of the incapacity of the General who commanded the Spanish quarter. The defences that covered this

The siege of
Arras, invested
by Condé in 1654.

The lines forc-
ed by Turenne.

quarter, formed a salient easily embraced ; and here Turenne resolved to penetrate with the regiment that bore his name.

Three false attacks were directed against the other quarters, to restrain them ; whilst Turenne carried sword in hand the quarters of the Spaniards, and compelled Condé to retire under Cambrai with the wrecks of his army. The Archduke sought refuge in Douai, under the protection of a squadron which carried him through the baggage of the French army.

The siege of Valenciennes. invested by Turenne in 1656.
The lines form ed by the great Condé.
On the 15th of June, 1656, Turenne suddenly invested Valenciennes, and covered his army, which was 25,000 strong, by lines of circumvallation. Marshal De la Ferté was encamped on Mount Azin, and by a single quarter invested the citadel on the left bank of the Scheldt. The king's household troops, and the Lorrains, had their quarters between the upper inundation and the Rouelle ; and the space between the Rouelle and the lower inundation, was invested by Turenne.

Bridges on boats, and dikes of fascines, were established across the inundations, to communicate between the quarters. These dikes and bridges were established with great difficulty ; for the enemy by means of the sluices of Bouchain, repeatedly swelled the waters.

Whilst Turenne was pushing the siege with the greatest vigour, the Prince of Condé and Don Juan of Austria assembled an army of about 20,000 men under Douay ; and about the 18th July came and encamped opposite and within half cannon shot of the quarters of the Lorrain and household troops, with their left resting upon the Scheldt and their right upon a brook.

Turenne seeing the Spaniards so near his intrenchments, now thought only of defending them ; he suspended the labours of the siege, keeping the garrison in check with a corps of 7 to 8,000 men, and distributed his army behind his intrenchments. A corps of reserve of infantry and cavalry, was destined to move to the support of the most threatened points.

Condé, after very closely reconnoitring the lines, did not deem it prudent to point his attack against the quarter of the household troops, nor against that in which Turenne commanded in person ; the exellent dispositions of this illustrious adversary, left him no hopes of success. But having perceived that Marshal De la Ferté who defended Mount Azin, was badly intrenched and not on the alert, he formed the project of attacking him in the night sword in hand. This consummate Ge-

neral passed the Scheldt, and at the first peep of dawn fell upon the intrenchments of Marshal de la Ferté, which he forced ;
making a great many prisoners, and among them the Marshal
himself.   It was in vain that Turenne strove to pass the reserve
across the dikes ; all the battalions that succeeded in crossing,
were charged and overthrown by Condé.   General Marsin attacked Turenne's quarters with 4,000 men ; but he was repulsed, and compelled to retreat.

Turenne finding that Marshal de la Ferté was taken, and that
his troops were flying towards Condé, evacuated his intrenchments ; and putting himself in battle array, retreated upon
Quesnoy.

The campaign of 1706 in Italy, presents an event of a similar nature to those under consideration, and deserves our attention.   The examination of this campaign and comparing it with
that of 1800, would form a valuable source of instruction for
the young officers and students.   They would behold how two
great Generals could by the force of their genius and character
bring a campaign to a close by a great battle, which made them
masters of all Italy.   But we have already stated in the First
Part, the reasons that prevent us from entering upon this wide
field of glory.

The siege of Turin, invested by the French in 1706.   (See PLATE III, figs. 1 and 2.)

We must take a retrospect of the origin of the movements
and manœuvres of the hostile General, to arrive at the lines of
Turin and there give battle to the French army.

In the month of May 1706, Prince Eugene took command of
the Austrian army, and moved to the Adige with 20,000 men.
At the same time, Vendome surrendered the command of the

The lines forced by Prince Eu-gene.

French army to the young Duke of Orleans, who was to be
under the direction of General Marsin.

On the 13th of May, Marshal De la Feuillade invested Turin
with 64 battalions and 80 squadrons, and prepared to lay siege
to it with 164 pieces of battering artillery.   The place was
circumvallated, and the lines fortified with all the skill of art.

The ground on the right bank of the Po being very much
broken, all this part was circumvallated by some slight intrenchments drawn upon the declivities of the mountains, and by
some redoubts or small forts placed upon their summits.   From
the Po to the Doire, a circumvallation and countervallation
were constructed with great care ; the part adjacent to the
Doire covered the attacks, and contained the park, ovens, (*fours*

de munition), &c.   In the fork formed by the Doire and the Stura, a circumvallation and countervallation were drawn; the intrenchments of the first, were almost a straight line; and they were carelessly constructed, because it was not supposed that they could be attacked.   The course of the Stura, and a few intrenchments upon its right bank, completed the circumvallation.

(See Fig. 1.)   The Duke of Orleans occupied the right bank of the Adige opposite Rivoli, and observed the movements of Eugene; his army was about 20,000 strong.

Prince Eugene perceiving that the Duke was making timid movements and had not a force capable of stopping him, formed the project of reinforcing his army, of passing the Adige and the Po and ascending the right bank of this river, and forming a junction with the Duke of Savoy who with 12,000 men was encamped at La Motte; and then with these united forces (amounting to 45,000 men, including 6,000 cavalry), to attack the French army in its lines.   The Prince was not able to put himself in motion 'till the beginning of July, when with an army of 32 to 35,000 men he passed the Adige and Tartaro, drove back all the French posts, effected the passage of the Po at Policella, and ascended the river; whilst the Duke of Orleans with 40 battalions and 57 squadrons coasted its left bank and endeavoured to impede his march, to give time to the Duke of Feuillade to capture Turin.

Eugene overcomes all obstacles.   On the 19th August he carries the important post of Stradella; on the 28th he crosses the Tanaro at Isola, below Asti, and forms a junction with the Duke of Savoy at the camp of Stellon.

On the 30th of August he places his army, now nearly 45,000 strong, in order of battle in the camp of Stellon, and throws two bridges across the Po.   The Duke of Orleans re-enters Piedmont with his 25,000 men, and joins the besieging army.

On the 4th September Eugene with his army crosses the Po between Carignan and Montcallier, and moves round the quarters of the French army, by marching upon the Doire towards Pianessa.   On the 6th, the whole army passes the Doire and takes post offensively between this river and the Stura, with its right resting on Pianessa, and its left at the Venery.

Eugene, after reconnoitring the French quarters, determined to attack the intrenchments still in an imperfect state between the Stura and the Doire.   He expected to easily carry them, because of their weakness ; and to thus command the intrenchments on the right bank of the Doire ; and having forced the line, to take all the attacks in reverse and cut off the retreat of the siege artillery and baggage.

Since the 30th of August, the French had vigorously attacked and continually assaulted the works on the fronts of attack of the citadel ; but they were repulsed by the garrison who were animated by the presence of an army of succour, commanded by a General whose talents and genius gave him a marked ascendancy over his adversaries.

As soon as the army of observation had taken post within the lines, the Duke of Orleans proposed in the council of war, to march out and fight the enemy ; observing that the army, which consisted of 97 battalions and 120 squadrons, was too scattered within the lines, &c.   Count Marsin being opposed to this admirable proposition, it was determined to await the enemy, to re-enforce the intrenchments between the Stura and Lucento, and to arm them with 40 pieces of cannon.

On the 7th of September at the first dawn of day, the attack took place.   After a most tremendous battle, the lines were forced from the right to the left of the enemy ; and Eugene gained possession of the two bridges across the Doire.   The efforts of the garrison, added to the first successes of the enemy, threw the French army into the greatest disorder.   They raised the siege, burnt their magazines, spiked and abandoned their artillery, and retreated under Pignerol by Canoret and Montcallier, after losing 8,000 men and all their siege equipage and train.

Attack on the lines the 7th September 1706. (See PLATE III, and its explanatory Table.)

These events, the success of which had transcended the expectations of the General, who had only calculated on probabilities, made him master of all Italy.   The famous battle of Marengo, after a series of operations of which modern military annals afford no examples, in a similar manner put the French in possession of this country.

At the siege of Phillipsburg in 1734, the army of observation remained within its lines, and Eugene was not able to force them.   It is proper to observe, that the besieging army had its

Siege of Phillipsburg in 1734 ; the succouring army could not force the lines.

communications secured ; and that the Marshals D'Asfeld and
Berwick had constructed the lines in the strongest manner.

Blockade of
Maubeuge by the
Prince of Co
bourg in 1793:
In the month of September 1793, the Prince of Cobourg,
commander of the Austrian army, moved with 60,000 men on
Maubeuge and formed the blockade of the place and of its intrenched camp, by a kind of investment consisting of lines of
The lines forc-
ed by the French
army.
circumvallation and countervallation.   The French army,
40,000 strong, commanded by General Jourdan, marched
against the Prince of Cobourg and attacked him at Wattignies ;
and forcing this part of his lines, compelled him to raise the
blockade.

Siege of Char-
leroi in 1746 ; the
army within its
lines.
In 1746 the French General, the Prince of Conti, invested
Charleroi and caused lines to be constructed by 20,000 peasants ; within which he shut himself up.   These lines were not
attacked.

Siege of Char
leroi invested by
the French in
1794 ; the suc-
couring army re-
pulsed   (See
PLATE   XK,
vol. I)
The siege of Charleroi by the French army in 1794, was
covered by the army disposed in quarters or intrenched camps,
the whole of which formed a line of circumvallation.   Just at
the moment that the fortress surrendered, an army of succour
of 100,000 men attacked the French army in its camps or positions ; we have already seen from the description of the battle of Fleurus, that this army was repulsed with immense
slaughter.

In this battle there was a peculiar circumstance of topography very favourable to the French army.   The investment being only on the left bank of the Sambre, the army was enabled
to concentrate on a semi-circular position.

We will now relate a few events in which the besieging
army covered the operation of the siege by an army of observation, which, stationed without the lines, followed the movements of the enemy.   This is the method now-a-days most
generally adopted.

Siege of Dun-
kirk, invested by
Turenne in 1658.
Turenne at the head of the combined armies of France and
England, invested Dunkerque in 1658, and opened trenches before the place.   Whilst the siege was pushing with vigour,
Condé and Don Juan assembled under Furnes an army of
Spaniards and other troops, and resolved to raise the siege.   On
the 15th June, the enemy having made a strong reconnaissance
with 30 squadrons, Turenne moved to the Downs and there intrenched himself.

On the 16th, the Spanish army consisting of 15,000 men, including 9000 cavalry, arrived and formed in order of battle within 4000 mètres (4500 yards) of Turenne's intrenchments. This General on seeing that the enemy were preparing to attack him, resolved to anticipate them. Leaving 4000 men in the trenches, he marched out of his intrenchments at noon day with 12,000 men, and surprised Don Juan in his position upon the Downs; and Condé, although he performed prodigies of valour, could not check the disorder that the Spaniards, warmly pursued by the British and French cavalry, carried into all the line. The victory gained by Turenne was complete, and enabled him to prosecute the siege of Dunkerque. *The prince of Condé's army repulsed by the army of observation.*

Of this battle it is to be remarked, that there were in the armies only 10 or 12 field pieces; that Turenne in forming his order of battle, had intermingled platoons of infantry among squadrons of cavalry; and that Condé in his order of battle, had covered his cavalry by his infantry, and supported them by matchlockmen posted in the ditches.

We have seen in the relation of the battle of Malplaquet (66), that Eugene and Marlborough preferred to meet and give battle to the French at Malplaquet, to awaiting them in their lines. *The siege of Mons, invested by Eugene and Marlborough in 1709: the army of observation beats the succouring army at Malplaquet.*

If Prince Eugene, in 1712, had not kept his army of observation too near the lines of Landrecies, Marshal Villars would not have succeeded in cutting his line of communication with Denain and capturing his magazines at Marchiennes. *The siege of Landrecies in 1712; the succouring army raises the siege.*

Marshal Saxe was covering the siege of Tournai with an army of observation enclosed within lines; but as soon as he found that the hostile army was advancing upon his quarters, he marched out to meet the enemy and fought the battle of Fontenoy. *The siege of Tournai in 1745: the army of observation gives battle and is victorious at Fontenoy.*

In 1793, the hostile armies of the coalition covered the siege of Valenciennes by two corps d'armée of observation. These corps masked all the debouchès by which the French army could reach the place. *Siege of Valenciennes in 1793; covered by an army of observation.*

In 1796 the siege of Mantua was pressing with vigour by a division of the French army, covered by an army of observation, when suddenly the enemy advance on all sides to raise the siege and envelop the French army whose situation became most critical. Napoleon, instead of enclosing himself within circumvallating positions in which he would have had to con- *Siege of Mantua, invested by the French army in 1796: the general raises the siege to march and fight the succouring army.*

tend with very superior forces, preferred to raise the siege and abandon his artillery, and to march against the divided forces of the famous and skilful Wurmser. But it belongs only to geniuses of the first order to conceive such splendid plans even in the very moment of danger, and to execute them with a rapidity and precision that secures success.

General reflections.
The exposition of these various events, proves that the General must be governed by circumstances in his measures for covering the siege. Nevertheless it may in general be laid down as a rule, that it is almost always dangerous to await the succouring army within lines ; for the greatest Generals have been beaten in them. And we may add, that the bad disposition of lines, the defects of their plan, and the little care taken in their construction, powerfully influence the fate of the army that defends them*.

* Maxim 1. An army covering a siege should never let itself be attacked by the enemy, but must anticipate him. It is by beating the army of succour that we make sure of the fall of a fortress ; and we are more certain of vanquishing this army by marching against, than by quietly awaiting in a position its approach.

2d. If the enemy present an imposing force, we must raise the siege, concentrate our forces, and attack him according to the established rules, by overwhelming one extremity of his line by an united effort.

3d. If we beat the army of succour, we can always resume and push the siege or blockade; and the army will be unable to return before the reduction of the place.

4th. When an army in consequence of preceding offensive movements and successes undertakes a siege, it should not cover it by a near position ; but should profit of its successes and push its enemy as far as possible ; for the longer and more extended the line is that must be traversed to succour a place, the more difficult it will be to succour it, and the greater time it will require. And the time that the army may gain by defending this line inch by inch, will be sufficient to reduce the fortress. If however the enemy at last succeed in getting sufficiently near to leave us to suspect the success of his enterprise, the army can suddenly and quickly raise the siege, call in the troops that formed it, and strike a last blow.

These maxims have been suggested by the admirable conduct of Napoleon at Mantua. By neglecting these maxims at Olmutz, Frederick lost all the fruits of the brilliant opening of the campaign of 1758. But they are not applicable to the circumstances of the siege of Prague. There, it was a beaten and refuged army that was to be captured ; by raising the blockade, he must have lost the fruits of the victory; the raising of the siege was therefore the last thing to be proposed.—*Jomini, vol.* 1, *p.* 152.　　　　　　　TRANSLATOR.

We must conclude from the preceding ; 1st, that lines are General conclusions on the advantages of lines, and on the conduct of the besieging general. weak, because of their great extent and circular form ; for when one point is forced, all the other parts are taken in flank and rear, and the place is succoured :

2d. The general battle is fought so near the operations of the siege, that this proximity renders it impossible for the army of observation to protect the raising of the siege by a retreat suitably regulated ; and hence it is that all the besieging train and equipage necessarily fall into the hands of the garrison, if they possess the least activity :

3d. Lines are necessary to stop small succours, and to prevent *soups de main.* If the General foresee that the succouring army will not be numerous ; and if he cannot divide his own army into two parts, which would be too weak to act separately ; he should in this case remain within his lines, and continually improve and strengthen them. He will keep out large detachments to gain intelligence of the enemy ; and as soon as he learns that the army of succour is assembling, he will form an active van guard which will keep in presence of, and observe and harass the enemy. Fields of battle will be reconnoitred between the fortress and the points of assemblage of the hostile forces ; and even defensive dispositions will be made on those positions which are susceptible of them. As soon as the van guard and other detached corps give advice of the march and movements of the army of succour, the General will choose his measures ; either he will remain in his lines and there form in order of battle, recalling the troops from the siege, and only leaving in the trenches the force necessary to restrain the garrison ; or he will march out to meet the succouring army, surprise it on the march, and give battle ; or he will raise the siege and send the artillery and equipages into some neighbouring fortress, and with all his forces march to destroy the succours, and then return and renew the siege.

From this plain exposition, we see that the tactics relative to sieges are a very difficult and complex part of war ; and it is not surprising that so many deservedly celebrated Generals have failed in operations of this nature.

127. Whilst the lines are constructing, the army establishing 127. The reconnoissances for choosing the front of attack : the operations prior to opening the trenches. itself in its quarters, and every thing preparing in the parks of artillery and engineers, the brigades of engineers will daily and nightly be moving about the place and reconnoitring it to de-

termine the fronts of attack. For this purpose a plan of the
fortifications and ground to a distance of 1500 mètres (1670
yards), is made with the greatest possible accuracy, and on a
scale of 5 centimètres (2 inches) to 100 mètres (111 yards).
As there are few fortresses of which there are not pretty accurate plans, advantage must be taken of these, which are verified
by new operations with the graphomèter or repeating circle, or
even with the circumferentor. As fast as the engineers construct the plan for determining the fronts of attack, they will
draw up military memoirs of all the circumstances that they
discover, on the nature of the ground and the advantages afforded by its form, on the supposed strength of the different
fronts that they have reconnoitred, and on the waters around
the place ; and they will add what they have seen themselves,
and the reports of the country people and prisoners. Now it is
that the use of the balloon will enable them to procure the most
valuable particulars ; by ascending in it to a certain height,
they will see into the interior of the place, discover the new
intrenchments upon which the garrison are working, look down
into the ditches and judge of the strength of the counterscarps
and the armament of the covert-ways, and discover the means
of making inundations, &c.

The general plan for determining the fronts of attack : When they have laid down upon the general plan for choosing
the fronts of attack, all the accidents of ground and all the parts
of the fortification whose figure and position they have been
able to determine ; and when the memoir of the reconnaissances
is digested, we are then able to select the fronts of attack.

the manner of selecting them. This choice consists in determining what part of the fortress
to penetrate. This selection is not indifferent ; by the manner
in which it is made, it is discoverable whether the engineer
has a coup d'œil sufficiently skilful and scientific to combine
together all the elements that can secure and accelerate the success of so grand an enterprise.

No army, whatever may be its numerical strength and means,
can attack and overthrow the whole perimeter of a place. The
attack must be confined to one or two fronts, against which the
trenches are opened and all the measures of the attack displayed. When two distinct attacks are made, one of them is the
real, and the other a *false* attack. This mode is frequently
adopted to weary out the garrison, and to advance the *real* attack with more expedition.

All the fronts of a place are not equally strong, nor so constructed as to oppose an equal resistance ; it is consequently very important to select the weakest.　But in this selection we must not only take into consideration the intrinsic strength of the works, but likewise the nature of the ground on which the trenches are to be cut, and the position of the front with respect to the ease of transport and supplies : this latter consideration often inclines us to prefer attacking a stronger front.

The General, after weighing with wisdom the reports and opinions of the chiefs of the engineers and artillery, decides definitively what fronts are to be attacked.

The fronts of attack being fixed, the officers of engineers will make a particular or separate plan, comprehending the fronts of attack and the collateral works that can see and influence the progress of the attacks.　All the accidents of ground, whether seen or guessed, are drawn with the greatest care ; and the covert-ways, the width of ditches and the thickness of the parapets will be laid down as exactly as possible.　The prolongations of the faces and capitals of all the works, will be marked out on the ground with the greatest exactness ; these lines are determined by the eye or by trigonometrical operations.　On each prolongation, at a distance of 50 mètres (55½ yards), two pickets are planted, called *directing pickets* (*piquets de repaire*); and the distance from these pickets to the outmost salients of the covert-way, is measured.　The positions of these pickets are laid down upon the plan with the same reference (*cote*) that they have upon the ground.　This corrected and detailed plan, is called the *directing plan of the attacks*.

The polygon formed by the directing pickets, and which embraces the prolongations of the faces and capitals of all the works of the front of attack, serves as a base for all the graphical operations to which the successive measures of the siege give rise.

It must be observed, that the trigonometrical operations and reconnaissances should be feigned all around the place ; in order that the besieged may not be able to judge which are the real points of attack.

The only manner of determining the prolongations of the faces of works and their capitals, is to draw them upon the directing plan ; this will indicate nearly the points of ground through which they pass, and then the prolongations found are

The directing plan of the attacks ; determining the prolongations of the faces and capitals of the works.

The modes of finding the prolongations of the faces and capitals of the work.

verified by seeing whether they coincide with those obtained
by the directing plan : these latter will be corrected according
to the observations best made and frequently repeated.   It is
chiefly at the rising and setting sun that the planes of the parapets, differently enlightened, enable us to distinguish the ridges
and consequently the prolongations of the covering lines, to
which we devote our attention when we cannot distinguish the
magistral lines.   As to the capitals, the salient angles of the
works and the point formed by the palisades of the salients of
their covert-way, will give them with sufficient accuracy.   But
if they be required with more critical accuracy, they may be
obtained by simple operations with the graphometer, and even
(PLATE IV) with the magnetic compass.   Let EA be the base included between the prolongations of the faces of the bastion (B) and drawn
at a distance of about 7 to 800 mètres (780 to 890 yards) ; find
with the graphometer the angles $eEA = e$, and $aAE = a$, which
these prolongations make with the base AE ; and we will have for
the value of the summit angle $= z = \dfrac{180° - a - e}{2}$;

and for the angle that the capital makes with the base

$= x = \dfrac{180° + a - e}{2}$.

If the operation be performed with the magnetic compass,
we will have for the angle that the needle makes with the ca-
pital $= y = \dfrac{e' - a'}{2}$ or $\dfrac{a' - e'}{2}$, calling a' and e' the angles that
the needle of the compass makes with the prolongations of the
faces ; this established, find on the base EA with the instrument
the point c of the capital.

The critical determination of the prolongations of the faces,
is of very great importance ; that of the capitals is not so much
so, because it is indifferent whether we advance upon the capitals themselves, or upon lines whose directions differ very little
from theirs.

The general
depot of engi-
neers in front of
the attacks : the
artillery depot.

Opposite the front of attack and in a place about 1200 mètres
(1335 yards) from the works and sheltered from their fire, will
be formed the *general depôt of engineers ;* and in this will be
assembled the necessary implements for opening the trenches,
and large collections of *fascines, gabions,* pickets, &c.   The
depôt of artillery will be situated in the vicinity of that of the
engineers ; and there will be collected in it the fascines, gabions,

pickets, &c., necessary for laying out and constructing the batteries ; and here the saucissons, &c., will be made.

All the preliminary particulars having been established in the best manner, the commandant of engineers will draw upon the directing plan of the attack the project of opening the trenches : by this is understood the *first parallel* and the boyaux of communication leading from the separate depôts to this parallel.

The project of opening the trenches.

128. Let us pause a moment in describing the operations of the besiegers, to consider their aim and situation, and the means to which they must have recourse.

128 The design of the besiegers, and the means that they are compelled to use to accomplish it.

In besieging a fortress, the object of the General is to get possession of a position that restrains or may favour his operations. As the besieged are eight or ten times weaker than the besiegers, the latter will carry it the moment that they find themselves opposed man to man to the former, as in the open field. But as the material constitution of the field of battle of the besieged, prevents the contact of the two hostile armies ; the besiegers are necessitated to procure the practicability of contact, by overthrowing all the obstacles that separate them from the besieged and clearing the way to get at them.

The besiegers cannot succeed in an attack by storm even by using their whole force.   If such attacks sometimes succeed, it is in consequence of circumstances that do not commonly exist ; such as a garrison that does not properly guard itself and may be surprised, a fortification accessible in certain points, or the cowardice or treason of a governor. It frequently happens in the case of a fortress surprised, that the garrison by fighting in order in the streets and squares, succeed in repulsing the enemy : this was actually the case at the famous surprise of Cremona.   Eugene penetrated into the place and captured the governor ; but notwithstanding the great advantages that he obtained at the beginning of the action, the garrison succeeded in driving him out of the place with great loss.

The attack by storm is impossible (Se Folard, Feuquieres, and De Cessac, on the surprise of fortresses and posts.)

M. De Bavière surprised Ulm, the capital of Suabia, by introducing into the town officers and soldiers in disguise.

Mentz might have been surprised in 1793 by a corps of grenadiers ; but General Custine did not stand in need of such a bold stroke ; the place was given up to him in consequence of an understanding that he had with the citizens.

Let us return to our subject.   If the besiegers hazarded an attack by storm, they would probably succeed in penetrating into the covert-ways and in getting possession of them. They would then have to descend into the ditches and raise ladders against the scarps, under the fire of untouched batteries and of covered and unapproachable musketry. The success of such an operation is evidently impossible ; and the elite of an army would be immolated in the attempt.

The attack by skill and industry is the only possible mode : the means that it uses.

As the conquest of a fortress must not cost the besiegers too great sacrifices of lives, it is absolutely necessary to adopt the method of an attack by skill and industry ; the execution of this requires indeed a considerable length of time—but it spares the blood of the assailants. With time and labour, this mode of attack has in all ages obtained for the besiegers the means of employing their active forces against the besieged.

The means used in attack since the invention and use of artillery, consist of ; 1st, selecting one or two fronts of attack ; 2d, silencing the fires of the batteries of these fronts ; 3d, making ways that lead under cover up to the foot of the ramparts ; 4th, opening these ramparts and making practicable breaches in them. When all these labours are completed in such a manner that the besieged cannot prevent the besiegers from circulating in them from the camps, it is evident that then the latter, who are seven or eight times stronger than the besieged, can invade the place and compel them to lay down their arms.

The kinds of batteries used in sieges: the general mode of posting them.

Experience has established 600 mètres (670 yards) or thereabouts, to be the distance at which cannon and mortar batteries should be posted to obtain accurate and effective fires.

Howitzer batteries are established at a distance of 300 mètres (335 yards) from the objects that they are to batter.

Stone mortars are placed near the works, and at a distance not exceeding 60 mètres (67 yards).

The effective range of grenades does not exceed 30 mètres (100 feet).

Observations on the effects of ricochet and direct batteries.

We have seen (52) that batteries are distinguished into direct, and enfilading which fire in *ricochet*. Formerly only direct batteries were used to combat the batteries of a fortress ; and the celebrated Vauban was the first who conceived the idea of enfilading and ricochet batteries. This mode of firing consists in seizing the prolongations of the covering lines of the faces and branches of works, and establishing on these directions batteries of cannon, mortars, and howitzers, which are fired with little charges under small angles of inclination ; their shot falling in the terra-plains under small angles of descent, make successive bounds or ricochets, destroying the wheels and carriages of all the artillery (*prennent en rouage*) mounted upon the rampart. Experience has constantly proved that these batteries produce so great an effect, that in a very short time they silence the fire of the place. Bombs are fired in *ricochet* by mounting the mortars upon cannon carriages, or even by fixing the bomb to the muzzle of cannon.

Batteries of cannon of heavy calibers, and mining, are the two means by which a breach is speedily effected in the most solid revêtement or in any kind of wall.

The means by which a breach is effected and made practicable, and by which all kinds of walls are overthrown.

Twenty-four and thirty-six pounders fired at a distance of 100 mètres (111 yards) with the maximum charge, shake and overthrow the thickest revêtements. We begin by making with cannon two vertical cuts including the portion of the wall that is to be battered down ; the foot of the wall is then sapped by a deep horizontal cut or groove at ¼ of its height ; and the firing is by volleys or salvoes at different heights, until the revêtement and parapet are crumbled into the ditch. In order to make the breach more practicable, a great quantity of howitzes are fired at its summit, and render the ascent more gentle and assailable.

We will at present consider mining only as the most expeditious means of making a breach, and of subverting all kinds of walls : this was the first light in which this arm was viewed.

(See Vauban's Treatise on Mines, Foissac's edition.)

To mine a revêtement, we begin by making with cannon a cavity at the foot of the wall, into which the miner introduces himself ; and whence he penetrates by cutting a branch into the thickness of the revêtement until he meets with the earth or even farther, according to the height of the scarp. Then two miners make on each side of it at right angles, a branch along the wall ; these two side branches are more or less protracted, according to the rules of the art. At the extremity of each branch, the miners establish a mine (*fourneau*) or chamber to receive the proper charge ; they then place the end of the saucisson in the centre of the powder, lay the trough (*auget*), fill up and ram the branches, and conduct the other end of the saucisson into the ditch : it is fired by means of a match, &c.

When the miner is set to work at the revêtement of a scarp, the entrance of the mine is covered by long planks covered over with tin and resting against the wall ; and the gap or chasm on the side of the flank, is masked by a traverse of bags of earth, &c.

By inspecting the plates of Vauban's Treatise on Mines, the students and young officers will immediately understand the labours and measures for making an offensive mine; they should likewise examine that plate in which all the mining implements are drawn with the greatest accuracy.

When mines are well calculated, they almost always subvert that portion of the revêtement which it was intended to overwhelm: and the breach is then made practicable with cannon and howitzers.

Consequence. It follows from what we have here laid down, that the execution of a siege is reducible to making practicable breaches in the body of the place, and making ways for the troops to advance and penetrate into the place in columns of attack. It is the arrangement, nature and construction of all the offensive works made before a besieged place, that constitute the theory of attack.

129. General description of the figure and arrangement of all the works used to reduce a fortress: the first parallel (PLATE IV) 129. It is proved by the experience of sieges, that the first offensive position that the besiegers should take against the besieged, is a continuous intrenchment drawn concentrically at about 600 mètres (670 yards) from the outmost salients and embracing the front of attack and the collateral parts which overlook the approaches of this front. At a distance of 600 mètres, the fire and sorties of the garrison are to be little feared; yet at this distance the attacking batteries may produce considerable effect. This first work is called the *first parallel*, and its wings are often supported by redoubts.

General profile of all the offensive works of the attack. The configuration of all the offensive works of the besiegers, is deduced from the very object to be obtained by them: 1st, They should cover the troops and be proof against artillery. 2d, They should be quickly laid out and constructed. 3d, They should be defended by forces superior to those of the enemy. It follows, that the general profile of all these works is without ditches; and that its terra-plain is sunk below the natural ground to a depth sufficient to immediately cover the workmen by the excavated mass formed into a parapet.

The first batteries, whether direct, or ricochet: the approaches by boyaux made zig-zag. We depart from the first parallel, 1st, to establish under its protection batteries of cannon, howitzers and mortars, to silence the fires of the place which impede the progress of the attack; 2d, to advance by *boyaux* laid out in zig-zag and defiled from the most advanced works, and leading to within 300 mètres (335 yards) of the salients.

The second pa-rallel: the new batteries.

When the besiegers find themselves at a distance of 300 mè-tres from the salients, they lay out and construct a *second pa-rallel*, whose wings are supported by redoubts furnished with artillery. Under the protection of this second parallel, they establish those direct and ricochet batteries that the case re-quires; hence they again debouche to move forward and gain the foot of the glacis ; always advancing by defiled boyaux laid out in zig-zag.

The third pa-rallel: the new batteries.

As soon as the besiegers have attained the foot of the glacis and arrived within 60 to 80 mètres (67 to 89 yards) of the sa-lients, a *third parallel* must be made and more strongly consti-tuted than the preceding. Under its protection new batteries of mortars, howitzers, and stone mortars are established, and their effects are much more effectual than those in the rear.

The crowning and capture of the covert way

They move from the third parallel to carry their approaches along the glacis, and to crown the covert way (*et faire le cou-ronnement du chemin-couvert*) ; this operation secures the pos-session of it.

Counter batte-ries and batteries in breach.

The crowning of the crest of the glacis, and the capture of the covert-way, place the besiegers in a position whence they uncover the ramparts and flanks that defend the ditches. They must therefore establish *counter-batteries* to ruin the flanks and silence their fires, and *batteries in breach* to batter down that portion of the ramparts which will afford the greatest facility for penetrating into the works. To attain this latter purpose, the besiegers may avail themselves of mining.

The open and subterranean de-scents of the dit-ches.

Whilst the breaches are effecting and making practicable, the besiegers sink into the glacis and construct in them galle-ries, either open at top, or subterranean, leading from the de-bouchès to the bottom of the ditch facing the centre of the breach. These galleries are called the *descents of the ditches* (*descentes de fossès*) ; when they are open at top, they are cover-ed over with blinds and raw bull's hides.

The passages of the ditch.

By means of these descents and of openings made in the counterscarp, a footing is gained in the ditches, into which the besiegers debouche ; and they make their way across them, by constructing a heavy epaulment leading to the foot of the breach and defending them from the fires of the opposite flank. The operation of the passage depends upon the nature of the

ditch.   If it be dry, it will be sufficient to construct a thick
epaulment of earth, or of bags of earth or wool, &c., and to cover it with raw ox hides when it is made of combustible materials.   When the ditch is filled with water, or capable of being
inundated by streams, a floating bridge must be constructed capable of resisting the currents.   This bridge rests upon the
breach or is fastened to it ; it is furnished with a thick epaulment carefully covered over with hides.

The assaults.   When all the works, the series of which we have just described, are completed, art has done every thing to bring the
assailants in contact with the besieged ; the assaults and definitive combats then take place, and lead to the catastrophe of
the siege.

Classing of the   It results from this general review of all the works and la-
works in a siege. bours of a siege, that they may be distinguished into three
classes ; the first includes the *parallels*, which successively support the batteries and approaches (*cheminemens*) and contain
the troops to repulse the sorties that the besieged continually
make to put the workmen to flight and level the works ; the
second class comprehends all the various kinds of batteries ; and
the third includes all sorts of communications, as boyaux, descents of ditches, and the passages of ditches, by means of
which the troops are carried from the first parallel to the foot of
the breach and artillery is transported to all the batteries.

130   General   130. The art of attacking fortresses has improved like all
reflection upon other parts of the art of war.   In all ages, the attack has been
the progress of
the art of attack- fashioned according to the material constitution of the fortresses
ing fortresses.   and the powers of the weapons used in their defence.   After
the invention and use of artillery, a great revolution took place
in the art of attacking towns ; the ancient method disappeared
to give place to the modern, which slowly improved ; but
which has at length attained that admirable order which we
have just sketched.

The first methods of attack consisted in choosing one or two
fronts of attack, by which it was proposed to penetrate into the place.   At a distance of about 500 mètres (560 yards) several small forts were constructed in the most advantageous situations, and contained the artillery destined to batter down the
place.   The trenches were then opened under the protection
of these forts, and were carried on in zig-zag boyaux towards
the place and in such a manner as to be always defiled from

the salients of the covert-ways.   Having attained these salients, they succeeded by force of labour, time and sacrifices, in crowning the covert-way and establishing batteries in breach, or in setting the miners to work.   Care was taken to make in each boyaux of the approaches, lodgements extending to the right and left in which platoons of matchlockmen were posted to sustain the workmen ; these were again supported by troops stationed in the boyaux in the rear.

This order had defects that greatly delayed the progress of the attack.   1st, The fort batteries were only direct and at a great distance, and they succeeded with great difficulty in silencing the fires of the place : they remained stationary during the whole period of the siege, and did not protect the zig-zag approaches.   2d, The sorties not being restrained by any considerable and well disposed forces, the enemy easily succeeded in taking the works in flank and destroying them before the besiegers could arrive from the tail of the trenches to cover the workmen and repulse the sortie.   3d, The crowning of the covert-way was always effected by storm, and cost the besiegers many lives.   Lastly, all the assaults were by storm, under the ill extinguished fires of the body of the place.

In the first sieges that Vauban had the conduct of, he perceived the defects of the arrangement of the works of the attack, and sought the means of improving them.   He devoted his attention to two principal points ; 1st, he saw the necessity of never abandoning the workmen to themselves, and of supporting them by bodies of troops always within reach to repulse the sorties : this was actually creating new siege tactics, infinitely superior to the ancient.   Vauban resolved this first part of the question by inventing *parallels* or *places of arms*, which are made as fast as the approaches are pushed towards the place.   These parallels embrace all the parts of the front of attack, and contain the troops to protect the labourers. 2d, He totally changed the disposition of the batteries, and invented the dreadful riocochet batteries ; he exploded the use of forts in which all the artillery used to be collected, and showed that attacks by skill and industry might be substituted for assaults by storm.

By the application of his methods in several famous sieges, this illustrious engineer proved that their application was gene-

(See Foissac's edition of Vauban's Treatise on the attack of fortresses.)

ral and susceptible of all the modifications required by ground and the irregularity of fortifications.

It was at the siege of Gravelines in 1658, and at that of Lille in 1667, that Vauban began to exhibit the advantages of his new method. At the siege of Maestricht in 1673, he completely displayed his theory, and with such success, that he took this important fortress in ten days after opening the trenches.

At the siege of Ath in 1697, under Marshal Catinat, Vauban for the first time made use of ricochet batteries; so surprising were their effects, that they carried consternation among the besieged.

The methods used by Vauban towards the end of his military career, have been followed by his successors without any great alterations. The successes that they obtained, and the glory with which they covered the French armies, astonished Europe and proved them deserving of general approbation.

In the application of the general principles, we will give the particular forms of all the works of the attack.

131. Preliminary dispositions before opening the trenches against a common front.

131. The dispositions for opening the trenches, consist in properly preparing all things necessary for this important operation, conformably to the project of opening the trenches. We will suppose that the front attacked is a common front, composed of two bastions and three ravelins, including the two collateral ravelins which overlook the attack.

Formation of the several depots on the capitals: reconnaissance for the first parallel.

From the general depôt of engineers, established on the centre of the attacks, implements, fascines, gabions, &c. will be drawn secretly and during the night to form *five separate depôts* on the prolongations of the five capitals of the front of attack and within 8 or 900 mètres (900 to 1000 yards) of the place. At the close of day the engineers will lay off on the ground and mark with pickets the intersections a, a, a, &c. of the first parallel with the capitals and prolongations of the faces of the works: to effect this, they will begin from the directing pickets P, P, P, &c.

The number of fatigue men and troops necessary for opening the trenches.

The Commandant of engineers and the Chief of the staff of the army, will concert together and regulate; 1st, the number of fatigue soldiers necessary for opening the trenches; 2d, the number of troops, of infantry and cavalry, to cover the work. The number of workmen is calculated at the rate of one man for every 15 decimètres (5 feet); accordingly, by dividing the length of the parallel as laid down on the directing plan, by 15, we find the number of labourers ; to which must be added the number of workmen required to cut the boyaux of communication that connect the depôts with the parallel.

The troops to cover the work, are estimated at the rate of one battalion for every 4 or 500 mètres (445 to 556 yards), according to the strength and vigour of the garrison.   To this force of infantry is added, one or two regiments of dragoons, and two squadrons of light cavalry. Therefore for the front of attack under consideration, there are required eight battalions of infantry, or even three regiments if the garrison be very strong ; and at least 2500 workmen.

Such are the preliminaries that constitute the first period of the siege, and which precede the operation of opening the trenches. This period cannot be calculated at less than ten days.

The first period of the siege is at least 10 days.

THE FIRST PERIOD OF THE DEFENCE.

The Conduct of the Governor during the first period of the Attack, &c.

132. We will only take a hasty glance of the dispositions that the Governor of a fortress should make during the first period of the siege.

132. What should be the conduct of the governor during the first period of the siege.

As soon as he is informed by the detachments which he daily sends out into the country, and by the movements of the hostile army, that he is threatened with investment, he should collect into the town all the cattle, forage, and corn, &c., of the surrounding country ; he must send out of the town under strong escort to the interior, all the useless mouths, old men, women, and children. Here, all private interests and considerations must yield to the safety of the public service. The Governor must supply himself with all the materials requisite for sustaining a long siege ; such as gabions, fascines, timber for blinds, &c.

All the ground without to the distance of 1200 mètres (1335 yards) must be levelled, the hedges cut down, the ditches filled up, and the houses demolished or burnt : finally, every thing that might cover the enemy within gun shot, must be removed or destroyed.

The labours outside the place.

The garrison will be organized in a manner suitable to the

The organization and instruction of the garrison.

defence; and there will be formed, after the example of Mons. De Chamilli at Grave, and of General Meunier at Cassel, companies of grenadiers and rangers (*chasseurs*) of the bravest men, to act without and achieve brilliant exploits.   The troops will be constantly manœuvring day and night, and will imitatively go through all the various kinds of actions that take place in the course of a siege.   All the officers will be made familiarly acquainted with the properties of the fortifications, by instructions given to them before the manœuvres.   The Governor should by his intelligent, active, and engaging conduct, win the confidence of his brethren in arms; like them he must sustain fatigues, share in dangers, and live with temperance.   It is by the practice of these military virtues that he will inspire all with enthusiasm and love of glory.   To his companions in arms he will talk of nothing but the signal service they are about to render to their country, by preserving a fortress entrusted to their loyal and courage.

He will also organize a division of light artillery, served by a company of horse artillery, to act without the walls.

The interior labours.
The place being provided with munitions of war and provisions in proportion to the defence which it should make, will be strengthened with all the slight fortifications capable of retarding the operations of the enemy.   Exterior posts will be occupied during the day, to annoy the besiegers and prevent them from reconnoitring too closely.   Finally, all parts of the fortifications will be renewed and repaired, and their armament (121) completed in every respect : the passages will be provided with barriers, the palisadings repaired, and communications of all kinds established at every point.

The exterior operations against the investing corps.
As soon as the investing corps appears in sight of the place, it will be reconnoitred by the cavalry and horse artillery, supported by light and heavy infantry disposed in *echelons* and so ambushed as to surprise the enemy's troops, who will probably at this moment fall into the snare.   In sorties, the troops must never commit themselves in face of a powerful enemy; but must manœuvre with skill to draw them into ambushes, and inspire them with high notions of the valour and enterprise of the garrison.   The exterior operations will be confided to an active and intelligent field officer who is perfectly skilled in the war of posts and stratagems.   This officer will unceasingly harass the enemy; at one moment he will attack them on this

point, and at the next on another.   He will surprise their night posts by laying ambushes that the enemy cannot discover, by reason of not being able to reconnoitre the ground ; and he will endeavour to maintain an exterior correspondence, to concert and facilitate the entrance of succours and convoys and the forcing of the investing posts.   This officer should particularly watch the enemy's reconnaissances about the place, and must post sharp-shooters in ambush to shoot down every person approaching to discover the form of the ground and nature of the works.

Lastly ; the Governor of an invested fortress must endeavour to discover what fronts the enemy intend to attack, and the day of opening the trenches.   If he succeed in gaining this intelligence, he will make dispositions to counteract the operation.   There are many indications by which the besieged may judge which are the fronts of attack chosen by the enemy ; such as, the posting of the grand park of artillery, the depôts of materials, the direction and nature of the communications, and the order of encampment behind the lines.   When the lines are too near the place, the tail of the camps is exposed to its fire ; and in this case we must fire at random (*à toute volée*), to compel the besiegers to distance their lines and quarters.

Within the fortress, all are in motion to organize the accessaries of the defence, and arrange with order all the branches of administration.   The souterrains are aired and put in a good state ; the magazines, caserns, &c., are covered with blinds and earth or dung ; and the posterns are unmasked, &c.   Finally ; the most regular service is established within the garrison. *The interior order.*

Commonly the service is performed by *thirds;* that is, one third of the garrison is under arms in presence of the enemy, whilst another third is held in readiness to march, and the remaining third reposes.   When the garrison is strong enough to allow the service to be performed by fourths, this order is preferable ; and in this case one half of the garrison reposes, whilst part of the other half is in presence of the enemy, and the other part ready to fly to arms. *The regulation of the service of the garrison.*

SECTION II.

The attack and the defence during the second period of the siege.

THE SECOND PERIOD OF THE ATTACK.

Description of all the Labours of the Attack, to the third Parallel; the various Measures of the Besiegers; the Batteries; the Journal of the Attacks, &c.

133. Detailed description of all the labours of the modern bastioned front.

133. Before we describe the measures for opening the trenches, we will make our readers acquainted with their profiles, and the manner of laying them out and protecting their construction.

Definition of trenches.

The term *trenches* (*tranchée**) is generical; and in attack, it signifies all the works that are executed before a place to approach and get possession of it at the least possible cost of lives and time.

The profiles of the trenches, and the manner of laying them out with fascines and with gabions. (See PLATE IV, and PLATE IV, 2d Part)

We have already made known (129) the general composition of the profiles of the trenches; they consist of a covering bank made of the earth taken from the interior ditch which serves as a terraplain, and into which we descend by a slope of 15 decimètres (5 feet) base, called the *reverse of the trench* (*le revers de la tranchée*). The bottom of the trench is always sunk 10 decimètres ($3\frac{1}{3}$ feet) below the natural ground; its parapet is made 15 decimètres (5 feet) high. The width of the bottom of the ditch varies according to the thickness of the parapet; it is at least 20 decimètres ($6\frac{2}{3}$ feet) in the profiles of the parallels, and 16 ($5\frac{1}{3}$ feet) in the boyaux of communication. All the profiles of the trenches have a *berm* which is 5 decimètres (20 inches) in those of parallels, and only 3 (12 inches) in those of boyaux. In the parallels, the berm serves as a banquette for infantry, and is ascended by a step likewise 5 decimètres (20 inches) wide. Instead of making a step, we may make this berm 10 decimètres ($3\frac{1}{3}$ feet) wide, so as to have a banquette capable of holding two ranks of infantry; and make an interior slope with a base of 15 decimètres (5 feet). The boyaux have no banquettes.

* In French this word (*tranchée*), when used in relation to sieges, &c. is generally in the singular.

TRANSLATOR.

The trenches are laid out with fascines so long as they are *Laying out the trenches with fascines :* not within musket shot ; that is, whilst they are more than 300 mètres (335 yards) from the salients. They are laid out by placing fascines in the given directions ; these fascines alternately cover each other nearly 2 decimètres (8 inches), and mark the foot of the interior slope of the parapet. The workmen, at the rate of one man to every fascine, are posted behind the fascines to excavate the trench and form the parapet.

When the musketry fires begin to take effect, the method of *with gabions, & flying saps :* laying out with fascines is abandoned for that with gabions; that is, the engineers quickly place the gabions next to each other upon the direction of the trenches, and the labourers, who are in the proportion of one man per gabion, immediately fill them with earth, and by this expeditious method cover themselves from the fire of musketry. As soon as the gabions are filled, they are crowned with three fascines which unite the gabions solidly together; and the parapet is then made of the proper height. This method of carrying on the trenches, is called *constructing with flying saps* (*tracé à la sape volante*).

When we are too near the fires of the place to work at the *with gabions, and whole saps (PLATE IV. 2d Part, fig. 2.)* trenches uncovered and with flying saps, the method of *whole saps* (*sape pleine*) is then used. This ingenious method of carrying on the trenches under the fire of the works, was little known before the time of Vauban who recommends the use of it from the 2d parallel.

The *whole sap*, is executed by squads of sappers equipped *The means and materials used in the whole sap : the progress that it makes in 12 hours.* with head pieces and musket proof cuirasses. Each squad consists of four men, who alternately conduct the head of the work. In constructing the whole sap, the sappers make use of the common gabion, the large filled gabion, and sap fagots or bags of earth.

The *stuffed and rolling gabion* (*le gabion farci et roulant*) is *The stuffed gabion, or mantelet.* a large gabion made like the common kind, and is 20 decimètres (6⅔ feet) long, and 15 (5 feet) in diameter; it is filled with fascines, or wool, or hair, so as to be proof against the shot of rampart guns.   There is attached to it a staff with a hook, by which the sapper rolls it before him and fixes it in such position as he thinks best.   This stuffed gabion has taken the place of the *mantelet* invented by Vauban.

Bags of earth are small sacks of coarse linen or cloth, filled *Bags of earth, and their use.* with earth and strongly sewed with pack-thread ; they are 55 centimètres (22 inches) in length, and 30 (12 inches) in diameter. They are used for filling up the intervals between the gabions; and are likewise very frequently used for crowning the parapet in the form of loop-holes.

Sap fagots, and their use.

The *sap fagot* is a piece of saucisson 20 decimètres (6⅔ feet) long, with a picket through its centre pointed at one end and handled at the other: they are used to strengthen the joints of the trench gabions, &c.

The manner in which a squad of sappers carry on the sap.

A squad of sappers who are to carry on a trench under the direction of an officer of engineers equipped with his headpiece and cuiràs, go to work in the following manner: The first sapper pierces the common trench at the point of departure, covers the opening with the stuffed gabion which he eloigns sufficiently to be able to place the first gabion; this he fills with earth by excavating a ditch 49 centimètres (19½ inches) deep and the same in width, and leaving a berm of 40 centimètres (16 inches). After the first gabion is placed, the sapper creeps on his knees into the ditch and places the second gabion, covering the joint by two bags of earth laid one upon another, or with a sap fagot; he then fills this second gabion. In the same manner he advances to place the third and fourth gabions, &c. As soon as the first sapper has placed the third gabion, the second sapper can enter the sap; he crowns the gabions with three fascines, and deepens and widens the work 17 centimètres (nearly 7 inches). When the second sapper has reached the third gabion, the third sapper comes into the sap, and increases its dimensions 17 centimètres. Lastly; the fourth sapper advances into the sap as soon as the third is sufficiently forward; and he likewise increases its dimensions 17 centimètres. In this state the sap is as deep as the trench, and is 10 decimètres (3⅓ feet) wide. It is now delivered over to the common fatigue-men, who complete it by making it of the form and dimensions prescribed by the profile.

A squad of sappers work only two hours at a time, and each sapper in his turn conducts the head of the sap. They are paid at the rate of two francs (37 cents) per mètre, and sometimes more; according to the dangers and difficulty of the ground. A sap pushed with activity, may advance in common ground 70 to 80 mètres (78 to 89 yards) in 12 hours' work.

Carrying on the trenches with the double sap.

We will find that when we are near the crest of the glacis, it is impossible to advance except in directions taken in flank;

so that the trench then becomes a ditch covered by two parapets.   In this case the trenches are carried on by the *double
sap (sape pleine double)*; that is, two squads of sappers advance
on parallel lines at a distance determined by the width of the
bottom of the trench, covering themselves in front with stuffed
gabions, which they place in the most convenient manner.   If
the trench is to be made 20 decimètres (6$\frac{3}{4}$ feet) wide at bottom, the sappers will place their files of gabions 40 decimètres
(13$\frac{1}{2}$ feet) apart.   After the sappers have excavated the sap,
there remains a mound in the middle of it which the common
workmen dig away to complete the trench.

Reflections on
the use of the
sap.

The trenches are carried on by the flying or whole sap from
the moment that the musketry fires begin to take effect;
this is the case, with respect to rampart guns, at a distance of
about 300 mètres (335 yards).   The approaches by the flying
sap are more expeditious than with the whole sap, the progress
of which is very slow.   But when we take into view that the
whole sap is pushed on day and night, whilst the flying sap can
only be carried on during the night ; we will not be surprised
that Vauban recommends it in preference, and assures that it
rapidly advances the attack.   The best way is to intermingle
the two methods ; to advance constantly with the whole sap,
and to use the flying sap whenever the fires of the place will
permit.

Principle in
laying out the
works of the at-
tack.

We have now only to lay down the general principle upon
which the application of the theory of attack is founded, and
which secures its execution and baffles all the efforts of the besieged.   As all the offensive works of the besiegers may be attacked suddenly and at any moment, by the besieged rushing
out unrestrained from their covert-ways ; and as these works
are laid out and constructed by officers and fatigue-men who are
not in a situation to fight ; it follows, that these works are abandoned the moment that the enemy appear.   They would therefore be levelled and destroyed by the besieged, if troops
were not properly posted to cover the work and repulse the
enemy at the instant of their sortie.

We must consequently lay down this general rule, *that all
works laid out and carried on within striking distance (sous l'action) of the besieged, must be properly covered or protected by
troops to prevent the officers and workmen from being cut down
or put to flight.*

134. The ope-
ration of open-
ing the trenches:
the manner of
conducting it:
the labours of
the first night.

134. Let us resume the train of operations of the siege. The project of the opening of the trenches is determined on (127), the preliminary dispositions are made, the troops and work-men are detailed and ready, the officers of engineers have marked on the ground with conspicuous pickets the intersections of the capitals and prolongations of the faces of the works with the parallel, the separate depôts are formed, and the day for opening the trenches is fixed.   As this operation would be op-posed by the garrison and would cost a great many lives if the enemy obtained a knowledge of it, it must be performed at night and with the utmost secrecy ; several similar operations must be feigned at different points, to divert their attention from the real point of attack.

Conduct of the
troops who are to
cover the open-
ing of the tren-
ches   (PLATE
IV, fig. 1.)

In conformity with the preceding principle, the opening of the trenches must be covered along their whole extent by troops who will repulse the enemy and encourage the labour-ers.   As soon as the night is sufficiently advanced to conceal the movements of the troops, the eight battalions will file off and proceed and take post 100 mètres (111 yards) in front of the parallel.   These troops I, I, I, &c. will lie flat on the ground, and send forward detachments posted in echelon with orders not to fire, but to charge with the bayonet and seize all patroles that they may meet.

The manner of
laying out the pa-
rallel, and the
order to be ob-
served to spee-
dily execute it.

The plan for laying out the parallel will show its length, which will be about 3,200 mètres (3560 yards, or about 2 miles) ; and the officers of engineers on duty for the night, will distribute the work among themselves.   We will here suppose that they are ten in number ; two of them will proceed to each depôt D, D, &c. with the labourers necessary for executing that part of the trenches with which they are charged.   As soon as the troops have taken their posts, each engineer forms his workmen in a single file, at the head of which he advances towards the directing picket a planted upon the capital on which he marches ; the two united brigades having arrived at a, one of them will wheel to the right, and the other to the left ; each engineer will then lay off with the fascines brought by the workmen the portion of the parallel with which he is charged.   As fast as the engineer places a fascine, he will cause a workman to lie down behind it, with injunctions not to stir 'till further orders.   When all the intermediate brigades which extend to meet each other, have united, and when the

wings are likewise correctly laid off, the commandant of engineers then gives orders to begin the work.   Each engineer immediately returns to his brigade, and in a low tone commands
" *handle your shovels*" (*haut les bras*) ; the workmen instantly
begin digging the parallel, taking care to leave a berm and interior slope ; to this the officers of the line will attend particularly.   In the same night an officer of engineers will be charged with laying out and executing the communications from the
parallel to the depôts placed on the bastion capitals.   By day
light the parallel, though very imperfect, will afford a shelter
to which the troops will retire.   Fresh workmen, each carrying
two fascines, will relieve those of the night ; and notwithstanding the furious fire of the fortress, the parapet will receive its
proper thickness, the banquettes will be formed, and all the defective parts will be corrected.   Two days are required to
complete the first parallel.

The *journal of the attacks* is the diary and plans which exhibit the daily progress of the siege.   The length or duration of
the siege, is the time that elapses from the opening of the
trenches to the reduction of the place.   The probable duration
of the siege is estimated by the time supposed necessary for
constructing the works, excluding all moral circumstances that
may influence the issue ; and we are able to determine this
with great exactness by the examination of numerous sieges.

The journal of the attacks ; man-ner of estimating the probable du-ration of the siege.

135. On the morning following the opening of the trenches,
the positions for ricochet batteries are reconnoitred ; and the
intersections of the prolongations of the faces of the works with
the parallel, are marked.   The artillery, in concert with the
engineers, decide the positions of the different batteries ; these
must be in *ricochet* (128, 129, and 130) to silence the fires of
all those works which overlook the approach of the attacks.
The batteries are laid out and constructed under the protection
of the first parallel.   As the besiegers use in their construction
materials which from their nature are indestructible, and as
they are free in their movements and in the choice of time, the
fire of the place and the vigorous sorties of the garrison may
indeed delay, but they cannot prevent the laying out and erec-
tion of the batteries : this is proved by all experience.

135 The object of the besiegers after opening the trenches : rico-chet batteries, their plan, posi-tion & construc-tion.

The batteries may be placed in the very parallels themselves,
and in this position their construction is more expeditious and
less perilous ; but they would here greatly impede the service.

It is better to make them 60 to 80 mètres (67 to 89 yards) in advance, and to communicate with them by boyaux. If the ground be irregular, the advantages of site will determine the position of each battery : it is sometimes proper to post them in rear of the parallel. When the ground does not afford a suitable position for a ricochet battery, we must defer constructing it until we are nearer the place, and even until we have reached the second place of arms.

The laying out, and composition of ricochet batteries. When the plan of the batteries is determined upon the directing plan of the attacks, they are laid out on the ground. To this end the artillery officer as soon as darkness permits, marks off on the ground the point of the prolongation of the covering line upon which the battery is to be established ; to this point he draws a perpendicular upon which he marks with gabions the interior line of the epaulment, and he places parallel another row of gabions to mark the epaulment ; and he then establishes the length of the epaulment on the right and left of the prolongation of the crest of the parapet. The cannoniers and fatigue-men from the line then excavate the outside ditch and form the coffer of the battery. When the fire of the place is very hot and the grape and musketry take effect among the workmen and cannoniers, they cover themselves with a gabionnade made in front of the battery ; and under this shelter continue the work.

The length of the epaulment of a battery depends upon the number of guns for which it is designed. The object of each battery being to strike by ricochets the wheels and carriages of the artillery of the ramparts, to harass and impede their service, and to annoy the besieged in the covert-ways and ditches, &c. it is composed in the following manner : 1st, two or three siege 12 pounders or 16 pounders are posted on the interior side of the covering-line, to ricochè the terra-plain ; 2d, two mortars are placed outside the magistral line, to fire into the ditches ; 3d, two howitzers of great ranges are placed inside the prolongation of the crest of the glacis, to fire in ricochet into the covert-ways and cut down their palisades, barriers, &c. The front of such a battery will be 45 to 50 mètres (50 to 55½ yards).

The height of the floor of batteries their construction : the time required for establishing them, and when they may be opened. When the platforms for cannon can be raised 7 or 8 décimètres (2⅓ to ⅔ feet) above the natural ground, the fire is more effective ; but on the other hand, the construction is more dangerous and requires more time. Commonly the platforms for

cannon and howitzers are established upon the natural ground ;
but those for mortars are always sunk below it, which expedites
the work.   When batteries are established at a distance from
the first parallel and their line of fire is consequently very much
lengthened, the platforms may be sunk below the natural
ground a quantity equal to the height of the genouillère.   In
the construction of such a profile, the natural ground forms the
bottom of the embrasure ; and the revesting of the cheeks with
saucissons is begun at the same time as the excavation.   As in
this case the earth for the coffer of the battery is taken both
from within and without, the work is less perilous and sooner
finished.   The artillery officer is governed in his choice of a
profile by the ground, and by the powers of the fires from the
fortress.

(See L'Aide
Memoire. the 630
and following pa-
ges)

Here we must recall to the mind all that was said on batteries
in the Second Part (Chap. VI, arts. 84, 85, and 86). For all the
important details relative to the quantity and dimensions of the
materials necessary for the construction of batteries, the number of workmen, and the arrangement of the labour, we refer to
the admirable particulars given in L'Aide Memoire, by General
Gassendi ; an invaluable work which officers of artillery and
engineers should constantly study.

(See the Se-
cond Part, Chap.
VI, 84, 85 & 86)

Experience has constantly shown that 40 hours work is sufficient to construct a ricochet battery.   Accordingly, during the
second night the formation of the coffer and epaulment is laid
out and forwarded with activity ; on the second day they labour at the revêtement of the merlons, genouillères, &c., and
prepare the timbers for the platforms ; in the third night the
platforms are almost completed, the artillery is brought to the
batteries, and the powder magazines are constructed ; in the
morning of the third day the platforms are completed and the
ammunition is brought up, the batteries are armed, and their
embrasures are unmasked.   At meridian a signal will be made
to open the fire of all the batteries upon the defences of the
place.   As ricochet firing is with small charges, which must be
varied until we find that the shot or howitz grazes the crest of
the parapet and plunges into the terra-plain as it describes the
descending branch of its trajectory, we must begin firing in
day-light, to regulate the charge and mark the directions of the
fire upon the platforms.   Moreover, all the batteries must be
unmasked at once ; so that the besieged will be compelled to

divide his fire on each of them, and not be able to concentrate it against a single battery. Without this precaution, the first firing will scarcely be of any effect; and the besieged would gain confidence when we should astonish and intimidate them from the very beginning of the firing. This was the case at the siege of Atb, where Vauban unmasked his ricochet batteries all at once, and in a few hours silenced the fires of all the defences.

136. Carrying forward the trenches from the first parallel : the directions in which they should be advanced : approaches in zig-zag on the capitals.

136. While the batteries are constructing, the officers of engineers will attend to the debouching from the first place of arms to advance towards the place. As these approaches may be made in several directions, those which are most advantageous must be selected; that is, those which lead to the most advanced salients by the shortest way, are the easiest laid out, least exposed to the enemy's fire, and least mask the batteries established in rear. Now it is evident that the capital of a salient is the only line among those which can be drawn from the place of arms to the works, that fulfils these conditions : 1st, it is the shortest; 2d, it cannot be defended by the musketry of the works, except the angle be obtuse and the fires greatly obliqued; and cannot be defended by artillery, except by the single piece posted in the salient; 3d, the embankments raised upon the capitals and which extend to the right and left only a certain distance, are not crossed by the horizontal projection of the lines of fire from the direct or ricochet batteries, unless they are very near the salients. Consequently the relief of these masses of earth never masks the fire of the batteries, and the capitals are generally the most favourable directions to carry on the trenches in.

The figure of the approaches on a capital : approaches in zig-zag.

The most simple method of making approaches on a capital, is to make the trench in a right line, covering it on each flank with a parapet. The trench would in this case be like a double sap; its front would be covered by single or tambour traverses, on which gabionnades would be constructed whose relief would defile that portion of the trench in rear. We should indeed be compelled to adopt this method of carrying on approaches, if there were none better; for it is evident that it is defective, slow, and perilous. The narrow front of the trench would be always uncovered; it would be swept in all quarters, and would be continually enfiladed and exposed to the ricochets of balls, bombs, and howitzes. To obtain a form of approaches more advantageous and expeditious, a method was invented from the birth of the art of attacking modern fortresses of advancing towards the salients by a disposition of trenches, all whose parts are defiled from the most advanced salients. What we have laid down on defilement (104), demonstrates that the form of such approaches must be a zig-zag disposition of boyaux. Each boyau crosses the capital and extends beyond it 30 to 50 mètres (33⅓ to 55¼ yards) at the most; its prolongation passes within a distance of 30 to 40 mètres (33⅓ to 44¼ yards) from the most advanced collateral salient: by this direction each boyau is defiled and most advanced towards the salient that is to be approached. Its advancement is in proportion as the angle that each boyau makes with the capital, is more or less acute; and this angle depends upon the situation of the collateral parts of the fortification from which the boyau must be defiled. The further we are from the place, the more acute is the angle that the boyau makes with the capital. But in proportion as we advance, these angles increase; and when we are within 60 to 80 mètres (67 to 89 yards) of the salients, we can no longer approach in zig-zag, but must advance in the direct method just described.

The debouché of each zig-zag boyau towards the place, is covered by prolonging the following boyau to the rear 4 or 5 mètres (4¼ to 5½ yards): these returns likewise facilitate the communication.

The boyaux or approaches are laid off from the first parallel, and are laid down on the directing plan; in the night they are marked off on the ground.

Manner of laying out the boyaux on the directing plan, and on the ground.

Let us suppose that we are to approach on the capital of the ravelin of the front of attack; we must take the point of departure *b* at 30 to 40 mètres from the capital, and thence draw the defiled direction *bm* upon which we mark the length *bc* of the first boyau: from the point *c* we draw the defiled line *cn*, and take upon it *cd* for the length of the second boyau. Lastly; from the point *d* draw the defiled line *do*, and upon this take *de* for the length of the third boyau, the head of which will be at a distance of about 300 mètres (335 yards) from the place; here the second place of arms must be established.

To lay off upon the ground the project laid down upon the directing plan, of which the engineer officer will take a rough draught (*croquis*) with the measures accurately noted, there are two methods ; both of which should be always used together to attain correct results. The first consists in endeavouring to discover at night by lying down on the ground, the most advanced salients ; and laying off the boyaux with fascines or gabions outside of these salients. But it is a more certain method to advance towards night-fall a few platoons of grenadiers who lie down flat on the ground, whilst the engineer plants the pickets c, d, e, marking the extremities of the boyaux that are to be executed during the night : he will make non-commissioned officers of the sappers lie down near the pickets. At the moment of beginning the work, these non-commissioned officers will stand up and serve as points of sight for placing the fascines, gabions, and workmen.

The second method consists in taking on the directing plan the length of the boyaux, and making a clew of cord of the same length to measure upon the capital the lengths ax, xy, yZ, &c. ; and with these particulars going in the night and planting the pickets x, y, Z, &c. and the picket of departure b. The first cord is tied to the picket b, and by passing it through the picket x its other extreme gives the point c : this point c will be easily put in the alignement bx, for it is easy even in a dark night to mark off by stakes the line bx, or by two dark lanterns at x and c. By recollecting the length of the boyaux and the quantity that they should extend beyond the capital, we may do without these cords whose use might seem impracticable. The use of this method must not prevent the engineer from verifying whether the directions of the boyaux pass without the salients, which he must endeavour to reconnoitre in spite of the darkness.

Progress of the attacks : continuation of the journal of the attacks : labours of the 2d, 3d, 4th, & 5th nights.

During the second, third, fourth, and fifth nights, the direct and ricochet batteries will be completed, and will fire upon all the defences of the front of attack. On the second night the engineers will debouche from the first parallel, to lay out with fascines and construct the first boyaux of communication on the capitals of the two bastions ; these two approaches will suffice for the moment. They will likewise debouche from the two extremes V of the parallel, to begin the grand communication Vu which is to connect the first with the second place of arms. These two communications on the wings will be profiled like the first parallel, with banquettes to fire from. As the batteries are opened from the third day, it will be practicable during the fourth and fifth nights to advance more rapidly, and to construct during the fifth the extremities *u* of the last boyaux which bring the besiegers to within at most 300 mètres (335 yards) of the salients. The distance to the salients of the covert-way must be greater than the distance to the first parallel ; in order that if the besieged make a sortie upon the heads of the approaches *u*, the grenadiers who advance from the first parallel will be able to arrive before them.

137. In laying out and constructing the first parallel, the operation may be covered and secured by a disposition of troops. But these measures cannot be perfectly repeated after we have arrived within the effect of musketry ; here all the approaches and works must be covered by dispositions in the rear. These reflections show, that the heads of the approaches must cease to be carried on when the protection from the works in rear ceases to be effectual ; that is, when the enemy can fall on the heads of the trenches before the troops can arrive from the parallel in the rear. It follows, that when the heads of the approaches are arrived at 300 mètres from the first parallel, it is necessary to establish a second place of arms to protect the ulterior works.

137. Situation of the besiegers when arrived at half the distance included between the first parallel and salients : the protection that this parallel affords the approaches.

The communications between the first and second parallel consist of 3 or 4 boyaux laid out with fascines. It will perhaps be possible to make the openings (*amorces*) of the second parallel on the fifth night ; these openings will be made with gabions, that is, with the flying sap, and will be very useful to post platoons of grenadiers in.

The necessity and position of the 2d parallel : its first openings may be on the fifth night.

When laying out and constructing the last boyaux to reach the position for the second parallel, the sorties of the besieged become very frequent and dangerous. In order to repulse them, detachments of grenadiers are posted in front and on the flanks of the work, and lie flat on the ground ; these restrain the sorties until the troops from the parallel can come up. As soon as a sortie takes place, the engineers quietly withdraw the labourers, to unmask the fire of the parallel. Whilst this is doing, the cavalry *C* turn the trenches and come on at a gallop to take the sortie in flank and cut off their retreat ; the troops of the parallel advance at the same time at the charging step, and attack the sortie in front with the bayonet. When these measures and manœuvres are ably executed, the besieged very rarely succeed in injuring the works.

The measures of the besiegers when the garrison make sorties to destroy the works.

Remark upon
the time required
to arrive at the
second parallel.

We see that five days are strictly necessary to gain the position for the second parallel. If the sorties be made with vigour, and if we have not been able to establish some ricochet batteries from the first parallel, the labours that we have just described will not perhaps be completed until the close of the sixth or even seventh day : but it will be impossible for the besieged to further delay the advance of the besiegers, which each day becomes more imperative.

The theorick
redoubt, placed
in the centre of
the attacks be-
hind the first pa-
rallel.

In important sieges which may last a month or longer, it is proper to establish on the centre of the attacks in rear of the first parallel a redoubt that may be called the *theorick redoubt*, with 30 mètres (100 feet) face. In its terra-plain a lodgement will be constructed and covered with blinds and bomb proof, to contain the plans, instruments, head pieces, &c., of the artillery and engineer officers. These officers will here daily labour at drawing up plans of attack, laying down plans of the works already executed, and measuring the work and settling the accounts of the workmen (*faire les toises et les decomptes des travailleurs*); and in this redoubt the general officers of the day assemble to give orders and establish concert between the operations of all arms.

Continuation of
the journal of the
attacks. Labours
of the sixth
night carrying
on the second pa-
rallel with the
flying sap; its
profile ; the mea-
sures of the be-
siegers.

On the sixth night the engineers, after reconnoitring the points of intersection of the second parallel with the capitals, proceed to construct it with the flying sap as correctly as possible.

The order to be observed in laying out and constructing this parallel, is nearly the same as that for the first place of arms, except that each workman brings a gabion ; these gabions are passed by hand to the engineer officer or to a non-commissioned sapper who lays out the work under his direction, in order that they may be placed together upon the direction in which the parallel is to be run (133). The brigades of labourers will extend to meet each other, and will connect and correct the portions of the work done during the night. As soon as the parallel is laid out and corrected, the workmen will rise up and fill the gabions as quickly as possible : two gabions are arranged to every two men, one of whom breaks, and the other shovels the earth.

To prevent the besieged from harassing the operation by sorties which at this distance are always dangerous, the work, and especially its wings, are covered by detachments of grena-

diers posted 50 paces in advance of the parallel and lying flat
on the ground.   These detachments must make head against
the sorties, vigorously charge them, and give time to the troops
posted in the boyaux to arrive to their assistance and drive the
enemy into his covert-ways.

When we have been able to establish from the first parallel
the batteries on the wings which ricoché the faces of the ravelins and other collateral works, we must take care that the prolongations of the wings of the second parallel do not mask the
fires of these batteries.   But if the laying out of these same batteries have been delayed until the second parallel, it must embrace the prolongations of the faces of all the collateral works
that bear upon the attacks.   Its length in the first case will
be about 1800 mètres (2000 yards), and in the second 2400
mètres (2680 yards) : this length shows that this work will require 4500 gabions and 2400 labourers.   The flanks of the attacks being very much exposed to insult by sorties from the
collateral works, the wings of the parallel are terminated by
two pentagonal redoubts made like the parallel with the flying sap.   These redoubts are each armed with five or six
pieces of small caliber firing with grape or canister (*cartouch*),
and sweeping the approaches of the flanks.

By break of day the parallel will be in a state to receive
some platoons of grenadiers ; and the labourers will be relieved
by fresh workmen, each of whom will bring two fascines to
crown the gabions.   If during the night we were not able to
finish some parts of the parallel, they will be completed with
the whole sap.   During the fifth day the crowning with fascines will be effected, and the trenches will be profiled.

The dimensions of the second parallel are the same as the
first, except that of the bottom, which is 23 to 25 decimètres
($7\frac{2}{3}$ to $8\frac{1}{4}$ feet) ; this makes the quantity of earth for the embankments greater, and the thickness of the parapets is in-
creased.

When we have not been able to establish all the ricochet batteries at the first parallel, and when it is necessary to advance
them to produce greater effects, this important work is attended
to as soon as the second parallel is sufficiently strong.

These new batteries may be placed in three different positions with respect to the place of arms ; they may be posted in
the very parallel, or in advance, or in rear : the ground and

circumstances will guide the artillery and engineer officers in determining their situation.

If the ricochet batteries be posted in the parallel, their construction will be more expeditious and less dangerous; but they will greatly embarrass the movements. If they be carried forward, their fire is less protracted and less effective, the laying them out is retarded one day, and their construction is more exposed to the fires and sorties of the besieged. Lastly; if they be placed in rear of the parallel, they must be sufficiently elongated from it to prevent their fire from being masked by the parallel; and this cannot be done except on irregular ground which affords some advantageous positions. Generally, the best situation for these second batteries is a little in advance of the second parallel, or in the parallel itself; but their fire must not embarrass the approaches.

Continuation of the Journal of the attacks. The works of the 6th, 7th, and 8th nights. During the seventh and eighth nights these new batteries are laid out and constructed; the redoubts on the wings of the parallel are completed and armed; and the two grand communications connecting the two parallels, are also completed. On the morning of the eighth day these batteries will be armed, and their fire opened upon the defences.

The approaches in advance of the second parallel. On the 7th night the officers of engineers will conduct the squads of sappers into the second parallel, and will debouche by whole saps on the five capitals at the same time. These approaches will be regularly carried on night and day with the whole sap in zig-zags (133) defiled from the salients; but the officers will at every favourable moment, in order to expedite the work, carry on the approaches with the flying sap. Under the protection of the new batteries, the approaches will on the eighth day reach by two or three zig-zags the points of the capitals distant from the salients nearly 120 or 130 mètres (133 to 145 yards).

The half places of arms: their necessity and advantages: their situation and extent The approaches in advance of the second parallel can no longer be protected by platoons of grenadiers posted and lying down at the head and on the flanks of the approaches; the troops remain in the second parallel and in the boyaux as fast as they are finished, and do not stir from these positions except to repulse a sortie and cover the labourers. It follows that when the heads of the approaches have arrived within a distance of 120 to 130 mètres of the salients, they cease to receive from the parallel a protection sufficiently immediate to prevent the besieged from attacking them before the troops can come up to cover the sappers. It therefore becomes necessary to support the approaches by *half places of arms* (*demi-places d'armes*), occupied by grenadiers; and in which the materials for the ulterior trenches are deposited. These half places of arms should embrace the prolongations of the branches of the covert-ways, and include the prolongations of the flanks of the bastions.

The extremes of the half places of arms are armed with batteries of howitzers and mortars, which ricochè the branches of the covert-way and the flanks of bastions.

The extremes of the half places of arms are armed with howitzer and mortar batteries

On the ninth night the half places of arms will be constructed with the flying or whole sap, and the approaches will be continued in zig-zag upon the capitals of the collateral ravelins to within 100 mètres (111 yards) of the salients; and an opening (*amorce*) will be made of a parallel whose extremity will return towards the redoubt of the wing of the second parallel, in order to be flanked by it. In the day the work will be completed; and batteries of howizers will be formed and ready to fire next morning. The approaches will be continued in shortened and defiled boyaux to within 80 mètres (89 yards) of the salients; and at night-fall an opening will be made of the third parallel on the three centre capitals.

Continuation of the journal of the attacks. Labours of the ninth night and ninth day.

The third parallel, and the laying it out.

On the 9th in the evening every thing will be prepared to construct the third parallel during the tenth night and tenth day. The materials will be transported into the half places of arms and boyaux; the half places of arms will be occupied with grenadiers, as likewise the wings of the second parallel and the openings of the wings of the third which were enlarged during the ninth day. Lastly; two corps of cavalry will take post on the flanks, and during the night will be stationed behind the wings of the second parallel to take in flank any enemy's corps that endeavour to penetrate between the second and third parallels. During this night the squads of sappers will be relieved every hour, in order that the work may be pushed with the greatest activity. Eight squads are requisite; these will advance to meet each other, and will by day light have executed 600 mètres (667 yards) of the work; that is, at least one half of the parallel. The work will be continued during the tenth day; and at night the whole of the parallel will be completed.

Continuation of the journal of the attacks. Labours of the tenth night and tenth day: measures of the besiegers to establish the third parallel at the foot of the glacis.

Labour of the
eleventh night
& eleventh day. Lastly; in the course of the eleventh night and eleventh day
the besiegers will complete the parallel and arrange it relatively
to their ulterior operations. It is obvious that the parallel will
be laid out with the whole sap in 24 hours; because each brigade of sappers will execute 160 mètres (180 yards) of sap
in this interval of time. If the defence be not active, and if
the fire of the place permit carrying on the parallel during the
night with the flying sap, it will be possible to complete the parallel by the evening of the tenth day.

THE SECOND PERIOD OF THE DEFENCE.

The Conduct of the Governor during the second period of the siege.

138. The con-
duct of the Go-
vernor from the
opening of the
trenches, to the
establishment of
the third paral-
lel. 138. When the Governor of the fortress perceives that the
moment for opening the trenches has arrived, he must be very
vigilant and form ambushes to surprise or drive away all who
approach the place. During the three first hours of each night,
he will illuminate the whole circumference of the place to a
distance of 600 mètres (667 yards) by throwing from mortars
fiery balls or pot-grenadoes (pots à feu), to discover whether
the enemy are at work on any of the conjectured fronts of attack. An intelligent Governor, acquainted with the properties
of his fortress and the proportions of strength of its different
fronts, has many means of discovering what fronts the enemy
will select. But to ascertain the moment of opening the trenches,
is very difficult.

Disposition of
the artillery of
the place rela-
tive to the open-
ing of the trench-
es. Besides the pieces disposed on all the works to fire in barbette, there must be a general disposition made of the artillery
relatively to the opening of the trenches. All the disposeable
artillery must be brought forward on the fronts and covert-ways
of those parts liable to be attacked; the small pieces and howitzers will be posted in the covert-ways, to fire in ricochet over
the palisades; and the heavy pieces that are to fire in ricochet,
will be posted on the terra-plains in rear of the parapets, in order that the ball or bomb may pass over them.

The measures
of the besieged
at the moment of
the opening of
the trenches: the
sorties from the
place. As soon as it is perceived by the light of the fiery balls that
the besiegers are manœuvring and labouring to establish themselves on some point, a most furious fire, both direct and ricochet, will be opened upon them from all the works. Engineer

officers with patroles, supported by detachments, will proceed to closely reconnoitre whether the enemy's dispositions *are real*; and when they are satisfied that the enemy are opening the trenches, the fire will be renewed with the greatest fury and most accurate direction. A sortie will be made on the flanks of the work with light artillery and howitzers, sustained by infantry and cavalry, to take in flank and obliquely (*écharper*) the troops that cover the work, and to put the labourers to flight. Two thirds of the garrison will be under arms and employed in making a vigorous sortie, which may be attended with the greatest success. After having harassed the besiegers by a fire of two hours, the cavalry and horse artillery, supported by a body of light infantry, will debouche from the collateral parts and advance upon the flanks of the work to check and repulse the hostile cavalry. At the same instant the infantry of the line will make a sortie from the covert-ways, flanked by light artillery, and will attack in front the enemy's corps that cover the workmen; taking care however not to commit themselves too far. After the besiegers have sustained several discharges of musketry and of artillery firing with grape, the light cavalry will glide through the flanks and intervals to attack and put the labourers to flight by scouring (*parcourant en fourrageurs*) the whole length of the line. If this manœuvre be conducted with the daring skill necessary to its success, it will cause the enemy great loss, and will reduce his labours for that night to very little. As soon as the sortie has returned into the covert-ways, the fires of the place and of the exterior batteries established to take obliquely (*écharper*) the flanks of the attack, will be vigorously renewed. Manœuvres of this kind can only be executed during this first night. We have already seen that the besiegers adopt such measures and have such numerous forces at command, that it will be impossible to contend with them; and that it is only practicable to retard their works and cut off a great many of their men.

When once the first parallel is laid out and executed, the besieged should then only act against the besiegers and their works with their fire; and this fire is reduced to that of the batteries. The howitzers and mortars that are mounted upon cannon carriages, should be posted in the salient places of arms to fire *in ricochet* upon the capitals; the heavy mortars

Measures of the besieged after the opening of the trenches; the manner in which they should use their fire.

will be on the curtains of the front of attack and of the contiguous fronts; their fires will be directed sometimes against one point, and sometimes at another. All the pieces of heavy caliber will be mounted upon garrison carriages, or upon barbettes constructed on the terra-plains of the works on the front of attack and contiguous fronts. This method of using the artillery is evidently the most advantageous during the first moments of the siege.

The directing plan of the defences. The governor will cause the chief engineer to draw up the *directing plan of the defence* (*le plan directeur de la defense*), upon which will be written a list or explanation of the works, &c. The prolongations of the faces and capitals of the works of the front of attack, will be laid down on this general plan; and every morning the works constructed by the besiegers during the night, will be laid down upon it. Besides this general plan of the place and its environs, there will be constructed upon a greater scale a separate plan of the attacks, including only the front of the attacks and the collateral works which overlook their approaches. On this plan the prolongations of the faces and capitals will be traced with great accuracy, as well as the disposition of the batteries and their successive changes; the opening of the trenches will be accurately drawn, and also the precise position of all the works of the besiegers. Lastly; the plans of the new works proper to be undertaken to strengthen the fortifications, will be laid down upon this plan.

As soon as day light enables them to judge of the position and extent of the first parallel, the besieged know by the directing plan of the defences the position of the ricochet batteries that the besiegers must establish. All their artillery is in consequence so disposed, that the greatest possible number of barbette batteries firing direct, and of mortar and howitzer batteries, will be brought to bear upon and scour these positions. This is the only epocha at which all the artilery must be brought into action without respite. Ammunition must not be spared during the thirty-six hours that the enemy will take to construct their direct or ricochet batteries. But circumstances will soon change; and then the artillery and ammunition must be used with as much parsimony as it is now lavished.

From the opening of the trenches the besieged should foresee the critical position in which they will be placed after the besiegers have constructed their batteries; it will then be no longer possible to make use of cannon mounted on garrison carriages and on barbettes. The cannon must then be placed in embrasures, and covered with traverses and paradoses made of gabions 15 decimètres (5 feet) high and 10 (3½ feet) in diameter. Each gabionnade is made of two tiers of gabions, the first composed of four rows, and the second of three; the gabions are bound together with fascines, &c. These traverses and paradoses, placed on the terra-plains against the batteries, arrest the shot in its descending branch and destroy a great portion of the ricochets. The situations in which embrasures should be constructed, are designated by the positions of the enemy's batteries which must be combatted from several points, especially from the collateral parts and from those parts that the enemy cannot enfilade by effective ricochets. The construction of the embrasures and traverses will be carried on with the greatest activity, in order to change the defensive system of the artillery as soon as the enemy unmasks his batteries; for it would be vain and wasteful to contend against the artillery of the besiegers with artillery almost uncovered and exposed to ricochets (*prise en rouage*). As the besiegers debouche on the second night from the first parallel to carry their approaches forward, the heads of the boyaux must be unremittingly battered from all parts by direct fires, and the capitals swept and crossed by ricochet fires of howitzers and mortars posted in the salient places of arms: this will produce great effect, because the fires are as yet unimpaired and are wholly directed against these approaches.

From the moment that the front of attack is determined, the besieged will attend to strengthening the fortifications. The parapets are made thicker and are again cut or smoothed; the banquettes are formed, and the plunges or superior slopes are well levelled, &c.; the palisadings, the barriers and fraises of the covert-way, are put in the best condition; and the communications across the ditches, composed of bridges, caponnières, &c., are established in the best manner.

If the ravelins and bastions of the front of attack are not already intrenched, their intrenchments must be laboured at with the greatest activity. These intrenchments will be constructed of earth, and will be fraised and palisaded, &c. ; their scarps will be revested with fascines or saucissons, and their counter-scarps with planks supported by piles.   The same preparations will be made in the re-entering places of arms : if their capacity permit, a redoubt of earth will be made in them with 10 to 12 decimètres (3½ to 4 feet) commandment over the crest of the glacis.   If circumstances and the nature of the works do not permit these additions to be made of earth, there will be substituted in their place redoubts or tambours made of strong palisades placed together, and behind which a banquette will be raised with its breast height strengthened with a layer of sods or clay mixed with cut straw.

The frame tambours with which the salient and re-entering places of arms are armed to cover their stairs. (PLATE IV. Second Part, fig. 3.)
When the re-entering places of arms are provided with a redoubt, the stairs of their gorge is perfectly secured and requires no addition ; care is merely taken to cover the stairs of the salient places of arms by tambours of timber (*tambours en charpente*), which are likewise used in the re-entering places of arms when these are not capable of containing a redoubt.

The frame tambour with which salient and re-entering places of arms are armed, is a redan constructed of large oaken planks 20 centimètres (8 inches) thick, and 40 decimètres (13¼ feet) high ; they are planted upright and close together, so as to rise 22 décimètres above the ground.   Loop-holes are made in the planks at 2 feet apart ; and on the extremes of the faces of the tambour against the counterscarp, doors are made for the passage of troops.   The summit of the tambour is furnished inside with a small pentice 20 decimètres (6⅔ feet) wide, to defend it from grenades : this pentice in the salient place of arms causes the grenades to roll into the ditch, and in the re-entering place of arms causes them to fall into a small ditch made directly beneath its edge.

The second palisading planted on the terra-plain of the covert-way   Its advantages and defects.
When the common palisading with which a covert-way is armed, is thought inadequate to protect the retreat of the troops from the covert-way and to deprive the besiegers of all hopes of carrying it by storm ; the besieged may arm their covert-way with a *double palisading* planted upon the terra-plain, and uniting with the palisades of the traverses and forming a second intrenchment.   Behind this palisading a banquette will be made, with steps to ascend it ; and the breast height will be strengthened by fascines planted upright against the openings, and by a layer of sods or clay, &c.   This palisading contains

single barriers, established on the outside against the traverses, for the troops to retreat through.

The advantages of this double palisading do not compensate for its inconveniences : 1st, It greatly impedes and embarrasses the manœuvres and circulation in the covert ways.   2d, It increases and multiplies the dangerous splinters produced by ricochets and howitzes.   3d, As it must be erected from the beginning of the siege, it will be in a great measure destroyed by the time that the attack upon the covert-way takes place.   4th, The besiegers on arriving on the crest of the glacis, have a plunging, enfilading and reverse fire into it ; whilst their sappers, covered by it from the fires of the place, cut it down.   5th, When the besiegers descend by storm into the covert-way, the double palisading is more favourable to them, than to the besieged.   If the intermediate traverses have a passage between them and the counterscarp, the retreat of the besieged will be sufficiently secured.

We described in the first period of the defence, all the precautions to be taken in the interior of the place ; these are completed when the front of attack is known by the opening of the trenches.   Blindages are immediately erected on this front of attack, together with powder magazines for the daily service ; the powder and all other munitions of war and provisions are removed from the front of attack, and distributed on those points least exposed to the fires of the besiegers.   The quarters that the garrison should occupy are determined ; and their duties of labour and combat are so regulated, as to enable them to sustain the fatigues and privations to which they are about to be condemned.   Lastly ; special care must be taken that the places that the garrison occupy during the hours of repose, are healthy and free from contagion. *The dispositions in the interior of the place.*

The besieged must not only attend to making those interior intrenchments, cuts (*coupures*), &c., which increase the strength of the permanent works ; but they must advance outside, to act with more effect against the approaches of the besiegers and eloign their parallels from the body of the place.   The two kinds of works erected for this purpose are called *flèches* and *counter-approaches.*   The flèches are constructed at the tail of the glacis and upon the capitals, and are formed by two faces about 30 mètres (33½ yards) long, whose directions are enfiladed and flanked by the faces of the bastions and ravelins.   These *The exterior works that the besieged may construct ; the flèches, and lines of counter approach.*

flèches are constructed with gabions, which are ranged in two or three rows to expedite the construction ; their ditches must be fraised and their gorges palisaded, to compel the enemy to attack them by storm before they begin the third parallel. As the flèches occupy the lowest points of the glacis, they will very little mask the fires of the place ; and they will greatly annoy the enemy in pushing on their boyaux, which must be defiled from them.

Counter-approaches are works thrown forward on the flanks of the attacks, and by means of which the boyaux of the besiegers may be enfiladed and scoured by cannon firing grape, and even by rampart guns. A line of counter-approach debouches from the covert-way in a direction defiled from the trenches of the besiegers, to reach a position for a battery that is to be constructed during the night ; it is made with gabions 10 decimètres (3⅓ feet) high, if the fire is to be in barbette ; and with gabions of this dimension and of 20 decimètres (6⅔ feet), if the battery is to be with embrasures and covered on its flank by an epaulment. The boyau leading to this battery is made like a trench, and is single or double, according as it is to be covered on one or both sides. Frequently the counter-approach consists of only a boyau, lined with infantry to enfilade the trenches. When a counter-approach is no longer useful, it is levelled and the materials carried away.

The sorties, or the tactics for the exterior defence of a besieged place. That part of the war of sieges which treats of the manœuvres that the garrison should make outside to retard the works of the attack, is of the greatest importance. This branch of grand tactics is totally neglected in time of peace, and very few Governors have been distinguished in it. We cite as examples to imitate, the admirable manœuvres of Chamilly at the siege of Grave, those of Guèbriant at Aire, &c. A Governor who thinks that he should always remain within his works and act against the enemy with the fires of his intrenchments only, sees fortification in too narrow a point of view, and neglects one of its chief advantages ; he does not keep alive in his garrison that activity which arises from offensive operations. A Governor who always remains close within his works and does not know how to manœuvre outside, under the protection of the place, with sufficient skill and without jeoparding himself make havock among the besiegers and destroy and level their works, does not conduct himself like a General; for he entirely abandons the defence to the artillery and engineer officers.

The French garrison of Mentz and Cassel, though besieged by more than 120,000 men, made continual sorties and retarded at each step the progress of the attacks. All the arms were combined to attack the enemy without, to repulse them, and to level their works. At the siege of Grave, Chamilly repeatedly fought with his cavalry on the glacis. But what shall we think of the last siege of Mantua, where 8000 Frenchmen opened the trenches and succeeded in establishing batteries in breach against a garrison of more than 6000 men, who only ventured one sortie, and were then repulsed!

Sorties should be conducted according to the general principles of attack. The manœuvres that we have described for a vigorous sortie against the first parallel, show that as long as the besiegers have not advanced beyond the second parallel, they have the advantages of position and numbers; consequently at this distance the sorties must be seldom, and must be made with great forces and prudence. They are combats in which the besieged, concealing their order of battle and their central lines of action, endeavour to surprise the besiegers, put their workmen to flight, spike their cannon, and destroy a part of their works. Nothing has a greater tendency to inflame the courage of a garrison than achieving some brilliant exploit, ending in the capture of several pieces of artillery brought off in triumph into the works and there placed in battery against their former masters.

The besieged are better able to oppose the establishment of the second parallel, than the first; because its position is known, as likewise the moment that it is begun. Consequently the same manœuvres that we have described will be repeated against this parallel, and to greater advantage. As the distance of the parallel does not permit it to be covered, except by a few platoons of grenadiers who will suffer severely from the musketry of the covert-way; these troops will be easily overthrown by the sortie and driven beyond the trench, where the besieged will form in order of battle and make head against the reinforcements, to give time to the labourers under the direction of the engineers to level the saps and particularly the redoubts on the wings. But it will be here, as it was at the first place of arms; the besieged can only for a short time retard

The manœuvres and sorties at the epoch of drawing the second parallel.

the laying out of the parallel, and they will soon find themselves reduced to the use of their fires only.

The use of the fires at the epoch of the second parallel. Although the first batteries of the besiegers have at the epoch now under consideration silenced a great part of the batteries of the besieged; nevertheless the latter must endeavour to re-establish in battery as many pieces as possible, to act against the new batteries that the besiegers are about to construct to obtain more effective fires. Frequently in abandoning their first batteries, they afford a moment of intermission of which advantage must be taken to re-kindle the fires of the place. The collateral parts that the besiegers have not been able to ricoché and counterbatter, must now be armed in a formidable manner, and should without intermission fire direct and ricochet upon the attacks.

If the fires of the besieged artillery diminish in proportion to the progress of the besiegers, they on the other hand acquire fresh strength from the musketry fires; the proper use of these at the second parallel, may compel the besiegers to construct it with the whole sap. Excellent marksmen, supported by the fires of the covert-way, will be advanced on the flanks of the attack to take in flank and enfilade the boyaux, &c. Platoons of rangers will go out at night to ambush themselves and fire upon the labourers carrying on the approaches with the flying sap, and to fall upon them unexpectedly and put them to flight. During the day the infantry posted in the salients of the covert-way, will keep up a constant fire upon the heads of the saps; and in order that the fire may be the more effective during the night, the directions of the fire will be marked in the day time by iron stakes planted in the ground. Such a fire, though scattering or occasional, produces far greater effects than a volleying fire (*feu roulant*) from the covert-way, which the enemy will quickly learn to despise; it will render them much more timid and cautious.

The sorties at the epoch of the half place of arms. After the establishment of the second parallel, the sorties assume a different character. Prior to this epoch they could produce no effect; the enemy, discovering them coming on from a distance, had time to prepare to receive and repulse them before they could reach the works. But at the epoch of laying out the half places of arms, the besieged are so near the works of the besiegers, that they must constantly attack them by small sorties that strike terror among the labourers. But as the ene-

my will soon become accustomed to this *petite guerre*, real sorties will be made from time to time to endeavour to destroy and
fill up the works and spike the cannon, &c.

Finally ; at the epoch when the besieged behold themselves
about to be enveloped by a third parallel, they must redouble
their vigour and activity. They must most carefully examine
the properties of the fortifications, whose influence becomes
more effectual and immediate at each step of the besiegers. Indeed the further the besiegers advance, the more difficult they
find it to defile themselves ; the directions of their boyaux are
almost at rectangles with the capitals, and they consequently
approach more slowly, circumspectly, and perilously : their
progress therefore becomes more laborious (*plus industrieuse*).

SECTION III.

The Attack and the Defence during the third Period of the Siege.

THE THIRD AND LAST PERIOD OF THE ATTACK.

*Description of the Works, Measures and Manœuvres of the Be-
siegers from the third Parallel, to the Reduction of the
Place.*

139. When the besiegers have completed the third parallel,
occupied it in force, and crowned their parapets with loop-holes
made with bags of earth, they no longer fear the sorties of the
garrison; these are now enveloped in such a manner, that they
cannot sally out of their covert-way, nor advance from the
collateral parts upon the flanks of the attacks. The besiegers
will labour to establish new batteries whose effect will far sur-
pass that of those in the rear, the fires of which have now
become annoying to the troops in the parallel. In consequence
of the perfection to which artillery has attained, these batteries
have the great advantages of silencing a large portion of the
musketry fires, protecting the species of approaches which the
besiegers must now make, and showering such a quantity of
projectiles upon the defences, that the besieged will be so harassed and tormented as to be unable to make much use of musketry. These batteries will be armed with howitzers, mortars, and stone mortars : and when the distance is too great to

139. The bat-
teries of howit-
zers, mortars and
stone mortars,
used by the be-
siegers after es-
tablishing the
third parallel.

use the stone mortar, a substitute will be found by loading the mortar with grenades to shower into the re-entering places of arms and other parts of the covert-way.

The situation of these batteries. (PLATE IV. fig. 2.)

The batteries of the third parallel are placed at about right angles with the prolongations of the faces and flanks of the works and of the branches of the covert-way, in order to enfilade and ricoché them, and to destroy any batteries that the enemy may endeavour to preserve ; and also to avoid masking the debouchés and embarrassing the approaches on the edges of the glacis. These batteries may be placed in the parallel ; but it is preferable to carry them a little in advance, to give them a better direction and prevent their interfering with the manœuvres of the troops and other dispositions of the attack.

In the front of attack under consideration, there will be four great positions B, B, B, B, on the right and left of the capitals, that will be occupied with batteries ; each battery will have two faces, united by a curve. The faces will be occupied with howitzers, and the centre by mortars or stone mortars.

Continuation of the journal of the attack. The labours of the 12th and 13th nights

As the construction of these new batteries will afford a respite to the besieged, they will avail themselves of this favourable moment to re-establish and bring into action part of their artillery. The besiegers cannot therefore debouche from the third parallel until these new batteries are opened ; which should be the case by the end of the 13th day : consequently the besiegers will not be able to debouche from the third parallel, under the protection of their batteries, before the fourteenth night.

140. General reflections on the method of conducting the attack in advancing from the third parallel.

140. We will now attend to the general considerations on the manner of conducting the attack from the third parallel. At this epoch the strength and arrangement of the front attacked, and the position of the besiegers in relation to the besieged, influence the choice of the means for hastening the catastrophe of the siege.

The object of the besiegers in advancing from the third parallel.

The aim of the besiegers after strengthening their parallel and after their batteries are in full activity, is to become master of the covert-way and thence uncover the scarps. This is a very nice operation, and requires to be conducted with great skill.

The crowning of the covert-way and the causes which decide the besiegers in their choice of the means for effecting it.

They are masters of the covert-way when they succeed in crowning it with a trench which the besieged cannot attack. This trench is provided with traverses which defile its different parts from the plunging fires of the principal works. To effect this coronation, the besiegers bear in mind that in advancing from the third parallel they are upon the ground of the fortifications, and that then the positive defence of the place begins and is in proportion to the good or bad disposition of the works. They must also take into their calculations the strength and valour of the garrison. Lastly; a succouring army threatening the army of observation, or the badness of the season, may determine the besiegers to make sacrifices and to attempt by a bold stroke to abridge the siege.

These motives may often decide the besiegers to effect the crowning of the covert-way by storm ; that is, by the flying sap. This was the method always followed before the time of Vauban ; but this celebrated engineer caused it to be abandoned for that by gradual approaches. The present state of fortification and artillery has rendered the attack by storm easier than it was in the time of Vauban, and its success almost certain. This has resulted from the imperfections of fortification, and the powers of artillery fires which have become so multiplied as to compel the besieged to abandon the defences and deprive them of the means of resistance. Nevertheless, the besieged by taking precautions may render an attack by storm very dangerous ; and may force the enemy to approach step by step.

The attack of the covert-way by main strength the preparatory means that the operation requires.

When the besiegers have determined on crowning the covert-way by storm, they take measures accordingly from the laying out of the third parallel which is advanced within 60 to 70 mètres (67 to 78 yards) of the salients ; care being taken to give it a configuration a little convex in front of the re-entering parts. They approach as near as possible to the batteries of these re-enterings, in order to establish stone mortars and fire without remission into the salient and re-entering places of arms and render them untenable. They will make steps in those parts of the parallel which are on the right and left of the capitals, so that the elite troops that are to assault the covert-way may debouche with ease. These parts disposed in steps will be 12 mètres (40 feet) long, that the troops may debouche with a front of a company.

As soon as the parallel and batteries are completed, all the materials necessary for crowning the covert-way are transported to the reverse of the parallel and into the boyaux in rear. The troops that are to make the attack, are held in readiness ;

The measures for the attack of the covert-way by storm.

and likewise the labourers, in the proportion of one man per gabion. All these preparatory dispositions being made, the batteries will during the 13th day keep up a tremendous fire upon all the defences, to batter down the palisadings, frame tambours, &c. and drive the enemy from behind them. Towards night and while there is yet day-light enough to conduct the operation with order and without confusion, platoons of grenadiers will move out of the parallel, advance towards the salients, and shower grenades into the salient places of arms and branches of the covert-way. At the same instant the picked troops will debouche from the parallel and storm the covert-way. The sappers, conducted by engineer officers, cut down the palisades and facilitate the entrance of the troops, who will pursue the besieged to the re-entering places of arms, and display along the covert-way to fire upon any troops that show themselves upon the defences. Part of the troops will avail themselves of every shelter, such as the defiles of the traverses, the profiles of the outlets (*passages de sortie*), and the first gabionnades of the coronation, to thereby cover themselves and support those who remain uncovered.

As soon as the attack has succeeded and the enemy are repulsed, the labourers come out of the parallel and begin crowning the salients of the covert-way ; that is, the engineers construct with the flying sap a trench 6 mètres (20 feet) from the crest of the glacis, embracing the salient angles and extending as much as possible along the branches of the covert-way. As fast as this work is carried on, the workmen fill the gabions and quickly cover themselves. As these lodgements upon the salients are taken in flank and enfiladed by the collateral defences, they are defiled from them by traverses placed at intervals ; the defiles of these are also covered by other traverses constructed on the reverse of the trench, with sufficient length to serve as paradoses when the trenches are seen in reverse. These lodgements are not for the moment extended more than is necessary to enfilade and take in reverse the palisadings of the covert-way.

Whilst the salients are thus crowning, other workmen lay out and execute the communications with the third parallel ; these must be configured as we shall immediately describe. At the end of 2 or three hours work the lodgements will be sufficiently strong to receive the fresh troops who are to support them, whilst the elite troops will gradually retire from the covert-way.

During the night the lodgements and works laid out will be strengthened ; and the parts which could not be constructed with the flying sap, will be completed with the whole sap. These labours would be very dangerous if they were not covered by the furious fire of all the batteries. The reason that during this night the lodgements must only be extended along the branches a little beyond the traverses of the salient places of arms, is that they would mask the fires of the mortar, howitzer and stone mortar batteries, whose directions must be regulated before night-fall. Care must be taken to well-cover the extremes of the lodgements by returns of strong gabionnades.

When the attack of the covert-way by storm succeeds, it so greatly advances the labours that the besiegers will on the following night (the fifteenth night) become masters of the whole covert-way. The description of the manœuvres for this operation, show that it is of a nature to succeed only in particular circumstances, and that the besieged may be able to defeat it with great slaughter of the besiegers. Therefore the attack by gradual approaches is the only mode that should be recognized by theory, when the question is the probable duration of the siege.

Reflections on the attack of the covert-way by storm.

Let us follow the regular progress of the attack by gradual approaches advancing from the third parallel, which we will here suppose to be drawn 180 mètres (200 yards) from the salients without any alteration in its concave figure. The approaches in advance of this parallel can no longer be made by defiled boyaux ; and recourse must be had to direct approaches upon the capitals or other directions least exposed to flank and reverse fires, and which will least mask the fires of the batteries of the parallel. The approaches will be carried on with the double sap (sape pleine double), and the several parts will be defiled and covered from direct fires by winding or tambour traverses (traverses tournantes ou en tambour) surmounted with a gabionnade to give them the proper relief.

The attack of the covert way by industry ; the approaches from the third parallel.

Instead of debouching directly upon the capitals from the third parallel, a method has been invented of debouching in portions of circles of about 50 to 60 mètres (56 to 67 yards) chord and 25 (28 yards) sagitta. The convexity of these circular portions is determined in such a manner as to defile them

Debouching from the third parallel in circular portions ; their advantages.

from the salients; they are disposed with steps and provided with loop-holes. The advantages of these circular approaches are obvious; 1st, by their convex form they afford excellent cross-fires into the re-enterings, and oppose a front to the branches of the covert-way; 2d, they contain platoons of grenadiers to repulse the sorties and support the sappers; 3d, they afford valuable situations in which to deposit all the materials for the trenches.

Continuation of the journal of the attacks. Labours of the fourteenth night and of the fourteenth day.

On the 14th night they will debouche from the third parallel to construct with the whole sap the three circular portions; this will be effected by squads of sappers who will advance to meet each other. This night will be sufficient to lay out and rough form them; in the day time they will be completed and fitted to receive the troops. These circular portions will bring the besiegers within 45 or 50 mètres (50 to 55 yards) of the salients.

Labour of the 15th night, and of the 15th day.

On the 15th night the besiegers will debouche from these circular portions to advance upon the three capitals by *double direct saps* (*sapes double et débout*); platoons of grenadiers will line the circular portions, and the batteries will unceasingly fire into the works and covert-ways. During this night it will be practicable to execute 15 to 20 mètres (17 to 22 yards) of work; and to thus get within 30 mètres (33 yards) of the salients. The sappers cover the debouches and approaches of this night by one or two tambour traverses, which they construct by wheeling to the right and left round a solid mass; which is then covered with a gabionnade to give it the necessary relief. During the 15th day the labours of the preceding night will be completed.

The situation of the besiegers when they are within 30 mètres (100 feet) of the salients, or within reach of grenades. The last half places of arms.

When the heads of the saps have arrived within 30 mètres of the salients, they are no longer adequately protected by the circular portions; besides, they are almost within range of grenades (which is 26 mètres (86¼ feet)); and the besieged will dreadfully annoy the trenches with these kind of projectiles, if precautions be not taken against them. To attain this double end of protecting the approaches and sheltering them from grenades, half places of arms must be made embracing the salients; and the enemy must be driven from the salient places of arms and branches of the covert-way. This latter may be effected in two different ways; 1st, by terminating the half places of arms by *trench cavaliers* (*cavaliers de trenchée*), which by their relief will have a plunging and enfilading fire into the branches of the covert-way; or, 2dly, by arming the wings of these half places of arms with batteries of *stone mortars* which will render the covert-ways untenable. The trench cavaliers make part of Vauban's theory; he employed them with great success. Latterly however it was perceived that these long and difficult labours might be dispensed with, by substituting for them batteries of stone mortars posted on the wings of the last half places of arms.

Trench cavaliers and batteries of stone mortars.

The trench cavalier is a lofty gabionnade made of several tiers of gabions, and from the top of which the besiegers plunge and enfilade a branch of the covert-way. Steps are made inside to ascend from the bottom of the trench to the banquette; and the summit of the parapet is made in loop-holes with bags of earth. Each trench cavalier is covered from the fires of the collateral works by a *return* of the same height as itself, and of sufficient length to serve as a parados if such be necessary. The return is made with banquettes, and is armed like the cavalier if it be useful.

Description of the trench cavalier. (PLATE IV, Second Part, Fig. 5.)

When each circular branch of the last half places of arms has attained the prolongation of the crest of the glacis, a perpendicular is drawn to this prolongation and will indicate the most advantageous direction on which to establish the trench cavalier; its length must at least be equal to the width of the covert-way. But this direction can only be thus taken when the salient angle is acute or right, and when the collateral works do not take it in reverse. If the contrary by the case, the cavalier must be drawn about parallel to the crest of the glacis, and in such a manner that its return will perfectly defile its interior.

The plan and construction of trench cavaliers.

Fig. 5 of Plate IV, Second Part, shows better than words can describe, how the cavalier and its epaulment are raised: the gabions are placed according as the cavalier is to be 2, or 3, or 4 gabions in height. One, or two, or three rows of gabions are placed in the bottom of the trench and filled up with earth; and upon this base is arranged the successive courses of gabions necessary to attain the required height. After the mass is raised, the interior steps and breast height are formed. When the salient angle about which the besiegers wind, is very obtuse and very much flanked (*débordé*) by the collateral works, it is often impossible to construct trench cavaliers; in this case there must be substituted in their place mortar and stone mortar batteries firing grenades.

Continuation of the Journal of the labours of the 16th night and following day.

On the 16th night the sappers being arrived within 30 mètres (33 yards) of the salients, quit the direct approaches to embrace the salients by the last half places of arms, and to construct the trench cavaliers. These labours are completed during the day ; and the half parallels are lined with grenadiers.

Labours of the 17th and 18th nights ; the fourth parallel.

The 17th and 18th nights will be devoted, 1st, to raising the trench cavaliers ; 2d, to connecting them by a fourth parallel if the re-entering be great, and if the vigour of the garrison forces a recurrence to this method.

Remarks on the fourth parallel. & on the new batteries of the attack.

When the disposition of the fortifications and the attitude of the garrison necessitate a fourth parallel, it must be remarked that the probable duration of the siege will be necessarily increased. This parallel will by its relief mask the fire of the batteries of the third parallel, so that it will be requisite to transport these batteries into the fourth parallel ; this operation will occupy at least two days, and will afford a respite to the garrison and the means of rekindling their fires. In this progress of the attack, it will be best to approach on the capital of the re-entering to communicate from the third with the fourth parallel.

The fourth parallel, with a view to carry the covert way by storm.

A fourth parallel is often made with a view to crowning the covert-way by storm. In this case, this operation becomes easier under the protection of the trench cavaliers and batteries of the fourth parallel. When the attack on the covert-way is by storm, the fourth parallel is made with steps ; and the precautions that we have described, are taken.

Continuation of the attack by gradual approaches. Labour of the 19th and 20th nights ; the crowning of the salients of the covert-way.

On the 18th the fires of the trench cavaliers or of the batteries of stone-mortars being in full activity, it will be practicable to push forward the approaches and attain during the night of the 19th, the three salients of the front attacked. These approaches may be made on the capitals by direct double saps, as previously ; but it is preferable to debouche from near the cavaliers by simple saps uniting together within 6 mètres (20 feet) of the salients, and enclosing a trapezoidal mass covering part of the last half place of arms and serving as a place of deposite for materials for the trenches. The sappers directed upon each salient, after uniting, glide parallel to the crest of the glacis and extend as far as possible, covering themselves with numerous winding traverses.

During the 19th day and 20th night the salients will be embraced in such a manner as to discover through the openings of the ditches the scarps and collateral flanks ; the wings of the coronation will be supported by long and high returns that will cover them from the fires of the collateral works.   They may easily advance far beyond the salient of the ravelin ; but opposite the bastions, the coronation will with difficulty attain the prolongation of the magistral.

As the lodgements upon the crest of the glacis are enfiladed and frequently seen in reverse, they are covered by winding traverses sufficiently numerous and crowned by a gabionnade, and by masses constructed opposite the defiles of the traverses and of sufficient length to serve as paradoses.

The winding traverses, and masses established on the reverse of the trenches to cover the defiles of the works and serve as paradoses.

When the trench cavaliers or wings of the last half places of arms are not connected by a fourth parallel, the re-entering place of arms is enveloped by a *concave circular portion* joining the salients of the bastions with the salient of the ravelin. On the centre of this circular portion a heavy battery of mortars and stone-mortars is established, and directed against the re-entering place of arms, the ravelin and its redoubt, and the bastions.   But when a fourth parallel is made, the direct approaches are pushed on to the salient to crown the faces of the re-entering place of arms and join the other parts of the coronation.

The circular concave portion embracing the re-entering place of arms.

As soon as the re-enterings and salients are seized, a small battery of one or two six inch howitzers may be immediately established to fire upon and destroy the frame tambours that cover the stairs (*pas de souris*).

Batteries of 6 inch howitzers posted in the salients and re enterings, to destroy the frame tambours.

During the 21st and 22d nights the circular concave portions will be constructed, the salient of the re-entering place of arms will be seized, the crowning of the whole covert-way will be completed, and heavy batteries of mortars and stone-mortars will be established.

Continuation of the journal of the attacks. Labour of the 21st and 22d nights.

From the 22d day the positions for the different batteries will be prepared, &c.

141. After the crowning of the covert-way is effected and strengthened, the besiegers are in an offensive position alarming to the besieged ; the latter have been driven from the covert-way and compelled to retreat into the redoubts of the re-entering places of arms ; and the besiegers uncover the scarps of the ravelin and bastions.   In consequence of this position, the besiegers should have in view three things ; 1st, to counter-batter the fires of the flanks of the body of the place which enfilade the

141. Position of the besiegers after they have crowned the covert-way : their objects : the ulterior labours.

ditches; 2d, to overwhelm the scarps of the ravelin and bastions by batteries in breach, or by mining; 3d, to make communications suitable for gaining the breaches, to assault the works and come in contact with the besieged man to man.

The two first will be attained by *counter batteries* and *batteries in breach.* Both of these are constructed in the coronation opposite the objects that they are to batter; their terraplains are covered by traverses sufficiently high and long to defend them from flank and reverse fires; and they are more elevated than the bottom of the trench in rear, in order to better uncover and have a lower plunging fire against the scarps.

When the tracé and the relief of the fortification do not allow the besiegers to uncover the revêtements sufficiently low to batter them in breach from the crest of the glacis, the batteries in breach must necessarily be brought down into the covert-way, where their construction will require more time and be more perilous. It must be remembered that the line of fire of a battery cannot be greatly inclined below the horizontal; the angle of fire beneath the horizon for batteries in breach firing with the maximum charge, cannot exceed 7 degrees (old measure).

The parapet of the trench is made use of for the epaulment of these batteries; their terra-plains are raised with the earth taken from the communication which passes in their rear; and their platforms, embrasures, &c., are made like the batteries of which we have before spoken (135).

The third object is attained by means of two kinds of communication, called the *descents of the ditch,* and the *passages of the ditch.* The first are distinguished into two kinds—*open to the heavens (à ciel ouvert),* and *subterranean.* These descents are galleries leading from a certain point of the glacis in a gentle slope down to the bottom of the ditch, and debouching opposite that part of the breach by which the works are to be assaulted. When the ditch is full of water, the debouché of the descent is on a level with the water.

When the bottom of the descents is one uniform slope, its inclination is about 6 to 8 centimètres per mètre (2½ to 3¼ inches in 40 inches); but when the descent is steeper, the ground is disposed in steps. This latter disposition is inconvenient; and as the besiegers are free to make the opening of the descent wherever they choose, the first method is to be preferred.

As the enemy throw great quantities of grenades, stones and fire works into the works, it is necessary to blind those parts of the descents that are open at top.   To this end the gallery is covered over with hurdles and several layers of fascines, and the whole is supported by a disposition of blinds.   The blind is a simple frame composed of two uprights united together by two cross pieces ; the ends of the uprights extend 30 centimètres (12 inches) beyond the cross pieces, and are sharpened to a point ; the uprights and cross pieces are square by 18 by 18 (7½ by 7½ inches) ; and the frame is 22 decimètres high and 12 wide (7½ by 4 feet.)

The manner of blinding the descents of ditches open to the heavens. Description of the blind. (PLATE IV. Second Part, fig. 7.)

The manner of disposing the blinds along a descent 20 decimètres (6¼ feet) wide, is very simple.   Against each profile of the descent a file of blinds is vertically established and sufficiently apart that the interval which separates two blinds is covered by another blind laid horizontally, whose interior angles receive the points of the vertical blinds, and thus unite them.   This system, strengthened by pegs and brackets, supports the hurdles and fascines ; the whole is then covered over with raw hides.

When the bottom of the ditch to be attained is very deep, it is obvious that the excavation would be immense if the descent must be made open at top.   In this case the debouché of the gallery is more or less eloigned from the crest of the glacis ; and after making in the glacis the opening of the descent and conducting it open at top as far as possible, it is then carried on like the gallery of a mine, with a width of 15 decimètres (5 feet).   This construction is the same as that of the branch of a mine, of which we shall speak hereafter.   For this purpose frames 22 decimètres high and 15 wide (7½ feet by 5) are used, and placed square upon the direction of the gallery at a distance of 10 decimètres (3¼ feet) from each other.   As fast as the frames are laid, a coffer work of planks is made to support the lateral and superior earth.

The descent of the ditch by subterranean galleries : their construction.

When the descent of the ditch has reached the counterscarp, they cut through it to get into the ditch.   It is proper to make at this debouché a spacious place of arms, to receive the materials for the passage of the ditch, and to facilitate the debouching of the column marching to the assault.   If it be intended to break through the counterscarp by a mine, it must be fired before the head of the gallery has attained the counterscarp.

Breaking thro' the counterscarp : the debouché of the descent of the ditch made with a place of arms.

The descent of the ditch by mining. It is sometimes practicable to do without the descent, and to succeed in debouching into the ditch by more expeditious means. These consist in making an overloaded mine under the banquette of the covert-way, and calculated of such power as to overwhelm the counterscarp and mingle its ruins with those of the breach. The shaft or crater (*entonnoir*) produced by the explosion, will enable the besiegers to descend through it by sap into the ditch.

The passages of the ditch. By the *passages of the ditch*, is understood the works that must be made across the ditch to gain the breach and make the assault. Sometimes, owing to particular circumstances, no such dispositions are made in the ditch, and the troops debouche uncovered from the place of arms and mount to storm the breach. But such cases are rare ; and if the enemy make even but a little resistance, and if the opposite flank can open its fires, the attack must be repulsed with great loss. To carry on the operations with more method, the besiegers must join the debouché of the counterscarp with the breach by an epaulment carried on to the top of the breach and masking the fire of the opposite flank : the assault may then be made, and the besiegers establish themselves by storm within the work.

The passage of a dry ditch. If the ditch be dry and there be earth in its bottom, the passage is made by sap. If the reverse be the case, the epaulment is made of bags of earth which are passed down by hand to the sappers from the opening of the descent : when the sappers gain the ruins of the breach, they make use of them for the epaulment. Thus we see that the passage of a dry ditch is nothing more than a common trench made with the whole sap ; and to which is added a large epaulment, or an epaulment made of materials brought from the circular portions.

The passage of a ditch filled with stagnant water. When a ditch filled with stagnant water is to be passed, the difficulty is not much greater than if the ditch were dry. From the debouché of the counterscarp loads of fascines are thrown in and loaded with stones, rubbish, and earth, &c. ; each layer of fascines is pegged with small pickets. In proportion as any part of the bridge rises to the water level, an epaulment is made next the flank. This work is continued until they reach the breach, upon which a lodgement is effected by the whole sap. When this epaulment is made of fascines or bags of wool, it must be covered with very raw hides to prevent the garrison from setting it on fire.

The passages of ditches that are most difficult, are where they contain running waters which the besieged by means of sluices may let in at pleasure, or when they contain stagnant waters which the garrison can at any moment swell.

In the first case the bridge must be so constructed as to resist the currents that the enemy can produce at any moment; and in both cases, it must be a floating bridge. This bridge will be made of fascines laid in successive layers, and connected together by small pickets. After three or four layers of fascine-work are established, five or six rows of sleepers 2 decimètres (8 inches) thick are laid lengthways with the bridge, and traversed at intervals of 12 decimètres (4 feet) by large spindles 10 decimètres (3½ feet) long : these spindles running through the layers of fascines, consolidate the work. The thickness of this fascine-work should be such as to enable the bridge to support the weight of heavy artillery and of a column of infantry. As fast as the bridge is built, its epaulment is likewise made with fascines or bags of wool.

In proportion as the work is advanced, it is supported against the current by anchors thrown out above the stream, and by buttress piles driven with the hand rammer (*mouton à main*) : these two species of supports should both be used at the same time, if the current be strong. One of the ends of the cable of each anchor will be fastened to the sleepers on the side looking up the current, and the other end to the superior surface of the bridge; in order that the cables may be veered out and the bridge possess the power of rising or lowering, according as the level of the waters is swelled or diminished.

Instead of a fascine bridge, a *raft* (*radeau*) may be constructed along the counterscarp and surmounted with an epaulment. When it is completed, it is brought by a movement of conversion with its head towards the breach, and kept in that situation by the anchors and piles of which we have spoken. Lastly; there are cases in which it is practicable with proper precautions to throw a ponton bridge across in a few minutes, surmounted with a parapet of several rows of gabions stuffed with wool and 22 decimètres (7½ feet) high. The engineer who directs the works, must determine according to local circumstances and the nature of the defences which of these methods should be adopted.

We have now completed the description in detail of all the

works of a siege ; we will therefore continue without interruption the journal of the attacks on the bastioned front that we have taken as a term of comparison.

Continuation of the journal of the attacks. Labours of the 23d & 24th nights, and 24th day.

The batteries in breach against the ravelin faces, and the counter batteries against the flanks of the body of the place and against those portions of the faces of the bastions that enfilade the ditches of the ravelin, are begun from the 22d. These latter batteries are armed with 24 pounders, in order that they may batter in breach after counter-battering the enemy's artillery. The length of the half-moon faces always allows these batteries to be established in the coronation of the covert-way ; and it will suffice to raise the bottom of it a little higher, when requisite. But when the batteries in breach against the ravelin faces do not fire sufficiently low, the besiegers must descend into the salient places of arms and into the branches of the covert-way to construct their batteries.

On the 22d the openings of the descents of the ditch will be laid out. In the course of the 23d night the counter-batteries and batteries in breach will be completed ; and the openings of the descents of the ditch against the ravelin and bastions, will be made.

The 23d day and 24th night will be employed in completing all these labours, in arming the batteries, and continuing the descents of the ditch.

On the 24th day all the batteries will be completed and armed. The counter-batteries may open their fires in the morning, but the batteries in breach cannot be brought into action before night or next morning ; and if the besiegers have been compelled to descend into the covert-way to establish their batteries in breach against the ravelin, their construction cannot be completed before the 26th night.

Whilst the batteries and counter-batteries are ruining the defences, the descents of the ditch are continued, and all the materials are brought forward for the passage of the ravelin ditch.

Labours of the 25th and 26th nights, and of the 26th day.

On the 25th night they will debouche into the ravelin ditch opposite to the breach ; and a place of arms will be made in the counterscarp. The 26th night will be employed in making the passages of the ravelin ditch, and in reconnoitring the breach, &c. In the course of the 26th day the passages of the ditch will be completed, and the breach made practicable by firing a great many howitzes, &c. against its summit.

In the course of the 26th day and 27th night every prepara-Assault on the ravelin the morning of the 27th. Labours of the 27th night, and of the 27th day. tion will be made to assault the ravelin.   On the 27th, at break of day the troops for the attack will debouche from the places of arms of the counterscarp, rapidly mount the breach, drive the enemy from the salient, and compel them to retreat into the redoubt.   During this attack by storm, the engineers, followed by the sappers, will lay out with the flying sap a lodge- ment around the counterscarp, and will connect it with the epaulments of the passages of the ditch.   As fast as this work is completed, the troops will retire to it for shelter.

During the 28th night the lodgements in the ravelin terra-Labours of the 28th night, and of the 28th day. plain will be extended to the ditches of the cuts (*coupures*). Fougasses will be made for overwhelming the counterscarps of the ravelin cuts ; and the besiegers will advance by saps along and into the body of the parapets, to take in reverse the re- doubts of the re-entering places of arms.   They will continue to batter in breach the faces of the bastions, and approach by zig-zags in the ditches of the ravelin in order to debouche into the ditch of the body of the place.   They will descend by wide cuts (*coupures*), made opposite the defiles of the traverses, into the re-entering places of arms ; and lastly, they will crown the counterscarp.   In the course of the 28th day they will descend by wide cuts into the ditches of the redoubts of the re-entering places of arms ; and the miners will be set to work at the redoubt- scarps.

During the 29th night they will labour with the greatest ac-Labours of the 29th night and 29th day: the assault on the redoubts of the re-entering places of arms. tivity at the batteries in breach against the redoubt of the ra- ve in : and they will complete the mines for overwhelming the ravelin cuts (*coupures*) and the scarps of the redoubts of the places of arms.   At daylight the mines will be sprung, the re- doubts will be assaulted, and the besiegers will establish them- selves in them.   During all this time the descents of the ditches of the body of the place will be continued, and will be proper- ly directed in order to debouche opposite the breaches made through the openings of the ravelin ditches.

In the course of the 30th night the batteries in breach againstLabours and progress of the 30th and 31st nights, and 31st day. the ravelin redoubt are completed ; these batteries will be opened at break of day, and the lodgements in the re-entering places of arms will be strengthened.   The descents of the ditches of the body of the place, are pushed forward with vi- gour ; and the besiegers descend from the ditches of the ravelin cuts (*coupures*) into the ditch of the redoubt. During the 31st night they continue to batter in breach the redoubt of the ravelin, and to make the breaches practicable; they debouche into the great ditch, and labour at the counterscarp places of arms and at the epaulments of the passages of the ditch. On the 31st, at break of day it will be practicable to assault the ravelin redoubt, and to establish themselves in its terra-plain in the course of the day.

Observations on the breaches made in the bastions through the openings in the ditches of the ravelin.
When the batteries established in the coronation of the salient ravelin place of arms do not effect breaches sufficiently wide and of a nature to ensure the success of the assault; and when it is foreseen that the enemy will make a great resistance to the passages of the ditch of the body of the place, and to the attack on the bastions; the besiegers must display greater powers of artillery. They must as soon as they are masters of the redoubts of the places of arms, establish fresh batteries in breach against the faces of the bastions, either in the coronation of the covert-way against the traverse of the place of arms, or in the covert-way itself, or in the terra-plain of the redoubt along its gorge; and here they will post two or three 12 or 16 pounders to counter-batter the fires of the curtain and tenaille. It must be again observed, that though the breaches made in the faces of the bastions through the openings of the ravelin ditches may be practicable from the 27th or 28th at farthest; nevertheless if the bastions be intrenched it will be impossible to carry them, because the besiegers cannot work at the passages of the great ditch so long as the enemy have possession of the ravelin and of the redoubt of the re-entering place of arms. The flanks of the ravelin redoubt take these breaches in reverse; and the attack by industry on the body of the place, cannot be attempted until this redoubt is taken.

Remarks on the intrenchments of the bastions, which protract the defence beyond the 30th day.
If the bastions of the front of attack were not properly intrenched, the besieged would not be able to stand an assault; they would therefore be compelled to capitulate the moment that the besiegers had secured their debouché into the ditch, that is, on the 30th or 31st day after the opening of the trenches. But under the protection of the intrenchments in the bastions, the besieged must sustain and may repulse with advantage any assaults by storm on the body of the place; and by taking their measures with ability, they will force the besiegers to attack by gradual approaches, and thus protract the defence.

Labour during the 32d and 33d days.
During the 32d and 33d days the besiegers will labour with

vigour at the passages of the great ditch and their epaulments. The breaches will be made easy of ascent, by firing great quantities of howitzes into its crest and at the ressaults or projections formed by the ruins. If it be necessary to mine any part, it will be done from the 31st, in order that the mine may be sprung on the 33d. Finally; in the course of the night between the 33d and 34th, every preparation will be made for the assault of the bastions.

Every preparation being completed for storming the bastions, on the 34th at break of day the troops will debouche from the descent, form in the ditch behind the epaulment, bravely mount the breach, and attack the besieged by storm in the terra-plains. They will maintain their ground whilst the engineers are constructing a lodgement upon the top of the breach, behind which the troops will retire as fast as it can shelter them. During the whole day the besiegers will labour at the lodgement on the breach and at the communication to the rear.

Assault on the bastions on the 34th, at break of day.

On the night of the 34th day they will debouche from the lodgement on the breach into the terra-plain of each bastion; and they will crown with the whole sap the counterscarp of the intrenchment. During the 36th day they will labour at the batteries in breach against the intrenchment, or they will set the miners to work at it.

Labours of the 35th and 36th days.

In this posture of affairs the besieged can no longer defend themselves against the besiegers, to whom they have no further obstacles to oppose. In a few hours they will be in contact man to man; and the garrison must suffer all the severities of the custom of war in such cases, if they do not hasten to capitulate. The capitulation will take place on the morning of the 37th.

The forced capitulation on the 36th, or 37th day at farthest.

Thus the probable duration of the siege of the modern bastioned front, left to its own positive strength, should be calculated at 36 days of open trenches.

The probable duration of the siege, is 36 days of open trenches.

THE THIRD AND LAST PERIOD OF THE DEFENCE.

The conduct of the Governor of a Fortress during the third and last period of the attack.

142. The epoch of the establishment of the third parallel is followed by that in which the defence should acquire new vigour. At this moment, when the besiegers set foot upon the

142. The conduct of the governor from the epoch of the third parallel, to the capitulation.

ground of the fortifications, the Governor should under its protection, now become so much more effectual, display all the activity of his garrison and all the resources of his genius.   Hitherto he has economized his ammunition and other means of defence ; but now he must no longer spare them, and must dispute every inch of ground included within his field of battle. The intrinsic and relative strength and value of all the works, are now brought into their fullest effect.   The general description of the attack has just shown that the arrangement of the different parts of the system under consideration, is such, that the progress of the besiegers becomes in proportion as they advance, slower, more difficult and more dangerous ; they are at each step compelled to have recourse to new and more complicated measures of ingenuity and industry.   'Tis by deeply studying the protecting and conservating properties of the fortification, and teaching them to the officers of the line, that the chief who conducts a defence may hope to retard the imperative march of the attack and make great slaughter and destruction of the enemy.

The opposition of the besieged to the establishment of the third parallel ; the use of the artillery and sorties.
The besieged must exhaust all their efforts to retard the laying out and establishing of the third parallel.   If the besiegers venture to execute it with the flying sap, the labourers will be overthrown and put to flight by the smallest sortie ; for the enemy cannot cover the work by a disposition of troops, without exposing them to destruction from the fire of the works.

Whilst the besiegers are opening (*amorcera*) the parallel with the whole sap, a few pieces of artillery that have been concealed from them will be opened against the heads of the saps ; these pieces will be chiefly posted in the collateral works.   The salient places of arms, and the collateral ravelins, will be armed with howitzers to fire obliquely at the parallel.   All the pieces that can be brought into action, will fire with canister to scour the ground of the parallel.   Excellent marksmen will line the covert-way and keep up a continual and well-directed fire on the heads of the saps ; they will be relieved every half hour, in order that they may clean and put their arms in order.   Potgrenadoes will be thrown out to illuminate and discover the works and approaches of the besiegers.

As soon as the besieged perceive that the besiegers have succeeded in laying out rather considerable portions of the parallel, they will prepare to make a vigorous sortie to level the

works. Bodies of infantry, and even of cavalry, will debouche
from the collateral works to cover the flanks of this operation ;
and the elite troops will sally out of the covert-way against each
portion of the parallel and put the labourers to flight.   They
will firmly maintain their ground on the flanks whilst the workmen destroy the gabions, level the trenches, and speedily retire under the protection of the troops, who will retreat as soon
as the enemy advance from the half places of arms.   They
will not restrict themselves to one single and vigorous sortie ;
they will continually make small ones which will be mere incursions or alarms, but will be sufficient to put the labourers to
flight.   It is the proximity of the labours that thus enables the
besieged to harass and impede the work by constant sorties,
which may be made almost without danger. Frequently these
sorties will be merely feints to draw the enemy out of their parallels and cause them to sustain severe and previously prepared
fires.

After the besiegers have established and strengthened the
third parallel, they no longer depend upon the efficacy of their
batteries in the rear ; they now labour to establish new ones.

*The position
of the besiegers
after the estab-
lishment of the
third parallel ;
the new batteries
of the besieged.*

This is an invaluable moment for the besieged, who for two
days enjoy a species of tranquillity on their ramparts; they
should take advantage of this respite to re-establish in battery
on all points as many pieces as possible, and to keep up the
most furious and incessant fire upon all the works.   This is the
moment when neither artillery nor ammunition are to be spared :
it is a moment that never will return, and the besieged must
profit of it accordingly.   They must never forget, that it is
their duty and honour to delay as long as possible the surrender
of a fortress whose works must become a heap of ruins, whose
artillery will be destroyed, and whose ammunition and provisions
will be exhausted. During this epoch the parapets will be repaired,
the palisadings and frame tambours will be again put in good
condition, and the intrenchments and cuts (*coupures*) will be
completed : finally ; the fortifications must, as it were, be restored to their primitive condition of strength and freshness.

The besieged will construct in the salients of the collateral
works blinded batteries, which will produce great effects against
the third parallel and ulterior approaches : they will preserve
the use of these batteries to the end of the siege.   During all
the time that the enemy take to construct their new batteries.

the besieged will incessantly fire at their position with how-itzers and mortars; they will bring forward mortars into the re-entering places of arms, and fire them loaded with grenades, &c.

The conduct of the besieged in an attack by storm upon the covert-way.

If the enemy take great pains to complete the third parallel; if they make it with steps (*gradins*), and establish in it stone-mortar batteries, &c.; it is a certain proof that they intend at-tempting to crown the covert-way by storm. The besieged should make their dispositions accordingly. They must during the night illuminate the parallel, and post chosen troops in the re-entering places of arms and ditches; the parapets of the co-vert-ways and works will be lined with infantry, the collateral covert-ways will be held by detachments of grenadiers, and all the batteries that can bear upon the debouchès of the parallel and upon the covert-way will be loaded with canister; finally, platoons of grenadiers will be posted in the ditches of the rave-lin and bastions, to shower grenades into the covert way.

The moment that the enemy debouche from their parallel, all the fires of artillery and musketry will be directed against them; the troops who occupy the salients and branches of the covert-way, after firing a volley close to the enemy's breasts at the in-stant that they reach the crest of the glacis, will retire behind the second palisading if there be one, and there continue their fire. If there be no second palisading, they will retreat, some into the re-entering place of arms, the others into the ditch by the tambour of the salient place of arms. After these troops have retreated from the covert-way, all the fires of the place will be directed upon the enemy who have penetrated into the covert-way, and upon their workmen; and the grenadiers will shower their grenades from all quarters. Lastly; when the fires have thrown the troops and labourers into disorder, the elite of the garrison will sally out of the re-enterings and at-tack the besiegers in the covert-way; whilst the grenadiers from the wings will advance on the glacis at the charging step and take the coronation in reverse, and overthrow the troops and works; the workmen will at the same time level the rough drawn crowning.

Remark on at-tacking the co-vert-way by storm

In operations of this nature, the besieged have every advan-tage; accordingly they very seldom succeed when the garrison conduct themselves properly. We have seen that Vauban abolished this method of crowning the covert-way, in consequence of the great sacrifices that it requires.

Let us return to the defence against the attack by gradual approaches of the covert-way. All the mortars and howitzers, which should be very numerous, will unceasingly fire upon the batteries and approaches ; and stone-mortars will be transported into the salient places of arms, if they can throw the stones as far as the circular portions. Small sorties, and now and then strong and vigorous sorties, must be constantly made during the night against the heads of the saps ; and chosen marksmen will keep up a continual fire on these heads with rampart guns. Covered batteries with oblique embrasures will be constructed beforehand, to be ready for the moment that the enemy begin raising the trench cavaliers ; these batteries will produce great effect.

The measures of the besieged against the attack on the covert-way by gradual approaches.

As soon as the besiegers are within reach of grenades, they will be showered down like hail upon their labourers and troops in the trenches ; and when the openings of the descents of the ditch are discovered, bombs, howitzes, and incendiary shot will be showered at them.

The use of grenades.

When the enemy seize the salients, the besieged will retire from traverse to traverse into the re-entering places of arms ; and the traverses will one after another be battered down with cannon, to prevent the enemy from covering themselves by them when executing the descents of the ditch or establishing batteries in the terra-plain of the covert-way.

The moment that the enemy crown the covert-way step by step, is that in which a skilful use must be made of the artillery, and the most perfect concert exist between the arms of artillery and engineering. Oblique embrasures in the curtain of the front of attack and in those of the adjacent fronts, must be opened to obliquely cut with their fires the lodgements on the salients of the bastions. Similar embrasures must be opened in the collateral ravelins and in their redoubts, to enfilade or take in reverse the wings of the coronation and the positions of the counter-batteries. These batteries may be blinded : and the enemy may be compelled to descend into the covert-way to establish their batteries. The batteries on the flanks will be covered with traverses and paradoses, and will even be blinded. These batteries will be unmasked at the very moment of the coronation, to fire direct during the construction of the counter-

The use of the artillery after the besiegers have crowned the covert way.

batteries.   The besieged will endeavour to make blinded batteries in the flanked angles of the bastions, to take in reverse
the crowning of the ravelin covert-way, &c.

The defence of the ditches depends upon their nature.   If
the ditches be dry, their defence will be offensive as in every
other part of the fortification ; and whilst they are principally
contending against the besiegers with artillery and musketry
fires, the besieged sally out upon the passages from the collateral ditches and from behind the tenaille.   These sorties must
be in strength when it is expected to be able to level the epaulment and cut down the sappers.   Commonly however, they are
made with few men ; but are often repeated.   These bold
strokes will greatly retard the progress of the works.   As soon
as the debouché of a descent is discovered, a position in the
fortifications must be sought whence it can be battered with a
blinded battery that the enemy cannot counter-batter.

The case of a ditch filled with stagnant water, does not afford the besieged any advantage ; its defence is entirely by artillery which must by some means be established against the
debouché of the descent, and by the fires of the opposite flank.
As the epaulment may be made of earth, the garrison cannot
burn it.   Accordingly ditches filled with still water are not advantageous, except when the body of the place is badly planned and liable to be carried by storm after a breach is practicable and without it being necessary to raise an epaulment.

Ditches that may be filled with water at pleasure, and especially those into which considerable currents of water may be
introduced by means of *influent* and *refluent sluices* (*écluses de
chasse et de fuite*), are the most advantageous; they afford the
besieged great means of defence : 1st, The garrison may first,
as in common cases, harass and impede the construction of the
besieger's bridge and epaulment by their fires and by sorties :
2d, They may make fire-works of such an incendiary nature as
to succeed in burning the epaulment, and even the bridge itself if it be floating and composed of materials of less specific
gravity than water : 3d, They have in letting in and drawing
off the waters, or manœuvring the sluices (*le jeu des eaux*), a
last resource that may dishearten the enemy.   In this case, if
the besiegers have constructed a massy bridge, at the moment
that they have reached the breach the influx sluices will be
opened and the reflux sluices shut ; the waters will rush with

such violence against the bridge as to probably carry it away, together with part of the ruins of the breach. If however the bridge resist the shock, the manœuvre will be repeated again, and as often as necessary. When the waters have swelled to their greatest height, the refluent sluices will be opened and the influent shut, to be opened however again; and thus very rapid torrents are successively produced and will wash away the foot of the breach, and which the bridge, however well it may be constructed, will resist with great difficulty. These difficulties that the besiegers will have to contend with, will be still greater when they are obliged to construct a floating bridge in a dry ditch attacked every moment by armed men or floods of water.

The *assault* is the operation by which the besiegers gain possession of a work by penetrating through the breach. The besieged should therefore constantly attend to rendering the access of the breach very difficult ; they must throw at its foot a great quantity of combustible materials, which they will set fire to at the proper moment ; they will cover the breach with caltrops, and roll down bombs and howitzes. Lastly ; they will make mines under the breach which will be sprung the moment that the assaulting column gains the top of it. *The assault and defence of the breach.*

The measures for defending a breach are of two kinds. The first is adopted when the breach is not intrenched in rear ; that is, when it is not supported and protected by an intrenchment that cannot be carried by storm. The second is used when the breach is supported by a strong intrenchment. In the first case, the defence is by main strength by troops suitably armed and disposed. At the moment that the enemy debouche into the ditch, the breach is crowned by troops armed with muskets and grenades, and who make the greatest possible resistance. These troops are supported by a corps in deep order consisting of the strongest men covered with defensive armour, and armed with long reaching weapons, such as partisans, pikes, and sithes, &c. The moment that the column of attack appears upon the top of the breach, the first troops will retire, whilst the main body will furiously charge the assailants and endeavour to repulse them into the ditch. This manœuvre must be repeated with fresh troops as often as the assailants renew the assault. *The measures of the besieged at the moment of an assault.*

But when the assailed work is provided with a redoubt or an intrenchment capable of checking the assailants, the manœuvres are very different, and are of a nature analogous to the defence of a covert-way attacked by storm.   The parapet of the intrenchment is lined with infantry, and if possible provided with a few small pieces loaded with grape shot and pointed at the debouché of the breach; there will be behind the infantry two ranks to load their arms.   Platoons of infantry and grenadiers will be posted on the flanks and behind the breach, to receive the first shock of the enemy's column; but as soon as it has gained the summit of the breach and they have fired their last volley, they will quickly retire into the redoubt or intrenchment.   All the fires of the intrenchment will now be opened upon the enemy, and upon the workmen that are making a lodgement in the terra-plain.   If the enemy appear to be shaken by the fires of the flank which takes the breach in reverse, and by the fires of the intrenchment, troops will sally out by the flanks of the breach and attack the enemy and their labourers, and charging them with the bayonet throw them into the ditch.   If this attack succeed, they will level the coronation of the breach, and spread over it fresh combustible materials, caltrops, &c.   Lastly; it is in a defence of this kind that mines are advantageous; because the besieged have all the means and leisure of springing them at the proper moment; but in the defence by main strength, it frequently happens that they explode too soon or too late.

Reflections upon the defence of breaches,   by main strength, and by industry. Defences by main strength rarely take place, especially in the body of the place; because the position of the besieged is much more critical than that of the besiegers.   If the latter do not succeed, they retire and make new dispositions for a fresh attack; and so on until they do succeed.   The besieged on the contrary can only delay the fall of the place a few minutes; and if they do not succeed in their defence, they cannot retreat without the greatest difficulties and dangers.   When this contest is within the body of the place, the retreat of the besieged is followed by the loss of the fortress and all the horrors of a storm.   Hence it follows that a work of fortification is no longer tenable when it can be assaulted by a practicable breach; and the assault upon it by storm should not be sustained, except in consequence of calculations foreign to fortification.

The defence by industry must always be adopted in a work provided with an interior intrenchment.   By this method an able Governor succeeds in withstanding one or more assaults upon the breach of the principal work ; and thus more or less protracts the probable duration of the siege, without jeoparding the fate of the garrison.

Finally ; after successively abandoning the advanced parts of the fortification, the besieged will at length be only separated from the besiegers by the last intrenchment of the bastions ; and the commander of this valiant garrison will find himself compelled to accept an honourable capitulation. He will march out at the head of his troops, through the breaches and over the ruins, glorious monuments of his courage and talents and of the valour of the garrison !

CHAPTER V.

The relation between the Attack and the Defence ; General Conside-
ration of this subject ; the general principles of Attack and De-
fence ; Examination of the Bastioned Front that has been de-
scribed ; the Theory of Commandment ; Determination of the
Relief of all the Parts of the System ; the Strength of the
Assailable Fronts, respect being paid to the Collateral Fronts ;
Parallel between the Attacks of the Bastioned Front in its se-
veral conditions ; Principles on the General Figure of an En-
ceinte, &c.

143. The rela-
tion between the
attack and the
defence, to com-
pare together the
fronts of attack
of the systems of
fortification.

143. THE relation between the attack and the defence is established by approximation, by means of the general methods
that we have just described.   Their arrangement is founded
upon indisputable principles of tactics, and deduced from numerous military facts which have ever confirmed it.   It is
therefore by establishing the nearest relation between the attack and the defence of a front of attack, chosen in any particular system, that we succeed in ascertaining the *probable du-*
ration of the siege ; and consequently the most important element of the strength or value of this front of attack.   But this
instrument or means of investigation, although it affords a general approximation, requires to be used with ability in particular cases ; the manner of using it constitutes an essential part
of the military coup d'œil of an engineer.

Reflections on
the progress of
the attack and
the defence gene-
rally.

To form an exact idea of this manner of analyzing the several systems of fortification with a view of comparing them, we
must draw some general results from the examination of the
march of the attack and of the defence.

There are two remarkable periods of the attack and of the
defence distinguished in the siege of a fortress.   The *first* is
from the opening of the trenches, to the establishment of the
third parallel ; the *second* commences with the third parallel,
and terminates at the moment of the definitive capitulation.

The properties
of the works of
the attack during
the first period

During the first period of the siege, the works of the attack
envelop the defensive polygon by concentric parallels whose
fires converge upon the defences.   Under the protection of these
powerful fires, the approaches are carried on with rapidity by

constantly advancing with a front. This power that the besiegers possess of surrounding the defences, enables them to seize the prolongations of the faces of the works, and to establish upon them ricochet batteries, whose effects, combined with those of batteries with direct and curvated fires (*batteries à feux courbes*), soon ruin the batteries of the besieged that are open at top. They annoy the terra-plains so dreadfully, that the service on them is very perilous and often impracticable ; all the buildings in masonry that can be perceived from without, are immediately ruined from the first parallel by the direct batteries ; and all the fires of the defences being open to the heavens, the besiegers silence them before they can act against the works of the second period. Lastly ; the enemy surround and easily repulse all the exterior operations of the garrison.

In examining the measures of the defence during the first period of the siege, we see that the fires of all kinds upon the works of the besiegers are divergent, and can only batter them direct ; that the sorties must be few, and timid ; that the curvated fires, so advantageous to the besiegers, are of little avail to the besieged ; that the besiegers can with ease construct and repair their works ; that the besieged are constantly restrained and annoyed in their movements and manœuvres, whilst the besiegers enjoy a freedom very favourable to all their operations ; and lastly, that in the present state of the material of the defence, the besieged cannot preserve fires sufficiently numerous and effective to use during the last period of the siege.

The general properties of the fortification during the first period of the siege

We must observe that in proportion as the besiegers approach the salients of the front of attack, the disposition of their works becomes less favourable to them ; the length of the parallels diminish, and they lose their enveloping nature ; they flatten, and the extent of their front tends to an equality with that of the front attacked. The boyaux are shortened, the angles that they make with the capitals become greater and greater, and the approaches become slower. At the third parallel, at which the second period begins, the properties of the works of the attack are so changed, that this parallel is almost rectilinear, and even convex towards the fortress ; and the defiled zig-zag approaches can be carried on no further. It follows from these facts, that when the besiegers set foot upon the ground of the fortification, they experience great difficulties to establish their works, and that the defence must naturally assume the ascendant over the

The properties of the works of the second period of the siege

X

attack. But if the besiegers lose advantages in the form of their works, they acquire new ones by the power of the curvated fires that they shower down upon the defences; and which compensate for the loss of the first. Under the favour of these fires, they baffle all the measures of the garrison.

The properties of the fortification during the second period of the siege.

All the properties of the fortifications display themselves as the siege advances; and when the enemy begin to occupy the ground of the fortifications, they exert their utmost force. After the third parallel, the works of the attack are cut obliquely and taken in flank and reverse; the approaches must be made direct; and if the besieged could make use of and manœuvre their artillery, the defence would have greatly the ascendancy over the attack.

144. Consequences or general principle of the attack, and of the defence.

144. From these considerations we must conclude; 1st, that the march of the attack is necessarily imperative, and that the defence cannot arrest its progress; that the incurvated fires used in the attack (whether ricochet or with elevated trajectories) annihilate all the fires of the defences when these are open to the heavens, and render the defences almost untenable; and this superiority of the fires increases from the beginning to the end of the operation : that from the first parallel, or at least from the second, the direct fires demolish all the buildings in masonry that can be seen from the without, and even the covered masonry is not secure from being greatly damaged by the curved fires.   2d, That the march of the defence is essentially timorous; that its fires are of little annoyance to the enemy, very little injurious to their works, very divergent, and almost extinct at the moment that they might be very effectual; and that the besieged cannot uncover any of their constructions in masonry.   Lastly; that the besieged should defend their artillery from the curvated fires of the besiegers, and should find means to shelter their troops in the terra-plains of the works, &c.

145. Examination of the bastioned front; completion of the description given in Chap. III (114, 115, &c)

145. We may now analyze the bastioned front that we described in the third chapter (118 and 119), and thus establish the mediate and immediate relation between all the elements of the system, and expose their advantages and defects.

The distant, & the near, defence.

The *distant defence* (*défense eloignée*), is that part of the defence which relates to the first period of the siege; and the *near defence* (*défense rapprochée*), is that which relates to the second period of the siege (143).

The enceinte, its composition & configuration.

The enceinte being the principal obstacle that must be preserved as long as possible, it must be constituted with great strength and resistance ; accordingly, it consists of vertical scarps of solid masonry, &c.   This masonry must not be discoverable from the country ; and it is for this reason that the summit of it is placed in the plane of defilement of the covert-way.

The masonry of the enceinte is well covered during the *distant* defence ; but this is not the case in the *near* defence. The moment that the besiegers effect a lodgement on the salient of the ravelin, they uncover and ruin the scarps of the bastion faces &c.   This disposition is therefore very defective, and requires correction.

Reflections on the masonry of the enceinte: its defects.

The bastioned enceinte, such as we have drawn (116), fulfils the greatest part of the conditions prescribed by the science of defence ; but its figure is more favourable to the near, than to the distant defence.   It affords along the whole extent of its front during the latter part of the last period of the defence, an immediate flanking of musketry and artillery fires ; but beyond the covert-way the artillery fires cross on the capitals with very little effect, and the musketry fires are inefficient, by reason of the great obliquity of the bastion faces.

The properties of the enceinte in relation to its ground plan ; length of the side of the polygon.

We now perceive the reason for fixing the length of the side of the polygon between the limits of 260 and 360 mètres (290 and 400 yards).   This length must afford bastions sufficiently spacious to construct an intrenchment in, and flanks of sufficient length to vigorously defend the ditches and the crowning of the covert-way ; the musketry of these flanks must also act effectively on the trench cavaliers and coronation of the salient place of arms. The flank should always be of greater extent than the enemy's counter-battery ; and the flanked angle must never be less than 60 degrees (old measure).

From the origin of the art, acute salient angles were banished from fortification ; none are now admitted of less than 60 degrees.   Three great defects or inconveniences induced their interdiction ; 1st, they produce outside a large sector destitute of fires : 2d, they narrow the terra-plain so much, that it is impossible to post artillery in the salient angle : 3d, they are easily ruined by the artillery from the moment that they are uncovered.

Why the angle of 60° is the smallest salient angle that can be used.

Flanks drawn about perpendicular to the lines of defence, have an excellent direction for defending the ditch and crest of the glacis of the salient place of arms ; but their prolongations

The disposition of the flanks.

are easily seized by the enemy, who from the site of the half places of arms sweep them in *ricochet*, and annihilate their artillery by vertical fires. It is therefore indispensable that the artillery of the flanks be covered and preserved unimpaired until the crowning of the covert-way.

The trace of the curtain.

We have already said that the first tracé of the curtain (116) was best, because it affords a greater place of arms between the tenaille and the body of the place for the sorties, &c. to debouche from. And we will add, that the portion of the flank retrenched in the second tracé, defends advantageously the crowning of the salient place of arms by slightly obliquing the directrices.

The width of the terra plain of the enceinte.

The width of the terra-plain of the body of the place, is fixed at 12 or 14 mètres (40 to 47 feet), measuring from the covering line; in order to have 7 or 8 mètres ($23\frac{1}{3}$ to $26\frac{1}{4}$ feet) for the service of the artillery, and 6 or 7 mètres (20 to $23\frac{1}{3}$ feet) for transport and the movements of troops.

The intrenchments in the bastions: the tenaille and its advantages.

The permanent intrenchment of the bastion, is one of the constituent elements of the modern bastioned front. In this system, in which the enemy cannot penetrate into the place but by the faces of the bastions, they cannot turn the intrenchment by its gorge. Under the protection of this redoubt the besieged sustian one or several assaults, and compel the besiegers to attack by gradual approaches; and consequently force them to carry the ravelin redoubt, which sees the breach in reverse, before they attempt to assault the bastion.

We said in describing the tracé, that the chief use of the tenaille is to cover a portion of the enceinte and the communication with the ditch. Its other advantages are; 1st, it affords a kind of place of arms whence to debouche to any of the outworks; 2d, it affords a scouring (*rasant*) fire on the terra-plain of the ravelin redoubt, and favours the retreat of the troops defending the ravelin.

Reflections on the tenaille.

The introduction of the tenaille into the bastioned system, has modified the enceinte, and should cause it to be beheld in a different point of view; for by its relief it offends against the general principle that led to the invention of the bastioned figure, and which inculcates *that all parts of the ditches must be seen and flanked by the enceinte*. We said that this mask (118) produced a dead part that the flanks cannot discover; therefore the principle quoted is no longer observed, and is changed into the following : *An enceinte being beyond insult and secure* New principle on the general disposition of the enceinte. *from an attack by storm, part of this enceinte is covered and shielded from the effects of batteries in breach, in order to flank and defend the parts exposed to the artillery of the besiegers.* This *dead space* that the relief of the tenaille produces in front of its scarp, is a defect in the system ; and of which daring besiegers may take advantage. They may bring forward troops and oc-cupy it by debouching from the ravelin ditch, and thus cut off the retreat of the troops defending the ravelin redoubt ; and they may thence march to assault the bastion or curtain, if they have been able to make a breach through the opening (*trouée*) between the tenaille and the flank.

If the enceinte and the tenaille were the only constituent The ravelin & its redoubt : their advantages. elements of the system, the progress of the besiegers would be very rapid. Their advance upon the capitals of the bastions would be opposed by few obstacles ; because the cross-fires of artillery are there scarce and of little effect, and the musketry fires are almost nothing. This defect increases in proportion as the enemy advance ; because the lines of fire become more and more oblique. At the distance of the half places of arms, the besiegers could counter-batter the flanks and destroy their fires ; and by a single operation they would at the same in-stant crown the whole covert-way, batter in breach the faces of the bastions and the portion of the curtain facing the openings of the tenaille, and thus render nugatory the intrenchments of the bastions.

All these considerations show the importance of the ravelin, the necessity of covering with it the shoulders of the bastions and the openings between the tenaille and the flanks, and the advantage of carrying its salient as far out towards the country as possible. The tracé of the ravelin should be such, that the besiegers will be forced to make a separate attack upon it be-fore they can attack the enceinte ; and in this disposition, the besieged will devote all their attention and employ all their strength to defend this outwork.

Next to Vauban, Cormontaigne devoted most attention to the properties of the ravelin of great dimensions. He has shown that in high polygons the half-moons or ravelins are in relations of defence ; that they form re-entering spaces occupied by the bastions ; and that with them the bastioned system assumes a new aspect favourable to the defence. We will display hereafter these admirable advantages, which have for several years excited the attention of engineers. In the plan of the ravelin of the front described, its faces fall nearly at right angles on those of the bastions ; its redoubt is well constituted, and allows it to be defended inch by inch ; cuts (*coupures*) are made in it a little in rear of the prolongation of the faces of the reentering place of arms, in order to stop the enemy and prevent

(PLATE II.) them from gliding by sap into the body of the parapet to take in reverse this same place of arms and its redoubt. As the flanks of the redoubt from the manner in which they are drawn see in reverse the breaches of the bastions, the besiegers are forced to attack this redoubt and make a breach in it either by mining or by battering ; but as the first method gives rise to a war of stratagem (*guerre de chicane*), which might retard the operation, the besiegers are compelled to mount a battery in

The thickness of the terra-plain of the ravelin. breach of 24 or 16 pounders in the ravelin. It is this measure of the enemy that determines us to make the width of the ravelin terra-plain not more than 10 mètres (33¼ feet), so as to force them to cut away the parapet to form their epaulment and gain the necessary space for the terra-plain of their battery ; and they are then seen in reverse by the salient of the bastion, and by the salient place of arms of the collateral ravelin. The ditches of the redoubt are flanked by a part of the faces of the bastions that cannot be counter-battered except from the very terra-plain of the ravelin, and on which blinded batteries may be constructed that will produce great effect on the passage of the redoubt ditch.

Rule respecting the width of the terra-plains of works that cover them. In general, whenever a work covers another, the terra-plain of the first must be reduced to its smallest width ; in order that the besiegers cannot establish themselves in it without cutting down the parapet to construct the epaulment of their battery. The celebrated Coehorn adopted this principle in his system.

Plan of the gorge of the ravelin and of its redoubt. The gorge of the ravelin and of its redoubt, is terminated by lines of fire drawn through the flanked angles of the bastions and the extremes of the ravelin faces ; in order that no part of their terra-plains can be seen and taken obliquely by the musketry fires of the coronation of the bastion salient places of arms.

The defects of ravelins of great dimensions. All ravelins have two essential defects ; 1st, they enable the enemy when they are established upon the crest of the glacis, to see through their ditches portions of the enceinte ; 2d, their ditches are not flanked, except by a portion of the face of the bastion that is counter-battered and battered in breach by the same battery. These defects exist in a greater degree in ravelins of great dimensions. As these are more salient, their places of arms are sooner crowned; and their faces being longer, the batteries plunge with more ease at the foot of the bastion scarps. To these must be added, that as the flanked angle of great ravelins is as acute as possible, they are more easily ricoched, and it is easier to embrace in the attack the prolongations of the faces of the collateral ravelins. Although it is true that the bastions may be battered in breach before the capture of the ravelin and its redoubt, yet it is not possible to storm them; because the bastions are intrenched, and the flanks of the redoubt see the breach in reverse. Nevertheless these breaches are very harassing to the besieged, who are fatigued and wearied by continually guarding them. Accordingly, as merely respects its positive strength or value, the bastioned system has not been very sensibly improved by the use of the great ravelin. And it is indispensable to so modify it, as to remove this radical defect.

We can now perceive and appreciate the relation between the redoubt of the ravelin and the enceinte; it defends the breach of the bastion, and suspends the march of the attack as long as the obstacle that it opposes is unconquered. Accordingly many officers have very judiciously thought, that batteries secure from ricochet and vertical fires should be constructed on the flanks of the redoubt; for they otherwise can only be used for musketry, which cannot produce sufficient effects.

The relations of the redoubt with the enceinte.

By recalling to mind what we said (116) about the dimensions of ditches, we may now find a complete explanation of it. Their breadth should be such, that the counter-battery of the attack will be ever inferior to that of the opposite flank; and this width should be sufficiently great to prevent the ruins of the breach from ever occupying more than the half of it, in order that the operation of the passage of the ditch may be longer and more difficult. With respect to the depth of the ditch, after attending to the equalization of the excavation and embankment, the following must be considered; 1st, the efficacy of the lines of fire from the flanks against the passages of the ditch: 2d, the difficulties that the besiegers must experience to carry on their descents of the ditch: 3d, the positions of the batteries in breach. When the counterscarps are of little height,

The dimensions of the ditches of the enceinte: their width and depth.

the descents of the ditch are made open at top and are quickly executed.   This is the reason that 50 decimètres (16⅔ feet) is the least height for the counterscarp of a principal work. When the ditches can be made deep and have counterscarps of about 60 or 70 decimètres (20 to 23½ feet), they oppose two great obstacles to the besiegers.   These are compelled to make subterranean galleries, and frequently two together, to debouche in force into the ditch ; they are also compelled to lower their batteries in breach down into the covert-way terra-plain, so as to uncover the scarps sufficiently low to be able to ruin them.

The ditch of the ravelin, or half-moon.   When the ditch of the body of the place is deep or contains water, that of the ravelin is not excavated to its level ; its bottom is at such a height as to be well defended by the enceinte, to be always dry, and that the relation between the width and the height of the relief be correct.   When there is a ressault or ascent to the ditch of the ravelin from that of the body of the place, ramps or stairs are made and covered by caponnières to maintain the communication.

The ditch of the ravelin redoubt.   In this system, the ditch of the ravelin redoubt is not made so deep as that of the ravelin or enceinte.; the portion of it in front of the flanks, is a little lower than the part in front of the faces.   This arrangement affords a kind of place of arms which favours the retreat of the troops defending the ravelin, and prevents the besiegers from turning them by the ditch of the redoubt when they are retiring through the gorge.   The cuts (*coupures*) made in the ravelin deprive the enemy of the power of plunging into that part of the ditch where the postern debouches.

The covert-way.   The theory of the attack has demonstrated to us the necessity, 1st, of the garrison being able to freely sally out from their field of battle, to operate without : 2d, of covering the masonworks and defending them from the attacks of the besiegers' batteries : these ends are obtained by the use of covert-ways. Moreover, this defensive enclosure with which the counterscarp is enveloped, greatly increases the strength of the system ; for the crowning of the covert-way, whether effected by storm or by skill and industry, is an operation that costs the besiegers much time and great sacrifices.

The width of the terra-plain of the covert-way.   The width of the terra-plain of the covert-way, is in general about 10 mètres (33½ feet). This is too little, for in most cases the enemy, lodged on its crest, plunge at the ramparts sufficiently low to batter them in breach. When the ditches are so deep that the enemy are forced to lower their batteries down into the terra-plain, it is then best that the covert ways should be narrow, so that they cannot construct their batteries without cutting away the parapet ; and if the revêtement of this parapet be built of masonry 10 decimètres thick ($3\frac{1}{3}$ feet), the construction of these batteries will be very long and perilous*. But in case a narrow covert-way would enable the enemy to discover two-thirds of the height of the rampart, it is then best to sufficiently increase the width of the terra-plain ; and if this width make the slope of the glacis too gentle, we must increase a little the relief of the enceinte or of the work.

The stages of the attack show, that it is in making approaches on the glacis that the besiegers must lose most time and lives. This is a period of the siege in which the influence of the fortification is most powerfully felt. The glacises must accordingly fulfil several conditions ; 1st, their slope should be such, that when their plane is prolonged it must not leave below it any line of fire. If the hinge or axis of the glacis be parallel to the covering line of the work, it is not through this latter that the plane of the glacis should pass, but through the lowest line of fire : 2d, the slope of a glacis must not be too great, in order that the lines of fire may be effective and not inclined more than 7 or 8 degrees : 3d, this slope should be so regulated, that when the approaches have arrived within grenade distance, the besiegers will not be able to plunge into the covert ways without making their cavaliers of a height that will expose them to almost inevitable destruction. By regulating this slope in the proportion of 8 or 10 centimètres per 2 mètres ($3\frac{1}{5}$ to 4 inches in 80 inches or $6\frac{3}{4}$ feet), the cavaliers will be at least 28 decimètres ($9\frac{1}{5}$ feet) high, and their construction very dangerous.

The glacises and their slope.

Cormontaigne applied to the covert way this principle—That all assailable works to be capable of being defended, should be supported by an interior intrenchment. The most favourable position for the redoubts that support the covert ways, is obvi-

The redoubts of the re-entering places of arms.

---

* The enemy may, to uncover the bottom of the scarp, make a mine under the crest of the glacis. The explosion of this mine will blow down a portion of the counterscarp and covert-way terra-plain, and will form a chasm through which the besiegers may batter the scarp. The only delay will be the time required to sink the shaft of the mine.

                    TRANSLATOR.

ously the terra-plain of the re-entering places of arms, which are flanked by the ravelin and bastion, and are in the most re-entering part.   We have drawn the faces of the redoubts in such a manner as to defile them from the lodgement that embraces the salient place of arms ; consequently the besiegers cannot seize the prolongations of these faces to ricoché them, and the place of arms is more spacious and better defended by the musketry of the redoubt.   The small flank of 8 to 10 mètres (9 or 11 yards) that sees in reverse the ravelin breach, if mounted with a covered battery of two small pieces, will render the assault of it almost impracticable.   Thus the redoubts of the re-entering places of arms compel the besiegers to attack by gradual approaches, by preserving to the besieged the power of offensive returns against the besiegers when these have penetrated by storm into the covert-way ; and by their relation with the ravelins, they retard the assault upon them until the besiegers have carried and established themselves in these very redoubts.

The traverses of the covert-way.   All the traverses interposed along the branches of the covert-way, have this general and principal property—they cover the different parts of the covert-way from the ricochets to which they are exposed even from the first parallel.   The traverses which close the salient place of arms, together with the frame tambour, secure the communication with the ditch ; they should be attached to the counterscarp, and established upon the prolongations of the parapets.   Those of the re-entering places of arms enclose them, and form a continuous intrenchment ; they likewise are attached to the counterscarp, because their defile is sufficient for the retreat of the troops.   As respects the intermediate ravelin traverses, whose defiles are seized by the enemy in both kinds of attack, it is proper to leave between them and the counterscarp a passage through which the troops may retire or debouche.   As the besiegers cover themselves by these traverses to make their descents and to construct their batteries in breach in the terra-plain, they should in consequence not exceed 30 decimètres (10 feet) in thickness, except those of the re-entering places of arms which must be cannon-shot proof.

It follows that it is useless to make banquettes to any of the traverses, except to those of the re-entering places of arms ; and even the palisadings and single barriers may also be suppressed, for they only embarrass the movements and cause dangerous

splinters. The last sieges of Valenciennes, Quesnoi, &c. proved that these palisadings, and the barriers of the defiles, can
now be of no use.

It has been long acknowledged that the organization of the
covert-ways is not sufficiently strong ; and the more the attack
is improved, the more manifest is this weakness. Many examples taken from the last war, have shown the necessity of making dispositions in the covert-ways that will enable the defendants to resist, and for a longer time to counterbalance, the great
powers of the present mode of attack.

It is by communications that the relations between the different elements of a system of fortification, are established (116);
it is by means of these that troops, artillery, ammunition, &c.
are transported from the interior of the field of battle to any
point.

From these considerations it follows, that all communications
ought to be easy and convenient, and disposed under the relation
of the retreat of the troops. When the communications to the rear
are not perfectly secure, the troops have not confidence enough
to make an obstinate defence. This principle does not apply
to a war of sieges only ; its application is necessary and general to all the dispositions of an offensive or defensive war. These
communications should consist of ramps, wide posterns, blinded
caponnières, subterranean galleries, barriers and passages of the
covert-ways, &c. It would be proper to adapt the ramps and
passages to the manœuvres of cavalry ; a kind of force not sufficiently used in the defence of places, where they might be very useful to continually throw the workmen into disorder, &c.

All the elements of the bastioned front whose chief properties
we have just examined, are arranged in the horizontal projection
in such a manner that the besiegers are obliged to attack them
one after another, under pain of being taken in reverse in their
assaults and compelled to retrace their steps. They protect
each other without the possibility of their own safety being
jeoparded ; and this arrangement or relation of defence, is
founded upon the general principle (93. Second Part)—*That
every part of a fortification which flanks a more exposed part,
must not be under the necessity of attending to its own immediate
defence.*

Reflections on the covert-ways, with respect to the present state of the attack.

The communications.

The general arrangement of all the elements of the bastioned front.

146 The relief of all the elements of the bastioned front, to complete the description in Chap III (117) The theory of commandment. (PLATE II, Second Part.)

146. In describing the relief of the bastioned front (Chapter III. 117), we explained the reasons that determined engineers to establish the relief of all the elements according to a certain law. We now know that the arrangement of their vertical projection, like their horizontal projection, should be deduced from the rules of attack and defence. The relation of defence can only exist between the elements of the system in proportion as they protect each other, and act with the greatest possible effect against the works of the besiegers. This leads us to the consideration of the vertical projection of the lines of fire, and to deduce the relief from the efficacy of the lines of fire viewed in their vertical plane. On this subject we have two principles to establish, to serve us as guides.

First principle; respecting lines of fire, to be effectual.

We showed in the Second Part (105), that fires inclined below the horizon beyond a certain limit, lose their efficiency. Musketry fires may be inclined below the horizontal about 30 degrees; but we have seen in the First Part (Chap. VII.), that artillery cannot fire direct when the piece is inclined more than 10 degrees beneath the horizon. Accordingly we will lay it down as a principle, that the direct and plunging fire of artillery can only be effectual when it is included within an angle of nearly 9 degrees; that is, within an angle whose tangent equals $\frac{1}{7}$ of the radius.

Second principle; on the height at which a direct line of fire must pass above a line of musketry fire in its front, so as not to annoy the defenders.

The second principle that we will lay down, will establish the height at which a line of direct fire must pass above a covering line in order not to incommode its defenders who are simultaneously to use their fires; this height must be at least 10 or 12 decimètres ($3\frac{1}{3}$ to 4 feet.)

Third principle; on the commandment.

As all the works of a system should co-operate in the general defence, their respective commandment should be such as to enable them to act with their fires against all the works of the attack. Hence it follows, that the outmost works should have least commandment; in order that they may not mask the fires of the works in rear, by which they must be commanded when the besiegers succeed in getting possession of them.

This third principle is not general; it is liable to great exceptions.

This last principle is liable to many exceptions; it is differently modified in each system, and is only generally true as it relates to the commandment of principal works over their covert-ways. Thus in the system under consideration, the tenaille has very little relief, although it is preceded by the ravelin, &c. The interior redoubts of the principal works have little commandment over them, and their fires cannot be simultaneous. In Vauban's Systems of Bastioned Towers, the counter-guards entirely cover the towers, &c; and in Carnot's system, the *face-coverings* (*couvre-faces*) completely mask the principal work.

From the preceding principles we will deduce the general relation that should connect the respective commandments of the elements of the bastioned front. We shall distinguish in this system three principal works; 1st, the covert-way; 2d, the ravelin or half-moon; 3d, the enceinte. The secondary works are, the tenaille, and the interior redoubts of the principal works. In examining the manner in which the principal works present themselves to the attack, we see that the covert-way of the ravelin is the work that is first attacked, and consequently that it should have the minimum of commandment above the plane of site; that the covert-way of the body of the place, including the re-entering place of arms, should have a little greater commandment; that the ravelin should command the whole covert-way; and finally, that the body of the place should command the whole. General idea of the commandment of the elements of the bastioned system.

Before Vauban and Coehorn had effected in fortification and in the wars of sieges, a revolution similar to that which the princes of Nassau had brought about in tactics and field operations, engineers followed no rule in establishing the relief. They gave the enceinte a very considerable commandment over the country, and made it more than 100 decimètres (33½ feet) above the plane of site. This enormous relief necessarily enabled them to discover all the works of the besiegers; but it was accompanied by two great defects; 1st, the lines of direct fire were so plunging during the near defence, that they could not be effectual; 2d, the mason-work by being greatly raised above the plane of defilement of the covert-way, was exposed from the first parallel to the batteries of the besiegers. Coehorn and Vauban partly remedied this radical defect; they diminished the commandment of the enceinte over the plane of site, in order to obtain more scouring and effective fires. The manner in which the relief of fortifications was considered before the time of Vauban and Coehorn.

Vauban reduced the commandment of the body of the place to 70 decimètres (23½ feet), and by this correction obtained profiles more scouring or rasant and less exposed to be battered down from a distance by the enemy's artillery. But as he revested the exterior slope of the parapet with masonry, he ex- Rasant fortification: the exterior revetement of the parapet in masonry; the watch towers of freestone.

posed to the besiegers a mass of mason-work 40 decimètres
(13⅓ feet) high ; moreover, he added to the salient and shoulder angles watch-towers (*guerites*) constructed of free-stone in
a very costly manner.

It followed from these dispositions, that from the first or second parallel the besiegers could level the defences and crum-
ble the parapets into the ditches ; and that they were singularly
aided in their reconnaissances by the watch-towers, which enabled them to seize with exactness the prolongations of the faces
and the distance of the collateral works.

Rasant fortifi-
cation after the
time of Vauban.   To complete the correction of the general profile of the enceinte, and of the other parts of the system, the engineers who
succeeded Vauban modified it by the principles that we have
deduced from the attack : 1st, they entirely conceal the masonry from the view of the besiegers, by placing the summit of the
scarp or its coping (*tablette*) in the plane of defilement of the covert-way : 2d, they construct in earth, with exterior slopes, all
the parts of the relief that are above this plane : 3d, to shield the
fortification as much as possible from the besiegers' batteries,
and to render its fires very scouring or rasant, they have often
reduced the commandment of the enceinte to 50 decimètres
(16⅔ feet).   But in consequence of this ill calculated reduction,
the fires of the principal works cannot act direct against the
works of the attack from the second parallel, except by extin-
guishing the fires of the works in their front.

Necessary dis-
tinction between
the plane of fire
for artillery, and
the plane of fire
for musketry.   In all permanent works of fortification, and even in field
works, there must be distinguished as we have before observed
two planes of fire ; one for artillery, and the other for musketry.   Before the besiegers have brought their batteries into action, these two planes are contained in each other and pass
through the covering line ; but the instant that the enemy's artillery is unmasked, the plane of artillery fire sinks 10 or 12
decimètres (3⅓ to 4 feet), in order that the artillery may be covered, &c.   This consideration shows that when the radical
or origin of the lines of fire is determined, the covering line
must be raised 10 to 12 decimètres above it.

Examination of
the relief of ra-
sant fortification,
the command-
ment of whose
enceinte is fixed
at 50 decimètres
(16 2·3 feet) a-
bove the plane of
site.   Let us now suppose the commandment of the enceinte of the
bastioned front to be 50 decimètres (16⅔ feet) above the plane
of site, and then examine whether the lines of artillery fire can
preserve their efficiency and act simultaneously with the musketry fires of the covert-way.   We will take a profile in a ver-

tical plane perpendicular to the face of the bastion, and construct upon this plane of projection the direction of the line of artillery fire.

(PLATE V. fig. 1.)

Then as the radical a of the line of fire should be placed in the vertical ab, distant 20 centimètres (8 inches) from the covering line and 10 decimètres ($3\frac{1}{3}$ feet) lower, this point will be elevated 40 decimètres ($13\frac{1}{3}$ feet) above the ground line ; and ab will $= 40$ decimètres.　But as this line of fire should pass through the point c elevated 12 decimètres (4 feet) above the crest of the parapet, we will therefore have $cd = 36$ decimètres (12 feet) ; and as $bd = 500$ decimètress (167 feet) nearly, we will find by calling x the distance from the crest of the parapet to the point where the line of fire strikes the ground, 40 x—36 $x = 500$ dts. $\times 36$ and $x = 450$ mètres (500 yards) : this shows that the artillery will cease to batter the works with effect at the distance of the second parallel.

If we now give the enceinte the commandment of 65 decimètres ($21\frac{2}{3}$ feet), which we admitted in the third chapter (117) in describing it ; we will find $x = 94$ mètres ($104\frac{1}{3}$ yards). This shows that this is the smallest relief that can be adopted ; and it must be increased to 70 decimètres ($23\frac{1}{3}$ feet) in order that the lines of fire may strike the foot of the third parallel. In this hypothesis the lines of fire preserve their efficiency in proportion to their inclination beneath the horizon, since the angle will be such that its tangent will be equal to $\frac{1}{30}$ of the radius.　Supposing that the slope of the glacis is 8 centimètres per 2 mètres ($3\frac{1}{4}$ inches in 80 inches or $6\frac{2}{3}$ feet), the line of fire will be a little plunging on the surface of the glacis ; and this is proper.

The relief of a rasant enceinte whose commandment is 65 decimètres above the plane of site.

Let us now suppose that we have to arrange the relief of a system of fortification whose horizontal projection is drawn : the method that we shall follow for the bastioned front, may be applied, with necessary modifications, to all systems.　After distinguishing the component elements of the system into principal and secondary works, we will determine what are the works whose fires should be simultaneous and effective during both the distant and near defence.　It will therefore be indispensable to draw the foot of the glacis, at which the third parallel is established, or nearly so ; and to draw the lines of fire so that they will strike the foot of this parallel.　These being established, let us consider that part of the bastioned

Method of determining the relief of all the elements of the mentioned front : that is, the relation that should exist between the planes of defilement of all its elements. (PLATE V, fig. 2.)

front and the part of the attack included between the capital of
the bastion B, and the capital of the ravelin D. The face of
the bastion will batter the portion mP of the parallel; and the
face of the ravelin will batter the other portion nP. This
shows, that the lines of fire of the bastion should pass over the
redoubt of the re-entering place of arms without restraining its
musketry fires; the same rule holds with respect to the ravelin
and its covert-way.

Commandment
of the covert
ways of the ra-
velin, and of
those of the body
of the place.   As in this system the covert-ways are the parts first attacked,
they must therefore have the smallest commandment; and as
the besiegers seize the covert-way of the ravelin before that of
the bastion, it is proper to make the commandment of the covert-way of the body of the place a little greater than that of
the ravelin covert-way. And this is the reason that in the description we fixed them respectively at 25 and 30 decimètres
($8\frac{1}{4}$ and 10 feet); taking care to make them unite in the crotchet
of the traverse of the re-entering place of arms next to the
ravelin.

Let us now draw two vertical sections; one perpendicular to
the face of the ravelin, projected on vz, and passing through
nearly the middle z of the parallel; and the other perpendicular to the face of the bastion, cutting the middle of the face of
the re-entering place of arms and whose direction is rx. Let
(Figures 3 & 4.) us then construct upon these two profiles the vertical directions
of the lines of fire whose positions are known; for they must pass
through the points q and z of the parallel or foot of the glacis,
and through points elevated 10 to 12 decimètres above the crest
of the glacis ($3\frac{1}{2}$ to 4 feet.)

To calculate vn in order to find the height of the radical or
source of the line of fire, we have the proportion $140:110::x:36$
decimètres, and $x = 46$ decimètres nearly; therefore vo, the
height of the covering line, is at least $= 55$ decimètres ($18\frac{1}{4}$
feet).

In the same way is calculated the height rm of the radical of
the line of fire of the body of the place; and we will find for
the height of the plane of defilement above the plane of site,

$$rc = rm + 10 \text{ decimètres} = \frac{230 \times 40}{146} + 10 = 73 \text{ décimètres} \left(24\frac{1}{3}\right.$$

feet).

Thus, according to this very simple calculation, the commandment of the body of the place over the ravelin will be 18 decimètres (6 feet).

The plane of defilement of the re-entering place of arms, is determined by raising the vertical ys containing the direction of the covering line until it meets at s the line of fire mo; then take $sk = 10$ decimètres ($3\frac{1}{3}$ feet) and through the point k draw the direction of the plane of defilement: the height ky is thus calculated; $ky = 63$ decimètres $\times \dfrac{166}{240} - 10$ decimètres $= 33$ decimètres .5 ($11\frac{1}{8}$ feet).   That is, the redoubt of the re-entering place of arms will only have a command of 4 decimètres (16 inches) at most over the covert-way of the body of the place, and of 8 decimètres ($2\frac{3}{4}$ feet) over that of the ravelin, when its fires and that of the bastion are to be simultaneous.   If it be not intended to preserve this advantage, the direction of the plane of defilement may be placed in x, the centre of sk; and we will then have $yx = 39$ decimètres (13 feet) nearly, for the expression of the commandment.

As the ravelin redoubt should command the ravelin and be itself commanded by the body of the place, its plane of defilement may be made to pass through the centre of the commandment of the body of the place over the ravelin; this will make the height of its plane of defilement above the plane of site $= 64$ decimètres ($21\frac{1}{3}$ feet).

If the intrenchment of the bastion should not have a height depending on the exterior form of the site, it will be sufficient to give it 10 to 12 decimètres ($3\frac{1}{3}$ to 4 feet) command over the bastion; the height or reference of its plane of defilement will be 85 decimètres ($28\frac{1}{3}$ feet).

In the chapter describing the system (117) we were not able to say any thing definite on the relief of the tenaille; we merely pointed out that it occasioned a dead space along its scarp, that might be dangerous; and that it should not mask the fires of the flanks that defend the approaches of the breach.   Accordingly the relief of the tenaille should be such as to satisfy the three essential conditions that caused its introduction into the system: 1st, it must not mask the fires of the flanks which defend the breaches and the ditches of the faces of the attacked bastions: 2d, the tenaille should cover as much as possible the masonry of the curtain and flanks: 3d, its terra-plain must be defiled from the commanding points occupied by the besiegers when they become masters of the covert way and ravelin.

Students and young officers will not be able to perfectly understand what we are going to lay down on the relief of the tenaille, until they have studied the tenth chapter, in which we will treat the elements of defilement : they will then return to this chapter, to resume the examination of the tenaille and draw its tracé.

1st. To prevent the tenaille from masking the fires of the flanks that defend the faces of the bastion, that part $R'r$ of the line of defence which is drawn from the flank to the breach of the opposite bastion, will be regarded as the line of fire of a covered battery ; the lines mq' and mq will be drawn, and taken as the horizontal projection of the covering line of the tenaille. This covering line projected on mq' should be 12 decimètres (4 feet) lower than the plane of artillery fire passing through the flank $R'T'$ and through the line of fire $R'r$; and this will be the case, if after determining the point m at 12 decimètres below the line of fire $R'r$, we draw mq' in the angle formed by the horizontal and the parallel to the plane of fire. We must now determine the point m by making a projection on the vertical plane passing through $R'r$. Upon this plane draw the line of fire $R'r$, the position of which is known by the relief of the flank and the depth of the ditches ; project through m the vertical which will meet the line of fire, and beneath this point of junction lay off 12 decimètres to find the point m in the covering line of the tenaille. If through this point we draw an horizontal, it may be considered as the direction of the plane of defilement of the tenaille ; but by this construction the tenaille would not cover the flanks exposed to the enemy's counter-batteries, as much as it is possible to make it.

2d. In order that the flanks may be covered as much as possible by the relief of the tenaille, draw mq' parallel to the plane of fire as directed above ; this will not prevent the first condition from being fulfilled.

3d. Lastly ; the terra-plain of the tenaille must be defiled from the lodgements of the enemy in the ravelin redoubt and on the salient of the bastion. To effect this, raise the outer extremity of the plane which passes through the covering line mq' until it passes above the enemy's most commanding lodgement ; this inclined or rampant plane will then be taken as the plane of defilement, and the terra-plain should be parallel to it in order that the third condition be satisfied, as we shall see in the sequel.

The same operation being repeated on mq, the arrangement of the tenaille will be complete : we see that the terra-plain will thus form a gutter (*gouttiere*) on the perpendicular. In the place of the lines mq' and mq, which are not the true covering lines, we may substitute without any sensible error and without injuring the arrangement, the figure of the covering line given in the horizontal projection.

It is of importance to remark in determining the command-ment of works, that the lines of fire must be efficient upon the covert-way. For this purpose the line of artillery fire oa, drawn 10 or 12 decimètres above the counterscarp M, should not be inclined more than one sixth ; that is, the angle nos should not exceed 9 degrees ; and when it does happen to be greater, the relief above the plane of site must be diminished, or the width of the ditch must be increased. In the front under examination, the relief of the ravelin may be 60 decimètres (20 feet), and that of the bastion 76 (25¼ feet), without the lines of fire ceas-ing to be effective on the covert-way. Remark on the efficiency of the lines of fire on the covert ways. (PLATE V, fig. 1.)

147. Independent of the *positive strength* of a fortified front, which depends upon its constitution and arrangement in its hori-zontal and vertical projection ; it possesses a *relative strength*, resulting from its relation with the collateral fronts that have necessarily a more or less distinguished influence over the at-tacks. Indeed we have seen in the preceding chapter, that in conducting the attacks against the bastioned front the collateral ravelins operate so powerfully against the wings of the attacks, that it becomes indispensable to batter them *in ricochet ;* that it is necessary to inundate their covert-ways and re-entering pla-ces of arms with curved fires ; and that it is necessary to cover the trench cavaliers, the lodgements, and the counter-batteries by traverses or epaulments of greater or less extent, according as the sally or projection of the ravelins is greater or less. To be fully convinced of this truth, it is necessary to compare the probable duration of the siege of the bastioned front, considered in the three principal stages of improvement through which it has passed. 147 The rela-tive strength of a fortified front. In con equence of its relation with the collateral fronts which have an influence on the progress of the attacks.

By supposing the front to be composed of small bastions, without a tenaille and a ravelin, such as it was before Pagan and Vauban; we will observe, 1st, that whatever may be the an- Attacks on the bastioned front, composed of small bastions and destitute of tenaille and ra-

gles of the polygon, it is always practicable for the besiegers to cover themselves from the collateral fronts which cannot take in reverse nor much injure the works and lodgements on the glacis ; 2d, That the fires upon the capitals are little effective, as we previously remarked in Chapters III. and IV. Consequently the progress of the approaches will necessarily be more rapid during the distant defence, and the probable duration of this part of the siege will be shorter.

On the tenth night at farthest, the third parallel will be completed and the mortar and howitzer batteries established.

On the twelfth night the trench cavaliers will be ready, &c.

On the fourteenth night the covert-way will be crowned along its whole extent, because the besieged are not intrenched in the re-entering place of arms.

On the 16th night the batteries in breach and counter-batteries will be opened ; the former will make a wide breach in the shoulders of the bastion and in the curtain, and by which all the interior intrenchments may be turned.

On the 18th night, at break of day, the general assault may take place.

Thus the probable duration of the siege cannot be estimated at more than 17 days.

If we suppose the front to be covered by a small ravelin, the attack will necessarily progress slower ; for the ravelins afford cross-fires on the capitals, and delay the works ; and the lodgements on the salients of the bastions are enfiladed or obliquely scoured by the fires of the collateral ravelins. But as their sally is inconsiderable, it is very easy to guard against their fires.

On the 12th night the third parallel and its batteries will be completed.

In the 14th night the trench cavaliers will be commenced ; but their construction will be slower and more dangerous.

As the sally of the ravelins is inconsiderable, it will be practicable to seize the three salients at the same time.

In the 18th night the covert-way will be completely crowned, &c.

The effects of the collateral ravelins which enfilade the lodgements upon the salients of the bastions, will render the establishment of the counter-batteries longer and more perilous.

On the 21st, the batteries in breach and counter-batteries will be in full fire.

From the 19th, the besiegers will have descended into the terra-plain of the re-entering place of arms, to there establish a battery in breach against the shoulder of the bastion ; this battery will at the same time batter the curtain in breach, through the opening of the tenaille, &c.

On the 23d the breaches will be practicable ; and as the intrenchments may be turned by the breach of the curtain, the besieged cannot stand the assault.

The probable duration of the siege may therefore be fixed at 23 days; surpassing that of the front in its first state, by only five days.

The probable duration of the siege, calculated at 23 days.

Let us now return to the bastioned front that we have described, to use it as a term of comparison : it is the third stage to which the system was brought after the time of Vauban, by the genius of Cormontaigne. We must bear in mind that we supposed the angle of the polygon to be such, that the collateral ravelins only enfilade and do not take in reverse the trench cavaliers and the wings of the coronation of the covert-way ; and that their faces can be embraced to *ricoché* them.

Attack of the front with great ravelins. su h as we have described & examined.

This great separation (*écartement*) of the collateral ravelins, only takes place in the heptagon and lower polygons. The ravelins being very much advanced into the country, form considerable re-enterings, and enfilade and more effectively command the cavaliers and the lodgements ; the besiegers find it more difficult to seize at the same time the salients of the bastions and that of the centre ravelin ; and they find it impossible to crown the whole covert-way by a single operation, because of the great effects of the ravelin and its redoubt and of the redoubt of the re-entering place of arms, &c. They must carry all these works one after another, and they will be able to batter in breach only the faces of the bastions ; this renders the intrenching of them useful, and enables the besieged to sustain several assaults on the body of the place. This disposition has increased to 36 days the estimated probable duration of the siege.

This prolongation of the probable duration of the siege of the modern bastioned front, is owing, all other things being equal, to, 1st, the great sally of the ravelins ; 2d, the redoubts constructed in all the principal works.

148 Reflections
en the openings
of angles exceed
ing those of the
heptagon: the
relation of de-
fence that arises
between the front
of attack, and the
collateral fronts.
148. It is now easy to conceive that the greatness of the angles, when they exceed those of the heptagon, gives to the collateral fronts a position in relation to the front of attack that
must have a powerful influence over the dispositions of the attack.   There is in proportion to this influence, a relation of
defence between the front of attack and the collateral fronts ;
and the effect of this relation is to increase the positive strength
of the front of attack in proportion as these angles are great.

The chief ad-
vantages result-
ing   from   the
greatness of the
angles of the de-
fensive polygon
The measures of the theoretick attack show at the first glance,
the advantages derived by the defence from increasing the
greatness of the angles of the defensive polygon.   The flanked
angles become more obtuse ; the parallels must be more extended, in order to be able to seize the prolongations of the
faces of the collateral ravelins ; the besiegers are frequently
compelled to await the epoch of the second parallel, to establish
their ricochet batteries ; and in this last position, the flanks of
these batteries are exposed to the collateral parts whose fires
annoy the troops and dismount their guns.

But what it greatly concerns us to remark, is, that the flanked angles of the bastions may become so obtuse, that the prolongations of their faces will fall upon and be intercepted by
the salients of the ravelins.   When this is the case, it becomes
very difficult to ricoché the faces of the bastions.   The ravelins
are not much thrown asunder, and enter into immediate relations of defence ; they completely cover the body of the place
and include between them such great re-enterings, that they
envelop and take in flank and reverse the works of the besiegers
as soon as they debouche from the third parallel.

The attack of a
bastioned poly-
gon, higher than
the heptagon.
In polygons higher than the heptagon, the collateral ravelins
have so great an effect upon the wings of the attacks, that the besiegers are under the necessity of including them within the front
of the attack, in order to seize them before crowning the salients of the two bastions.   Without this preliminary attack, the
trench cavaliers and counter-batteries would be so enfiladed
and taken in reverse, that their construction is regarded in theory as impracticable.   The third parallel must therefore embrace the collateral ravelins ; and the front of attack must include five salients.   This will produce such an extent of
trenches, and require so many bloody lodgements to be made,
that the besiegers must in this case endeavour to penetrate into
the place by a front different from the common bastioned front.

To abridge the labours, the besiegers should prefer to the common front of attack, that which is included between the capitals of the ravelins of two contiguous fronts.   By this selection the collateral works will be two bastions, which having little sally, will have but a slight influence on the wings of the attack.   The besiegers will advance into the re-entering formed by the two ravelins, to penetrate into the place by a single bastion, whose two faces will be simultaneously battered in breach as soon as the besiegers have crowned the salients of the two ravelins.

The front of attack included between the capital of the rave-line o' two adjacent fronts.

We will now succinctly describe the regular attack of this new front, supposing it to be part of a dodecagon.   The works of the two first periods are the same as in the first case ; but as the faces of the collateral bastions and those of the assailed bastion cannot be effectively ricoched, there will consequently be direct and cross-fires upon the five capitals ; the effect of which must necessarily retard the progress of the attack.

The attack of this new front, considered as part of a dodecagon (PLATE V. fig. 5.)

On the 12th night the third parallel will be completed, and all the cannon, mortar, and howitzer batteries will be begun, to enfilade the faces of all the works, counter-batter the faces of the bastion and annoy the besieged in their terra-plains.

Journal of the attacks.

In the 14th night all the batteries will be brought into play ; the besiegers will debouche in circular portions or trenches upon the three capitals, and will make direct approaches on the capitals of the re-entering places of arms.

The 15th, 16th, 17th, and 18th nights will be required to approach within 30 mètres (100 feet) of the ravelin salients, and to embrace them by half places of arms whose wings must be armed with trench cavaliers.   The besiegers will experience great difficulty in raising these trench cavaliers, which will be taken in flank and reverse by the redoubts of the ravelins and by the collateral bastions.   If it be impossible to construct them, batteries of stone-mortars, covered by high and strong epaulments, will be made in their place.

In the 19th and 20th nights they will join the wings of the half places of arms, or of the trench cavaliers, by a fourth parallel convex towards the salient place of arms ; it will be armed with stone-mortars, to inundate the three places of arms.   The communications from the third to the fourth parallel will be completed,

On the 21st night they will seize the two salients and crown a portion of the branches of the covert-way; endeavouring to extend as far as possible beyond the salient of the ravelins: they will cover themselves by winding traverses and paradoses.

In the 22d and 23d nights they will descend by wide cuts (*coupures*) into the terra-plain of the salient places of arms; they will crown the counterscarp, and begin the batteries in breach and counter-batteries against the ravelins and bastion. They will also begin the fifth parallel that is to join the extremes of the coronation of the salient places of arms.

The 24th and 25th nights will be employed in completing these batteries and the fifth parallel, which will be made a little concave; and in making the communications from the fourth to the fifth parallel, and in arming this parallel with stone mortars.

During the 26th and 27th days they will batter the ravelins in breach, and counter-batter the faces of the bastion; and they will debouche from the fifth parallel to raise trench cavaliers upon the prolongations of the branches of the covert-way of the three places of arms. If this labour cannot be accomplished, they will debouche from the fifth parallel in circular portions or in direct double saps, to join the salients of the three places of arms and crown all the covert-way. They will also begin the counter-batteries.

During the 28th, 29th, and 30th nights they will complete the counter-batteries, which will be opened on the evening of the 29th: they will descend by cuts into the terra-plains of the re-entering places of arms, and set the miners to work at their redoubts; they will open the descents of the ditch. And lastly; they will commence the passages of the ditch of the two ravelins.

The 31st and 32d nights will be devoted to completing the passages of the ditches of the two ravelins, and to working at the descents of the ditch of the bastion.

In the course of the 33d night every thing will be prepared for the assault of the ravelins; and at break of day the besiegers will effect a lodgement on their terra-plains, and in those of the redoubts of the re-entering places of arms.

The 34th and 35th nights will be employed in constructing the batteries in breach against the redoubts of the ravelins, in rendering the breaches of the bastion practicable, and in beginning the two passages of the great ditch.

During the 36th and 37th nights they will complete the passages of the great ditch, and assault the redoubts of the ravelins.

On the 39th night they will prepare to assault the bastion at break of day.

On the 40th day they will assault the bastion and effect a lodgement on its terra-plain.

In the course of the 41st and 42d days they will strongly establish themselves on the terra-plain of the bastion ; and they will labour at the batteries against the intrenchment of the bastion, or set the miners to work.

On the 44th day the breach in the intrenchment of the bastion will be practicable, when the capitulation will take place.

As every thing is in favour of the besieged at the epoch of the attack of the bastion ; and as they can move in force on a narrow front where the enemy cannot display, we may calculate the probable duration of the siege at a few days more. But this depends upon the obstinate defence, good conduct, and valour of the besieged ; and upon moral causes that we leave out of view. We calculate that a work is in the power of the besiegers the moment that, in consequence of the works of the attack, we place the besiegers in contact with the besieged.

It follows from this exposition, that when the angles of the polygon are sufficiently great to compel the besiegers to attack a single bastion, the defence is protracted 8 days ; and that the conduct of the attack is more difficult, and the losses of the besiegers much greater.

The relative strength and advantages of fronts of attack of high polygons, increase with their angles ; and when several fronts are displayed upon a right line, they afford a much more decisive result. The circumstances of the attack and of the defence in this case, tend to favour the besieged in a much more striking manner : 1st, the capitals of the ravelins being parallel, these are in more immediate relations of defence, and form an advanced and formidable front that completely covers the enceinte ; and the works of the attack being no longer enveloping, are parallel to the front attacked. 2d, The prolongations of the bastion faces fall upon the ravelins and cannot be seized without great difficulty ; and the flanked angle is so obtuse, that its prolongations pass without the sphere of the attacks : the bastion faces cannot therefore be *ricoched*. 3d. The attack

Conclusion.

The strength of front on a right line. (PLATE V, fig. 6.)

must include four ravelins, because the two collateral take in reverse and command the trench cavaliers and the lodgements upon the ravelin salients of the front of attack. 4th. During the near defence the besiegers will be compelled to make their approaches in a deep re-entering, where they will be seen in flank and reverse by the collateral bastions, and plunged by their intrenchments or cavaliers; they will be enclosed and surrounded in a very narrow space, in which they will be opposed by every kind of stratagem, and where all the fires of the front of attack, and especially of the collateral parts, concentrate.

Finally; the besiegers will not be able to counter-batter the flanks of the bastion of the front of attack until they have gained possession of the whole covert-way, down into the terraplain of which they will be obliged to lower their counter-batteries and batteries in breach; in order to shield themselves from the reverse and plunging fires of the collateral bastions.

The probable duration of its siege.

By drawing the plan of the attack of a front adjacent to two other fronts situated on a right line, we will readily discover that the probable duration of the siege will be greatly increased; that it will at least be as much as 50 days of open trenches; and that it may be extended to 60 days by making skilful use of blinded batteries.

The strength of fronts drawn on a curve concave to the exterior.

If after examining a part of a convex enceinte, and a portion of a rectilinear enceinte, we now consider an enceinte that is concave towards the exterior; we easily perceive from the reasons above laid down, that in this latter case all the elements of the bastioned front are disposed in a manner still more favourable to the defence. If the besiegers attack one of the fronts of the wings, they will present their flank to the fronts of the centre, and their rear to the fronts of the other wing; such an attack will therefore be impracticable. The besiegers must therefore attack the fronts of the centre; but then when they reach the position for the half places of arms, they advance into a re-entering space where they are enveloped, and their disposition swept by flank and reverse fires which they can neither ricoché nor counter-batter. They can neither ricoché the faces of the bastions, nor even those of the ravelins, if the convexity be a little considerable. In such a disposition, the besiegers occupy the central position of a curve whose perimeter, defended by the besieged, is secure from an attack by storm. Hence it follows, that all the fires of the defences converge upon the attacks; whilst the fires of the latter diverge, and cannot counter-batter without exposing their flank or rear. Accordingly we have a right to conclude that fronts thus disposed, are impregnable.

149. We deduce from the preceding, this important conclu- sion—that the configuration of an enceinte which is most favourable for its defence, is that which is least convex towards the exterior, or that whose several fronts form with each other the most obtuse angles. Consequently in planning enceintes and detached works, we must display the attackable fronts on very flattened curves, and in preference, on a right line; and when the ground or local circumstances permit, we should make the fronts unassailable by disposing them in the middle of a curve concave to the exterior.

Exclusive of the demonstrations drawn from the theory of the attack, these truths will become obvious to the students by the mere application of the general principles of tactics.

A front is more advantageously attacked in proportion as it is easily enveloped; and if during all the periods of the seige, the besiegers be constantly able to envelop the defences, without the besieged possessing the same advantage in respect to the works of the attack.

The convex enceinte affords the besiegers these advantages. They avail themselves of them to ricoché and enfilade from a distance, and when near, all the works; to surround the sorties, and to crown at once the covert-way; and to penetrate into the place by two bastions, &c.

When the figure of the enceinte is very flattened, or rectilinear, or is concave, these inestimable advantages are transferred to the side of the besieged. The attacks of the besiegers are then no longer so enveloping, they advance with a front nearly equal to the front of attack, they cannot *ricoché* the faces of the works, and they are compelled to confine their attack to a single bastion, &c. During the period of the near defence, the besiegers advance into a re-entering space where they are in their turn enveloped and surrounded by the besieged, and their works enfiladed and taken in reverse; and the besieged preserve this advantageous attitude to the last moment.

Vauban had a presentiment of the theory that we have just laid down. His great experience in the wars of sieges, had convinced him of the difficulty of conducting attacks against fronts on a right-line ; and he expressly recommends avoiding them.

This celebrated engineer made some admirable tracés, which have served as models to his successors : that of the crown-work of Haurs, at Givet, is one of the most remarkable. He knew so well how to take advantage of all the circumstances of this varied site, and apply the principles of regular fortification to the accidents of ground, that not one of the bastion-faces can be *ricoched ;* their prolongations fall either upon the river, or upon anfractuosities. In applying to such a site the principles that we have just explained, it would be practicable to display the general tracé on a curve concave to the exterior. The enemy in this case not being able to attack the wings of the crown, placed upon the sides of the declivity, would be compelled to attack the centre of the disposition.

We might also refer with deserved praise to the admirable tracé of the double crown of Belle-croix, at Metz, planned by the famous Cormontaigne. Its arrangement and order leave nothing more to be desired for the instruction of the students of artillery and engineers.

CHAPTER VI.

*General Reflections on the several Systems of Fortification;
Brief Descriptions and Examinations of the Principal Systems invented and used since the use of artillery and invention of Bastioned Enceintes.*

150. We said (Chap II. 113.) that it was in the fourteenth century that bastioned fortification originated; and that it consisted at first of small bastions that were substituted for the ancient towers. But for a long time there were no rules established respecting the dimensions and proportions of the several parts of the front. Errard of Bar-le-Duc, one of the corps of engineers formed by Sully, was the first who laid the foundations of the science by endeavouring to establish it upon a few principles deduced from the tactics of sieges. He regulated the extent of the front by the range of the matchlock, established a ravelin in the re-entering place of arms, and adopted a regular method for drawing the enceinte.

150. General reflections upon the several systems of fortification. (See St. Paul's Treatise. Bousmard's Essay on Fortification, and Mondor on the architecture of fortresses. (See PLATE VI)

Errard's system, exhibited in Figure 1, is only adapted to the hexagon, and is defective in every respect. Its bastions are small and narrow; the flanks are directed against the curtain, and against each other; and they only defend the ditches very obliquely. The tracé cannot be generally used; and the batteries in breach may open the enceinte at any point.

Errard's system: examination of it. (Fig. 1.)

In about the same age, the Italian engineers cultivated fortification with success. They drew many plans of enceintes, which were judiciously disposed and superior to the tracés used in France. Many engineers, and among others Deville and Marollais, proposed systems better planned than that of Errard.

In these tracés, the exterior side was about 300 mètres (335 yards); the lines of defence were plunging (*fichantes*); and the flanks perpendicular to the curtain. But their construction was embarrassing, and could not be adapted to particular cases.

(Figures 2 & 3)

The bastioned enceintes were no sooner generally used, than it was proposed to modify the bastion in a manner that has been the subject of great controversy. The Chevalier Deville was one of the first who introduced the *orillon*. The orillon is a

The invention of the orillon: its use and tracé.

kind of exterior traverse advanced on the line of defence a little beyond the flank, to defile one piece of artillery from the opposite counter-battery. As this piece cannot be counter-battered, it sees the breach in reverse and defends it at the moment of the assault. The first orillons were very large, and occupied two-thirds of the flank ; in consequence of such immense dimensions, they greatly weakened the retired flank. The contour of the orillon is formed by three distinct lines : 1st, the prolongation of the bastion face beyond the shoulder angle ; this quantity varies in the different systems ; in Deville's system it is 10 to 12 mètres (11 to 13½ yards), in Coehorn's 17 (19 yards), and in Pagan's and Vauban's it is reduced to 0. 2d, the front of the orillon, which is either circular or rectilinear ; 3d, the reverse of the orillon ; that is, the interior line drawn from the flanked angle of the bastion opposite to the point of the flank which marks the thickness of the orillon, and which is more or less protracted into the interior of the bastion, according to the position of the retired flank.

Vauban's correction of the orillon. (Fig. 5.) Vauban very soon perceived that the great thickness of the orillons weakened the flanks ; he corrected this defect by reducing their thickness to 18 mètres (20 yards) at most, and making the reverse line 14 mètres (15½ yards), &c. Coehorn, in his first system, made the orillon 30 mètres (33⅓ yards) thick ; but in his second system, he reduced it to 15 mètres (16¾ yards).

The fausse-braie : its use & tracé. (Fig. 3.) The engineers towards the end of the sixteenth century, and among others Marollais, imagined that by doubling the rampart they would double the strength of the body of the place ; and for this purpose constructed *fausse-braies*. That is, to the first enceinte *P*, they adapted a second enceinte *P'*, having a rampart *R* of about 3 or 10 mètres (9 or 11 yards). This fausse-braie was made as high as the crest or cordon of the rampart.

Examination of the fausse-braie. It is very easy to perceive that fausse-braies, the building of which was so very expensive, are destitute of real strength, especially in the present state of the attack. If the enceinte *P* be not revested, the fortress ceases to be secure from an attack by storm : and if it be revested, its escalade will become practicable in many circumstances. But let us examine the effects of the fausse-braie on the attacks.

During the distant defence it will be of no effect against the

besiegers, because it does not command the crest of the glacis.
During the near defence it may be of some service against the
attack of the covert-way by storm, at the moment that the assailants penetrate into it ; but after the coronation is effected,
the besieged in the fausse-braie will be exposed to an enfilading
and plunging fire in flank and front, and will be compelled to
abandon it by the mere power of musketry fires.   As soon as
the batteries in breach and the counter-batteries are established,
the scarp P will be battered down by the first firing upon the
fausse-braie, which will become untenable throughout its whole
extent : it thus gives the besiegers the advantage of making the
breaches practicable in a short time.   Consequently the fausse-
braie has no other effect, than to render the attack of the covert-way by storm a little more perilous.

After the invention of the great orillon, they called that part
of the flank which was behind the orillon, the *covered flank*.
It was proposed to make this covered flank of several stories or tiers retired towards the interior of the bastion ; and
subsequently, to casemate these flanks, in order to prevent the
men from being destroyed by the ruins and splinters of the superior flanks falling into the inferior terra-plains.

The covered flank: the retired flanks of several stories, & the casemated flanks.

These flanks of several tiers are subject to the same defects
as the fausse-braies ; those that are higher than the counter-
battery, are seen and battered down from the half place of arms,
and are ruined by the epoch of crowning the covert-way.   The
flanks or low places of arms being below the counter-battery,
they cannot prevent its construction ; and they are destroyed
the moment that it opens its fire.

Examination of the flanks of several stories, and of the casemated flanks.

Casemated fires should only be used when they cannot be
counter-battered from the country and from those points of the
fortification of which the besiegers become masters before the
epoch at which these fires are brought into action.   It is in this
manner that Vauban used them in his second and third systems.

Reflections on casemated fires.

The combination and use of bastions, orillons, fausse-braies,
and of retired flanks of several stories or casemated, gave rise
to the multiplicity of systems that appeared in the fifteenth
century.   They composed several classes, under the denomination of the *French, Italian, Spanish, Dutch*, &c., methods.

All these methods partook of the defects of Errards' system :
1st, Their tracés produced bastions whose interior capacity
was very narrow and did not permit the display of the artillery

and infantry service. 2d, The flanks were badly directed, and their fires almost entirely extinguished by an immense orillon. 3d, All parts of the front might indifferently be battered in breach ; because the body of the place was only covered by a weak ravelin.

151. Towards 1640, Count Pagan, a young general of rare merit, appeared in the career of science. He had in the reign of Louis XIII. co-operated in the conduct of more than twenty sieges, and had witnessed military operations with the eye of an observing and scientific soldier. The artillery used at this period in besieging fortresses, was very heavy, and had suddenly given the attack a great superiority over the defence. Pagan perceived that the material of the defence no longer opposed a resistance proportioned to the violence of the attack; and that a new method of fortifying was urgently required.

151. The progress of fortification at the epoch that Count Pagan developed his system.

He adopted the bastioned system, and endeavoured to find a tracé free from the minute and tedious methods of the systems hitherto used. These methods could have no weight in the eyes of a soldier instructed by long experience.

Pagan's bastioned front. (PLATE VI, fig. 4.)

The tracé of the bastioned front of Pagan, differs very little from that of Vauban, and from that which we have adopted as a term of comparison (114 and 115). He fixed the exterior side of the polygon according to the range of the matchlock, and within the limits of 240 and 390 mètres (270 to 434 yards) ; he took this exterior side as the base of the tracé, and by means of the perpendicular raised upon the centre of the front, drew the lines of defence rasant : then taking upon the lines of defence the faces of the bastions, of proper length to produce spacious bastions and good flanks, he let fall perpendiculars from the shoulder angles upon the lines of defence. By this simple tracé, which was applicable to all cases, he obtained the arrangement of the horizontal projection of the regular bastioned front. For an exterior side of 390 to 312 mètres (434 to 347 yards), he allowed 58 mètres (64½ yards) for the perpendicular, and 120 to 100 mètres (134 to 112 yards) for the faces of the bastion : these produced flanks of 45 mètres (50 yards), capable of contending against a counter-battery.

The orillon, & the covered flanks.

Pagan, like his predecessors, overloaded the flanks of the bastion with an enormous orillon that occupied one half of the flank ; and behind this square orillon, he made three covered flanks retired into the interior of the bastion. The first of these flanks

was lower than the counter-battery; the two others commanded it.

He understood the importance of the ravelin, and he substituted for it a more considerable work which he considered as
one of the constituent elements of the front; he directed its
faces upon the shoulder angles of the bastions, but he did not
give it a sufficient sally.

The ravelin, & the intrench-ments of the bas-tions.

Finally; this great engineer, whose conceptions were always
grand, was too much experienced in sieges not to perceive the
utility of intrenching the bastions; he therefore constructed
small bastions within the great ones.

Although Count Pagan's system was a great step towards the
improvement of the science, yet it has great defects; 1st, its
line of defence is too long for the musketry fires to act with effect against the trench cavaliers and crowning of the salient
place of arms: 2d, the flanks are perverted by the orillon, and
by the covered flanks of three tiers, which obstruct the interior
of the bastions: 3d, the dimensions of the ravelin are too small;
the whole covert-way may be crowned at a single operation;
and the curtain may be battered in breach through the opening between the ravelin and the shoulders of the bastions, and
thus the intrenchments of the bastions may be turned.

Examination of Count Pagan's system.

152. Immediately after Count Pagan, and towards the year
1650, there appeared in the military world two engineers of
the first talents, and equally celebrated in the attack and defence of fortresses. Coehorn and Vauban were rivals in talents
and in fame; they both served their country with devotion, and
each of them far extended the boundaries of the science. Vauban, serving under a conquering and ambitious government,
naturally paid more attention to improve the methods of attack,
than the means of defence; accordingly, by his inventions he
raised the attack to its highest pitch.

152. The sys-tems of Coehorn and Vauban.

Coehorn, whose country was almost always upon the defensive, followed a course opposite to that of his rival; he endeavoured to improve the material of the defence. He ad-
mired Vauban's ingenious methods of conducting attacks; and
he improved them by inventing the small portable mortar for
throwing from small distances immense quantities of grenades
and driving the besieged from behind their parapets. His country, and the different sites upon which he had to exercise his
talents at fortifying, being of a marshy nature and affording we-

ters for the ditches, he naturally sought to discover a system adapted to this local circumstance.   This manner of viewing fortification and making it consist in applying to each site the defensive system best suited to the ground, is common to both him and Vauban, and proves the comprehensive genius of these two illustrious engineers.   The circumstances in which Coehorn was placed, restrained his genius to a particular case ; but he treated it in such a manner as to justify the belief, that on any other site he would have displayed the same ability as in the defences of Manheim, of Bergen-op-zoom and other places in Holland.   His defence of Namur in 1692, obtained for him the eulogiums of Vauban, who conducted the siege according to his new tactics.   These encomia inflamed his love of glory, and directed his talents entirely to this career ; and he obtained in it such great success and general applause, that impartial nations have ever pointed to him as the worthy rival of Vauban. If the French engineer had the honour of inventing *ricochet* batteries, Coehorn completed the theory of the attack by the happy invention of small grenade mortars, to cripple the besieged during the epoch of the near attack and defence.   It is true that the French have not made much use of this invention ; but he knew how to derive great advantages from it in many sieges.

The principles on which Coehorn arranged his system.   In his system, Coehorn leaves his predecessors far behind ; he advances in a new direction, constantly applying the most luminous principles : *To cover and flank in the most effective manner, by works spacious and favourable to an active and obstinate defence ; to dispose those works that are most advanced and upon which the enemy must establish themselves, in such a manner that they will not find sufficient space upon them for their batteries, and will be compelled to transport to them large quantities of materials,* &c.   These are the fundamental principles upon which Coehorn founded the arrangement of the elements of his system, both in its horizontal and vertical projection. He adopted also a third general disposition, which was to establish the terra-plains of covert-ways and the bottoms of dry ditches in such a manner, that the besiegers could not dig down into them 7 or 8 decimètres ($2\frac{1}{3}$ to $2\frac{3}{4}$ feet) without coming to water.

The application of these general principles was favoured by a marshy site, affording waters for the ditches at any point that the engineer wished to introduce them.

We will give but a very brief description of Coehorn's system, such as was adopted in fortifying Manheim and several places in Holland; a detailed description would carry us far beyond our prescribed limits. Those students who are desirous of fully understanding this admirable system, may consult the description and examination of it that is to be found in Gousmard's General Essay upon Fortification; a work whose merit has been attested by public opinion.

A general idea of Coehorn's system. (PLATE VI. fig. 6) (See Bousmard's General Essay on Fortification.)

Coehorn draws his bastioned polygon on the interior side of the hexagon, which he makes 297 mètres .5 (332 yards); he protracts the radii 146 mètres (163 yards), makes the demigorge of the bastion equal to one fourth of the side; and describes the flanks concave, by taking for a centre the summit of the flanked angle: by this construction, the exterior side of the polygon will be found to be about 448 mètres (493 yards). This tracè produces great acute bastions B, B, in which this able engineer made several dispositions. At the shoulder angle he established a great orillon O, made of masonry and surmounted with a parapet terminating at the vertical wall pqr. Beneath the part mr, a casemate is constructed for 6 pieces of artillery with embrasures on a level with the natural ground. That part of the orillon revêtement that the enemy can see, is built with peculiar art; it is composed of relieving vaults (voutes en décharge) formed by counterforts abutting against the piers of the souterrains: the counterforts are connected and united together by concentric walls convex to the interior. This construction is admirable for resisting batteries in breach and the pression (poussée) of the earth, and for stopping the enemy's miners. The same kind of revêtement is continued along the face of the bastion 8 or 10 toises (52 to 65 feet); the remainder of the bastion, both faces and flanks, is constructed of earth. The thickness of the rampart at the level of the waters, is 14 to 15 mètres (15¼ to 16¼ yards); it is arranged entirely for musketry, with a banquette and terra-plain of about 3 mètres (10 feet). The gorge of the bastion face is a wall, against which is built a crenated gallery; and behind which there is a dry ditch 32 mètres (36 yards) wide. From this dry ditch, raised about 5 decimètres (20 inches) above the level of the waters, the ascent to the terra-plain of the bastion is by stairs of free-stone; the troops debouche from the gallery by gates.

The horizontal projection of the system: the tracé of the enceinte: that of the orillon.

The interior of the great earthen bastion is occupied by an

The capital bastion.

intrenchment called the *capital bastion* (*bastion capital*), the face of which is drawn 32 mètres (36 yards) from the gorge of the earthen bastion, and the flank at 30 mètres (34 yards) from the flank of the great bastion. The flank is terminated by the prolongation of the rasant line of defence. This disposition produces a dry ditch between the two parallel flanks. The capital bastions and the curtains, are revested in masonry; but its height does not exceed the lowest crest of the parapets of the works in earth.- Along the faces of the capital bastion, there is a *mine gallery* (*galerie de mines*).

The part *rst* is enclosed by a wall 40 decimètres high (13½ feet) which together with the face *mr* of the orillon, is covered by a ditch filled with water. This ditch is crossed by two fixed bridges *p, p*, each furnished with draw-bridges fitted to two gates in the wall *st*. Between these two gates and in the wall *rs*, there are embrasures for cannon.

The tenaille is with flanks, and its curtain is broken. As the line of defence is very long, the flanks of the tenaille are to furnish effective fires on the ditch of the salients of the low bastions: accordingly the tenaille is only disposed for the use of musketry. There is a wet ditch before the flank and orillon; and against the orillon, at the origin of the tenaille face, there is a vaulted passage to communicate with the great ditch.

The communications.

The communication with the dry ditch of the curtain is by a postern placed under the centre of this curtain; and with the dry ditch of the flanks, by a postern placed under the break of the same curtain. From this dry ditch we enter through gates into the souterrains and casemates of the orillon, and from these casemates into the crenated gallery of the gorge of the low bastion. A subterranean gallery whose bottom is 10 decimètres (3½ feet) below the level of the waters, crosses the dry ditch along the capital and forms the communication between the crenated gallery and the mine gallery of the capital bastion. Under the break of the curtain, there is a casemate to defend the dry ditch of the flanks; the postern passes through it.

The great wet ditch.

The great ditch is filled with water; it is 48 mètres (54 yards) wide opposite the flanked angle: the counterscarp is directed upon the shoulder of the opposite bastion.

The low and capital half-moon.

In planning the ravelin, Coehorn left far behind the notions of his predecessors; he made it of great dimensions and with a great sally; its gorge covers all the masonry of the orillons.

At the extreme of a demi-gorge of 110 mètres (122 yards), he draws the faces so as to make the flanked angle 70° degrees. This low ravelin is made of earth, and disposed entirely for musketry ; the thickness of its rampart is therefore only 14 mètres (15½ yards).

The capital ravelin or half-moon (*la demi-lune capitale*) is drawn at 32 mètres (35½ yards) from the gorge of the earthen ravelin ; one half of its faces, measuring from the flanked angle, is arranged for artillery. The gorge of the capital ravelin is provided with a crenated caponnière made of brick walls, covered over with planks and earth ; these form the terra-plain of a second tier of fire, whose parapet is a continuation of the walls of the caponnière. In front of the caponnière there is a palisading with a banquette, &c.

At the extremity of the faces of the low and capital ravelins, the dry ditch is crossed by a wet ditch defended by a covered caponnière with banquettes which furnish a double tier of fires. At the gorge of the extremities of the earthen ravelin faces, there is a crenated gallery ; its gates are placed behind the caponnière and before the wet ditch : its use is to defend the ditch, to afford debouchés there, and to favour the retreat. The troops pass from the interior of the capital ravelin behind the caponnières, &c.

The dry ditch of the ravelin is crossed along the capital by a crenated caponnière, constructed and arranged like that already described which crosses the dry ditch of the bastions. It leads into a great caponnière that occupies the flanked angle for a length of 20 mètres (22¼ yards), also pierced with loopholes and covered over with planks and earth. The communication from the interior of the capital ravelin to these caponnières, is by a postern, &c.

The capital ravelin is revested with strong masonry as high as 40 decimètres (13¼ feet) above the level of the waters.

The bastion is covered with a counter-guard whose gorge is the edge of the great ditch ; its thickness is only 18 mètres at the level of the waters. Accordingly it is only disposed for infantry. Its ditch is 28 mètres (31 yards) wide, and debouches into that of the ravelin ; they are both wet ditches. *The counter-guard of the bastion.*

Finally ; all these described dispositions are enveloped by a covert-way 24 mètres (26¾ yards) wide and free throughout its whole extent, except at the re-enterings, which are made into *The covert-way.*

large re-entering places of arms, provided with a crenated brick redoubt. The gorge of this redoubt is on the prolongation of the crest of the covert-way ; and the interval between this gorge and the counterscarp, is closed by a traverse cannon-proof. The traverses and the redoubt are covered by an inclined palisading ; and the whole covert-way is palisaded as usual. In order to better defend the approaches of the redoubts and of the traverses of the re-entering places of arms, Coehorn sinks *defensive coffers* in the glacis of the faces of the re-entering place of arms. These coffers are 25 decimètres wide by 20 deep (8⅓ by 6⅔ feet), and are placed 15 mètres (16⅔ yards) from the crest and parallel to the faces ; they rise about 80 centimètres (32 inches) above the ground, so as to be able to defend with their loop-holes the approaches of the place of arms. The descent into these coffers is by covered cuts (*coupures*) made 6 mètres (20 feet) from the re-entering angle.

The relief and commandment of the elements of Coehorn's system. (PLATE VI, fig. 10*.)
The depth of the ditches

The relief and commandment of the elements of Coehorn's system, are regulated from the plane of the water level, which is supposed to be 13 decimètres below that of the natural ground.

The dry ditches and terra-plains are 50 centimètres (20 inches) above the level of the waters, and afford consequently little excavation for the construction of the works. The wet ditches are about 20 to 25 decimètres (6⅔ to 8⅓ feet) deep below the level of the waters ; their width and depth vary according to the equalization of the excavation and embankment. The terra-plain of the capital ravelin, and those of the covert-ways, are a little raised above the level of the waters.

Figure 10* represents the relation of all the planes of defilement. It shows, that the capital bastions and orillons command the whole system in such a manner as to produce effective fires of artillery and musketry on all the exterior points ; that the masonry of the capital works is covered by the works made of earth ; and that they defend the latter by lines of fire whose effects are certain, by reason of the width of the dry ditches. The flanks of the tenaille are made very low, to un-

---

* The figure referred to in the original, is Fig. 7, which seems to be Coehorn's second system ; and the reference in page 205, for *Coehorn's* second system, is to Fig. 8, which is *Vauban's*. We have changed the references, in the first case, to Figure 10 ; and in the second, to Figure 7. The small scale on which these systems are drawn, greatly obscures the description.   TRANSLATOR.

mask the fires of the flanks in rear ; its faces are higher, so as
to cover and defile the flanks. Lastly.; the middle of the faces
of the low hastions, and of the earthen ravelin, is not so high as
the salients, in order to unmask the artillery fires of the capital
works.

The complete examination of this system would lead us into
too long investigations ; we shall therefore confine ourselves to
a few general observations, and recommend to the students to
apply to it the knowledge that they have acquired, to determine the probable duration of its siege. *Examination of Coehorn's system.*

By comparing this system with that which we have taken as
a term of comparison, we will observe ; 1st, That the capital
works are the only ones whose artillery has a direct effect upon
the attack ; and as these works have but a little sally into the
country, their fires do not cross so effectively on the capitals as
in the first system. 2d, As the tracé makes the bastions acute
in all polygons, it follows that all the faces of the works may
be ricoched, and that their perfect parallelism will facilitate
the reconnaissances to determine the position of ricochet batteries. 3d, The capital ravelins have little power over the coronation of the salient places of arms, because they are not further advanced than the ravelin redoubts of the common system,
whilst the salients are considerably advanced by the counter-
guards : it follows from this latter observation, that the front of
attack will be in all cases an ordinary front, composed of two
bastions and a ravelin. 4th, The three salients of the front of
attack are almost on a straight line, from which the re-entering
places of arms are very little distant ; hence, the crowning of
the covert-way may be effected by a single operation : but this
coronation must include five salient and four re-entering places
of arms, to obtain for the attack the means of taking in enfilade
and reverse all the parts of the front attacked. *Comparison of this system with that taken as an unit of force.*

In attacking this system, the first parallel must be established
at a distance of 600 mètres (670 yards) from the capital works ;
the prolongations of the faces of the works must be exactly
seized, and ricochet batteries established even against the collateral rav   ochet battery should be composed
according   attained by it ; the terra-plains of
capital   ed   annon ; the dry ditches,
the c   re-entering places of
a   d howitzes. *The opening of the trenches, and the first ricochet batteries: the approaches, to the crowning of the covert way.*

The effect of the artillery and musketry on the approaches not being greater than in the common bastioned system, the progress of the attacks will be the same, and will meet with the same obstacles in both cases. As the low ravelins and counterguards are not made for artillery, the trench cavaliers will be easier established, and the crowning of the covert-way of the four re-entering places of arms may be a little more quickly effected.

Reflections on the effects of the artillery of the besiegers.

If we now examine the effects produced by the batteries of the first and second parallels, and by those of the third which enfilade all the works and dry ditches, it will be evident from the known and confirmed effects of modern artillery, that the casemates which defend the ditches of the bastions will be battered down by the ricochet batteries ; that the crenated gallery at the gorge of the earthen bastions will be beaten down and probably ruined ; that the caponnières and coffers will be rendered untenable (*hors de service*) ; and that the terra-plains of the flanks and orillons will be untenable, and the redoubts of the places of arms battered down. It is true that a greater quantity of artillery will be required to attack this system, than that with which we are comparing it ; for it will require about 120 pieces, including 50 mortars and howitzers. But on the other hand, more must be used for its defence ; because a great deal of artillery must be posted in the dry ditches, to act against the enemy by elevated firing. This is the only means that the besieged have to enfilade the coronation of the covert-way.

The means that the besiegers should use to carry on the siege, after crowning the covert-way.

As soon as the besiegers have completed the crowning of the covert-way and constructed their long winding traverses and paradoses, they turn their attention to counter-battering the flanks, and to battering in breach the capital works. When these two ends are effected, they advance by the common methods, by means of passages of the ditch and epaulments, to gain and assault the breaches. But in the system in question, where the flanks and capital works are covered by works of earth, these earthen works must be either destroyed by making openings in them through which to discover the capital works, or seized to establish batteries in breach upon them.

Bombs fired horizontally, to produce fougasses in the banks of earth.

When Coehorn invented and planned his system, he did not think it was possible to destroy works made of earth ; he saw the enemy compelled to attack them by the common methods, and he organized them in such a manner as to make an active and artful defence under the favour of defensive caponnières, crenated galleries, and casemates.　Cormontaigne was the first who pointed out the great effects of bombs fired horizontally ; and it has been since often observed, that bombs and howitzes bursting in masses of earth produce great effects in them, and in a short time level the parapets of intrenchments.　The howitzes are loaded with 4 pounds of powder and fired by volleys or salvoes into the masses of the parapets, where exploding, they form in consequence of being thus overloaded, craters or tunnels (*entonnoirs*) that facilitate the entrance into the intrenchment.　This mode of attacking intrenchments was frequently used in the last war.

We can conceive however that it is practicable to mount mortars and heavy howitzers upon common gun carriages, and to fire the bombs horizontally, like ball.　Besides, bombs may be fired by affixing them to the muzzle of common cannon.　By loading the mortars and howitzers with one-fifth or a quarter of their total charge, the bombs and howitzes at a distance of 200 to 300 mètres (222 to 335 yards) will penetrate 12 to 15 decimetres (4 to 5 feet) ; and if the shells be charged with 10 to 15 pounds of powder, and if the lines of least resistance be horizontal, they will produce tunnels (*entonnoirs*) of 20 to 30 decimetres (6⅔ to 10 feet) in diameter.　If therefore batteries armed with mortars and howitzers firing horizontally, fire by regulated salvoes against the works made of earth, it will probably be practicable to level a portion of the work in a short time, and to discover through the chasms that which is behind it.　But in the present state of our knowledge respecting the effects of artillery, we cannot calculate upon the efficiency or certainty of this mode.　It would be proper to make experiments to dispel all doubts on this important question ; and to examine whether labourers, having earth and fascines at hand, cannot during the night repair the breaches made by the bombs. If this manner of using bombs were introduced into the attack, it would become necessary to increase the thickness of the parapets, and to revest them with something capable of withstanding the effects of these fougasses fired by the besiegers.

If we admit that by firing bombs horizontally, a chasm may be made in two or three days in works of earth 18 mètres (20 yards) thick ; then the attack on Coehorn's system will advance with great rapidity.

First method of attack, ly the horizontal firing of bombs.

On the 12th day after the opening of the trenches, the besiegers will debouche from the beginning of the trench cavaliers and from the fourth parallel, to seize and embrace the salients of the salient places of arms. On the 15th day they will seize the salients of the four re-entering places of arms, crown the whole covert-way, and commence the batteries against the three salients. The 16th and 17th will be employed in completing all the works of the coronation; and in laying out all the other batteries on the extremities of the branches and on the faces of the re-entering places of arms, to counter-batter the artillery of the place and level those parts of the earthen works that mask the flanks and capital works. More than 100 pieces of artillery, of which 60 will be mortars and heavy howitzers, are requisite to effect this purpose. Batteries will be established; 1st, against the flanked angle of the low ravelin, to level its rampart, uncover and ruin the caponnières, and batter down the traverses and redoubts of the re-entering places of arms: 2d, against the extremes of the faces of the same ravelin by means of the openings of the ditches of the counter-guards, to level them, uncover the capital ravelin, and batter it in breach by substituting cannon in the place of the howitzers and mortars: 3d, against the *exterior* faces of the two counter-guards, to uncover the flanks of three stories, counter-batter and batter them down upon each other, and batter in breach the stone tower whose ruins will mask the debouché established beneath the face of the tenaille. It must be observed, that it is not expedient to level the *interior* faces of the counter-guards, the earth of which should be preserved for making the approaches*, &c.: 4th, against the low faces of the bastions, through the openings included between the counter-guards and ravelin and through the openings of the ravelin ditches, in order to uncover the capital bastions and the break of the curtain and batter them in breach, together with the orillon, which must necessarily sink beneath the united efforts of cross batteries posted in the re-entering places of arms and opposite the openings of the exterior faces of the counter-guards.

On the 18th all these batteries will be completed; and during the 19th and 20th they will fire without intermission, to make the chasms and breaches that we have mentioned. From the 17th, the besiegers will have descended into the covert-ways through four blinded openings or cuts made behind the traverses

---

* That is, the parapet is to be levelled, and the rampart preserved.
                                                        TRANSLATOR.

of the re-entering places of arms, to make four passages of the ditch or fill it up in four places; two of these passages will be directed towards the interior faces of the counter-guards, which being untouched, will cover the operation; and the two others, facing the origin of the openings at the flanked angle of the ravelin.

On the 19th the passages of the ravelin ditches will be completed; and the besiegers will glide into that part of the body of its rampart that is unimpaired, by saps in cremaillère, to gain the openings of the extremities of the faces and debouche in front of the breaches in the faces of the capital-ravelin. On the 20th they will assault the capital ravelin; and they will glide by saps in cremaillère into the body of the rampart of the interior faces of the counter-guards, in order to gain their extremities.

On the 21st they will begin the passages of the great ditch; and they will establish batteries on the terra-plain of the capital ravelin, to complete the ruin of the orillon and break of the curtain. On the 23d the passages of the ditch and their epaulments will be completed; and as breaches are already made in the faces and flanks of the capital bastions, and in the breaks of the curtains, the definitive assault may take place on the 24th at farthest.

Labours of the 21st, 22d, 23d and 24th days.

If the practicability of making breaches in works of earth by horizontally battering them with bombs, be not admitted; the besiegers must proceed by the common methods hitherto used. By employing mines, the necessary chasms may be made in the ramparts of the low ravelins and counter-guards, to uncover the capital ravelin, the flanks of three stories and the orillon. But this method would be much longer than the first, and would protract the siege to at least 30, and probably 36 days. If the method of offensive mining be not practicable, the besiegers will then adopt the most common methods; they will attack the low ravelin and counter-guards and establish themselves in them, and there construct batteries in breach and counter-batteries to make a breach in the capital ravelin and counter-batter the three story flanks of the bastions. They will then assault the capital ravelin; and they will construct in it batteries in breach against the orillons, to complete their destruction. After this, the passages of the great ditch may be made, and artillery brought up to batter in breach the low bastion* ; but it will be more easy

Second mode of attack, according to the methods now in use.

---

* This should most probably be " high bastion."—TRANSLATOR.

to fill up the ditch of the orillon, and set the miners to work at the face and at the break of the curtain. As soon as the mines are sprung, the capitulation will take place. Following this mode of attack, the probable duration of the siege cannot be calculated at less than 40 to 45 days.

Examination of the advantages & defects of Coehorn's system.

Coehorn has shown in his system, how the advantages of dry ditches which procure an active and brilliant defence, may be preserved to a fortress on a marshy site ; and he has established this remarkable maxim—that every site should be fortified by means analogous to the nature of its topography. If in this system, currents of water capable of acting with violence against the passages of the ditch, could be obtained, they would greatly increase its strength. Nevertheless the examination that we have sketched of it, shows that its accessory works, such as the crenated galleries, casemates, caponnières and coffers, do not contribute to lengthen the probable duration of the siege. All these means are destroyed at the very moment that they are about to be used. The plan of attack likewise shows some essential defects in the disposition of the trace : 1st, The great orillon or stone tower is ill placed at the shoulder of the low bastion ; because it is battered and ruined from the crowning of the covert-way, and it masks the fires of the opposite flank that should batter the dry ditch of the bastion, which is without defence the moment that the enemy penetrate into it. 2d, The ravelins and counter-guards leave between them a very dangerous opening, and form inconsiderable re-enterings ; this enables the besiegers to crown the re-entering and salient places of arms at almost the same time. 3d, The covert-way is not strongly occupied ; the redoubts of the re-entering places of arms are ruined and extinct at the moment of the coronation. 4th, The communications across wet ditches with the outworks, are difficult ; and the execution of a retreat very dangerous.

To remedy all these essential defects, the orillon should be established at the shoulder of the high bastion, the low bastions converted into an enceinte for musketry and enclosing dry ditches 40 mètres (45 yards) wide, the faces of the counter-guards protracted to the prolongation of the gorge of the low ravelin, the ravelins laid out upon the counter guards in order to mask the opening and make its flanked angle 60 degrees to give it a greater sally ; all the communications, galleries and caponnières, should be vaulted and bomb proof, and their bottoms raised above the level of the waters ; lastly, the re-entering places of arms should be intrenched with redoubts secure from an attack by storm.

Coehorn's second and third systems (PLATE VI, fig. 7*.)

Coehorn, in his second system, corrected the greater part of the defects of the first by more skilful dispositions, which favour the display of an active and artful defence. The first enclosure is a capital bastioned enceinte, whose flanks, covered by the orillon, have three tiers of fire ; and whose curtain and shoulders are covered by a wet ditch. The low bastions and curtain, connected together, constitute the first low enceinte whose gorge encloses the great dry ditch : it is provided with galleries, as in the first system. The counter-guards are connected together to form the third enceinte ; the salients and re-enterings are occupied by crenated redoubts covered by inclined palisadings ; these redoubts must be strongly constituted, and have ditches full of water. Lastly ; these three concentric enceintes are enveloped with a covert-way. Coehorn gives to the capital enceinte a greater relief than in the first system, in order that the glacises and country may be effectively defended by the direct fires of this principal enceinte.

The superiority of this system over the first, is obvious. A great train of artillery is requisite to attack it ; but like the first, it is greatly exposed to ricochet firing. It will not be estimating its strength too highly, to calculate the probable duration of the siege, by the first methods, at 40 days of open trenches ; and at 60 days, by the methods most commonly used.

Coehorn's third system being in every respect inferior to the second, we refrain from describing it ; contenting ourselves with a reference to Bousmard's work. His second and third systems have never been executed ; probably because he did not compose them until after he had fortified according to the first, most of the places that he constructed.

It is evident that these two systems of Coehorn, are less expensive than the bastioned system with which we have compared it ; since their construction only requires for all the works outside the capital enceinte, the removal of earth, the expense of which is very inferior to that of masonry. And as the strength of these two systems is at least equal to that of the modern bastioned system, they should be preferred to the latter whenever the site for the projected fortress is of the same nature with that for which Coehorn composed them.

Reflections on Coehorn's systems.

* In the original the reference is Figure 8 ; but it must be a mistake.
TRANSLATOR.

Vauban was born in 1633, and from his earliest youth was brought up in camps. The sight of the first fortresses and the first sieges in which he served, decided his predilection for engineering and fortification. From that time he devoted his attention to mathematics, all the branches of drawing, the arts of building, and to drawing plans and estimates of works, &c.; and in a short time his happy genius, aided by an unconquerable love of study, made him an engineer of the first order. He assisted at more than 50 sieges, and acquired in them an experience that enabled him to improve the theory and quicken the march of the progress of fortification, especially of that part relating to the attack of fortresses. He lived under a king who was seduced by the love of power and a passion for conquest, and whose armies were almost always on the offensive. He was therefore led to chiefly study the art of attacking places; and, as we before observed, he produced a complete revolution in the tactics of the wars of sieges. Stimulated by humanity, he unremittingly studied the means of sparing blood, and of rendering sieges less slaughterous by protecting the organic forces by the resources of art.

Vauban had not only hostile fortresses to conquer, intrenched camps to force, and attacks on posts to direct; but he had likewise to create and establish the defences of the frontiers, by erecting fortresses, forts and intrenched camps, repairing ancient fortresses and erecting new ones, and fortifying the seaports, and putting them all in a situation to resist the enemies of his country. The vigour of his genius was as great in this part of fortification, as in the attack. He first examined what the material of the defence consisted of; and reflecting that he had in a little time captured the fortresses that he had besieged, he sought the means of increasing their powers of resistance. His first system was not exclusive; he modified it according to the ground; sometimes combining its elements one way, and sometimes another, to obtain the desired end.

Vauban took up fortification at that point of improvement to which Count Pagan had brought it; and finding that the general dispositions of this great soldier and able engineer were such as he could desire, he devoted his attention to introduce into it only such modifications as he thought necessary. He suppressed the triple story flanks, reduced the orillon to its proper thickness, and made his retired flanks concave. Like Pagan, he took the exterior side for the base of the tracé of the enceinte, and made the fortification rasant ; but he reduced the greatest side of the polygon to 350 mètres (390 yards), to diminish the length of the lines of defence. He arranged the tracé of the enceinte by making the perpendicular, not of a determined length for each kind of polygon, but a determinate portion of the length of the side depending on the species of the polygon ; vizt, for a square one-eighth, for a pentagon one-seventh, and one-sixth for a hexagon or any higher polygon. When the position of the line of defence was thus determined, he took two-sevenths of the side for the length of the bastion faces ; and then drew the orillon and retired concave flanks. Towards the latter part of his life, he suppressed the orillons, and drew the flanks rectilinear.

But the greatest improvements that Vauban made to Pagan's system, were in the outworks. To him we are indebted for the invention of the tenaille whose properties we have discussed (145). He increased the dimensions of the ravelin, whose faces he directed 10 mètres (11 yards) above the bastion shoulders ; but he made it with flanks, which diminished its strength by uncovering the opening included between the tenaille and orillon or straight flank. He determined the ravelin flanked angle by describing from the flank angle, as a centre, with its distance from the shoulder angle, an arc of a circle cutting the perpendicular at the summit of the flanked angle. Inside the ravelin he made a redoubt, which at first consisted only of a crenated wall ; but it was subsequently properly constituted and intrenched.

The tenaille; the ravelin and its redoubt. (Figure 5.)

Lastly ; he organized his covert-way, provided it with traverses, and enlarged the capacity of the re-entering places of arms.

The covert-way.

The examination of this system is that which we described (147) ; it makes the strength of the system 25 days of open trenches at most. The advantages and defects of this system are easily inferred from what we have said on the system adopted as a term of comparison or unit of force.

Examination of this system. (See 147.)

When Vauban had applied his new theory to the siege of several places, and even of some that he had himself fortified agreeably to his first system ; and had perceived and ascertained beyond doubt from several facts the advantages of ricochet batteries, he was astonished and became convinced of the

Vauban's second and third systems, called the systems of mantioned towers. (Figs. 8 & 9.)

weakness of fortresses. And he was the more struck, as at this period the armies of Louis XIV were obliged to stand on the defensive against the armies of the greatest part of the allied powers, and as the political state of Europe inspired a presentiment that France would soon be compelled to cover her frontiers and defend her fortresses.

It was at the beginning of the war of 1688 that Vauban began to think seriously of improving the fortification of fortresses, to take from the attack part of the great advantages that it had just acquired over the defence. He proposed to construct at Befort and Landau, fortifications arranged according to a new tracé, which is now styled the Second System. Having afterwards induced Louis XIV to order the construction of a new fortress upon the Rhine, he fortified New Brisach according to a third system, which is nothing more than the second modified in the tracé of the body of the place.

It was the intention of Marshal Vauban in these two last systems, to correct several defects in the system of fortification hitherto used. All its parts that were easily reconnoitred, were ricoched; all its defences were ruined at the epoch of the near defence, and there were no longer any effective fires to defend the terra-plains of the outworks. Fortresses surrendered before the assault on the body of the place, because there was no longer any artillery to defend the ditches of the enceinte, and the consequences of an assault might be dreadful for the besieged. Lastly; the terra-plains of all works afforded so little space, that intrenchments could not be constructed in them to protect the retreat and preserve the power of offensive returns.

To remedy so many defects, Vauban conceived the following dispositions; 1st, to separate the bastions from the enceinte and make them spacious, so as to be able to stand several assaults and make in them an active defence by means of intrenchments that might be raised on their terra-plains: 2d, to introduce into his system casemated batteries that the enemy could not destroy from the covert-way, and which would defend the ditches of the enceinte: 3d, to constitute his enceinte in such a manner, that the enemy could not ricoché its batteries.

(PLATE VI.) He effected these several dispositions in his second system:
(Figure 8) 1st, by an enceinte composed of bastioned towers united to-

gether by a curtain : 2d, by full detached bastions or counter-guards, including a wide tenaille between their flanks : 3d, by a ravelin and covert-way, disposed in the ordinary manner. The bastioned towers are vaulted bomb-proof, and have beneath them great souterrains whose floors are 20 decimètres (6⅔ feet) above the bottom of the ditch : these souterrains extend along the flanks, in each of which there are two embrasures to enfilade the ditches. The bastioned towers are crowned with a platform of free-stone, and by a brick parapet pierced with embrasures.

The ravelin is of 90 mètres (100 yards) capital, and its faces are directed to 20 mètres (22 yards) above the shoulder angles ; it is with flanks.

The communications are composed of posterns, wooden bridges, and ramps.

In this second system, Vauban allowed for the interior side containing the curtain, only 234 mètres (260 yards) ; this gave an exterior side of about 330 mètres (368 yards).

He drew his third system by taking for base the exterior side, (Figure 9.) which he made 350 mètres (390 yards), &c. By this, he enlarged the dimensions of all the elements. Not content with having casemates with two pieces of cannon in the flanks of his bastioned towers, he obtained others by bastioning the curtain and constructing casemates for two more pieces under the small flanks. The descent to these souterrains is by posterns leading from the slope of the rampart. In this system the ravelin capital is 110 mètres (122 yards), and its faces terminate at 30 mètres (33⅓ yards) from the shoulders ; it is provided with a redoubt, whose flanks of 8 to 10 mètres (9 to 11 yards) see in reverse those parts of the faces of the counter-guards which are opposite the openings of the ditches. All the communications are the same as in the second system.

The relief and commandment of all the elements of the system, are regulated as follows : the covert-way is raised about 20 decimètres (8⅔ feet) above the plane of site, and is commanded by the ravelin by 20 decimètres (6⅔ feet); the body of the place commands the ravelin by 20 decimètres, and its redoubt by 10 decimètres (3⅓ feet); and the terra plain of the bastioned towers is raised 13 or 14 decimètres (4⅓ or 4⅔ feet) above the terra-plain of the small bastions and of the curtain : this shows that the relief of the body of the place above the plane of site, is 66 decimètres (22 feet). In the second system in which the ravelin has no redoubt, the relief of the body of the place above the plane of site, is only 56 decimètres (18¾ feet).

The general advantages of the two systems, under the relation of their attack & defence.

In examining the arrangement of these two last systems, we perceive their superiority over the first, from the greatness of the detached bastions or counter-guards, which are capable of being strongly intrenched ; from the largeness and sally of the ravelins, which in the third system enclose an excellent redoubt and almost entirely cover the body of the place ; from the power that the besiegers have of standing an assault in the ravelins and counter-guards, without running the risk of seeing the place carried by storm. These remarkable advantages approximate the third system to that which we have taken as a term of comparison, particularly when we examine the influence of the collateral ravelins on the attacks and crowning of the covert-way.

The attack on these systems : the probable duration of the siege

As the disposition of the third system assimilates it very nearly to the bastioned system that we have taken for the foundation of our studies, we should accordingly assimilate their attacks. We must suppose that the besieged have made cuts (*coupures*) in the ravelins, and likewise in the counter-guards, and surrounded the stairs of their gorge by a strong covert-way. These being granted, the theoretick march of the attack will be exactly the same in the two systems compared, up to the establishment of the trench cavaliers. As the sally of the ravelins in the system compared, is less, the trench cavaliers are laid out and constructed with less losses and more expedition ; the salients of the three re-entering* places of arms may be seized at almost the same time ; and the re-entering places of arms not being intrenched, the operations of attacking and crowning the covert-way will be less dangerous and more rapid. This will also be the case with respect to the construction of the batteries in breach and counter-batteries ; these works will be easier established than in the system taken as a term of

Labours of the 30th night. Assault on the counter-guards.

comparison. It follows from these observations, that on the 30th day of open trenches the counter-guards will be assaulted and a lodgement effected in their terra-plains by a sap, the figure of which will depend on that of the intrenchment. These lodgements will be strongly covered on the side of the cuts.

* This should most probably be salient.   TRANSLATOR.

In the 31st night the miners will be set to work at the cuts of the counter-guards, or at their redoubts; and on the 32d, at break of day, these intrenchments will be forced. The besiegers will then make their way by saps into the body of the flank parapets, to take the tenaille in rear.

As the ravelins have flanks and do not cover the openings between the flanks and tenailles, batteries in breach will be erected against the curtain as soon as the covert-way is crowned; these breaches will be practicable on the 27th.

During the 33d and 34th days batteries will be constructed on the gorge of the counter-guards, to batter in breach those parts of the curtain next to the flanks of the bastioned towers : the ruins of these breaches will mask and render nugatory the casemated batteries. The besiegers will carry on their approaches towards the opening of the tenaille, and begin the passages of the great ditch with double epaulments.

The passages of the great ditch, and their double epaulments, will reach the foot of the breaches on the 36th at farthest ; and if the besieged have not hastened to beat the chamade on the 35th, the definitive assault will be made on the 36th, at break of day, by four columns moving simultaneously against the four breaches.

It follows from this sketch of the attack against Vauban's third system, that its strength is in equilibrium with that of the modern front to which we have compared it. The defence of the second system, whose elements are less perfect and not so well disposed, cannot be protracted beyond 30 to 32 days of open trenches.

It is not unworthy of remark, that the strength of the systems of the three most celebrated engineers, are about the same. The differences between the ratios of their respective strength, depend upon slight gradations that are difficult to be estimated in theory, and which may vanish or increase with moral or other causes. Nevertheless it is thought by the most experienced engineers, that Vauban's third system is superior to that of Cormontaigne.

The arrangement of Vauban's third system, presents general dispositions worthy of an engineer most consummately skilled in the art of war. The body of the place is covered by a system of outworks that are easily communicated with ; these are of great capacity, which allows making in them the necessary interior intrenchments and dispositions for the most active defence and for repulsing attacks by storm. The whole strength of the system depends on those great counter-guards, closely supported by the body of the place and preceded by great ravelins which cover their shoulders and flanks, and whose redoubts take in reverse the breaches made in the faces of these counter-guards through the openings of the ditches. However, the general disposition offends in a very essential point : the ravelin flanks which can be of no real use, uncover the openings between the tenaille and the flanks, and consequently the opposite part of the curtain : this is the only part of the body of the place that can be seen from the coronation of the covertway.

The new and secondary means used by Vauban, consisting of bastioned towers and casemated batteries, do not correspond with the excellence of the general dispositions. The bastioned towers and their platforms are ruined from the first period of the siege ; after a few days they are reduced to a heap of ruins that the besieged must clear away. The casemated batteries are likewise of no service ; 1st, because they are counter-battered from the gorge of the counter-guards, or masked by the ruins of the breaches : 2d, because being in enclosed souterrains, their fire is uncertain and inconstant, by reason of the suffocation occasioned by the smoke. In consequence of these weaknesses, the ditch of the body of the place is not flanked ; and the place must capitulate as soon as the counter-guards are occupied by the besiegers and the breaches in the body of the place are practicable. It is probable that in attacking the common front, it would be necessary to attack the two collateral ravelins ; their power over the wings of the attack is such, as may decide the besiegers to direct their attack against two ravelins and a single counter-guard. In this case, the besieged will be able to defend the ditch of the body of the place, by opposing a great resistance to the construction of the epaulments. The bastioned tower of the front of attack not being counterbattered from any point, the besiegers can do nothing more than to mask the casemated batteries of its flanks by the ruins of two mines made in the gorge of the counter-guard.

The improvements that may be made to Vauban's third system. This examination of Vauban's third system, shows that by slight alterations its strength may be increased to a degree exceeding that of any system hitherto used. The first alteration might be ; 1st, to increase the capacity of the bastioned towers, in order to make their parapets of earth ; 2d, to procure a circulation of air in the casemated batteries, that their firing may be without remission ; 3d, to suppress the ravelin flanks, in order that they may cover the openings of the tenaille.   The second alteration would be more extensive, but would not change the principles of the arrangement of the system ; it would be, 1st, to suppress the bastioned towers and small bastions, and substitute in their place common bastions including a tenaille ; these bastions and the opening of the tenaille would be perfectly covered by the counter-guards ; 2d, to increase the dimensions of the ravelin, and draw it like that in Cormontaigne's system ; 3d, to intrench the re-entering places of arms with strong redoubts ; 4th, to make intrenchments in the bastions of the body of the place, to compel the enemy to make complete passages of the great ditch.

By examining the advantages that would be acquired by Vauban's system, by virtue of the alterations and modifications that we have just suggested, it is easy to perceive its superiority over the system that has served us as a basis.   In the first, when the besiegers have taken the counter-guards, an untouched bastioned body of the place presents itself before them, and cannot be battered in breach except across a narrow and deep ditch.   At the same epoch in the second system, the besiegers will be masters of the bastions, and will have nothing more to conquer than a weak intrenchment, the last hope of the garrison, who cannot risk an assault upon it.   Accordingly the probable duration of the siege is at least six days more in Vauban's system, than in the other ; and considering the power that the besieged have of harassing the enemy in their labours on the counter-guards, we may without danger of exaggeration increase this excess of defence to ten days.

The strength of Vauban's system, corrected and modified.

153. After Vauban's systems, the system which was and is still most used, is that of Cormontaigne, which we have chosen for the particular subject of our studies.   Its author borrowed the plan of the body of the place from Pagan's system, and of the ravelins whose terra-plains are narrow, from Coehorn's system ; and he took the redoubts of the re-entering places of arms from Glasser and Rosard.   The great ravelins sallying out into the country and provided with redoubts with flanks, and the permanent intrenchments of the bastions, are improve-

153. Cormontaigne's system ; its advantages & defects.

ments of his own.   To this celebrated engineer was reserved
the honour of discovering the new advantages acquired by the
modern bastioned front when it is contiguous to collateral fronts
that make with it very obtuse angles, or which are on the same
right line.   But if the salient ravelins produce a better general
arrangement, they greatly increase a defect already existing in
the system : they are more exposed to ricochet batteries ; and
they uncover at a greater distance the opening through which
the bastions of the front of attack are battered in breach.   It
occurs in consequence, that the breaches in the body of the
place are practicable ten or twelve days before it is possible
to assault them, if their assault be deemed impracticable until
after the taking of the ravelin redoubt ; and that this is the
case, is not quite certain.   Besides, the existence of a breach
in the body of the place for several days, keeps the garrison in
perpetual alarm, and affords the Governor a plausible pretext
for surrendering.

154. The systems that have appeared since the days of Vauban and Coehorn (See *L'Architecture des Fortresses, by Mandar.*)   154. Since the time of Vauban and Coehorn a great number
of systems have appeared, few of which deserve attention in
relation to the progress of the science ; but their study may be
useful to noviciates, by making them acquainted with several ingenious means used in this multitude of combinations.   All these
systems are divided into three principal classes as respects the
figure of their enceinte.   The first class comprehends those
with circular enceintes ; the second consists of the bastioned
systems, and is the most numerous ; and the third class includes
those whose enceinte is an angular polygon with acute salients
and rectangles of defence.

Blondel's system (1683)   At the time that Vauban and Coehorn devoted their attention to improve the form and arrangements of fortification, several other writers also pursued the same subject.   In 1683,
Blondel proposed a bastioned system with flanks of several
tiers ; its merit is very moderate, for it is far inferior to Vauban's
systems.

Landsberg's system (1712 to 1758.)   Landsberg, a celebrated engineer in the Dutch service, and
the worthy successor of Coehorn, had acquired great experience
in the wars of sieges.   His theory, added to long practice,
enabled him to investigate the composition of the systems in
use in his days.   In his numerous systems he sometimes adopts
a figure with tenailles, and sometimes the bastioned figure ; he
disposes all the parts for artillery principally, and is of opinion

that musketry is of little avail in the defence of fortresses.   Finally ; he proposes and adopts casemated redoubts and defensive caserns, to form an interior defence ; taking care to always cover these defences with parapets.

Sturm, whose systems are but modifications of those of his predecessors, makes the tenailled enceinte the base of his systems ; he covers it with several outworks whose disposition is more or less complex.   In his systems he makes use of timber batteries covered over with earth, of blinded galleries, and of coffers.

Sturm's system (1720)

Glasser is distinguished by his endeavours to strengthen the bastioned enceinte, which he covers by ravelins with redoubts, by counter-guards with narrow terra-plains, by a continuous enclosure, and by a covert-way whose re-entering places of arms are intrenched.   But what most distinguishes his compositions, are the casemated fires that he uses to defend the ditches. The salients of bastion and ravelin ditches, are crossed along the capitals (*traversés en capital*) by casemated caponnières that the enemy cannot counter-batter but from the ditch itself, and which defend the breaches.   Glasser conceived the ingenious idea of covering the casemated artillery by parapets of earth made in the casemate.   His systems do honour to their inventor, and are very strong.

Glasser's systems (1738.)

Rosard, an engineer in the Bavarian service, acquired his first knowledge of fortification in the French engineer corps ; he composed two bastioned systems which resemble those of Glasser.   He carefully intrenches his bastions, and raises commanding cavaliers upon the curtains ; he covers the body of the place by intrenched ravelins, by tenaillons and counter-guards (this disposition of outworks is very defective); and he intrenches the re-entering places of arms of the covert-way.   This able engineer disposes on the capitals a system of advanced lunettes, covered by an advanced covert-way, and with which the garrison communicate by subterranean galleries.   The flanks of the body of the place are the only parts that are casemated, and in such a manner, that the smoke produces no inconveniences.

Rosard's system (1731.)

Frederick Augustus II, king of Poland, successfully cultivated the science of fortification ; he is the author of many systems, whose combinations are very different from those of his predecessors.   Augustus abandons the bastioned for the te-

Systems of Augustus II. (1737)

nailled system, and intrenches the gorge of the tenailles to procure an interior defence.   In the re-entering angle of the tenailles he constructs casemated redoubts of several tiers, to flank the exterior and interior of the tenailles.   The enceinte is differently covered in his various systems, which are very complex.   Casemated batteries of a single tier are used in these ingenious systems, to defend the ditches and act against the batteries in breach : the redoubts of the re-entering angles are casemated with three tiers.   It is probable that these were the first casemates of this kind that were introduced into the systems.

Belidor's systems (1740) Belidor, whose knowledge in all branches of engineering was most extensive, composed several systems ; they are founded upon the bastioned enceinte covered by outworks more or less complex, and in which there are low casemated flanks.   On the capitals of the bastions and in advance of the covert-way, he establishes detached lunettes with retired flanks, and covered by a glacis likewise detached.   Belidor's systems are not judged capable of making a better defence than Cormontaigne's.

Filey's system (1746 to 1762.) M. de Filey, an engineer of the first talents, and a Lieutenant General in the French army, published in 1762 his system of fortification, which he calls " *Mézalectre.* "   The basis of this system is the bastioned figure, which he modifies in a peculiar manner and covers with ravelins and counter-guards.   The modification is founded on the curtain, which is broken into the bastion form and the salient of which reaches into the ravelin. The flanks of the curtain thus arranged, defend rectangularly the faces of the bastions, and the flanks of the bastions defend the ravelin.   The re-enterings formed by the mézalectre, are covered by a tenaille whose parapet is a crenated wall.   The gorges of the bastions are intrenched with a small bastioned front whose flanks are casemated and covered by a redoubt, the parapet of which is a crenated wall.   Behind the gorge of the mézalectre, cavaliers are raised and cover spacious souterrains.

The strength of this system, whose characteristics are simplicity, is inferior to Cormontaigne's ; the attack upon it may be directed against the mézalectre, without the besiegers being compelled to attack the bastions and their intrenchments.

Reflections on he preceding systems. It may be observed of the systems that we have just described, that after Vauban and Coehorn, the plan of their authors, or

of the most of them, was to introduce into their systems covered or casemated batteries to act against the batteries in breach
and against the passages of the ditch.   Glasser, and Augustus
II, founded the success of their systems on the more or less fortunate use that they made of this species of defence.   The
combinations in fortification of posterior ages, are gradually
more and more of this character, by reason of the constantly
increasing powers of ricochet and curvated fires.

In 1767, M, De la Chiche perceived the necessity of making
great changes in the arrangement of the horizontal projection of
fortification.   He adopted the bastioned system ; but he draws
it by allowing ¼th of the front for the perpendicular, and diminishes the length of the bastion faces in order to procure greater
flanks.   He covers the ravelin by a flêche placed in the salient
place of arms, and makes the tenaille with flanks ; he constructs
redoubts in the re-entering places of arms and defiles their
faces ; and strengthens by an intrenchment the terra-plain of
the salient place of arms opposite the bastion.   By these dispositions in the horizontal projection, M. De la Chiche places
his bastions in deep re-enterings into which the besiegers cannot advance without first taking all the outworks : their communications are secured by the use of blinded, frame, and terraced galleries.   With respect to the composition of his primitive profiles, this writer follows a new method ; and it is by
reason of this arrangement in its vertical projection, that his
system is totally different from the preceding and from all the
systems hitherto used.   His scarp-revêtements are made of
casemates, covered over with a parapet of earth through which
there are air-holes (*soupiraux*) for the escape of the smoke ; this
revêtement is pierced with embrasures 7 decimètres (28 inches)
wide at the exterior.   At the foot and in rear of the scarp and
counterscarp revêtements, there are crenated galleries with air-
holes which debouche either into the upper casemates, or into
the covert-ways.   The flêche, the ravelin and its redoubt,
and the bastion faces and flanks, are with casemated revêtements.   The curtains are likewise casemated ; but they are
open at the gorge and have only a simple superior banquette.
The covert-way is raised so as to conceal all the masonry of
the works, whose relief is regulated according to the rules of
defilement.

Chiche's system (1767.)

We see that this system is arranged to afford, 1st, uncovered and superior fires, to act during the exterior defence in proportion as the circumstances of the attack will permit; 2d, great quantities of covered fires, to be used curvatedly before the coronation of the covert-way, and to fire direct during the near defence of the covert-ways, ditches and breaches. Its inventor thinks that the air-holes are sufficient for the escape of the smoke.

The examination of this system depends upon the great question—of the effect of the attacking batteries upon casemates and even covered casemates; and upon the practicability of constructing batteries in breach and counter-flank on the coronation of the covert-way, in the face of casemated batteries that are lower than the coronation. None of the casemated batteries in this system act on the flanks or rear, or have a direct and plunging fire on the coronation of the covert-way.

General Montalembert's system. (See this writer's works) Of all modern writers who have published systems of fortification, General Montalembert has the most novel and varied plans for using casemated fires. He has invented or improved several kinds of casemates, and introduced them into fortification either to correct the old systems, or to make part in the disposition of his own. General Montalembert has acquired by his labours well-merited honour, and secured to himself the lasting admiration and gratitude of all officers whose studies are directed to the progress of the science. He not only devoted his attention to permanent fortification, but he also contributed to improve field fortification, which should possess a certain degree of strength. His profiles for wooden casemates and defensive caponnières, may be frequently used in defensive war and in establishing winter quarters, &c.; as has been observed by M. De Cessac, who does full justice to the merit of General Montalembert.

The author of Perpendicular Fortification has opened a new field by his investigations. He perceived that the weakness of the present fortifications was occasioned by the want of coverts in the fortresses, to shelter the troops and material of the defence; and his object in his systems, is; 1st, to construct at the same time the material and accessaries of the defence; 2d, to shield all his artillery and means of defence from the destroying effects of the curvated fires of the attack; 3d, to combat, both during the distant and near defence, the artillery of the besiegers with a more numerous artillery, which shall be capable of counter battering the former with certain advantages.

In his tracés, he abandons the bastioned figure and substitutes in its place the tenailled figure whose salient angles are 60 degrees and the re-entering 90 degrees. 'Tis in consequence of this tracé that his method is styled *Perpendicular Fortification*; because in it, the lines of defence are at right angles with the faces. It follows from this disposition, that the regular polygons that are to be thus fortified, cannot be lower than a dodecagon. The lengths of the side, and of the radius, are deduced from the length of the line of defence, which cannot exceed 300 mètres (335 yards).

The tenailles are separated from the capital enceinte by casemated flanks that defend the ditches; the gorge is occupied by a casemated tower several tiers high. The tenailles are covered by a general enclosure of earth, whose re-enterings are occupied by casemates; these are themselves covered by a lunette with casemated flanks, placed in the re-entering of the counterscarp.

The faces of the general enclosure are occupied (*coupées*) by two casemated traverses, which fire into the country and into the terra-plains of the works.

It is in the arrangement of his profiles that General Montalembert differs from all that have been hitherto proposed or practised. He has improved the existing casemates and made them convenient for service; he varies their form and dimensions for each particular case, and completely removes all objections to them on account of smoke; and he introduces them into his systems in the most ingenious and diversified manner, regarding them as the basis of his defences.

The profiles of the tenailles and capital ramparts, are composed of a casemated scarp of two stories; each casemate of which is 50 decimètres (16½ feet) wide, and is destined to contain one piece of artillery. Behind this scarp is the embankment of earth, forming a counter-guard to cover the capital rampart. Between these two scarps there is a dry ditch, that is flanked by the fires of the two casemated stories of the capital rampart. This latter rampart, and likewise the tower, command the country by a third tier of fire, also casemated; and behind this casemated scarp is the bank of the earthen rampart. To acquire a just and exact idea of the arrangement of

(PLATE I. 1. 7.)

(See Montalem-
bert's works, and
Mandar's Essay
on Fortification.)
Montalembert's systems, we must consult his works, or at least the Historical Abridgment in Mandar's Essay on Fortification.

The investigation of Montalembert's system, like M. De la Chiche's, depends upon the reciprocal effect of the casemated and attacking batteries. Facts seem to demonstrate that all the parts of systems with casemated batteries which are above the covering banks of earth, would in a short time be demolished and ruined by the direct batteries of the attack established from the second parallel. With respect to the lower batteries which can only act directly against the terra-plains and ditches, it is not at all proved that they can prevent the establishment of counter-batteries which will command them from the crest of the covert-ways, or from the terra-plains of the face coverings (*couvre-faces*). It is probable that they would be totally unfit for service before they could destroy the epaulments by means of howitzes, &c. Besides the besiegers may use the powerful weapon of horizontal bomb and howitze firing, to lay open the earthen face-coverings and unmask the embrasures of the casemates. Engineers likewise allege the immense expense of constructing such works, and the enormous quantity of artillery that it would require to arm fortresses built according to these systems.

But if inland fortifications should not be composed of whole systems of casemates of several tiers; yet this latter is the fittest fortification for forts to defend ports and harbours; and by firing red-hot shot, they are perfectly secure against the attacks of fleets and floating batteries. In this view of the subject, General Montalembert has greatly contributed to the progress of the art, and has rendered signal service to his country.

Reflections up-
on direct & ver-
tical casemated
fires.
It is a truth at present generally received, and Montalembert greatly contributed to establish it, that casemated fires are easily executed; that they should be used in various circumstances; and that their combination with the other elements of fortification, is the only mode of composing systems capable of opposing a resistance proportioned to the exigencies of war and to the violence of the attacks, which appears daily to increase.

During the period of the distant defence, the casemated fires can only be curvated or vertical; but as soon as the besiegers are within the limits of the near defence, these fires should be at the same time both direct and vertical. And in order that they may possess a certain efficacy, they must be so disposed that the besiegers cannot counter-batter them, or not until they have spent a great deal of time and experienced great losses, &c.

Virgin, a celebrated Swedish engineer, after observing in several sieges of the war of 1740 the causes of the weakness of fortresses, perceived that the violence of the attacks was a consequence of the improvements in artillery, and of the manner in which the besiegers might use it to compel the besieged to abandon their defences and silence their artillery.   Convinced of the necessity of making great changes in fortification, Virgin conceived systems founded on the great and copious principle of reverse and casemated fires : he disposes his casemates for curvated fires, and lavishes them in all parts of his systems.   He adopts by preference the bastioned system, but modifies it in such a manner as to unite the reverse defences of the works with the interior defence.   He endeavours to so dispose all his works, that they will protect and support each other with such efficacy as to compel the besiegers to envelop by their attacks a great portion of the perimeter of the enceinte.   Virgin's systems are complicated and overloaded with elements ; their expense would be great, and they would require an immense quantity of artillery for their defence.   It is impossible to form an exact idea of these new systems without their author's work, which deserves the study and attention of those officers and artists who particularly cultivate the science of fortification.   It is to be regretted that this work is so scarce.

Virgin's system (178] to 1788.) (See this author's work ; and the Abridgment of Mandar.)

Reveroni, an officer of engineers, embraces Montalembert's principles, on the necessity of shielding the artillery from the ricochet and vertical fires of the besiegers ; but he proposes to cover the casemated batteries without losing the advantage of acting against the works of the attack.   To obtain this advantage, upon which the basis of his system is founded during the distant defence, he has conceived the perfectly novel idea of making the casemates with vertical embrasures, from which pieces of artillery are run out at pleasure to fire in barbette, and then run back into the interior of the casemate to be reloaded to continue the fire.   This manœuvre is executed by means of a very ingenious swipe-gun-carriage (affût à bascule), turning upon an axis of rotation by the very effect of the recoil.   If experience prove that the fire can be executed with ease and promptitude by means of such a carriage, it would be sufficient

Reveroni's system (1794.) (See the author's memoir, entitled Inventions Militaires, &c ; and Mandar's Essay on Fortification.)

to give the casemated scarps very little commandment over the earthen face-coverings, and to make them bomb proof. The same casemates contain low batteries to act against the crowning of the covert-way, terra-plains and ditches. The system, in its vertical projection, is founded on the combination of the profile of çasemated batteries ; and its horizontal projection consists of a bastioned and casemated enclosure, behind which there is an earthen intrenchment, also bastioned, and raised with the earth taken from the ditch. The body of the place is covered by counter-guards of earth, at whose extremities the ravelin faces terminate. This ravelin is with orillons and retired casemated flanks of two tiers, to defend the counter-guard ditch and terra-plain, and take in reverse the face of the casemated bastion ; the interior of the ravelin is occupied by a casemated redoubt, &c.

Carnot's system (1797)? The last system to which we shall refer, is that of Carnot. This veteran officer of engineers, after giving proofs of the greatest talents in conceiving and forming plans of campaign and their general conduct, devoted his science and attention to fortification, and exhibited in an accurate and luminous manner his opinion of the necessity of changes in the present dispositions of fortification.

(PLATE VII.) In adopting most of Montalembert's ideas on casemated fires, Carnot does justice to the labours and talents of this officer. Like him, he takes casemated and covered fires for the basis of the vertical projection of his system, and the tenailled tracé for that of the horizontal projection ; but his method is essentially different as respects the disposition of his batteries and the manner of combining them with the elements, to obtain the least complicated arrangement.

Experiments made at St. Omer having proved that the use of blinded batteries is easy, and that they are perfectly strong against the shocks and blast of heavy artillery ; Carnot makes use of them, but only in those parts of the ramparts where they cannot without great difficulty be counter-battered.

The following are the principles upon which the arrangement of Carnot's system is founded : 1st, The distant defence must not be much attended to, for it is impossible to arrest until after a certain point, the advance and progress of the attack. In this respect all the systems are about equally strong, provided they afford cross-fires upon the capitals, and vertical fires.

These fires can never produce any great effect so long as the besiegers have not reached the third parallel; and it is here that Carnot differs totally from Montalembert. 2d, All the batteries and constructions in masonry must be carefully concealed; and all the means of defence must be chiefly applied to the near defence. 3d, It must not be attempted to bring into play an immense quantity of artillery, to act directly; but rather an artillery so well covered and disposed, that in defending the approaches of the works it cannot be counter-battered, except from the narrow and confined ground on which the besiegers are taken in flank and reverse. Let us examine briefly how this writer endeavours to fulfil these important conditions, without which the defence must remain in its present state of weakness.

The capital enceinte of the system is a tenailled tracé, with re-entering angles of 90 degrees, and salient angles varying from 60 to 80 degrees. This body of the place is enveloped with a common counterscarp and ditch. The re-enterings are occupied by casemated batteries of two tiers; the lower one is defended by an earthen caponnière, which at the same time masks the debouché of a wide postern. This same casemate is continued beyond the counterscarp, to preserve two pieces of cannon which take in reverse the salients of the tenailles. The upper casemate only extends to the prolongation of the covertway, so as to be able to defend the ditches of the outworks.

Upon each tenaille salient is erected a bastioned tower casemated bomb proof, with an embrasure on the capital and two on each flank; and beside each bastioned tower, there is a blinded battery of three or four pieces of cannon.

The body of the place, thus constituted and armed, is perfectly covered: 1st, By two counter-guards, or face-coverings, terminated by two flanks whose profiles are on the line drawn from the extremity of the flank of the bastioned tower to the flanked angle of the collateral counter-guard. The bastioned tower is by this plan embraced by the face-covering, whose relief completely covers it from all direct views; but the flanks of the face-coverings do not mask the fires of the bastioned-tower-flanks, which see in reverse the faces of these counter-guards. 2d, The profiles of the counter-guards are united by a covertway which forms the re-entering place of arms; and the counter-guards are likewise enveloped by a covert-way whose ter-

ra-plain is very narrow and provided with a single banquette.
3d, The terra-plain of the face-coverings likewise consists of
only a single banquette for musketry, in order that the besiegers
may experience the greatest difficulties in establishing upon
them batteries in breach and counter-batteries. 4th, The
ditches of the face-coverings unite tangentially with the surface
of the glacis of the re-entering place of arms. 5th, The long
branches of the covert-way are enfiladed and even taken in reverse by the blinded batteries contiguous to the bastioned towers. 6th, Finally; casemates with reverse fires may be made
in the counterscarp of the salient place of arms; but this disposition does not appear necessary against an attack by storm,
and is superfluous against an attack by gradual approaches.
Nevertheless it is proper to remark, that the ditch of the counter-guards is only defended by fires that are uncovered at top;
and if it be intended to flank them by covered fires, there must
be constructed on the faces of the tenailles, not common blinded batteries with wide embrasures, but blinded batteries sunk
in the body of the parapet, and the merlons of which, 14 decimètres ($4\frac{2}{3}$ feet) thick, should be made of heavy timbers.

If this system, organized principally for the near defence, do
not appear to furnish sufficient artillery fires during the period
of the distant defence; more may be obtained by raising cavaliers on the salients of the tenailles, and by disposing the flanked angle of the counter-guards to receive artillery.

The admirable disposition of the covert-ways in relation to
the debouchès for sorties, deserves our attention. The ascent
from the caponnières that cover the re-entering angle, to the
re-entering place of arms, is by wide ramps; this re-entering
place of arms is covered on all sides. From this latter the infantry, and even the cavalry, defile into the ditches and covert-
ways of the counter-guards; and the several columns then move
out to form along the branches of the covert-way, by the great
debouchè included between their extremities.

There is in Carnot's essay many remarkable advantages,
which must make his much superior to all modern systems.
There is great simplicity in all its dispositions; its artillery-
fires are covered during the principal period of the defence; it
affords the sorties the greatest facilities for assembling and debouching; its defence is maintained with a moderate quantity
of artillery, proportioned to the means of a state; the expense

of its construction is moderate, and does not exceed that of any of the systems hitherto used ; lastly, the arrangement of the system is of general application, and may be adapted by the art of defilement to the most irregular sites and to those which are most influenced by circumjacent ground.

This mere glance of a system that is reserved to be perfected by its inventor, suffices to show in what manner casemated and blinded fires, whether direct or reverse, may be introduced into the dispositions of fortification. We will here conclude this enumeration of the principal systems, the single object of which is to excite the curiosity of the students, and to induce them to make these systems the subject of their profound study at a future day ; and to confirm them in this opinion—That in the arts, as in all branches of precise science, a man of genius may always make new combinations and hope to be useful to his country.

This brief exposition of the principal systems of fortification, and of the efforts that are daily made to raise it from the state of weakness into which it has fallen in consequence of the violence of the attack, proves that there are yet great improvements to be made in the arrangement and combinations of the fortification of fortresses. The defence can never resume an attitude capable of inspiring the defenders with confidence, until the effects of the vertical fires from the half places of arms are moderated ; and until the besieged can themselves make use of these fires to arrest the progress of the approaches, and to compel the besiegers to cover themselves with blinds in all parts of the third parallel, &c.

General clus on on strength of fo fication in present state.

CHAPTER VII.

The additional works used for increasing the Strength of the Fronts of Fortresses; Inundations and use of Waters; Advanced Ditches and Advanced Covert-ways; Tenaillons and Counter-guards; Horn and Crown Works; Lunettes, considered under different points of view; the Defence obtained by Casemates and Crenated Galleries; General Reflections on Detached and Advanced Works.

The additional works used to increase the strength of a fortified front. SEVERAL kinds of works are introduced into the arrangement of systems of fortification applied to different sites, either to increase the positive strength of a fortress, or increase the strength of certain separate fronts, or to modify the whole fortification according to peculiar circumstances; or lastly, to occupy particular positions that would have a dangerous influence over the defensive polygon. For instance, if a place be situated on a river or creek, it is obvious that advantage should be taken of its waters to give to the fortification (all other things being equal) a new increase of strength. This is effected, 1st, by producing inundations that will make some parts inaccessible; 2d, by making such dispositions of the waters, as to carry torrents into the ditches, inundate the foot of the glacis, and even the terra-plains of the covert-ways when the besiegers establish themselves in them.

If the construction of a place have rendered an advanced ditch (*avant-fossé*) necessary, it may be supported by *flèches, lunettes,* or advanced *covert-ways,* &c. And these additional works may likewise be employed to increase the extent of a fortress that is too small for its garrison and the importance that it should possess in the organization of the frontier. If it be practicable to introduce waters into an advanced ditch, it will be capable of a better defence.

Finally; the other additional works are adapted to the enceinte, and make with it one and the same system. They are likewise used outside and in various modes, according to their destination. They consist of *counter-guards* or *face-coverings, tenaillons, horn-works, crown-works,* several kinds of *lunettes, casemates with reverse fires, crenated galleries,* and *defensive mines* and *subterranean war.*

155. We showed in the Second Part, what advantageous resources might be derived from the proper use of waters in field fortification. These resources, frequently afforded by the sites of fortresses, become in the hands of an able engineer the most economical and efficacious means to increase the strength of fortified fronts, by forming inundations or ponds, rendering the ground impracticable for trenches by irrigations, organizing waters so as to fill the ditches at pleasure, or forming in them floods and currents to overwhelm the bridges and works of the besiegers.

155 The manner of using waters to increase the strength of fortifications.

The increase of strength obtained by waters, is at a very moderate expense, and does not require any increase in the numerical force of the garrison. The establishment of these kinds of defences, requires on the part of the engineers extensive theoretical and practical knowledge of the construction of hydraulic works. The students will acquire this knowledge in the theoretical course on civil works, and in the schools of application.

The first use that can be made of the waters of a river that traverses a site, is to form inundations to cover more or less extended fronts and render them inaccessible. These inundations, kept at the greatest height, procure two other advantages ; 1st, of forming a grand reservoir, whence waters may be drawn and conducted to other parts that are capable of containing them: 2d, of enabling us to raise in the midst of the waters *works of earth that are inaccessible (pièces en terre inaccessible),* and which take in reverse the adjacent assailable fronts.

Upper and lower inundations; insulated or inaccessible works.

It is easy to produce an upper inundation, as it is sufficient for this purpose to construct a refluent dike (*reversoir*) that will cause the waters to flow back and raise them to their greatest height. But a lower inundation requires the construction of a small fortress or fort situated down the stream, to contain the causeway (*barrage*) that is to cause the waters to flow back beneath the glacis of the place. It rarely occurs that such extensive means are employed.

The artificial works by which water defences are obtained, consist of dikes, sluice-bridges (*ponts éclusés*), *sluices*, dams (*batardeaux*), refluent dikes (*réversoirs*), and over-falls (*déversoirs*). The placing of these various works requires great attention on the part of the engineer ; and they should be so established,

Artificial works to create water defences.

that the defenders cannot be deprived of them at any period of
the siege.   Consequently they must be shielded from the view
of the besiegers, even when the latter are established upon the
covert-ways.

Accordingly when the place is seated upon both banks of the
river, the inundation may be supported by a sluice-bridge (*pont-
ecluse*), serving as a communication between the two quarters of
the town.   But if the place occupy only one side of the river,
it becomes indispensable to occupy the other side with an outwork to cover the bridge and all the dispositions for manœuvring
the waters, and to prevent the enemy from attempting to attack at this point.   A sufficient space will be left between the
place and the river, to cover this part of the enceinte by a covert-way and glacises.   This kind of esplanade will be of the
greatest use during the siege.

Sluice bridges,
sluice dykes, and
sluices under the
terra-plains.

An inundation is formed by means of sluice-bridges or dikes
with sluices, or by a disposition of sluices established under the
terra-plains of a work.   A sluice bridge is commonly founded on
piles, as is likewise its ground-frame (*radier*); its piers are of masonry.   At 3 decimètres (12 inches) from the starlings (*avant-becs*)
or projectures up and down the stream, grooves are made 2 decimètres square (8 inches) to receive beams furnished with iron
clasps ; these beams slide horizontally by means of a peritro-
chium (*treuil*) and its appurtenances.   These dispositions,
which are those most commonly followed, are susceptible of improvements.   The students will read with attention the Memoir on this subject by M. Curel, Director of Fortifications, inserted in the second number of the *Memorial de l'Officier du
genie*.   The sluices made in dikes or causeways, are constructed
in the same way, and are manœuvred with beams.   This is a
simple and adequate mode to swell or draw off an inundation ;
these manœuvres are only executed gradually.

Sluices with flood-gates (*vannes*) and provided with peritro-
chiums to work them, are frequently made in souterrains constructed under the terra-plains of bastions, to convey water
from one front to another, and to turn mills.

The batar-
deaux or refluent
dikes.

The batardeaux, or dikes, are masses of masonry 20 decimètres thick (6⅔ feet), crossing the ditches at the most suitable
points for the purpose of there introducing and supporting the
waters drawn either from the inundation or from the full unassailable ditches.   They are placed in front of the curtains,

or on the capitals of the bastions, or on the prolongation of their faces ; this depends upon local circumstances and the necessity of shielding them from the views of the besiegers when they have crowned the covert-way.   In these batardeaux narrow cuts (*pertuis*) are made to receive flood-gates, which are manœuvred by means of a jack (*cric*) or other mechanical powers.   These cuts (*pertuis*) are generally very narrow, and can only gently fill or evacuate the ditch.   When it is required to animate a large volume of water with great velocity, influent and refluent sluices must be made in the batardeau ; these, by forming at once great openings, produce violent floods of waters that rush against the besiegers' works in the ditches and carry them away together with frequently part of the breaches, which thus become inaccessible.   It is obvious that these dispositions by which a dry ditch is converted into a wet ditch at pleasure, and vice versa, cannot be effected by batardeaux with the common openings (*pertuis*).   There must be established above and below, and frequently at some intermediate point, influent sluices and refluent sluices ; but these sluices cannot be made with beams, because the manœuvre must be quickly executed. They must therefore be provided with flood-gates that can be raised in an instant.

Influent and refluent sluices. The turning-gate (See Bousmard's *Essai sur la Fortification.*)

In the place of a sliding flood-gate (*vanne à coulisse*), we may substitute the turning-gate proposed by Bousmard ; a very ingenious invention.   This turning-gate which must be manœuvred in each opening of a sluice, is divided in its width into two unequal parts by a vertical upright with an inferior pivot and a superior trunnion.   This vertical axis rests by its pivot upon a socket soldered to the threshold, and its trunnion is received into the upper head-piece fitted into the piers.   The wider part of the gate plays in a groove facing up the river, whilst the other part plays in a groove looking down the stream.   A small flood-gate (*vantelle*), manœuvred by a jack, is constructed in the larger side of the gate.   It is now easy to understand how simple is the manœuvring of this gate.   The pressure of the water being stronger on the side of the upper groove, keeps the gate shut ; but by opening the little flood-gate this pressure becomes greatest on the side of the lower groove, and the gate opens and places itself in a line a little oblique to the current : by shutting the little flood-gate, the pressure of the water shuts the gate.

The manner of
using the waters
against the be-
siegers.
Suppose all the dispositions for using the waters to be completed ; it is then easy to perceive how they should be used
against the besiegers. After combatting against them by the
ordinary modes in dry ditches, the besieged wait for the moment when their bridge and epaulment will have nearly gained
the breach ; the refluent sluices, situated below, will then be
shut ; and the influent sluices, situated above, will be opened.
The waters will rush with violence against the works of the
besiegers, and will accumulate in the ditches 'till they reach
their greatest height ; the refluent sluices or drain-gates will then
be opened, and the rapid draining off of the waters will carry
away the works and a great portion of the ruins of the breach.
This manœuvre will be repeated until the ditches are cleared ;
and then the war of dry ditches will be renewed.

Overfalls.
Overfalls (*deversoirs*) are constructions of a peculiar kind
made in causeways and batardeaux to let off the excess of waters ; its face that looks up the stream, is vertical and tangential
to the curve of the summit which descends down the river by a
gentle slope to unite tangentially with the ground-frame upon
which the waters fall. The overfalls are about 70 to 80 decimètres (23 to 27 feet) thick at their base, according to their
height. Their construction is very nice, and requires the section or cut to be very carefully and accurately made, so that
the waters may not suddenly carry away the back of the over-
fall. The materials used for this work should be of the largest
kind, and united together with pozzulana cement.

An improve-
ment in bat-
ardeaux   (See
St. Paul's work)
St. Paul proposes to make the batardeaux, placed opposite
the curtains, of sufficient thickness to serve as bridges of communication during the distant defence ; and to make inside of them
a gallery that would be an excellent communication during the
near defence. This modification, which would cost little,
would be of great use.

The depth of
the ditches, and
the general slope
that they should
have to be de-
fended by waters.
If the place be situated upon both banks of the river, the
ditches up the stream adjacent to the inundation will be filled
with water and excavated to contain 20 to 25 decimètres depth
of water (7 to 8 feet). But if the place occupy only one bank,
the ditches that border upon it may likewise be excavated to
contain 20 to 25 decimètres depth of water. At this point will
be established the refluent dyke (*reversoir*) and sluices, for
letting in the waters and carrying them in torrents into the
ditches of the attackable fronts. These latter ditches will be

made with a regular declining slope, or successive ressaults, if circumstances so require, from above to below the stream ; that is, from the rushing in of the waters, to their evacuation by the refluent or drain sluices whose height must be properly calculated.   Such are the general ideas that we should have of the use or manœuvres of waters in a fortress.

156. When the site upon which one or more fortified fronts are established does not allow making the ditches of the depth required by the equalization of the excavation and embankment, either by reason of the ground being low and wet and precluding sinking into it, or because of hard rocks, or because the ditches would in other respects be too deep ; in this case earth must be brought from without to form the glacises. The most natural method that suggests itself, is to make an advanced ditch at the foot of the glacis to increase at the same time the strength of the fortification.

156 Advanced ditches ; glacises and advanced covert-ways.

When it is practicable to introduce waters into the advanced ditch, and the enemy cannot drain it, it makes a good defence if it be sufficiently wide.   The only defect of it is, that it restrains the offensive movements and manœuvres of an active defence.   To remedy this great defect, several wooden bridges of proper width are thrown across the advanced ditch at the most advantageous points for a retreat ; these are supported by flêches, and covered by an advanced, or parts of an advanced covert-way.   The flêches F, F should be placed inside in the re-enterings, to prevent their being carried by storm and to defend the salients and branches.   The bridges P, P, placed on the right and left of the flêches, will be covered by an advanced continuous covert-way, or by what is still better, simple places of arms Q, Q that will contain and secure the sorties : the terra-plains of these places of arms, or advanced covert-way, will be under the fire of the covert-way of the body of the place.

The wet advanced ditch, supported by flêches and portions of an advanced covert-way (PLATE VIII, fig. 1.)

When water cannot be brought into the advanced ditch F, (fig. 2), the protracted glacis (glacis coupé) aMN, or the flat bottomed ditch (fossé en fond de cuve) bRN, will be substituted for it.   This disposition in affording the necessary earth, is favourable to the besieged ; the enemy will find great difficulty in getting over its reverse RN.   When it is designed to make an advanced covert-way in front of the protracted glacis, it is disposed like txyzv.

The protracted glacis, a substitute for the advanced dry ditch. (Fig. 2.)

The communi-
cations across the
glacis, and the
defects of this
disposition.

Whenever flêches or other works are established in advance of the glacis, it is customary to communicate with them by double caponnières covered by tambour traverses and strongly palisaded. These communications open at top, are very unfavourable to the defence ; they facilitate the approaches of the besiegers, and furrow the glacis with cuts that incommode the manœuvres of the besieged. In general all these advanced works are from their nature weak and of little advantage, and are only suitable for great fortresses whose numerous garrisons should act without against the besiegers.

157. Tenaillons:
counter-guards or
face-coverings.

157. In all systems, the use of *tenaillons* and counter-guards or face-coverings, as out-works, is to cover a principal work that is found to be too much exposed to batteries in breach.

The tenail
lon: their de-
fects (PLATE
VIII. fig. 3)

Tenaillons were most commonly used to cover the faces of small ravelins ; and we see that the tenaillons T, T, cover the faces of the ravelin O ; but they leave its flanked angle uncovered. This kind of outwork still exists on the fronts of certain fortresses ; it is surprising that they have not been corrected and converted into real face-coverings. The old engineers did not reason upon the strength of this accessory ; for the interval included between the heads of the tenaillons, forms an opening through which the batteries of the coronation of the covert-way batter in breach at the same time, the body of the place, the tenaillons, and the flanked angle of the ravelin ; so that the assaults may be regulated to carry all the works at once. This proves that tenaillons do not protract the probable defence a single moment. In 1708, the fortress of Lille was attacked and taken by a front covered with tenaillons.

The counter-
guard : its posi-
tion : its dimen-
sions and value.

The *counter-guard* is evidently superior to the tenaillon, and is in the modern system an essential element of the ravelin whose name it has assumed ; whilst the latter has taken that of *redoubt*. The old engineers generally established the counter-guard on the bastions, and made use of it whenever they could not cover the bastion faces from without ; and in such cases the counter-guard, properly speaking, was a face-covering. The dimensions of the counter-guard vary in the different systems ; in general its thickness should not exceed 20 mètres (22 yards), nor should that of the ravelin, which has taken its place in the common system. It was in this manner that Coehorn, and many other writers, introduced it into their systems ; but Vauban in his second and third systems (152), makes its terra-plain very spacious, and considers it only as a great bastion detached from the enceinte.

The value of the counter-guard depends upon its relation with the other elements of the system into which it is introduced ; it holds a distinguished place in Coehorn's system, in Vauban's two last systems, and in Carnot's. Cormontaigne considers it in his system, as that constituent element which gives to his dispositions the most remarkable properties ; with him it is the real ravelin.

In the examination of Cormontaigne's system (153), we observed that the ravelins produced an essential defect in the disposition, and in the manner in which the outworks covered the capital enceinte. It would seem necessary, according to this remark, to introduce the counter guard into the system. But if after the method of the ancient engineers it be placed on the bastion without making any change in the position of the ravelin ; that is, if after their way the counter-guard H be placed upon the ravelin E, the advantages that will be derived from it will not compensate for its expense ; nor will it sensibly protract the probable duration of the siege. Indeed the counter-guard thus disposed, enables the besiegers to batter in breach the body of the place from the coronation of the ravelin salient ; so that after taking the ravelin E, and its redoubt S, they may storm the bastion without attacking the counter-guard. If the practicability of this operation be contended against ; it must nevertheless be remarked, that the counter-guard greatly diminishes the re-entering included between the two ravelins ; and that in two or three days at farthest after the crowning of the ravelin salients, that of the covert-way of the counter-guard may be effected and this work battered in breach. Therefore on the supposition of a like attack, the counter-guard will not delay the assault of the bastion more than three or four days.

In order to shut up all the openings that expose to view the body of the place, and to completely cover it, the ravelin D must be moved out upon the counter-guard G, and the shoulder of the redoubt R covered by a caponnière M. In this tracé, the dimensions of the redoubt R and the width of its ditch, and the width of the ravelin terra-plain D, must be a little increased ; in order that its salient may be sufficiently advanced to make the re-entering, formed by the two ravelins, deep enough ;

The situation of the counter guard in the common system (PLATE VIII, fig. 1)

and to prevent the besiegers from seizing for several days the salient of the counter-guard *G*.

By this arrangement the general properties of the system are not impaired ; the body of the place is perfectly covered, and the besiegers cannot batter it in breach until they have gotten possession of the counter-guard and ravelin redoubt ; this they will effect by a single operation. In this tracé, the counter-guard protracts the siege eight or ten days ; this is obtaining a grand advantage.

The modern system thus disposed, might be improved by two modifications that would cost but a trifling expense : 1st, That part of the counter-guard facing the flanked angle of the bastion and as far as the line drawn from this angle to the salient of the ravelin covert-way, should be raised in such a manner as to perfectly cover a blinded battery *B*, constructed on the flanked angle of the bastion. 2d, Under the part *K* of the counter-guard and facing the ditch of the ravelin, there should be made a casemated battery to defend this ditch and act by curvated fires against the lodgement in the salient place of arms. There will be between these two batteries an immediate relation ; for as the blinded battery *B* cannot be counter-battered but with great difficulty, it will take in flank the lodgement in the ravelin covert-way, and it will take in reverse the breach in the ravelin. The besiegers will therefore find great difficulty in establishing batteries in breach against the ravelin, and counter-batteries to ruin the casemates *K*, which will consequently render the passage of the ditch and the assault on the ravelin very difficult to execute. It cannot be doubted that the modern system thus arranged, would acquire a new degree of strength, which in high polygons will increase the probable duration of the siege about 15 days.

158. Horn-works, and crown works, used as detached, and out-works.

158. Although the custom of using horn and crown-works, as outworks and additionals to an enceinte, has been long exploded ; we will nevertheless say a few words on these works which were very much multiplied in several fortresses, in which they were established in direct opposition to sound principles.

The horn-work. (PLATE VIII. fig. 1.)

The horn-work consists of a bastioned front terminated laterally by two long branches ending at the enceinte when it is an outwork, or united by a gorge properly arranged when the work is advanced or detached ; the works *F*, *M*, *N*, are half horn-works. The front of a horn-work cannot be less than 200 mètres (223 yards); otherwise the half-bastions and ravelin would be so small, that even a moderate defence could not be expected from them ; and however inconsiderable might be the relief, the flanks could not effectively defend the faces of the bastions.   The wings of this work should not be longer than 160 mètres (178 yards), in order that the musketry fires of the enceinte may be effective upon the half-bastion capitals and upon the coronation of the covert-way of the salient places of arms.

The beginning of the seventeenth century witnessed the origin of this kind of work, which engineers then adopted for outworks; they lavished them with such profusion and with so little judgment on the fronts of enceintes, that caprice and the love of novelty seem to have entirely directed their arrangement.   We will refer as an instance to Sedan, where there are on the same front three horn-works, each of 150 mètres (168 yards) front, and distant about 40 mètres (45 yards) from each other.

There are but two modes of disposing a horn-work as an outwork.   The first is to rest the wings upon the two bastions of a front, giving them the necessary divergency to make the front at least 220 mètres (223 yards) : this is the disposition of *N*, in the figure.   The ravelin *S* occupies the interior of the work, and is not supposed to have any counter-guard ; the covertway of the branches unite with that of the bastions ; and the re-entering is occupied by a redoubt.

The position of the horn-work adapted to the enceinte as an out-work.
(PLATE VIII, fig. 1.)

It is easy to discover the weakness of this disposition of the horn-work : 1st, the head of the work being very narrow, is easily embraced by the attacks; its small ravelin, little advanced into the country, will be taken at the same time with the work itself.   2d. As soon as the besiegers have crowned the salients of the horn-work, they can through the opening of the ditches of the branches batter in breach the faces of the two enceinte bastions, and at the same time penetrate into the terra-plain and ditches and carry on their approaches in safety to the crowning of the ravelin covert-way.   They may communicate by a cut from their third parallel to the approaches in the ditches, and make their way without resistance into the covert-way of the body of the place : and in this attitude they may attack the ravelin by its gorge, and assault the bastion. If the bastion be well intrenched, and if it be deemed impracticable to attack the ravelin by its gorge, its covert-way will be

Examination of this disposition.

crowned and it will be battered in breach; the general assault will then take place.

We see that in this case the horn-work, the expense of which is very great, affords no satisfactory result; and that its resistance is inferior to that of the ravelin of great dimensions.

The second mode of disposing the horn-work on the enceinte, is to place it upon two ravelins, that it may embrace the bastion : this is the disposition F, in the figure. This disposition is not so very defective as the former, because the enemy are obliged to attack the two ravelins before they can penetrate as far as the bastion ; nevertheless its defects are obvious and numerous : 1st, The head of the front is necessarily narrow, and is abandoned to its own strength, as in the first case. 2d. From the crowning of the salients the ravelins will be battered in breach, and will be taken by assault as soon as the work itself. 3d. The enemy carry on their trenches in the terra-plain of the work with the greatest ease, and without the sorties ever being able to harass their flanks ; they are covered by the relief of the branches from all collateral fires.

It was by taking advantage of all these defects, which are inherent in the horn-work, that the French captured the fortress of Tournai with so much ease in 1746.

It follows from all this, that the horn-work whose wings project out from the body of a place, rather weakens, than strengthens a fortified front ; and that when its wings rest upon the ravelins, it only protracts the defence 5 to 6 days. It is therefore with good reason that this work has been laid aside, even when it is requisite to increase the interior space of a small fortress in order to make a more vigorous defence by the manœuvres and strength of the garrison.

The crown-work considered as an out-work on a front; the manner of disposing it on the enceinte. The crown-work that is placed on a front as an outwork, consists of a central bastion, two half bastions, and two branches which terminate in the ditch of the enceinte ; and in order that these branches, which are only 180 mètres (200 yards) long, may include the extent of the two fronts and about 450 mètres (500 yards), they are made very divergent.

The crown, like the horn-work, may rest its two branches upon two adjacent bastions, or upon two ravelins. The simple or single crown-work thus contracted, possesses the same defects as the horn-work ; there is indeed a slight difference between them, in consequence of a slight increase of strength in the front ;

but this increase of resistance is more than counterbalanced by the enormous expense of these works.

We must conclude from what has been said of single crown-works and horn-works, that they should not be adopted for the outworks of the enceinte of a place.

Conclusion on the value of crown and horn works, as outworks.

Since the principal defects of these works result from connecting them with the enceinte, and their chief advantage is to procure for the garrison interior space favourable for the defence ; it follows that they should be *completely detached* from the enceinte, in order that there may be no communication between their respective ditches. By this disposition, which places these works beyond the tail of the glacis, the result will be ; 1st, that the capture of these works will occasion no immediate injury to the body of the place ; 2d, that the near defence, which is the most important, will not be diminished ; 3d, that the flanks of the attack will not be covered, except during the short space of time that the besiegers will take to traverse their terraplain ; 4th, that there will be obtained between the detached work and the place, a portion of glacis that will be covered and very favourable to the defence.

These works, considered as detached or advanced works. (PLATE VIII, fig. 4.)

When it is apprehended that a detached work may be attacked by its gorge and carried by storm, several means may be used to render such an attack impracticable : 1st, The glacis, after the manner of Cormontaigne and Vauban, may be prolonged to the foot of the gorge, which being revested and surmounted with a strong palisading, will be sufficiently high to render its escalade impossible under the fire of the covert-way of the place. 2d, The covert-way of the branches may be joined with that of the place. 3d, Crenated galleries and casemated batteries with reverse fires, of which we will say more in the sequel, may be used.

Remarks on the gorges of detached works, & on the ditches of the branches. (Fig. 4.)

In any case, the ditches of the branches must unite or be lost in the glacises ; in order that the fires of the place may enfilade them, and the enemy find no cover in them. If this condition cannot be fulfilled, recourse must be had to another mode ; a casemated and crenated traverse T may be established in the ditch, and will defend it until the enemy have destroyed this traverse by the counter-battery A of the coronation of the salient place of arms.

When the detached work is displayed upon several fronts and is composed of two, three, or four, &c. central bastions, and

Complex crown, & crowned works.

the wings terminated as before by two half-bastions and two branches ; the work is then said to be a double, or triple, or complex crown.

But if a work containing several central bastions be terminated by two half bastions whose ditches communicate with those of the place, so that the counterscarp and covert-way of the place form the gorge of the work ; this kind of outwork is called a *crowned* work (*ouvrage couronné*).

The tracé of complex crown, & crowned works. A complex crown, and a crowned work, being unattackable by their wings and by the re-enterings that they form with the enceinte, they should be as little convex as possible ; and even all their fronts should be displayed upon a right line, in order that these fronts may possess the great advantages appertaining to such a disposition.

The strength that detached works afford to enceintes. Detached works whose tracés and relief are well arranged, more than double the strength of the fronts that they cover, and of the adjacent fronts, either by their intrinsic value, or by the advantages that they obtain for the defence in other respects.

Advanced works used to occupy particular positions. Crown and born-works are specially used to occupy in advance of certain fronts of a fortress particular positions that would be favourable to the enemy, and to compel them to open their trenches at a greater distance.

They are likewise used for têtes de pont on the bank E, to cover the dispositions for the use of waters.   Lastly ; they are used to envelop suburbs which it is of importance to preserve, and not to devote to the flames the moment that a place is menaced with siege.   In any of these circumstances, the gorge of these works should be prepared in such a manner and according to the ground, that they will be secure from an attack by storm and from any bold stroke.

When the positions occupied by advanced works are considered as a kind of intrenched camp that is to be defended by a numerous garrison or corps d'armée, the bastions or other elements that compose the enceinte may be detached from each other ; in order to preserve intervals to carry the troops rapidly into the outworks, and to be able to execute with ease all the movements of attack and retreat to which an active defence founded upon tactics gives rise.

These general principles will suffice to guide the young officer in the examination of these great works, of which he will find models on several points of the frontiers ; and will teach him the importance of constantly uniting the study of fortification with that of tactics.

159. Of all the works that can be disposed on the front of an enceinte to increase its strength, lunettes have been preferred; and they are daily used by modern engineers. Sometimes they enter into the systems in a regular manner; at others they occupy particular positions, and are a kind of observatory post to watch the first measures of the besiegers ; and sometimes a single lunette covers a front of attack. The general properties of these works are easily perceived : 1st, advanced lunettes are less expensive than the other kinds of outworks : 2d, they compel the enemy to open their trenches at a great distance : 3d, the cannon of these lunettes have an advantageous position during the distant defence : 4th, if they be properly disposed, they will not mask the fires of the place : 5th, they protect the sorties ; and they have between them and the place, an esplanade very favourable for the manœuvres of even cavalry : 6th, they form a first enceinte, which when it is taken is more embarrassing and injurious to the besiegers than useful : 7th, they enable the war of stratagem to be begun at a far greater distance ; and this species of war, in well ordered dispositions, is ever advantageous to the besieged.

We showed in the Second Part (91), that a lunette is a small detached bastion enclosed by its gorge. The lunettes adapted to an enceinte vary in their dimensions according to the system and its arrangement ; their faces should be at least 40, and may be as great as 70 mètres (45 and 78 yards) ; and their flanks may be from 20 to 30 mètres (22 to 33 yards). They are designed to contain 150 to 200 men. The lengths of the faces and flanks are deduced from the position of the lunette at the foot of the glacis ; its terra-plain must be sufficiently elevated for the relief of its gorge to place it beyond an attack by storm. When this gorge is not sufficiently secured, the besiegers will not fail to venture a *coup de main* as soon they have completed their third parallel.

As the lunettes adapted to an enceinte should form with it the best regulated system, they should fulfil by their disposition and tracé several conditions ; 1st, the besiegers must be compelled to attack them before they can approach on the glacis ; 2d, the attack upon them must be by gradual approaches ; they must consequently be secure from being carried by storm ; 3d, their position must be such as to allow making them of the proper dimensions and relief ; 4th, they must be under the most immediate protection of the place, in order that their glacises and ditches may be flanked by the fires of the covert-ways of the front that they cover.

First disposition of lunettes in a single line: its defects.

There are three principal modes of disposing a row of lunettes about the modern bastioned enceinte.   The first is to place them upon the capitals of the re-enterings ; but in this situation they cannot fulfil any of the general conditions just laid down : 1st, They do not form salients into the country that the besiegers are compelled to attack before they can attack the ravelin salients, unless they be thrown very much forward ; and then they will no longer be protected and sustained by the enceinte : 2d, They mask the fires of the place, and their ditches will not be defended by it if their flanked angle be not very acute ; and in this case it will not be susceptible of any defence.   In this disposition, the lunettes may be carried by storm and quickly connected with each other by a parallel that will graze the salient of the bastion or ravelin, according to the front of attack that the besiegers have chosen.

The second disposition of lunettes : its defects (PLATE VIII, fig. 5.)

The second disposition that may be made of lunettes, is to establish them at A on the ravelin capitals.   In this situation they possess a few of the general properties that are requisite to their making a good defence : 1st, they form salients A, which the besiegers are forced to carry before they establish the third parallel : 2d, they do not mask the fires of the place.   But they have in this situation several essential defects ; 1st, as they are very far from the bastion covert-ways, they cannot be defended by musketry ; they must therefore be flanked by the artillery fires of the bastions ; this necessary condition makes their flanked angle very acute in all orders of polygons : 2d, the distance between the lunettes will be so great if the polygon be not of a high order, that they will not be in relations of defence ; and the attack directed against a common front will be only opposed by a single lunette, enfeebled by its tracé and distance from the enceinte ; this distance will exceed 300 mètres (334 yards), measuring from the covert-way of the bastions.

If the lunettes be disposed upon the ravelin capitals of a high polygon, the disposition will be improved.   The capitals being less divergent and tending to parallelism, the distance between the lunettes is diminished ; their flanked angles become less acute, and they are brought into relations of defence ; and the flanks of each lunette will defend the salients of the collateral lunettes. If the attack be directed against a common front, it will be opposed by three lunettes that will reciprocally support each other ; and if it be directed against the front included between two ravelins, the besiegers will probably be compelled to make separate attacks upon four lunettes, &c.: but in any case, this disposition will have the essential defects of the lunettes being necessarily thrown too far forward, of being badly supported by the body of the place, and of being attacked and carried all at the same time. This latter circumstance greatly lessens the reciprocal protection that lunettes afford each other in high polygons.

Finally ; the third disposition that may be made with a single row of lunettes, is to place them on the bastion capitals and at a distance of about 250 mètres (280 yards). By this disposition the lunettes *D, D* will fulfil all the conditions prescribed by the defence : 1st, they will be sufficiently eloigned to allow their relief to be properly arranged, and to form salients beyond which the besiegers cannot pass to attack the ravelins without first forcing them ; 2d, they will be under the immediate protection of the enceinte and ravelins, which will flank them even with musketry ; 3d, their flanked angles will always exceed 60 degrees, and in high polygons will be nearly rectangular. If the polygon be of an inferior order, the lunettes will not be in relations of defence ; but this advantage is acquired as soon as the polygons are of a superior order. When the attack is displayed against a common front, as in inferior polygons, it will have to contend against two lunettes ; and when it is directed against two ravelins to reach a single bastion, it will have to embrace and capture three lunettes.

Third disposition of lunettes in a single row : its advantages.

To make a complete disposition of lunettes forming a real enceinte, all whose elements will reciprocally protect each other in any polygon, the two latter dispositions must be combined together ; that is, lunettes must be established upon the ravelin and upon the bastion capitals. In this tracé the lunettes will be in relations of defence, and their flanks will defend the salients of the collateral lunettes. An important observation must be here made ; in high polygons the lunettes *A* on the ravelin capitals may have such a sally beyond the lunettes *D* on the bastion capitals, that they will form two rows of lunettes

The complete disposition of lunettes upon all the capitals. (PLATE VIII, fig. 5.)

and compose two distinct defensive enclosures which the besiegers can only force one after another. Therefore as the interior
lunettes are not seized at the same time as the exterior, the
former can effectually flank the latter, agreeably to the principle laid down in the Second Part (93). This mode of posting
and drawing the lunettes of the first line, will be regulated by
those in the second, as is shown in Plate VIII.

*The ditches &
gorges of lu-
nettes.*

The ditches of lunettes that are 12 to 15 mètres (40 to 50
feet) wide, are conducted like a glacis from the flanked angle to
the gorge ; in order that they may be perfectly scoured by the
fires of the works in rear that are to defend them.

The gorge of lunettes should be arranged with such care, that
the enemy cannot force them by a *coup de main.* For this
purpose, after prolonging the planes of the glacises till they meet
the gorge of each lunette, this gorge must be about 20 decimètres (6⅔ feet) high ; it will be crowned with a strong palisading
provided with a banquette. These simple arrangements will
render the attack of it by storm impracticable. But when
the exterior foot of the gorge is not sufficiently low to give it the
proper relief, the interior of the lunette is made full (*plein*), or
it is enclosed by a wall surmounted with a strong palisading
and provided inside with a banquette of earth to secure it from
ricochet shots, which would infallibly destroy it and occasion
dangerous splinters. Lastly ; to defend the gorge of the most
advanced lunettes, other means may be used ; such as crenated
galleries, casemates with reverse fires, &c.

*The covert
ways of lunettes
(PLATE VIII,
fig. 5.)*

Each lunette, like every other permanent work, should be
surrounded with a covert-way ; and this covert way, when the
lunettes are placed upon the bastion capitals, may be prolonged and united with that of the ravelins, as is shown in Plate
VIII. But when lunettes are established upon all the capitals
and form a system whose elements are in relations of defence,
the covert-way may be a general one, and may be displayed
in a continuous manner on all the lunettes. It becomes in this
case an advanced covert-way, sustained by lunettes and forming
an outwork capable of an active and vigorous defence.

Instead of connecting together the lunette covert-ways, or of
uniting them with that of the principal enceinte, engineers prefer isolating them to preserve intervals of great value for the
general defence, and which cannot impair the particular defence
of the lunettes. In this tracé, the branches of the covert-way of

each lunette are terminated by re-entering places of arms furnished with redoubts, and bounded inside by a profile directed
towards the flank.   These profiles may be flanked by casemated
batteries placed beneath the lunette flanks, to arrest the enemy
should they endeavour to turn the re-entering place of arms.

The method most generally used to communicate between The communi-
cations that con-
the place and the advanced lunettes, is by double caponnières nect the lunettes
with the place.
directed on the capitals and covered at intervals by tambour
traverses.   These communications are palisaded, and lead to a
stairs (*pas de souris*) or postern which affords an entrance into
the lunette terra-plain.   It has been proved by experience
that these communications open at top are exposed to great inconveniences ; 1st, they are ill secured and can make but a
faint resistance against an attack by storm ; 2d, they may
serve as trenches to the besiegers, if the garrison have not time
to destroy them ; 3d, they cut up the glacis and greatly incommode the manœuvres of a sortie, especially of cavalry.   If at
the siege of Grave the glacises of the place had been furrowed
by such deep cuts, M. De Chamilly would have found it impossible for his cavalry to execute those fine manœuvres by
which he obtained such great successes, and the glory of being cited as a model for the imitation of governors of fortresses.
At the last siege of Mayence, when it was defended by the
French, the besieged cavalry frequently made brilliant charges
on the glacises to disperse and strike a panic into the workmen.

The best communications are subterraneous galleries made
30 decimètres (10 feet) wide for the passage of artillery, and
leading from the enceinte ditch to a souterrain against the gorge
of the lunette ; the ascent to whose terra-plain is by a ramp.
If it be feared that the besiegers will gain possession and take
advantage of these subterranean communications for the purposes of subterraneous war ; they may be made in any other
directions than the capitals, and disposed in such a manner as
to be of positive advantage to the besieged.

As the lunettes should be commanded by the bastions and The relief or
ravelins, those of the first line may have 30 to 35 decimètres (10 commandment of
lunettes.
11¾ feet) commandment above the plane of site ; and those of
the second line 35 to 40 (11⅔ to 13¼ feet).   When enceintes
are covered by such outworks, it is proper to increase a little
their relief.

The increasing
value of lunettes,
resulting from
the increasing
greatness of the
polygonal angles.

All that has been said respecting the properties acquired by great ravelins in proportion to the greater opening of the angles of the polygon, has an immediate application to lunettes disposed around an enceinte. In proportion as the angles of the polygon increase, they form greater re-enterings, afford each other a more effectual reciprocal protection, and the relation of defence is established between a greater number of them. Accordingly if we suppose the polygon to be only an octagon, the besiegers may attack a common front and have only three lunettes to carry. But if the polygon be as high as a dodecagon, the attack will be directed against a single bastion, and they will be compelled to attack five lunettes; and if the collateral fronts and the front of attack be on the same right line, the approaches could not be carried on upon the glacis without previously taking seven lunettes. These truths are obvious from the mere measures of crowning the covert-ways, &c.

160. The defence obtained
by casemates &
crenated galleries. General reflections.

160. Before discussing advanced lunettes totally detached from the enceinte, we must describe some means or accessories of defence, whose consideration is of the greatest importance to obtain for detached works a strength proportioned to the object that they are to fulfil in a defensive system. These accessories consist of *crenated galleries, defensive caponnières,* and *casemates.*

These latter were used by the ancient engineers, as we remarked in describing their systems ; and Coehorn is particularly distinguished by the ingenious manner in which he combined them in the arrangement of his system. Modern engineers have perceived the necessity of making use of them in many circumstances ; and some have even founded their systems upon them.

Montalembert is of this number ; and of all writers on fortification, he has most studied to improve and diversify casemates. Indeed the officers of engineers generally acknowledge, that the only method of raising fortification from its present state of weakness with respect to the attack, is to introduce into its arrangement covered fires ; but in a judicious manner, consistent with the expenditures that the state can afford, and with the quantity of artillery that it is able to assign for arming its frontiers.

161. Casemates,
and the manner
of using them.

161. All souterrains arranged for furnishing covered fires either during the *near* or *distant* defence, are called *defensive casemates.*

We deduced from the theory of the attack and from the powers of the besieging artillery, this incontrovertible fact—that uncovered casemates destined to act during the period of the distant defence, are inadmissible, and cannot sustain the shock of the besieging artillery. And we also concluded from the same theory, that casemates destined to defend the ditches cannot fulfil their destination when the besiegers have a plunging fire into them from their lodgement on the crest of the glacis.

But whenever the casemated fires cannot be counter-battered, and can act in flank and reverse upon the lodgements and troops of the besiegers, they are the most powerful and effectual and cheapest means of defence.

Casemates with reverse fires, & casemates for vertical fires.

Casemates are also of great utility for using curvated fires, which during the distant defence afford ricochets, and produce showers (*gerbes*) of stones and grenades during the near defence. In the modern system that serves us as a subject of comparison, such casemates might be constructed in the curtains and in the flanks; they would be covered by the tenaille. All kinds of casemates would be almost already constructed, if the scarps and counterscarps of the fortification were profiled with relieving vaults.

The reproach of ancient casemates was, that they were not properly constructed to allow the escape of the smoke produced by the combustion of the powder; this poisons the air of confined places, and renders them uninhabitable if currents of air cannot be introduced. Accordingly engineers have devoted their attention to making vents or air-holes (*events*) in the top of the vaults, and through which the smoke may escape; but in this respect those casemates that are open at the gorge, are the best and most exempt from this defect. In the last profiles that Montalembert composed, he made a narrow ditch behind the casemates sunk in terra-plains, in order that their gorges may be open. And experience has proved, that currents of air rush through the embrasures and carry off the smoke with sufficient rapidity to allow the service of the artillery to be quick and constant.

The evacuation of the smoke from casemates.

The figure of all kinds of casemates is similar to that of a bomb-proof souterrain, having its front wall pierced with embrasures; this wall should never be a pier of the vault. Frequently a single souterrain contains many guns; but they are more generally semi-circular vaults with full centres and separa-

The figure of casemates: their dimensions: their embrasures (See PLATE I, fig. 8.)

ted by piers, and each containing one piece of artillery or three loop-holes for large muskets, as is shown in Plate 1, Fig. 8.

The dimensions of embrasures are according to the kind of artillery that they are to contain. The choice of this artillery depends upon the effects to be obtained for the defence ; sometimes only musketry fires are required ; at others, showers (*gerbes*) of fire are necessary to scour certain parts and act against the troops ; sometimes it is requisite to contend against artillery of heavy calibers, to retard its establishment and destroy the epaulments ; and lastly and most frequently, it is necessary to act against the saps, lodgements, passages of the ditches, &c. It follows, that the artillery proper for the defence of fortresses should be in relation to the defence, and is necessarily subordinate to fortification. These two branches of war should act in concert to improve the defence ; for whatever dispositions may be made in fortification, and however excellent they may be in themselves, they can nevertheless be of no service unless properly armed.

In all kinds of casemates this important condition must be fulfilled—the muzzle of the gun in battery must be on a level with the exterior side of the facing wall. By this disposition two great results will be obtained ; 1st, the greatest part of the smoke will be driven outwards; 2d, the figure of the embrasure will resemble that of a loop-hole, and will be much more advantageous. To satisfy this condition, at least in a near degree, the three following elements must be combined together —the carriages, the length of the chace of the piece, and the thickness necessary for the facing wall.

Of the gun-carriages in use, the navy carriage and the Montalembert and the Meusnier carriages are perfectly suitable for the service of casemates by making them of the dimensions proper for each caliber. The artillery necessary for the armament of all kinds of casemates, may consist of garrison 8 and 12 pounders, 6 inch howitzers, mortars, and stone-mortars. Let us examine whether the common cannon and howitzers are sufficiently long for their muzzles to reach the exterior side of the merlons; for this purpose it is necessary to fix the thickness of the facing wall. We will admit two thick-

(See PLATE IV. and its explanatory table, in the First Part)

nesses ; one for casemates that may be counter-battered, and which may be fixed between 20 and 30 decimètres (6¾ to 10 feet) ; and another for reverse batteries, of 80 centimètres (2⅔ feet). The first kind of battery will be armed with 8 and 12 pounders ; and when bombs and howitzes are to be fired, they will be affixed to the muzzle of the gun.   But siege 12 and 8 pounders are only 5 feet 2 inches and 4 feet 8 inches (5¼ and 5 feet Eng.) long, from the front of the trunnions to the muzzle. If from this length we take one foot for the front of the carriage, there will remain 4¼ and 3⅔ feet (4¼ and 4 feet) for the portion of the chace that strictly can enter the embrasure : therefore it is not possible for the chace of cannon to be of sufficient length for the muzzle to project out of the embrasure. But if the chace enter 4 or 5 feet, this will be enough to expel the greater part of the smoke outwards.   In facing walls of 20 decimètres (6⅔ feet), this result would be obtained by making the cannon 2 feet longer.

With respect to the howitzers with which the second kind of casemates should be armed, they have only 10 inches (10⅔ inches) chace, whilst 36 (39 inches) are requisite.   The howitzer thus lengthened, would be a thick short cannon, or kind of caronade, firing almost always with canister ; and to fire howitzes from it, they would have to be fixed to the muzzle, the limb of which should be made with a cavetto to facilitate the fixing of the shell.   Casemates with reverse fires intended to play upon troops, may also be armed with large blunderbusses (*espingoles*) mounted upon crotches or *chandeliers* with a double movement of rotation, one horizontal, and the other vertical : this weapon is about 3 feet in length, and when loaded with 10 or 12 balls produces great effects at small distances.

The figure and magnitude of the embrasures of casemates, depend upon the object that these batteries are to fulfil.   If they are to batter fixed and determined points upon which the enemy must establish themselves, and scour the ditches with showers of fire ; the horizontal angle of fire should in this case be very small.   And as the extremity of the chace extends beyond the exterior side of the facing wall, which is not at most more than 80 centimètres (2⅔ feet), the exterior opening will be only a little greater than the diameter of the chace ; and the interior opening will have the necessary width for facility of manœuvring.   The embrasures will therefore in this case be really loop-holes.

The figure & magnitude of casemate embrasures.

But when casemates are destined to contend directly with the hostile artillery and batter the ground outside, they must have a field of fire equal to that of common embrasures, and have the

same form or opening.   They will therefore, if all the circumstances be the same, possess the same inconveniences ; and they
will have a very great exterior opening.

The facing walls of these batteries being 27 to 37 decimètres (9 to 12½ feet), and the horizontal angle of fire being supposed to be 15 to 20 degrees in order that the extreme lines of
fire may effectually cross each other at a distance of 15 mètres
(17 yards) when the directions are distant 60 decimètres (20
feet) ; the exterior opening will be 210 to 266 centimètres (7
to 9 feet) ; supposing the centre of rotation to be 3 decimètres
(12 inches) from the inside wall.

(See PLATE
IX. fig. 1.)
To improve the figure of these embrasures and prevent them
from being a kind of wide tunnel affording the counter-batteries a great chance of embrasure shots, we must endeavour to
bring them into the form of musketry loop-holes.   If the muzzle were on a level with the exterior side, and if the centre of
motion of the carriage-frame could be at the same point ; the
cannon would then be manœuvred similar to the manner of
musketry, and the embrasure would be the smallest possible and
about 6 decimètres (2 feet).   But as this plan cannot be executed, Meusnier has substituted for it the ingenious method of
making the centre of motion 10 decimètres (3⅓ feet) in front of
the inner surface.   An iron working pintle is fixed in the ge-
nouillere wall, and is embraced by a stirrup-iron (etrier)
attached to the beam (fleche) of the carriage, whose head enters
into the wall 6 decimètres (2 feet).   By its motion upon the
pintle, the piece is brought into any position included within
the angle of fire, and the exterior opening is very much diminished.   With these data it is easy to draw the plan of the embrasure.   If the piece be supposed to be a 12 pounder, the
chace of which is 5 feet in length and will enter into the embrasure 4 feet, we perceive that the embrasure must be widened without and within ; that its exterior opening will be 130
to 172 centimètres (4½ to 6 feet), and its interior opening 65
centimètres (2½ feet) ; and that this embrasure will be far better than the common kind.

The batteries of the sea-coast forts at Cherbourg, were drawn
according to Meusnier's method ; and the dimensions of the
stones were cut with such accuracy and precision as to leave
nothing to be desired, and to serve as a model of stone-cutting
which young engineers should imitate in like constructions.

The embrasures of casemated batteries that are to fire curvatedly and with high trajectories, are masked by advanced works over which they fire; their embrasures may consequently have the width necessary for working them.   The upper part of the vault is raised 6 or 8 decimètres (2 to 2⅔ feet), so as not to incommode the fire under the angle of 45 degrees; and the front of the battery is a genouillère wall 6 decimètres high (2 feet), and the same in thickness.   In revêtements built with relieving vaults (*voutes de décharge*), a vault of the first or second story may be immediately converted into a casemate for two mortars or two stone-mortars, by merely taking down that part of the facing wall included in the centre and between the piers as far as 3 decimètres (12 inches) above the ground of the battery.   Virgin uses casemates of this kind in his system.

The embrasures of masked casemates, for mortars & stone mortars.

162. A *crenated gallery* is a vaulted passage constructed in the body of a wall, either of the scarp, or counterscarp, or gorge, and in which a disposition of loop-holes (*creneaux*) is made: they defend the ditches or approaches of walls.   The ancient engineers often used crenated galleries to defend the ditches; and there is still a great many of them existing in the fortresses of Bergen-op-zoom, Luxembourg, &c.   Errard constructed some in the Castle of Sedan of great dimensions, and with embrasures opposite the bastion-faces.   The dimensions of the galleries existing in most fortresses, are only 14 decimètres (4⅔ feet) in width and 20 in height (6⅔ feet); these are evidently too small, and are inadequate for the service of the defence.   It would be proper to make their width 24 decimètres (8 feet), and their height 22 decimètres (7½ feet).

162. Crenated galleries: their dimensions

The crenated gallery that is frequently made in the counterscarp of a work, has its debouchès at the landing places of the stairs (*pas de souris*) of the re-entering places of arms: the centre lines of its loop-holes are 10 decimètres (3⅓ feet) distant apart.   The use of this gallery is to defend the ditch by a covered fire of musketry that the enemy cannot counter-batter.   It also favours a subterranean war; but on this latter point opinions are various, as we shall explain.   The crenated gallery, considered solely as a means of defending the ditches, cannot accomplish this object except in works liable to be carried by storm or by a sudden and impetuous attack of a daring besieger who is willing to make sacrifices to bring the siege to an end.   But in works whose ditches are well flanked, and

The crenated gallery of the counterscarp: its use: its value.

which must be attacked by industry and gradual approaches, the crenated gallery can be of no use ; and in this single respect will be more injurious than useful, by affording advantages to the besiegers when they get possession of it.

163. The chief use of casemates with reverse fires and of crenated galleries to complete the defence of works detached from the enceinte. (See PLATE VIII.)

163 Casemates and crenated galleries may be combined in all sorts of ways in the new or modified systems ; but their principal use in the present state of fortification, is to complete the defence of works detached from the enceinte, as we before said (155). If the gorge of the detached horn-work M cannot be sufficiently raised, it may be carried by storm ; and it may even happen that this gorge has no relief whatever, and is perfectly open and level with the glacis. In such a case, it is indispensably necessary to envelop this gorge with a ditch, which the fortress will not be able to look into ; but which may be defended by counterscarp crenated galleries gg, by crenated caponnières P, P, and by casemates with reverse fires n, n lodged in the re-enterings and scouring the ditches of the wings and gorge. The communication from the ditches of the place to the counterscarp gallery, is by a subterranean gallery along the capital. By means of these dispositions, the besiegers will be compelled to crown the covert-way by the common methods. The double caponnière P, P that crosses the middle of the gorge ditch to communicate with the stairs or ramps that ascend into the terra-plain of the work, may consist of a single vaulted caponnière 30 decimètres (10 feet) wide and crenated on both sides ; or of a double caponnière open at top, and under the glacis of which two crenated galleries are made, with a small ditch in front to prevent the enemy from gaining the loop-holes : in either case, the small ditches are flanked by two loop-holes of the counterscarp-gallery.

When it is designed to incur the expense of a counterscarp-gallery, and of a reverse battery n, n; such a disposition will at once deprive the enemy of all desire of attempting to storm the work. But when we intend to confine ourselves to a more simple, and generally sufficient defence for detached works, we content ourselves with the double caponnière P, P, and with the half caponnières o situated towards the extremities of the branches : the communication with them is by the posterns t. These half caponnières should not be only made open at top ; they should have beneath their parapet a crenated gallery that may be made sufficiently wide to contain small howitzers.

They will cover the stairs that communicate with the covert-way. It is likewise proper to make under the parapets of the double caponnière, crenated galleries for a howitzer and some musketry.

164. If crenated galleries, caponnières, casemates with reverse fires, and covered fires in general be sometimes necessary to secure the defence of detached outworks, they are indispensable to complete that of advanced works that cannot be effectively supported and flanked by the fires of the enceinte, and which have no relations with the place but to be supplied with troops and ammunition and supported immediately by sorties acting in mass against the works of the attack.

164. The use of casemates, crenated galleries, &c. to complete the defence of advanced works detached from the enceinte.

The advanced works of which we have spoken (155), possess properties that deserve the study of engineers. When they are judiciously established on the avenues of the attackable fronts of a place, they keep the enemy at a distance from the principal enceinte, compel them to open their trenches very far off, increase the capacity of the fortress, and compel the enemy to conduct the siege according to rule, and deprive them of the hope of reducing the place by the immoderate and barbarous use of incendiary batteries. General Darçon seems to have foreseen prior to the breaking out of the last war, this new mode of carrying on sieges. He proposed throwing up in advance of enceintes, detached works that could only be taken by gradual approaches, would compel the besiegers to open their trenches at a great distance, and would deprive them of the power of destroying at first sight the buildings and coverts of a place. We will describe with some care the means proposed by this officer, and of which he has himself made several times use; but before we commence this discussion we must lay down the principles that should govern in the arrangement of advanced works: 1st, The communication between them and the place must be secure. 2d, Their constitution must be such as to render an attack by storm impracticable. 3d, Their gorges must be prepared with such skill, that in affording a sufficient resistance they will preserve to the besieged the power of offensive returns. 4th, Their debouchès should favour the acting in mass of the sorties that should at every moment threaten the works of the besiegers. It follows from these conditions to be fulfilled, that these kinds of works, with the exception of a few particular cases, are only suitable to great fortresses with

The importance and advantages of advanced works.

The principles regulating the disposition, &c. of advanced works.

numerous garrisons; they may however be adapted to fortresses of a moderate size, whose capacity it is requisite to enlarge. Lastly; they are a means of forming permanent intrenched camps beneath the cannon of a place.

165. Crows and horn works, considered as advanced works: the dispositions to which they give rise.

165. When the advanced work is a horn or crown-work distant 4 or 500 mètres (445 to 556 yards) from the place, it so far eloignes the first batteries of the besiegers, that they cannot hope to gain possession of the place without laying regular siege to the advanced work. But as at this distance the work is only protected by the heavy artillery of the place, and as its gorge may be enveloped in the night and attacked by storm at the first onset; it is indispensable that this gorge should be provided with means of defence to render such an attack impracticable for even the most daring enemy. If the extent of the gorge be about 240 mètres (267 yards) or upwards, it may be bastioned in the common manner and even covered with a covert-way. Such a disposition makes a complete fort of the work; but the expense of it is very great, and the resistance is diminished, because, 1st, the parapets will mask the terra-plain from the views of the place, and will render nugatory the effect of the batteries on this terra-plain; 2d, the besieged will lose the power of offensive returns; 3d, and in consequence of such

The crenated galleries, and casemates with reverse fires.

a disposition, the branches will not be flanked. It is therefore better to use crenated galleries and casemates with reverse fires, made in the re-enterings of the counterscarp; and to leave the gorge and terra-plain exposed to the effect of the batteries of the place, and without coverings that would favour the enemy when they carry the work by gradual approaches.

The crenated gallery or casemate made on the scarp of the gorge: its construction.

However, if this kind of defence, supported by covered fires arranged in the ditches, do not appear sufficient; the resistance may be increased by constructing along the scarp of the gorge a crenated casemate whose facing wall will be only 6 decimètres (2 feet) thick, and with its loop-holes on a level with the counterscarp or natural ground. The fires of this casemate will be most effectual against an attack by storm, and will scour the approaches of the counterscarp. This disposition in increasing the difficulties of an escalade, supplies the place of the fires of a covert-way, without having any of its inconveniences. As this crenated casemate is covered from the direct views of the enemy, it may be so constructed as to be easily battered down by the fires of the place, or intermediate works, of which we will speak directly.

This crenated casemate should have its gorge enclosed, to defend the inside of the arches from ricochet shots ; but instead of a wall of the same thickness as the facing wall, timbers joined together may be used and pierced with loop-holes on a level with an earthen glacis. These interior loop-holes will serve to defend the terra-plain until the besiegers have established themselves on it in force, and brought up cannon on the ramparts to overwhelm the casemates.

In order that an advanced work may make the most obstinate defence and be only taken by a regular attack and gradual approaches, it is necessary that its interior should be provided with casemated traverses ; under cover of these, the garrison may defy the ricochet and curvated fires by which modern artillery annoys the besieged without respite, and renders the terra-plains untenable as soon as the besiegers have occupied the half places of arms.

Casemated traverses to serve as shelters for the garrison.

When a work is in a very advanced position, it appears necessary to complete the defence and support it and protect the manœuvres of the troops by an intermediate work, situated in the most advantageous manner. This work will be effectually defended and flanked by the works of the enceinte, and will consequently be secure from an attack by storm, even if it be only made of earth. It will be armed with batteries to fire canister, and with batteries of heavy calibers to batter down the crenated casemate of the gorge when such a measure becomes necessary. Finally ; it is from this intermediate work that the communication, whether open at top or subterranean, should lead to débouche into the gorge ditch of the advanced work. This communication, if open at top, will be a double capounière ; or a subterranean gallery 30 decimètres wide (10 feet), like those of detached outworks.

The intermediate works necessary to support advanced works.

166. The great expense of works of a continuous extent, and the great numbers of troops and artillery requisite for their defence, make it preferable to use *lunettes or detached bastions* which are adapted to all local circumstances and favourable to the manœuvres of sorties, and whose construction requires but a moderate expenditure that may be restricted at pleasure ; and whose arrangement is such, that the capture of one work does not bring on the loss of the whole system. If the front of the

166. The advanced positions occupied by lunettes or detached bastions in relations of defence.

position that is to be held by a disposition of lunettes, be very narrow, a single lunette may suffice ; but if this front be considerable and exceed 600 mètres (667 yards), several lunettes will be requisite on the first line, and must be supported by others that are intermediate or in second line. These latter lunettes should form with the first, re-enterings of sufficient depth to prevent the besiegers from enveloping them at the same time, either by a sudden, or regular attack ; they are intermediate works, and should be armed as precedingly described (165).

Lunettes with casemated reverse fires, safety redoubts, and casemated traverses. (See PLATE IX.)

The lunettes proposed by General Darçon may be regarded either as detached outworks, or as advanced works occupying particular positions and almost independent of the place. They were employed under this first point of view at Metz and Landau ; those constructed around the fortress of Besançon, occupy particular positions and commanding heights from whence the enemy might destroy the town by simple batteries. The lunettes established in advance of the exterior front of the citadel, whose capture would be followed by that of the town, are to eloigne the first batteries of the besiegers, whose effects would be terrible upon works and parapets of masonry.

In the organization of these lunettes, General Darçon proposed to obtain a work of moderate capacity, of mediocre expense, and of quick construction ; one that would be secure from an attack by storm when in advance of the principal works, and which would be in itself sufficient, and would resist any onset or storm even when very advanced or its gorge supported by natural obstacles, such as a declivity, a river, &c.

The accessories by which this engineer expects to obtain these various advantages, consist of :

Casemates with reverse fires made against the salient of the counterscarp.

1st, *Reverse fire casemates* C, C, constructed against the salient of the counterscarp, and by which the ditches are enfiladed throughout their whole extent. These casemates should be armed with light pieces firing with grape, or with heavy blunderbusses loaded with many balls.

The defensive safety redoubt (PLATE IX, figs. 2, 3 and 4.)

2d, A *safety redoubt* R ; this is a round tower built of freestone, of about 15 mètres (50 feet) exterior diameter, and the height of which (nearly 50 decimètres (16¼ feet)) is determined in such a manner that its cornice is covered by the relief of the work. This redoubt is of two vaulted stories ; the first is a ground floor, the summit of whose vault is in the plane of site : it contains a stairs to ascend to the second story, and may con-

tain a powder-magazine, a wood-magazine, a cistern, and sinks :
the entrance is by a crenated iron door.   The upper story is
vaulted bomb-proof by a pointed vault (*voute d'arête*), formed
by two semi-circular vaults crossing each other at right angles :
four interior piers sustain the pressure of these vaults.   This
mode of construction was at first followed ; but the necessity of
establishing a pillar in the middle, was soon perceived ; this
produces an annular vault cut by four semi-circular arches with
full centres or elliptical.   The tower walls between the piers
of the vaults, are only 60 centimètres (2 feet) thick ; and 20
loop-holes are made in its perimeter.   The heads of the semi-
circular arches are left open above for the escape of the smoke ;
and pillars in the form of corbils support the cornice in this
part, and form a kind of machicoulis whose parapet is a strong
plank *m, m,* moveable and supported by iron corbels.

    The communication from the ground floor of the redoubt to *The gallery leading from the* the counterscarp casemate, is by a subterranean gallery 20 *redoubt to the* decimètres wide passing under the work ; the extrados of this *casemate* vault is on a level with the ditch.

    3d, A casemated traverse placed along the capital, and about *The casemated traverse made on* 30 decimètres (10 feet) in width.   This traverse is terminated *the capital in the terra-plain of the* circularly towards the redoubt whose fires enfilade it, and from *work.* which it is separated by an interval of 35 decimètres (12 feet) ; two passages *p, p,* (fig. 2) pass through this casemate to commu- nicate from one part of the terra-plain to the other.   Its use is to cover the garrison when it is not necessary for them to fight.

    From the bottom *S* of the traverse, the descent is by a stairs *The communi- cations between* of free-stone as far as the intrados *K* of the grand gallery ; the *the traverse and the galleries and* remainder of the communication is by wooden steps *KM,* which *redoubt.* turning upon two trunnions may be lodged in a recess made in the pier.   By these means the communication may be broken off, and the retreat into the redoubt is secured.

    The chief means of defence in the organization of these lunettes, *The general form of lunettes ;* show that their general form is that of a redan, with interior *their dimensions, and those of their* flanks superadded.   The measure of the flanked angle, and the *ditches.* direction of the flanks, are determined according to local and other considerations.   The faces of the lunettes may be made 200 to 300 mètres (223 to 335 yards) long, measuring from the casemate : but this latter dimension cannot be exceeded, if it be intended to preserve the efficacy of the casemate reverse fires. Their ditches are 12 to 15 mètres (40 to 50 feet) wide ; and their

depth at the salient is at least 33 decimètres (11 feet), in order
that the counterscarp casemate may be covered over with a
bed of masonry and earth at least 20 decimètres (6⅓ feet) thick.

The ditches of lunettes that are in advance of principal
works, with which they are in immediate relations, lead from
the salient up to the glacis by a gentle slope, so as to produce no projection or ressault that might impair the effect of
the protecting fires ; like those constructed at Metz and Landau. But when the lunettes are very advanced and are isolated works, the ditches are nearly of the same depth throughout
their whole extent ; and they debouche either on declivities or
on ground in rear of their gorge : it was thus that the lunettes
constructed on the heights of Bescançon, and in advance of the
succouring front of the citadel, were arranged.

The gorges of
lunettes; their
profiles, & com-
muni-ations with
the rear. (Fig. 2.)

The profiles of lunette gorges are constructed either with
sods, or dry walls, or common masonry ; their direction ends
at the centre of the redoubt, in order that its fires may scour
them and cross those of the counterscarp casemate.

The gorge of lunettes, considered as detached outworks, is
only secured by the redoubt ; and the communication between
them and the principal works, is by a subterranean gallery
having its outlet on the ground floor of the redoubt. But when
the lunette is an advanced work, the redoubt is enveloped by
a circular glacis resting against its profiles. A cut is made in
this glacis and leads into this species of place of arms, from
which the entrance into the redoubt is by an iron gate : on the
right and left there are ramps to ascend the terra-plain of the
work.

The palisading
which surrounds
the work. (Fig.2)

Lunettes made of earth and whose ditches are of slight depth
towards their shoulders, are enveloped by a straight palisading
planted at the foot of the scarp ; and in order to conceal it from
the view of the enemy, a small ditch is made from one third of
the face with a counter-slope to the first (à contre pente du
premier), and in which the palisading is planted. This little
ditch and palisading wind round the shoulder angle to envelop
the profiles and gorge, and unite with the barrier and palisading included between the redoubt and profile of the ramp.
But when the lunettes are isolated and the ditches are of about
the same depth throughout their whole extent, there is then no
little ditch with a counter-slope ; and the palisading is placed
along the foot of the scarp and profiles. When the ditches are

cut in rock, or rocky soil, the palisading is useless; because the slope of the scarp may be one-fifth of the height. The detached lunettes established on the heights of Besançon, are of this kind.

The glacis by which the work is covered.

These lunettes have no covert-way; they are covered by a rasant glacis that masks the relief and increases the depth of the ditch.

Four uses or small mines to increase the strength of lunettes.

When the counterscarp casemate and the terra-plain traverse are constructed, branches of mines (*rameaux de mines*) of masonry are made in front of the salient and under the terraplain; in order to be able to spring fougasses when the enemy attempt to establish themselves upon the salient to destroy the counterscarp casemate, and when they penetrate into the terraplain to attack the traverse.

Reflections on the construction of lunettes, and the time required for their execution

The lunettes that we have just described, possess as respects their general figure, the simplicity of field works; but the accessories by which they are distinguished, are very far from this character; they are of the most complex kind of permanent constructions, and their building requires the most minute attention and considerable time and expense. Experience has proved that with the greatest industry in rocky ground, at least five months labour is required to construct a lunette of 100 mètres (111 yards) face; and that its expense will be about 60,000 francs ($11,100). In light ground that does not require mining or blasting to excavate it, three months labour may suffice; and the expense will not exceed 50,000 francs ($9,250).

The value of lunettes, as outworks connected with the enciste.

General Darçon's lunettes. used as outworks under the immediate protection of the principal works, are a substitute for the common lunettes. To compare their respective values, we must form some idea of their degrees of resistance and the expenses of their construction. The common lunettes, well revested, and with gorges of sufficient relief, cannot be taken by storm; and the besiegers are under the necessity of crowning their covert-way and battering their scarp in breach, &c.

The lunettes that we are considering, afford the same results as the common lunettes during the period of the distant attack; but they have the advantage over the latter, of affording secure shelters for the garrison. During the distant attack which may last about eight days, the besiegers will dismount all the batteries open to the heavens and throw great quantities of bombs to destroy the redoubt, and will incline the fires of their ricochet batteries to strike this redoubt whose thin walls will be easily pierced, and the upper vault of which will be infallibly ruined in a short time. Accordingly when the besiegers gain the third parallel, the redoubt will be defenceless. If the besiegers intend to continue their attacks by gradual approaches, they will push forward against the salient a branch of a mine ; at the end of which they will make an overcharged chamber, whose effects will ruin the reverse fire casemate. In this posture of affairs, they should not hesitate to carry the lunette by storm.

But if without having recourse to offensive mines the besiegers wish to carry the work by storm, they may effect it with 2,000 men. Eight hundred men, led by the engineers and engineer soldiers, will move upon the salient and throw against the casemate embrasures bags of earth, which will form a mass and mask their fires. The engineer soldiers, supported by 200 men, will descend into the ditch and prevent the enemy from removing this mask ; whilst the other columns will storm the scarp, mount into the terra-plain, and move upon the gorge against the traverse and redoubt. A lodgement will then be immediately effected in the work and will be connected by communications, made with the flying sap, with the third parallel.

It may even be possible to carry the work by the gorge, which is very accessible and only defended by an already ruined redoubt.

It follows from this exposition, that the resistance of the common lunette is superior to that of the lunette under consideration. And as to the expense, there is little difference between them.

The value of the lunettes considered as advanced and isolated works. This writer thinks that these lunettes when too far advanced to be under the immediate protection of the enceinte, or occupying positions where they must depend upon their own strength, are secure from an attack by storm, and must require the preparations and slow procedures of an attack by gradual approaches. An hypothetical attack by storm will enable us to judge whether its success is probable. Let us first suppose that the lunette is constructed on common ground ; it will therefore be accessible on its whole perimeter, and the columns of attack will be able without difficulty to descend into the ditches. During the night there will be established at a distance of 4 to 500 mètres (445 to 556 yards), three field batteries ; one upon the direction of the capital, and the other two upon the prolongations of the faces. They will ricoché the barbette batteries ; and by obliquing the fire a little, the shot will strike directly the cornice and upper vault of the redoubt, which towards the close of day will be partly ruined and defenceless. During the day 800 bags of earth will be prepared ; and 3,000 troops, destined to storm the work, will be ready and posted in columns on the proper directions. Every thing being thus prepared, after a very hot fire of the batteries which will be brought up within 300 mètres (235 yards), the columns will move forward ; one of 1,000 strong will advance upon the salient, and will mask with bags of earth the casemate counterscarp ; the attack will be thus reduced to that of a field work. The engineer work-men and artillery soldiers will quickly make a passage and ramp in the scarp, to bring up 4 pounders on the rampart which will be covered with a simple gabionnade ; these will hast-en the reduction of the redoubt. If the gorge were not bet-ter prepared and secured than those of the lunettes raised about Bensançon, the troops should penetrate into the work by the gorge and the lengthened slope of the profiles : such an attack would be almost certain of success.

Finally ; If the scarp were cut out of rock or revested, the attack would be conducted in nearly the same manner. It would be longer and more difficult, but not more murderous. The greatest efforts should be directed against the gorge, and the troops should be provided with small ladders to mount the berme. The columns should penetrate into the ditches through their debouchès on the ground of the gorge.

We see from the preceding, that an attack by gradual ap-proaches would be carried on with the greatest rapidity against the kind of lunette that we are examining. Seven or eight can-non, and 2 mortars and 2 howitzers, would suffice for this short siege, which could not be protracted beyond 7 to 8 days ; these would be consumed in conducting the approaches and con-structing a globe of compression, which would destroy the coun-terscarp casemate, give an entrance into the ditch, and compel the enemy to capitulate.

General Darçon knew how to appreciate this new invention in fortification ; but he thought that the strength of these lunettes depended more upon opinion, which exaggerates every thing, than on reality. If he have exaggerated their real value, it must be attributed to motives of policy, and to the necessity of deceiving the coalesced enemies of France and calming the general inquietude.

The Polytechnick School will ever boast the honour of having had General Darçon for the founder of that part of education which relates to the science of fortification. His ceaseless industry, his military works, and his knowledge in all the branches of the science of war, have rendered him famous throughout Europe and deserving of his country. The celebrated *Prames* that he built in the Bay of Algesiras, would alone crown his name with immortality.

The safety redoubts and reverse glacis, proposed by Reveroni.

M. De Reveroni, an engineer officer, has proposed an ingenious mode of using the safety redoubts as detached outworks. At the tail of the glacis of the enceinte he makes a short glacis (*glacis coupé*) with a counter-slope to the common glacis whose relief is 25 decimètres (8½ feet), and forming the same re-enterings and salients as the covert-way. The relief is regulated by an artificial plane of site, which passes 16 decimètres (feet) beneath the crest of the short glacis (*glacis coupé*). At the foot and in the salients of this declivity, whether natural or artificial, he places the safety redoubts; they are open at the gorge, with their flanks pierced with loop-holes for blunderbusses and for small pieces firing grape. These covered fires which the enemy can neither counter-batter nor silence, scour the reverse of the short glacis (*glacis coupé*) and take in flank and reverse the aproaches of the enceinte glacis. The redoubts are covered by flêches of earth, which are flanked by the enceinte in the most effectual manner. That part of the redoubt which faces the place and is open, is masked by a small court formed by a crenated brick wall. The communication with the redoubt is by a subterranean gallery.

The manner in which detached lunettes should be organized.

General Darçon in disposing his advanced and isolated lunettes, did not sufficiently consider the relations that they should preserve with the principal works that they cover; he left their gorge in an alarming state of weakness; and he made their dimensions so small, that the means of defence are too much concentrated for any good results to be expected from them. Advanced lunettes should be organized and disposed according to the principles above laid down; they should have good flanks to post artillery upon, and should possess sufficient capacity to display within them their means and manœuvres of defence. Their ditches should surround the gorge, and be defended by casemated batteries made in the counterscarp; their scarp should be revested, to render an escalade under the fire of the casemates impossible ; the approaches of the gorge should be scoured by the grazing fire of a casemate raised on the scarp of the gorge ; casemated traverses will be made on the terra-plains to shelter the garrison ; and the lunettes of the first line will be sustained by intermediate lunettes, from which the sorties will be made, and which will contain the debouchês of the galleries of communication. From the interior of the casemated traverses there will be communications leading under the ditches to the reverse fire counterscarp casemates ; and a subterranean war may be organized under the glacises of the lunettes of the first line. In this case, the counterscarp gallery will form the general communication with all the reverse fire casemates. By means of such arrangements, the garrison may bid defiance to the incendiary batteries of the besiegers, who will be forced to besiege the lunettes in form before they can undertake any operations against the body of the place. The consequence will be another advantage of great importance ; the troops will become inured and experienced during the defence of the advanced lunettes ; and the inhabitants, for a long time accustomed to a fire that does not annoy them, will bear it more patiently when the enemy attack the body of the place and burn their houses.

We will not further extend these general reflections on advanced works ; all officers who pay attention to fortification and its relations with tactics, acknowledge their importance. Every thing leads us to presume, that for the future the arrangement of advanced outworks will afford more security to the defenders ; and that the defence will resume the measure of resistance that it has lost by the successive improvements in artillery and mining, and in the modes of using them.

CHAPTER VIII.

Illustrations of the Art of Mining; the Principles and Facts on which it is founded; Mining, applied to the Attack and Defence of Places; Subterranean War; Systems of Defensive Mines.

SECTION FIRST.

The Experimental Theory upon which the Art of Mining is founded.

167. Mining applied to the attack and defence of places.

167. IN describing the origin of the art of mining (112 and 128), we said that this ingenious art was for a long time only used to open breaches and demolish large masses of masonry. Before the time of Vauban, mines were very seldom made under breaches, and especially under the exterior works of the besiegers. But after the attack had made such great progress and acquired such great advantages over the defence, it was perceived that mining might be a great resource for the besieged, and become in their hands a powerful and tremendous means of defence. The application of this art to attack and defence, gave birth to the *arm of mining*, which is a branch of engineering; we described its troops (*personnel*) in the First Part.

Definitions of mines, and of subterranean war; its use.

At first all this kind of works of the besiegers, were called *mines*; and those made by the besieged against the besiegers, were named *counter-mines*. But since the art of mining has been adapted to the defence by permanent dispositions and placed in relation with the other parts of fortification, the works of the besieged ought to be called *mines*, and those of the besiegers, *counter-mines*. The dispositions of the besieged are now distinguished as *defensive mines*; and those of the besiegers as *offensive mines*.

Subterranean war consists in the application of the art of mining to attack and defence. At first this art was in favour of the besiegers; but the progress that it made, and the panic that the first defensive mines spread among the besieging troops, convinced engineers that it was the most effectual means of replacing the defence in a respectable attitude.   Perhaps the great effects of subterranean war are more in imagination, than reality.   But this power of the imagination produces real effects ; because it is founded on the organization of man, who dreads more those dangers that he cannot estimate, than those that are much greater but with which he is acquainted.   By subterranean war the besieged transform the combats under the canopy of heaven, to subterraneous battles in which the besiegers cannot display and use their strength ; and in which they are obliged to grope their way through unexplored passages, where they are every instant surprised and checked by a vigilant enemy who has foreseen and arranged every thing against them.

What we have said (128) is sufficient to enable us to understand what is a mine in general.   A chamber of a mine (*fourneau de mine*) is a hollow made in a mass of earth or masonry, and filled with powder.   It is communicated with by means of galleries and branches which are strongly rammed or barricaded, as we will more fully describe hereafter : the charge is fired by help of a saucisson or other means.

General idea of a mine: the chamber, galleries, and branches ; and barricading or ramming, &c.

168. The practical theory of mining and its application to subterranean war, is founded on several facts discovered by observation and with which it is of great importance to be well acquainted, in order to be able to form an idea of the means that the arm of mining employs in this species of war ; which in proportion to its good arrangement, increases the value of fortifications above ground.

168. The facts upon which the practical theory of mining is founded, as applied to the attack and defence.

When a mine is properly prepared beneath the surface of the earth, which we will suppose to be horizontal, and loaded with a sufficient quantity of powder and fire conveyed to the centre of the charge, this first general effect is observed—that if from the centre of the chamber a perpendicular (which is called the *axis of explosion* or *line of least resistance*) be drawn to the plane of the earth, the explosion forms a cavity $ABCD$ of a determined figure around the axis FG, and the earth is thrown up like a spout (*en gerbe*).   Part of the blown-up earth falls down again into the excavation and forms around its circumference the ridges (*levres*) L, L of a certain height, as is shown in the figure.   It must be remarked that this relief or height of the ridges, is very favourable to the besiegers.

First fact observed in springing mines (PLATE X, 6g.)

The charge of a mine capable of producing an outward explosion. The first experiments made by miners, showed immediately that the charge for a chamber capable of producing an explosion should vary according to, 1st, the nature of the ground; 2d, the length of the line of least resistance; and, 3d, the greatness of the excavation intended.

The crater: its figure. The crater or *tunnel* (*entonnoir*) is the excavation produced by the mine, supposing that none of the earth blown up falls back again. When it is desired to know the form of the crater, all this earth must be carefully thrown out of it. It is difficult to determine its exact figure, because it is very difficult to precisely excavate it; and the figure varies with the nature of the ground, which is itself very variable. When the ground is homogeneous, the crater is a solid of revolution whose meridian curve may be deduced from the hypotheses on the ignition of powder, its manner of acting, and the quality of the ground.

Figure of the crater in common ground. (Fig. 1) In common ground whose particles are susceptible of a certain cohesion and compression, the crater is widened towards the plane of explosion; it narrows towards the centre of the powder, and terminates a little below it like the reversed bottom of an oven.

Vauban's opinion of the figure of the crater. Vauban considered this crater as an inverted cone, having its summit or apex in the centre of the powder; and on this supposition calculated the volume of the excavation.

Opinions of Generals Vallière & Cormontaigne. General Vallière, a General of artillery of great merit and distinction, after Vauban, examined with great care the generating line of the craters of several mines made for experiment in homogeneal ground; and he thought that he discovered in them several properties of the parabola, and thence concluded that the figure of the crater was a paraboloid whose focus (*foyer*) is the centre of the powder. This figure is adopted by Cormontaigne.

Belidor's opinion. Belidor is of a different opinion from General Vallière. It follows from his theory, that the crater is a reversed cone, having its apex below the centre of the powder and very much rounded. In practice he considers this cone as perfect.

The opinion of modern miners. The figure of the crater of a mine is now considered as of little importance. It is sufficiently approximated by substituting for it that of an inverted cone, truncated by a plane passing through the centre of the powder.

Figure of the crater in incompressible earths. The figure of the crater is modified according to the quality of the ground; it is such as we have described in adhesive and compressible earths. But there are two species of soil that

are incompressible—sand, and rocks.   In the first the crater is
very little widened towards the exterior, and is a kind of pit.
In rock, the crater is very irregular ; and it frequently happens,
especially when the charge is not very strong, that only fissures
are formed, through which the elastic fluid escapes.

In common adhesive and compressible earths the dimensions
of the crater, that is, the magnitude of the inferior and superior
circles, depend upon the charge.   Suppose the explosion to
take effect ; if the charge be small, the superior diameter will
be a radius less than the axis of explosion : if the charge be increased, the diameter of the crater will also increase, and extend
until its opening becomes double the line of least resistance ;
whilst the diameter of the inferior circle will be nearly equal to
this line ; so that as respects the profile, a line drawn through the
upper edge of the crater and through the centre of the powder, will
be inclined 45 degrees towards the line of the earth.   It was only
these moderately charged mines that the ancient miners used ;
and they may be taken as a term of comparison, and as proof-mines
(*fourneaux d'épreuve*).   Their use is adapted to the besieged,
because they throw up a sufficient extent of ground without producing too great coverts or consuming a great quantity of
powder.

Dimensions of the craters of mines loaded with moderate charges, to produce craters of a diameter double the line of least resistance.

The volume of craters of common mines may, without any
very sensible error, be calculated by that of a cylinder whose
base is the superior circle of the crater, and whose height is
half the line of least resistance ; and as these craters are similar solids, the charges for the same soil are in the same proportion as the cubes of the axes of explosion.

The volume of the crater: the ratios of the charges.

Tables have been calculated according to these principles,
and show in an approximating manner the charges for moderate
chambers in grounds of various natures.   But whenever mines
are to be made in ground whose nature is not well known, one
or several proof-mines should be first made to ascertain the
charges proper for the mines.

Tables of charges for mine-chambers.

TABLES

Of Charges for Chambers of Mines, to form in different soils Craters whose superior diameter shall be double the axis of explosion.

Charges beneath a Line of Least Resistance of 10 feet (10⅜ feet).

Pounds

Common soil mixed with gravel	102
Strong sand or tophaceous soil	136
Strong clay or loam	145
Quick-sand	153
Old masonry	161
Free-stone or rock	177

Charges for Chambers beneath a Line of Least Resistance of one mètre (3⅓ feet).

Hectogr.

Soil mixed with sand	12.5
Common earth	15.
Strong sand or tophaceous soil	20.
Clay or loam	21.2
Old masonry	24.
Rock	25.

The quantity of Powder required for blowing up a Cubic Mètre (nearly 37 cubic feet).

Hectogr.

Soil mixed with sand	7.
Common earth	8.
Strong sandy or tophaceous soil	10.6
Loamy or argillaceous soil	11.2
Old mason work	12.6
Rock	13.5

N. B.　These weights are French.

Second fact in the effect of a mine, observed by Vauban Rule for the distance between independent chambers.

Vauban was the first who observed that the effect of a mine was not wholly outward, and that the explosion produced an interior action which broke through and destroyed the walls or sides of cavities, such as galleries and branches, when they

were too near.   This effect operates in all directions, whether
laterally or vertically below the chamber; the distance to
which it extends varies greatly, according to the nature of the
soil.   Vauban adopted it as a rule, never to make chambers
nearer together than the line of least resistance ; and experiments made since his time have proved that chambers, branches
and galleries to be secure from the effect of another mine,
should be separated apart twice or at least once and an half the
line of least resistance : this limit depends upon the nature of
the ground that separates the chambers from each other, and
upon other circumstances relating to the disposition and springing of the mines.

Belidor, whose memory is honoured by artists and philoso- *Facts observed by Belidor; globes of compression, or over loaded mines.*
phers, devoted his attention to the art of mining, and was the
first to suggest a theory explaining all the phenomena that
occur in springing mines.   He pushed his researches farther
than any of his predecessors, especially in examining the interior action of mines.   He thought that by overloading the common chambers, the commotion would be greater and capable of
acting against hollow spaces at greater distances, and of producing wider craters than those of mines moderately charged.
Chambers thus overloaded, he called globes of compression
(globes de compression).

Experiment ought, and indeed has confirmed Belidor's suppositions ; he burst through galleries at a distance of quadruple
the line of least resistance, and produced craters whose diame-
ters exceeded five times this line.   The charges were increased
to as much as ten times the common charge ; but it was remarked that the widenings of the craters did not follow in the same
ratio, and that they did not exceed the sextuple of the line of
least resistance.   These experiments were repeated at Potsdam
by the celebrated Lefebvre, by order of the great Frederick ;
the results were nearly the same.

The discovery of globes of compression or overcharged cham- *The proper-
bers, and the experiments at Potsdam, led to perceive that ties of globes of compression ; the
these species of mines are more favourable to the attack, than advantages deri-
to the defence.   By their greatly extended spheres of action, ved from them by the attack.*
they reach the previously arranged dispositions of the besieged,
overwhelm their galleries, and destroy their chambers; and
are a powerful weapon with which to attack the covert-ways
and overwhelm the counterscarps into the ditches.   The be-

sieged cannot employ them with the same success, because they would destroy their own works, and they cannot spare the enormous quantity of powder that they require.

Belidor made another interesting experiment; by placing barrels of powder along a gallery at certain distances from each other, he succeeded in bursting the top of the gallery and converting it into a kind of trench.

General Mares-
cot's experi-
ments on the
empty spaces left
around the box
of powder in a
mine (See his
Memoir in those
of the Institute,
8th year, (1800))

It was known by experiment that when a space was left in the barrel of a musket between the charge and the ball, the shock was greater and would frequently burst the musket. General Marescot having reflected on this fact, thought that the same phenomenon must occur in springing mines; and that greater craters ought to be obtained, all things else being equal, by leaving certain intervals around the box containing the powder. This General proposed in 1800 to determine by curious experiments, the effects of air in the action of mines.

After disposing the chambers agreeably to his plans, he perceived that a certain quantity of air, included between the box and the sides of the chamber, greatly increased the effect; and that beyond a certain limit, this increase not only ceased to be progressive, but even decreased and ultimately became nugatory. In a chamber charged with 100 pounds and occupying $1\frac{1}{2}$ cubic foot, and with 10 feet ($10\frac{3}{4}$ feet) of line of least resistance, the greatest effect was procured by a capacity of 27 cubic feet. The effect was the same as if the chamber were loaded with 196 pounds, or the same as that of a common chamber at a depth of 13 feet (nearly 14 feet) and charged with 219 pounds of powder. The details of these curious experiments are contained in a memoir inserted in the Memoirs of the Institute for the year 1800.

The experi-
ments that re-
main to be made
on overloaded
mines.

It yet remains to be proved by experiments accurately made, to what point an increase of charge produces an increase in the widening of the crater and of the radius of rupture. It is probable, that this charge is not far from twelve times the common charge; that this maximum charge would not produce a crater of a diameter seven times greater than the common crater; and that the radius of rupture would not exceed five or six times the axis of explosion.

The charge of
a chamber in
made ground, the
tenacity of which
has been de-
stroyed.

Many experiments, which require to be repeated very carefully in various kinds of soil, have caused it to be admitted as a principle, that one half of the effort of the charge is exerted in common soils to vanquish the resistance opposed by the tenacity of the earth ; and that in very dense and tenacious ground, two thirds of the charge are spent to overcome this resistance. This proves, that in made ground or ground whose tenacity is destroyed, only one half or one third of the common charge is requisite to form a crater.

In mines made in common soils, the branch leading to the chamber must be rammed for a length equal to nearly twice the line of least resistance ; in order that its effort may be in the plane of explosion.   But frequently it is not possible to effect this ramming (*bourrage*), either because the mine must be immediately sprung, or because it is made in the bottom of a shaft or pit.   It was of great importance to know in what manner to act in these cases, which frequently occur in sieges.

The effects of globes of compression induced M. Mouzé, formerly commander of the miners, and whose discoveries and works on the art of mining will form an era in this science, to suppose that an overcharge should produce a diminution in the length of the ramming effected vertically or in the direction of a common branch.   The admirable experiments that he made on this subject, and which it is very important should be completed, prove that an increase of the charge will supply the place of ramming.

Mouzé periments ramming.

These curious experiments, which were directed with the ability by which M. Mouzé is distinguished in practice and in theory, must one day be the subject of the meditations of young officers and students.   We shall restrain ourselves to presenting the chief results in the following Table, with this observation—that these data, deduced from experiments, are consequences flowing from General Marescot's theory.

TABLE

Of Experiments, establishing the relation between the Ramming and the Charge.

Experiment	Charge		Ramming.	
1st	Appointed	or = 1	Complete	or = 1
2d	Increased	or = $1\frac{1}{2}$	Reduced to $\frac{2}{3}$ or = $\frac{2}{3}$
3d	Increased	or = $1\frac{1}{2}$	Reduced to $\frac{1}{3}$ or = $\frac{1}{3}$
4th	Double	or = 2	Suppressed	or = 0

Experiment has shown, 1st, that by properly establishing the dimensions of the profile across a common branch, the same effect may be obtained by diminishing the ramming, provided that the charge be increased in a certain proportion ; 2d, that there is an increase of charge which allows the total omission of ramming, and that it is nearly equal to the common charge for full ramming ; 3d, that by these means chambers may be made in the bottom of shafts, and will form as great craters as if full branches were used.

Examination of the various circumstances that accompany the springing of a mine, made in different soils.

The miners skilled in natural philosophy, and the engineer officers who were witnesses of a great number of experiments with mines, were sufficiently near to examine with care the various circumstances accompanying the springing or explosion of a mine. These circumstances vary and are modified by the nature of the soil, of which we will admit three principal kinds , to which may be referred and compared the mean effects produced in intermediate species. These three kinds are, rock, sand, and common homogeneous earth, tenacious and compressible.

In rock, as soon as the energy of the powder is sufficiently exerted to produce an effect and shiver the ledges of rocks, it forms clefts on every side through which the fluid endeavours to escape ; and if the charge be strong enough to produce an explosion, it takes place at the very instant of inflammation. The fragments of rock are blown to a distance, and the crater is very irregular and of greater or less width.

If the chamber be in a sandy soil whose particles have no adhesion, the fluid at the moment of inflammation forces its way through these particles ; and the explosion; if the charge be moderate, forms a crater very little widened and resembling a pit. In order that the explosion may embrace a greater space of ground, the charge must be increased.

Lastly ; in tenacious and compressible soils three remarkable effects take place before the total effect, and which it is possible to observe notwithstanding the rapidity of the phenomena : 1st, at the very instant that the ignition of the powder takes place, a rumbling noise is heard, and a quaking or trembling of the earth is felt : 2d, the ground surrounding the axis of explosion is observed to rise up and form a spherical calotte, which gradually enlarges until the moment that a smoke is perceived issuing from the perimeter of its base : 3d, the explosion follows closely after these two circumstances, and the ground corresponding to the calotte is thrown up like a spout ; part of it falls back into the crater, and the remainder falls and forms ridges or lips about the excavation.   The violent *commotion* produced by the explosion, gives to the particles of earth adjacent to the focus a great vibratory motion, which extends to a greater or less distance in proportion to the tenacity, density, and elasticity of the soil ; and which fills up the empty spaces that are within its sphere of action.

From the preceding facts many consequences are deduced, which are of great importance to the attack and defence : 1st, The chamber of a mine established in a sandy soil, should, compared with a mine in common ground, be overcharged, if it be intended to produce widened craters, unlike pits.   2d, Mines made in rock should likewise be overloaded, and their branches should be harder rammed and for a greater length.   3d, The total effect of a mine consists of two separate efforts, one exterior, and the other interior ; the first produces a crater, and the second occasions a commotion, which acting against the interior hollow spaces, bursts in the sides of branches, galleries, &c.   Experiment has proved that the hollow spaces included within the sphere of action of the interior shock of mines, may be preserved by ramming them and making the whole mass nearly homogeneous.

Important consequence : deduced from the preceding facts.

169. The theoretical explanation of all the phenomena that occur in mines, is yet far from possessing that degree of precision which is satisfactory to minds accustomed to the rigorous demonstrations of numerous physico-mathematical truths. It depends upon the nature of the forces produced by the inflammation of the powder, and their manner of acting against the circumjacent ground.

169. Explanation of the phenomena and facts observed in springing mines. (See Belidor and Marescot's Memoirs & Mouzé's Manuscripts.)

The nature of the forces of inflamed powder, can only be deduced from the hypotheses established respecting its inflammation ; and the action of these forces against the earth, depends upon the very nature of these earths, which are of infinite variety.   Hence it follows, that their effects are infinitely diversified ; and that each particular case requires a particular explanation.   Accordingly, experiment is the surest guide that an officer of miners can follow in applying the theory to the art.

We know from what was said in the First Part (47) respecting the inflammation of powder, that its change from a concrete body to the state of an elastic expanding fluid tending to occupy a space 15 to 20,000 times greater than its primitive space, gives birth to repelling forces composed of forces of percussion and pression.   These forces rapidly increase ; and in a very short instant of time, their combined action produces the total power.

If the phenomenon of combustion took place in vacuum, the elastic fluid would rapidly expand and occupy the space required by its nature.   But if circumjacent bodies confine the fluid and oppose a strong resistance to its expansion, it then acts against them by virtue of the forces that we have defined : this is proved by experience, by the discharge of cannon, and by the explosion of a powder-magazine.   In this case the air alone resists the action of the powder, which communicates to it a motion of transition capable of overwhelming and shivering strong obstacles, and a motion of vibration which will make stringed instruments resound at a great distance.

The effect of a mine in soil indefinitely tenacious and compressible.

To judge of the effect of a mine in a common soil whose particles are adhesive and compressible, we may first suppose that the ground is indefinite in every direction, and then examine what should occur in consequence of the inflammation of the charge.   The first stratum of earth in contact with the chamber will be beaten back and compressed in all directions, as well by the successive commotions, as by the force of pressure. This motion will be communicated immediately from one stratum to another to a certain distance, beyond which there will be no sensible motion ; but there will be a vibratory motion that will extend farther, in proportion to the elasticity of the earth : this is the tremulous motion that the spectators feel under foot, and which alarms the troops who are exposed to it. Accordingly there must be formed about the chamber, 1st, a hollow sphere whose small diameter, which is variable and difficult to determine, depends upon the compressibility of the earth ; 2d, a sphere whose particles are convulsed, and whose diameter is also very difficult to determine ; 3d, and lastly, a great sphere including the motion of vibration.

(See General Marescot's Memoir in the 11th No. of the Journal of the Polytechnick School.

General Marescot distinguishes accordingly three concentric spheres in the mass of earth in which a mine is sprung: 1st, The *sphere of activity*, extending from the centre of the chamber as far as the point where all effect ceases : 2d, The *sphere of friability*, extending from the sides of the chamber as far as the limit at which the particles cease to receive a motion of translation, and at which the tenacity is not destroyed : 3d, The *sphere of rupture;* this is that portion of the sphere of friability within which galleries may be injured, souterrains burst in, revêtements overwhelmed, and cavities filled up, &c.   The radii of these spheres are difficult to determine ; but by experiments well directed and made in various soils, we may arrive at a knowledge of the sphere of rupture, which is the most important.

When the tenacity and compressibility of the soil are not sufficiently great for the radius of the empty sphere to embrace the whole extent required by the energy of the powder, it produces crevices and clefts of greater or less depth, and through which the fluid penetrates and expands.

If we suppose the sphere of activity to be cut by a plane passing without the sphere of friability, there will be no other effect in this plane than the mere vibration of the particles ; which effect will be felt at great distances.   A chamber at a depth of 30 decimètres (10 feet) and loaded with 100 pounds of powder, is felt at a distance of more than 200 mètres (223 yards) ; and a miner at work under ground, can be heard at a distance of upwards 30 mètres (100 feet).   These effects vary in proportion to the elasticity of the soil.   If this plane of intersection become tangential to the sphere of friability, the effect will be still inward ; there will be on this plane only a quaking, which will be stronger in proportion as it is nearer the point of contact ; and only the particles that are adjacent to this point, are impressed with a small degree of motion.

Finally ; if the plane *P, P* cut the sphere of friability, the phenomenon is no longer wholly interior, but exerts itself without by an explosion.   This plane is then called the *plane of explosion ;* and the perpendicular *So* drawn from the centre of the powder, is called the *axis of explosion* or *line of least resistance.*   The particles in the section *ab* of the sphere made by the plane, will evidently remain stationary ; whilst those situated within will be projected out of the plane with a violence greater in proportion as they are near the axis of explosion : there will therefore be produced a spout of earth and a crater. If through the circumference of rupture *ab* a conical surface be drawn enveloping the empty sphere *QtRu,* which is always of a small radius, we will have the form of the crater, nearly.

Supposition of a plane cutting the sphere of activity.

The plane, and the axis of explosion : the phenomenon supposed to occur in vacuum (PLATE X, fig 2)

The axis of explosion = H.

But in consequence of the tenacity of the earth and the lateral pressure of the elastic fluid, the rectilinear sides aQ, bR will assume the curved figure ayQ, bxR : this is the reason that the crater profile was called a parabola.

Remark upon the figure of the sphere of friability.

When the soil is indefinite and nearly homogeneous, the sphere of friability is spherical ; but in the event of an explosion, the vertical radius SM beneath the chamber necessarily diminishes and becomes SM' ; that is, there is formed a species of ellipsoid whose lesser axis is vertical : this part of the theory is confirmed by experiment.

The radius of friability $Sb = M$; the radius of the circle of friability $ob = N$: the relation connecting these elements.

The line Sb drawn from the centre of the powder to the circumference of the rupture, is called the radius of friability ; and the line ob is designated the radius of the circle of friability. The relation between these lines and the axis of explosion, is shown by the equation $M^2 = H^2 + N^2$ .... (1).

Reflections on the magnitude of the crater in soils of various compressibility.

It must be remarked, that the magnitude of the crater does not always extend as far as the circumference of rupture projected in ab. That this may be the case, the tenacity and compressibility of the earth must be such that the calotte df , $a'fb'$, &c., which rises up as the inflammation takes place, will widen to the circumference of rupture ab before any lateral crevices are formed, running from the sides of the hollow sphere towards the plane of explosion included within another circumference of rupture projected in dg or $a'b'$: in this case the crater is $dQuRg$ or $a'QuRb'$. Experience proves that this is the case in most soils.

Consideration and influence of the atmospheric pressure in the springing of mines.

When the mine acts outwards in the plane of explosion, the pressure of the atmosphere opposes the formation of the crater and modifies its opening. Indeed as soon as the ground begins to rise up around the axis and to form the calotte, the atmosphere resists with its weight the formation of the crater. This pressure reacts upon and violently repercusses the elastic fluid when it endeavours to escape through clefts in the circumference of rupture.

The atmospheric pressure $= b =$ a stratum of common earth 725 centimètres (24 feet) thick.

The weight of the atmosphere is considered as equal to that of a stratum of common earth 725 centimètres (24 feet) thick ; and to reduce the question to the case of soil ordinarily tenacious and compressible, this stratum is supposed to be tenacious and only 362 centimètres (12 feet) $= \dfrac{b}{2}$.

In supposing that the explosion of the mine takes place in atmosphere, we will consider the phenomenon as occurring in vacuum ; always substituting for the atmospheric pressure a stratum of earth 362 centimètres (12 feet) thick.   This is as if a new plane of explosion $P'P'$ were to cut the sphere of friability 362 centimètres above the first plane of explosion ; in this case the crater would be $IQRK$; therefore the real crater would be $rQRz$.   The line Sz drawn from the centre of the powder to the edge of the crater, is called in General Marescot's theory, *the radius of explosion.*

The phenomenon of an exploding mine in the atmosphere. (Fig 2.)

The radius of explosion $Sz = R$. The radius of the crater or $= T$.

We see from what has been just laid down respecting the formation of the real crater, that there is around its surface a solid of revolution generated by zRb and whose particles are violently convulsed ; and that if a plane zX ended at a point of the crown zb, it would be broken to pieces.   This is the reason that the chambers of mines must be made at such a distance from works that are to be preserved, that the side of the crater shall be sufficiently distant.   It is proved by experience that the width of the crown of common chambers, may be from 20 to 30 decimètres ($6\frac{1}{2}$ to 10 feet).

Consequences and important result.

To find the relation between the real radius, the radius of the circle of friability, and the radius of friability, General Marescot observes that for the first instant the effect in vacuum is the same as in air ; consequently the masses must be equal ; that is, the excavation $aQRb$ is equal to the excavation $rQRz$ added to the pressure of the artificial stratum substituted for the atmosphere : this gives $T^2 (H+b) = N^2 H \dots\dots\dots\dots (2)$.

The relation between the radius of the crater, and that of the circle of friability.

This equation, combined with the equation (1), will give the radius of friability when the radius of the circle of the crater and the axis of explosion are known.

The radii of rupture are included between the radii of explosion and the radii of friability, and depend on the solidity of the bodies to be destroyed : there remains to be made a great many experiments on this important subject.   Nevertheless the few facts known seem to indicate that the radii of rupture are in direct proportion to the radius of explosion and the elasticity of the medium, and in inverse proportion to the tenacity and resistance of the body, &c.

The limits of the radii of rupture.

The bases of the experimental philosophy of mines, are as yet established on too small a number of facts to strictly determine the relations that exist between the charge and the ele-

The relation between the charge and these elements.

ments just discussed. General Marescot, after investigating the greatest number of experiments that afford certain results, found that for the same medium a constant quotient nearly equal to $\frac{1}{14}$ is obtained by dividing the charges by the product of the square of the crater radius multiplied into the radius of explosion : whence he deduced this important relation $\frac{F}{T^2 R} = \frac{F'}{T'^3 R'}$ $= \frac{1}{14}$. And to extend it to all media, he introduces into it in direct proportion the tenacity combined with the density and inertia, a quantity expressed by P; and in inverse proportion the elasticity E: when we have $\frac{FE}{T^2 RP} = \frac{F'E'}{T'^2 R'P'}$ . . . . (3).

Experiment must determine E and P relatively to various media ; and then by a single trial well made in a single soil, all the elements of the second member of this fundamental equation will be known. By combining the equation (3) with the equations (1) and (2), we easily attain a solution of the most important questions in subterranean war.

We will here subjoin a table of results, sufficiently verified by five very interesting experiments, in which General Marescot has determined by calculation those elements which are not yet determined by experiment. For instance, all the radii of rupture, excepting mines 4 and 5, are not the immediate product of trials ; they were calculated according to the hypotheses that the media and bodies to be burst through, are similar. The examination of these experiments will show how many important points remain to be fixed and determined, before the bases of the practical theory of mining can be established.

Mines.	Charges. F.		Axes of Explosion. H.		Radii of the Craters. T.		Radii of Explosion. R.		RADII OF RUPTURE. In the horizontal direction.		RADII OF RUPTURE. In the vertical direction, from top to bottom.		RADII OF RUPTURE. In the vertical direction, from bottom to top	Radii of friability. M.		Radii of the friable circles around the craters. N.	
	Fr	Eng.	Fr.	Eng.	Fr.	Eng.	Fr.	Eng.	Fr.	Eng.	Fr.	Eng.		Fr.	Eng.	Fr.	Eng.
No.	pds.	pds.	feet.	feet.	feet.	feet.	feet.	feet.	feet.	feet.	feet.	feet.		ft.	feet.	feet.	feet.
1	100	108	10	10$\frac{5}{7}$	10	10$\frac{5}{7}$	14.0	15	17.6	18$\frac{3}{4}$			Nearly equal to the radii of explosion.	20.5	22	18.0	19$\frac{2}{7}$
2	172	185	12	12$\frac{6}{7}$	12	12$\frac{6}{7}$	17.0	18$\frac{3}{14}$	21.4	22$\frac{3}{4}$				23.3	25	20.0	21$\frac{3}{7}$
3	416	441	16	17$\frac{1}{7}$	16	17$\frac{1}{7}$	22.5	24$\frac{1}{6}$	28.4	30$\frac{1}{2}$				29.7	31$\frac{3}{4}$	25.0	26$\frac{5}{7}$
4	3600	3877	12	12$\frac{6}{7}$	36	38$\frac{4}{7}$	38.0	40$\frac{5}{7}$	48.0	51$\frac{3}{7}$	38.0	40$\frac{5}{7}$		62.2	66$\frac{2}{3}$	61.0	65$\frac{1}{3}$
5	3000	3231	15	16$\frac{1}{14}$	33	35$\frac{1}{3}$	36.3	38$\frac{3}{4}$	48 0	51$\frac{3}{7}$	38.0	40$\frac{5}{7}$		55.0	59	52.8	56$\frac{1}{2}$

RATIOS,

Given by several writers, agreeably to many experiments, respecting the resistance occasioned by the tenacity, weight, inertia, &c. of Virgin Media: this is P and P'.

		Ratio.			Ratio
No. 1.	Common earth a little mixed with gravel ..	1.00	No. 4.	Quick sand	1.50
2.	Strong sand, tophus, soil mixed with these..	1.30	5.	Old masonry, well built	1.58
3.	Strong clay, loam, fresh masonry	1.40	6.	Free stone, and rock	1.75

The practice of mines requires the solution of several important questions, which are determined more conformably to
the laws of nature and in a more satisfactory manner by General Marescot's theory, than by Belidor's theory, the only one
hitherto known.

First question.   The position of a chamber being given, find
the proper charge for blowing up a point situated in the plane
of explosion ?

The point against which the power of the mine is to act being placed at the extremity of the radius of explosion, the quantity R, and likewise H, are known ; and we have therefore only
to disengage F from the equation (3) ; this gives $F = \dfrac{T^2 R}{14}$:
T and R will be expressed in feet, and the weight of the charge
will be expressed in pounds.

Second question.   Find the radius of the crater that will be
formed by a given charge under a determined axis of explosion ?

We have for this the two equations $R^2 = T^2 + H^2$, and
$R = \dfrac{14.\,F}{T^2}$, from which we deduce $\sqrt{T^2 + H^2} = \dfrac{14\,F}{T^2}$;   an
equation that will show what T is.

It follows from the value of T, that under the same axis of explosion the radii of the craters should increase or diminish indefinitely like the charges. This result was not known before Belidor ; and experience can only verify this important fact to a
certain limit, variable in each kind of soil.   It is probable that
this limit would be obtained by a charge 15 to 20 times stronger
than that of the simple chamber.   When the force of the powder becomes very superior to the forces composing the resistance of the earth and the pressure of the atmosphere, the effect
will be so rapid that the lateral action of the powder will not
have time to co-operate in widening the upper part of the crater ; and it will be constantly the same, whatever may be the
increase of the charge.

It results from the values of F, that the charges are proportional to the products of the square of the crater radius into the
radius of explosion.   It had been hitherto thought, that they
were merely as the squares of the radii of the crater.

If the case were simple chambers, that is, if $H = T$; we

would have $F = H^3 \times \dfrac{\sqrt{2}}{14}$. Or, $F = \dfrac{H^3}{10}$ nearly.   Accordingly when the radii of the craters are equal to the axes of explosion, the charges are proportional to the cubes of these same lines, or to the cubes of the radii of explosion; the solids being homogeneal.

Third question.   The charges being equal, find for the same soil the ratios of the radii of the craters?

The equation (3) gives $T : T' :: \sqrt{R'} : \sqrt{R}$; that is, the radii of the craters are in inverse proportion to the square roots of the radii of explosion.

It follows from this latter proportion, that when the axes of explosion increase, the radii of the craters diminish. But we *Consequence & remark.* must not hence conclude that there will be a crater always formed ; for when the expanding forces of the powder cannot vanquish the resisting forces, the effect will be reduced to an interior compression or to the formation of a calotte outside around the axis of explosion ; and this effect will be in proportion to the charge.

It is probable that experiments well made and sufficiently diversified, will show that the action of a mine on a point situated *The effect of the action of a mine on a point within its sphere of activity.* within its sphere of activity, is in a direct proportion to the charge and elasticity of the medium, and in inverse proportion to the tenacity and cube of the distance of this point from the centre of the powder.

Such are the principal bases upon which the theory of mining is founded; it cannot be raised from the state of imperfection in which it still is, without a complete system of experiments planned and directed by an able officer of miners, who, like M. Mouzé, must be skilled in theory and consummate in practice, and possessed of extensive knowledge in fortification and the other branches of military science.

SECTION II.

Application of the experimental Theory of Mining to the defence and attack of Places ; Subterranean War.

170. The art of Mining applied to the attack and defence of *170. General considerations.* places, is founded on the general principles that were deduced from the experimental theory just developed. This art should be to the besiegers a violent means of overwhelming all obsta-

cles opposed by the defences, whatever may be their nature; and to the besieged, a system combined beforehand, by which they can at pleasure get under the besiegers' works above ground, to establish mines and blow them up.

Defensive mines; their use. *Defensive mines* consist in making under the exterior of a place and in the interior of the fortifications, such dispositions, that at any moment chambers or mines may be made to blow up the works of the besiegers and compel them to undertake a subterranean war.

Offensive mines; their use. *Offensive mines* consist of all the subterraneous works and mines that the besiegers make to destroy, 1st, the defensive mines; 2d, to overwhelm the scarps and counterscarps.

Consequence. Hence it follows, that defensive mines should in general produce moderate effects, and often little felt outside; whilst offensive mines should extend their effects as far as possible, either to destroy the defensive mines by violent inward concussions and form great craters, or to effect the passage of ditches and make breaches.

171. Galleries, branches, and shafts of mines. (PLATE X, fig. 9.) 171. It is by means of subterranean communications, called *galleries*, *branches*, and *shafts*, that the troops gain the different points where chambers are to be established.

There are four kinds of galleries or branches distinguished in respect to their dimensions :

1st, Grand galleries, 20 decimètres high by 12 decimètres wide (6$\frac{2}{3}$ feet by 4).

2d, Half galleries, 14 decimètres high by 10 decimètres wide (4$\frac{3}{5}$ feet by 3$\frac{1}{3}$).

3d, Great branches, 10 decimètres high by 8 decimètres wide (3$\frac{1}{3}$ feet by 2$\frac{2}{3}$).

4th, Common branches, 8 decimètres high by 7 decimètres wide (2$\frac{2}{3}$ feet by 2$\frac{1}{3}$).

The construction of galleries, branches and shafts. The galleries are constructed of masonry or wood; the branches and shafts are made always with wood, unless the shafts are a species of ventilator to supply currents of air in permanent galleries.

Their construction with wood requires timbers of various dimensions; these are small rafters or thick sleepers to form the frames of shafts and the sashes (*chàssis*), planks for the tops of galleries and branches, and boards for the coffer-work of the shafts and galleries. The thickness of these timbers varies a little, in proportion of the dimensions of the shafts and galleries and the favourable or unfavourable nature of the soil.   There are two kinds of frames for shafts—those with ears (*oreilles*), and the common frame.   We shall not enter into the details of executing a shaft or gallery ; their modes of construction are simple and described with the greatest clearness in the memoirs and works of several officers, the study of which we cannot too strongly recommend to the student.   We will merely observe, that when the depth is not too great, and especially when galleries in mason-work are to be constructed, it is preferable to work open to the light of day ; in order to avoid making shafts and wooden galleries, whose previous establishment is necessary before the masonry can be begun.   The subterraneous modes should not be adopted, unless the depth require too great excavations.

(See Mousé's and Delox ve's Memoirs, and Etienne & Bousmard's works)

The piers of galleries of masonry vaulted with full centres, are commonly made of a thickness equal to the radius from the centre of the intrados ; that is, about 7 decimètres ($2\frac{1}{4}$ feet).

In galleries made of masonry, preparations are made to defend them inch by inch; these are barricaded and crenated doors to arrest the progress of the hostile miners, and chamfers (*coulisses*) 2 decimètres (8 inches) square to barricade and isolate the parts that are to be abandoned.   Lastly ; shafts may be made in them, and covered over with planks easily removed.

(PLATE X, fig. 9.)

172. When a chamber is to be established under any given point and at a given depth, a branch is made from a gallery or shaft in the direction of the point that the centre of the powder is to occupy ; but instead of strictly following this direction, the branch is obliqued to the right or left, so that its centre line will pass 15 decimètres (5 feet) from this point : a rectangled return is then made, and at the end of this the chamber of the mine is established.   This mode is adopted in order to more easily and solidly buttress the chamber.

172. The position of the chamber with respect to its branch : the box : the chamber : the charge : the ramming : the mode of communicating the fire : the smoke.

The chamber is the space that is hollowed out at the end of the branch, to lodge the powder in ; it may be made more spacious than the volume of powder requires, for theory teaches that this empty space increases the effect.   When the powder is placed in the chamber without being enclosed in a separate box, the coffer-work and the top and floor of the chamber must be made with great care, and the powder must be surrounded with hay or straw to preserve it from dampness.

The capacity of the chamber.

Most generally a box or chest is placed in the chamber, and the bags of powder are emptied into it.   Its form should be spherical to be most conformable to the laws of inflammation, which propagates itself from the centre to the surface ; but in practice, it is made of a cubical form.   To determine its capacity, and consequently its side, we must know that 10 cubic decimètres of powder weigh about 100 hectogrammes (22 lbs. avoirdupois, Eng.) ; or what is the same, that 75 pounds of powder (81 pounds) occupy a cubic foot (1.225 cubic foot).   Now if the charge expressed in hectogrammes be divided by 10, and the cube root be extracted, we have the measure of the side of the chest.

We have seen by the theory, that the ramming of the branch of the mine is important ; and that it should be effected on a length at least double the line of least resistance.

When the powder is placed, the door of the chamber is shut with strong planks buttressed against the uprights of the sashes of the returning branch ; the branch is then filled up with bags of earth strongly rammed against each other ; and care is taken to lay pieces of timber across the ramming at intervals of 2 mètres (6½ feet) from each other and pressing against the uprights of the sashes.   The extremity of the ramming is closed by planks strongly buttressed against the pier of a gallery, or by buttresses sunk in the ground.

The communication to the powder is by means of a *saucisson*. This is a long linen bag filled with powder, running along the branch into the centre of the powder ; its other extremity extends into the gallery, along which it is continued if thought expedient.   Formerly the saucisson was made 7 to 8 centimètres (about 3 inches) in diameter ; but 12 to 15 millimètres (about ½ inch) is sufficient, in order to diminish the suffocating vapours which diffuse themselves through the galleries and poison the air in them for a long time.

To preserve the saucisson and to prevent it from being damaged by the ramming, it is enclosed in a trough (*auget*) made of deal boards and nailed against the uprights of the sash of the branch.

To convey fire to the powder of a mine, it would be sufficient to prolong the saucisson ; but as this mode would poison the air of the galleries, the saucisson terminates at the extremity of the ramming, and at this point the fire is communicated.   By these means no more smoke gets into the galleries, than is driven through the trough by the explosion.　As it would be very dangerous for a miner to apply the fire directly at the extremity of the ramming, recourse is had to the fire-table or fire-pan (*planchette ou moine*).　The fire-pan is a piece of tinder or spunk 2 or 3 centimètres long, by 1 thick (nearly 1 inch by ¼ inch) ; one of its extremities is fixed to the sheet of paper that covers the priming of the extreme of the saucisson, and communicates the fire to it.　The moment that the fire-pan (*moine*) sets fire to the mine, is known by the time that the piece of spunk or touchwood, equal and similar to the fire-pan and lighted at the same instant as the latter, takes to burn : this latter piece of touchwood is called the witness (*temoin*).

The fire-table (*planchette*) is a more certain mode of firing the powder ; it is composed of a box without bottom or lid, with horizontal grooves in it in which a shelf (*tablette*) with a ring plays, and which can be easily drawn out of the grooves without moving the box.　In using this machine, the miner lights a pellet made of good matches and places it upon the drawer ; he covers the priming-powder (*pulverin*) with the box, upon which he lays a strong plank to give it stability and prevent the pellet from falling out of it.　He ties to the ring of the drawer a well untwisted pack thread about three or four times longer than the line of least resistance : this cord is supported by small props or crotchets fixed in the uprights of the branches.　By pulling this cord, the shelf is drawn out of the box, and the burning match falls upon the priming-powder.

The greatest difficulty that occurs in the practice of mines, is occasioned by the smoke which in consequence of the explosion penetrates through the ramming of the branches, and spreading along the galleries strikes the miners senseless.　The hostile miners have therefore time to dig down into the crater and branch and gain the gallery, before it has become habitable. Many able miners have sought means to guard against these inconveniencies, and many experiments have been made on the subject ; but as they have afforded no very satisfactory results, we are now reduced to use the *mouse* (*souris*), a very ingenious method of conveying fire to the powder without employing a saucisson, the smoke of which spreads by means of the trough through the galleries.

The mouse is a pellet of burning match, and is conveyed to the powder in the chamber through the ramming of the branches.

[marginal note: Conveying fire to the powder by means of the mouse & alleviating the inconvenience of the smoke.]

It is attached to a very short small chain, and the chain is connected with a cord well untwisted and very flexible.   To convey the mouse, a trough very smooth inside is placed against
each upright of the branch, and these two troughs are united
together at the distance or height of the charge by a semi-circular trough ; a piece of saucisson leads from the centre of the
powder into the semi-circular trough.   When the troughs are
established and the priming laid, the mouse-cord is placed in
the trough against its interior side ; and the ramming is then executed.   When the mine is to be fired, the small mouse-chain
is tied to the cord, and this cord is drawn through by its other
extremity ; the mouse enters the trough and is drawn through it
with ease, and in a moment reaches the powder.   As soon as
the mine has sprung, the miners hasten to stop up the mouth of
the troughs, for fear of smoke being driven back through them.
The only disadvantage of this method is, that we must be provided with troughs so well made that the mouse will experience no difficulty in its progress.

173. The execution of subterranean war is founded on the
art of arranging and distributing mines to act outwardly against
the ground on which the besiegers must approach and establish
their batteries ; and compelling them by these means to descend under ground and approach subterraneously, to destroy
the works of the garrison and combat their miners.

In this contest, where every thing is already disposed in favour
of the besieged, the two contending parties may use *simple* and
overcharged mines ; the first is best suited to the defending party ;
1st, because their outward effects, which are adequate, do not
produce too deep craters ; 2d, because they may be so disposed as not to injure any other parts of the fortification ; 3d, they
consume less powder.   But the overcharged mines are the weapon for the assailing party ; they strike objects at a greater
distance, produce immense craters, and create violent inward
concussions capable of overwhelming the piers of galleries,
branches, &c. at a distance six times greater than the axis of explosion.   By means of these mines, counterscarps and scarps
are blown down into the ditches.

There are likewise distinguished in the art of mining as applied to the attack and defence, *fougasses*, and *camouflets*, with
single and overloaded chambers.   Fougasses are small mines of
little depth, and whose line of resistance is only 18 to 20 deci-

172. The dispo-
sition and distri-
bution of mines
for carrying on a
subterranean war.

Fougasses and
camouflets (See
Marshal   Vau-
ban's Treatise on
Mines, Foissac's
edition.)

mètres (6 to 6½ feet); they are used to defend large posts, and in advance of the front of attack of a fortress that has no permanent defensive galleries.   But the besieged must have time and means to prepare this kind of defence between the opening of the trenches and the arrival of the besiegers at the foot of the glacis.   The offensive mines of the besiegers are but a species of overloaded fougasse.

To establish a fougasse, a common shaft is sunk to the necessary depth, and in one of its sides the fougasse chamber is made for containing the box of powder : to this box the tarred trough containing the saucisson is affixed. This trough leads out into the covert-way or ditch or into the inside of the works by means of a trench 8 or 10 decimètres (about 3 feet) deep, along the bottom of which it is laid.   As the resistance of the soil is diminished by the sinking of the shaft, the fougasse chamber must be strongly braced and buttressed, and the branch rammed with great care.

Fougasses may be loaded with bombs filled with powder; and this ingenious method may be varied in many ways.   When only a single bomb is used to charge the fougasse, the shell itself is the best of boxes.   But when the simultaneous effects of several bombs are to be combined together, they must be enclosed in a box with a double bottom ; the upper compartment will contain the bombs, whose fusees will pass through apertures made in the division ; the lower compartment will contain the priming into which the saucisson leads ; it may even be filled with powder to produce an overcharge.   Frequently this lower compartment contains the complete charge, and the bombs are only loaded with what is required to burst them.

To estimate the effects of bomb fougasses, artillerists have ascertained the exact quantities of powder contained in each kind of bomb.

A bomb of 8 inches (8½ inches) weighs about 43 pounds (46½ lbs.); it requires 4 pounds (4½ lbs.) of powder to fill it ; but 1 pound will burst it.

A 10 inch (10½ inch) bomb weighs about 100 pounds (108 lbs.), and contains 10 pounds (nearly 11 lbs.) of powder ; but 3 pounds will burst it.

A 12 inch (13 inch) bomb weighs 148 pounds (160 lbs.), and will contain 17 pounds (18⅓ lbs.) of powder ; but 5 pounds (5½ lbs.) are sufficient to burst it.

Lastly ; the 18 inch (19$\frac{3}{4}$ inch) bomb, or *comminge*, weighs nearly 530 pounds (571 lbs.), and contains 40 pounds of powder ; a charge of 13 pounds (14 lbs.) will burst it. .

It is easy to calculate according to these data the effects of a bomb fougasse, either single or compound. Fougasses charged with a single comminge may have a line of least resistance of about 18 to 20 decimètres (6 to 6$\frac{3}{4}$ feet), and will produce a crater of about 40 decimètres (13$\frac{1}{4}$ feet).

The use of the camouflet. The *camouflet* is a small fougasse hastily made to act against the enemy's miners who are heard at work, to suffocate them and poison their branch. The *camouflet* is also used. to act against the sides of the crater of a mine that has been sprung, and which the enemy are hastening to crown and descend into. But to gain the necessary time for establishing a camouflet, a sortie must frequently be. made to throw into the crater loaded bombs with fusees that will burn a certain time.

The disposition of mines in several tiers. . Mines are disposed in one, two, or even three imaginary planes in the earth parallel to the surface of explosion, which is supposed to be plane. These separate dispositions in each plane, are called the first, second, and third tiers. The communication with each tier of mines, is by galleries or great branches properly arranged. The mode of disposing the centres of the chambers in each tier, depends upon the object to be attained. Sometimes a great area of ground is to be at once blown up, as for instance the ground occupied by a circular portion or grand battery ; at other times the ground is only to be blown up by portions and by successive explosions, as when a moderate battery, or a trench cavalier, &c. is to be destroyed ; frequently a point is to be overwhelmed several times, as for instance a trench cavalier, the head of a sap, &c. ; lastly, perhaps a line occupied by a portion of the parallel, or coronation of the covert-way, is to be blown up.

Mines arranged together, and isolated mines, disposed in one single tier. (PLATE X, figs. 3, 4 and 5.) These various ends are obtained by the effects of *mines placed together* and of *isolated mines* disposed in a single tier, and by their combination in several tiers.

Mines set together (*fourneaux accolés*) are such as are placed in the same plane and at such a distance from each other, that their craters burst into each other ; so that on these mines being simultaneously sprung, they blow up a mass (*onglet*) of earth common to both their craters. These mines are generally separated apart by a distance equal to the axis of explosion ; accordingly if the brace of mines F and F' (fig. 3) be sprung together, they will blow up the common mass MOM', and the surface projected in MP. The configuration of the earth after the explosion, is profiled nearly like *abcde*. But if the mines be sprung one after another, that is, F' after F (fig. 4); we see that the line of least resistance of F' will be $F'P$, and not the perpendicular to the plane of explosion. Its effect will therefore be laterally directed against the first crater; and the mine F' can only be considered as a kind of fougasse, or camouflet. The effect after the first explosion is profiled nearly like *abcdef*; and after the second explosion, it is like *ghklmnf*.

Mines placed together at the distance of the axis of explosion, cannot be sprung separately without great precautions in the construction and ramming of their branches; and even then the common charge must be diminished. To certainly prevent the interior concussion produced by the explosion of one mine from injuring the neighbouring mines and their branches, their respective distances must be at least once and an half the axis of explosion; and in practice, to be secure from any accident, it is adopted as a general rule, that these distances should be double the line of least resistance. *Isolated mines* or chambers are such as are disposed according to this principle on each plane of tier.

The difficulty of springing separately mines placed together.

We see that when the mines are placed together, they blow up at the same time a common mass in consequence of their craters, supposed to be right truncated cones, penetrating into each other. If therefore these mines were charged as if they were not combined, they would be uselessly overcharged; it is therefore proper to reduce their charges in relation to the volume of the common mass (*onglet*). Its volume is calculated either by common or descriptive geometry; and the half of the charge for this volume, gives the quantity that is to be diminished from the ordinary charge. When the mines are isolated, their charges are not to be reduced.

The charge for mines placed together.

Mines placed together may be disposed in any figure whatever drawn on the plane of tier; the only condition required for their explosions to be effectual, is the interval of the fires (*compassement des feux*); that is, the length of the saucisson leading from the common focus to each chamber, must be exactly the same. Thus for example; if from the focus S (fig. 6) fire is to be conveyed at the same instant to the four mines F,

The only condition to be fulfilled in springing mines placed together, however numerous and of whatever disposition. (Fig. 6.)

a double trough *xyz* may be used, affording a length of saucisson equal to *Sr*.

Application of mines placed together to blow up part of the ground occupied by a battery or lodgement. (Fig. 6.)

Let us make an application of mines placed together; and suppose the point *C* be the centre of a besieging battery of 4 pieces. By blowing up the ground around the point *C* to a distance of 45 decimètres (15 feet) in all directions, the battery will be totally destroyed and the cannon buried in the earth, &c. This effect may be obtained by the four combined mines *F*, established in the angles of a square whose side is 30 decimètres (10 feet); the line of least resistance is supposed to be 30 decimètres. We see from the projections of the craters, that the two centre pieces will be blown up and the two extreme pieces buried; and that the ground included within the curve *abcdefgha* will be so rent, that the enemy will be obliged to carry fresh earth to it, to re-establish their battery.

Reflections on the use of these mines.

Formerly great use was made of these mines, considered as defensive mines; but at present they are only used to overwhelm scarps to a great extent, and to form deep and continuous craters at points where it would be dangerous to wait until the besiegers are established to act against their works open to the heavens.

The advantages of isolated mines over the preceding.

To show the superiority of isolated mines over mines placed together, let us suppose that the four mines *F* in fig. 6, are isolated. We might begin by springing a fougasse situated at the centre *C*, and then spring each mine separately; the battery would sustain such injury from each mine, that it would be rendered unserviceable four times in succession. This shows that the besiegers will lose more time than in the first case.

Disposition and combination of isolated mines in the same plane or tier.

Isolated mines in the same plane may be combined in an infinity of ways, either to blow up several times the same point of the surface of explosion, or blow up successively the different parts of a line, or to volcanize the ground on which the enemy must establish their batteries.

Disposition and combination of isolated mines in three planes or tiers.

The defence by the springing of mines situated and combined in different planes of tiers, is generally limited to three tiers; and the depth between the third plane and the plane of explosion, is about 80 decimètres (26¾ feet). Frequently only two planes are used, including a depth of about 50 decimètres (16⅜ feet).

The manner of repeatedly blowing up the ground around a point, considered as the

Having shown in what manner mines may be properly disposed in one plane or tier, to act several times successively

centre of a battery, or cavalier, or part of a parallel. by mines disposed in three tiers or planes. (Fig. 7.)

against the ground around the point C in the plane of explosion P, P; we will now show how by disposing mines in three tiers, they may be isolated and combined in such a manner as to produce around the point C explosions, each of which will suffice to strike a panic into the troops and labourers, and greatly injure the exterior works of the attack   We will suppose that the mines may be sunk to a depth of 80 decimètres (26¾ feet) under ground.

The plane of the first tier will be 30 decimètres (10 feet) below the plane of explosion PP; and in this plane will be placed the four isolated mines M, M, M, M, situated on the ridges of a pyramid rectangular to its summit c.   The mines of the second tier will be placed on the central lines cN of the faces of the pyramid, isolating them from the mines M of the first tier.   And as they are adversely below the first, it will be sufficient to eloigne them once and an half the line of least resistance $SC = 30$ decimètres.   To obtain their vertical and horizontal projections, let fall on the vertical plane of projection the face cOO of the pyramid, by turning it round its vertical projection Co; the mines M will assume the position M': then from these latter points with a radius 45 decimètres (15 feet) or once and an half the line of least resistance, cut at N the line Co; through the point N draw $u'u'$ parallel to uu, and this will be the direction of the plane of the second tier whose line of least resistance QC will be equal to 50 decim. .4 (16¾ feet). The mines of the second tier being thus projected in N, those of the third will be placed on the ridges of the pyramid and distant from these once and an half the line of least resistance; that is, 75 decimètres .6 (25¼ feet).   To obtain their projections, draw through the points C and M' of the turned down plane the right line CM' which is the position of the ridge, and from the point N cut it again in O' with the radius $NO' = 75$ decimètres .6; then raise the point O' to o, and this latter point will be the vertical projection of the mine of the third tier. The line $u''u''$ parallel to the plane of explosion, shows the direction of the plane of the third tier.

(Fig. 7.)

The mines being isolated in each plane of tier and with respect to the several tiers, they should be sprung successively; and when the mines of one tier are exhausted, the mines of the next tier below are then sprung; and so on.   It would be well to commence by breaking up the ground around the point C with

The mode of springing these mines.

a fougasse that would not injure the chambers M in the first tier. After the total effect of all the mines, consisting of 12 successive explosions, the ground around the point C will be completely volcanized on a square of about 28 mètres (31 yards) side.

It is to be remarked with respect to the charges for the mines in the second and third tiers, that their charges must not be calculated according to the lines of least resistance obtained by their projection or calculation. They must be diminished a certain quantity, on account of the ground being convulsed and its tenacity destroyed by the mines in the upper tiers. Accordingly, the mines N must not be charged according to the line of least resistance CQ; but according to the line of least resistance $= SQ + \frac{1}{2} CS = 20$ decimètres .4 $+$ 15 $=$ 35 decimètres .4 nearly (12 feet). In the same manner the mines O will be loaded according to a line of least resistance $= RQ + \frac{1}{2} CQ = 25$ decimètres .1 $+$ 25.2 $=$ 50 decimètres .3 nearly (17 feet).

The charges for the mines in the second and third tier.

When the ground in front of the crest P of the glacis PP' is to be blown up without injuring it, we must remember that the ground about the circumference of the crater is violently convulsed; and that consequently we must sufficiently eloigne from the crest P, the point C that is to limit the effects of all the mines, and draw it at a distance of at least 5 or 6 mètres (16¾ to 20 feet). The plane CV will be drawn through the point C making an angle of 45 degrees with the plane of explosion CP'. This latter plane will be turned down in CKV, and upon this plane the mines will be disposed in two or three tiers or planes, as in the preceding case.

The disposition of mines to blow up several times the ground in advance of a glacis crest, without injuring the crest. (Fig. 8.)

It must be remarked with respect to the two preceding dispositions, that the last is not so advantageous as the first; because the mines that are to act last, are most advanced towards the country, and consequently most exposed to the offensive mines; whilst the reverse is the case in the first disposition, where the mines of the first tier are further advanced than those of the second, and these further than the third; which is conformable to the rules of defence*.

When overloaded mines make part of the arrangement of a defensive system, we must determine, according to the relation of the crater radius and the axis of explosion, the inclina-

Observations on the disposition & plan of overcharged mines

---

* This must be understood when only one (the inner) face of the pyramid, is used.   TRANSLATOR.

tion of the plane upon which the centres of the mines are to be drawn. If the mines are to be isolated, they should be distant apart a length equal to the radius of friability ; that is, at least twice and an half the axis of explosion. But most generally they are placed together and sprung simultaneously. In practice, in disposing and combining mines, attention must be paid to the quality of the ground ; and several experiments should be made to ascertain the distances that ought to be between the mines and branches, and the quantity of ramming necessary to insure the complete effect of the mines.

174. As subterranean war (170) depends upon the immediate and rapid execution of mines properly arranged, there is required an establishment of galleries, half-galleries, and branches, whose disposition and tracé form what is called a *system of defensive mines*. This part of subterranean war has for a long time exercised the ingenuity of many distinguished officers. The galleries that we have described (171) and which make part of the arrangement of a system of defensive mines, formerly called *countermines*, have various denominations according to their use, their position with respect to the fortification, and their respective positions.

174. Definitions and disposition of subterranean communications for carrying on subterranean war (PLATE X, fig. 10)

Those galleries that are inside a work and under its terraplain, were formerly called great galleries (*galeries majeures*) ; they are now called *scarp galleries*. They are generally disposed parallel to the faces and in relation to the mines made under the ditches and breaches.

The great or scarp galleries

The magistral, now called the *counterscarp* gallery, is made against the inner side of the counterscarp, and has several debouchès into the ditches. Several writers have proposed to detach it from the counterscarp, and carry it forward to beneath the banquette of the covert-way.

The magistral or counterscarp gallery : its position.

The enveloping galleries (*galeries d'enveloppe*) are those which in several systems extend under the glacis parallel to the faces and branches of the covert-way, at a certain distance beyond the crest of the glacis: there are sometimes two of them.

The enveloping galleries.

Galleries of communication are those which lead from the magistral to the enveloping galleries, and from one enveloping gallery to another.

Galleries of communication.

Transverse galleries are those that connect together the longitudinal galleries, which are substituted for galleries of communication in those systems where enveloping galleries are not used.

Transverse galleries.

Listening galleries.
Listening galleries are longitudinal galleries leading out into the country in certain directions from the magistral and transverse or enveloping galleries.

Definition of a system of defensive mines.
Formerly they called *systems of counter-mines*, what are now styled *systems of defensive mines.* These consist of the more or less advantageous combinations that the engineer miner may make of the various kinds of galleries, to organize the subterranean war of a front of attack.

The necessity of permanent galleries in organizing subterranean warfare.
It was long a subject of dispute, whether it was proper to establish in time of peace the principal galleries that make part of the arrangement of a system. By some it was contended that if this was done, the enemy would obtain a knowledge of them and conduct their attack accordingly. Their opponents alleged the impracticability of constructing such great subterranean works at the moment that a fortress is threatened, or even in time of war. At present all military engineers and miners are of opinion, that it is necessary to construct the principal galleries in a permanent manner ; and that in new places, they should be constructed at the same time with the fortress.

The relation between subterraneous fortification and exterior fortification.
Subterranean fortification is evidently an appendage of exterior fortification, and is one of the chief accessory means to greatly increase the resistance of the latter. It is a tremendous obstacle that the besiegers must vanquish before they can succeed in taking and crowning the covert-way.

Consideration of the measures of the attack in organizing subterranean fortification.
The organization of subterranean fortification is, like exterior fortification, deduced from the means of attack that the besiegers may employ. These means consist of, 1st, the trenches and batteries, whose progress and plan may be modified to a certain extent ; 2d, the use of overloaded mines or globes of compression, which are the real countermines ; and by the use of which the besiegers may, with time and fortitude, destroy the defensive mines and branches, and even the galleries.

The proper situations for subterranean war.
The works for subterranean war are not of a nature to be far distant from the fortification ; 1st, because it would be difficult to establish in galleries of too great extent, the circulation of air necessary in subterranean tactics; 2d, because beyond the third parallel the position of the besiegers' works is so uncertain, that we cannot calculate to injure them by mines, which the besiegers have every opportunity to destroy. But this is not the case during the period of the near defence ; here the works of the attack are confined, the progress of the besiegers

has become slow and cautious, the forms of their works have become more complex, and their position is foreseen with sufficient accuracy to be able to rightly establish the mines. It follows from these considerations, that the contests of subterranean war should not be carried beyond the glacis : and this is also the opinion of the ablest engineers and miners.

A fortification to be susceptible of dispositions for subterranean war, must possess several essential conditions to ensure the efficacy of subterranean fortification : 1st, the fortress must be sufficiently strong in itself to prevent the enemy from attempting it at the first onset : 2d, the nature of the fortifications must be such, that the time elapsing between the opening of the trenches and the third parallel, must be sufficiently long for executing all the labours requisite to arrange the mines, the listening galleries, and the service of subterranean tactics: these works cannot be begun until the front of attack is known, and the directions of the trenches accurately determined : 3d, the strata of earth through which the galleries and branches pass, must be dry and free from water or springs. This kind of war is not adapted to all fortresses ; because of the great supplies of timber, gun-powder, and implements required for its execution. But it is strictly applicable to fortresses of the first and second orders, especially when they are reduced to two or three fronts of attack ; or in the case of well-constituted detached works, which the enemy are compelled to reduce by gradual approaches.

Preliminary conditions that a fortress must fulfil to be susceptible of subterranean warfare.

As all the dispositions for executing a subterraneous war have their origin in the great or counterscarp gallery ; it follows that if the covert-way be liable to be taken by storm, the besiegers may make such an attack after forming the third parallel, and thus capture the whole system of mines prepared under the glacis. In the present state of fortification, the covert-ways are not sufficiently strong and secure ; and whenever the fronts that they cover can be ricoched, they may be considered as liable to be carried by storm in consequence of the great power that the attack at present possesses over them. Accordingly it has become necessary to improve this essential part of fortification.

Consequences and important reflections on covert-ways.

Systems of defensive mines are formed by the combination and use of several kinds of galleries, to establish under the glacis and inside of works a permanent disposition enabling the

The relation of systems of defensive mines with the measures of the attack.

besieged to organize a subterranean war even at the very moment of siege. It is in respect to this kind of defence, as of all others, its arrangement must be deduced from the measures of the attack ; and consequently from the exterior progress of the besiegers, and from a knowledge of the effects of offensive mines. These latter mines are the globes of compression with which the besiegers endeavour to destroy the defensive mines, before they carry on their approaches on the ground under which they know that they are established.

The principal sieges at which defensive mines were employed.

Amongst the sieges that were longest protracted by the use of mines, that of Bergen-op-zoom in 1747, is distinguished. The springing of defensive mines and the subterranean tactics, confined the besiegers more than a month on the glacis without their being able to crown the covert-way or batter in breach the body of the place. But in this siege, as in all those preceding, simple mines only were used. It was at the siege of Schweidnitz, in 1762, that the Prussian engineer Lefebvre made a trial for the first time of the use of overcharged mines ; he expected from the experiments made by order of the great Frederick, that their effects would procure him great advantages. It was fortunate that this defence was conducted on the part of the Austrians by the celebrated Gribeauval. This attack and defence, conducted by two officers so eminently skilful in the war of sieges, has presented facts and results that have greatly improved the practical theory of subterranean war.

The principal results drawn from experiments and from what occurred at Schweidnitz.

Three principal results are deduced from the experiments made relative to the circumambient action of overcharged mines, and from what occurred at the siege of Schweidnitz.

1st, Overloaded mines, or globes of compression, act with effect against galleries or branches that present a flank to their action, and are capable of destroying them at a distance of 5 or 6 times the axis of explosion. They are therefore a terrible weapon in the hands of the besiegers when the arrangement of the systems of defensive mines presents a flank to the exterior progress of the attack.

2d, The action of overcharged mines does not produce any great effect against those galleries and branches that point directly or very obliquely towards them ; especially when care is taken to ram a proper length of the most exposed parts. This important fact was very remarkable at the siege of Schweidnitz.

3d, It is not a very easy operation for the besieged to establish globes of compression in ground guarded by listening galleries skilfully disposed, that compel them to sink their shafts and attacking galleries to a great depth.

The moment that the besiegers find themselves compelled to undertake a subterranean war, they must dig down under the ground on which they are to approach, and drive the besieged from their mines.   To effect this, there are two modes, which they will use according to their knowledge of the arrangement of the defensive mines.   If they know that the subterranean defensive system is composed of enveloping galleries, they must endeavour to ascertain their position and make above them portions of parallels or lodgements, and burst them in with a few barrels of powder; they will also use globes of compression which take these galleries in flank and break them open in every quarter: they will then penetrate into the galleries and expel the enemy from them by main force.   But if they cannot thus attack the defensive mines, they can then only sink shafts and galleries to establish globes of compression and destroy and disorganize the mines of the besieged. *The procedures of the attack with respect to subterranean war.*

We see from the relation that exists between the attack and the defence in subterranean war, that if its elements be well disposed, it will suspend for a more or less considerable length of time the exterior efforts and necessarily rapid progress of the besiegers; and that the effects of globes of compression, estimating them at their just value, are not of a nature that should cause to be abandoned this powerful means of strengthening the attackable fronts and detached works of a fortress.   But in order to obtain these advantages in favour of the defence, the elements for executing a subterranean war must be arranged according to subterraneous tactics founded on a practical theory that requires to be perfected by well directed experiments. *The advantages of the besieged in subterranean war.*

The galleries composing a system of defensive mines, possess properties dependent on their position with respect to the fortification and exterior march of the attacks. *Characteristics of the various kinds of galleries*

The counterscarp gallery is the general debouché of all the other parts of a system.   'Tis through this that the passages lead to all the other parts, and air is conveyed and circulated to sustain the lives of the defending troops.   It should therefore have numerous outlets in the ditches.

The counter-scarp gallery: its position.

Military writers have differed in opinion respecting the position of the great gallery. Some would have it under the crest of the glacis or beneath the banquette of the covert-way; in order that when the enemy get possession of it, it may not favour their passage of the ditch. Others think that it should be made against the counterscarp, so as to preserve it 'till the last moment; taking care to make loop-holes in the roundings of the counter-scarp, and a species of place of arms to maintain a post in. As it is evident that in any other position the gallery would be more easily destroyed by offensive mines and would tempt the enemy to try to carry the covert-way by storm, all opinions are now united on this important point.

The advantages of substituting relieving revetements for great galleries.

General Marescot's idea of substituting for the great gallery, vaults with relieving revêtements (*revêtemens en décharge*), is most admirable.

These vaults would serve for galleries, magazines, places of arms, &c.; and they would afford invaluable shelters for the daily manœuvres of the defence.

Longitudinal galleries.

The longitudinal galleries, which include the listening galleries (*écoutes*), are from their position the most advantageous, because they present but a point to the offensive mines. Care must however be taken to dispose them in such a manner, that the besiegers cannot take them in flank.

Enveloping galleries.

Enveloping galleries are now generally proscribed; because the besigers may attack them from above ground at as many points as they choose, and because they present a flank to offensive mines.

Transverse galleries.

Transverse galleries are necessary to form currents of air in the longitudinal galleries; but they have the essential defect of presenting a flank to the march of the enemy. They must accordingly be protected by listening galleries, and covered by a disposition of mines whose last explosions will destroy and render them impracticable to the besiegers.

The distance under ground at which galleries are uninhabitable.

Experience has proved that in most soils galleries cease to be habitable at a distance of about 35 to 40 mètres (39 to 44¼ yards) from their debouchès in the open air; because at this distance the air becomes unfit for respiration, lights extinguish, and the men are soon struck senseless to the earth.

Consequence respecting the disposition of galleries.

This fact shows that in the disposition of galleries, the ventilator or some other means must be often employed to introduce fresh air; but it is preferable to combine the longitudinal and transverse galleries in such a manner as to procure currents of air, which enable the miners to circulate through them and work at all points.

The following are the general principles that should guide an officer in arranging a system of defensive mines: General rules for arranging a system of defensive mines.

1st. To arrange the system correlatively to the fortifications above ground, and place them in the most immediate relations.

2d. To give to the general tracé of the galleries a disposition favourable to a subterranean war whose execution must be prompt and very simple.

3d. Never to present a flank to the march of the attack; but to establish the mines in such a manner that they will form salients and re-enterings where the enemy may be always anticipated and easily cut off. This arrangement will diminish the success of their globes of compression as much as possible.

4th. To combine the longitudinal and transverse galleries to obtain currents of air, &c.

5th. To dispose the same galleries in such a manner, that those which lead to one disposition of mines, shall be independent of those that lead to another disposition.

6th. To dispose the mines in such a manner, that the enemy can never penetrate into galleries that can be no longer used; that is, the last explosions of a first disposition must destroy the galleries that lead to it, or they must be destroyed by the first explosions of the following and less advanced disposition.

7th. To embrace sufficient space before the salients, in order to be certain that the enemy will come in contact with the listening galleries and mines, even when they carry on their approaches on other directions than the capitals, and on directions different from those followed when there are no mines.

8th. To oppose the greatest obstacles to the construction of cavaliers, counter-batteries, batteries-in-breach, descents of ditches, &c.

9th. To establish mines under the breaches, to make them precipitous.

10th. Lastly; to establish under the ditches, galleries of communication leading to and uniting in a great souterrain under the gorge of the bastion.

175. The most celebrated writers who have written on subterranean war and proposed systems of defensive mines, are, 175. The systems of defensive mines hitherto invented & used.

Goulon, General Vallière, Belidor, Cormontaigne, and Rugy. Among the most modern writers are distinguished, the Prussian engineer Lefebvre, Etienne, Mouzé, and General Marescot. The numerous Memoirs of Mouzé, and those of General Marescot, contain new discoveries and principles that establish the practical theory of the art upon more certain bases, and render it of more easy application.

Goulon's system.   Goulon's system is solely composed of one counterscarp gallery made under the terra-plain of the covert-way, and from which listening galleries lead as far as the foot of the glacis. Galleries of communication are made under the ditches, and communicate with the great gallery. He justly rejected the use of enveloping galleries. But the defective position of his magistral gallery, and the weakness of the listening galleries in which even the air cannot circulate, render his system very weak, especially when the front of attack can be ricoched.

Vallière's system.   The system reputed to be General Vallière's, is composed of a magistral gallery made under the terra-plain of the covert-way, two enveloping galleries (one of which is 30 mètres and the other 100 (33 and 111 yards) distant from the salients), and galleries of communication; some of the latter lead under the capitals of the re-entering places of arms, whilst the others are parallel and at 20 mètres (22 yards) from the capitals of the salients. By these dispositions the glacis is divided into squares of 40 mètres side (44¼ yards), and under which mines are established in several tiers. What we have said suffices to show the weakness of this system, whose enveloping galleries are easily attacked and ruined by the besiegers, and whose capture must be followed by the loss of the mines before it is possible to make use of them.

Belidor's system.   Belidor proposed another system. He places the great gallery beneath the terra-plain of the covert-way, and an enveloping gallery at the foot of the glacis; but the first is 33 decimètres (11 feet) above the latter. The galleries of communication lead from the enveloping, and passing under the great gallery, debouche into the ditch. Listening galleries (écoutes) lead from and cover the enveloping gallery. This system possesses this advantage over the others—that the listeners which cover the enveloping gallery, render the attack upon it longer and more difficult: but when once this attack succeeds, all the rest oppose but a feeble resistance.

Cormontaigne's
memoirs on
mines.

All Cormontaigne's memoirs on mines suppose the establishment of longitudinal and transverse galleries, forming squares of about 40 or 50 mètres (44¼ to 55¼ yards) side. Under these squares dispositions of mines are made in several tiers, which volcanize the ground so repeatedly, that if this plan were executed the exterior march of the attack would become absolutely impracticable. The attack in its present state, armed with overcharged mines, pays no respect to these preparations so formidable in appearance, and enveloped with transverse galleries, which the besiegers meet and take in flank before they are exposed to the action of the combined mines.

Delorme's sys-
tem.

Not one of the systems that we have just described, has been fully executed. Delorme, a French miner, has displayed under the glacis of the double crown of Belle-Croix, at Metz, an immense system of galleries whose use and properties he has not made known. These galleries form squares of 60 mètres (67 yards) side, and are doubtless intended for mines disposed in several tiers agreeably to Cormontaigne's plans. This complicated and expensive display of galleries, is not at all combined according to the rules of the attack, which might be carried on in directions where it would be very difficult for the besieged miners to much retard the approaches. Besides, the globes of compression would be most efficient against such a system.

De Rugy's sys-
tem.

M. De Rugy, commandant of miners, caused to be constructed at Verdun a more complete and better combined system. He rejects the enveloping galleries used by Vallière, Cormontaigne, Belidor and Delorme, and follows Goulon's method. His system, the combination of which is simple, consists of a great gallery placed against the counterscarp, and listening and transverse galleries, which lead to the execution of the following disposition of mines; 1st, a disposition against the howitzer batteries of the third parallel: 2d, two dispositions, each of three tiers under the capitals: 3d, a disposition beneath the trench cavaliers and stone-mortar batteries opposite to the re-entering places of arms: 4th, a disposition under the batteries-in-breach and counter-flank batteries: 5th, a disposition beneath the breaches, to blow up their ruins. This system would sufficiently satisfy all the conditions of the defence, if it did not invariably suppose that the march of the attack is confined to fixed and unchangeable positions; and as this is not the case, the besiegers may take the parts of this system in flank, avoid them, or destroy them by globes of compression.

Remarks on the nature and use of mines made under the coronation of the covert-way.

In the systems hitherto used, and in those that we have just sketched, mines are disposed against the crowning of the covert-way and against the breach and counter-flank batteries. But it is conformable to the progress of the present state of the attack, to consider this operation as impracticable ; because the besiegers by means of offensive mines will have destroyed this last resource, if the besieged wait until they effect the coronation. It is therefore better to regard these mines as a means of breaking up the earth, without injuring the crest of the glacis. The besiegers will in this case experience infinite trouble to establish their lodgements and batteries of breach and counter-flank upon ground thus volcanized.

Mouzé's systems. (PLATE X, fig. 11.)

Subsequent to all the systems that we have described, appeared the learned Memoirs of M. Mouzé, which have irradiated this branch of fortification with more luminous and certain principles. For a long time a few of these manuscript memoirs were known to several officers ; and we have now arrived at a period when we shall behold them generally diffused, and become the subject of the studies of young officers. Mouzé in the application of his general principles for establishing subterranean war, does not carry his operations further than the foot of the glacis. He uses a great gallery made against the counterscarp, longitudinal and transverse galleries, and galleries of communication, which he combines and directs in such a manner that the enemy cannot take them in flank and attack them without first sustaining the effects of dispositions of mines. Upon each salient that the enemy must crown, he makes three dispositions ; two of which, A, A and B, B, advanced, are of two or three tiers of isolated and independent mines. The third disposition R, R is against the crowning of the covert-way, if made by gradual approaches ; or to break up and volcanize the ground at a distance of 6 mètres (20 feet) from the crest of the glacis. When an attack by storm on the covert-way is dreaded, a disposition Q, Q is made to blow up the enemy's lodgement and defend the counterscarp gallery. The front of each advanced disposition A, A, B, B, is sufficiently extended to prevent the besiegers from taking it in flank. The two first tiers of mines, f and f', are independent ; but those f'', of the third tier, are not. It is necessary in order to establish this latter disposition, to eloigne the mines of the two first tiers further from each other; this will leave too great wedges (*quilles*) of earth untouched. If the mines *f''* of the third tier be isolated, mines set together must be placed in the first and second tiers.

Mouzé ingeniously proposes to direct under the capital of the salient, the gallery *G G*, consisting of two galleries established against each other, and having a common pier. This gallery along the capital leads to a souterrain which serves as a general depôt for the first disposition and produces a current of air, without which the service would here be difficult and dangerous. The souterrain *a* might without any inconvenience have a shaft debouching on the surface of the glacis.

In the transverse galleries and opposite the galleries of communication, shafts *x, x,* &c. are excavated; and from these great listening branches *xc* lead and by a gentle slope gain the lowest points that the enemy can reach, keep them in check from their first works, compel them to make vast excavations to establish their globes of compression and to keep them at such a distance that they will not be able to affect the mines of the first tier. These listening branches *xc* might, by giving them the proper slope, be made on the prolongation of the galleries of communication; but it is better to make them independent by means of shafts.

From the souterrain *S*, constructed under the gorge of the bastion, to the foot of the glacis, the galleries communicate and combine with each other in an easy and simple manner; and there must be in them a free circulation of air. The besieged by means of the listening galleries can anticipate the enemy in every quarter; so that the latter cannot advance their works without first (if we may so express it) pulverizing the ground on which they are to approach and establish their lodgements and batteries.

General Marescot, in his last Memoir on Subterranean War, applies it by a very ingenious system to the defence of a fortified front. He suppresses the counterscarp gallery, to substitute in its place a relieving revêtement, the numerous advantages of which we have already shown. From the bottom *M* of the relieving vaults, a plane *MN* is drawn with a gentle slope as far as the foot of the glacis, and to as great a depth as the soil will permit; that is, 11 to 13 mètres (36⅔ to 43⅓ feet). It is upon

Marescot's system. (See No. 11 of the *Journal de L'Ecole Polytechnique*.) (PLATE X, figs. 12 and 13.)

this plane thus disposed, that this author establishes all his permanent and listening galleries. He suppresses the enveloping, and even the transverse galleries ; retaining only the galleries of communication and listeners.   These are disposed in the lozengal form, as is shown in the figure ; and in this disposition, they always present themselves directly or obliquely to the action of the offensive mines.

The lozenges are so drawn as to make their angles sufficiently acute, and that the listeners will not be at a greater distance than 20 to 25 mètres (67 to 83 feet) ; in order that the hostile miners may be closely watched and always anticipated.   The galleries of communication unite together in a kind of small circular souterrains, which are favourable for the execution of a subterranean war.   The intermediate souterrains may without any inconvenience have small air holes debouching on the surface of the glacis.

General dispo-
sition   of   the
mines in this sys-
tem.   (Fig. 13.)

In this system, the approaches of the glacis may be defended by three dispositions of mines.   The first, in three tiers, will be directed against the third parallel ; the second, likewise of three tiers, will act against the fourth parallel and trench cavaliers, &c. ; and the third, of one or two tier, is to blow up the batteries of breach and counter-flank, and to volcanize the ground in front of the crest of the glacis.   The mines in the first and second disposition, are arranged in parallel files on the directions of the listeners and on the intermediate lines.   The half-galleries and branches of each tier, are independent of each other ; and the listeners may be sufficiently prolonged to watch the first labours of the enemy, and anticipate them in establishing their globes of compression against the first disposition. With respect to the second, shafts must be made in the galleries to sink the listening branches as low as possible.

It will be very instructing for the students to compare together these two systems that we have described ; and to remark how their inventors have by very different combinations succeeded in conforming to the most general principles, and in rendering the subterranean tactics of the defence far superior to those of the attack.   We could not follow more luminous courses to introduce the students to the study of this interesting branch of fortification, in which there yet remains doubts to be cleared up ; and consequently many difficulties to vanquish, and numerous glorious labours to accomplish.

CHAPTER IX.

The Principles upon which must be founded all Improvements in the Systems of Fortification.

176. HAVING completed the description and examination of the elements constituting fortification, and which now make its arrangement very complex ; we will briefly take a general review of this arrangement, to ascertain the extent of knowledge to which officers of the line should attain, and from what point officers of engineers and artillery should set out to enter into those more profound and detailed considerations that are the subject of instruction in the schools of practice.

176. General reflections on fortification and the combination of elements that should constitute its arrangement.

All that we have developed in the preceding chapters, has led us to consider that the arrangement of a complete system of fortification requires the combination of four essential elements, vizt. : 1st, The *covering masses*, consisting of revêtements, parapets and traverses : 2d, *Casemates, crenated galleries* and *blindages*, to obtain covered fires : 3d, *Galleries of defensive mines :* 4th, *Bomb-proof buildings*, including magazines of all kinds, and defensive caserns whose use we are about to describe.

The four elements of which a system of fortification must be composed.

Defensive caserns are those that are established on the fronts, and which for instance, close up the gorges of bastions and serve at the same time as an interior intrenchment and as quarters for the troops. Nothing has as yet appeared of a satisfactory nature on this important object of defence ; but the encouragement held out by government, and the zeal of a great number of enlightened officers whose attention is occupied by the progress of the science, will doubtless soon lead to the invention of plans founded upon economy, salubrity and strength.

Reflections on defensive caserns.

In the disposition of the covering masses in the ancient systems, the direct fires were only attended to ; and there are even some modern systems, all the parts of whose tracés are exposed to enfilading fires. This is the case with Carnot's ; the merit of this scientific system depends on covered and concealed reverse fires, and on the manœuvres for operations without. The other modern systems, excepting Carnot's and Montalembert's, are arranged in relation to ricochet fires, and to shield

The disposition of covering masses with respect to direct and ricochet fires.

the body of the place from the terrible effects of these fires whose execution has been so perfected in theory and practice. Indeed experience has confirmed what the theory of projectiles indicated ; that by varying the charges and the small angles of inclination, three enfilading batteries may be established on a length of 500 mètres (556 yards), whose effects might be simultaneous without injury to each other; that is, the face of a work may be ricoched by three batteries established at the points where its prolongation cuts the three parallels of the attack.

Consequences.
We must therefore in the modern bastioned system endeavour, 1st, to arrange the tracé in such a manner that the body of the place will be secure from ricochet fires ; 2d, to find means of preserving artillery and troops upon the terra-plains of those works whose faces are enfiladed.

Near vertical
fires ; shelters on
the terra-plains
The prodigious use made of near vertical fires is another improvement in the attack that necessitates making coverts (abris) on the terra-plains of works, and without which the necessary service of the defence cannot be there performed.

Casemated or
blinded traverses, and blinded
batteries, made
upon all the terra-plains.
Two dispositions on the terra-plains will render the service of the defence in them practicable : 1st, Casemated traverses will shelter the troops there from all fires ; they may in these prepare for battle, and move out at any moment that it is required to open fires on the trenches.   2d, Blinded batteries will preserve their artillery, which will then only be counterbattered by direct batteries.   It is not a numerous, but a well disposed artillery that produces great effects on the works of the attack.

Reflections on
the troops sheltered in the terra-plains ;   the
service of troops
in a work.
It has been objected, that it would damp the courage of soldiers to keep them thus continually lying close within blinded or casemated traverses.   But fortification only fulfils its object in proportion as it secures the troops from inevitable destruction when they are not fighting.   There are certainly occasions enough to inure them to dangers, by operations and sallies against the enemy ; and it is surely more advantageous to lose men in sorties to level the works of the attack, than to expose a brave soldiery to be maimed and destroyed in works ploughed and cut up by ricochet and vertical fires.   The troops who defend an assailed work, act against the enemy with their fires, and sometimes with their swords and bayonets ; their fire should therefore be regulated in such a manner, that one third of the

troops fire, whilst the other two thirds are reposing or cleaning their arms.   Hence, the coverts or shelters of a work should contain at least two thirds of the proper garrison.

We have repeatedly said, that casemated batteries should only be employed when the masonry parapet cannot be counter-battered; but they may be made use of to advantage by establishing their vaults behind a bank of earth 6 mètres (20 feet) thick, with embrasures made in it.   The piers of the vaults will be prolonged as far as the slope of the earth, to support the timbers of the top of the embrasures.

The kinds of casemated and blinded batteries. (See Mandar's and Bousmard's works.)

The blinded batteries of which Count Carnot made a trial at St. Omers, are of this description ; except that they were constructed with timbers.   They resisted the concussions of the artillery.   Both have the inconvenience of very widened embrasures, which in weakening the epaulment increase the number of embrasure shots.   Therefore, batteries, the front of whose embrasures consists of a mass of heavy timbers joined together, should be preferred to them.   This mass should be 13 decimètres ($4\frac{1}{3}$ feet) thick ; and the embrasures are cut in the form of loop-holes, in order that the chace of the piece may extend beyond the exterior of the epaulment.   When the piece is a howitzer, or a mortar mounted on a carriage, the embrasure is made with a suitable opening.   If it be intended to make use of General Meusnier's carriages for batteries of an extensive field, a working pintle is placed 4 decimètres (16 inches) from the genouillère.   These batteries have the advantage of being sunk into the parapet, of not being exposed to ricochet fires, and of presenting to the exterior an opening of so small a surface, that the embrasure shots may be regarded as nothing.   They however require great quantities of large timber for their construction ; the epaulment pieces must be 50 decimètres ($16\frac{3}{4}$ feet) long, and square by 40 by 40 centimètres (16 by 16 inches).   Accordingly for one battery there will be required a length of timber of 812 decimètres (271 feet) ; and for the 20 batteries necessary on a front of attack, there will be required 16,240 decimètres (5,420 feet).   This quantity of heavy timber should not discourage us, for it may be obtained from about 300 trunks of trees (*pieds d'arbres*).

(PLATE XI, fig. 1.)

If the enemy attempt to burn with hot shot the wooden parapets of the batteries, it is proved by experience that this is easily prevented : for by making the timber parapets 48 to 50 inches thick (51 to 54 inches), shot of heavy calibers can never penetrate through them.

Recapitulation of the value of the systems of fortification now in use.
The relation established between the attack and the defence, shows, 1st, that the great powers of vertical fires are much more favourable to the attack, than to the defence ; and that they secure to the former a rapid and imperative progress ; 2d, that all the systems oppose about an equal degree of resistance during the first period of the siege, provided they afford cross-fires upon the capitals, &c. If on one hand those systems whose batteries are open to the heavens, are exposed to rico-chet and vertical fires ; on the other, systems with *casemated galleries* and *constructed in masonry* are speedily ruined, and their fires extinguished from the second parallel.

Important consequences.
It follows, that it is chiefly for the period of the near defence that a system should be constituted and organized.

General principles on the organization of systems of fortification.
We may deduce from the preceding the following principles, to guide officers in the arrangement of a system :

1st, If the system be open to the heavens, the body of the place should be defiled in the best possible manner from the ricochet fires that take effect from the first moment of the siege to the last.

2d. The system should possess covered artillery fires, to be used during the period of the near defence. These fires should be shielded from the direct batteries of the attack, and should take in flank and reverse the lodgements upon the crest of the glacis : it should only be possible to coun-ter-batter them from the very positions that they batter.

3d. Each part of the system should have coverts properly disposed for the protection of the troops who defend it ; in or-der that they may be secure from vertical fires during the time that they are not required to act.

4th. All the intrenchments that make part of the system, should be beyond the reach of insult ; and the besiegers must be under the necessity of attacking them by gradual approach-es.   If this condition cannot be strictly fulfilled, the attack by storm should necessitate great sacrifices on the part of the enemy.

5th. All those parts that are not efficaciously flanked by the parapets, must be flanked by crenated galleries that the enemy cannot counter-batter.

6th. Subterranean war will be used as a necessary element.

and disposed with such art that it will be impossible for the besiegers to establish breach and counter-batteries without first
undertaking and sustaining the long and painful operations of
subterraneous war, or being compelled to have recourse as a
substitute to offensive mines.

7th. The enemy should not be able to discover the body of
the place until they have made themselves masters of the outworks.

8th The covert-ways should facilitate and protect sorties,
and favour the manœuvres of an active defence.

9th. The relief and commandment must be arranged in such
a manner, that all the parts will be covered as well as possible,
and without impeding the display of the artillery and musketry
fires deemed necessary for defending the exterior ground and
the interior of the works.

By applying to modern bastioned fortification these general
principles, we shall discover the causes of its weakness :

Application of these principles to modern bastioned fortification.

1st. It is only in very high polygons, and in fronts disposed
on a right line, that fortification acquires the advantage of
having the body of the place secure from ricochets, and of
forming considerable re-enterings. The near works of the attack may then be seen in flank and reverse, the covert-way
cannot be seized and insulted throughout its whole extent, and
the manœuvres of a sortie are efficiently protected.

2d. The fortification being entirely open to the heavens, batteries cannot be preserved unimpaired for the most critical period of the siege, from the commencement of which the troops
in it are exposed to ricochet fires, and during the near defence
to vertical fires that render the terra-plains untenable. The
defence can therefore be but feeble and spiritless, because it
will be excessively perilous. Accordingly the covert-ways are
not secure from being carried by assault, and the troops in them
are broken at the moment when they should contend with the
bayonet.

3d. The body of the place is discovered and battered in breach
through the openings of the ditches of the ravelin and of its redoubt, and of the tenaille, even before these works are carried.

4th. The flanking is imperfect and bad in front of the tenaille,
and in the ditches of the ravelin and of its redoubt.

177. The improvements that might be introduced into the arrangement of modern bastioned fortification.

177. To form an idea of the improvements of which the modern bastioned system is susceptible, we will resume the general march of the attack, and show how the defects that we have just exposed may be corrected and the system acquire the general and essential properties of a well-arranged system.

As from the first days of the siege the prolongations of the faces of all the works may be seized and ricoched by batteries that will plough up their terra-plains, &c. ; it is necessary to mask the most important prolongations, and consequently to so arrange the tracé of the horizontal projection that the ravelins will intercept the directions of the bastion faces in all polygons of a medium extent. And as the ravelins and their covert-ways are necessarily very much exposed to ricochets, traverses vaulted bomb-proof must be established in them to contain two-thirds of the garrison and cover the flanks of the batteries. Their salients must also be occupied by blinded batteries made of timber.

The first mode of correcting the tracé, to defend the bastion-faces from ricochets (PLATE XI, fig. 2) (See the Supplement to Bousmard.)

There are two modes of shielding the bastion-faces from ricochets ; and both methods are very ingenious. The first was proposed by Bousmard, and consists in detaching the ravelin from the body of the place and carrying it forward 55 to 60 mètres (61 to 67 yards) in front of the crest of the glacis ; taking care to unmask the flanks of the redoubt, so that they will take in reverse the approaches of the bastions and collateral ravelins. The ravelin covers the whole front, and the bottom of its ditches is in the prolongation of the glacis of the body of the place. The flanked angles of the bastions are curvilinear ; and the bastion faces are convex to the exterior, and are drawn as if they were each the evolute (*développée*) of the opposite flank, which is preserved concave. The gorge of the ravelin, and of its redoubt, are provided with crenated galleries communicating with the body of the place. These counterscarp galleries have manifold uses ; 1st, they make part of the subterraneous warfare ; 2d, they afford secure communications during the whole duration of the siege ; 3d, they enable the garrison to blow up the ravelin and ravelin-redoubt terra-plains at the moment that the enemy gain possession of them, &c. The ravelin itself is a complex work ; and is, with respect to the redoubt, two tenaillons covered by a redan : the faces of this redan are the only parts that the enemy can protract. By this modification of the modern system, many other advantages, independent of the consideration of ricochet fires, are obtained. The ravelins, even in medium polygons, form sallies that place the bastions in so great a re-entering, that the march of the attack must be sustained by six parallels before the covert-way of the body of the place can be crowned. But we must remark, 1st, that the musketry of the bastions cannot be effective against the crowning of the ravelin salient, because the length of the line of fire exceeds 300 mètres (335 yards); 2d, that the bastion faces do not take in reverse or even enfilade the branches of the ravelin covert-way; nevertheless we must observe at the same time, that these parts are taken in reverse by the flanks of the collateral ravelin redoubts, which should be armed with batteries firing canister; 3d, that the inside of the terra-plains are not provided with shelters to cover their separate garrisons and their service; 4th, that it is practicable (leaving out of view subterranean war) for a daring enemy to carry the ravelins by storm from their fourth parallel : this latter consideration shows that the crenated counterscarp galleries are indispensable.

The second method of shielding the body of the place of the bastioned system from ricochets, is contained in Mouzés memoirs. It consists in obtaining for polygons of moderate extent, for instance the enneagon, the decagon, &c., the properties of very high polygons; and for these latter, those of fronts disposed on a right line. To effect this, it is sufficient to increase the number of the polygonal sides and diminish the length of the exterior side, without disturbing the flanking and other relations of the disposition.

Second method of correcting the trace of the modern system. (PLATE XI, fig. 3.)

Let the line bd be the base of the ravelin, which must not exceed 200 mètres, in order that the bastion faces may afford effective fires on the coronation of the ravelin salient. On bd the equilateral ravelin bgd will be constructed, and bg will be the covering line. Through the points b and d of the covering lines of the bastion faces, draw the lines of defence bo, do, making the diminished angles 18° 30′ as in the common tracé. Inside of the point b take $bc = 30$ mètres (33 yards), to obtain the shoulder-angle and flank, &c. ; and without the point b take a quantity ba which must not be less than the distance included between the ravelin covering line and the crest of the glacis : we will suppose this distance to be 40 mètres (44½ yards). Through the flanked angle a and the angle g of the ravelin draw the right line *gam*, which will give the flanked angle of the bastion and the angle of the defensive polygon. The tracé and calculation show that the exterior side is equal to 282 mètres (314 yards), that the flanked angle is 112 degrees, and that the angle of the polygon is 148°. Accordingly the result of this tracé is a polygon of 11 sides, nearly equivalent to the common nonagon ; and the bastions of which are retired into such great re-enterings, that their faces are intercepted by the salients of the ravelins. The farther the point *g* is removed into the interior of the ravelin, the higher will be the polygon and the better will the bastion faces be defiled. This tracé is adapted to all local circumstances, and these the engineer should know how to seize with ability ; and if it increase the number of capitals, this inconvenience vanishes before the great advantages that make it so superior to the common tracé.

Coverts to protect the troops & favour the sorties ; the great counterscarp gallery ; the counterscarps with relieving vaults.

In proportion as the attacks approach the place, the ricochets become more effectual and the vertical fires more numerous ; but the sorties also become more vigorous and frequent. Hence it follows, that there should be *coverts* (*abris*) properly disposed to cover the troops on duty in the terra-plains, and for the corps of reserve that are to make sorties. The coverts for the reserves and *bivouacs* may be made in the counterscarp gallery; by making it 25 to 30 decimètres (8½ to 10 feet) wide and with numerous debouchés into the ditches : this gallery will at the same time answer for organizing the subterranean war. But it is far preferable, on account of the reasons already explained, to construct the counterscarps with relieving vaults which will afford more spacious coverts and be more favourable for the manœuvres of the troops. With respect to the coverts of the terra-plains of the covert-ways and other works, they can only be composed of traverses vaulted bomb-proof and terraced on the side facing the enemy's artillery. In many circumstances these masses may be organized into defensive traverses, either by crowning them with parapets, or making loop-holes in their piers, or making in them low crenated galleries.

The alterations to be made in the covert-ways, and in other parts of the system : reflections on the attacks from the half places of arms.

The ravelins in the bastioned system, and the branches that form the salients in the angular systems, are inevitably exposed to ricochets. This cannot be remedied but by traverses, which will at the same time defile them and serve as coverts. The salient of each ravelin must completely cover the redoubt by its relief, and will be armed with blinded batteries ; that portion of the ravelin faces corresponding to the line of fire of the redoubt faces, will have less relief than the salient; it will unmask the blinded batteries of the redoubt that will take in reverse the glacis and salients of the collateral ravelins.

To advance regularly in the improvement of the various elements of the system, let us follow the measures of the attack, whose march is from its nature imperative. As soon as the besiegers have laid out the half places of arms, they establish mortar and howitzer batteries that more powerfully ricochè the covert-ways, &c. ; they endeavour to sieze the prolongations of the bastion flanks, to ricochè them at the same time ; and the proximity of the works aids them in this operation, &c.

It follows, that it is much better to draw the flanks in concave curves ; that they must be covered by a traverse established at the shoulder-angle ; and that they should be armed with batteries covered at top. These batteries should be casemated, and their embrasures made in a parapet of earth 6 mètres (20 feet) thick (176).

Correction of the flanks : drawing them in concave curves.

After the establishment of the third parallel and of the numerous direct and enfilading batteries that are upon it, the besieged will be overwhelmed by vertical fires ; the covert-ways will be ricoched, and being without protecting coverts, they cannot be defended with vigour and cannot resist an attack by storm.

The covert-ways as hitherto arranged are thought by all engineers, and other military men, to be in a state of weakness that we have constantly pointed out to our readers. Notwithstanding the improvements that Cormontaigne introduced in the re-entering places of arms, they do not sufficiently protect the garrison in their manœuvres, nor furnish fires capable of overawing the movements of the attack. Accordingly the covert-ways are regarded as an insecure element, even to secure the execution of a subterranean war.

The arrangement of the covert-ways. (See Bousmard's Supplement, and le No. 2 du Mémorial du Génie.)

It seems from the fruitless efforts that have been made to improve the organization of covert-ways, that their imperfection belongs to their very nature ; and that in all probability it is only by constituting them under the relation of the tactics of the troops, that we can succeed in arranging them in such a manner as to deprive the besiegers of all hopes of carrying them by storm. By adopting relieving revêtements for the counterscarps, we have already improved the covert-ways in some degree, for the corps of reserve are under cover and always ready to act ; but they are insufficient, because their debouchés are inadequate and insecure.   The covert-way is so confined and the defiles of the traverses are so narrow, that no manœuvres for offensive returns can be executed in them : and if the besieged attempt to withstand the first impetuosity of the enemy, they will run the risk of not being able to retreat. Vauban accordingly expressly recommends abandoning the covert-way, and to make use of the fires only.

What is very embarrassing in the arrangement of a covert-way, is that it is assailable immediately and in a moment : it is therefore no more than a kind of weak field intrenchment.   To raise it above this class of intrenchments, it is necessary that the fires of the principal works that it covers, completely batter its terra-plain ; and that the troops be able to re-enter it, to attack the enemy and drive off their workmen.

Important reflections on the defence of the glacises.

A covert-way to be properly arranged, must be able to contain and cover a sufficient number of mortars and stone-mortars to fire with grenades, stones, &c. and inundate the works of the besiegers from the third parallel.   This idea of Coehorn, is that of a great soldier who strongly perceived the necessity of defending the approaches of the covert-way with arms easily fired, of short ranges, and consuming little ammunition.   If this plan could be executed, the defence would then make use of the same weapons as the attack ; the besiegers would be obliged to blind their batteries and other principal works ; and they would sustain great losses of lives and time, and would consume far greater quantities of materials.

The width of the terra plains of covert-ways, and of ditches.

Opinions still differ as to the width that the terra-plain of the covert-way should possess ; in the common system this width is only 10 mètres (33½ feet).   A covert-way so narrow cannot be advantageous, except in this case, depending on the relief ; that is, when the besiegers cannot from the coronation of the covert-way plunge the scarp sufficiently low to effect a breach.   They are in this circumstance compelled to lower their battery down into the terra-plain ; which being narrow, occasions great difficulties, especially if the breast-height be made of masonry and its foundation be lower than the banquette.   Excepting in this single case, the narrow covert-way possesses no advantage.   By making it wider, the besiegers will be always compelled to bring down their batteries into the ter-

ra-plain, the manœuvres for offensive returns may be executed
in it, and coverts may be disposed on it sufficiently capacious to
contain the troops and mortar and stone-mortar batteries whose
advantages we have just described, and which would be too
distant if they were placed in the principal works.   Agreeably
to these considerations and those relative to the formation of
breaches, the width of the ditches of the body of the place in
front of the salients may be reduced to 18 or 19 mètres (20 or
21 yards) ; and that of the ravelin ditch, to 13 or 14 (14½ to
15½ yards).   Consequently the covert-way may be made 22
mètres (24½ yards) mean width, without the crest of the glacis
ceasing to be plunged by the covered battery of the bastion
salient.

The width of
the ditches of the
body of the
place and of the
ravelin.

To organize the covert-way it must be remarked that according to the tracé and the rélations between the dimensions of
the elements of the front, the salient and two re-entering
places of arms unite together in a single one T, formed by two
faces enfiladed by the blinded batteries of the ravelin redoubts.
These batteries are themselves covered by the part gu of the
ravelin faces, whose relief is greater than that of the remainder
uz.   The interior of this place of arms is occupied by a great
casemated redoubt P ; the casemates of which, open at the
gorge, are armed with howitzers, stone-mortars, &c. firing with
small charges and continually showering grape-shot and grenades
upon the works of the attack.   As their embrasures are 40 centimètres (16 inches) above the terra-plain of the covert-way,
their flanks defend it by direct and curvated fires.   These
flanks, which are 20 mètres (22 yards), take in reverse the
breach of the ravelin.   The lodgements upon the crest of the
glacis and in the interior of the covert-way, are taken in reverse
and enfiladed by the flanks of the bastions and of the tenaille.
The salient places of arms are occupied by a casemated redoubt R, but without a superior terra-plain ; like the redoubt
P, it is armed with six pieces of ordnance to shower howitzes,
grenades and stones upon the approaches along the capital, upon
the trench cavaliers, &c. Four traverses K, 18 to 20 mètres (20 to
22 yards) long and 7 or 8 (8 or 9 yards) wide, occupy the terra-plain of each branch of the covert-way.   These are vaulted
bomb-proof, and covered with earth and terraced on the side
towards the salient place of arms ; their face which fronts the
crest of the glacis, is each pierced with two embrasures for small

Organization of
the covert-way :
remarkable alter-
ation in the sa-
lient of the bas-
tion. (PLATE
XI, fig. 4.)

(Figures 4 & 5')

mortars or stone-mortars, which greatly multiply the curvated
fires of short ranges.   Each traverse may contain 50 to 60 men;
its floor is sunk 6 decimètres .6 (26 inches).   The ascent to the
traverse is by the ramps Vu leading to the landing place S,
which communicates with the two divisions of the traverse;
and from this traverse the ascent into the crenated tambours
T, is by two gates r furnished with doors.   These tambours
flank the traverse, and are constructed of two rows of heavy
timbers and with two gates.   The landing place S, the tambours, and the portion uo of the ramps, are blinded; so that
more than 108 men may be stationed under these coverts.

As the part xyz (fig. 4) of the salient is the only part that is
palisaded, as much timber is not required for arming this covert-way as is necessary for the common covert-way.   We
are supposing that the scarp and counterscarp revêtements
are with relieving vaults; and that casemates have been made
for heavy musketry, as recommended (115).   These casemated fires will act direct and with great effect on the covert-way
terra-plain, and will combine with the fires of all the other
parts of the system.

The attack of this covert-way by storm.   It appears certain that an attack by storm cannot succeed
against a covert-way thus protected by concealed and open
fires, which cross each other on the terra-plain and take in reverse the crowning of the glacis crest; and in which covered
and fresh troops may debouche from all quarters to fall upon
the enemy and their labourers, and where even the cavalry
may manœuvre.

Improvements indicated by the operations of the siege following the capture of the salient places of arms, of the rave- lin salient, and of the redoubt P of the re-entering place of arms. (Fig. 4.)   When the besiegers have succeeded in establishing themselves in the salients of the covert-way, they will plunge the
scarp of the ravelins and the faces of the attacked bastion.
They may therefore effect breaches in them all at the same
time; and then descending into the ravelin ditch, carry on
their approaches against the bastion.   This great advantage is
possessed by the besiegers in the common bastioned system;
but they are easily divested of it by raising a caponnière X
with a relief that will not mask the flanking fires of the bastion,
and that will cover its scarp.   A similar caponnière Y will in
the same manner mask the opening of the ditch of the ravelin
redoubt, through which the enemy could discover the bastion
scarp to a sufficient depth.   As the works X and Y form by
their relief coverts of which the besiegers may take advantage,

they are defended by the crenated counterscarp galleries : besides, the scarp of the work X is flanked by the flank of the
opposite bastion.

After the capture of the redoubt P, the besiegers will batter
in breach the bastion faces, and counter-batter its flanks ; and
if the tenaille leave an opening opposite the curtain, they will
make a breach in it with a battery posted at the extremity of
the ravelin face.   This latter breach will be the more advantageous to them if they can make it practicable, for by it they
may turn the intrenchment of the bastion.   To compel the besiegers to attack the bastion by gradual approaches and effect a
lodgement on top of the breach after several assaults, the passage between the shoulder angle and the tenaille-gorge must be
only made 5 or 6 mètres (16⅖ to 20 feet) wide ; and this gorge
must be made parallel to the circular flank, but only for an extent of 10 to 12 mètres (33¼ to 40 feet).   By this single modification the enemy will be unable to discover the curtain, which,
together with the flanks, will be entirely masked by the tenaille.

The best figure for the tenaille is that with flanks, adopted
first by Vauban, and subsequently abandoned ;   and which
Bousmard has again proposed to adopt and make it with casemated flanks F, whose embrasures are cut in a parapet of earth
6 mètres (20 feet) thick.   As the gorge of the tenaille is revested with relieving vaults, it may be established within 6 or 8
mètres of the enceinte ; in order to make the flanks of greater
length, and the better to cover the curtain without lowering the
tenaille too much.   There are two ways of arranging the relief
of the tenaille flanks F : 1st, they may be made as high as the
flanks H, which they will completely mask ; and in this case the
casemated batteries F will be the only flank fires that can be used
until the enemy have gained possession of the re-entering place
of arms T and the redoubt P.   In this latter conjuncture the
besieged will cut down the superior portion of the tenaille
flanks, in order to plunge and discover the bottom of the ditch,
flank it by the lines of fire HI, and counter-batter the breach
and counter-flank batteries established in the terra-plain of the
redoubt P : 2d, the superior part of the tenaille flanks will be a
little below the line of fire HI, in order to unmask the fires of
the bastion flanks ; and in this second case, the casemated batteries F will be on a level with the terra-plain of the redoubt
P ; and they will act simultaneously with the batteries H of the

The form of the
tenaille : its re-
lief (See Bous-
mard's Supple-
ment (Fig. 4)

flank.   The terra-plain P of the redoubt, and the passage of the ditch, will be defended by two tiers of fire difficult to contend against.   To deprive the enemy of all hope of being able to debouche from the ravelin ditch and form under the covert of the relief of the tenaille, its scarp and the counterscarp of the ravelin redoubt will be provided with a crenated gallery.

The rampart of the ravelin re-doubt: reflec-tions upon terra-plains supported by relieving vaults.   The centre of the ravelin redoubt shall be empty, and its rampart sustained by a relieving revêtement.   By this mode of construction, which we unceasingly recommend the use of, and which will be repeated under all the terra-plains, from that of the covert-way to the intrenchment of the bastion ; the besieged will be able by small mines, made under the piers, to blow down all those parts of the terra-plains upon which the enemy are compelled to establish their batteries of breach and coun-ter-flank.   By these measures, if they be ably executed, the besiegers will be reduced to effect all the breaches by offensive mines ; and the besieged will preserve to the last moment the use of their covered batteries, which take all the works of the besiegers from the fourth parallel in flank and reverse.

Improvements to be made in the scarp profiles, with respect to making breaches in them (PLATE XI, Fig. 6.)   We have a few more observations to make on the plan and construction of general profiles, in respect to effecting breaches in them.   In walls profiled in the common manner, breaches are soon practicable ; the parapets are soon crumbled down, and the fires that defend the ditches are necessarily extinguished.   Al-though this operation is more difficult when the revêtements are with relieving vaults, nevertheless the besiegers succeed with sufficient despatch in crumbling down the upper part of the wall into the ditch ; and consequently in tumbling down the parapet.   In order that the plan and construction of a profile may afford a resistance superior to that of the common plans, the two following conditions must be fulfilled, viz : 1st, the be-siegers must not be able to effect a practicable breach with can-non ; 2d, they must not be able to tumble the covering mass down into the ditch.   The first condition cannot be always ful-filled ; but the second can be complied with in every case.

Let P be a profile whose scarp is supposed to be battered by the battery B, lowered down into the covert-way ; the width of the ditch is about 18 mètres (20 yards) : a profile is required to be constructed that will fulfil the two preceding conditions, and also that relating to the commandment.   Let us suppose that the commandment is to be at its maximum, having regard to the width of the ditch ; and let us take hK equal to 10 decimètres ($3\frac{1}{2}$ feet) on the counterscarp, and draw the horizontal KY, above which make the angle VKY whose tangent will be $\frac{1}{4}$ of the radius ; this right line will be the direction of the plunge of the parapet. If then through the point b of the battery the extreme line of fire bo be drawn, making with the horizontal an angle whose tangent will be also $\frac{1}{4}$ of the radius, the portion of the scarp oa will be the only part that can be ruined. And if through the point o we draw om making with the vertical an angle of 45 degrees, this line will be the boundary of the mass that can be crumbled into the ditch. Therefore, if measuring from the point n the parapet be made with an additional thickness nc of 6 mètres (20 feet), it will remain untouched, and the fortification will be only weakened in its scarp even after a breach is effected. If we now suppose that the ditch may be excavated the quantity $os = 7$ mètres ($23\frac{1}{2}$ feet), a height sufficient to render an escalade impracticable ; we will have a scarp that can only be ruined by mining, and the upper part of which oa may be replaced by a slope of earth oh. But as this construction will always require a relief of 120 to 130 decimètres (40 to $43\frac{1}{3}$ feet), it is better to make a revêtement with relieving vaults along the whole height, to prevent escalade and obtain the covered fires so useful for defending the terra-plain of the covert-way. It is proper to remark that in profiling the revêtement with relieving vaults, the line om cannot be inclined $45°$; the inclination om' will be given to it, of 30 to 35 degrees. In this case the breach will not be practicable, and the additional thickness of the parapet must be lessened. We have here again a proof that narrow and deep ditches are the most advantageous ; provided that the lines of direct fires are effective on the covert-way terra-plain. All these considerations lead to this conclusion—that the vertical and horizontal projections of fortification must be so arranged, that breaches cannot be effected without having recourse to offensive mines.

All these means of improvements, and the modifications that we have introduced into the form and disposition of the elements of the bastioned system, are founded on the principles developed by Count Carnot in the sketch of the system that he has proposed. These principles are the basis of the art of combining and disposing covered fires to resist with a moderate quantity of artillery the violence and multiplied fires of all kinds made use of by the besiegers, and the effects of which are now known and estimated in theory. We have insisted on the necessity of modifications and additions in relation to the manœuvres of the troops and to those tactics that are peculiar to the war of sieges, so much neglected, and the importance of which is acknowledged by all enlightened minds.

Conclusion. We must conclude from all that has been developed, that an engineer cannot render his defences of any strength or value, but by combining in them covered fires and defensive mines ; the works must be supposed to be defended by troops and miners perfectly skilled in the practice of sieges, and whose devotion and patience is unlimited, and their officers instructed in those tactics . peculiar to sieges and so fruitful in combinations.

CHAPTER X.

General Reflections on Irregular Fortification; the Causes of this Irregularity; the Principles of Defilement; Application of the Principles and Rules of Defilement to a Fortified Front.

178. WE explained in the Second Part (106 and 107) the causes that produce irregularity in fortification, and the effects arising from *commandment.* We said that commandment assumed a peculiar character in permanent fortification ; and this is in consequence of the nature of the contest, which gradually displays itself by means of industry and ingenuity. Hence it follows, that if the defenders be not shielded in their works from the influence of the exterior commandment, their means of defence will be destroyed from the very first onset; and the service within will be so impeded, that the progress of the attack will be astonishingly rapid. As commandment in horizontal fortification affords the besieged great advantages, so would exterior commandment procure much greater advantages for the besiegers if modern engineers did not, as in the infancy of the science, possess the means of defending fortification from its influence.

We know that there are two principal causes that produce irregularity in fortification. The first is the irregularity of the site upon which the works are built ; the second is in consequence of the commandment of the ground without. 'Tis this latter that is the origin of the art of defilement.

It is not our intention to treat irregular fortification in detail ; this must be the subject of particular studies, in the course of which the students will daily go, under the guidance of an able master, and study nature and topography under the relations of fortification. We will confine ourselves to a few general illustrations showing how the general principles and rules composing the theory of regular and horizontal fortification, are applied to the varied sites proposed to be occupied by fortresses or permanent works. Irregular fortification is, properly speaking, the art of fortifying ; and this art is founded on the theory that we have established. Judgment and the *coup d'œil,* assisted by those geometrical operations to which the particular problem gives rise, determine the greater or less excellence of the arrangement of the system. 'Tis the variety of sites that makes fortification so difficult a science, and requires such long and tedious study ; a science that requires consummate practice, and frequently a superior genius.

179. Fortification, with respect only to the irregularity of the site upon which it is displayed. 179. When an engineer is about to establish a fortress on an irregular site. he reconnoitres it in the most minute manner and determines the topography by plans made with great accuracy, by levellings, and descriptive memoirs which complete what drawing fails to represent. He examines and sounds all the surface of the site, to ascertain the nature of the strata of earth and the depth at which water is found. These various particulars being perfectly ascertained, he next examines what resources can be derived from currents of water, to form inundations, ponds, and manœuvres of waters (manœuvres d'eau) ; he takes advantage of declivities and other accidents of ground, and determines the points at which it is practicable to organize an exterior subterranean war. After this general view, he proposes to render unattackable as many points as possible, by placing the unattackable and assailable fronts in relations of defence. He must never forget, that the assailable fronts should present fronts drawn on curves little convex ; and that when circumstances permit, they should be displayed on a right line, and even on concave curves.

After this general coup d'œil embracing the general relations of all the parts of the system and seizing at the same time the particular relation of the attack and of the defence, and which constitutes the genius of the engineer ; he will draw the defensive polygon whose extent and interior space must be proportioned to the garrison intended for its defence ; that is, to the rank that the fortress is to occupy in the defensive system of the frontier. This primitive polygon then undergoes the following modifications ; vizt. : 1st, It must be adapted in such a manner to the peculiar form of the ground, that each part shall be most favourably situated and afford the best respective defence : 2d, It must be arranged under the relation of the expense and construction ; for the embankment must be always equal to the excavation : 3d, It must be modified in relation to the second cause of irregularity that gives rise to introducing defilement into the system.

Having thus drawn the outline of his work, the fortifying

officer will examine in detail the accessible and attackable fronts
to fortify them, not according to one uniform system, but according to systems that he will compose with the elements described, and which must be adapted to the different natures of
the ground.   On such a front or part of the enceinte, he will
make numerous casemates, crenated galleries, &c., because the
depth of the ditches will be slight and the relief inconsiderable;
whilst another part will be inundated and unsusceptible of subterranean war ; another part will likewise be unsusceptible, on
account of the ground beneath the glacis being composed of
strata of hard rock in which trenches cannot be cut ; and another part will admit the organization of an exterior subterranean war of greater or less extent.   Lastly ; it will be proper
and natural to nearly equilibrate the strength of the different
attackable fronts.

180. We found it easy to represent horizontal fortification by
an horizontal projection on the plane of site and by general profiles.   The same method might be used in irregular fortification ; but it would be wearisome from the multiplicity of profiles and elevations that would have to be constructed.   A more
simple and very ingenious method has been invented to represent the relief of ground, and to determine that of fortification
even in the retirement of the closet.   By this method, and
with the elements of the topography accurately established, an
engineer may determine the project of a fortification and completely constitute and arrange it, without ever having been upon the ground.

180 Method of representing ir-regular fortifica-tion without using the profiles and elevations. The plane of compari-son, and the nu-merical heights or references.

This method is that used for representing the configuration of
the bottom of roads and harbours.   Having placed an inanimate
body in any given position, this point is drawn and constructed
in an horizontal projection ; the sounding-line is then used, and
thus the depth of the bottom of the road or bay below the surface of the water at this point is found.   The numerical depth
or reference that is the measure of the vertical let fall from the
point in question, is written or set down beside its horizontal
projection.

The same operation being repeated at a great number of
points, the whole of these numerical references (*cotes*) gives a
very exact idea of the surface of the bottom of the sea ; for the
horizontal projection of all the points of its surface is given,
and also the value of all the vertical ordinates.

. The same mode is followed with respect to an irregular site upon which a fortification is to be constructed. An horizontal plane is imagined to pass above its most elevated point ; and this plane, taken as a plane of projection, is called the *plane of comparison :* it is constructed by the common methods of topographical drawing. Then through the principal points of the ground, imaginary verticals are drawn cutting the plane of projection at points whose positions are known. The heights of these verticals are then determined by levelling, and their numerical references are set down beside each corresponding point. The whole of all these references shows the surface of the ground.

The use of the plane of comparison

It is easy to understand the use that may be made of the plane of comparison. For let us suppose that we have drawn on this plane a fortification whose relief is known ; then if beside the different points of the horizontal projection we place the numerical heights or references of the verticals raised from these same points to the plane of projection, the whole of these references will exhibit the relation of the relief of the works with the ground ; and by adding the references relative to the bottoms of the ditches, magistral lines, and covering lines, we complete the representation of the fortification. Accordingly whenever the plan and arrangement of a fortification is to be established upon an irregular site, we must begin by constructing a plane of comparison ; then draw the horizontal projection of the works agreeably to the principles that we have already taught and shall further establish, and determine the relief by means of the numerical references that we succeed in finding by the methods of defilement that we are about to explain. By assuming the hypothesis that the irregularity in fortification does not arise from the influence of exterior commandment, but solely from the irregularity of the site itself, the trace and the relief are easily enough arranged. The ground occupied by the fortification is divided into parts sensibly uniform ; and for each of these parts an artificial plane of site is adopted that is as near to the ground as possible, because it is either tangential to its surface, or cuts it to make it more regular. In passing from the artificial plane of site of one part, to that of another adjacent, these planes are connected in the most advantageous manner ; in order that the fronts may preserve the most efficient relations of defence. When the whole of the artificial

planes of site are thus established, they are laid down by
the references of three points on the plane of comparison; in
order to arrange the relief of each front in relation to its plane
of site, in the manner that we have described for horizontal
fortification, and as we shall explain in the general hypothesis
that we are about to discuss.

181. The second cause of irregularity is of most important
consideration; giving rise to very curious applications of descriptive geometry, without the aid of which the engineer could
not succeed in determining the forms and proportions proper
for the works in order that they may possess in the defence
the same advantages as a system displayed upon an horizontal
site. The greatest number of frontier fortresses are situated
upon the banks of streams or rivers, where they are overlooked
by the heights of these banks; others are seated upon the declivities of mountains whose tops look down upon them; finally, there are others that are partly situated upon the plain, and
partly upon heights. If upon such sites, fortifications nearly
regular were displayed, by placing all the covering lines in horizontal planes; it is evident that these planes would cut the
commanding heights, from all the upper parts of which the enemy would have a plunging fire into the terra-plains and interior of the field of battle, and would even discover a more or
less considerable portion of the scarps. A fortification thus arranged, would be an absurdity; and would be almost utterly
incapable of defence.

181. Irregular fortification with respect to the influence of the commandment of the exterior ground.

The ranges and effects of the missile weapons of the ancients,
were favoured and increased by commanding heights; and as
the distances at which their weapons took effect were inconsiderable, the besieged might be reached by them without their
being able to return a shot, because they had to fire up. But
what is true with respect to ancient weapons, is not so with
regard to modern artillery; because this arm strikes at very
great distances. Nevertheless, beyond a certain limit fixed by
experience, its effects become uncertain and are not to be depended upon, except to produce conflagrations. This distance
beyond which artillery ceases to be of sure effect, may be established at 1,000 to 1,200 mètres (1,112 to 1,335 yards). But
at this distance in firing upwards, provided the inclination of
the line of fire be not too great, the shot possess an efficacy and
power of destruction which counterbalances that of shot fired

Reflections on the effects of missile weapons hurled from above down upon a commanded fortification; and fired up against the besiegers' works.

downwards. And we may add, that in this case the trenches of the besiegers being carried on against the slope (à *contre pente*), they will be very much exposed, and their parapets must be higher, and their disposition will be more difficult to regulate.

Consequences.;   By resuming the consideration of what we have laid down, it follows, 1st, that commanding heights have little influence at a distance of 1500 mètres (1670 yards); 2d, that heights at this distance, and even within it, will not be injurious to the defences, provided that their tracé and relief be arranged in such a manner that the disposition of the whole shall be the same as in fortifications upon horizontal sites.

The use of defilement.   It is by the art of defilement that this result is obtained; it consists in, 1st, disposing the tracé and relief in such a manner as to shield the service of the garrison from the views of the besiegers; 2d, concealing from them all parts of the field of battle, except those wherein missile weapons are used; 3d, arranging these latter parts in such a manner, that the missile weapons in them will be as effective as in horizontal fortification.

General idea of a defiled fortification.   It is easy to imagine a defiled fortification fulfilling all the conditions that we have just laid down. If, in an horizontal fortification, we suppose the plane of site to turn upon an hinge or axis and become tangential to a commanding height; and likewise, that all the horizontal planes of defilement become parallel to this plane of site, preserving the same respective commandments; we will then have a fortification whose parts will be all defiled, and which will preserve nearly all the properties of horizontal fortification. The plane of site becomes in this case a plane whose position is known; and upon which all the relief is regulated according to the commandments (likewise known) of all the planes of defilement.

The artificial plane of site, and plane of defilement inclined to the horizon.

Choice of the artificial plane of site.   The chief merit of this method consists in the choice of the plane of site, and of the line to serve it as an axis; for when once the position of this plane is known, those of the planes of defilement, which are parallel to it, are deduced from the rules taught in horizontal fortification to establish their relation.

The mode of finding the numerical references of the rampant planes, by means of real-s of defilement. (PLATE XII, fig. 1.)   Let *A* be the ground upon which a fortification *S'S* is to be established, and which is commanded, and let *SB* be the axis (*charnière*) of the rampant plane or of the artificial plane of defilement; then raise this plane until it touches the ground, and suppose *C* the point of contact. As the ground is represented by horizontal curves (this is a very ingenious method of establishing the topography of a particular site), we will find the references of the three points S, B, and C; and consequently the plane of site will be determined.   Now to find with ease the references of all the points belonging to the inclined or rampant plane (*plan rampant*); we may effect this by means of a *scale of defilement* (*echelle de défilement*), drawn on the plane, and the horizontal projection of which must be determined. This scale is most generally constructed on the projection of the line of the greatest declivity.   This is the name of the line perpendicular to the horizontal drawn on the rampant plane.   The projection of the horizontal line upon the plane of comparison, is found either by a simple calculation by means of the references of the three known points, or by a vertical projection. Indeed let there be a vertical plane passing through the line SB, considered as the common intersection of the two planes of projection; and construct on this plane the vertical projections SC', SB' of the two right lines SC, and SB: through the point B' draw the horizontal $B'K$, which will give in E the vertical projection of the point of the right line SC that is at the same height or of the same reference as the point B.   Therefore this point drawn down to E' in the horizontal plane, will give the means of drawing the projection BE' of the horizontal.   If then at any point of this horizontal a perpendicular XY be raised, it will be the line of greatest declivity; and upon it the scale of slope or defilement will be constructed.   For this purpose, through the points C, B, and S let fall upon XY perpendiculars that will give the points b, g and a, which will be marked with the références 31, 45 and 55.   If we divide the interval ba into 24 equal parts, the point g will be found at the 14th division and will have for reference 45.   We shall thus have a graduated scale by which may be instantly found the reference of any given point taken in the rampant plane.   Thus for instance, if it be desired to know the reference of the shoulder angle Q in the proportion that it is in the rampant plane; draw the horizontal QT, and the reference indicated by the scale of site will be that of the point Q.

The choice of the plane of site is a very delicate operation depending on the *coup d'œil*, because dependent upon circumstances relating to the arrangement and construction; and from which are deduced the data that make the question determinate,

Continuation of the considerations on the choice of the artificial plane of site.

or indeterminate.   There follow from this consideration several preliminary problems, respecting which we must say a few
words previous to discussing the general questions of defilement.

The first ques-
tion.   Determin-
ation of the plane
of site subjected
to pass through a
given point : the
conical surface :
the line of appa-
rent   contour.
(PLATE   XII,
fig. 3.)
     The first preliminary question that it is proper should receive
our attention, is that in which the position of the rampant-plane,
necessitated to pass through a given point A, is to be found. If
through this point we imagine tangents to the surface of the
ground, which is known by the formation of the plane of comparison, a conical surface will be generated whose points of
contact will be the line of apparent contour.   It will be easy
to project this curve upon the horizontal plane and upon any
vertical plane whatever.   Indeed let AP be the horizontal
projection of a ridge ; then if through this line a vertical plane
be drawn, it will cut the ground following the curve mno, to
which the tangent An will be drawn to project at n' the point
of contact n.   In the same manner will be determined a series
of points, through which a curve will be drawn ; this curve
will be the horizontal projection of the apparent contour.   Now
to ascertain the form of the conical surface, it must be cut by
a vertical plane whose direction is XY ; and upon which it is
easy to draw its intersection with the conical surface.   Let us
draw a point ; for instance, that belonging to the ridge projected in AM ; we must construct like as before the section of
ground qst, and draw the tangent As ; then through the point e
raise the vertical ef in the vertical plane passing through AM ;
by laying off this length ef on the vertical eg considered in the
vertical plane of which XY is the direction, we will have a
point of the vertical section aaa : its other points will be found
by similar constructions.   If now we draw to the vertical section aaa tangents xy, they will be the directions of as many
rampant planes passing through the point A : this shows that
the problem is susceptible of several solutions.   But among all
these tangents we must choose that which gives the most suitable rampant plane under other relations, exclusive of the defilement.   If the artificial plane of site is necessarily to touch the
ground in two points, the problem would be determinate ; because the tangent uv is the only one, or is unique. When the point
of the vertical section through which the plane of site is to pass, is
known, we can find on the plane of comparison the point of the
ground corresponding to it.   For this purpose, draw the horizontal projection AK of the ridge passing through the point b ;

construct the section of the ground, and the projection K of the point of contact G will be that of the point sought.

When the tangents drawn to the vertical section do not give a suitable rampant plane, a plane is chosen that is not tangential to the surface of the exterior ground and which cuts it at a certain height. Let us suppose that hl is the direction of this plane; it is evident that all that part of the ground which commands the plane of site, must be cut down and carried away: this part is shown by the extreme ridges that pass through the points g and g', and by the portion of the vertical section included between these two points. To lay off on the ground its intersection by the rampant plane, we must project this curve upon the plane of comparison. This projection is tangential to the two extreme ridges AM, AM'; and the points of contact are found by their constructions s in the vertical plane passing through the ridge. Let us also construct the two points situated on the right line projected in AP: by carrying the height dc from d to d', we will have on the vertical plane the direction Am' of the rampant plane; and the two points m' and o' projected at m'' and o'', will be the two points sought: and in the same way as respects the others. In this manner we will obtain upon the plane of comparison the curve $m''p's'q'o''$, which being laid down upon the ground will show the earth to be cut away.

The case when a rampant plane that cuts the ground must be chosen.

The case in which the rampant plane is made to pass through a right line whose position is given, frequently occurs in practice. This is the case whenever an axis or hinge is taken either for the plane of site, or plane of defilement.

Second question. The plane of site is supposed to be obliged to pass through a right line whose position is known. (Fig. 2.)

The problem in this case is determinate, and is treated like the preceding. Let the position of the right line GE be given; its direction R is sought upon the vertical plane, and through this point the tangent RR' is drawn to the vertical section and gives the position of the rampant plane, which is the only one of its kind. By finding the reference of the point of ground situated in the ridge that passes through the point of contact, we determine the rampant plane on the plane of comparison.

As early as 1775 M. Monge and General Meusnier instructed the students of the school of engineering in the methods of determining artificial planes of site subjected to pass either through a given point, or through a right line. Meusnier composed on this subject a manuscript memoir to guide the students. He

The solution of the two preceding questions by Monge, and by Meusnier

treated it with that judgment and acuteness that was his chief
characteristic ; and which, joined to ceaseless industry, raised
him to merited celebrity in the mathematical sciences and in
their application to the arts and inventions of several kinds.

Meusnier, in his manuscript memoir, defines the ground by
horizontal sections, made by planes rising gradually from the
lowest points to the summits of the commanding heights. He
draws these sections upon the plane of comparison, by drawing
curves through the points that have the same reference. He
then cuts the conical surface with an horizontal plane established at any selected height, and constructs the section upon the
plane of comparison.   To this curve he draws a line that touches
it in two points ; and the ridges that pass through the two points
of contact, show the two points of ground through which the
rampant plane must pass.

The case of the rampant plane being made to pass through
a right line taken as a hinge, and whose slope is sufficiently
great to be calculated, is treated in this memoir in a peculiar
and most ingenious manner, easily applied in practice.

Let A and B be the two salients of the covert-way of a fortified front ; through these points, whose references are 100 decimètres and 60 decimètres ($33\frac{1}{3}$ and 20 feet), the plane of site
must pass ; and let us suppose that the horizontal curves of
which we have spoken, have been drawn as correctly as possible upon the plane of comparison. This being granted, then
the right line AB which is the hinge of the rampant plane, will
be considered as a scale divided in proportion to the slope ;
that is, into 40 equal parts from A to B. These divisions will
be protracted until the reference is equal to that of the highest
horizontal curve : in the present example, this will be to reference 10.   This first operation having been executed with care,
through each point of division of the scale MN tangents will be
drawn to the curves of the same reference ; and of all these
tangents that only will be retained which makes with the right
line AB the smallest angle. Thus for instance, for the point of
the scale whose reference is 20, we will have the right lines
as, $a's$, &c. ; but the tangent as only will be preserved, as it
makes the smallest angle.   In the same way for the point marked 50, the horizontal tangent bp will only be retained ; and so
on.   After all these successive operations, we have a series of
horizontal tangents oq, bp, as, &c. ; from which the tangent bp,

making with the line *AB* the smallest angle, will be chosen: it will give the point *b* of the ground through which the rampant plane should pass. Indeed as all the other tangents make with *AB* greater angles, they will be beneath the plane; therefore it will touch the ground at the point *b* only, situated in the tangent that makes the smallest angle with the hinge.

If we suppose that the right line *MN*, which is to be the hinge of the rampant plane, is horizontal, this method becomes impracticable. We must in this case draw to all the horizontal curves the tangents *mn*, &c. which are parallel to it; draw a curve through the points of contact, and construct this curve upon a vertical plane perpendicular to the hinge. From the direction of this same right line in the vertical plane, a tangent is drawn to the curve; and the point of contact will give the point of ground upon which the rampant plane should rest.

The case when the right line that serves as a hinge for the rampant plane, is horizontal.

182. Defilement is the art of arranging the works of a fortification in such a manner, that, 1st, all the service within them shall be shielded from the view of the besiegers; 2d, the besiegers shall only see such parts of the field of battle as it is absolutely impossible to conceal from them, and which are least destructible; 3d, all the missile weapons shall have the same effect against the works of the attack, as if the fortification were horizontal. Now we know from what has been said (181), that all these conditions will be fulfilled by exactly establishing the topography of the site, by the formation of a plane of comparison; and by skilfully choosing artificial planes of site, upon which the fronts and other works that enter into the composition of a fortress are arranged.

182. The use of defilement: its definition.

In all questions of defilement, there are three data considered; 1st, The *exterior ground* from which the enemy's lines of fire are projected; this ground is included within a circle of about 1500 mètres radius (1670 yards): 2d, The *interior ground*, which is the space to be defiled: 3d, The covering masses, composed of the parapets, traverses, paradoses, &c. that are used to intercept the enemy's lines of fire. Of these three data, the exterior ground is known by the plane of comparison; and as the lines of fire are supposed to be rectilinear, cases of defilement are treated in the same manner as those of shadows. The ground without is the luminous body, and its rays are the lines of fire; the covering masses are the opaque bodies,

The three data that enter into the general questions of defilement.

and the ground defiled is the space included within the shadows of the covering masses.

The two general questions of defilement. All particular cases of defilement are included in two general expressions :

1st, The exterior ground and the covering lines being given, the form of the terra-plains is to be so determined that they will be defiled.

2d, The exterior ground and the principal points of the horizontal projection being given, the position of the covering lines is to be determined in such a manner that all the conditions of defence shall be fulfilled and at the minimum of expense.

The first question. The covering lines are given. The solution of the first question is effected by imagining a plane resting upon the exterior ground and upon the covering lines, and always tangential to both. The successive intersections of this plane, which is continually changing its position, will be the ridges or generating lines of the *surface of defilement :* and if through the foot of the parapets and parallel to it a curved surface be drawn, it will contain the terra-plain of the work, &c. It must be observed that the exterior space is a surface parallel to that of the ground ; but higher by about 20 decimètres (6¾ feet).

In particular questions, the surface of defilement is generally composed of one or more planes whose positions are known ; and the graphical constructions by which the projections of the defiled surface are determined, become more or less easy.

The second question. The principal points of the horizontal projection only are given. In the second general question it is supposed that the principal points of the tracé are laid down upon the plane of comparison, and that the corresponding points of the natural ground belong to the surface of defilement. Through these latter points a surface will be drawn enveloping the natural exterior ground ; and this will be the *artificial surface of site,* which should contain the terra-plains of the most advanced works. And if the covering lines of these works be placed in a surface of defilement parallel to and 25 decimètres (8¼ feet) above it, we will then have the relief, &c.

In particular cases we substitute for the surface of the site, one or more planes tangential to this surface and properly chosen. The surfaces of defilement then become planes of defilement which are placed in relation with the planes of site, according to the rules given in horizontal fortification relative to the defence and the expense of the construction.

When the artificial planes of site, and the relation expressive of the commandment of the elements are determined, we draw the scales of defilement by which we obtain the references that give the relief, &c.

When a fortification is displayed upon an irregular site influenced by commanding heights, it seldom happens that a single plane of site can satisfy all the conditions. In such cases several are adopted, which have with respect to each other known positions; and sometimes there is an ascending or descending ressault between one plane and another. In the first case, the lower part is covered on its flank, and there is no modification to be made; in the second case, it is indispensable to place on the direction of the ressault a bomb-proof traverse of sufficient elevation to cover the flank of the higher fortification. Passages with ramps are made in the body of the traverses, to communicate from one part to another.

The respective positions of the different planes of site belonging to the same fortification.

In passing from one rampant plane to another through the intersection of these two planes, it may happen that this intersection forms either a gutter, or a ridge. If it form a gutter, a traverse sufficiently high must be interposed in its direction; but if it be a ridge, the two parts will be defiled as if the plane were not changed. It is easy to ascertain upon the plane of comparison, whether the rampant planes cut each other in gutters or ridges. For this purpose, we have only to draw the projections of the lines of greatest declivity; if these lines converge from the interior to the exterior, it will be a ridge; if they diverge, it will be a gutter; finally, if the lines of greatest declivity be parallel, the rampant planes will be lost in each other, or be parallel.

183. We will now apply the general rules that we have laid down, to two particular cases that the students may vary at pleasure.

183. Application of the general principles to two particular cases.

The gorge of the salient is supposed rectilinear, and its horizontal and vertical projections are QMR and qmr; it is also supposed that the common intersection XY of the two planes of projection, is perpendicular to the capital, and that it passes through the salient angle. This granted, the section of the conical surface by the vertical plane, must be constructed by the means already described. This curve is $abcde$, and is supposed not to extend beyond the prolongations of the two faces.

First state of the question: a salient whose covering lines and their position are known, is to be defiled from front, but which are embraced by the prolongations of its faces. (PLATE XII, fig. 4.)

If the direction *fh* of the plane passing through the covering lines be constructed in the vertical plane, and this direction pass above the section of the surface of defilement ; this will show that the work is defiled, and that it is sufficient to establish its terra-plain in a parallel plane.   But if, as in the case considered, the direction of the plane of defilement cut the section *ace*, the work will not be defiled and will be plunged from the height *B*.   It is required to construct its terra-plain in such a manner as to leave it no longer under the influence of the commanding height.   For this purpose, imagine that the conical surface of defilement, all the ridges of which pass through the summit *M*, is prolonged into the interior of the salient ; it will there form a conical concave surface, easily constructed : and if through the foot of the parapets a surface parallel to it be drawn, this should contain the terra-plain.   To simplify the construction and form of the terra-plain, substitute for the irregular conical surfaces the two tangential planes whose directions are *fc'* and *hc'* ; or else the surface whose direction is the mixed line *fbcdh*.   On this supposition the surface of the terraplain will be composed of two planes forming a gutter, or of a conical concave surface terminated by two planes that are tangential to it.   It now only remains to draw the projections of the ridges of the two points of contact *b* and *d*, and of those of the curve *bcd*, to obtain the section *qzvur* of the interior surface by the vertical plane passing through the gorge.   At 25 decimètres (8¼ feet) below this line, the parallel *sotxp* will be drawn, and will be the vertical boundary of the terra-plain, &c.

Second state of the question : there are supposed to be collateral heights that take the faces of the salients in reverse. When the prolongations of the faces do not include all the commanding heights, and when there are collateral heights *A* and *C* ; these heights take in reverse the troops and artillery stationed along the faces.   In this case, we cannot cover ourselves from these reverse fires but by interposing in the terraplain of the work a mass called a *traverse*, which will intercept the lines of fire from the right and left.   To determine the direction and height of this traverse, we must begin by performing all the operations relative to the preceding case ; then draw the vertical projection *q'm'*, *r'm'* of the two right lines about 10 decimètres (3¼ feet) above the covering line.   Through the directions *f'* and *h'* of these right lines, tangents will be drawn to the collateral parts *a'b'd'*, *a''b''d''* of the section of the surface of defilement, and they will be the directions of two tangential planes of defilement passing through the right lines $q'm'$ and $r'm'$.   It is obvious that these two tangential planes will cut each other in a right line, the direction and height of which above the horizontal plane will be those that the traverse should possess.   This line terminating in the vertical plane passing through the gorge, may therefore be considered as the summit of the traverse which will be made of proper thickness, according to the nature of the materials of which it is to be constructed and the resistance that it must oppose.   If this traverse be constructed of earth, the face corresponding to the gorge will be made of sods ; the two other faces will have the slope of falling earths.   There will be one or two communications made under the traverse, to pass from one part of the work to the other ; and a powder-magazine will be made in the body of it. When the direction of the traverse makes with the capital so great an angle that it is too close to one of the faces of the work, its direction must be changed and its height raised to the lateral plane of defilement resting upon the face from which it is necessary to distance the foot of the traverse, in order to obtain sufficient terra-plain and that the service of the garrison may be unimpeded.   This remark shows that when there is only one lateral height, the traverse along the capital may be placed in such a direction as is most advantageous with respect to the manœuvres of the garrison ; and that its height is determined by the single consideration of one lateral rampant plane.

In both the cases that we have just considered, it is necessary, in order to be able to fulfil all the conditions of the defilement, that the prolonged faces do not cut the earth ; for if this were the case, the terra-plain would be defiled, but the troops stationed on the banquettes would be plunged and taken in flank by the enfilading fires of the enemy.

We have by a few words caused our readers to anticipate (178), how a work under the influence of commanding heights might satisfy the conditions prescribed by the rules of defence. Those preliminary ideas may now be completed and illustrated by the application of the methods that we have described ; and which it is easy to regulate in one single system of operations, to attain a solution of all particular cases.   After establishing the topography of the site by the formation of the plane of comparison, and drawing upon this plane the horizontal projection of

Application of the preceding principles to the arrangement of fortifications, whose tracé is known, in relation to its defilement.

the defensive polygon, the different points of ground will be selected that should belong to the artificial planes of site ; and the respective positions of these several rampant planes will be determined.   If these planes be tangential to the exterior surface, all the terra-plains will be placed in parallel planes, &c. But if any of them cut the exterior ground, either the portion of ground above them must be cut away ; or the terra-plains must be excavated accordingly, and traverses used to prevent the works from being seen in reverse.   Each plane of site being determined and its references marked upon the plane of comparison, their intersections or the ressaults that they form will be examined (179); and the directions and heights of the traverses will be determined, and likewise of the paradoses that the passage from one plane of site to the next renders necessary.   These operations having been laid down upon the plane of comparison, or executed on the ground by the modes known in practice ; the scales of defilement will then be formed, in order to afterwards establish the relief of each particular front.   This relief will be arranged by determining the relation of all the planes of defilement in the manner taught (146) for horizontal fortification.   The crest of the glacis will be placed in a plane of defilement 25 to 30 decimètres ($8\frac{1}{3}$ to 10 feet) above the plane of site, and the slope of the glacis will then be arranged as we have described.   The tracé of the third parallel will then be drawn ; and the commandments of the ravelin, of the body of the place, and of the other elements, will be determined by separate profiles.

This general explanation will suffice for the present to show how the principles of regular fortification are applied to the various cases of irregular fortification.   It frequently occurs that the rampant planes that have been chosen, produce too great or too little reliefs : which is against the rules of defence. This consideration leads to treating under another point of view the question relative to the choice of a plane of defilement.

184.   As the relief of a work should be regulated by the rules of defilement, by the rules prescribed by the tactics of defence, and by those depending upon the construction and expense ; it follows that the fulfilling of so many conditions renders the question very difficult and complex in practice.   And accordingly, when an engineer accomplishes the arrangement of all the elements of a fortress in such a manner as to obtain

184 The defilement of works, by introducing the consideration of a maximum & minimum of relief.

the maximum of strength at the minimum of expense, he leaves to posterity a lasting monument of his talents and science.

Therefore before proceeding to the choice of artificial planes of site, the engineer should fix the limits of the maximum and minimum, within which he may restrain the relief, independently of the circumstance of defilement. These limits being established, he can only choose from among the rampant planes those that will give to the body of the place planes of defilement which pass between the determined limits.

The questions precedingly treated accordingly assume this condition, that each plane of site must be deduced from a plane of defilement fulfilling this condition—that the relief must not exceed established limits.

When the relief is regulated according to the plane of defilement of the body of the place, the exterior ground must be a parallel surface to that of the ground, but higher by about 50 to 60 decimètres ($16\frac{2}{3}$ to 20 feet); in order that the plane of site resulting from it, may be nearly tangential to the surface of the ground.

Remark respecting the surface of defilement.

In the first case, where the plane of defilement of the principal works must pass between the limits m'' and m' of the maximum and minimum of relief, the point A is selected inside at a given position and through which the plane of defilement must necessarily pass. This point must be chosen with that accurate *coup d'œil*, which all officers entrusted with the conduct of such plans should possess.

The first case ; the plane of defilement must pass through a given point and between limits fixed for the relief. (PLATE XII, fig. 5)

Through this point A, chosen as correctly as possible, the ridges of the conical surface of defilement will be drawn ; and this surface will be cut by a vertical plane of which XY is the ground line : the points of the maximum and minimum of relief will be projected upon the two planes at m, m' and m''. These being established, the vertical section ooo of the surface of defilement will be constructed; and through the projections of the point A, and through those of the points that establish the maximum and minimum of relief, right lines will be drawn which will determine their directions t and t' upon the vertical plane. It is now plain that of the tangents to the curve ooo, we can only choose such as VV that pass between the limits t and t'.

If the plane of defilement be compelled to pass through a right line AF whose position is given, the problem will be de-

Second case ; the plane of defilement is compelled to pass

terminate ; but it will not be always practicable.   Indeed we
must find the direction K of the right line in the vertical plane,
and through this point draw a tangent KP to the curve ooo ;
and as this tangent is the only one through which the plane of
defilement can be drawn, it follows that if it do not pass between the limits t and t' the problem will be impracticable.   It
will therefore be necessary to change the position of the right
line AF.

Lastly ; we will suppose that the plane of defilement, always
restricted to passing between the points of the maximum and
minimum of relief, must also be parallel to a line whose position is given.   This is a case that frequently occurs in practice
when part of an enceinte of little extent in breadth, but great
in length, is to be defiled.   It is requisite in this case, that the
plane of defilement should be parallel to the direction of the
ground along which the tracé of the fortification is to be laid
out.

The solution of this particular case, is not more difficult than
the two preceding ; only that we must take care to give the
surface of defilement a different generation, by enveloping the
exterior ground with a cylindrical surface, all whose ridges are
parallel to the line AF, to which the plane of defilement should
be parallel.   The section ooo of this surface by the vertical
plane passing through XY, is not more difficult to construct than
that of the section of the conical surface ; and is deduced from
sections of ground by vertical planes containing the ridges.
This granted, then through the points m of the maximum and
minimum of relief draw parallels to the right line AF, and draw
their directions in the vertical plane : we will suppose that
these directions are the points t and t'.   These graphical operations being performed, all the tangents drawn to the curve
ooo, and which like VV pass between the directions t and t' of
the sytems of the maximum and minimum of relief, will satisfy
the conditions of the problem, and may be taken for the direction of the plane of defilement.   Then from all these tangents
that one will be chosen which gives the most advantageous artificial plane of site under those relations which are independent
of defilement.   The direction of the plane of defilement in the
vertical plane being known, we will easily find it upon the horizontal plane.   For this purpose, take on the direction in the
vertical plane two points, through which draw two right lines

parallel to the line whose position is given ; and find the points
at which these right lines, which are in the plane of defilement,
cut the horizontal plane : the line drawn through these two
points, will be the intersection sought.

The art of conducting the laying out of the boyaux of trenches
before a front of attack, is founded upon defilement ; and consists in conducting the boyaux in such a manner, that the rampant plane which passes through the summit of the profile of
the trenches and at 20 decimètres (6¾ feet) above the foot of
its reverse, shall graze the most commanding points of the fortification and leave below it the most salient parts.   It would be
possible to construct an instrument that would be of great
assistance to engineers in laying out the direction of boyaux.
It might consist of a truncated cone whose side would have the
same inclination as the rampant plane, and which is known by
the profile of the trench.   This cone, of about 3 decimètres
high (12 inches), should revolve round a vertical axis, and have
a transom or cross-staff (*alidade*) fixed to its surface which would
turn in the tangential plane.   The use of this instrument would
be very simple.   At the point of departure of the boyaux and
covered by an opening or ditch (*amorce*), the engineer would
establish the foot of the instrument perfectly vertical, and then
turn the cone and cross-staff, or alidada, until he perceived that
the visual ray rested upon the most commanding point : he
would then fix the body of the instrument ; and by directing the
cross-staff upon the ground itself, the visual ray would trace upon it the direction of the boyau, which will be always right if
the visual ray directed towards the most advanced parts of the
fortification leaves them inside.

Application of
defilement to the
laying out of
trench boyaux.

185.   We showed in the Second Part (104), that the influence of commanding heights produces modifications in the tracé.
This truth has now become most striking from the preceding
exposition of the general rules of defilement.   The two causes
that produce irregularity in fortification, combine together in
its arrangement, in the same manner that they do in the formation of general orders of battle.   In these, the General who is
endowed with an able *coup d'œil*, retires the weak parts from
the points advantageous to the enemy ; whilst he boldly advances on those parts of the site that are favourable to the action and display of his moving forces.   It may be truly said

185. The com-
bination of the
two causes of ir-
regularity, or the
influence of com-
manding heights
over the tracé.
(See the Second
Part) (104).

that he draws a moveable fortification, which varies in form every moment of the battle.

The arrangement of the tracé of a fortification, with respect to defilement.

When we only consider in the tracé of a fortification the irregularity of the site itself (179), we adapt the tracé to the peculiar form of the ground, with a view to have the smallest relief without impairing the efficiency of the commandment. But when to this first difficulty must be added the consideration of the defilement, the question becomes more complicated ; and we must then endeavour to dispose the tracé in such a manner as to experience the fewest difficulties possible in the operations of the defilement, without however deviating from the other general conditions.   A slight change in the direction of one part of the enceinte, or in that of the branch of a work, though often indifferent in relation to the other conditions to be fulfilled, may lead to operations of defilement extremely simple and easy ; and which, without this modification in the tracé, might have been impracticable.

Consequences and rules deduced from the cases of defilement.

The cases of defilement that have been treated, lead to important consequences which furnish some rules proper to direct us in laying out works of fortification, with respect to their defilement.

First consequence.

It is as easy to defile from a great height that is distant, as from a small one that is near ; that is, the influence of commanding heights is in direct proportion to their vertical elevation above the site upon which the tracé is to be displayed, and in inverse proportion to their distance.

First rule.

This obvious consequence (181) leads to this first rule—*That the parts of a fortification must be eloigned as far as possible from the heights to which they are exposed.*

Second consequence.

The questions treated (182), lead also to the following consequence ; The faces and branches that form the salients of the works, must embrace as much as possible by their prolongations the whole extent of the commanding height that possesses an influence over them ; they should never plunge into the ground.   When this condition cannot be fulfilled, the faces and branches must be directed in such a manner that their prolongations will fall upon low-grounds, water-courses, and anfractuousnesses, &c.   Traverses must likewise be used with skill, to cover the works from lateral heights.

Second rule.

From this flows the important rule—*The salient angles must be made as obtuse as possible:* this second rule is contained in the first.

These general rules are liable to exceptions in practice. We shall see in the sequel, that there are cases where the parts of a fortification should converge towards the commanding points, instead of retiring from them.

Remark on the application of these rules in practice.

186. In the same manner that the directions of the faces and branches composing the elements of a fortification may be varied in relation to the commanding heights, and thus their defilement facilitated ; we may also vary within certain limits the directrices of the tracé of an enceinte or of part of an enceinte, in order to facilitate the defilement of all the parts ; provided that the relief be arranged according to the rules of the defence and construction.   But this question, taken in its generality, is so complicated, that to attain some results it is necessary to simplify its data.   It is supposed, 1st, that the enceinte is simple : 2d, that the systems of the maximum and minimum of the relief are given, and situated in planes parallel to the plane of the ground upon which the tracé is to be laid out : 3d, that there is considered only one commanding point, or one commanding line, on the exterior ground.   These being granted ; then if we suppose a plane of defilement properly chosen, it will cut the planes containing the systems of the maximum and minimum in two lines, whose projections upon the ground will include a *zone* which M. Say calls the *fillet of defilement* (*bandeau de défilement*), in his interesting Memoir on Defilement. This zone is obviously the only part of the ground upon which the fortification can be displayed ; and the nearer the tracé is to one of the limits of this zone, the nearer will be the relief to its corresponding limit, &c.   Hence it follows, that the narrower this fillet is, the more we will be straitened to display the tracé ; and the wider it is, the more easy will be this operation.   It is therefore important to find out the causes that increase or diminish the width of the zone of defilement.

186. General considerations on the direction that must be given to the directrices of the tracé of enceintes, with respect to commanding heights from which the fortification is to be defiled.

Consequences.

We will first suppose that there is only one single commanding point to be considered on the exterior ground ; and we will see at once that two causes produce the variation in the breadth of the zone of defilement : 1st, The distance of the commanding point, which, according as it is more or less considerable, evidently produces a zone of greater or less width : 2d, The direction of the zone in respect to the commanding height. In-

The magnitude of the zone of defilement, when there is but one single commanding point.

deed if we project upon the horizontal plane the line drawn from the commanding point to the point of departure of the zone, we find that its width becomes nothing when it is directed upon the commanding height ; and that it increases until the angle becomes a right angle.   This likewise demonstrates the first rule, and shows that whenever a commanding point through which the plane of defilement must pass, influences a portion of an enceinte, all its parts must be retired from this point as far as possible ; and that if the direction of the works be rectilinear, this line must be drawn perpendicularly to the projection of the line drawn from the commanding point to that from which the directrix must be drawn.   Nevertheless if .the ground be acclivous along the general direction of the directrix, this latter may be inclined towards the commanding point.   If on the contrary the ground be declivous, the angle of departure must be made obtuse ; that is, the directrix of the tracé must more or less diverge.

First state of the case : the direction of a directrix of the tracé with respect to a commanding point.

When, instead of a commanding point, we have to consider a commanding line through which the plane of defilement must pass ; we must imagine that the prolongation of this line cuts the planes of the maximum and minimum of relief.   This shows that the zones of defilement pass through the horizontal projection of that part of the prolongation of the commanding line included between these planes ; that the breadth of these zones is greater in proportion as the commanding line is less inclined upon the plane of the earth, and as their directions tend more and more to become perpendicular to the horizontal projection of the commanding line ; and that consequently, the defilement and tracé are regulated with the more ease in proportion as these circumstances exist in a greater degree.

Second state of the case: the directrix of the tracé is supposed to be displayed facing a commanding line through which the plane of defilement must pass.

The preceding considerations furnish some general rules proper to serve as guides in practice : 1st, Works whose salients are obtuse, have in general a disposition favourable for the defilement ; and as this same disposition concurs to increase their intrinsic and relative strength, it follows that it accords with all the principles.   2d, When part of an enceinte is to be displayed before a chain of heights, whose crest inclines towards the ground upon which the tracé is to be laid out, the directrix of this tracé must converge towards the point where this crest meets the plane of the ground : but if this crest be not sensibly inclined upon the plane of the ground, the directrix of the tracé

General results deduced from the preceding considerations.

should tend to become parallel to it. 3d, Lastly, and to complete what we said in the Second Part (104); when part of an enceinte or other defensive disposition crosses a valley commanded by collateral heights, the works in the bottom of the valley must be thrown back as far as possible ; their salient angles must be made sufficiently obtuse for their faces and branches to converge towards the most advanced works upon the heights ; and the lines that transversely descend the sides of the hills, must be drawn in cremaillère, &c.

187. That our readers may better understand this subject, we will now apply these principles to the particular defilement of a common fortified front ; reckoning among its elements the advanced lunette situated upon the bastion capital.

187. Application of the preceding principles to the defilement of the elements of the modern bastioned front.

As the arrangement of the relief must be deduced from the very operations of defilement, we must evidently begin with the most advanced elements ; because they become so many commanding points from which the works in rear must be defiled. This shows that the lunette must be first treated ; then the ravelins, and their redoubts ; and finally the bastion.

To defile the lunette, we must according to the local circumstances fix the position of the hinge or axis of the artificial plane of site, to afterwards determine its position by Meusnier's and Monge's method, precedingly described (181). This hinge must occupy the lowest part of the plane of site ; in order to avoid the necessity of excavations, or to excavate as little as possible, and give the work the greatest commandment. To this effect, draw through the points c and d of the branches of the covert-way, given by the perpendiculars ac and bd, an indefinite right line GG bounding the ground that possesses a lateral influence ; and through this right line protracted 7 to 800 mètres (780 to 890 yards) on the right and left, a vertical plane will be drawn and upon it will be constructed the section ttt of the ground that is turned down (*rabattue*): this section will show the general direction OO of the ground. If the right line mn be parallel to the line OO, it will be taken for the hinge ; if it be not, it will be oscillated in the vertical plane about the point x of the capital until it becomes parallel. If this change in the position of the hinge sink one of the points n or m more than 5 decimètres (20 inches), it must be raised to this depression ; in order that the ravelins may completely enfilade the ditches. In any other case this depression may be as great as 1 mètre .5

Defilement of the lunette. The horizontal projection of the crest of the covert-way is supposed to be given : that of the covering line is not. (PLATE XII, fig. 6.)

(5 feet), to preserve 10 decimètres (3¼ feet) of commandment. The plane of site being thus established, the scale of declivity will be drawn ; and if the reference that it gives for the point of the salient, differ more than 2 mètres (6¾ feet) from that of the corresponding point of ground, the plane may be raised as high as this difference, and thus the relief of the work increased.

(Figure 7.) To determine the plane of defilement of the lunette, we must through the point *M*, supposed to be the lowest of the face, draw along the perpendicular direction *AB* a vertical plane upon which the profile will be constructed. Through the crest *c* of the covert-way the parallel *co* will be drawn in the direction of the plane of site, and this will determine the summit *o* of the scarp ; through this summit draw the line *on* inclined towards the horizon 45 degrees, and through the point *K* elevated 10 decimètres (3¼ feet) above the counterscarp draw the line *Kr* making an angle of 9°, 30′ with the horizon ; these two lines will cut each other at *m*, and *mo* will be the exterior slope of the parapet. By drawing a vertical at 60 decimètres (20 feet) from the point *m*, it will cut the line of fire or plunge at *r* ; and this point will be the direction of the covering line. Through this point will be drawn the line *VV*, parallel to *AB* ; and this will be the direction of the plane of defilement of the lunette, which will have the minimum of relief.

Defilement of the ravelin. The horizontal projection of the covering line is supposed to be given. (Fig. 6.) The defilement of the ravelin *D*, is also reduced to selecting properly the position for the hinge of its plane of site. Through the extremes of the faces two perpendiculars will be raised, upon which about 40 mètres (44½ yards) will be laid off to find nearly the points of the crest of the covert-way. Through these points *E* a vertical plane will be drawn cutting the ground, and upon which the section will be constructed to a distance of 800 mètres (890 yards) on the right and left. We will therefore have the general direction of the ground ; and the right line *E′E* will be oscillated until it becomes parallel to it. This latter line, which will be the hinge sought, must touch the ground at one of the points *E*, or be depressed at most 1 mètre .5 (5 feet).

Construction of the profile of the left face (Fig. 8.) The plane of site and its scale of declivity being determined as precedingly, the height of the plane of defilement remains to be established ; and likewise the position of the glacis crest, and that of the scarp and counterscarp. These projections can only be obtained by the formation of a profile arranged agreeably to the rules of the attack and defence.   Through the lowest point E' and perpendicularly to the direction of the left face of the ravelin, draw a vertical plane $E'F$ that will cut the capital of the adjacent bastion at a point that will be the *point to be battered (point à battre)*; upon this plane the section of the ground and the direction of the plane of site will be constructed.   This being granted ; the lines of artillery fire which must pass through the point to be battered and at 10 decimètres ($3\frac{1}{4}$ feet) below the covering line, must also pass 13 decimètres ($4\frac{1}{3}$ feet) above the crest of the glacis : and besides this first condition, it is necessary that these lines of fire when inclined $\frac{1}{6}$th should pass 10 decimètres above the summit of the counterscarp. Hence it follows, that by supposing the width of the covert-way terra-plain to be 10 mètres ($33\frac{1}{4}$ feet), the lines of artillery fire inclined $\frac{1}{6}$th will cut the vertical from the glacis crest at 31 decimètres .6 ($10\frac{1}{2}$ feet) below this crest ; and as the lines of musketry fire pass 23 decimètres ($7\frac{2}{3}$ feet) above this same crest, the portion of the vertical included between these two lines of fire will be 54 decimètres .6 ($18\frac{1}{4}$ feet).   We must now draw the curve that is the locus (*lieu*) of the foot of the glacis crest.   For this purpose, take upon the vertical oo which contains the direction of the covering line, several very approximated points $m, m,$ &c. which will be considered as the directions of the covering line ; and through these points the lines of fire mt will be drawn, passing 10 decimètres ($3\frac{1}{4}$ feet) above the point to be battered.   To all these lines the parallels $pn, pn,$ &c. will be drawn 54 decimètres .6 ($18\frac{1}{4}$ feet) below them ; and through the points $m,$ &c. the lines of fire $mq, mq,$ &c. will be drawn inclined one-sixth.   At the points of intersection $q, q,$ &c. the verticals $qr, qr,$ &c. of 0 mètres .66 (nearly 27 inches) will be raised ; and the points $r, r,$ &c. will be the points of the curve sought.   This curve will cut the plane of site at the point T, which will be the foot of the crest s of the glacis ss'. If we lay off from T to Q the width of the terra-plain, we have the counterscarp.   Raise the vertical Qx of 10 decimètres ($3\frac{1}{4}$ feet) and draw xM inclined one-sixth ; the point M will be the direction of the covering line, through which the direction ZZ of the plane of defilement will be drawn.

The position of the scarp remains to be found.   This should be established in such a manner, that after a breach is formed there will remain 40 decimètres ($13\frac{1}{4}$ feet) thickness of parapet

Through the summit Q of the counterscarp draw the line of fire Qg inclined one-sixth, and cutting in g the line inclined 45 degrees drawn through the point of the plunge distant 40 decimètres (13½ feet) from the vertical oo: through this point g a vertical will be drawn, giving the position of the scarp; and the point y of intersection with the line inclined 45 degrees, and drawn through the point of the plunge distant 60 decimètres (20 feet) from the line oo, will be its summit. But from the preceding construction it may happen that the ditch will not have the proper established width of 20 mètres (22 yards). In this case a second operation will be requisite to establish the scarp, counterscarp, and crest of the glacis. This new construction is performed by taking upon the plane of site several successive and very approximated points that will be considered as the summits of counterscarps and as belonging to so many profiles, whose scarps will be determined as we have just explained. Through all these latter points a curve age will be drawn, and will be the locus (lieu) of all the scarps; then on all the lines inclined one-sixth and passing through the summits of the counterscarps, will be laid off the length of the hypotenuse of a rect-angled triangle one of whose sides is 20 mètres (22¼ yards) and whose hypotenuse is inclined one-sixth on this side. Through all the points thus found the curve hef will be drawn; it will be parallel to the first, and will be the locus for the counterscarps of a ditch 20 mètres wide: the intersection e of this curve with the plane of site, will be the summit of the counterscarp, whose particular profile will be constructed.

If the width, instead of being too little, were too great, it must be diminished by approximating the counterscarp and suitably lowering the covering line.

Construction of the profile of the right face. (Figs. 6 and 9.) The profile of the left face being constructed, we proceed to construct that of the right face. It would be the same as the first, if the capital of the right bastion were placed in the same relation with the right face, as the capital of the left bastion is with respect to the left face; and also, if the scale of declivity were parallel to the capital. As this is not generally the case, the profile of the right face is different from that of the other face; because the covering line is determined. To construct it, we must through the extremity of the face draw the vertical plane through EF perpendicular to the direction of the face; and construct upon this plane the direction of the plane of site, the section of the ground, and the direction of the covering line.

Through the direction of the covering line draw a line of fire passing 10 decimètres (3¼ feet) above the point to be battered situated on the capital of the collateral bastion ; this line of fire should be elevated 48 decimètres (16 feet) above the foot of the crest of the glacis.   If therefore the parallel *Kl* be drawn, elevated 48 decimètres (16 feet) above *PP*, the vertical *yv*, drawn through its point of intersection with the line of fire *Mt*, will be the exterior limit of the foot of the glacis crest.   Through the direction *M* of the covering line draw the line of fire *Mè* inclined one-sixth, and cut by the parallel *nr* elevated 10 decimètres above *PP ;* and the vertical *xz* drawn through the point *q* will be the limit of the counterscarps.   Accordingly if we draw the vertical *y'v'* at 10 mètres (33¼ feet) from *xz*, it will be the interior limit of the glacis crest : therefore the space *TT'* is the only one upon which the foot of the glacis crest can be found.   To find this point, construct as precedingly the curve *hef* which is the locus of the counterscarp summits for a ditch 20 mètres (22¼ yards) wide ; and the point of intersection *e* with the plane of site, will give the summit of the counterscarp ; and then by laying off 10 mètres (33¼ feet) from *e* to *e'*, we will find the foot of the glacis crest.

If by this operation the point *e* do not fall within the limits, but fall on this side of the limit *y'v'*, the ditch must be widened and the parapet heightened : and then perform upon this profile an operation to find the profile adapted to the true width of the ditch ; and from which the precise quantity that the covering line is to be raised, will be deduced.

The defilement of the ravelin redoubt is effected by establishing its terra-plain in a plane parallel to that containing the ravelin terra-plain, and 10 decimètres (3¼ feet) above this latter.

Defilement of the ravelin redoubt : the covering line is given.

In the defilement of the bastions we must not only consider the commanding ground that is in front, but likewise the terra-plains of the ravelin redoubts, that are two collateral commanding points from which they must be defiled.   The hinge of the rampant plane that is to contain the terra-plain, will be that which passes through the most commanding point of each redoubt.   But we will first suppose that these two points are lowered down into the plane of site of the ravelin covert-way ; and it is through these two new points that the rampant plane

Defilement of the bastion.

tangential to the ground will be drawn. The plane will then
be raised parallel to itself until the hinge rests upon the commanding points of the terra-plain of the redoubt in their true
position ; and this plane, thus elevated, must contain the terra-
plain of the bastion.   To find the most commanding points of
each redoubt in relation to the bastion, we must therefore consider these redoubts as lowered down into the plane of site ; and
draw the scale of declivity of the plane of site of each ravelin
covert-way. If these scales of declivity diverge towards the
country, the intersection of the two planes will form a gutter ;
and the point that the scale last abandons in departing parallel
to itself from the intersection, will be the most commanding
point. But if the scales of declivity converge towards the
country, the intersection of the two planes of site will be a salient
ridge ; and the most commanding point of each redoubt, will be
that through which the line passes that is parallel to the scale
of declivity and nearest to the intersection. These two points
of the hinge being thus known and marked with the references,
the rampant plane will be drawn tangential to the ground ; and
it will then be raised parallel to itself until the hinge has gained
its true position. It is in this raised plane that the bastion terra-
plain will be established.

Defilement of
the salient and
re-entering pla-
ces of arms.
(Fig. 6.) The two re-entering places of arms P, P, and the salient
place of arms S, will be in the same plane of defilement. They
will be defiled from the ground in front comprised between the
two perpendiculars xv drawn to the faces of the bastions through
the intersections of the branches of the covert-way with the
counterscarp. Through these perpendiculars vertical planes
will be drawn, and upon which the directions y of the bastion
covering line will be drawn ; at 10 decimètres (3⅓ feet) below
these points will be drawn the line of artillery fire inclined one-
sixth, which will determine the height of the counterscarp at x.
Through the one of these two points that is nearest the plane
of the bastion terra-plain, and in the vertical plane of which
xx is the direction, a parallel to the plane of the bastion terra-
plain will be drawn ; and this line will be the hinge through
which the plane of site will be drawn tangential to the ground,
or a plane parallel to the bastion plane of defilement, if this latter leave below itself all the exterior commanding points.

It must be observed with respect to the bastion B, which has
in its front a lunette L, that the places of arms must be defiled

from the terra-plain of this work (*piece*); if they be not, the rampant plane must be raised a sufficient quantity, &c.

It must likewise be observed, that the terra-plain of the ravelin covert-ways being determined by previous operations, it must be united with that of the bastion covert-way: but two things may happen; 1st, the plane of the place of arms may be higher than the other; and in this case, if the ressault or rise exceed 5 decimètres (20 inches), the plane must be lowered to this difference; always taking care that the highest extreme line of fire does not pass at more than 10 decimètres (3½ feet) above the summit of the counterscarp: 2d, The terra-plain of the place of arms may be lower than that of the ravelin covertway; in this case, the first plane must be raised to a level with the latter.

To find the plane of the terra-plain of the redoubts of the *Deflement of the redoubts of the re-entering places of arms*, it must be observed that their covering line should be 23 decimètres (7¾ feet) below the bastion plane of fire; or what is the same, that their plane of terraplain must be 48 decimètres (16 feet) below it. Accordingly on the vertical plane passing through *yv*, the bastion line of fire inclined one-sixth will be drawn; and a line will be drawn parallel to and 48 decimètres below it. This latter line will be considered as the hinge of a plane drawn through the most commanding point of that portion of the glacis crest included between the capitals of the bastion and ravelin. It is evident that this plane will be determined by making it pass through the horizontal that makes the greatest angle with the hinge, since this hinge is declivous towards the summit of the angle. This plane being thus determined, its scale of declivity will be constructed; which will give the references of the directions of the verticals raised through the angles of the redoubt. Then take the difference between these references and those of the directions of these same verticals on the plane of the terraplain of the place of arms, and we will have the height of the verticals included between the two planes. Through the summit of the smallest of these verticals draw a plane parallel to the plane of the terra-plain of the place of arms; and this latter plane must contain the terra-plain of the redoubt, in order that it may be defiled and that its highest point be 48 decimètres (16 feet) below the bastion plane of fire.

We have nothing to add to what we have already said re- *Deflement of the tenaille.*

specting the defilement of the tenaille, in Chapter V. (146), where it is completely described.

Defilement of the bastion cavalier.

The plane of defilement of the bastion cavalier, when there is one, is parallel to that of the bastion ; its height above the latter depends upon the commandment and range to be gained over the country without.

The particular methods that we have now described, afford an idea of the manner in which the students for the artillery, and engineers, apply the general rules of defilement under the direction of M. Dobenheim.   This veteran officer of engineers, possessing the greatest talents, is generally acknowledged as a most able professor of fortification, and the fittest man to guide young officers in the study of this science.

General reflections. (See the works of St Paul, and Bousmard, & the Memoir by Say.)

This general exposition is sufficient to introduce the students into those applications, which, properly speaking, constitute the art of fortification.   The students and young officers who are ambitious of extending their knowledge in this branch, in relation to its practice, will consult the works of St. Paul and of Bousmard ; and they will read with interest the Memoir of Say, inserted in the fifth number of the Journal of the Polytechnick School.

We should omit a duty, the performance of which is dear to us, if we did not seize this occasion to pay to this young engineer the tribute of praise due to his talents and devotion to his country.   Say fell at the siege of St. Jean D'Acre, covered with wounds and with glory ; he died with his General, the virtuous Caffarelly-Dufalga, whose name awakens every liberal idea, and whose memory will never cease to be honoured by letters, arts, and friendship.

CHAPTER XI.

*The Materials and Stores necessary for the Defence of a For-
tress ; the Data according to which the quantity of Artillery,
the Strength of the different Arms and Services composing the
Garrison, the quantity of Supplies, &c. are calculated ; the
Situations for the several Depots and for lodging the Troops.*

188. IN Chapter IV (124 and 135), in which we established
the relation between the attack and the defence, we supposed
that the fortress was suitably armed and provided with a garrison proportioned to all the exigencies of the defence and to the
tactical manœuvres ; and that it was furnished with all those supplies and provisions and ammunition that the conduct of a regular
siege renders indispensable. We could not then exhibit the data
upon which the calculation of the quantity of these objects, is
founded. We propose in this Chapter to supply the omission
by a few general sketches, without entering into details that
are contained in many excellent works ; which the students
and young officers may consult when their residence in fortresses,
and the sight of these admirable productions of the art of fortification, inspire them with the noble ambition of extending their
knowledge in this branch of science.

189. The arming with cannon, the strength of the garrison,
the supplies of arms, ammunition, provisions, &c. are the result of an immediate reconnaissance made by the General or superior officer charged with the defence of the fortress threatened. When the General of an army is upon the defensive and
occupies a position, his walls are his soldiers and artillery ; and
he covers the line of operations by which he is continually
receiving reinforcements in men and artillery and the supplies
for daily subsistence. But this is not the case with a General
shut up in a fortress ; he must provide it with every thing for
a vigorous defence, establish them in safe situations, and distribute them in the best manner.

The Governor to whom the defence of a menaced fortress is
intrusted, will first devote his attention to inspecting the nature, strength, and disposition of his fortifications. This reconnaissance is not the result of that prompt and rapid coup d'œil

*188. General
reflections on the
elements neces-
sary for the de-
fence of a for-
tress.*

*189. Reconnais-
sance of a fortress
for an approach-
ing defence.*

by which the General of an army seizes the advantages of a field of battle, and posts his army accordingly; but it is the fruit of the engineer'and artillery officer's long labour and meditation in the solitude of the closet, and executed by mock representations on the ground. Accordingly, the officer of engineers and the officer of artillery, who should be the soul of the Governor's council, will furnish him with plans and memoirs, agreeably to which will be determined, 1st, which are the assailable fronts, and to what period the probable duration of the siege may be protracted; 2d, what quantity of artillery is requisite for the defence, either during the operation of the investment, or during the operations of a siege in form. These being established, the Governor will determine the services of the garrison according to the rules of siege tactics. He will consider the extent of the exterior fortifications, to fix the number of troops necessary to guard against all kinds of surprise; and then descending to the detailed operations of the siege, he will divide his garrison into three corps; one will be charged with all the labours, the second will be assigned to the artillery and service of the mines, and the third will be reserved for acting against the enemy with their fire-arms, swords, and bayonets. This last corps will keep up a constant and regular fire upon the trenches, repulse the enemy in all their attempts to storm the works, execute all the sorties against the working parties, and sustain all assaults. The general service will be so arranged, that each labourer will have at least 10 hours rest out of 24; and each soldier 12 out of 36. It must be reckoned in· calculating the strength of the garrison, that their numbers will be reduced to two thirds towards the end of the siege; for sickness and wounds will occasion great losses. Hence it follows, that one half of the garrison should be sufficient to repulse the besiegers in their attacks on the covert-way and in the assaults.

He must likewise, in calculating the quantity of artillery and strength of the garrison, never lose sight of this important truth —that a besieging army, however strong it may be, for instance of 80,000 men, cannot provide for more than two attacks. And if this army do not exceed 45 to 50 thousand men, it can only form one single attack.

After the Governor has established the principal elements of which we have spoken; that is, the quantity of artillery, the strength of the garrison, the presumed number of attacks, and the probable duration of the siege ; he thence deduces the quantities of ammunition and provisions, and of all the other supplies necessary for the defence of the place.   He will hence learn the spaces of coverts or shelters requisite to contain all these stores, and for the portion of the garrison that reposes.   This last consideration shows how much superior, all other things being equal, the great fortresses are to the medium and small fortresses, in consequence of the facility with which all the dispositions of the defence may be made in them and concealed from the knowledge of the besiegers and defended from their artillery.

190. It is as yet a very indeterminate question what quantity of artillery a fortress should be provided with, to make the greatest resistance.   But if we consider that this quantity must be proportioned to the means of arming all the frontiers of a state, and to the necessarily limited portion of the munitions of war that it is possible to place in each threatened fortress ; and that reason and experience coincide in establishing it as a principle, that it is not the greatness of the quantity of artillery that can protract the duration of the siege, but a well disposed artillery defended from the fury of that of the besiegers ; we will see that it is practicable conformably to long experience to assign to each fortress the quantity of artillery necessary for its defence, by founding the calculation on the extent of the perimeter that is assailable, and on this principle—that a fortress is never exposed to sustain more than two simultaneous attacks. In this question of the application of principles, as in all others relating to the arts, the general principles admitted must bend to particular cases ; they are only, as it were, a species of magnetic compass to direct the matured *coup d'œil* of the engineer and artillery officer.   Fortresses have consequently been divided into eight classes, in relation to their extent and the probable duration of their sieges.

190. The rule by which the quantity of artillery for a fortress, the strength of the garrison, &c. are calculated.

The quantities of cannon assigned to the various classes of fortresses, can therefore only be approximations, as we have already said, which are modified for each particular case ; and which afford the probability of a general armament and supply upon the frontier.

The arming of the eight classes of the fortresses with artillery.

The places of arms and places of depôt that compose the three first classes, may be considered as polygons of 18 to 25 sides. The fortresses of the fourth and fifth classes descend to dodecagons and decagons. The sixth class includes the hexagons and octagons. And the seventh and eighth classes comprehend those that are equivalent to the pentagon and square.

TABLE

Of the mean quantities of Artillery necessary for arming Fortresses.

Cannon, Mortars, Howitzers and Stone Mortars		1st, 2d & 3d Classes	4th and 5th Classes	6th Classes	7th and 8th Classes
Cannon Garrison Pieces,	24 p'drs 16 p'drs 12 p'drs 8 p'drs 4 p'dr	1 10 15 20 10 } 140	6 30 33 15 6 } 100	3 13 13 12 8 } 61	2 6 7 6 6 } 35
Field Pieces,	12 p'drs 8 p'drs 4 p'drs	6 8	2 4 4	... 3 4	.. 2 4
Mortars, ...	12 inch 10 inch 8 inch	6 10 } 30 20	4 7 } 26 15	2 5 } 17 6	1 2 } 9 6
Howitzers, ...	8 inch 6 inch	24 } 34 20	10 } 26 16	6 } 16 10	1 } 4 3
Stone Mortars, ...		10	8	6	4
Total quantities of ordnance,		220	160	100	50

Besides the kinds of artillery mentioned in this Table, we have shown the importance and even the necessity of founding for the defence of fortresses a great number of small Co ehorn-stone-mortars, for throwing showers of grenades. And in the place of the arquebuses with rests, which are no longer manufactured, we must substitute four-pounder field-pieces, or *rostaing pieces;* these are transported by hand into the most advanced and most exposed works. Let us now see whether this general project of armament is capable of fulfilling the conditions prescribed by the rules of defence.

Disposition of the artillery at the various epochs of the siege, in a fortress of the first order.

The moment that a fortress is threatened the artillery must be posted on the ramparts and in the advanced works, for the two-fold purpose of preventing attacks by storm, surprise or escalade, and to act against the operations of the investment. It is therefore necessary that all the artillery should be distributed at this moment along the whole assailable part of the perimeter, to scour the ditches and batter all points of the coun-try.

Let us imagine a fortress of the first class, assailable on all its ambit, and all the barbettes and flank embrasures of which are completed ; we may distribute in the following manner the 200 pieces of ordnance allotted for its armament :

The 24 pounders will be mounted on the most commanding points of the enceinte, in order to overlook far into the country. Each bastion will be armed with two 16 pounders, one 12 pounder, one 4 pounder or 1 howitzer, and with one mortar to throw fiery balls. The barbettes of the ravelins of gates, will be armed with 12 and 8 pounders. Each salient ravelin place of arms will be provided with one 8 inch mortar for throwing pot-grenadoes. The remaining 60 pieces, consisting of 12, 8, and 4 pounders and field-pieces and howitzers, will be held in reserve, either to arm the flanks in case of an esca-lade, or to mount in the advanced works, or to act without in attacks upon the investing troops.

When the besiegers, after reconnoitring, have selected the fronts of attack, the armament will be changed. At least two-thirds of the artillery will be disposed upon these and the col-lateral fronts, the advanced works of which take in flank and obliquely (*écharper*) the enemy's dispositions. It is obvious that 120 pieces of artillery well disposed, will constitute a most formidable armament, whose effects will be as efficient as if we had an unlimited quantity of artillery at command. The field pieces will be always in reserve, to follow the sorties, or to be used in the advanced posts. The mortars will be esta-blished upon the curtains and in the ravelin terra-plains, to fire over the parapets and throw fiery balls during the night.

When the besiegers' batteries are in full fire, the most ex-posed artillery will be withdrawn and placed in reserve, and posted on the collateral works. The position of the batteries will be frequently changed, in order to deceive the enemy ; and only a well served artillery, defended from ricochets, will be shown.

Finally ; when the enemy establish their third parallel, the greatest possible quantity of artillery will be brought forward, and its fires will be no longer economised ; it will contend to the last moment against the besieging artillery. It is obvious that the quantity of artillery that we have just allotted, will be sufficient to arm the flanks, and also the covered and casemated batteries, if there be any on the fronts of attack. At this epoch of the siege, when mortars, howitzers, stone-mortars and 4 pounders are the most useful artillery; it may happen that according to the mode of armament laid down, these pieces will be too few in number; whilst there will be a superfluous quantity of heavy pieces. We are therefore of opinion, that the number of heavy pieces should be diminished by 15; and that there should be substituted in their place, 4 mortars, 6 howitzers, and 5 stone-mortars.

Disposition of the artillery in a fortress of the third order. This same reasoning may be applied to a place of any other class; for instance to the octagon, the project of whose armament is 100 pieces of artillery. We see that 33 pieces will be mounted upon the barbettes of the eight bastions, and of the two ravelins of the gates; and that there will remain 28 pieces in reserve, either to arm the flanks or advanced works, or to operate without. We must also observe that it would be expedient in this scheme of armament, to diminish by 10 the number of heavy cannon; and to substitute in their place at least 6 howitzers and 4 mortars.

Reflections on the mode of using the artillery. It will not be superfluous to say a few words on the manner in which the Governor should use his artillery during the siege. He will only use random-firing with full charges (*tir de plein fouet*) in firing upon the camps, parks, depôts, &c during the period preceding the opening of the trenches. After the trenches are opened, he will only use these fires to penetrate the imperfect parapets of the besiegers, to retard the construction of ricochet batteries and other works (by horizontal howitze and bomb firing), and to contend during the first moments against the formidable artillery of the besiegers. But as soon as the latter have unmasked their ricochet and direct fires, very little artillery must be suffered to remain upon the enfiladed branches and faces, and it must be there covered by traverses, paradoses, &c. From time to time, and but for a few minutes only, some pieces will be brought forward to fire direct and by salvoes against the trenches, saps, &c.

Notwithstanding that after the first five days of open trenches the direct fire with full charges (*tir de plein fouet*) is no longer regularly used, the artillery fires will not in consequence cease. There will be substituted for this kind of firing, ricochet fires, of which the besieged should (after the example of the besiegers) make habitual use. This fire possesses this triple advantage; 1st, the cannon are never exposed to the enemy's artillery, because they may be placed upon the curtains and other parts that are not enfiladed, and even in the covert-ways : 2d, this fire does not incommode the works in front, because the trajectories pass above the parapets : 3d, This fire consumes a great deal less powder, because the charge is not at the utmost more than one half the common charge : Finally, of all the advantages obtained by ricochet firing when well understood and directed, the greatest is the preserving of the cannoniers and artillery for the end of the siege.

It would be superfluous to insist further upon the importance of this mode of using artillery, for here all the military concur ; and it is chiefly on these considerations that the possibility of defending a fortress with a moderate quantity of artillery, is founded.

After the armament of the place with artillery, it concerns the governor to determine the *strength of the garrison.* This is not an easy matter ; and the various writers who have written upon this subject, have no invariable rules. The most certain data upon which we can depend to arrive at this estimate, must be drawn from the service of the defence. We must distinguish three kinds of *service ;* and even *four,* when a subterranean war is to be carried on : 1st, the service of the artillery : 2d, the musketry service : 3d, the service at the interior and exterior works or labours : 4th, the service of the mines. The services being thus classed, we must remember that their duties vary at the different epochas of the siege ; and that it is a knowledge of these duties that partly leads to that of the strength of the garrison. The extent of the perimeter that is to be defended, is also an essential datum to be considered ; and attention must be paid to the probable duration of the siege, for the longer the siege, the greater are the losses ; and notwithstanding these losses, the strength of the garrison must suffice to repulse the assaults of the besiegers to the last moment.

The memoir for the defence, composed by the officers of artillery and engineers under the direction of the commandant of the fortress, will exhibit the number of men necessary for each service for each principal epoch, and even for each day of the siege. This memoir will determine ; 1st, the service of the artillery, the labours of the artillery, and the mode in which the fire must be executed each day and each night ; 2d, the

The basis on which the calculation of the strength of the garrison is founded.

works of fortification to be erected ; 3d, the service of the infantry, including the use of their fire, and their sorties to level the works of the attack.   In all that we are about to say we will take it for granted that this memoir is digested with proper skill, and that the case is a common octagon with fronts arranged like that which we have taken as a term of comparison.   We will also suppose, 1st, that the place is only on its guard, and expected to be invested ; or, 2d, that the investment is effected, and that the siege is regularly carrying on.

Calculating the strength of the garrison under the apprehension of surprise and investment.
If the fortress were only menaced with an attack by storm, and even with a blockade, and this is the case with all fortresses in the vicinity of a hostile corps d'armée ; the strength of the garrison should be calculated in relation to this particular circumstance, and would be inferior to its state on the footing of a siege in form.   This calculation must be made agreeably to the efforts that the garrison must display, to repulse a daring and enterprising enemy.

The manner in which the troops of the various arms should do duty in a fortress menaced and besieged.
The practice hitherto has been, to relieve the troops on duty only every 24 hours ; but engineer and artillery officers have long concurred in the expediency, we might say the necessity, of changing an arrangement that fatigues the troops, makes the service languish, and that is at variance with the physical organization of man.   They wisely propose to relieve every 12 hours the corps employed on actual duty, and to assign them six hours of bivouac only ; that is, in 36 hours a soldier will have 12 hours actual duty, 6 hours bivouac, and 18 hours of positive rest.   By this arrangement the bivouacs will consist of one half of the troops on actual duty, the soldiers will be fatigued as little as possible, and the enemy will always find them fresh and ready to make a vigorous resistance.   It is agreeably to this principle that we will now estimate the number of men necessary for the service of the artillery, infantry, and cavalry.

Calculation of the strength of the artillery troops : principle on this subject.
To estimate in general the force of the artillery troops, we must know that the cannoniers attached to the service of a piece can fire in 24 hours 100 to 120 rounds ; of which number 30 or 40 will be fired during the night.   It follows that when there are several pieces upon a battery or barbette, they may be all served by one set of men or *section* (*atelier*), if they all together are not to fire more than 120 rounds in 24 hours. This now is the case, for all the barbette batteries are but in

positions of observation.   Accordingly it will be sufficient for
the day and night service to have in each bastion and in the
ravelins of the two gates, one gunner and four matrosses (ser-
pans); there will also be a bombardier on duty in each bastion
during the night.   These form one relief (relais) of 18 gunners
and bombardiers and 64 matrosses.   The two other reliefs will
compose a portion of the reserve, and of the bivouacs, if any
be established : the strength of this reserve will be 40 gunners
and bombardiers and 240 matrosses.   These matrosses should
be sufficiently numerous to transport the reserve 8 and 4 pounders to the flanks at the moment of an alarm.   Each flank must
be armed with two pieces, to fire with grape into the ditches.
As, on the supposition of an attack by storm, all the artillery
of the flanks must be brought into action at the same time ;
this service will require 34 gunners, 16 bombardiers, and 150
matrosses.   The remaining 12 gunners and 50 matrosses will
be kept in reserve to supply casualties (remplacemens); the
other 100 matrosses will serve with muskets.   These details
of the defence, show that the artillery service of observation
(surveillance) will require at least 60 gunners and bombardiers
and 300 infantry-men.

We know that to perfectly guard a fortress, it is necessary ;   Calculation of
the strength of
the infantry.
1st, To establish without patroles and scouts of cavalry and in-
fantry ; this, for the octagon, will require at least 100 dragoons
and 100 foot rangers (chasseurs à pied); there will be therefore
for the three reliefs, 300 cavalry and 300 rangers : 2d, To
guard the covert-ways and support and protect the scouts
(eclaireurs), and likewise the bombardiers posted in the salient places of arms.   For this purpose, a detachment of 20
men will be stationed in each re-entering place of arms, and
will guard the whole covert-way.   The aggregate of these detachments will compose a force of about 300 men ; and for the
three reliefs we will have 900 men : 3d, To line the flanks of
the bastions with infantry in two ranks, and keep up a warm
fire into the ditches : this service will be performed by 50 men,
who will be on daily guard in each bastion.   The three reliefs
make 150 men, and the whole will form a force 1200 strong :
4th, To have a reserve of 500 men, for repulsing the enemy
who may succeed in mounting the ramparts or in establishing
themselves in some outwork.

By recapitulating these forces of the several arms, we have, of

Artillery ....   60 ⎞ gunners and bombardiers.
Infantry .... 2800 ⎟
Dragoons ....   300 ⎬ 3460 men.
Foot rangers......   300 ⎠

This estimate shows, that a fortress of the medium order, with a garrison of 3500 men, is perfectly secure from a coup-de-main : this garrison could even sustain a siege in form for upwards of 15 days[*].

Calculation of the strength of the garrison in case of a regular siege. It is insufficient that a threatened fortress should be secure from an attack by storm ; for when once enveloped and invested, the besiegers must be compelled to open their trenches at a distance, and the garrison should be able to force them to have recourse to all the slow and laborious methods belonging to the tactics of the attack of fortresses.   But this garrison on the establishment of observation that we have just considered, would soon be reduced to extremities ; they could not furnish men for the execution of the tactics of the defence, and could not attain the maximum of the probable duration of the siege. We must therefore, as in the preceding case, consult the memoir for the defence ; and from the duties therein prescribed, deduce the strength of the different services.

Calculation of the strength of the artillery troops on the siege establishment, On the supposition of a real investment by the enemy, the barbettes of the eight bastions and of the eight ravelins will be each armed with 3 pieces of cannon ; they will be served by 20 gunners and 90 matrosses.   By adding 20 bombardiers and 60 matrosses for the 16 mortars, the whole will compose a brigade or relief of 40 gunners and bombardiers and 150 matrosses.

For the reserve of 12 pieces there will be 15 gunners and 150 matrosses, to convey them to the points at which they are wanting as soon as it is suspected that the enemy are opening the trenches before any front ; or to be employed in sorties against the nocturnal cordon.

According to these data the three brigades, or reliefs, and the reserve, will form a force of 135 gunners and bombardiers and 600 matrosses.

Let us now examine whether this force is sufficient during the other periods of the siege.   There are two, on which the

---

* There are several inaccuracies in the summing up of the preceding and following estimates ; but as they are merely formulæ, we have given them as in the original.   TRANSLATOR.

memoir for the defence lays particular emphases; the one that commences with the opening of the trenches, and that which begins with the drawing of the third parallel. At these two moments the besieged should bring into action all the artillery that they can, agreeably to what we said in the fourth chapter.

As soon therefore as the opening of the trenches is discovered, the reserve will move and take post in battery on the front of attack; and the greatest part of the heavy artillery will be withdrawn from the unassailed fronts and placed on the front of attack. The 8 inch mortars will also be withdrawn, and a great many of them will be mounted on gun-carriages to fire bombs horizontally. The ravelins and even the bastions of the collateral fronts will be armed with 12 and 8 pounders, to take obliquely and ricoché the works of the attack. The 8 inch mortars, the howitzers, and the 4 pounders, will be carried into the covert-ways to open a ricochet fire upon the boyaux of the trenches, &c. There will consequently be 76 pieces of ordnance in battery on the front of attack and on the two collateral fronts, and of which 43 will be cannon. The distribution and posting of this artillery, depends upon the disposition of the fortifications, and on the choice that the enemy make of the front of attack. We must observe that as at present each piece does not fire more than 50 rounds in 24 hours, one section (*brigade*) may serve two pieces: the service will consequently require 38 sections, or 38 gunners and bombardiers and 150 matrosses. And for the three reliefs, we must reckon 120 gunners and bombardiers and 450 matrosses. But when we reflect that from the opening of the trenches the labours of the artillery on embrasures, epaulments, traverses, paradoses, &c., are very great; we will perceive that this number must be necessarily increased by three brigades or reliefs, composed of 90 gunners and bombardiers and 900 matrosses.

As during the last period of the siege the service of the artillery may be performed with one third fewer gunners, the preceding calculation will guarantee the service during the whole period of the siege. Accordingly the strength of this service may be estimated at 210 gunners and bombardiers and 1300 matrosses and labourers. When the principal works are completed, 700 of the labourers will be returned to the infantry; and there will remain only 600 men attached to the service of the artillery.

After the fourth day of open trenches the ricochet fires of the besieging artillery will assume such an ascendancy over

Remark on the use of the artillery after the ex-

tablishment
the batteries of
the attack.
of that of the place, even though lowered below the covering-line and placed in embrasures, that its use must be positively changed. The pieces must be posted on all those points where the enemy cannot ruin them, and from which they can keep up a ricochet fire crossing on the trenches. A few pieces only will be brought forward from time to time, to fire direct and with full charges with ball and horizontally with bombs upon the heads of the saps: these pieces will be blinded and covered by traverses. By thus using the artillery, it will be preserved for the latter part of the siege; the ammunition will be economised; and the besiegers will be constantly annoyed in their works. The mortars may be placed in the ditches, if they be dry.

The service of
the engineer
troops, includ-
ing the miners:
calculation of
this force.
Next to the artillery, the most efficient means of defence are the mines; this service is part of the duty of the troops of the engineer corps. The strength of this service is estimated according to the nature of the works to be executed during the investment and after the opening of the trenches. Forty miners will be sufficient either to organize a grand subterranean war, if there be permanent galleries already existing under the assailable fronts; or to make on all these fronts the shafts, the openings of galleries (*amorces de galeries*), and the branches, proper for a *petite guerre*. As soon as the opening of the trenches is known, they advance from the first general dispositions to make the disposition of mines and fougasses. The number of these will be proportioned to the nature of the ground and the quantity of labour that can be performed during the time that elapses between the opening of the trenches and the establishment of the third parallel. To these 40 miners must be attached at least 160 matrosses drawn from the infantry.

To execute the ordinary works which must be begun as soon as the opening of the trenches is discovered, there is necessary; 1st, one company of 100 artificers, of whom three-fourths will be carpenters and one-fourth blacksmiths; 2d, one company of terrace-makers, of 200 men. To these 300 military artificers of the engineer corps, will be added every day and every night the number of workmen furnished from the infantry and necessary to execute with dispatch the flêches, the lines of counter-approach, the bastion and ravelin intrenchments, the frame-tambours of the places of arms, the bridges of communi-

cation, the ramps, &c.   These common labourers will work
under the direction and conduct of the engineer soldiers. Their
number during the first six days will be about 500, and they
will be relieved every twelve hours ; but as after this period
these great labours will be completed, these workmen will then
be returned to the infantry.

The engineers' service may therefore be estimated at 500
men, including 40 miners.

The strength of the infantry during the investment, must be
adequate to resist an enterprising enemy, and to act without
against the troops distributed around the place to ascertain the
strong and weak points of the fortifications. There must therefore be both day and night, an interior service of observation,
and an exterior service.

Calculation of the infantry force during the time of the invest-ment.

The interior service of observation will be   performe 1st,
by detachments of 50 men, posted in each re-entering place of
arms ; 25 of whom will occupy the salient places of arms ; 2d,
by detachments of 20 men posted in each bastion, to line the
flanks and guard the ditches ; 3d, by a detachment of 150 men,
to maintain order within.   This service will therefore be performed night and day by a relief or brigade of 900 men* ; and
the three brigades will be 2,700 strong.

_ The service without will be performed by eight detachments,
each of which will take post 500 or 600 mètres (about 600
yards) in advance of each front and connect with each other,
and form a kind of cordon to prevent the investing troops from
approaching and closely reconnoitring the place.   Each detachment will consist of, 1st, 15 ranger-riflemen and scouts ;
2d, 10 dragoons or mounted rangers ; 3d, 100 infantry ;
making together 125 men.   The exterior cordon will therefore
be formed by 1000 men, forming one relief or brigade ; and
the three reliefs will be 3,000 strong.

---

* Agreeably to the preceding data, the relief would be 1,110 strong ;
and the three reliefs would make a force of 3,330 men.

The difference may have been occasioned by considering this merely as
a general view of the manner of posting the troops on duty, or from considering one or two fronts as unassailable.

TRANSLATOR.

By recapitulating the different forces that we have just calculated, we will have, of

Artillery...... 210 gunners and bombardiers, 600 matrosses.

Engineers .. $\begin{cases} 40 \text{ miners} \dots\dots\dots\dots 160 & \text{do}, \\ 300 \text{ artificers.} \end{cases}$

Ranger-riflemen.......................... 300

Dragoons and mounted rangers............. 350

Infantry of the line 5100

550	6510

7060 men.

But we stated above that the corps of infantry must furnish at the moment of the opening of the trenches to the artillery and engineers, two detachments that will not be returned to the line before about the eighth day of open trenches. These two detachments consist of 700 men for the artillery and 1500 men for the engineers ; making together 2200 men. Consequently after the opening of the trenches there will only remain 2800 men to perform the proper duties of infantry ; and this body, divided into three reliefs or brigades, will give 933 men for each. And this force is sufficient for the service after the opening of the trenches and during the first six days ; for as there is no longer any exterior observation, it is sufficient for the garrison to be upon their guard in the covert-ways and upon the ramparts. The covert-way of the front of attack will be occupied by 400 men ; 150 men will be on guard in the salients of the remainder of the perimeter ; 200 men will be in observation upon the ramparts ; and 150 men will keep guard at the gates and in the interior of the fortress. This detail shows that 900 men will be sufficient for this service.

It must be observed that during the first six days the infantry may be said to have nothing to do ; and that after this period the greatest portion of the troops detached from this corps for the service of the artillery and engineers, daily return to their duty ; so that by the eighth day the infantry service will be re-enforced by 1800 men, affording a relief of 600. At this epoch, when musketry begins to take effect, there may be 1000 men on guard in the covert-ways of the front attacked ; of whom 300 will keep up a constant fire upon the trenches. When sorties are to be made, whether strong or slight, the bivouacs, the reserves, and a portion of the troops of the ordinary guard will be put in motion.

It follows from this, that the garrison for the octagon is at the utmost 7000 men; and that it may be reduced to 6000.

The strength of garrisons for polygons higher than the octagon, is calculated according to the same principles, and by finding for each epoch of the siege what should be the separate strength of the different services to make a vigorous resistance. It must however be remarked, that the strength of garrisons do not increase in proportion to the number of the fronts. Thus, the force for a dodecagon will not be 14,000 men, but only 9000; and that for a polygon of twenty-four sides will not even be 18,000 men, but only 12,000. This is in consequence of the impossibility of attacking a fortress on more than two fronts at a time; there are therefore not many more men requisite for the defence of the fronts of attack of a great fortress, than for the defence of a moderate fortress. This important truth shows how erroneous is the opinion that it requires an army of 18 to 20,000 men to defend a fortress of the first order, such as Strasburg, Lille, and Mayence, &c. There is no fortress, however high its polygon may be, that cannot be vigorously defended and its siege protracted to the maximum of its duration by a garrison of 12,000 men. And this garrison will be able to cope for five or six months with an army of 80,000 men with 200 pieces of artillery.

Strength of the garrisons of polygons higher than the octagon.

191. The probable duration of the siege, the strength of the garrison, and the quantities of artillery and musketry that must act during the whole course of the siege, are contained in the memoir for the defence; and are the elements by which all the chief supplies of munitions of war and provisions with which the place should be provided, are calculated. We will suppose for the octagon, that the probable duration of the siege is 50 days of open trenches; for we suppose that the 40 miners will carry on a subterranean war that will protract the siege 15 days.

191. Calculation of the supplies of all kinds, with which a place should be provided.

The quantity of powder necessary for the artillery service, may be thus calculated:

The quantity of powder necessary for the defence of the octagon.

For the ten days of Investment.

For 60 pieces of ordnance, firing together 300 rounds per day, at the rate of 1¼ kilo-

	Kil'gr.	Pds. Eng.
gramme (nearly 3¼ lbs. avoirdupois English) per round	4,500 =	9,900
For sorties and bold strokes	300	660

First night and first day of Open Trenches.

For the 60 pieces of ordnance at 20 rounds each, and at 1½ kilogramme per round	1,800	3,960
For the seven nights and days following, at the rate of 25 rounds per piece and 2 kilogrammes (4¼ lbs. Eng.) per round	21,000	46,000
For the seventeen days and nights following, at the rate of 40 rounds per piece, and of 1½ kilogrammes per round	61,200	134,640

On the twenty-sixth day, the epoch at which the enemy form their third parallel, the mortars will fire 25 rounds per day ; the stone-mortars and the howitzers will fire 100 : several batteries will fire with full charges upon the saps, new batteries, cavaliers, &c.

For the ten nights and days following.

Thirty pieces of cannon at 50 rounds each, and at 2 kilogrammes per round	30,000	66,000
Twenty mortars at 20 rounds each, and each round of 4 kilogrammes (9 lbs.)	16,000	35,000
Twenty stone-mortars and howitzers at 80 rounds each, and at 1 kilogramme (2¼ lbs. nearly) per round	16,000	35,000

On the thirty-sixth day of open trenches the coronation of the covert-way is effected ; and the garrison contend against the breach and counter-flank batteries, and against the passages of the ditch, &c. The consumption from this period to the conclusion of the siege, is one fourth greater than on the preceding days. Accordingly we have for the 15 last days of the siege .... | 100,000 | 220,000

Total for the consumption of the artillery..	250,800	551,160

The quantity of powder necessary for the infantry or musketry service, may be thus calculated : it must be laid down as a fact, that an infantry soldier can fire 50 rounds in a guard of 12 hours ; and that 1 kilogramme (about 2¼ lbs.) of powder will afford 80 rounds.

	Kil'gr.	lbs. Eng.
For the 1000 men on guard outside during the ten days of investment, at 20 rounds each, for the nightly guard.............	2,500 ⇌	5,500
For bold strokes (*actions de vigueur*)	500	1,100
For the service of the 100 ranger-riflemen, at the rate of 50 rounds per day during the 50 days of open trenches	3,300	7,260
It may be calculated that the rolling fire from the covert-ways and other works, kept up by 500 infantry who during 40 days will fire 80 rounds per day, will consume in this vigorous defence	20,000	44,000
For the bivouacs	4,000	8,800
For sorties and daring strokes	5,000	11,000
Total consumption by the infantry	35,300	77,660

The quantity of powder required for the service of the mines, cannot be calculated without detailing the operations of the subterraneous war carried on and executed by the 40 miners. These successive operations will show the quantity and kind of mines, fougasses, and camouflets, that it is expected to be able to spring under the glacis, ditches and breaches. The number of these principal mines cannot be estimated above 40 ; ten of these will be made under the breaches ; and the remaining 30, one third of which will be overcharged mines, will be made under the glacis and under the coronation of the covert-way, &c. We will suppose the line of least resistance of the mines under the breaches, to be about 50 decimètres (16⅔ feet); and that of the other mines, to be 40 (13⅓ feet). Agreeably to these suppositions we will have,

	Kil'gr.	lbs. Eng.
For the 20 common mines made under the glacis, the charge for each being 80 kilogrammes (176 lbs.)	1,600 ⇌	3,520

	Kil'gr.	lbs. Eng.
Amount brought forward	1,600 =	3,520

For the 10 overcharged mines, 150 kilogrammes for each (330 lbs.)	1,500	3,300
For the 10 mines made under the breaches, with a charge of 160 kilogrammes (352 lbs) each	1,600	3,520
For the fougasses and camouflets	1,500	3,300
One-tenth for saucissons, &c.	600	1,320
Total for the mines	6,800	14,960

Thus for a defence of two months, including the consumption of the subterranean *petite guerre* organized at the very moment that the place is threatened, the octagon must be provided with 290,000 kilogrammes (about 640,000 lbs. Eng.) of powder. If the place were mined, the consumption of powder for the service of the mines would be greatly increased, and would amount to at least 20,000 kilogrammes (44,000 lbs. English).

The quantity of powder requisite for the defence of a fortress of the first class. It may be perceived by the application of these rules to the octagon, that if the case were that of a fortress of the first order, of 20 to 25 fronts, the supplies of powder would amount to about 600,000 kilogrammes (1,320,000 lbs. Eng.) for a defence of five months.

The supplies of projectiles. As the memoir for the defence exhibits the service of the artillery each day, it is easy to calculate the supplies of projectiles of all kinds. For the octagon, which we have taken as an example, these supplies should be as follows:

| 16,000 cannon balls for each caliber, and for the 5 calibers .... | 80,000 |

12 inch bombs, at the rate of 800 per mortar 1,600 ⎫	
10 inch bombs, at the rate of 900 per mortar 5,400 ⎬ = 19,000	
8 inch bombs, at the rate of 1000 per mortar 12,000 ⎭	

| 8 inch howitzes, at the rate of 4,500 per howitzer .... 24,000 ⎫ = 74,000 | |
| 6 inch howitzes, at the rate of 5,000 per howitzer .... 50,000 ⎭ | |

| Fiery-balls, carcasses, and pot-grenades.......... | 4,000 |

Tumbrel-loads (*tombereaux*) of stones, for 20,000

rounds of stone-mortars, and at the rate of 15 rounds
    to the tumbrel   1,333
Of grenades there must be a very great quantity, both
    to throw by hand, and to load howitzers, mortars
    and stone-mortars with : it will not be too much to
    have 80,000 ; of which number 10,000 should be
    large, for rolling down breaches   80,000

The supplies for the works of the defence, consist of ; 1st, timber The supplies for the labours and works of the defence.
for palisadings, barriers, gates, fraisings, tambours, bridges of
communication, blindages, covered batteries, small powder-
magazines made in the works, and the timber requisite for the
service of the mines and artillery : there will be required at
least 4,000 trunks of trees 60 decimètres long (20 feet) by 130
centimètres (4½ feet) in circumference: 2d, gabions, fascines,
pickets, and withes (harts) : we must reckon 4,000 gabions of
all dimensions, 20,000 fascines of 2 mètres (6½ feet) in length,
and 150,000 pickets : 3d, bags of earth to line the parapets,
&c. ; of these there will be at least 12,000 necessary : 4th,
the implements and machines requisite for executing the
works and manœuvring the sluices, &c. : 5th, the various weapons used in the defence ; viz. :

Spare muskets ; as many as foot soldiers   7,000   The supplies of fire arms, and of wielded and defensive weapons.
    Rifles or Carabines ; one-tenth as many as spare
    muskets   700
    Blunderbusses (Mousquetons) ; one-half as many as
    horsemen   200
    Pairs of Pistols ; one-half as many as horsemen   200
    Miner's Pistols ;   100
    Miner's Blunderbusses, or Air Guns, (fusils à vent)   100
    Bayonets of Reserve ; one-third of the number of
    muskets   2,000
    Infantry Sabres ; for one-fourth of the infantry ·····   1,700
    Cavalry Sabres ; as many as horsemen   400
    Halberd's or Pikes ;   1,500
    Sithes, hafted backwards, ...   1,000
    Breach Swords or Knives (couteaux de breche)   250
    Breast Plates and Helmets (plastrons et calottes) ; half
    as many as there are horsemen   200
    Cuirasses and Head-Pieces, for the assaults, &c.   250

The artillery is supplied in a suitable manner with gun-carriages, wagons, machines, and implements and stores (*objets d'armement*) for the pieces. For the cannon and howitzers, there must be as many spare carriages as pieces ; and for the mortars and stone-mortars, one-half as many more beds as there are pieces.

There must be at least 12 carts, drawn by 3 horses, to transport ammunition ; and 3 sets of 10 horses each, to draw the heavy pieces to their different positions : this makes 66 draft horses.

Fire-works (*artifices*) are of great importance in the defence of places ; they consist of ;

Tarred *tourteaux*, of which there must be about 30,000
Tarred *fascines*,   do.   do.   at least 7,000
Tarred *dry chips and shavings* ; there must be, wagon
    loads, ... 3
Small *hand fire-balls*, there must be .... 3 to 4,000
Fusees *for bombs*, ... 20,000
Fusees *for grenades*, ... 80,000
Fire or " *thundering*" *barrels**, *for breaches*, ... 35
Fire-rocks (*roches à feu*), to light the fire-works, .. 20

When we know the strength of the garrison and the probable duration of the siege, we have all that is necessary to calculate the quantity of provisions with which a fortress threatened with siege should be supplied. This quantity should be calculated as if the garrison were complete during the whole period of the siege, in order to have a surplus to provide for what is called the *longest holding out of the place* (*la plus tenue de la place*). The allowance of food for a soldier in a besieged town, is composed of ; 1st, one ration of ammunition bread, in weight 1 kilogramme ($2\frac{1}{4}$ lbs.) ; 2d, one ration of salted bacon (*lard salé*), weighing $\frac{1}{16}$ of a kilogramme (about $3\frac{1}{4}$ oz.) ; 3d, one ration of salt beef, weighing $\frac{1}{4}$ of a kilogramme (9 oz.) ; 4th, one ration of wine of $\frac{1}{6}$ litre ($\frac{1}{3}$ of a pint), or one litre ($1\frac{1}{16}$ quart) of beer ; and 5th, one ration of brandy of $\frac{1}{12}$ of a litre (upwards of $\frac{1}{2}$ a gill).

The ammunition sack of corn, containing $\frac{2}{3}$ wheat and $\frac{1}{3}$ rye, weighs 100 kilogrammes (220 lbs.), and yields 99 kilogrammes of flour, including the bran. This quantity of flour produces 135 rations of baked bread.

* *Barils foudroyans.*

The number of rations for the octagon that we have taken as an example, will be,

1st, ... 7,000 rations.
2d, One-fifth of this quantity for the officers, sergeants, servants and followers 1,400
3d. One-tenth allowed for loss or waste .. 840

Total for one day, ... 9,240 rations.

And for sixty days, ... 554,400 rations.

Therefore there will be required a supply,
. of flour, of about, ... 4,000 sacks.
Of salt bacon (*lard salé*), nearly 26,000 kilog. (57,200 lbs.).
Of salt beef . . . . . . 105,000 kilog. (231,000 lbs.).
This quantity of salt provisions will require about 400 oxen; but 50 live oxen will be kept to supply the sick with fresh meat: the numbers of these, towards the end of the siege, may amount to 1200.

For wine, we may calculate 70,000 litres or 250 muids . . . . . . : (66,000 gallons).
For brandy, 28,000 litres or 100 muids (26,400 gallons).
Besides these several kinds of food, every day dry vegetables are distributed to the troops; such as peas, beans, and lentils, in the proportion of $\frac{1}{4}$ kilogram (4$\frac{1}{4}$ oz.) per ration. The troops are also allowed 35 grammes of rice and 20 grammes of salt (1 oz. and $\frac{1}{2}$ oz. nearly).

To these stores are added, sheep, poultry, and calves, which are kept for the sick.

Vinegar is an article of great use; there must be a sufficient quantity laid in to allow $\frac{1}{16}$ of a litre ($\frac{1}{2}$ gill) to every room containing five men. This quantity may be estimated at about 25 muids (6,650 gallons).

Lastly; all the necessary supplies of spices will be provided; and care must be taken to furnish the apothecary's department with linen and medicines.

The new processes for purifying air, will be of great utility in a besieged place. This discovery, so beneficial to humanity, will secure to its distinguished author the gratitude of all men entrusted with the care and preservation of their fellow men; and in this respect, none can more deeply feel its importance than engineer and artillery officers. It will be proper to fumigate twice a day the hospital, and all other places in which men are crowded together. .

The baking ovens. The ovens (*fours de munitions*) are established in a building containing every thing for baking. This building must be vaulted bomb-proof and situated far from the attacks; and should contain a sufficient number of ovens to daily bake the quantity of rations required, that is, about 9,000. An oven of 40 by 44 decimètres (13¼ by 14¾ feet) will bake 400 rations, and supply eight batches or bakings in 24 hours: there will consequently be four ovens required for this service, one of which will be a relief or spare oven.

This bakery must be provided with all the proper utensils for working and making bread, and with the necessary supplies of fuel, which may be estimated at 300 cords and 20,000 fagots.

The supplies of forage and oats. The supplies of forage consist of, hay, straw, and oats.

The rations of hay and straw are each of 5 kilogrammes; that of oats consists of 3 litres (3⅓ quarts).

Accordingly to feed 500 horses 80 days, there will be required,

Of hay 40,000 rations, or 200,000 kilogrammes (440,000 lbs. English).

Of straw 40,000 rations, or 200,000 kilogrammes (440,000 lbs. English).

Of oats 40,000 rations, or 120,000 litres (31,875 gallons).

192. The situations for the supplies, and for lodging the troops in. 192. We will only awaken the attention of the reader and student to the mode of placing and distributing the supplies within the fortress, and of quartering the troops that are not on duty. What we have already said (135, 141, and 145) sufficiently shows the importance of this subject, and how much attention the Governor should bestow upon it; for if the enemy succeed in blowing up the powder-magazines, in setting fire to the other stores, and constantly annoying the garrison and giving them no rest, the fortress will soon be compelled to capitulate, even before the fortifications are sufficiently ruined to be carried by assault.

Therefore souterrains must be made under the bastions, powder-magazines must be built bomb-proof, and likewise stores for the provisions, ovens, and an hospital. The interior space of any polygon affords sufficient room for all these establishments, and for the blindage coverts for quartering the troops in. When all the souterrains, buildings, sheds, &c. are inadequate and not adapted to the different kinds of supplies, a suppletory method must be had recourse to. Thus, in case there are not enough of powder-magazines, we must, after the example of M. De Chamilly, at Grave, form a substitute by constructing a gallery under the parapet of the curtain of a front : and if there be no hospital in the place, the Governor will cause the ground-floors of several houses to be blinded, and devote them to this service.

The stores of liquors will be deposited in the dampest souterrains ; and the other supplies will be placed in those souterrains that are driest and best aired, and beneath the blindages of several solid edifices, distant if possible from the front of attack. In great fortresses, the firewood is stored in covered places secure from the fires of the attack ; but in moderate sized fortresses, this article of the first necessity must either be placed in souterrains, or in the cellars of houses. With respect to the forage, it should be bundled up and well tied or corded, so as to reduce the space occupied by 1,000 kilogrammes (2,200 lbs.) of hay to one cubic mètre (about 37 cubic feet) : the forage thus arranged, will be stored in souterrains or under blindages.

Finally ; the one half of the garrison that is not on duty, should be so lodged as not to be annoyed during the time allowed them to repose and refresh themselves. Thus in the octagon, there must be coverts for about 3,000 men, including 100 officers ; but if there be a deficiency of space, one half of the bivouacs will have no shelters ; and in this case it will be sufficient to lodge 2,500 men and 80 officers. At least 4 square mètres (44.5 feet Eng.) should be allowed for lodging every three soldiers ; and the same space should be allowed for each officer : there will therefore be required a superfices of at least 3,500 square mètres (40,850 square feet). Great care must be taken not to crowd the troops in souterrains, where the damps and confined air produce diseases that frequently kill more men, than the fire and the steel of the enemy. If there be a deficiency of vaulted caserns, buildings are blinded ; and if the resources of the place in this respect be inadequate, recourse is had to blindages raised against the sides of walls, against the interior revêtements, of ramparts and in dry ditches opposite to the attacks. In great fortresses, the troops may be encamped or barracked upon the esplanades and in dry ditches distant from the attacks. The air must have a free circulation in these coverts, to refresh the men that are to repose in them.

Although the number and quantity of men and stores to be lodged and covered, is great enough to alarm the imagination of a person unacquainted with the resources of a fortress, even of a moderate size, but judiciously constructed ; yet it is easy to convince ourselves of the practicability of effecting this, by referring to fortresses of various orders.

When these fortresses have been constructed by able engineers, the Governor finds in them all the necessary permanent dispositions and localities adapted to the temporary dispositions relative to a state of siege ; and if he have the assistance of active officers of engineers well acquainted with all the resources and localities of the place, in a very few days the provisions and stores will be secured and the garrison will have comfortable coverts. It is with all these conservating means that the commander of a fortress may set at defiance the tremendous powers of modern artillery ; and, if he know how to inspire his troops with confidence and love of glory, may make a most obstinate and brilliant defence.

(See La Defense des Places, by Vauban. Foissac's edition : the Memoire by Cormontaigne: L'-Ouvrage de Bousmard ; L'-Aide Memoire d'-Artillerie ; and Le Manuel de D'Artilleur ; &c)

We will here conclude our discussion of a subject, which completes the circle of knowledge that it was our purpose to unfold and illustrate. We have not entered into details, however important they may be, because we should have trespassed beyond those limits that we prescribed to ourselves. But as the students and officers of all arms may one day deserve the honour of defending a fortress, we thought that it would be proper to present them with a description of the chief points of the defence, in order to induce them to read and meditate the authors who have written upon this subject. The admirable Memoir by Cormontaigne, worthy in every respect of this scientific engineer ; Vauban's work on the Defence of Fortresses ; Bousmard's work ; the Artillerist's Note Book ; and the Artillerist's Manual, &c. &c.; are sources from which they may draw the completion of their education and instruction.

CHAPTER XII, AND THE LAST.

The Gates of Fortified Towns ; their Situation ; their Architecture ; their Bridges and Profiles.

WE will in this last chapter give some particulars and description of the gates of fortified towns, and of the various kinds of bridges and profiles attached to these constructions. It is necessary that students and officers who have studied a course of fortification, and who frequently see for the first time a fortress, should be able to judge under what aspect they behold it ; and by what works the communication between the interior and exterior is maintained.

193. It is obvious, and is a necessary consequence of the theory of the attack, that the gates must be established with judgment and as seldom as possible on assailable fronts. We have seen that when these grand communications are disposed upon the flanks of the attack, we may debouche through them with infantry, and even with cavalry, to take in reverse the works of the besiegers. If the fronts on which gates are made be exposed to attack, it is proper that they should be flanked by unassailable works. The cannon of the works must completely enfilade the high roads that lead to the gates, in order that the enemy may derive no advantage from them.

193. The situation of gates in a fortified town, under the relation of defence.

When the fronts upon which gates and outlets are to be established, are determined, the opening in the body of the place should be made upon the centre of the curtain, as being the part best covered and least exposed to batteries in breach.

The passage out of a fortress is by a vaulted-way which has two fronts ; one interior, and the other exterior. The architecture of the former is generally costly and loaded with ornaments. The extrados of this vault is 10 decimètres (3¼ feet) below the terra-plain ; and it is so constructed as to allow the rain waters to run off, and to prevent their filtration. The exterior opening is most generally with a full centre ; but the arch may be made flat (*anse à panier*). It is 40 decimètres (13¼ feet) high under the key-stone, and 31 decimètres .7 (10¼ feet) wide between the two frames (*tableaux*). Two vertical grooves are made in the upper part, to lodge the plyers (*flèches*) of the draw-

The gates made in the body of a place : the arrangement and character of the architecture of their fronts. (PLATE XIII, figs. 1 and 4.)

bridge, of which we shall speak hereafter. The characteristics of the architecture of the front of the gate, should be solidity and strength ; delicate profiles and useless ornaments should be banished. They are an ill-judged expense, without any reasonable object. Two plain lateral pilasters surmounted with military trophies, a cornice of a handsome model, and a device suited to the subject, are the only ornaments that the engineer architect should permit. The masonry of the gates should be very little raised above the covering line, in order that it may not serve the enemy for a point of sight : and it would be a still greater error to construct and raise buildings above the gates, as is the case in several fortresses.

194. The draw-bridges, and fixed bridges.

194. The passage from the threshold of the gate of a fortified town, is over a *drawbridge* to a *fixed bridge* that crosses the great ditch and rests upon the gorge of the ravelin.

The gate constructed on one of the ravelin faces.

The gates of the ravelins are made open at top ; they are formed by two plain pilasters, generally crowned with a cominge or large bomb ; and the passage through the rampart is built with two plain profiles, which sustain its relief. The

The passage across the glacis.

passage across the ditch of the ravelin is by another drawbridge and another fixed bridge, which rests against the counterscarp. Finally ; we gain the plane of site, or country without, by a passage across the glacis formed by two profiles supporting their relief. Care is taken to configurate the direction of these profiles in such a manner, that the barrier placed in the direction of the covering line will not be seen from without.

Construction of the fixed bridges.

The fixed bridges (*ponts dormans*) may be made of masonry ; and this method is proper and economical when the fronts are not assailable and not too much exposed to bombs. In this case a few mines are made in the centre piers, to at once blow up the bridge if the events of the war render such a measure necessary. But it is in all cases preferable to adopt such a construction, that the bridge may be readily removed without its ruins encumbering the ditch. This condition, so essential to the defence, is fulfilled by wooden bridges established upon simple piers of mason work whose centres are 5 métres (16¼ feet) distant apart. The chief timbers for constructing a fixed bridge, are the *sole pieces* (*semelles*), the *corbils* (*corbeaux*), the *string pieces* (*longerons*), the *planks* (*madriers*), the *kerb pieces* or *pavement guards* (*garde pavés*), the *upright rests* (*montans d'appui*), the *riband* and *under riband pieces* (*les lisses et les sous-lisses*), the *bracing pieces* (*les liens*), &c.

The purpose of a *drawbridge* (*pont levis*) is to establish or to interrupt at pleasure the communication between the fixed bridge and the opening of the gate, whether of the body of the place, or of an outwork. Accordingly the drawbridge serves as a bridge when in an horizontal position, and as a shutter when it is in a vertical position. Drawbridges, and their use: description of them (See Bossut's *Mechanique*)

The table (*tablier*) of a drawbridge is a kind of moveable flooring *T*, serving as a bridge to pass over the interval left between the fixed bridge and the scarp of the work, and which masks the opening when it is drawn up. It is generally 4 mètres long, by 3 mètres .58 wide (13½ by 12 feet); there are distinguished in the table; 1st, the heel (*talon*), and the head (*tête*); the length of these two principal pieces is equal to the width of the table, and they are in thickness 9 inches by 9 (9¾ inches by 9¾): an interior groove of 2 inches is made in these pieces, to receive the planks of the flooring: 2d, the 7 sleepers 6 inches by 7 thick, and united with the head and heel pieces on a level with the groove: 3d, the flooring of planks, which are nailed to the sleepers: 4th, the two trunnions let into the upper side of the heel piece at 3 inches from the edge, and strongly secured by iron hoops and bolts with screws and nuts: the trunnions of the table are thus placed, in order that when it is vertical its centre of gravity may be outside their axis, and that it may have a constant tendency to fall down: 5th, the top flooring, made of fir planks. The table of the drawbridge, and its component pieces, and its other pieces. (PLATE XIII, figs 2 and 4.)

The trunnions rest upon sockets (*crapaudines*) fixed in the lateral part of the casing (*battée*) of the drawbridge. The sockets of the trunnions of the table

The extremes of the head-piece are furnished with *connecting staples* or *headed bolts* (*gaches d'attache ou de boulons à tête*) fixed in the lower side; and these pieces of iron catch hold of the chains of the plyers: they are thus disposed, in order that the table may be completely lodged in the fore-part of the gate. The connecting staples of the table.

The table being solidly made and furnished with iron hoops and stirrups to ease the tenons of the sleepers, it is laid resting on one side upon the first pier of the fixed bridge, and on the other upon the sockets that receive the trunnions. To ease these trunnions and the assemblage, a bolster piece (*chevet*) is placed under the heel piece or *talon*, and rests upon corbels of free-stone.

The swipe to put the frame in motion. (Figs. 3 and 4.) The method most used to manœuvre the table, is by a swipe (*bascule*) *B*, composed of several pieces joined together and arranged as exhibited in figures 3 and 4. Two beams of about 25 feet (27 feet) long, and 12 by 13 inches thick (13 by 14 inches), are crossed in the middle by 2 trunnions ; and are connected together in the after part by 3 transoms (*entretoises*), 2 long pieces (*potilles*), and 4 guards (*guettes*). Their forepart is called the plyers (*flêches*); and the other is called the branches of the swipe. The plyers decrease in thickness at 6 inches from the trunnions to their extremes, where they are only 9 inches square in thickness. Their angles are cut off to give them the figure of a truncated pyramid of an octagonal base. The trunnions which traverse the axis of the branches, rest against the first transom ; their distance to the extremities of the plyers, should be exactly equal to the distance from the axis of the trunnions of the table to the connecting staples ; and the distance between the axes of the plyers, is equal to the distance between the two connecting hooks or crotchets of the head piece.

The extremities of the plyers are armed with stork's-bill hooks (*crochets à col de cigogne*), to receive the chains ; and the ends of the branches are armed with two hoops (*frettes*) and two ring-bolts (*arganeaux*) provided with working-chains.

When the swipe is made; it is put up in the upper part of the gate by passing the plyers through the apertures and vertical grooves that have been made to receive them : the trunnions of the swipe are received into two sockets cramped or sealed in the piers at a proper height and in an horizontal line. When the plyers are horizontal, they rest against the roof of the casing or opening to the drawbridge. The plane that passes through the axis of the swipe trunnions and through that of the trunnions of the table, is always more or less inclined to the horizon, according to the construction of the gate.

Manœuvring the drawbridge. When the swipe is put up and in an horizontal position, two chains are affixed at one end to the capping iron-work (*armures*) of the plyers, and at the other to the connecting-staples of the head-piece of the table ; the swipe and the table then form one system or whole, and the swipe cannot turn upon its trunnions without turning the table upon its trunnions. If therefore a force be applied to the manœuvring or working-chains of the swipe, it will descend, and the draw-bridge or table will be drawn up and will shut the opening of the gate by lodging in the casing (*battée*) destined to receive it.

In former times, engineers frequently established the swipe of the drawbridge in a different manner.   They made under the passage a cellar, in which they disposed the swipe in such a way that the plyers rested against the lower side of the draw-bridge ; and the swipe by descending from the horizontal to the vertical position, raised the table.   This method possesses the advantage of shielding the plyers from the artillery of the besiegers ; but it is subject to a great many inconveniences, which have caused the drawbridge with plyers to be preferred*.

Another of placing swipe.

* The following note on foundations established under water, a case that very frequently occurs in harbour defences, having been omitted in the third chapter, it is here inserted.

In some cases, when there is a great depth of water, and the bed of the river is tolerably level, or where it can be made so by any contrivance, a very strong frame of timber about four times as large as the base of the piers may be let down with stones upon it round the edges to make it sink: after fixing it level, piles must be driven about it to keep it in its place ; and then the foundation may be laid in coffers, which are to be kept steady by means of ropes tied to the piles.

This method has frequently been used in Russia ; and though the bed of the river is not very solid, yet such a grate when once well settled with the weight of the pier upon it, will be as firm as if piles had been driven under the foundation : but to prevent the water from gulling under the foundation, and to secure it against all accidents, a row of dove-tailed piles must be driven quite round the grating: this precaution being taken, the foundation will be as secure as any that can be made.

The French engineers make use of another method in raising the foundations of masonry under water ; which is, to drive a row of piles round the intended place, nearer to, or farther from, each other, according as the water is more deep or shallow : these piles being strongly bound together in several places with horizontal tie-beams, serve to support a row of dove-tailed piles driven within them : when this is done, and all well secured according to the nature of the situation and circumstances, they dig the foundation by means of a machine with scoops, invented for that purpose, until they come to a solid bed of gravel or clay ; or if the bed of the river is of a soft consistence to a great depth, it is dug only to about six feet and a grate of timber is laid upon it, which is well secured with piles driven into the opposite corners of

195. Calcula-
tion of a draw-
bridge with ply-
ers to satisfy the
condition of equi-
librium   (See
Brissut's Mechan-
ieks, and Fran-
cœur's Statics.)

195. A drawbridge is calculated in such a manner as to place the machine in equilibrium ; and that the power having only to overcome the friction, two or four soldiers at most can draw it up.   We will suppose that the drawbridge is 11 feet (11$\frac{1}{4}$ feet) wide by 12 long (13 feet), and that the length of the plyers is equal to that of the table ; and in this case, the only one applicable to practice, the figure of the drawbridge will be that of a parallelogram.   This established, then we have the formula

$$\frac{b}{2}\,\pi + B) = \frac{f}{2}(F + T + 2\,C),$$ statics of the course, (page 133).

of which we must make a particular application. Here the quantity B is not the whole swipe, but only the branches with their iron-work ; π is the indeterminate weight of the connecting pieces

each square, not minding whether they exceed the upper surface of the grate much or little.

When the foundation is thus prepared, they make a kind of mortar called *beton*, which consists of 12 parts of pozzulana or Dutch terrass, 6 of good sand, 9 of unslacked lime, the best that can be had, 13 of stone-splinters not exceeding the bigness of an egg, and 3 parts of tile dust, or cinders, or else scales of iron out of a forge : this being well worked together must be left standing for about 24 hours, or 'till it becomes so hard as not to be separated without a pick-axe.

This mortar being thus prepared, they throw into the coffer a bed of ruble-stone, not very large, and spread them all over the bottom as nearly level as they can ; then they sink a box full of this hard mortar, broken into pieces, 'till it comes within a little of the bottom ; the box is so contrived as to be overset or turned upside down at any depth ; which being done, the pieces of mortar soften, and so fill up the vacant spaces between the stones ; by these means they sink as much of it as will form a bed of about 12 inches deep all over ; then they throw in another bed of stone, and continue alternately to throw one of mortar and one of stone 'till the work approaches near the surface of the water where it is levelled, and then the rest is finished with stones in the usual manner.

Belidor says, (*Second Part of his Hydraulics*, vol. ii. p. 188), that Millet de Montville, having filled a coffer containing 27 cubic feet with masonry made of this mortar, and sunk it into the sea, it was there left standing for two months, and when it was taken out again it was harder than stone itself.

We have hitherto mentioned such situations only where the ground is of a soft nature : but where it is rocky and uneven, all the former methods prove ineffectual ; nor indeed has there yet been any one proposed which can be always used upon such occasions, especially in a great

of the swipe, consisting of 3 transoms, 2 long-pieces (*potilles*), and 4 guards.   We will suppose that $\frac{b}{2}$ = 78 inches is the arm of the lever of the system formed by the timbers or pieces of the swipe ; and that this distance is equal to half the length of the branches : this nearly is sufficient in practice.   The equation will therefore become, 78 inches $\times \pi = T \times \frac{f}{2} + F \times \frac{f}{2} + C \times f - B \times \frac{b}{2}$, in which f is the length of the table, and b that of the swipe.   As each term of the second member results from the sum of several partial momenta, easily determined ; it follows that we may find π.   By allowing that the cubic foot of oaken wood weighs 70 pounds, (75lbs) we will have :

depth of water.   When the water is not so deep but that the unevenness of the rock can be perceived by the eye, piles strongly shod with iron may be raised and let fall down, by means of a machine, upon the higher parts, so as to break them off piece by piece, 'till the foundation is tolerably even, especially when the rock is not very hard; which being done in either this, or any other way that can be thought of, a coffer is made without any bottom, which is let down and well secured, so as not to move from its place : to make it sink, heavy stones should be fixed on the outside ; then strong mortar and stones must be thrown into it ; and if the foundation is once brought to a level, large hewn stones may be let down so as to lie flat and even : by these means the work may be carried on quite up to the surface of the water.   But when the water is so deep, or the rock so hard as not to be levelled, the foundation must be sounded, so as to get nearly the risings and fallings; then the lower part of the coffer must be cut nearly in the same manner, and the rest finished as before.   It must however be observed, that we suppose a possibility of sinking a coffer; but where this cannot be done, no method that we know of will answer.

The manner of laying the foundations of piers of harbours in different depths of water, and in various soils, requires particular methods to be followed.

When the water is very deep, the French throw in a great quantity of stones at random, so as to form a much larger base than would be required upon dry land; this they continue to within three or four feet of the surface of the water, where they lay the stones in a regular manner, 'till the foundation is raised above the water : they then lay a great weight of stones upon it, and let it stand during the winter to settle; as likewise to see whether it is firm and resists the force of the waves and winds : after that, they finish the superstructure with large stones in the usual manner.

1st, $T \times \frac{f}{2}$ = the momentum of the heel-piece, *plus* the momentum of the floorings, *plus* that of the head-piece = 453 pounds (weight of the heel-piece and of the 2 iron hoops) $\times 1\frac{1}{2}$ inch + 3,610 pounds (weight of the floorings and 7 sleepers, to which is added 40 pounds for bolts and nails) $\times 69$ inches + 475 pounds (this is the weight of the head-piece, added to 70 pounds for the two hoops or bands and the connecting staples), $\times$ 137 inches = (after working the several products) 679+249,090+65,075 = 314,844.

2d, To find the term $F \times \frac{f}{2}$, we must observe that the plyers are truncated pyramids forming a volume of 6 *solives* (21 cubic feet) and a weight of 1,260 pounds : we will add to this

As this method requires a great quantity of stones, it can be practised only in places where stones are in plenty ; and therefore the following one is much preferable. A coffer is made with dove-tailed piles of above 30 yards long, and as wide as the thickness of the foundation is to be ; then the ground is dug and levelled, and the wall is built with the best mortar.

As soon as the mortar is tolerably dry, those piles at the end of the wall are drawn out, the side rows are continued to about 30 yards farther, and the end enclosed ; then the foundation is cleared and the stones laid as before. But it must be observed, that the end of the foundation finished is left rough, in order that the part next to it may incorporate with it in a proper manner : but if it is not very dry it will incline that way of itself, and bind with the mortar that is thrown in next to it : this method is continued 'till the whole pier is entirely finished.

It must likewise be observed, that the piers are not made of one continued solid wall ; because in deep water it would be too expensive : for which reason, two walls are built parallel to each other, and the interval between them is filled up with shingles, chalk, and stone. As these walls are in danger of being overset or thrust out by the corps in the middle, together with the great weight laid at times on the pier, they are tied or bound together by cross walls at every 30 or 40 yards distance, by which they support each other in a firm and strong manner.

In a country where there is a great plenty of stones, piles may be driven in as deep as they will go, at about two or three feet distance ; and when the foundation is sunk and levelled, large stones may be let down, which will bed themselves : but care must be taken to lay them close, and so as to have no two joints over each other ; and when the wall is come within reach, the stones must be cramp together. *See Encyclopædia Britannica*, art. *Architecture*, Part II, *Aquatic Buildings*.

TRANSLATOR.

100 pounds for the hoops or bands and stork-bills ; and because this weight is situated at the extremity, we will suppose, without any sensible error, that the centre of gravity is in the middle of the plyers : accordingly we will have $F \times \frac{f}{2} = 1,360$ pounds $\times 72$ inches $= 98,920$.

3d, The term $C \times f$, which is the momentum of the chains, $= 105$ pounds $\times 144$ inches $= 15,120$.

4th, The term $B \times \frac{b}{2}$ expresses the momentum of the branches of the swipe ; *plus* the momentum of the iron-work of their extremities, consisting of the hoops, ring-bolts and small working-chains ; *plus* the momentum of the two bolts, of 4 cramp-irons (*crampons*), and of 2 stop-locks (*serrures à bosses*) : we will therefore have : $B \times \frac{b}{2} = 1,972$ pounds $\times 78 + 86$ pounds $\times 156$ $+ 36$ pounds $\times 120 = 171,552$.

Agreeably to the preceding calculations, we have, $\pi \times \frac{b}{2} =$ $428,884 - 171,552 = 257,332$ or $\pi = \frac{257332}{78} = 3299$ pounds.

Accordingly, in order that the machine may be in equilibrium, the connecting pieces must weigh about 3,300 pounds.

By making the three transoms, the two long pieces (*potilles*), and the four guards, 11 and 12 inches square, their volume will be about 16 solives, which will weigh 3,360 pounds and establish the equilibrium required in the particular case that we just have treated.   To put the machine in motion, it will be only requisite to apply to the chains of the swipe a force sufficient to vanquish the friction : this force will not exceed that of two men.

196. The manœuvring of a drawbridge by a swipe, is subject to great inconveniences : 1st, The drying of the swipe, and the variations daily produced in the weight of the table by rain, drought, mud, &c. continually destroy the equilibrium and render the working of it very difficult : 2d, The plyers must be renewed every ten years, and frequently repaired ; the lodging of the plyers in the front of the gate, greatly disfigures it : 4th, Finally ; the plyers are greatly exposed to the artillery and liable to be broken from the first days of the siege : this defect is of great importance, especially in large posts that may be surprised and attacked by storm.

196. The inconvenience of a drawbridge with plyers & swipes.

Various substitutes have been proposed for the plyers and swipe ; a description of them is to be found in Belidor. We must describe M. Dobenheim's method of remedying the greatest inconveniences.   In it are united safety, facility of manœuvre, the power of re-establishing the equilibrium at any moment, and the invaluable advantage of the manœuvre being little exposed to the hostile artillery.

197 The means used by Doben-heim as substitutes for the plyers and swipe of a drawbridge. (PLATE XIII, Fig. 5)

197. In the thickness of the two frames or walls (*tableaux*) of the gate and at 6 feet (6½ feet) from the front wall, a square niche of 3½ feet (3¾ feet) side and 13 inches (14 inches) deep, is cut.   Each nich *bd* is to contain a cast-iron pulley 30 inches (32 inches) in diameter, 5 thick, and with a furrow (*gorge*) of 4 inches.   The centres of the two pulleys are in an horizontal line, and are 12 feet (nearly 13 feet) above the table.   The vertical planes perpendicular to this horizontal line, and which pass through the centres of the pulleys, should likewise cut the connecting staples of the table : they are called the *planes of manœuvre*.   The pulleys revolve about an axis 2 inches in diameter, one of the ends of which rests upon a socket lodged in the bottom of the niche, and the other upon an eye made in a strong plate of iron solidly fixed and sealed on the front of the niche.

The drawbridge is worked by two chains composed of links 10 lines thick and 2½ inches long, by 1½ interior width. These chains, affixed to the table in the common manner, pass by two loop-holes through the frame of the gate to the niches and around the pulleys that we have described.   These chains draw up the table in the following manner :

The first iron-bar for working the bridge :

A bar of iron of the same length as the table and two inches broad by one thick, is connected by an hook (*guinguerlot*) to the end of the chain at a distance of five or six inches from the pulley : the other end G of the bar has an eye that is traversed by a bolt sealed in the wall, and about which it can freely turn, keeping always in the plane of manœuvre.   The point of rotation G is so situated, that in the initial position FG the bar is little inclined and makes almost a right angle with the end of the chain.

The second.

At 12 inches (13 inches nearly) from the point G there is another bolt I fixed like the first in the wall, and about which turns a second iron bar similar and of equal length to the first. A chain FH connects these two bars ; its length is that of the chord of an arc of 45 degrees, whose radius is equal to the length of the bars.

The bars are pierced with horizontal holes to receive pintles (*clavettes*); they are loaded with cubic blocks of cast-iron of about 10 inches (10¼ inches) side. These blocks weigh about 300 pounds (325 lbs.), and are pierced with rectangular holes.

The weight with which the bars are loaded.

The bars being in their initial position, they are each loaded with from one block to four; and these bars are placed in such a way, that the machine is in equilibrium when the second bar is vertical.

Loading the bars.

The drawbridge is manœuvred by applying to the second bar a power capable of overcoming the friction : that of one man on each side is sufficient. As the momentum of the table diminishes in proportion as it rises; in the same way the momentum of the powers produced by the weight of the blocks, also gradually decreases. Thus, when the table is raised to the height of 45 degrees, the bar IH has gotten into a vertical position ; and the power of the bar FG is then sufficient to complete the movement.

Manœuvring the drawbridge.

The system of bars and blocks that is substituted for the plyers and swipe, is situated in a recess of about 15 inches (16 inches) made in the profiles of the passage of the gate. The bar RS, upon which the working bars slide, is established to prevent the blocks from rubbing against the wall. Two riband pieces ML, NO, are also established to facilitate the manœuvre.

The situation of the bars and blocks in the profiles of the passage of the gate.

Weight of the Tables.		Number of blocks upon each bar.	
Of 1,430 lbs. and under, (1,540 lbs.)		1 block for each bar.	
1,430 do. to 2,750 lbs. (1,540 to 2,962 lbs.)	2	do.	do.
2,750 do. to 4,060 do. (2,962 to 4,375 lbs.)	3	do.	do.
4,060 do. to 5,250 do. (4,375 to 5,670 lbs.)	4	do.	do.

The number of blocks required to load the bars.

The machinery (*la manœuvre*) of a draw-bridge of common dimensions and made agreeably to these principles, would amount to at least 1,100 francs ($203½) ; whilst the expense of a swipe with plyers, would not at farthest exceed 600 francs ($111) : but with respect to duration and other advantages, the mode proposed by Dobenheim is far superior.

We should be gratified to be able to complete this Third Part, like the two others, with a description and illustration of a few celebrated and instructing sieges ; but this would render the work too voluminous. Besides it must be remarked, that

Reflections.

there is a great difference between the description of a siege, and that of a battle. In the latter, the action passes quickly; and the imagination supported and heated, seizes with avidity all the details. In a siege, every thing on the contrary passes slowly; and the details are tedious and innumerable. Its description, which is composed of two long memoirs, one of the *defence* and the other of the *attack*, is protracted to such a length, that the journal of a great siege would furnish matter enough to fill a volume; and in combats and operations of this nature, the particular cases bear such a strong resemblance to the description that is the subject of the fourth chapter, that it appears to us superfluous to extend this elementary treatise.

Conclusion and end of the treatise.

198. We will here conclude the theoretical and descriptive illustration of those principal branches of military science that should form the subject of a treatise purely elementary and founded upon descriptive geometry. We hope that this compendium, in which we have endeavoured to display to our readers the immense and almost boundless regions of this science, will serve them as a guide in the profound study of its several branches; and that the principles we have here laid down will be found by them to be more unquestionable and certain, in proportion as they become more familiar with them by practice and by the study of those admirable works that are extant.

On this important subject our readers may consult the judicious and interesting account contained in the second number of the Topographical Memoir, and in Mandar's work. They will likewise find in the third number of the Topographical Memoir, a catalogue of the best maps that a soldier can refer to.

We have now only to remind the students that they should do honour to the study of the arts and sciences by unlimited devotion to their country, and by a morality worthy of the education that they have received.

If the government have lavished upon them so many means of instruction, it is in order that they should bring with them into the public service the most distinguished talents, united to the purest moral character. They will doubtless consummate these paternal views, and be ever animated and guided by gratitude, a sense of duty, and love of glory.

END OF THE THIRD AND LAST PART.

APPENDIX.

—◆—

A SUMMARY OF THE PRINCIPLES AND MAXIMS

OF

GRAND TACTICS AND OPERATIONS.

———

PRELIMINARY NOTICE.

MOST military writers have rather treated of great details, evolutions, and manœuvres, than of the real and important combinations of the science. Lloyd, Tempelhoff, and Jomini, are exceptions to this remark. Lloyd is generally profound on lines of operations, stratagic movements, and dispositions for battle. Tempelhoff writes with uncommon minuteness, and describes perfectly the tactics of Frederick, his orders of battle, his grand stratagic movements, and the causes of his superiority; and he proves that these principles and causes have been greatly misunderstood.

Among late writers, Bulow is distinguished by a novelty and ingenuity that would have done him honour, had it been exercised on true principles and sane combinations. His foundations being radically wrong, his superstructure must of course be fallacious; and the reader is left to regret that so much time and talents have been wasted on fanciful and deceptive theories. This author pretends to demonstrate by high sounding scientific terms, and by angles, segments and peripheries, that war may be made *geometrically*. He considers lines of operations under an aspect repugnant to the most universally received principles; and he discusses them in a language that none but mathematicians can understand*. His principles to be practised, must be inverted, or they will lead an army to inevitable destruction. Among the novel sophisms with which his work abounds, is that the base of operations should form an obtusangled, or at least a rectangled triangle with the army or summit (*objective angle*) of the line of operations! And he zealously contends that *retreats* should be divergent, or " *excentric;*" as if a beaten army were not weak enough already, without further reducing it by division and detachments. His principles have been the ruin of many armies; for they were the evil genius of Mack, Wurmser, and others.

* Jomini, vol. i.

General Jomini has transcended all writers on war, and has exhibited the most extraordinary powers of analysing and combining military operations. His work forms an epoch in the history of the science, and should be read by every person ambitious of extending their knowledge, or of understanding military history. This writer has enlightened the annals of his own and former times, by referring events to principles and causes; and he has reduced the hitherto mysterious science of war to a few self-evident principles and axioms. From a work of such excellence, the following summary is chiefly taken; and it is hoped that it will both serve as an introduction to what is emphatically called the *sublime of war*, and induce the reader to consult the original and other celebrated works. The only merit to which this summary can lay claim, is that of a judicious selection; and if it be such, the end proposed is attained.

SECTION I.

The Fundamental Principles of Military Operations ; their Division into three Branches ; Sketch of the two Campaigns of the Great Frederick in 1756 and 1757, to serve as illustrations ; the Battles of Kollin, Rosbach, and Leuthen ; Reflections on these Campaigns ; Maxims ; Definitions of Lines of Operations and Lines of Manœuvre ; Reflections on the Lines of Operations, offensive and defensive, taken by the Great Frederick, and by the French and Austrians, during the seven years war ; on the Lines of Operations taken in several of the Campaigns of the French Revolution—by Napoleon in Italy in 1796—on the Rhine and Danube and in Italy, in 1799—by Napoleon in Italy, and by Moreau in Germany, in 1800—by Napoleon against Prussia in 1806 ; Reflections and Maxims ; Configuration of Frontiers ; Retreats ; the Retreat of the Great Frederick after the Battle of Hohenkirchen, &c.

THE science of war is founded upon *concentration of force* and *celerity of movement.* Consequently the great art is, to put the greatest mass of troops in simultaneous action against such a point of the enemy's line of battle or operations as threatens his flanks and rear ; and where, if successful, he can hardly escape capitulation or destruction, and being cut off from his communications. Now these points are *three*—the *extreme right*, the *centre*, and the *extreme left*. The centre should only be attacked when the line of battle or operations is very extended, and when the wings cannot support the centre. In this case, the centre is the most favourable point ; for being weak, it will be easily broken ; and the two wings will then be isolated, and may be crushed in succession. Where this condition of weakness or extension of the centre does not exist, then the attacks should be carried on against a single, or both extremities of the line ; according as the forces on the offensive are capable of a single or double attack. A double attack on both extremities of a line, requires vast numerical superiority ; and the attacks should be connected by a corps posted *in observation intermediately,* and facing the front of the hostile line of battle or defence. Such attacks, if upon a line of battle, must be simultaneous ; if upon a line of operations, they must be also simultaneous, and the direction of the two armies must be converging. Unless this be the case, the enemy may gain the initiative or first move, and carry all his forces against one of the armies, surprise it on its march, and beat it ; and then move against the other, without danger from the first, which will have been repulsed back out of striking distance.

From the preceding considerations we draw this maxim, equally applicable to attacks on lines of operations or lines of battle—

Carry the mass of your forces against the decisive point of the enemy's line, and there put them simultaneously into action. If this decisive point be an extremity, take care to give your movements such a direction as to get well upon the flank, or rear (if possible), of the enemy; in order that, if victorious, you may cut him off from his base of operations and communications, and that he shall be separated from his frontier and resources; and thus his destruction be inevitable. If the movement be against the extremity or rear of the line of battle or of operations, a corps must be left on the refused flank of the attacking army, to maintain and secure its own communications, and to provide for the case of defeat.

An assailed extremity can only be supported by troops arriving from a great distance in succession, and which are consequently exposed to be beaten successively as fast as they come up. A centre, on the contrary, may be supported simultaneously from both wings, *provided these wings be not too far extended or divided.* Besides, the attacked extremity may often be crushed before any battalions can arrive to its support, even should the latter be within supporting distance of the former.

These considerations have naturally led to the division of the science into three grand branches:—

1st. The art of choosing the best possible line of operations by which to invade or defend a country. This is called the *Plan of Campaign.*

2d. The art of carrying the greatest possible mass of force in the shortest possible time to any given or decisive point of this line of operations. This is called *Stratagy,* which is really only the means of executing this second combination.

3d. The art of directing this force, when brought together, to the greatest effect against the enemy's line of battle or position; in order that the whole force may make a simultaneous and combined effort against the decisive point of the position or line of battle. This latter is called *Grand Tactics,* but is properly the *Art of Combat.*

The uniting of forces against a decisive point, is best effected by superior celerity, and by choosing such a line of manœuvre or operations, that the forces will have a shorter distance to traverse than the enemy, who will consequently be incapable of anticipating or avoiding the blow. Stratagem is often used to effect this union; and marches may be stolen even upon the most wary and skilful adversary. But the best possible mode of accomplishing any plan of operations, is to assume the initiative or offensive, and not to give the enemy time to combine any movements against us. This attitude must be maintained; and when arrived upon the decisive point, the troops must promptly make an impetuous combined and simultaneous effort to crush the hostile forces, which should be alarmed on several points in rear and front and flank by detachments of light troops, thrown out for the purpose of masking the operation and disquieting the enemy for his communications.

Before we proceed to the discussion of lines and bases of operations, we will, in order to familiarize the subject and mode of reasoning, take a view of the lines of operations that were taken by the great Frederick, and his enemies, in the celebrated campaigns of 1756 and 1757.

The Campaign of 1756.

Bohemia forms a central salient line intersected by the Elbe, which became the central point of demarkation of the bases of operations. Silesia and Moravia were the Prussian left line of operations; Saxony formed their right line; and Lusatia their central line of operations. This centre had only two bad communications, by Zittau and Gabel, &c. It was therefore difficult for the king to move with as much advantage upon this line, as by the left on Moravia, where he might strike decisively at the heart of the Austrian States. The right line of operations led the Prussians only to Prague, and should have been only accessary; because it presented almost insurmountable difficulties, and successes on this line led to nothing *decisive;* and it had not, like the *left* line, a base covered by fortresses*.

The theatre of offensive operations for the *Austrians*, was naturally the reverse. Their right, opposed to the king's left, would always encounter obstacles in the Silesian fortresses; and victories on this line would be won to no purpose. They had therefore every inducement to make their attack by their left through Saxony on the right of the Elbe; because here they assailed the weakest part of the Prussian frontiers.

Bohemia afforded the Austrians the most advantageous defensive line. Its configuration, salient into the centre of the whole theatre of operations, enabled them to assemble their masses concentrically upon the Elbe, and to carry them offensively in the same manner against Dresden or Silesia, with equal facility. The chain of mountains that separates this country from all those adjacent, was for the most part in the hands of the Austrians, and afforded them great offensive and defensive advantages. These positions could only be turned and rendered nugatory and the Austrians compelled to fight on less advantageous ground, by an operation in mass against Moravia.

We will not, like Lloyd, enter into a long description of the theatre of

* See Maps of Bohemia, Silesia, Moravia, Saxony and Lusatia, especially those by Julien, Muller, Petri, and Backenberg.

war, which would answer no purpose; roads are to be found every where when grand stratagic movements are to be made. Nor is it necessary to enumerate the camps that were not occupied; because a good camp does not decide the fate of a war.

It is generally known that there were eight tolerable fortresses in Silesia; these were however always favourable for covering the depots and communications, and had too great an influence on the operations of the seven years' war. At that period, armies of 100,000 men were afraid of advancing for fear of having their retreat cut off by the garrison of Schweidnitz, 6,000 strong*!

Neisse and Glatz were the most advantageous fortresses for the Prussian offensive operations; Schweidnitz only feebly covered the outlets of the defiles leading from Bohemia into Silesia, by Friedland. Glatz possessed this advantage in respect to the defiles leading from Konigsgratz (in Bohemia) to Neisse. Custrin and Glogau covered the Oder on the side of Poland, and, together with Breslau, Brieg, and Kosel, secured the bridges over this stream and made the Prussians master of both its banks. Stettin and Colberg were important points in relation to Russian disembarkations.

On the side of Saxony, the Prussians possessed Dresden; all the rest of the country was open. The Austrians had only the fortresses of Olmutz and Prague on all their frontiers. Egra had no influence upon the operations of this war.

When the king found that a league was formed against him by Austria, France, Russia, Sweden, and the Empire, he resolved, after vainly striving to negotiate, to anticipate his enemies and beat them down in succession before they were ready or concentrated, and to carry the war into their own territory before they could invade his. He was early ready with 120,000 men, before the Austrians were at all prepared; their troops were only marching from Flanders, Italy, and the frontiers of Turkey, to unite at Vienna; the Russians were still behind the Dwina, and scattered over their vast empire.

Frederick might have profited of these incalculable advantages to have crushed the weak corps of Bohemia or Moravia, and then gained possession of Vienna and the line of the Danube as far as Lintz or Passau. But he preferred to take possession of Saxony, which would afford him great resources, and which covered his states towards the Elbe, where they were most exposed. And he thought himself the more authorised to do this, because he had information of the Elector's secret adhesion to all the plans formed for his ruin.

On the 29th August, 1756, an army of 70 battalions and 80 squadrons entered this Electorate at three points. The right wing, commanded by the Duke Ferdinand of Brunswick, marched from Magdeburg by Halle, Leipsic, Borna, Chemnitz, Freyburg, and Dippodiswalde upon Dresden;

---

* This was the reason gravely alleged in a council of war by Prince Charles of Lorrain, for not attacking Breslau in 1757.

which was the rendezvous for the army. The centre, commanded by the great Frederick in person, marched from Wittenberg on the left of the Elbe by Torgau, Meissen, and Kesseldorf, to Dresden. The left, under the orders of the Duke of Bevern, marched from Franckfort (on the Oder) by Elsterwarda, Bautzen, Stolpen and Lohmen, where it encamped on the right of the Elbe opposite Pirna.

The army was united near Dresden on the 6th of September. This march seems to have been very well combined. There were only 15,000 men in Saxony, and these were not together in a body; and even if they had formed a corps d'armée, they would have still been inferior to either of the Prussian columns, and could not have moved against one without being turned by the two others: this will be evident by inspecting the map.

The event proved the wisdom of these dispositions. The Saxons were compelled to abandon the country, and to retire with 14,000 men into the famous camp of Pirna. They chose this position because they believed it impregnable, and because it secured their communications with Bohemia, whence they expected succour, and whither they might retire in case of necessity. The Elector, encouraged by these advantages, refused all Frederick's propositions.

The king, who had not anticipated this resistance, and who meditated the invasion of Bohemia, had ordered Marshal Schwerin to penetrate into this kingdom by Nachod, with 33 battalions and 55 squadrons. Finding however that the Saxons rejected all his offers and were too strongly posted to be forced, he was obliged to change his plan. He thought that it would not be safe to advance into Bohemia whilst the Saxons were masters of the Elbe and his rear; because he had no magazines in this country, and the scarcity of transport would prevent him from carrying after him the little provisions that he had on hand. He therefore resolved to reduce the Saxons before undertaking ulterior operations.

For this purpose, the king detached a considerable corps, under the Duke Ferdinand of Brunswick, to Johnsdorf, to prevent the Austrians from succouring their allies, and to secure at the same time the passages into Bohemia. This division was subsequently commanded by Marshal Keith; and was succesively increased to 28 battalions and 69 squadrons. Marshal Schwerin received orders to take post at Aujest, facing Konigsgratz, in order to draw to this point part of the Austrian forces, and thus weaken their efforts to release the Saxons from blockade.

The empress queen, either desirous of concealing the schemes that she had formed against the king, until all her allies were ready to act; or guided by the slow and irresolute councils of her ministry, had not yet united any considerable corps in Bohemia. Nevertheless, on hearing of the movements of the Prussians, she ordered two camps to be formed of all the troops that were then in the neighbouring provinces. The smallest corps, commanded by Prince Piccolomini, was to take post at Konigsgratz, in opposition to Marshal Schwerin; the largest corps was assembled at Kollin, under Marshal Brown, and was destined to march with all possible expedition to the succour of the Saxons.

The respective positions of the hostile corps at the opening of this campaign by the Austrians, afforded Marshal Brown a fine opportunity of applying the fundamental principle of war—*concentration of force.* The distance from Kollin to Konigsgratz is about 25 miles, and from the latter to Aujest (Schwerin's post) is 12 to 15 miles; whilst from Kollin to Pirna is upwards of 100 miles, and through a difficult country. The Marshal could in two days have united his corps with Piccolomini's, and then have fallen upon Schwerin's corps; after which he might have succoured Pirna with his united force. But this was not the only opportunity that the Austrian commanders neglected in this and the subsequent campaigns.

The Empress Queen finding the situation of the Saxons to be critical, and that they must be soon reduced by famine; and aware that the fate of these troops would decide whether Saxony or Bohemia was to be the theatre of war, directed Marshal Brown to succour them at all hazards. The Marshal accordingly quitted his camp at Kollin on the 23d of September, and marched to Budyn on the Eger, in order to be near enough to concert measures with the Saxons for raising the blockade. He advanced on the 30th September to Lobositz, where he was met by the King, who had marched upon him. The Prussians attacked the Austrians on the morning of the 1st of October, and, after a severe contest, repulsed them from the field; the loss of each party was about 3,000 men.

Marshal Brown next attempted to succour the Saxons by the right bank of the Elbe; but here again he was frustrated by the measures of the King, the strength of the investing posts, and the badness of the weather, By this attempt he exposed himself to be cut off ; for had the Prussian army that was encamped at Lobositz, crossed the Elbe in his rear at this town or Leutmeritz, he would have been cut off from his base and compelled to fight with all the great chances against him.

The Saxons, having waited in vain for succour, capitulated on the 18th of October; it was stipulated that they should be disbanded, and should not serve against the King; that the Prussians should remain in possession of Saxony; and that the King of Poland should be free to retire to his kingdom. Frederick, having thus accomplished his plans for this campaign, ordered his armies to retire from Bohemia. The army under Marshal Schwerin, retrograded upon Silesia, and took up cantonments on the frontiers of Bohemia from Zuckmantel to Greiffenberg. The forces commanded by the King cantoned in Saxony, and formed a cordon extending from Egra to Pirna, and thence, through Lusatia, to the banks of the Queiss.

Let us now examine whether the measures of the King in this campaign were wise and agreeable to the rules of the science.

In all military operations there is something to censure; one party is always in some measure wrong. We must therefore confine ourselves to determining, whether the combinations had for object the application of the rules of the science ; and whether they afforded the greatest chances of success.

It is indisputable that the King was ready to take the field with 122 battalions and 211 squadrons. By leaving 12 battalions and 30 squadrons in Prussia or Pomerania, exclusive of the garrisons of the fortresses, he would have had 110 battalions and 180 squadrons for the invasion of Moravia, where there were not more than 30 to 36 battalions, which would have been destroyed. There was not a greater force in Bohemia; and this weak corps would have been unable to communicate with the other hereditary states and forces of the House of Austria. The capture of Vienna and the occupation of the line of the Danube, would have neutralized the Empire; and the King might even have raised in it men and money. The spectacle of the House of Austria humiliated in its very capital, would have made the powers of the coalition tremble. This was the grandest and most decisive plan of operations; and it might have been executed without risk, for the King had no organized forces to fear. If this enterprise had no t succeeded, nothing could be hoped from the fate of the war when all the Austrian armies should be united and seconded by the armies of France, Russia, Sweden, and the Empire.

The invasion of Saxony made the King many enemies, and this too for an operation of a very secondary interest. To justify his combinations, Tempelhoff calculates the number of wagons that the King would have required to carry the subsistence of his army in an enterprise against Bohemia or Moravia. At the time that he wrote, this calculation was every thing, and all plans were subordinate to it. But this was only a proof that the science had retrograded. Many centuries before, Cæsar said that *war supported war;* and his rapid invasions of Gaul, Helvetia, and Italy, prove that his army lived upon the resources of these countries.

The Emperor Julian also made invasions. The Cimbri and the Huns in their invasions of Gaul, the Moors in Spain, Gustavus Adolphus and his successors in Germany, certainly did not carry with them bakeries and great magazines. The genius of Frederick might have calculated, that 90,000 men marching rapidly to decisive offensive operations, could very well be fed in a rich and fertile country supporting a population of 8 to 10 millions. It was only necessary to make 14 or 15 decisive marches; the magazines might then have been filled, and the troops regularly supplied.

The campaign of *Napoleon* in 1809, shows the justice of this reasoning. Tempelhoff, to excuse his king for not having struck a decisive blow at the House of Austria, makes a false application of the rules of the science. He says, that Frederick by pushing the Austrians back upon Vienna, would have been elongated from his base of operations and weakened; whilst the Austrians would have become stronger and stronger as they approached their base. The maxim is true; but its application is farfetched and erroneous. A remote line of operations certainly becomes weak in proportion to its greater distance from its frontiers; and this is the case especially in respect to debarkations, and invasions of a country that is not adjacent to the invading power. The incursions of Alexander, of Charles XII into the Ukraine, the lines of operations of the Austrians and Spaniards in Flanders for the three last centuries; and, in general, all expeditions that lead through several foreign countries, are of this character. But the case in question, was not of this kind. Vienna is only distant 12 marches from Neisse (in Silesia); and if an operation to the Danube is to be considered as a remote expedition, we must conclude that an army should never pass beyond its own frontiers. Besides, the object was to overwhelm small armies with a far superior mass, and not to drive them back upon the centre of their strength. By marching rapidly, the two corps of Moravia and Bohemia would have been crushed in succession, pursued, and the greater part of them destroyed. To censure such an enterprise, is nearly the same as to blame the conduct of the King at Rosbach, and to reproach him for having attacked with his mass the heads of the Prince of Soubise's columns; because in so doing he ran the risk of driving back these heads upon the centre and rear of the columns, which might then become themselves a mass.

The Campaign of 1757.

The coalition formed against Frederick, had become more formidable by the accession to it of Sweden and the Germanic Body. The forces of the coalition amounted to 400,000 men; whilst Frederick, and all his allies, could only muster 180,000 men to oppose them.

As several of his enemies, in consequence of their great distance, could not begin operations before the season was very much advanced, Frederick determined to take the field as early as possible, and to attack with his united forces the nearest and most formidable. He justly reasoned that if he was fortunate enough to strike a grand stroke at the Austrians on the opening of the campaign, he would delay, and perhaps prevent, the operations of the other confederates.

These motives, which must have determined the King to hasten the catastrophe by deciding the quarrel, led Maria Theresa to adopt the opposite system of policy. The Empress Queen determined to stand on the defensive until her allies had taken the field; for the King would then be compelled to divide his forces, and would be incapable of opposing a great resistance at any one point. While waiting for this favourable moment, she provided for the defence of her States.

In order to cover all the frontiers from the enterprises of the enemy, Marshal Brown divided his army into four corps. The left corps, commanded by the Duke of Aremberg, took post at Egra; the second, commanded by the Marshal in person, was at Budyn; the third, under the orders of Count Konigseck, was posted at Reichemberg; and the fourth or right corps was stationed in Moravia under Count Serbelloni.

The Marshal thought that he thus covered Bohemia, because each of these corps was considerable; and he supposed that they could easily gain a central position to check the Prussians in the event of their attempting to advance. Lloyd however thinks that the Marshal did not impute to them this design; for otherwise he would not, contrary to all military rules, have established his magazines upon the frontiers.

Frederick, having determined to penetrate into Bohemia, divided his army into four corps. The first, commanded by Prince Maurice, took post at Chemnitz; the second, commanded by the King, was at Lockwitz; the third, under the Duke of Bevern, occupied Zittau; and the fourth, under the orders of Marshal Schwerin, was in Silesia. Each of these corps being very considerable, the King thought that he might cause them to penetrate separately into Bohemia; but in order to prevent them from being beaten in detail, the two first were to form a junction in the environs of Lobositz, at the moment of debouching from the defiles; and the two others were to unite on the Isere, in the environs of Turnau. The four corps, which would then become *two*, would after this junction be able, without any risk, to march upon Prague, where they were to unite.

This plan was precisely similar to that of the armies of the North and of the Sambre and Meuse in 1794, of the Rhine and Sambre and Meuse in 1796, and of the Danube and Helvetia in 1799. They all had specious points of junction at a distance of nearly 100 leagues from their base, and in positions occupied by the enemy.

All the columns formed the junctions required, and then took up two converging lines of operations against Prague; to which place Marshal Brown retired on Frederick's passing the Eger and threatening to cut him off at Budyn, by passing the river above his left and marching upon his rear. The command of the Austrian forces at Prague, was now assumed by Prince Charles of Lorrain.

The column under Marshal Schwerin passed the Elbe on the 4th of May; and on the 5th the King with his column crossed the Moldau. The two columns united under Prague at midnight; and on the morning of the 6th, the Austrians were attacked in their position before this city, and beaten after a desperate contest. The loss of the Prussians was 12,200 killed and wounded, and 1,500 prisoners; that of the Austrians was 12,000 killed and wounded, and 4,000 prisoners. The Austrians retired into Prague; the vicinity of this fortress saved them from total destruction: their right wing retreated upon Beneschau.

The King immediately took measures to blockade Prince Charles in Prague; and notwithstanding that the latter had 50,000 men, the King completely invested him with 60,000, and repulsed the frequent attempts made to evacuate the place.

On the irruption of the Prussians into Bohemia, the Austrian corps in Moravia, commanded by Marshal Daun, was ordered to join the Grand Army at Prague. This General arrived at Bomischbrodt on the 6th of May, where he learned the fate of the battle. He remained a few days in this town and then retired to Kollin, for the purpose of avoiding a battle and joining the right wing that had retreated upon Beneschau.

The King, fearing that this army under Daun, which was now 40,000 strong, might annoy him in his operations before Prague and enable

Prince Charles to evacuate the place, resolved to compel it to retreat. For this purpose, he detached the Duke of Bevern with 25,000 men.

The Marshal, in order to receive the reinforcements that were marching to join him, retired successively from Kollin to Kuttenberg, Goltzjenkau, and Haber. Having received these reinforcements, he advanced against the Duke of Bevern, who was compelled in his turn to retire towards Prague, after several manoeuvres and narrowly escaping an engagement. Frederick, on learning the advance of Daun, marched on the 13th June with a reinforcement, and joined the Duke of Bevern at Malohtitz on the 14th. On the 18th, he attacked Daun near Kollin, and, notwithstanding his admirable dispositions for battle, was beaten with dreadful slaughter. Frederick lost nearly one half of the corps engaged; his loss was 13,700 killed, wounded, and prisoners; that of the Austrians was only 6000 killed and wounded.

The van guard consisted of 55 squadrons, under Ziethen. In the first line there were 23 squadrons on the right and 20 on the left, with 14 battalions between them, and 3 battalions flanking each wing. The second line was composed of 10 squadrons on the right, 10 on the left, and 7 battalions. Four battalions were in reserve. The Austrians occupied a ridge of heights nearly parallel to the Prussian line of march. Their right rested upon a wood, beyond which there was a plain nearly a 1000 paces wide, bounded by a ravine through which flowed a rivulet. The Austrian cavalry, under Nadasty, were stationed in this plain between the wood and ravine; a few battalions, in crescent, occupied the front of the wood; the remainder of the army, in two lines, occupied the slope and summit of the ridges, which were well garnished with artillery: their front and left were inaccessible.

The van guard, under Ziethen, was to advance beyond the enemy's right and attack their cavalry if they appeared; and then to cover the Prussian left and support the attacks. The army was to march by *lines and platoons* by the left, in three columns; and so soon as the heads of the columns had gotten beyond the hostile right, General Hulsen was to attack the posts in its front with 3 battalions of grenadiers, the 4 battalions of reserve and 14 pieces of artillery, supported by 5 squadrons posted in third line. On repulsing the enemy, Hulsen was to incline to the left and dislodge the enemy from the wood, and then take their army in flank and rear. The army was meantime to continue its march to the left, to support Hulsen in case he should be repulsed; if he succeeded, the battalions on the left were to form upon and overthrow the Austrian right. The line was to be successively engaged; so that the refused right wing would come into action only in consequence of the progress of the rest of the army. The cavalry was to form in rear of the left, to support Ziethen and the infantry; and was to decide, by a charge at a favourable moment, the advantages gained by the latter. Only 10 squadrons of cuirassiers were left on the right wing, for the purpose of checking any of the enemy's enterprises against this extremity. All the Generals were well acquainted with the ground, as the Duke of Bevern had been manoeuvring there some weeks before. Hulsen's attack, in 3 lines, upon the posts in advance of the hostile right, succeeded; he accordingly next directed his troops against the wood, which he warmly attacked. Ziethen's cavalry charged Nadasty's with such effect, that they did not again appear on the field. In pursuing them through the plain between the wood and the rivulet, the Prussian cavalry exposed their right flank to the fire of the numerous Austrian artillery and infantry posted in this wood; and by which they were so roughly handled, as to be compelled to retrace their steps. The attack on the wood by Hulsen, which should have preceded this charge of cavalry, was delayed by the necessity that this General found himself under of bringing his second line up into his first, to prevent himself from being outflanked by the numerous forces that the enemy opposed to him, in consequence of the rest of the army having *halted* and left him without support. Prince Maurice had improperly halted the army 1000 paces in rear of Hulsen; this delay enabled Daun to check Hulsen, who however maintained his ground. The King hastened to correct this mistake; and the columns were again moving forward, when another mistake decided the fate of the day.

The army had marched by *lines and platoons*, and was continuing to advance to support the attack, when a battalion or two were annoyed by the firing of the croats who occupied the foot and steep sides of the ridge upon which Daun was posted. General Mannstein, who commanded these battalions, ordered one of them to form line and repulse the croats; and neglected to instruct the succeeding battalions to continue their march to the left. As the orders of the King were to march upon the left, it was natural for the battalions to halt and form line on finding that those on their left had done so; and this was unfortunately the case. The engaged flank was, in consequence, not supported; and the flank which should have been refused, was engaged against impregnable positions and steep acclivities, where neither valour nor skill could avail. The King says that a reserve of four battalions would have secured the victory.

This battle, which, had it been fought according to the King's plan, would have been a model of the oblique order against an extremity of a hostile line, was lost by a subordinate not understanding the *spirit of the operation*; and by attention to miserable trifles, when the great object should alone have engrossed attention. Several Prussian regiments were with great difficulty withdrawn; they could hardly be persuaded that their King was defeated.

Marshal Daun, instead of following up his victory, remained in his camp; and though another successful battle would have ruined the affairs of Frederick, who had only 60 or 70,000 men to oppose the 100,000 men now under Prince Charles of Lorrain, yet the latter remained inactive until the latter end of August: and he even then avoided a battle at Zittau, when Frederick marched from Bernstadel to attack him in a position that he found to be unassailable.

The loss of the battle of Kollin, placed Frederick in a very critical position. The French army under Marshal D'Estrées, after taking possession of his Westphalian States and overwhelming the army of the Duke of Cumberland, threatened his hereditary States. The Prince of Soubise was leading another French army into the empire, to act in concert with the army of the Circles. The Russians had penetrated into Prussia on the North, with an army out of all proportion to that opposed to them under Marshal Lehwald; the Swedes had begun to operate in Pomerania; and Frederick had before him an army of 100,000 Austrians, which was daily reinforced. To all these formidable masses he could only oppose an army of 70,000 men, with which he was to baffle the plans of his enemies.

His destruction appeared inevitable; nobody perceived the possibility of arresting such a threatening torrent, or of diverting its course. The wise and prudent Germanic Diet, thinking that they might brave the King with impunity, put him to the ban of the empire. Frederick alone preserved unshaken his fortitude and presence of mind; he found in himself that confidence which cannot be defined, and which made up for all that his arms had lost. He was never greater than at this time. His plans, as grand as they were unexpected, stupified the moral powers of his enemies; he knew how to keep their armies separated apart a suitable distance, in order to carry his greatest force against that which was most dangerous; whilst with the residue of his troops he maintained an admirable defensive, held the others in check, and prevented them from undertaking any thing decisive. He was able to deceive them by flattering hopes, which made them lose sight of the ensemble and harmony of their operations.

It was natural for the imagination of the allies to become inflamed by the victory of the Austrians, and to consider as certain the conquests with which they had flattered themselves beforehand. The French accordingly prepared to act with vigour; and the army of the Circles thought itself able to take part in the expected catastrophe.

The essential point for the King, was to prevent the coalesced armies from taking such a direction as would permit them to combine their movements and enclose him within a small space, where they might attack simultaneously his front and flanks, whilst another army assaulted his rear. This he effected in a masterly manner. As the junction of the Austrian and combined armies could only take place in Saxony, it was of the highest importance to the fate of the campaign to prevent this operation.

After the battle of Kollin it was uncertain whether the Austrians would march upon Saxony, in order to meet their allies; or whether they would endeavour to re-conquer Silesia, the loss of which they so much regretted. The conquest of this Duchy would be attended with great difficulties; its fortresses were well supplied and would make a long defence, and could be supported by the army of Frederick. Tempelhoff also thinks, that the consideration of subsistence must have greatly delayed the operations of the Austrians. During this time, affairs might take a more favourable turn; and if the King could succeed in the course of the months of August and September in getting rid of the armies of France and the empire, he might arrive in Silesia soon enough to prevent the Austrians from undertaking a siege or making any progress.

The aspect of affairs would have been greatly changed, if Prince Charles of Lorrain had marched upon Saxony. The King would then have had to contend against three grand armies; one of which was to operate against the Duchy of Magdeburg; the other upon the Saale, towards Leipsick; and the third between the Bober and the Elbe. These armies would have been able to form a junction; and if the King had attempted to march with all his forces against one of them, the others would have been able to closely follow him, to take him in flank and rear, and to cut him off from all communication with his frontiers. Lastly; by manœuvring with sufficient prudence to prevent Frederick from forcing them to a battle in too disadvantageous a situation, they would have gotten possession of all Saxony, and taken up their winter quarters in his States.

If Lloyd had reflected that the preservation of this province was necessary to the safety of the Prussians, he would not have censured the King's conduct; and the preservation of it depended upon holding Dresden, the only fortress of importance in the whole country, and which is the key to it on the side of Bohemia. It was therefore the King's interest to endeavour to hold this fortress as long as possible, and to take such positions as would cover it against all the enterprises of the enemy. It was still more important to draw the attention of the Austrians to some other point, and to leave them some less dangerous advantages. In the posture of Frederick's affairs at this time, the loss of a battle under the walls of Dresden would have been attended by the most disastrous consequences; a defeat elsewhere, might not be important. Such doubtless were the motives that determined Frederick to divide his army, to leave the Duke of Bevern with the greatest portion of it on the frontiers of Silesia, and to march in person with the remainder into Saxony. He accordingly on the 19th June raised the siege of Prague, without loss, and sent his train down the Moldau and Elbe to Dresden. The King with his corps retired on the 20th upon Leutmeritz, whilst the Prince of Prussia and Duke of Bevern gradually retreated on Bomisch-Leypa, which they occupied from the 7th to the 27th July.

These positions, of the King at Leutmeritz, and of the Prince of Prussia and Duke of Bevern at Bomisch-Leypa, completely fulfilled Frederick's plans; which were—to prevent the Austrians from penetrating into Saxony by the left of the Elbe. He had also reason to suppose that they would not risk penetrating into Silesia with a portion of their force, whilst the other part remained to observe the King and Duke; because these two would have united and repulsed the corps of observation, and would then have fallen upon their rear. Lloyd has therefore erroneously argued, that the only measure that Prince Charles could adopt, was the invasion of Lusatia; and this was resolved upon, notwithstanding the almost insurmountable obstacles that it presented.

It has been said[*], that the plan of Prince Charles in invading Lusatia, was to cut off the King from Silesia. If the intention had really been to invade Silesia, the road of Lusatia was the longest; and was, in relation to subsistence, the most difficult. The country lying between Saxony, the

* By Lloyd.

Isere, and the Elbe, was exhausted by the long stay of the two armies; and the forage that yet remained, was about being consumed by the army that occupied it: the Austrians had no neighbouring magazines; they drew all their supplies from the farther part of Bohemia. By inspecting the maps it will be seen that the shortest road from Jung-Buntzlau to Silesia, is that which leads by Trautenau and Landshut. Accordingly when the Austrians had arrived at Munchengratz, they should have left the Duke of Bevern in the mountains and rapidly directed their march upon Silesia, in order to cut him off from Schweidnitz and even from Breslau. Tempelhoff pretends that they would not have been followed by the King across Bohemia, because his army could not have subsisted in this country without magazines and at so great a distance from his depots on the Elbe. He therefore thinks that the march into Lusatia, was in direct opposition to the interests of Prince Charles; and that the King in a great measure attained his object by keeping him in check in a corner of this province until the French and combined armies had approached sufficiently near to permit him to advance rapidly against them and get rid of them by the battle of Rosbach for the remainder of the campaign, and then to return with promptitude to the succour of his Silesian army, by fighting the battle of Leuthen.

It is certain that the invasion of Lusatia was not the best plan for the Austrians; but its results would nevertheless have been decisive, had Prince Charles marched and *fought*. If, on his arrival at Zittau, on the 15th August, he had known how to have engaged his army with *all the great chances* that were then in his favour, he would have gained a decisive battle that would have enabled him to march upon the Elbe and decide the fate of Frederick under the walls of Dresden.

Whilst these events were passing on the frontiers of Lusatia, the French army, under Marshal D'Estrées, had succeeded by the battle of Hastenbach (26th July) and the consequent capitulation of Closter-Seven, in beating and neutralizing the British army under the Duke of Cumberland, and in getting possession of all Westphalia.

The other French army, commanded by the Prince of Soubise, had formed a junction on the 21st of August with the army of the Circles at Erfurt, and was advancing to lay siege to Leipsick and drive the Prussians out of Saxony. Its movements were delayed by waiting for the co-operation of the army in Westphalia, now commanded by the Duke of Richelieu. As the King appeared to be entirely occupied with the Austrians in Bohemia, the combined Generals supposed that he had neither the time nor the means of opposing them.

Frederick knew well that unless he could check the armies of Soubise and Richelieu, they would soon be upon the Elbe and strike him most fatal blows. He therefore left the Duke of Bevern with an army of 56 battalions and 100 squadrons, to defend Silesia; and on the 15th August marched with 16 battalions and 23 squadrons from Bernstadel, where he had formed a junction early in July with the Prince of Prussia and Duke of Bevern, when the advance of Prince Charles by the right of the Elbe upon Lusatia had menaced the Duke's separate corps and required the King to march from Leutmeritz to his support. When the King joined Bevern, Prince Charles took up an impregnable position near Zittau, which the King vainly strove to attack. Frederick united his troops with the corps under Prince Maurice, which he had left to cover Saxony; and, having thrown two regiments into Dresden, resolved to march to meet the enemy with 28 battalions and 43 squadrons. On the approach of Frederick, the combined army retired beyond Gotha, whither the King pursued them, and spent two months in secondary operations. The King, finding that the combined army declined an engagement, determined to send his army of Saxony into winter quarters; he had scarcely done this before the combined army, after effecting a junction with the corps under the Duke of Broglie, advanced upon the Saale, determined to give battle, when it was most their interest to avoid it. Fearing to fight with the Saale at their back, the combined army re-passed this river on the 29th of October. Frederick crossed the Saale in pursuit of them in three columns, on bridges that he had caused to be thrown over at Weissenfels, Merseburg, and Halle. His columns, which together were only 22,000 strong, united on the 2d of November near Rosbach; and on the 5th, he fought the famous battle of Rosbach, where he attacked and defeated the hostile army 50,000 strong. The Prussian loss was only 300 killed and wounded; that of the enemy was 800 killed, 6,000 prisoners, and 72 pieces of cannon. The two armies had been several days encamped fronting and in sight of each other; on the morning of the 5th, the enemy marched by their right to make a detour of the Prussian left, attack their rear, and cut them off from the Saale. The King, seeing the enemy in motion, and having discovered their object, marched perpendicularly to his rear by his left (*by lines and platoons*), and fell with his cavalry upon the heads of their three columns, which vainly endeavoured to display to the front. Their cavalry was beaten off the field; the heads of the columns of infantry were disordered and broken by the Prussian cavalry and artillery, and were driven back upon their centre and rear with a vigour and skill that afforded them no respite; and as these heads were already greatly outflanked by the Prussian line, the succeeding battalions found it impossible to display with the Prussians on both their flanks. They next attempted to display upon their rear; but their cavalry, which was to cover this operation, being defeated by the Prussian cavalry, the confusion and rout became general. A strong reserve, under the Count St. Germain, had been detached early to amuse the Prussians by demonstrations, and to cover the march; but the King had left a small corps in his camp to keep this reserve in check under favour of the ground.

This battle is regarded as one of the most scientific of the seven years' war; and may be quoted in support of the maxim—

That a skilful General should always endeavour to attack his enemy in march; for by attacking the heads of his columns with his mass, he virtually assails an extremity of his line of battle, which can only be supported gradually and successively : his battalions must therefore be crushed in succession by a mass, if they attempt to support the heads of the columns.

The order of march of the Prussians in this battle and at Kollin, is a model of the march by *lines and platoons*, so much recommended by Frederick and Jomini. The Prussians had the advantage of a ridge of heights that concealed their march and formation, and from which the King calmly watched the enemy's motions. No sooner did he discover that their intention was to turn his left and rear by Merseburg, than he ordered his army to march by *lines* (broken into platoons) *by the left and rear*, and in this order gained the head of the roads by which the hostile columns were arriving to turn his rear. The enemy supposed that he was retreating, and hastened on their cavalry. His first line was composed of 21 battalions, with a reserve of 4 battalions in second line : the cavalry (43 squadrons) with a few pieces of artillery, formed the van guard, commanded by General Seidlitz, and begun the attack by taking the heads of the hostile columns of cavalry in front, rear and flank, and driving them from the field. They were sustained by the infantry, which on arriving upon the ground had, like the cavalry, only to make a conversion of platoons to the right, to be at once in line upon the heads of the columns, which they bore down by constantly advancing as they broke or outflanked the successive portions of the columns.

One cause of the complete success of the Prussians, was that the enemy had no van guard ; which should never be the case when near an enemy. Their columns were in consequence surprised on their march and had not time to change their direction, by inclining to the right and then forming line by a conversion of platoons, or to display out of striking distance of the Prussians. Besides, their order of march and formation was complicated and bad. The action lasted only an hour and an half.

Frederick having by this victory and his consequent pursuit to Querfurt, gotten rid of the combined army for the remainder of the season, set out from Leipsick on the 12th November with 18 battalions and 28 squadrons, to succour his Silesian army, which had just sustained a series of disasters.

After Frederick had marched from Bernstadel, the Duke of Bevern retired to Gorlitz, where he took post on the Landscroon mountain ; he detached General Winterfeld with a division to Moys, between the Neisse and the Queisse, to defend the passages of these rivers. Prince Charles advanced to Bernstadel, detaching at the same time General Nadasty with a large corps to Seidenberg, to observe Winterfeld and secure a passage across the Neisse, and to be ready to anticipate the Duke of Bevern in the event of his attempting to gain Silesia. Here the Prince had a fine opportunity of attacking the Duke with 80 to 90,000 men ; but the position appeared to him too strong !

The Prince having determined to invade Silesia and re-conquer that country, on whose resources he hoped to be able to live, resolved to manœuvre to compel Bevern to quit his post. He caused the division under General Winterfeld to be attacked on the Holtzberg mountain, near Moys, in order to cut the Duke off from Silesia; whilst at the same time he forced a Prussian division to retire from Bautzen, and thus cut off the communications of the Duke with Saxony. General Winterfeld, after an obstinate defence against a very superior force, was defeated and slain on the 7th of September; and the Duke of Bevern thus found himself obliged to evacuate his strong position of Gorlitz, where he could now no longer obtain supplies, and to retire upon Lignitz (on the Katzbach) by Naumberg, Buntzlau and Haynau. He arrived at the bad position of Lignitz on the 21st, having descended and crossed the Neisse below Gorlitz, in order to avoid the neighbourhood of the enemy. He neglected to take post at Schmotseifen or Lowenberg, either of which would have covered Silesia.

As soon as Prince Charles was informed of the march of the Prussians, he moved by Lauban, Lowenberg, Goldberg, Hundorff, Jauer and Nicolstadt, to Greibnig, where he arrived on the 26th. By the choice of this position, he cut off the Duke from his communications with Breslau, Schweidnitz, and Upper Silesia. The Duke, in order to re-establish by the right bank of the Oder his communications with Breslau and Upper Silesia, marched on the night of the 27th towards Glogau; and finding that he was only followed by a van guard, which moved on the right of the Katzbach upon Parchwitz, he effected on the 29th a passage of the Oder near Lampersdorf. He then ascended the right bank of this river, which he re-passed at Breslau on the 1st of October, and encamped on the banks of the Lohe with this town at his back.

Prince Charles thought it was useless to fatigue his troops by pursuing the Prussians from Lignitz, because they had a secure retreat under the cannon of Glogau, where they could supply all their wants. And as the Austrians had no depots upon this line, and it seemed to them impossible to establish any in the face of an enemy who held several fortresses in their rear, the Prince determined to march upon Breslau, which he hoped to reach and capture before the arrival of the Prussians, especially as its fortifications were very weak and the garrison very small. But on arriving upon the Schweidnitzwasser he found himself anticipated by the Duke, whose army was encamped between him and the town.

Instead of slowly marching upon Breslau, to anticipate the Duke, Prince Charles should have thrown bridges across the Oder near Parchewitz, and there crossed to the right bank; he could then have anticipated the Duke, and would have effectually cut him off from Breslau.

As the Prince could not long maintain his position before Breslau for want of subsistence, he determined with part of his army to lay siege to some fortress that would serve as a place-of-arms for the next campaign, whilst the remainder of his army observed the Duke. Neisse being situated near the Moravian frontier, might be attacked with more ease than any other, because all the necessary supplies could be drawn from Olmutz; it secured an entrance into Upper Silesia, and would facilitate the conquest of the county of Glatz in the following campaign. On the other hand it was argued, that Neisse was too distant and the season too far advanced to hope for success; that the Duke of Bevern could arrive there before the Austrians, and could take such a position as would cover the fortress; that the possession of that place would secure but a very small tract of country, whilst the enemy would still have Kosel, Brieg, and Glatz, as points of support; and that Neisse covered Moravia only, leaving Bohemia open to the Prussians.

It was then proposed to attack the Duke of Bevern before Breslau, which place would fall of itself in the event of his defeat. If the Duke were beaten, the Austrians would then be able to take some other places, whose feeble garrisons, when abandoned to themselves, would be easily reduced; and the Austrian army might then, under the protection of these fortresses, take up its winter quarters in safety.

This proposition was overruled, because, if unsuccessful, the army would find great difficulty in retiring into Bohemia across several very high mountains and over very bad roads; moreover, it was objected that the garrison of Schweidnitz (composed of 6,000 men) might cut off their retreat! It was therefore determined to besiege and reduce Schweidnitz before undertaking decisive operations against the Duke. The capture of this fortress promised several advantages; 1st, it would render the Austrians masters of the principal defiles leading into Bohemia, and of the towns and villages in its rear; 2d, it would enable them to keep a large part of their army in Silesia during the winter; 3d, its capture without loss of time, would enable them then to attack the Duke, or to boldly undertake any other operation, because their retreat would be secured.

Such were the reasonings of Prince Charles of Lorrain at the head of 85 to 90,000 men, and when there were only 30,000 men to oppose him; and such were too often the plans and motives that characterised the Generals of Maria Theresa. General Nadasty was in consequence detached with a considerable corps to besiege Schweidnitz, before which the trenches were opened on the 27th October. The fortifications of Schweidnitz being at this time very imperfect, breaches were effected and some of the works were carried by assault on the night of the 11th of November. Next day the Governor capitulated. Nadasty had formed *three* attacks, two of which only were real. The garrison, 6,000 strong, became prisoners of war. Great quantities of artillery, ammunition and provisions were found in the place.

Whilst these events were passing, the two armies remained quietly near Breslau—Prince Charles covering the siege—and the Duke fortifying his camp, which he would not quit for fear of losing Breslau and of being enclosed between the Army of Observation and the corps besieging Schweidnitz.

Encouraged by the reduction of this place, Prince Charles determined to attack the Prussians, notwithstanding that they were now well fortified:

He accordingly ordered General Nadasty to join him; this General arrived on the 17th, and took post with his corps on the Austrian right.

On the 22d the Austrians attacked the Duke of Bevern in his position behind the Lohe, over which, under cover of 60 pieces of artillery, they threw seven bridges in less than three quarters of an hour, notwithstanding the fire of the Prussians. The position having been forced, the Duke retreated into Breslau, after losing 6000 men : the Austrians lost 4000.

The Duke of Bevern was next day taken in reconnoitring. General Ziethen then assumed the command, and directed his retreat by the right of the Oder upon Glogau, where he repassed to the left bank and advanced to meet the army that the King was marching with from Saxony. The Austrians, instead of vigorously pursuing Ziethen, whom they had nearly cut off and could have easily destroyed, were satisfied with their laurels, and remained 8 or 9 days before Breslau. After the shameful capitulation of this ill fortified town, they were preparing to take winter quarters, when the arrival of Frederick deranged all their plans.

Frederick, having no longer any thing to fear from the combined army, had marched from Leipsick on the 12th November with 18 battalions and 28 squadrons, to arrest the progress of the Austrians in Silesia. He arrived on the 28th at Parchewitz, where he staid till the 3d of December. His corps was supported and lodged on this march by the Communes, because it was impossible to carry with it any thing more than the necessary ammunition, and there were no magazines on the route. However, this manner of living in good cantonments, enabled the Prussian soldiers to sustain the fatigues of so long and forced a march. But this was not the first time that the Prussian troops had lived at the expense of the cantonments, without issues of rations ; and it ought to prove, that an army marching to decisive operations may easily find provisions on its route until it has decided the fate of an Empire. There are however countries that are perhaps an exception to this rule—such as Russia, Sweden, Canada and the United States, and all other countries of thin and scattered population.

Fearing that the Austrian division that had remained in Lusatia, under the orders of Generals Marshal and Haddick, might annoy his march, Frederick had detached Marshal Keith with a small corps by the upper mountains upon Marienberg and Pasberg and thence into Bohemia, in order to draw the attention of the enemy to this province. This enterprise succeeded. The Marshal advanced by Commotau and Laun as far as Leutmeritz, where he destroyed the magazines, burnt the bridge over the Elbe, and raised heavy contributions ; and, on the approach of General Marshal, retired into Saxony, where he took up his winter quarters.

During his march on Parchewitz, the King had received the most disastrous news ; that of the capture of Schweidnitz, was immediately followed by intelligence of the battle of Breslau, the capture of the Duke of Bevern, the capitulation of this fortress, and the almost total desertion of the Silesian regiments (8000 men) that had been left in it. The army now under Ziethen, was reduced by death and desertion to nearly 15,000 men; the

Duke had weakened it by improperly detaching 15,000 men of its original force into the Silesian fortresses; it formed a junction with the King's corps at Parchewitz on the 3d of December. The strength of the corps brought by Frederick from Saxony, is estimated by Tempelhoff at 13,600 men, at the rate of 600 men per battalion, and 100 per squadron; so that the two armies combined, were about 29,000 strong. The King, in his memoirs, states that he had 33,000 men at the battle of Leuthen or Lissa.

The Austrian force was 80,000; and so greatly were they elated at their successes, that they nick-named the army of Frederick—"the Postdam parade!"

A series of good fortune seems to unnerve the greatest souls and deprive them of their natural vigour, and to sink them to the level of common mortals. Adversity can alone restore their force and energy. Such was the case of Frederick. He called together his Generals and staff, and informed them of all his disasters; he declared that he relied more than ever on their courage and unshaken fortitude and patriotism, to tear from the enemy all the advantages that they had gained. He directed them to communicate all these things to the officers and even soldiers of the army, that they might be prepared for the great events that were about to take place. He said that they must attack the enemy wherever they met them, without regard to disparity of numbers; and that their valour, which was capable of surmounting all obstacles and carrying any intrenchments or positions, was a pledge that they would again save their country as they had just done at Rosbach! He conversed with the common soldiers, ordered extra rations for them, and succeeded in raising their spirits and inflaming their courage. The King marched on the 4th December to meet the enemy. He formed his army in two lines; the first consisted of 23 squadrons on the right and 25 on the left, with 20 battalions between them; the second line was composed of 20 squadrons on the right and 16 on the left, with 10 battalions. The van guard consisted of 34 squadrons of hussars, 15 squadrons of cavalry drawn from the right of the 2d line, 4 battalions of flankers, 10 battalions of grenadiers with 10 twelve pounders, and 800 volunteers who opened the march. There was a reserve of 10 squadrons of hussars.

The march upon Newmarck was in four columns, by wings by the right. The first column consisted of the two lines of cavalry of the right wing, excepting the squadrons detached to the van guard; the second column consisted of the two lines of infantry of the right wing; the third was formed of the left wing of infantry; and the fourth was composed of the cavalry of the left wing, likewise in two lines. The heavy artillery was in two brigades, following the two infantry columns. The columns were all with their right in front; so that on arriving upon the two points of conversion, where the two lines were to wheel to the right into a new direction to gain the hostile extreme left, the four columns became *two*; that is, every column separated into two parts, by the portions of the columns that belonged to the two lines *respectively*, wheeling simultaneously to the right;

every column (now half column) on the left of the right column of each line, wheeled into the new direction and formed with the right but one column. Thus by a simple change of direction, the army marched by lines and platoons at whole distances; and on halting, formed line by a mere conversion of platoons to the left.

Four thousand croats were found in Newmarck, 200 of whom were sabred, and 800 taken by the hussars; the rest were dispersed. The Austrian bakeries here fell into the hands of the Prussians. The head quarters were established at Newmarck. The King now received certain advice of the Austrians having advanced from Breslau and behind the Lohe, and that they had encamped on this side (left) of the Schweidnitz-wasser (the Weisswitz). On the 5th of December, at break of day, the army resumed its march in four columns; and on passing the village of Borna, a league in advance of the hostile right wing, wheeled to the right into the new direction nearly parallel to the Austrian front, and thus converted the four columns into two; or, what is the same, into two lines marching by platoons. The baggage and train were left at Newmarck, which was guarded by a few battalions. The joy of the troops at hearing that the enemy were at hand, could not be expressed. A cloudy morning concealed the Prussian march, and enabled their cavalry van guard to surprise and overthrow the 5 regiments of Saxon and Austrian cavalry, under General Nostitz, that were posted near Borna. These regiments lost many killed and 600 prisoners, and were driven back upon the Austrian *right.*

The Austrian army had taken post on the left of the Weisswitz, with their left thrown back in potence upon the pond of Gohlau and this river; their front stretched from the division of cavalry that connected it with this potence, nearly in a right line towards Nipern and the wood of Lissa, upon which their right rested; the village of Leuthen was close in advance of their centre. Their army was in two lines, and occupied a front of 4 to 5 miles. Their right rested upon the ponds and village of Nipern, and upon the wood of Lissa, which they had strongly occupied; their centre was slightly concave, and could be supported by their right taking the attacking columns in flank, by debouching forward through the wood. Their left was not so well supported; and if the retired potence, whose farther left rested upon the pond and marshes of Gohlau, could be forced, the left would then be without support. Accordingly, against the left the King resolved to operate. At some distance in front of the Austrian army arose a ridge, of heights, upon which they had neglected to plant outpos's. These heights concealed the King's march, and at the same time enabled him to closely reconnoitre their whole position. The ground declined from their left; so that the left was the key, for it commanded the whole plain on which the enemy were formed.

As the Austrian army was in the angle formed by the Weisswitz and the Oder, they could only retreat by crossing the former river. They had thrown several bridges across, especially at the village of Lissa, more than a league in rear of their *centre.*

Meantime the Prussians were constantly marching to their right, upon the hostile left; they advanced as if at a parade. The retreat of the enemy's cavalry from Borna upon their right, and the pursuit by the Prussians, had induced Count Luchesi, who commanded this right, to suppose that the attack would be upon his extremity. He therefore repeatedly and urgently requested succour; and Marshal Daun with the reserve marched to his support. The Prussians now appeared upon the Austrian left; and the point of attack became unmasked. The van guard was ordered to attack.

The Prussians formed the open oblique order in two lines, *in echellon* by battalions, with their left refused. Each battalion was posted 50 paces in rear of that on its right; so that the extreme left battalion was 1000 paces in rear of the right. This disposition, though nearly the same as the oblique order, is better; because it has the advantage of preventing the possibility of the refused flank being engaged contrary to order. After the fatal error of this kind at Kollin, this precaution was indispensable*. Six battalions of the van guard formed a forward potence, to cover the right flank of the cavalry of the van guard.

Nadasty, whose corps formed the retired potence, now advanced with his division of cavalry to outflank the Prussian army; he succeeded in repulsing the Prussian cavalry; but he was himself soon forced to retire by the fire of the 6 battalions in potence forward on the right of the cavalry, and by the other van guard battalions. A battery of twenty 12 pounders was brought to enfilade the enemy's potence; and General Wedel, with the 4 remaining battalions of the van guard, carried the heights and grand battery on their left. Nadasty's potence, with his division of cavalry that connected it with the Austrian left, were put to flight after a short resistance. A few battalions attempted to re-form in rear of a ditch; but they were soon overthrown.

The Austrian reserve, which was marching to their *right*, was now countermanded to their left; and Esterhazy's corps of cavalry, and the second line of infantry, were marching thither.

During these events the Prussian army still continued to advance, by prolonging its movement to the right; and as the van guard followed the same direction, the enemy found themselves constantly outflanked on their left; while the right 6 battalions of the van guard took them in reverse by the disposition of their march, which formed, in respect to the rest of the army, a crotchet or potence thrown forward. In consequence, the hostile corps, which were arriving in succession to support the assailed flank, were beaten as soon as they attempted to form. Their left wing now retreated in disorder; the King judiciously ordered the grand battery of the van guard to incline to the left and follow the movements of the army. The Austrians attempted to establish on the right and in rear of the pond of Gohlau (which was in *rear* of their *left*) a line in retired potence, to cover their flank; but the grand battery which had now been directed to the left, swept the right of this line, which was at the same time exposed in front to the fire of the Prussian infantry.

* See the King's Memoirs of his own times.

The cavalry of the Prussian right, which had hitherto been paralized by the great number of ditches, hedges and underwood, at length found ground fit to act on in rear of the pond and village of Goblau. They fell upon the Bavarian and Wirtemberg infantry, and sabred a great part of them; taking 2,000 prisoners, and routing the rest.

Meantime the Austrian Generals endeavoured to form with the rest of their army another retired potence, whose salient angle rested upon Leuthen (this village was in the centre of the original line); and to concentrate upon the heights in rear of this village, all the artillery that they could collect. This village had been occupied from the beginning of the battle by a strong division of infantry, to which was now added the reserve which had returned from the right, and the fugitives from the left, who threw themselves into the houses and church-yard, and seemed determined to maintain them to the last. The Prussian army had now arrived in front of this position, determined to carry it at all hazards. Three battalions charged into the village, where the most dreadful combat took place. The King ordered all the remaining battalions to advance against this village; so that the left, which was to have been refused, became most warmly engaged.

At length the guard, under Captain Mollendorff (afterwards Marshal), penetrated into Leuthen, and by extraordinary exertions of valour compelled the enemy to abandon it. But the enemy, under favour of some ravines in rear of the village, and which they had lined with grenadiers and infantry, still maintained a desperate contest—but they were at length put to flight.

During the attack upon the front of the village, General Wedel charged in front the cavalry on the left of the hostile potence, whilst the Bayreuth dragoons assaulted their left flank; and, though exposed to a terrible fire of grape, the Prussians overthrew this cavalry and expelled it from the field. Wedel then charged the Austrian infantry, and captured whole battalions.

The fate of the Austrian right, was no better. This wing had marched to the left, whilst the other had re-formed upon Leuthen, and still held that post; it then made a conversion forward, so as to form nearly a right line with the retired potence that rested upon Leuthen. The cavalry of the Prussian left, that had till now remained where the line was first formed, marched against the cavalry of the Austrian right; and having outflanked and overthrown them, next fell upon the infantry of the left. These two attacks of cavalry greatly contributed to the evacuation of Leuthen.

The Austrians now made a third attempt to form about half a league in rear of their *last* position and nearly parallel to it, with their right upon a height; but the Prussians continuing to advance, they were again outflanked on their *right*; and as their cavalry had quitted the field, the Prussian cavalry charged their infantry and made a great number of prisoners. The rout was now general; all who could fly, directed their steps to the bridges over the Weisswitz, pursued by Ziethen's and Wedel's cavalry.

Night, which had saved the combined army at Rosbach, now again preserved the Austrians from total destruction.

Next day the army marched by *lines by the right* upon Breslau, whither the ruins of the Austrians had retired. In the afternoon Prince Charles, after leaving 18,000 men in Breslau, retreated by Borau and Schweidnitz into Bohemia. A few days after, Breslau surrendered with its garrison as prisoners of war; and soon after Lignitz, which the enemy had fortified and garrisoned, capitulated on condition that its garrison of 3,000 men should have free passage into Bohemia. The severity of the cold and difficulty of breaking the frozen ground, induced Frederick to grant these terms. Schweidnitz was blockaded by the Prussian cavalry during the winter, and reduced in the spring.

Tempelhoff estimates the loss of the Austrians by this famous battle, at upwards of 50,000 men; viz. 6,500 killed and wounded, 21,500 prisoners, 17,000 prisoners taken at Breslau, 2,000 prisoners taken by Ziethen in the pursuit, 800 taken at Newmarck on the eve of the battle, and 6,000 deserters. The battle lasted from 1 o'clock to 8, P. M.

Prince Charles of Lorrain returned into Bohemia with 9,000 regular infantry and 29,000 cavalry and light troops—the wrecks of an army of 90,000 men. The Prussian loss was 2660 killed and wounded.

On the 6th January, 1758, the army went into winter quarters.

It yet remains to take a view of the operations against the Russians and Swedes, in this memorable campaign.

As the Empress Elizabeth was a party to the treaty of Versailles, Frederick had early in spring marched an army of 30,000 men, under Marshal Lehwald, to the frontiers of Prussia towards Russia. A Russian army of 60,000 infantry, 15,000 cavalry, and 16,000 Tartars, Kalmucks and Cossacks, advanced in May in four columns against Prussia. Three of these columns traversed Poland; and the other marched upon and besieged Memel, which capitulated on the 5th of August. This column was co-operated with by the Russian fleet, with 9000 troops on board. As the Russians by the fall of Memel had acquired a place of arms that could be supplied by sea, and from which they could draw subsistence, their army, commanded by Marshal Apraxin, marched upon the Pregel, behind which Lehwald had taken post. On the 30th August Marshal Lehwald attacked the Russians near Norkitten and *Jaegendorf*, and was repulsed with the loss of 3000 men. The Russians lost 5000 killed and wounded. The ground was very woody; and as the Russians had changed their position during the night, the attack was made upon their centre, instead of their left flank, as intended. But the Russians being badly commanded, did not advance further; and on the 11th September they evacuated Prussia, except Memel, by returning into Poland.

On the side of Pomerania, the operations of the Swedes were very unimportant. Their army of 17,000 men, commanded by General Ungern, passed the Peene and got possession of Anclam, Demmin and the fort of Peenamunde. The only forces to oppose them, were 4 battalions under

General Manteufel, and 10 militia battalions that garrisoned Stettin. On the retreat of the Russians, the King was enabled to send against them Marshal Lehwald, who, before the end of December, drove them into Stralsund, and retook all the posts.

Lloyd has censured the Duke of Bevern for not taking post more to the left towards Griefenberg, instead of at Gorlitz; because the first position, which was not occupied, could not have been turned by the right. It is astonishing he should suppose that 80,000 victorious troops could not endeavour to gain the extremity of an army of 40,000 men and establish themselves in mass upon its communications, from fear of this army capturing *some flour*, when they would have been themselves in the fertile country of Silesia.

He thinks that the Duke of Bevern should from the beginning have taken a more *divergent* direction from the army commanded by the great Frederick; in order to have better covered the Oder. But this reasoning is in violation of all sound principles :—

There is in lines of operations, as in fields of battle, a key. In the former, the great stratagic points are decisive ; by the same reason that the points which command a weak part, are decisive in positions of battle.

By holding the sources of the Neisse and the Spree, the Duke occupied the most favourable intermediate point for co-operating with the King in Saxony, and for moving on Breslau, if requisite. If he had moved on Schweidnitz, he would have left an immense interval between the two armies ; and Prince Charles by leaving 30,000 men before the Duke, might have marched with 50,000 to Dresden to complete the ruin of Frederick, who was already pressed by 60,000 French and Imperialists. The corps thus opposed to the Duke of Bevern, would have had an interior direction with these 50,000 men ; and might, if necessary, retire upon them, or join them to form in mass and strike a decisive blow. In every respect it was better to suffer Prince Charles to march against the fortresses in Silesia, than to abandon to him the central line which covered the heart of the Prussian States and secured the communications between the two armies. Lloyd, notwithstanding all his talents and genius, has totally mistaken, or did not understand, the advantage of central positions. He has however justly censured two fatal errors of the Duke—1st. In quitting too soon the position of Bernstadel, which possessed the double advantage of covering the Oder, and securing his communications with the Elbe ; for notwithstanding the declarations of Tempelhoff, who as usual justifies the Prussians, he might have remained there 15 days longer, by living on the resources of the country :—2d. In awaiting an attack in his camp at Breslau, where he suffered himself to be turned by the Austrians ; he should have attacked Prince Charles while he was covering the siege of Schweidnitz, and before Nadasty had joined him after its reduction.

Bevern was detached by Frederick to occupy the Austrians in Silesia, whilst he liberated his right line of operations and Saxony from the combined army. His object therefore was to give to the coalesced armies an *exterior direction*, whilst his two armies preserved an *interior* direction that would enable them to maintain sufficient space to manœuvre in, and to form a junction in mass if requisite, to strike down one, or in succession both, of the hostile armies. The Duke was besides to prevent the Austrians *from* making any great progress in Silesia; so that at the return of Frederick, they might be easily expelled from this Dutchy. The length of time that the Prince of Soubise refused battle to Frederick, in Saxony, prevented the Duke from being able to maintain the defensive and fulfil his part of the plan.

The progress made by the Austrians in Silesia, is therefore to be attributed to the long absence of the King in Saxony; and proves, that when we are obliged to assume *two interior* lines to oppose two lines of the enemy, we must not place our two armies too far apart: otherwise, that which is weak and destined only to observe the enemy, may be overwhelmed; and the enemy will have time to make solid conquests, whose advantages may exceed those we have obtained on another point.

Perhaps the most central and best position for Bevern, would have been Bœmisch-Leypa; but his force was too weak. It was certainly too feeble to allow of detachments; for an army weaker than its adversary, cannot make detachments, because it would be thereby exposed to be beaten in detail by an already superior enemy.

No maxim can be more indisputable than, that small armies *should constantly act in mass*. 'Tis by the application of this rule that they alone can undertake any important enterprise; they must give up the notion of covering all points, and look only towards the chief object upon which the fate of the campaign depends. If they make detachments, they deprive themselves of all means of acting with vigour when a good occasion offers. A small army should have its eyes constantly fixed upon its adversary; not only to take advantage of his faults, but to draw him into them; as for instance, by inducing him to enterprize against fortresses, and to make diversions that weaken his forces by separating them. This is the moment that it may attack him with equal chances; if he be beaten, his detachments will be lost, or compelled to return.

An army thus situated, may also, by concealed and rapid movements, fall upon one of these detachments and ruin it before it can be supported. Prince Henry has given us examples of this kind in 1759, near Hoyerswerda, against General Wehla; and near Dommitsch, against General Gimmengen. Operations like these, re-establish an equilibrium of physical forces, and double the moral force of the inferior army, by destroying much of the confidence of its adversary.

The Austrians should have attacked the Prussians at Leypa, in July; and, instead of marching into Silesia in September when Frederick had proceeded to Saxony, where his fate should have been decided upon the banks of the Elbe, they should have manœuvred rapidly upon Zittau and

Lobau against the Duke's right, to cut him off from the King; and then, in concert with the combined army, have marched upon Dresden.

It has been said of the campaigns of the French Revolution, that they enlarged the scale of military combinations; but even at this period, armies were fighting from Moravia to the mouths of the Weser, upon a circular line exceeding 300 leagues. But in extending thus the scale of fine projects, the operations were without concert; the incoherence of the enterprises, was equal to the mediocrity of the results proposed to be obtained. To make war grand and sublime, it is not necessary that the scale of it should be so extended, nor embraced in its whole extent. The Emperor Napoleon did not occupy so long a line between Jena and Naumbourg, between Donauwert and Ulm. In operating on a line of 50 leagues, we may sometimes beat an enemy who operates on one of 100 leagues; but this does not prove that the first is right.

What spectacle can be more awful and sublime, than the campaign of 1757? We see Frederick assailed on the east, west, north, and south, by the forces of Russia, Austria, the Empire, France and Sweden (amounting together to 400,000 men); defeated at Kollin; General Winterfeld soon after defeated and slain at Holzberg; and the Duke of Bevern beaten at Breslau. Yet with one arm he strikes the allies in Saxony, and with the other destroys the colossal forces of Austria in Silesia! Effecting all this with an army, which, at the opening of the campaign, amounted to only 100,000 men.

By his judicious dispositions he drew the Austrians to select the line of operations on his left, against Silesia, whilst he flew to rescue Saxony from the combined army; then returning by Lusatia, almost totally destroyed the Austrians, throwing their wrecks into Bohemia. When all Europe looked for his downfall; when in the confidence of success they had put him to the ban of the Empire, he arose with ten-fold might, and scattering the hosts that surrounded him, showed himself most dreadful in the moment of adversity. He showed what it was to contend against a great Captain.

He divided his army into two corps with *interior* lines of operations to those of the enemy, to prevent that enemy *from acting on one line and in mass.* Had they done this, the King would have joined the Duke of Bevern, and would have struck one of the two armies to the earth before the other could come upon him. He would then probably have been able to vanquish the other. This was his system; and such has been the system of all great men similarly situated. Witness Napoleon at Ligny and at Waterloo. He would have been able to oppose his whole mass to an isolated part; and if the combined army had not so long deferred the invasion of Saxony, his success would have been more brilliant, for the Duke of Bevern would not have been beaten at Breslau, nor would Schweidnitz have been taken.

The conduct of Frederick, and the events of the campaign of 1757, lead us to establish the following maxims:

1. A double line of operations may be good when the enemy forms the like; but in this case, the enemy's lines must be exterior,

and ours interior. The enemy's divisions will thus be at a greater distance than ours, and cannot unite without fighting us.

2. An army whose lines are nearer to each other than those of the enemy, may by a stratagic movement overwhelm these in succession, by uniting against them alternately the mass of its force.

3. The better to secure the success of this movement, a small corps or division must be left before the enemy who are to be kept in check ; with orders not to risk a battle, and to restrict itself to checking the enemy and suspending his march by every possible means, such as by profiting of defiles, heights, rivers, &c. This division will have orders to retreat upon the army.

4. It follows that a double line of operations exterior to another, whose parts are nearer to each other, will be always disastrous if the enemy know how to profit of the advantages of his position and of rapidity of movement within his line.

5. A double line of operations against a single line, is still much more dangerous, whenever its parts are distant several days' march.

6. The inverse of the two preceding maxims is true ; that is—single lines of operations, and interior lines of operations, are always the most secure.   They afford no advantage to the enemy ; they, on the contrary, enable us to act in mass against his isolated divisions, if he have been so imprudent as to follow this system.

7. Lastly ; the conduct of Frederick in the campaign of 1757, demonstrates the correctness of two other maxims : First ; that two interior lines can sustain each other reciprocally, and make head against two lines exterior and at a certain distance ; care being taken to avoid being confined in too narrow a space by the enemy, where his divisions might attack simultaneously : Second ; care must be taken to avoid the dangers of an opposite fault—that of pushing their operations too far ; because the enemy would have time to overwhelm the division that has been weakened, to present a mass on the other point ; and he might be able to make progress and conquests that would be irreparable. The disastrous battle of Breslau, is a proof of this rule.

In lines of operations, two or three corps isolated on an exterior direction and together equal to the enemy's single line, cannot succeed if they are unable to fall simultaneously upon this mass ; because the enemy will bring into action twice or thrice as many men as any one of these corps. Therefore two interior lines are advantageous, because they can concentrate at pleasure and with more rapidity than the enemy, whom they will overwhelm with their united force, by bringing twice his numbers into action. Single lines, those whose parts are united and can reciprocally support each other, are for the same reason the best.

The combinations of the first line of operations of Frederick, in 1757, are not exempt from censure ; he did not select the best ; and he embarrassed it by two armies isolated at a great distance. This error would have been fatal to him, if he had had to contend with Napoleon, or with a General who merely understood the application of the principle of central masses. His secondary lines, after the battles of Kollin and Rosbach, as well as his manœuvres in this battle and at Leuthen, will undoubtedly be the instructing subject of the meditations of the military of every age.

———

Lines of Operations.

Lines of operations should be considered under two points of view ; 1st, as territorial lines of operations ; 2d, as lines of manœuvre.

Territorial lines of operations, are those that nature or art has formed for the defence or invasion of states. Those frontiers that are supported by fortresses, or defended by natural obstacles, such as chains of mountains, great streams, seas and other insurmountable obstacles, are the first combination of lines of operations ; but they are not the only one. The dispositions of the General to embrace these lines at the essential points of their display, to traverse them offensively, or cover them defensively, form a second combination still more important, and almost always decisive in operations. The latter is without doubt connected with the former ; but it presents itself under a totally different aspect, as being entirely intellectual ; and we think may be precisely defined lines of manœuvre, because it is really the basis of military tactics. A few examples will render this more intelligible.

The three great lines of operations of France against Austria, are by Italy on the right, by Swisserland and the Tyrol in the centre, and by Germany on the left. The most natural lines of operations by which to penetrate into Germany, are those of the Mayn and the Danube. The most natural lines against Canada, are, by the Champlain in the centre, the St. Lawrence on the left, and the River St. Francis, or (in the next century) the Kennebeck and Chaudiere on the right. These are what are called the physical part of lines. This part of the art cannot be subjected to many rules ; it is, as it were, governed by nature.

In 1757, Frederick penetrated into Bohemia (his central line) by four points. The French armies invaded Germany in 1796 and 1799, by two lines, subdivided. Napoleon never operated upon any other than one principal line. These were combinations of lines of manœuvre. This latter part of the art, has never been reduced to strict and rational principles; and its relations with the rules of the science, have not been determined. We will endeavour, as far as possible, to accomplish this desideratum.

Definition of Lines of Operations, considered as Lines of Manœuvre.

The relations of these lines with those that nature has formed, with the positions of the enemy, and with the plans of the General in Chief, form so many different classes, which derive their character and denominations from these very relations. It is important to detail this classification before we proceed further.

Single lines of operations are when an army acts upon a single line and on the same frontier, without dividing itself; that is, when it does not form two great separate corps d'armée.

Double or multiplied lines of operations are when an army, operating upon the same frontier, forms two or three corps that act isolatedly to attain one or several ends.

Interior lines of operations are those formed by an army to oppose several lines of the enemy, and to which an interior direction is given, so as to approximate them and connect their movements, without the enemy being able to oppose to them a greater mass.

Exterior lines produce an opposite result: these are the lines formed simultaneously by an army upon both the extremities of one or many hostile lines.

Lines of operations on an extended front, are those formed on a great contiguous extent by isolated divisions, having the same base and object. The lines formed by two separate corps upon a single and given extent of country, are included under this denomination; and in this case, they form double lines upon a great front.

Long or deep or remote lines of operations, are those which being far protracted from their base, present a great extent of country to be traversed to attain their end.

Concentric lines of operations are many lines, or a single line subdivided, leading from two distant points to gain a single point in front or rear of their base.

Eccentric lines are when a single mass departing from one point, divides itself to march upon diverging lines.

Finally; the last combinations that the general operations of armies exhibit, are *secondary lines* and *accidental lines of operations*. The first serve to designate the relations existing between two armies, when they act upon the same line of frontier. Thus, in 1796, the army of the Sambre and Meuse, was the *secondary line of operations* of the army of the Rhine. *Accidental lines of operations* designate the changes that events may produce in the primitive plan of campaign, when these changes are of a nature to give a new direction to the operations. These latter are rare, and are of the highest importance; they are generally the fruit of a vast and active genius.

A review of these several combinations, will show that the principles laid down by Jomini, differ from those of the authors who have hitherto written on this subject. The latter have only considered these lines under physical relations. Lloyd and Bulow, the only writers on this subject, have merely given it a value in relation to the magazines and depots of armies. The latter has even laid it down—

That there is no longer any line of operations when the army encamps near its magazines.

This paradox cannot deceive an enlightened mind; the following example will destroy it :

Suppose two armies, one encamped on the Upper Rhine in front of Brisach, and the second on the Lower Rhine in front of Dusseldorf or any other point of this frontier ; and admit that their great depots are established immediately beyond the stream ; which doubtless would be the most secure and advantageous position. Now the object of these armies is either offensive, or defensive ; they will therefore have *territorial lines of operations* and *lines of manœuvre.*

1st. Their territorial defensive line will extend from the point that they occupy, to that point of the second line which they should cover; and they would be cut off from it, if the enemy succeeded in establishing himself upon this point. If the army of Melas had had ten years' supplies in Alexandria, it would not have been the less cut off from its line of operations the moment that the enemy occupied the line of the Po.

2d. Their line of manœuvre would be double against a single line, if the enemy concentrated their forces to overwhelm one of these armies ; it would be a double *exterior* line against a double *interior* line, if the enemy formed likewise two corps and gave them such a direction as to be able to unite sooner.

It is obvious therefore, that Bulow has set out on principles absolutely false ; his whole work must necessarily partake of these errors, and contain dangerous principles.

We will now examine the most important lines of operations that were taken during the seven years' war, and subsequently, and apply them to the different classes that we have just described : and by comparing their results and causes, demonstrate the maxims that we have laid down.

Observations on the three lines of operations taken by Frederick in 1756, 1757 and 1758, and on his defensive lines in the following campaigns.

A plan of campaign should be founded on six primitive combinations ; 1st, the political situation of the two parties ; 2d, the position of affairs ; 3d, their relative strength in means of warfare ; 4th, the distribution and situation of their armies; 5th, the natural lines of operations; 6th, the line most advantageous by reason of circumstances.

It is not pretended that a plan of campaign should be limited by the strict balance of physical forces—that is, by the means of warfare. Nevertheless, it must be admitted that they should have great weight. These plans, which are nothing more than the selection of lines of manœuvre, are subject to many accessary considerations; but these considerations should ever be subordinate to those rules and invariable principles of the science, that are acknowledged as their basis. Boldness, and even daring, qualities often necessary and decisive, are always compatible with an observance of these rules, and with the application of these principles. The greatest proofs of this that history can furnish, are the operations of the Army of Reserve in 1800. No enterprise was ever more daring; none was ever more fruitful in grand combinations; and none was ever more wise and prudent, because it menaced the enemy with total ruin by the mere risk of the last troops of a rear guard.

By applying these maxims to the various lines of operations taken by Frederick, we will be convinced that the accidental plans which his genius conceived from the turn of events in the course of a campaign, were infinitely superior to his original plans for opening the campaign. We will now endeavour to prove this.

It is obvious from the description of the theatre of war, that Frederick had three lines of operations against Austria; his left line was against Moravia, his centre against Bohemia, and his right against Saxony. The first of these lines was the most favourable, under military relations; because its communications were less difficult. If Frederick carried his views as far as Vienna, against the centre of the power of his enemies, this was the shortest and least difficult line; if he limited his views to the provinces bordering upon his states, it was then the longest line of the three, because it was further elongated from Brandenburg—the centre of his power.

The King knew very well that a coalition was formed against him, though perhaps he did not know all the parties, and all its articles; but he was at least apprised of its being formidable. The preparations of Austria had given rise to several diplomatic communications; and Frederick, persuaded that they were attempting to cajole him, resolved, like an able statesman, to anticipate his enemies, and to attack the one that he feared most. But this was also a reason to strike the most deadly blows at the latter—blows from which they could not recover; and which would confound the coalesced powers, at least sufficiently long to suspend their hostilities.

It was certainly more probable that Frederick would have marched upon Vienna with 100,000 Prussians, that is, with 105 battalions and 160 squadrons, when he was assured of the inability of his other enemies for the remainder of the campaign of 1756, than that he would have been able to defend himself as he did afterwards with 80,000 men, when the Russians were masters of the kingdom of Prussia, the Swedes of Pomerania, the French of Saxony, and the Austrians of one-half of Silesia. Could Frederick have feared to leave 20,000 Saxons far off on his right flank, when their country was not at war with him? If he had pushed forward to the Danube, as he might have done, the intimidated Elector of Saxony would have broken the constrained treaties that bound him to Austria; he would have been careful how he provoked a Prince who had made the first power in Europe tremble in its capital.

When Frederick chose the right line of operations, and determined upon the invasion of Saxony, it is certain that there were not 30,000 Austrians in Bohemia, nor 20,000 in Moravia. If at this period he had assembled his army at Neisse, to menace both provinces at once and keep the enemy's forces divided; and had then vigorously operated by his left, he would undoubtedly have destroyed the feeble army of Moravia before it could have been supported; and in 15 days 80 battalions and 120 squadrons might, by masking Olmutz, have arrived before the gates of Vienna. The troops that defended Bohemia, would have found it very difficult to unite with the forces destined to succour the capital. Frederick would have risked by this enterprise only a retreat and the loss of a few thousand men; whilst its success would have overthrown the house of Austria. The difference between these hazards, was the strongest motive to attempt the enterprise. He who has meditated on the achievements of Napoleon, will not doubt that he would have at first chosen this line.

Perhaps it may be objected, that the 30,000 Austrians who were in Bohemia, might have jeoparded the safety of the Prussian army. Can it really be believed that they would have remained quietly in this kingdom for the purpose of cutting off the retreat of the Prussians, when Vienna was on the eve of falling? But let us admit this most improbable supposition; the 25 battalions and 40 squadrons that the King would have left in Moravia, would have been more than sufficient to cover his line of operations. To cut off his retreat, it would have been necessary to guard the three lines of Saxony, Bohemia and Moravia on a front of 150 leagues. One hundred thousand men, when commanded by a Frederick, are not easily cut off from so extended a frontier. If the Austrians had retired upon the Danube, the King could have united to his army the corps left in Moravia. With the mass of his forces he could then have fought a battle under the walls of Vienna that might have decided the fate of Austria; whilst its loss would only have cost the Prussians the evacuation of the invaded provinces.

At the opening of the campaign of 1757, the King might still have attempted this enterprise with success; the French had not yet taken the field against him; the Russians were still within their frontiers, and were little to be feared; and the army of the Circles was not yet in existence. The Prussian army was 100,000 strong, including 30,000 cavalry, the finest in the world; the Austrians were divided. By leaving a few garrison battalions in Saxony, Frederick would have had nothing to fear; he could have carried the mass of his forces against the extreme right of the Austrian line, the very lengthened front of which extended from the frontiers of Saxony along those of Bohemia, Silesia and Moravia, and no where presented a well supported defence.

At last, in 1758, this great man perceived that his natural and most advantageous line, was Moravia; and that by invading this province he would compel the Austrians to uncover Bohemia, in marching to succour their capital. He undertook this invasion with an army much smaller than the enemy's, which was encamped at Konigsgratz, and which was thus much better able to support this line than in the preceding campaigns. Besides, the presence of the Russians on the Oder, and of the army of the Circles in Saxony, had obliged Frederick to divide his forces, and to avoid too great an elongation from his centre. But notwithstanding this immense disparity of circumstances, if the King had not been so long in besieging Olmutz, if he had united his forces and attacked Daun when the latter took post at Predlitz, and if he had not most imprudently exposed all his resources in a single convoy, he would probably have thrown the Austrians back upon the Danube; but to effect this, he should have fought Daun, or harassed him without a moment's respite. This war of vigour was not at that time well understood, and the slaughter that it occasioned was exaggerated; and the King had not at this period sufficient means to re-enforce his army in proportion as it embraced a line of greater depth, and sustained great losses. Such probably were the motives that kept Frederick in a state of inaction during the finest moments of this campaign.

However this may be, the choice of the Moravian line of operations was enforced in 1756 and 1757, 1st. By the political situation of both parties, and especially by their situation at that time; because instead of five enemies, one only had taken the field; 2d. By their relative strength in means of warfare; for instead of having four armies to contend against, the King had then only one to vanquish; 3d. By the distribution and positions of the enemy's forces; because they were scattered and did not cover this province; 4th. By its being the natural line of operations; 5th. Because under all these circumstances, it afforded the most advantageous and brilliant chances.

When Frederick in 1758 carried thither the theatre of the war, this choice was then, on the contrary, only sanctioned by the consideration of its being the natural line of operations; all the other chances had become favourable to his enemies. If he had done in 1756 what he attempted in 1758, Austria would undoubtedly have been invaded and brought to the verge of ruin; part of her provinces would have repaid Prussia for the expenses of the war; and the latter would have acquired the superiority over her rival. We shall see in the sequel, other striking instances of the importance of the choice of lines of operations, and of their influence on the fate of armies and the destinies of empires.

Having examined what Frederick might and should have done in these three campaigns, let us now take a view of what he did.

As the invasion of Moravia was not attempted in 1756, that of Saxony was without doubt the most advantageous operation that remained for him to undertake ; not under relations purely military and topographical, but in respect to political advantages. Indeed if Saxony had been an Austrian province, it would have been far better to have invaded Bohemia ; because the disposition and configuration of their frontiers is such, that Saxony is necessarily in the power of the Prussians the moment that they are masters of Bohemia. But the question was not merely to force an Austrian army to evacuate Saxony ; the conquest of this country presented itself under a totally different aspect. The object of Frederick was to get possession of a country that covered the weakest line of his frontiers, and secured his hereditary States from invasion ; whose population recruited his armies, and whose very troops passed over to his service ; whose revenues he himself received during the whole course of the war, and whose resources he used to form his magazines ; in fine, of a country that was to him as a Prussian colony. Under this view it cannot be denied, that a *momentary* invasion of Bohemia could not be put in competition with the conquest of Saxony.

The King having become possessed of this Electorate in 1756, nothing existed to prevent him from carrying his operations into Moravia the following year, as he did when it was no longer the season. He was obliged to fight the murderous battles of Prague and Kollin, and to retire without having effected any thing ; whilst by marching from Neisse on Olmutz, he would certainly have beaten Daun, before Prince Charles could come up to his succour. And if this Prince had pushed forward to cover Vienna and the Danube, Prague and all Bohemia would have been in the power of the Prussians, as is attested by the subsequent operations in 1758.

It cannot therefore be denied that the King in this second campaign chose a bad territorial line. The movements by which he embraced its display, and which we will call *lines of manœuvre*, were also in some measure dangerous : they were *double* and far apart, as the following figure exhibits :—

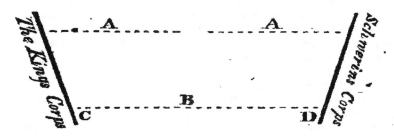

A great stream, the Elbe, flowed between the two corps d'armées, which were separated apart at least 15 marches. If the Austrians had occupied one of the two positions A, or B, and had carried the mass of their forces to a single bank of the Elbe (to C or D), and destroyed the bridges and guarded the whole course of this stream, they would certainly have destroyed one of these two corps. The other would have been forced to retreat, like the army of the Rhine in a similar situation, and on just such a line.

The only hypothesis that could render Frederick's dispositions defective, was that of the Austrians marching concentrically; but they had followed a system totally opposite. In their vain attempt to cover all points, whilst they really covered nothing, they had divided their army into four great divisions, whose extremes were much farther apart than the two Prussian lines. These four divisions had thus an exterior direction; and their reunion could only take place on a concentric point, chosen very far in rear of the frontier line. Frederick accordingly knew well how to take advantage of the errors of Marshal Brown. That in any other case this great man considered a double line as defective, is proved by his constantly censuring large detachments and double operations, and by his using all his science to force the Austrians and their allies to follow this system.

The territorial lines that the King assumed in the campaigns from 1759 to 1762, were always the same; for they were merely defensive. As the Russians then acted in concert with the Austrians, the King could not permit himself to be carried away by the allurements of a war of invasion; which, by leading him to a distance from his centre, would have enabled one of the three hostile armies to have struck him irreparable and deadly blows. As to his lines of manœuvre, they were always triple and *interior ;* to each of these lines he successively carried his mass, whilst the two others were maintained by well combined defensive dispositions. Figure 1, Plate XIV, shows the advantages of these dispositions.

The three interior lines A, designate the three Prussian armies; the four exterior lines B, indicate those of the enemy. The King carried with rapidity the mass of his forces upon that one of the three points A, where the danger was most pressing; and having there re-established his affairs, then flew to another point. After the battle of Hohenkirchen, he succeeded by a most masterly stroke in re-uniting his three corps in Saxony, and in compelling Daun to renounce all the advantages of his victory. Accordingly, after the campaign of 1758, the King always operated successively in Saxony, Silesia, and in the Mark of Brandenburg. He lost in 1757 the best moment of the war of invasion : of this he was conscious; and perhaps it was to this change of his system, that he was indebted for being able to maintain himself with so great glory against such disproportionate forces.

By referring to the different epochs of the seven years' war, we will be convinced that if the King was deficient in his first lines of operations and original plans, the choice of his accidental lines was always most able. Such were undoubtedly his marches against the combined army in Saxony, and his return into Silesia in 1757 ; the invasion of Bohemia after raising the siege of Olmutz; his movements after the battle of Hohenkirchen; and lastly, his march into Silesia in 1760.

There is doubtless merit in combining well a plan of campaign; but it very rarely happens that one of these plans can be literally executed in all its parts. An unforeseen event, such as the loss of a battle, may necessitate an entire change in the direction of the war. It is on these great occasions—in these critical moments, that genius appears in all its splendour. A common man is always at a loss—Frederick never was; he struck blows that are lessons of science to the soldiers who come after him.

The King, by his march into Bohemia, after raising the siege of Olmutz, has established this important maxim:—*That retreats should be directed parallel to the line of the frontier.* By its application, the Prussian army, instead of drawing the war into Silesia, transferred it into the enemy's provinces. If the Austrian armies had profited of this lesson in the wars of the revolution, it is probable that they would not have so hastily abandoned such vast extent of countries; and that the operations would not have been transferred in two campaigns from the banks of the Oise, to the heart of Germany and gates of Vienna.

After such proofs of the importance of accidental lines of operations, it would be superfluous to present further examples.

Remarks on the Austrian and French lines of operations in the Seven Years' War.

It is sufficient to cast our eyes over the General Map, to be convinced that Bohemia was the central point from which the Austrians could direct the mass of their forces with the greatest advantage.

The frontiers of the three lines form nearly a salient angle (See Fig. 2, PLATE XIV) towards the north, as Swisserland does towards the east, in relation to France. We will hereafter show how advantageous this configuration is for Bohemia, notwithstanding that Lloyd has asserted the contrary. This demonstration, confirmed by the most splendid operations of the war, will be the more interesting and convincing. It must, however, be here observed, that in consequence of this position the Prussians were compelled to take up two exterior lines of operations; whilst their enemies might make theirs *interior*, or even choose only a single line. Indeed, if the former had left Saxony or Silesia uncovered, the Austrian grand army might, by manœuvring with vigour and rapidity, have occupied that which was abandoned. This *central position* of the mass of their forces, was the more advantageous as a great stream intersected the salient angle and flowed in a diagonal direction towards Saxony and the centre of the Prussian states. The operations of the grand army against either of these provinces, were therefore favoured by the line of the Elbe; by means of which a single division might restrain one of the two hostile corps, at least long enough to enable the army to overwhelm the other. The King owed his safety to the erroneous operations of the enemy.

In 1756 the Austrian army was not ready to take the field; its only endeavours were to succour the Saxons. In 1757, Marshal Brown's dispositions for offence, or defence, were equally vicious. Instead of taking advantage of his central position to keep his forces united, he formed four great divisions on an extent of at least 80 leagues. Such a system answers neither the purposes of attack nor of defence. After the battle of Kollin, instead of operating in mass on the Elbe and against Saxony, whither the French army was marching, Prince Charles isolated his efforts from the chief object, and lost before the Silesian fortresses the most precious time.

Marshal Daun acted, in 1758, with more wisdom. After the raising of the siege of Olmutz and the march of the King against the Russians, he directed his forces against Dresden; but the French army was no longer in Saxony, and the Marshal wasted his time in unassailable positions. He detached 25,000 men against Neisse, as if this expedition were a matter of importance when he could overwhelm Prince Henry and carry the war immediately into Brandenburg. The taking of this double line, and the slowness of his operations, were the causes of Marshal Daun losing all the fruits of a good plan; they enabled Frederick to repair the losses of the battle of Hohenkirchen by a most skilful manœuvre.

In 1759, Daun manœuvres in Saxony; Dresden is taken; the Russians gain the battle of Kunnersdorf, and march towards this same province. This *concentric* combination of operations, the only one that took place in the course of this war, brought Frederick to the verge of ruin. But the timid slowness of the Marshal, spoils all; and proves by experience—

That two armies, under two different chiefs, manœuvring on the same frontier, are scarcely better than two exterior lines of operations.

The Russians return into Poland, not having been able to agree upon a plan of operations.

In 1760, the first dispositions of the coalition are still triple. The King, by marching too late into Silesia, draws all the enemy's forces down upon this province; but he preserves a *central position*, and beats Laudon at Lignitz. The Austrian and Russian armies, though only distant a few marches, cannot come to an understanding with each other, nor combine a single movement. The Russians march eccentrically, by elongating themselves from their allies, with a view to descend the Oder and make a diversion upon Berlin. Daun being thus isolated, is repulsed back into the mountains of Upper Silesia. After the Russians have set out for Poland, the operations become more active; the two armies march into Saxony, where the King gains the battle of Torgau over an isolated portion of the Austrian forces.

In 1761 the principal efforts are made in Silesia; notwithstanding that the possession of Dresden put it in the power of the Austrians to direct them with much greater success against Saxony, and even against Brandenburg. By his dispositions and by the camp of Buntzelwitz, Frederick checks Laudon and the Russians; whilst these, notwithstanding their immense superiority, do nothing but parading, encamping, and making demonstrations which result in nothing! Daun spends the whole campaign in Dresden, without effecting any thing against the point most favourable for the Austrian operations.

In 1762 Frederick gets rid of the Russians; he retakes Schweidnitz, and repulses Daun into the mountains. Prince Henry beats the double line of operations in Saxony; and Austria makes peace after seven campaigns, in which her Generals almost always acted the very inverse of what they should have done. They won many battles, without deriving the least advantage from them; whilst the single choice of the Saxon line for their principal operations, would have probably produced the ruin of Frederick.

The French Generals were neither more skilful, nor more fortunate. From the campaign of 1758 they chose two lines of operations—that of Hessia, and that of the Weser, on an extent of 100 leagues. The Duke Ferdinand of Brunswick, by manoeuvring upon the extreme left of this line, had only to contend against isolated corps, and was able to compel the enemy to retire beyond the Rhine.

When the Marquis of Contades, after the battle of Creveldt, assumed the command of the French army, he saw the advantages afforded him by the line of the Rhine, all the fortresses of which were in his possession; and beyond which his adversary had had the temerity to advance by his right, by placing himself between the North Sea, a superior army, and the French frontiers. The history of this campaign shows what advantages the Marquis might have derived from all these chances, if he had operated by his right with a little more vigour and rapidity. He occupied a position precisely similar to that of the Emperor Napoleon on the Saale, in 1806; but with greater advantage, because Wesel, which was on the line of the Rhine what Magdeburg was on the line of the Elbe, was in the hands of the French. Napoleon had not possession of Magdeburg.

The two French armies at the end of the campaign, lost all the fruits of their partial successes; for the Duke, by taking a central position, constantly prevented them from combining their operations. They accordingly wasted the time in movements without concert, in endless correspondence, and in forming memoirs and plans without results.

The Duke Ferdinand wishing at the opening of the campaign of 1759, to take advantage of his interior line, resolved to crush the corps d'armée in the country of Hessia, whilst the Grand Army was reposing quietly in winter quarters. The success of this plan would have caused the total ruin of Marshal Broglie's army. But the battle of Bergen averted this fate; because the Duke was not strong enough to repair his losses, and to renew the attack on the morrow of a check. At length the French perceived that it was more advantageous to operate united; and the two armies were concentrated in the country of Hessia. The conquest of this country, and of a great part of Westphalia, were the consequences of this single combination; whilst the loss of the too celebrated battle of Minden, whose results would have been incalculable if the armies had been isolated, would have been productive of no misfortunes but for the precipitate retreat of the Marquis of Contades, who very injudiciously re-crossed the Weser, when he might easily have maintained himself on the right bank. If this false movement had not taken place, the beaten army would have preserved its conquests; and might perhaps have made fresh acquisitions, by the single effect of its concentration.

In 1760 Marshal Broglie commanded all the forces united in the country of Hessia; and this single system was worth to the French army an honourable and successful campaign. Although Broglie did not know how to take advantage of his superiority, nor to undertake any enterprise of importance, yet his army made conquests and maintained them.

In 1761 the scene changed; and it might have been said, that the cabinet of Versailles was tired of forming good plans and combinations. The armies were re-enforced and increased to 199 battalions and 197 squadrons. France never before had such a formidable army on a single frontier. But it was *divided into two corps at a great distance*; one was commanded by Marshal Broglie, and the other by the Prince of Soubise. The war was carried on on paper; one General would form fine plans that did not however suit his colleague, and memoirs were substituted for battles; for before they had agreed upon an operation, the enemy had time to anticipate them and make tenfold changes of his dispositions. It then became necessary to have recourse to new plans and memoirs.

At length the French were forced to concentrate; but the command was left divided. The two armies attacked Duke Ferdinand; Broglie's commenced its operations a day too soon; and on the day fixed for the combined effort, the Prince of Soubise engaged too late. They were beaten! and how could it have been otherwise? Does not every page of history present similar results from like combinations.

By comparing the lines of manœuvre of the Austrians, Russians, and French, with those of Frederick, we will be convinced that they were combined on inverse principles; and this readily explains the difference of their results. And if, in his first campaigns, the King of Prussia had possessed the same talent of profiting of his victories as the Emperor Napoleon, these results would have been much greater and more decisive.

Review of some of the lines of Operations taken during the wars of the French Revolution.

The French lines of operations on the Rhine in 1796, were the counterpart of the Prussian lines in 1757, and of the lines of 1794; but their results, like those of the preceding year, were very different. The armies of the Rhine, and of the Meuse and Sambre, move from the two extremities of the base to take a concentric direction upon the Danube ; and they form, as in 1794, two exterior lines.

The Arch-Duke Charles, more skilful than the Generals of 1794, takes advantage of the interior direction of his lines, to give them a nearer concentric point. He seizes the moment when the Danube affords a strong defence to General Latour's corps, to steal a few marches and throw the whole mass of his forces upon the solitary right of Jourdan, which he crushes. The battle of Wurtzburg decides the fate of Germany, and compels Moreau, whose army is extended on an immense line, to concentrate in order to retreat.

At this time Napoleon begins his splendid career in Italy. His plan is to isolate the operations of the Piedmontese and Austrian armies ; he succeeds by the battle of Millesimo in forcing them to take up two exterior lines, which he afterwards beats in succession at Mondovi and Lodi. A formidable army is assembled in the Tyrol to save Mantua, and imprudently marches thither on two lines *separated by the lake of Garda.* The French Emperor, prompt as the lightnings of heaven, raises the siege and abandons his train and equipage, and marches with all his forces against the first column, which debouches by Brescia ; and which he beats, and throws back into the mountains. The second column arrives upon the same ground, and is beaten in its turn ; and is compelled to retreat into the Tyrol, to communicate with its right. Wurmser next commits a fresh error, by attempting to cover the two lines of Roveredo and Vicenza. Napoleon overwhelms the first, and repulses it back upon the Lavis ; he then manœuvres to the right, debouches by the gorges of the Brenta upon the left line, and forces the wrecks of this fine army to seek refuge in Mantua, which soon after capitulates.

In 1799 hostilities recommence. The French who were punished in 1796 for forming two exterior lines, now, notwithstanding, take up three lines upon the Rhine and Danube. An army on the left, observes the lower Rhine ; the army of the centre marches upon the Danube ; and Swisserland, that rampart formed by nature, and which ffanks all Italy and Suabia, is occupied by a third army, stronger than the two others. *These three corps could only unite in the Valley of the Inn, at a distance of 80 leagues from the base of their operations.* The forces of the Arch-Duke are equal ; he unites them against the centre, which he crushes at Stockbach ; and the army of Helvetia, is forced to evacuate the Grisons and eastern Swisserland. The army of the coalition commits in its turn the same error ; for instead of following up the conquest of this central rampart, which afterwards costs them so much, they take up a double line in Swisserland and on the lower Rhine. Their army in Swisserland, is overwhelmed at Zurich, whilst their second line is wasting its time near Manheim after miserable accessories.

In Italy, the double line of operations against Naples; is formed ; where

45,000 men are employed without an object, whilst upon the Adige, where the greatest blows should have been struck, the army is too weak and experiences the most dreadful disasters. On the return of the army of Naples to the north, it commits a fresh error by taking a direction divergent from the army of Moreau. Suwarrof profits of the central position in which he is left, marches against the first army, and beats it at a distance of a few leagues from the other.

In 1800, the whole aspect of affairs changes. Napoleon returns from Egypt; and the immortal campaign of 1800, exhibits the most masterly lines of operations, the plans of this illustrious man. The plan of the campaign on the Rhine, whose execution did honour to Moreau, was certainly the offspring of the same genius that planned the passage of the Alps. We recognize in it the same spirit and principles, so different from any thing preceding. One hundred and fifty thousand men defile along the two flanks of Swisserland, and debouche upon the Danube on one side, and upon the Po on the other. Immense countries are at once conquered by this skilful march upon the rear of the Austrian armies; and in this combination, the science is carried to its last degree of perfection. The two French armies form two interior lines, which communicate, and, in effect, support each other. The Austrian armies are, on the contrary, compelled to take an exterior direction, which disables them from communicating with or supporting each other. In the subsequent campaigns of this renowned soldier, we find the manœuvres against Ulm and Jena, founded upon the same principles as those of St. Bernard and Marengo. Finally; by a combination whose equal it would be vain to seek in the annals of war, the army of reserve cuts off a hostile army from its line of operations; whilst its own communications with the frontiers and with the army of the Rhine, which forms its secondary line, are perfectly secure. This operation is demonstrated by Plate XIV, fig. 3, which exhibits the situation of the armies: *A, A* are the armies of reserve, and of the Rhine; *B, B*, are the armies of Melas, and of Kray; and *C, C, C, C*, are the passes of the St. Bernard, the Simplon, the St. Gothard, and the Splugen. This figure shows that Melas was cut off from his base; whilst the Emperor, on the contrary, ran no risk, for he preserved all his communications with the frontiers, and with his secondary line.

This examination of the memorable events that we have now reviewed, is sufficient to convince any mind of the importance of the choice of lines of manœuvre in war. We see empires saved, or invaded, by the mere combinations of this choice; and battles lost and quickly repaired, when this choice was good; and when it is bad, we behold invasions made without success, and victories producing no results.

By comparing the combinations and results of the most celebrated campaigns, and by reviewing the series of important events that we have described, we will be convinced that all *successful* lines of operations are formed upon the principles *that we have laid down; because the object of single lines, and of interior lines, is to bring into action at the most important*

*point, by means of stratagic movements, a greater number of divisions,
and consequently a greater mass of force than the enemy.* And we will be
also convinced that all those that have miscarried, possess defects which
violate these principles; because double exterior lines, and all multiplied
lines, present weak and isolated parts to a mass that must overpower them.
In fine, we will find in them the proofs of the maxims that we have laid
down.

Configuration of Frontiers; Retreats and Accidental Lines of Operations, &c.

Having shown the advantages of single lines on a single frontier, and of
interior lines when they are double; it remains for us to exhibit the influence that the configuration of frontiers possesses over the direction of
grand operations, and to make a few reflections on eccentric lines. Lloyd
and Bulow have applied these to retreats; and the latter especially, has
inculcated that a retreat to be good, should be *eccentric*, like the following
figure:—

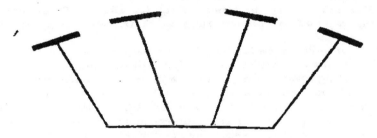

That is, the army that is beginning this operation to a given base, should
move upon several diverging lines; because it will thereby cover a greater
extent of frontiers, *and the position of its extremities will menace the enemy's
flanks.*

Lloyd, forgetting the principles upon which his best observations are
founded, praises the measures taken by Frederick for raising the siege
of Prague, and thence deduces the most false maxims. He says that
the King by dividing his army into several considerable corps, greatly
facilitated his retreat; and threw the enemy into such great uncertainty,
that they did not know upon which of them they should particularly fix
their attention. This author then deduces this general rule for retreats—
" Divide your army into as many strong corps as the nature of the coun-
" try will permit." According to his opinion, this disposition presents many advantages: viz.

" 1st. If the enemy form an equal number of divisions, they cannot act
" with vigour against any point; besides, the retreating army can prompt-
" ly re-unite its columns, and overwhelm separately those of the enemy:

" 2d. If they operate in mass, they can only do so against one division,
" whilst the others retire without danger. This division, supported by a
" strong rear-guard and avoiding a general engagement, will be able to
" move with more rapidity than a grand army; and will retire in *its* turn,
" without sustaining great losses."

All these ideas, newly dressed up by Bulow under the title of *eccentric
retreats*, are a violation of the principles upon which the maxims of Lloyd
are generally founded. It must be acknowledged that a retreating army
is already weak enough, without being divided. It is very probable that
in a state of division, it would be impossible to destroy all its divisions; but
one or two of them would be destroyed; and the result of the most unfortunate concentric retreat, could not be equally disastrous.

If, as is stated in the first part, the pursued body may unite and crush
the *divided* parts of the pursuing army; what is to prevent the pursuers
from doing the same? and why advise the retreating army to commit the
same fault! When a great river, or chain of mountains, crosses the *line of*
retreat, a divergent direction may be given to the columns, *in* order
to either speedily pass the bridges or defiles, or to seize and defend
them. Here the nature of the country forces a *seeming* deviation from
the rule. But the facility that these obstacles afford, of checking the
enemy's progress, and of concentrating in their rear, prove *its* univer-
sality.

What an air of importance is given by the help of these sounding words
" *flanks!*" to systems that are in utter violation of the principles of the science. A retreating army is always inferior in physical and moral strength;
for it retires only in consequence of disasters, or numerical inferiority.
And should this army be still further weakened by dividing, or scattering
it? We do not contend against retreats executed in several columns in
order to facilitate the retreat, when these columns can support each other;
we speak of those executed upon diverging lines of operations, in order to
remain divergent—of those represented by the figure.

Let us suppose an army of 40,000 men, in retreat before another of
60.000. If the former form itself into four isolated divisions of about
10,000 men each, the enemy by manœuvring upon two lines of operations
of 30,000 men each, will be able to turn, envelop, disperse, and destroy *in*
succession all these divisions. By what means could they escape this fate?
Only *by concentrating.* And as these means are the reverse of this writer's proposition, his system destroys itself.

We refer for the truth and *proof* of this reasoning, to the grandest lessons of history. When the first divisions of the Italian army were repulsed
by Wurmser, Napoleon concentrated them all at Roverbella; and with only
40,000 men, beat 60,000, because he had to fight with isolated columns.
If he had retreated eccentrically, what would have become of his army,
and of his conquests? Wurmser, after this first defeat, retreated eccentrically, by directing his two wings upon the two extremities of his line of
defence. The result was, that his right, though favoured by the mountains

of the Tyrol, was beaten at Trent; and Napoleon, by next directing his army upon the rear of the left wing, destroyed this latter at Bassano and at Mantua.

Would the Archduke Charles in 1796, when yielding to the first efforts of the two French armies, have saved Germany by an eccentric retreat? Was it not, on the contrary, to the concentric direction of his retreat that Germany was indebted for its safety? Finally; Moreau, who had marched on an immense extent of line by isolated divisions, perceived that this inexplicable system was only calculated to lead to destruction when it became necessary to fight, and especially to retreat. He therefore concentrated his scattered forces; and all the efforts of the enemy were incapable of checking such a mass, which was to be observed on all the points of a line of 80 leagues. Such examples are unanswerable.

Bulow has committed another capital error, by calling retreats *parallel*, when they take place directly from a given point to the line of the frontiers. These, on the contrary, are direct or *perpendicular* retreats. Lines of retreat are parallel when they pass over an extent of country situated along the frontiers; such was Frederick's retreat from before Olmutz (in Moravia), into Bohemia. In this case, the line of battle of the army, is perpendicular to that of the frontier; as is shown by the following figure:—

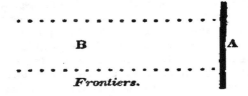

A, here represents the line of battle of the army; B, exhibits the lines that it is about to move on in retreat. But when the frontiers and the army are parallel, the line of retreat is necessarily perpendicular: the figure given by Bulow, is a proof of this.

From the preceding principles and exposition, follow these maxims:—

1st. Single lines of manœuvre on a single frontier, are the best: this is proved by the maxims and principles laid down, and by all the campaigns quoted

2d. Double lines against a single one, have never succeeded; the reason is obvious, and depends upon the general principles of all combinations.

3d. Lines upon two frontiers, and to which an interior direction has been given, have ever vanquished two exterior lines.

The success of all the grand stratagic movements of Frederick, and particularly that after the battle of Hohenkirchen; the disasters of the Austrians in the seven years' war; those of the French in the Hanoverian war; the defeats of the armies upon the Danube and upon the Rhine, in 1796 and 1799; and the immortal campaign of 1800—all equally prove the truth of this maxim. The invasion of Belgium in 1794, which succeeded in defiance of these principles, cannot be made an exception; because the Austrians did not take advantage of their central position, to overwhelm with their mass the hostile left, which was 15 days out of reach of support.

4th. The best direction for a line of manœuvre, is against an extremity, and thence against the rear of the hostile line of defence. The combinations of the campaign of 1800, have proved the truth of this in the most irresistible manner.

We find also another practical proof of this maxim, in the march of the grand army upon Donauwerth, where it gained the extreme right of Mack, and entirely cut off his communications with his secondary line (the Russian army) and base (Vienna). The admirable movement executed in 1806, by the sources of the Mayn and Saale against the extreme left of the Prussian army, was founded on the same principles and combinations, and produced the same result. And the memorable victories of Abensberg and Eckmuhl, present us with the most brilliant and incontestable proofs of the superiority of central masses, or interior lines, skilfully brought into action against divided corps d'armée.

The advantage of this direction does not solely result from the reason—that by attacking one extremity, we have only to contend against a portion of the hostile force; it results also from a more important one—the enemy's line of defence is thereby threatened with being reversed, and is no longer tenable. The army of the Rhine, after making demonstrations against Kray's left wing, marched rapidly along Swisserland, and placed itself upon the extreme right of his line of defence; and thus conquered, without a battle, the whole country between the Rhine and the Danube. The results of the combination which threw the army of reserve into the rear of Melas, by cutting his line, were still more splendid.

5th. The configuration of the frontiers may be of great importance in the direction of these lines. Central positions that form a salient angle towards the enemy, like Bohemia and Swisserland, (Fig. 3, PLATE XIV), are the best; because they are from their nature interior, and lead against the rear of the enemy, or against one extremity of his line of defence. The flanks of this salient angle are consequently so important, that all the resources of art and nature should be combined to render them unassailable.

6th. When these central positions do not exist. we may supply their place by the relative direction of the lines of manœuvre: as the following figure demonstrates:

B by manœuvring against the right flank of *A*, and *D* by manœuvring against the left flank of *C*, will form the two interior lines *E, E*, against one extreme of each of the two exterior lines *A & C;* which they may overpower in succession, by alternately carrying against them the mass of their forces. This combination presents the results of the lines of operations of 1800.

7th. The configuration of the theatre of war, may be of the same importance as that of the frontiers: we will now demonstrate this.

Every section of the globe forms a circle, and may therefore be considered as a square; consequently a theatre of war will always have four sides. To better illustrate this idea, we will refer to the theatre of war of the French armies in Westphalia, from 1757 to 1762, and of the Emperor Napoleon in 1806.

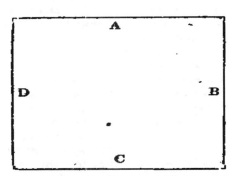

In this first seat of war, the side *A* was the North Sea; the side *B* was the line of the Weser, which was the base of the operations of the army under Duke Ferdinand; the line of the Mayn formed the side *C*, which was the base of the French army; and the side *D*, was the line of the Rhine, which was also guarded by the armies of Louis XV.

The French armies had therefore possession of two sides; and, in operating offensively, these armies had in their favour the North Sea, which formed the third side. They had therefore only to manœuvre in such a manner as to gain the side B, in order to be master of all the four sides; that is, to be in possession of the enemy's base and all his lines of communication. The following figure demonstrates this:

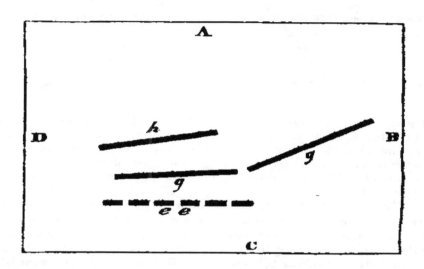

The French army by moving from the base *ee* to gain the position *gg*, would have cut off the allied army *h* from the side B, which formed its only communication and its only base. The latter would therefore have been thrown back upon the angle DA, formed towards Embden by the line of the Rhine and of the Ems, and by the North Sea; whilst the French army *gg*, would always be able to communicate with the Mayn.

The Emperor Napoleon's manœuvre against the Saale in 1806, was combined in exactly this manner. He occupied at Jena and Naumburg the line *gg*; and then marched by Halle and Dessau, to repulse the Prussian army *h* back upon the side A, formed by the sea. The fate that befell the wrecks of this army at Erfurt, Magdeburg, Lubeck, and Prenzlow, is well known. The great art is therefore, to so combine our marches as to get possession of the enemy's communications, without losing our own. We easily perceive that the line *gg* by the successive prolongation of its position, and by its crotchet left upon the enemy's extremity, always preserves its communications with its base C. This is an exact illustration of the manœuvres of Marengo and of Jena.

When the theatre of operations is not bounded by the sea, it will always border upon a great and neutral power, which will guard its frontiers and form one of the sides of the square. This is certainly not so good a barrier as the sea; but in general theory it must ever be considered as an obstacle upon which it would be dangerous for a beaten army to retire; and back upon which, on the other hand, a victorious army should endeavour to throw its adversary. The territory of a power that has an army of 200,000 men, is not to be violated with impunity; and if a beaten army take this course, it is not the less cut off from the base of all its operations, and from its communications. If it be a small power that is adjacent to the seat of war, it will be involved in it; and the side of the square will be thrown back to the frontiers of a great power, or to the sea.

To satisfy ourselves of the truth of these principles, it will suffice to cast our eyes over the theatre of war of the Polish campaign in 1806 and 1807. The Baltic Sea, and the frontiers of Austrian Gallicia, formed the two sides *A* & *C* of the preceding square. It was of great importance to each army, to prevent itself from being thrown back upon either of these obstacles; and the Russian army ran the greatest risks at Pultusk, and at Eylau, by exposing itself to this fate.

The configuration of frontiers, will doubtless sometimes modify that of the sides of the square; it may sometimes be a regular oblong, or a trapezium, as in the following figure:

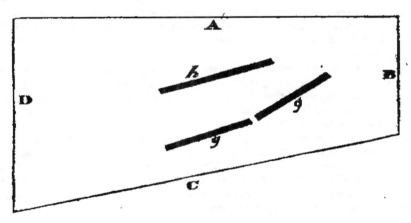

In this latter case, the army *gg* that is master of the sides *D* & *C*, would have still greater advantages; because its adversary's base narrowing towards *B*, he has much less means of regaining his communications. The front of this base being much less in extent, affords also much less resources for manœuvring, and would give the army *gg* the means of operating with more success; because the direction of its line *C*, naturally leads against the enemy's communications; and because the space that it would have to occupy to cut him off, is less extended, and could consequently be more easily guarded by concentrated forces.

The theatre of the Prussian and Polish war, that we were speaking of above, was exactly like this figure. The frontiers of Gallicia, extending as far as the Narew, formed with the line of the Vistula the shortened side *B*. And the manner in which the Emperor Napoleon embraced this line at Pultusk, and at Eylau, was precisely the same as that here laid down ; and would have been decisive, if skill could have commanded the elements.

These examples, we believe, are sufficient to demonstrate, that the manner of embracing a theatre of war may be reduced to a very few grand combinations, founded upon the same principle.

These combinations are :

1st. Direct your masses against the decisive points of the line of operations; that is, against the centre, if the enemy have committed the error of dividing his forces ; or against one of his two extremities, if he be in contiguous line.

2d. In this latter case, choose that extremity which will throw the enemy back upon an insurmountable obstacle, or which will lead your army upon the enemy's communications, without losing your own.

This manœuvre was applied by Napoleon at Marengo, at Ulm, and at Jena, as is shown by the line *gg* in the square. A corps must be left upon the flank or rear of the army, to maintain its communications and menace the hostile flank.

Consequently, movements between the enemy's forces and the sea, or a great river, are very dangerous. Such was Pichegru's movement in 1794, to turn the right of the Austrian general line of operations, by passing between this right and the North Sea; and such was Beningsen's movement on the Lower Vistula, in 1807, which came near ruining the Russian army. The fate of the Prussian army, in 1806, when thrown back upon the Baltic, after being cut off from its communications, is another proof of this truth. If the Prince of Cobourg had acted against Pichegru like a General, not one of the French army that executed this too daring movement, could have escaped; for Jourdan was not ready to co-operate simultaneously until one month after.

Retreats ; retreat of Frederick from Olmutz ; Washington's retreat from Trenton ; Frederick's accidental line of operations after the battle of Hohenkirchen.

An army compelled to retreat, is not always forced to regain its own frontiers; it may by a march parallel to its line of defence, change the direction of the operations, without carrying the war into its own country.

The accidental line of operations taken by Frederick in July 1758, by Leutomischel and Bohemia, after being obliged to raise the siege of Olmutz, is an admirable illustration of this principle. Instead of retiring upon the nearest frontier of his own states; Frederick saw that he was only compelled to change the theatre of the war; and he still maintained the offensive, by selecting the enemy's country (Bohemia) for this purpose. An ordinary man thus situated, would never have dreamed of such a manœuvre.

The accidental line of operations taken by General Washington in January, 1777, from Trenton by Princeton against New Brunswick, where the enemy's depots were, may be quoted with deserved admiration.

After capturing the Hessians at Trenton, Washington found it impossible to re-cross to the right of the Delaware, on account of the breaking up of the ice. Meantime Lord Cornwallis had collected his cantonments, and was advancing with a superior force upon Trenton. This was the crisis—here the talents of Washington bade equal defiance to the elements and enemies of his country. Retreat being cut off, he determined to reverse by Allen-Town the hostile line of operations, to strike down their rear guard (3 regiments) that was at Princeton, and then to move rapidly on Brunswick and capture or destroy their magazines, the loss of which would compel them to evacuate Jersey.

In pursuance of this plan, he decamped in the night, and next morning fought the battle of Princeton; and was moving upon Brunswick, when the retreat of Cornwallis to gain that place before him by forced marches, together with the arrival of re-enforcements at Brunswick, induced him to wisely renounce the latter part of his plans, and to retreat upon Morristown. Cornwallis was glad to gain Brunswick.

These events help to show the truth of the maxim—

That the best defensive positions, will not prevent the invasion of a country. It is by manœuvres—not by positions, that a country must be defended. This is another proof, that the use of masses against decisive points, alone constitutes good combinations ; and this use of masses should be independent of any localities.

The Accidental line of Operations after the Battle of Hohenkirchen.

The accidental line of operations taken by Frederick after his defeat at Hohenkirchen, near Weissenberg in Lusatia, 14 Oct. 1758, is among the most admirable of the kind in history. Instead of sinking under the prospect of ruin, his genius rose in proportion to the dangers that surrounded him ; and he proved that a great man is never conquered while his army remains embodied.

The King found himself at this critical moment beaten with the loss of 8000 men in the centre of his operations, and his left (Silesia) invaded and Neisse besieged ; whilst the combined army under the Duke of Deux Ponts threatened his right line, under Prince Henry, and occupied a large portion of Saxony and menaced Dresden. Unless Neisse could be succoured, it must fall; and with it, all upper Silesia. By attempting to succour it, the King would leave Marshal Daun at liberty to either follow him, or to unite with the combined army of the Circles and strike a decisive blow in Saxony; which would thus enable him, by the possession of Dresden, to carry the war in the next campaign into Brandenburg and the heart of the Prussian states. By delaying to operate, Daun would keep his impregnable and victorious position in advance of Hohenkirchen, and upper Silesia must fall. But the penetration of Frederick discovered the means of delivering his kingdom from such a complication of dangers. He founded the practicability of his schemes upon a knowledge of the character and talents of Daun, and the general rapidity of his own movements; and upon the reasonable expectation that Dresden would be able to hold out at least 3 weeks, and that the small army charged with the defence of Saxony, could in the last extremity throw itself into the place; for he correctly judged that Daun was unprovided with a siege train and equipage. The time thus gained, would be sufficient to raise the blockade of Neisse, and to return. Besides, the movements of the Russians, and Swedes, gave room to judge that they were about evacuating the Prussian states to go into winter quarters. The great distance of their frontiers, and the want of provisions, would at least compel the Russians to retire. And indeed the Russian General Fermor had quitted the camp of Stargard on the 16th of October, to march on Reetz. The Swedes had quitted their camp of Ruppin, and successively retired as far as Boitzenburg. The Russian General Palmbach was besieging Colberg; but the turn that the siege had taken, gave ground to suppose it would be soon raised.

Frederick therefore determined to unfurnish all this part of his frontiers, and to direct the corps of Generals Dohna and Wedel upon Saxony. He accordingly gave orders to these Generals, to march into Saxony without delay, and to only leave behind them a corps of observation of eight battalions under General Manteufel. The greatest obstacle to the King's plan, was the difficulty of becoming master of the road to Silesia, and of reaching Gorlitz before the enemy. The direct road to this town, leads through Weissenberg and Reichenbach, and was completely shut by the position of the Austrian army. Frederick could therefore only reach that place by a great detour on the Austrian right; and his first march must be forced and concealed, in order that the Prussian army should have less ground to traverse on the second day than the enemy, who could reach Gorlitz by one forced march. And as Marshal Daun had a division on the King's left, and numerous light troops almost in his rear, it was easy for him, by reason of the great proximity of the two armies, to be instantly informed of the least movement and to anticipate the Prussians.

It was therefore very important to deceive Marshal Daun in respect to the real plan of operations, and to lead him to suppose it to be directly the opposite. This the King did in a most masterly manner.

To execute the premeditated movement, it was necessary to disencumber the army of all its equipage. The camp was filled with sick; and Bautzen was crowded with the wounded of the battle of Hohenkirchen. Neither could be abandoned. A great number of country wagons was in consequence collected, which were loaded with all the wounded who could bear transportation. This convoy left Bautzen on the night of the 22d October, escorted by 2 battalions and 5 squadrons, and took the road to Dresden by Camenz, Konigsbruck and Radeberg. When the commandant of Bulow's Prussian regiment had arrived at Camenz, he learned that the Austrian General Nauendorf had advanced with four regiments of infantry as far as Konigsbruck, whither Daun had detached him to intercept the road to Dresden. The King having received intelligence of this, directed the convoy to resume its march that very night, and to march by Hoyerswerda direct upon Glogau. This was fortunately effected.

The provision and ammunition trains still remained, and their evacuation was of the greatest importance in the circumstances in which the army was placed; for it could not for a long time reach the magazines in Silesia, whilst those of Dresden could furnish nothing.

On the 23d at ten o'clock at night, General Bornstedt marched with these trains and the residue of the wounded, under escort of 4 battalions and 5 squadrons of hussars. This convoy coasted the left bank of the Spree as far as Kumereau, where it crossed to the right bank, and formed in order of battle.

The enemy were apprized at the moment of the march of these two columns, and might thence conclude that the army would not long delay to put itself in motion; but its direction was still uncertain. The second column appearing also to take the road to Glogau by Sagan, Daun thought that by occupying that to Gorlitz with a superior army, he had forced Frederick to abandon Saxony and the greater part of Silesia, and to retire upon this fortress of the second line. We are generally disposed to believe what we desire; and the Marshal's opinion seemed to be sanctioned by appearances. But what must have been his astonishment when on the 25th, at meridian, he discovered the whole Prussian army in his rear in possession of the direct road to Gorlitz, and threatening his great magazines at Zittau!

On the 24th at 6 o'clock in the evening, General Braun had marched with the baggage and 6 battalions and 5 squadrons of hussars by Salza and Leichnam to Neudorf, where he passed the little Spree and ranged his convoy in order of battle, whilst awaiting the army. The battalions that had occupied the villages in advance of the front and on the flanks, retired in the greatest silence into camp at 10 o'clock; the advanced guards of cavalry were left at their posts until the morrow. At 10 at night, the tents were struck, and the army began its march by *lines by the left*. Werner's hussars, Salomon's free battalion, and the 8 battalions that Prince Henry had brought from Saxony, formed the van guard which marched by Dresa, passed the Spree at Geilitz, changed direction to the right, and marched by Weigersdorf, Gros Raditz, and Diesa, to the camp of Ullersdorf. The first column, composed of all the infantry, followed the same road; the second, composed of the cavalry, passed the little Spree at Neudorf, where it was joined by the convoy under General Braun; the second column then marched by Barotsch, Tauban, Leipsche and Kolm, to the camp of Ullersdorf. General Bornstedt left Kumerau the same night with the provision park, and marched by Leiska, Tauen, Foertschen, Sproitz, and Kuna, to Jenkendorf, where he arrived at meridian on the 25th, and formed a barricade with the wagons.

The rear guard, consisting of 11 battalions and 20 squadrons, and of the cavalry guards, was commanded by Prince Henry. As soon as the army had quitted the camp, this Prince occupied until day break the hills called Spitzbergen; and then finding that the enemy remained quiet, he followed the route of the columns. The King encamped with his right at Diesa, and his left at Baarsdorf; the head quarters were at Ullersdorf. (*See the 19th Plate in Jomini's work.*) When we consider the Austrian position and the proximity of the two armies, it is astonishing how Frederick was able to gain a march upon them. The number and vigilance of their light troops, were ill employed on this occasion; for Daun only learned the departure of the Prussians when the heads of their columns had already gained Gros Raditz. Nevertheless he might still have anticipated the King at Gorlitz, if he had instantly put his army in march by the direct road; but he contented himself with detaching General Caramelli in pursuit of the rear guard. It was only in the afternoon of the 25th, that he detached to Reichenbach General Lascy with the grenadiers, the Duke of Ahremberg with the reserve, and General Esterhazy with two regiments of hussars, to observe the march of Frederick. When these Generals discovered the King's army at the camp of Ullersdorf, they could no longer doubt his plans; they determined therefore to decamp that night, and to occupy Gorlitz and the heights of Landskrone.

If the enemy had gained Gorlitz, Frederick would have run the risk of losing all the fruits of his fine march; he therefore did not delay a moment, and resumed his march at two o'clock in the morning.

By this bold and skilful march, Frederick rendered nugatory in a moment all the advantages that Daun had expected from the battle of Hohenkirchen, and from the position that he had taken after the battle. The Austrian General remained in his camp until the morning of the 26th, when he took up another near Gorlitz, with his right on the Burgberg near Jauernick, his centre on the Landskrone mountain, and his left at Markersdorf. Laudon's corps, which had followed the rear guard and the column of baggage, encamped on the 27th on the heights of Konigshain, upon the Prussian right.

Frederick next day began his march on Naisse, which he succoured. Daun marched into Saxony, after detaching a considerable corps to Neisse. The King soon returned, and expelled him from Saxony.

SECTION II.

Orders of March ; Detachments ; Convoys.

MARCHES are of two kinds—*route* marches—and marches *within* striking distance of the enemy. The *first* being executed out of reach of the enemy, should be on as many columns as the facility of subsistence, rapidity of motion, and the nature of the roads and country, require; for large columns cannot move with as much rapidity as small ones. Besides, the number and various directions of the columns, will leave the enemy in doubt as to their real direction, and will enable them to rapidly and alternately menace his flanks.

But when an army is *within striking distance* of the enemy, the desideratum of great celerity, must yield to the more important consideration of keeping in mass. For in this case, celerity unless accompanied by concentration, would frustrate its own ends, and draw down destruction on an army; because the object of celerity, is rapid concentration of force. Therefore when within three or four days' march of an enemy, the order of march by lines (broken into platoons at whole distances) by the flank, should be observed. This was the order of march of Frederick at Prague, Kollin, Rosbach, Leuthen, Zorndorff, and Kunnersdorf; and to this order he owed the ease with which he manœuvred upon the enemy's flanks, keeping his army in column until the very moment of attack, and then forming line with the swiftness of lightning.

His system of keeping his army always united, of opposing a mass to isolated parts, or a whole line to the single extremity of a line—this system, which is the admiration of warriors, could only have been executed by a similar order—by a mode of formation uniting promptitude, ensemble, and simplicity. We find only two instances in the seven years' war, in which Frederick attempted attacks by several columns at great distances from each other, and which were to attack simultaneously. And in both these instances (at Torgau, and at Namiest against Laudon, during the siege of Olmutz.) he miscarried. The late wars have afforded innumerable examples of the inconveniences of such a system.

Frederick's order of march was, as we have already described (pp. 397, 402, and 406), by the flanks of lines broken into platoons at whole distances, and the two or three lines (or columns) preserving a distance of 2 or 300 paces apart. The march was opened by a strong van guard of cavalry, supported by 7 or 8 battalions of grenadiers; then followed the two or three lines (or columns); the flanks were covered by a few battalions of light troops; and the rear was closed by the rear guard. The number of his columns consequently depended upon that of lines; and these never exceeded two, and a reserve. This order was suited to his oblique and perpendicular orders of battle against a hostile flank; for Frederick never used the parallel order. The columns were converted into lines by a simple conversion of platoons to the right, or left.

The following is a copy of the King's order of march from Meissen on the Elbe, to Silesia; issued as the orders of the day on the 2d October, 1760.

" The army will, as usual, march in three columns by lines. The first " column will consist of the first line; the second, of the second line; and " the third, of the reserve. The wagons, and hospital wagons, of regi- " ments, will follow their corps. The batteries of heavy caliber will " follow the infantry brigades to which they are assigned. On passing " woods, the regiments of cavalry will march between two infantry " corps.

" Each column will have a van guard of 1 light battalion and 10 squa- " drons of hussars or dragoons. They will be preceded by 3 wagons " carrying plank bridges. The rear guard is charged with taking up these " bridges after the army has defiled over them.

" The parks will be divided among the columns, to avoid the embar- " rassment resulting from a great many wagons being together in a body.

" If any thing should happen to the 2d and 3d columns, the King will be " instantly apprised of it; he will be found at the head of the first column. " Should any thing occur to the rear guards, the same will be instantly " communicated to Lieutenant General Zeithen, who will be with the " rear guard of the first column.

" The officers will take care that the soldiers march with an equal step, " and that they do not stray to the right or left, and thus uselessly fatigue " themselves and lose their distances.

" When orders are given to form the line, the wagons will file out of " the columns to the left, and will march to be parked, &c."

As the success of most attacks depends upon *surprising* the extremity of a line, or an isolated centre, all marches to attacks should be masked by either hollow ways, woods, mountains, or hills, or by demonstrations and false attacks. *Night* marches are much recommended, and are greatly prac- tised. We have seen by the description of the battle of Leuthen, that one great cause of Frederick's success, was the concealment of his march by a ridge of heights, and a demonstration made against the Austrian right. His march at Rosbach was concealed in the same manner.

The position of the baggage on marches near the enemy, varies accord- ing to the nature of the march. If the march be to the front, the equi- pages will be in the rear of the columns; if the march be by a flank and the enemy be on the outer flank, the baggage will be on the inner flank that is remotest from the enemy; if the march be in retreat, the baggage will be in advance of the army. In either case, it will be guarded by a strong detachment of infantry and cavalry.

Battalions are to a column, what a platoon is to a battalion. A column of 8, 10 or 50 battalions, displaying upon its head, should do it in the same manner as a battalion displays upon its first platoon. If the display be upon the 2d battalion, or upon the centre or rear, it is still the same; and in demonstrating this, Guibert pretends to teach us the Prussian tactics, and to extend and improve them.

His pages are doubtless instructive; and his manœuvres are excellent in a camp of instruction, to accustom officers to all the combinations of the manœuvres of troops, and to judge of distances. But that they are applicable to war, and preferable to the system of the great Frederick, is a question that all intelligent officers can decide.

Frederick in his instructions to his Generals, drawn up before the seven years' war, recommends this method of marching in lines, as the best; but he does not develope its mechanism or advantages. It would seem that he was afraid of giving them publicity, for he perfectly explains the marches by wings.

It is strange that Guibert has only made one application of this system; and that is to the insignificant operation of a parallel prolongation of direction (*See 4th and 6th Manœuvres, Plates VII and VIII of the Grand Tactics*); as if he were blinded by his system of Déployment, and did not perceive the incalculable advantages that the former affords for all marches and orders of battle. We will give the outline of these advantages.

1st. By means of this order of march, the army can effect all its movements and remain united. Columns on the right, or left, are therefore not exposed to be overwhelmed successively; because the army forms only two, at the small distance of a first line from the second.

2d. The enemy cannot penetrate between these columns, nor cut off one or two of them.

3d. By *taking the direction intended to be given to the line of battle*, the army on arriving upon the ground may be formed in a few minutes, or in the same space of time that the platoons require for wheeling up into line on the right or left.* It will be only necessary to protect the march of the columns by a van guard, which will fulfil the two-fold object of covering them, and deceiving the enemy.

4th. As the army has no other distances to observe than that of 200 or 300 paces between the two columns or lines, and the distances between the platoons, the precision and accuracy of this manœuvre is assured.

5th. The army having by a concealed march reached the height and direction of the enemy's flank, will rapidly form line, and will not give them time to form a crotchet, nor to effect an entire change of front; they will therefore be successively overwhelmed on one extremity of their line by a mass of forces that they cannot resist. This is proved in a striking manner by the battle of Leuthen.

---

* It is not pretended that all the platoons will wheel into line at the same minute along the whole line; but the signal to form line being given, there will be but a very short interval between the execution of the different brigades; and the conversion will certainly not require ten minutes to be completely executed.

6th. lastly; If the army do not wish to form two columns as long as its general line of battle, it may, according to the ground, form four columns, by doubling its lines or by marching by wings, without in the least increasing the difficulties of the formation.   These four columns having been formed by doubling the lines at *D* (Plate XIV. fig. 4.), on arriving near the height *E* where they should form, will again form two single columns ; the 2d column of each line will halt and protect the movement of the first whilst it marches by to get beyond the head of the second, which will then fall in after the last platoon of the first column. In this manner the two columns of each line will become one ; and will be able to form a continuous line by the simple conversion already mentioned. In this case if the march be by the right, the left column halts and covers the advance or unmasking of the right column ; if the march be by the *left*, the right column will halt until the left has advanced before it.

If the columns be formed by wings, they will be again formed into two lines or columns by a simple change of direction. executed at the same instant by the heads and tails of the columns.   The 2d line will in this case form the tails ; and by simultaneously wheeling into the same direction that the heads wheel, each half column will unite itself to the last platoon of the right or left column (according as the change is to the right or left,), and thus the two lines will form but two columns, with the distance of lines between them.   This order and mechanism of march, would be the same for a third or fourth line ; the only difference would be, that the columns will be divided into 3 or 4 parts instead of two, and the change of direction will take place at once at as many points as lines or parts of columns.   This was the order of march at Leuthen (*see page* 406).   Fig. 5, Plate XIV, illustrates this manœuvre: *A* is the village of Borna, on passing which the heads of columns changed direction to the right ; *C* is where the tails of the columns, or troops of the second line, changed direction. The van guard had precedingly changed direction.

Let us now examine the orders of march of Guibert, the difficulty of applying them, and their inconveniences ; and we shall be convinced that it was by a system completely the reverse, that Frederick moved his great masses with so much ease and precision.

Guibert has devoted many chapters and eleven plates to describe various orders of front marches, which in their essence are precisely the same ; because they only differ in the battalions of deployment, or in the directions of the right and left.   As it is almost indifferent which of these chapters we choose, we will take that which is the subject of his IXth Plate, or simple oblique order. ' The army that is here put in motion, is obliged to first open five marches, and to form five columns, each formed upon the right or left. These columns must in march strictly preserve their distances apart of half a league, and even a league.   When arrived upon the ground of attack, they must display by platoons on the leading platoon, with sufficient exactness for the leading platoon of a left column to find itself supported by the last platoon of the column on its right. This is vice versa, if the direction be by the left.

Officers accustomed to direct the movements of troops, will judge,

1st. Whether, in marching upon the enemy, five marches can be opened to within striking distance of him and across the various obstacles of ground; and this too without his discovering and repulsing an attack, that must fail the moment that it is discovered?

2d. Let us even suppose this to be possible; would it be practicable to conduct five columns out of sight of each other, and with a strict preservation of distances, so that they will arrive at the same minute along the whole front of attack; particularly when one column has less than half the distance to traverse that another has?

3d. Let us even accord the possibility of these two hypotheses, notwithstanding their improbability. Then how can the columns form a solid contiguous line, if either of them be the least delayed? and what length of time will they require to display upon their heads?

4th. Is it possible for them to display upon their centre, in order to accelerate the manœuvre, when to do this, half of each column must turn their backs to the enemy who are within reach? What would become of an army attacked in such a situation?

5th. What success could be expected from an attack in which at least one hour is required to form the line, when the success depends upon surprising the enemy's flank? Would he not have time to change front, to oppose an equal extent of line, and even to outflank the attacking army, by manœuvring in the direction of the attack?

6th. As the enemy can discover the march as far as the eye can reach, would he not have it in his power to re-enforce promptly part of his line, and to penetrate between the two nearest columns, which on being checked in their march and unable to display, would be taken in flank, front, and reverse, and would be in all probability destroyed?

7th. We have, contrary to all probability, supposed the possibility of opening the marches; but if it be acknowledged that this operation is impracticable before an enemy, we may then judge whether Guibert's system can be executed by columns marching at hazard in vague directions, compelled to subordinate their movements to the accidents of ground, frequently separated from each other by double the distance of deployment, some arriving much sooner than the others, and presenting isolated attacks destitute of strength and vigour. What would become of an army in this situation, if opposed by a Napoleon or a Frederick? The battle of Minden shows that this army would be destroyed.

Both the systems of Frederick, and of Guibert, and the principles that we have here laid down, are founded upon an order of battle *in displayed line.* But this is not the only order that can be employed with advantage. The order of a line of battalions formed in close column by divisions, at platoon or section distances, may be used with great advantage. As the battalion forms three or four divisions, it would in fact be a formation in three or four lines; but the regiments instead of being displayed, should be of three

divisions front. —————— —————— ——————

In this order they will be stronger, more concentrated, and more easily moved; and besides, this formation is not incompatible with marching by lines.

The difficulty of moving large masses during the late wars, was caused as much by the mode in which the armies were formed and constituted, as by ignorance of the true and solid principles of the science. This gave rise to the preconcerted orders of attack, founded on the last known position of the enemy, and executed by separate divisions moving towards one object; but whose movements were necessarily left to the sole direction of their respective chiefs after they had received the general plan.

We will conclude these remarks by acknowledging the utility of front marches and deployments, in two circumstances only:

1st. When an army is to take up a position positively parallel; this happens almost always out of reach of the enemy:

2d. When an army attacked on the heads of its columns, is compelled to display upon the attacked platoons, or at least upon those that follow. But in this case, the whole army is not compelled to display; it will be sufficient for the leading brigade or van guard to display. The army can and should endeavour to manœuvre upon a flank of the enemy, by a change of direction, instead of forming in parallel order by a deployment which most certainly cannot be executed.

And in the case of a front march, its execution should be totally different from the mode proposed by Guibert, the evils and dangers attendant on which we have described. A march to the front, should be executed in the manner of General Lehwald's march at the battle of Jaegerndorff; that is, on the same principles that the battalion column of attack is formed—by columns on the centre. This formation offers advantages directly opposite to the defects of Guibert's system. The two columns are within a short distance of each other, and can reciprocally sustain each other. On arriving upon the ground of formation, the right wing which has marched by the left, will display to the right; and the left wing which has marched by the right, will display to the left. All the platoons will arrive successively in line after each preceding platoon has formed; they are not compelled to observe distances, and their successive formation is protected.

The distance between the columns being that of the direction of the deployment, the ensemble and precision of this manœuvre leaves nothing more to be desired.

At the combat of Kampen (12th June, 1758), the Prussian and English armies, commanded by Duke Ferdinand of Brunswick, marched in columns of battalions on the whole extent of the line. Jomini thinks that this was the first time that an army marched in this order on the whole extent of its line; and he recommends this mode, because the formation is rapid, if the battalions be in columns of attack.

Detachments.

When an important object is to be obtained by a detachment, such as the destruction or capture of a convoy, post, bridge, or corps; the strength of the detachment should, if possible, be proportionate to the importance of the object to be attained, and not to the force to be vanquished. By following this rule, Marshal Daun captured the Prussian convoy and raised the siege of Olmutz; and by not observing it, the Marquis of Contades (in 1758) lost the opportunity of hemming in Duke Ferdinand between the Rhine and Meuse, by destroying his bridge over the Rhine at Rees. The detachment under Chevert, sent by the Marquis, was thrice as strong as General Imhoff's corps. Imhoff did not wait to be attacked, but advanced with his 3000 men, and fell upon the French and beat them. Chevert should have kept 7000 men to check Imhoff, and have despatched 3000 round his flanks to destroy the bridge, which was the *great object;* and which, if destroyed, would have forced Duke Ferdinand to a capitulation similar to that of Kloster-seven.

When detachments are made to guard baggage, convoys, &c. it is very advantageous to form the detachments of so many men from each battalion, particularly in the case of an inferior army; for a battalion of 600 men, will perform the same services as a battalion of 650 men. By detaching the surplus, we do not weaken ourselves; for the number of the organized corps that constitutes the real strength of the army, is not diminished.

Convoys.

It is better to supply the wants of a siege, or army, by small and constantly successive convoys, than by periodical and large convoys. Only one or two of the former can be captured or destroyed, and their loss will not be felt. But a large periodical convoy offers a temptation to the enterprise of the enemy, and is so great an object and so difficult to escort, that the enemy will venture much to destroy it; for its destruction will at once frustrate all the hopes and plans of the siege, or army. If the Prussian army when besieging Olmutz, had observed this rule, the capture of a convoy would not have forced them to raise the siege and to retreat.

SECTION III.

Sieges ; the Conduct of the Army of Observation ; Subsistence and Magazines ; the Passage of Rivers.

LLOYD lays down the following rules to determine when a siege should be undertaken :—

1st. When the fortress is situated upon passages leading into the enemy's country, so that it becomes impossible to advance without getting possession of i'.

2d. When it intercepts the communications, and the country does not afford the necessary subsistence.

3d. When the possession of it is requisite to cover magazines that we have formed in the country itself, in order to facilitate operations.

4th. When the enemy have in this fortress considerable depots that they cannot do without.

5th. When the capture of the fortress is followed by the conquest of a considerable extent of country, which will enable us to put the army into winter quarters in the enemy's territory.

6th. When its reduction will terminate the war.

The case of the blockade of Prague, was of the latter kind. The capture of the Austrian grand army, and the defeat of Daun, would certainly have prostrated the house of Austria. In decisive operations that do not admit of delay, fortresses may be masked by corps that will observe and restrain their garrisons.

Conduct of the Army covering a Siege.

In page 94 (Chap. IV, Vol. II) we have laid down the maxims for the conduct of the army of observation. The neglect of these rules at Turin, enabled Prince Eugene to beat the French and raise the siege (p. 90, Vol. II).

Subsistence and Magazines.

There is no subject on which there has of late been a greater diversity of opinion, that on the subsistence of armies. The late wars have given rise to maxims on this subject, which are in total opposition to all previously received. It has been inculcated that magazines should have no influence on invasions and operations. But these maxims must vary with the theatre of war. In a country like the Netherlands, thickly peopled and teeming with sustenance for animal life, and whose internal police embraces every town and village, requisitions are easily made and executed.

But we may be permitted to doubt the application of the following maxims and reasoning to a country like our own.

The experience of the last wars, says Jomini, has proved, that an army may derive its subsistence from the least cultivated countries. In the interval between the battles of Eylau and Friedland, in 1807, Napoleon subsisted 120,000 men during 4 months in a country already ravaged by war. We may hence judge whether for 15 to 20 marches, the calculations of bakeries and sacks of flour may not be thrown out of consideration. We are therefore authorized by the experience of late wars, to lay down the following maxims :—

1st. An army in march to undertake decisive operations, can always find resources while in motion. We may therefore, in proportion to these resources, dispense with the train of provisions and transports.

2d. But as it may nevertheless happen that this army may remain some days in position, (as the French army did at Austerlitz and Ulm,) it would be proper to have following it merely a supply of biscuit for seven or eight days; in order to secure at least the subsistence strictly necessary, and to gain time to establish the commissariat service.

3d. For this purpose, it is necessary as fast as the country is occupied, to require the disposeable flour and grain, and to form with them depots covered by the army. The number of these depots should be increased in proportion as the army advances.

4th. If according to calculations founded on an exact knowlege of the agriculture and produce of the provinces to be invaded or traversed, we can only derive from them a momentary supply; this supply will be always sufficient to support the army one month; and this period is commonly long enough to decide the success of an enterprise.

5th. When the principal and decisive operation is terminated, we may then organize magazines and regular administrations, to facilitate ulterior enterprises.

He quotes in support of these maxims many great operations; and among others, the march of Frederick from Saxony into Silesia, in November, 1757 (see page 405).

Armies compelled to canton themselves for subsistence, even in a country abounding in food, must unavoidably occupy a vast extent of ground; their lines must of course be considerably lengthened and exposed. If on the other hand they operate on a theatre exhausted of its products, or naturally sterile, or at a season of the year when all countries are comparatively so, their line must necessarily be still more protracted and weak. These considerations, founded on the nature of things, are not to be overruled by the success of any temporary deviations from them in unparalleled circumstances.

Tempelhoff says that in the campaign of 1757, the Prussian provision park carried *bread* for *six*, and *flour* for *nine* days. This supply for 15 days, enabled Frederick to undertake operations, which, without it, would have been impracticable.

The following maxims have the sanction of both prudence and experience :

1st. Form your depots in the rear of your line of operations and in places strengthened by art or nature, and which may be defended by a small corps or garrison.

2d. These places of depot should if possible be upon navigable rivers, or at least on practicable roads communicating with your line. When the line of operations is far protracted, transportation by land is very difficult.

3d. Multiply your magazines in proportion to the length of your line and the character of your operations. In long *offensive* lines of operations, two or three depots in the rear will at least be required. If the war be *defensive*, double or triple this number will be requisite; and they will be established on the intended direction of the retreat, should this become necessary.

4th. There must be always a supply in camp for 9 or 10 days; otherwise the best chances of war may be lost, and the army may be exposed to great inconveniences.

5th. The roads and communications to the magazines, will be made easy.

6th. On occupying a new line of operations, we must make ourselves perfectly acquainted with the productions of the country, both as to quantity and quality ; and we must quickly collect all the necessary supplies, and place them in such positions as will be covered by the army. The collections will be first made from those districts most exposed to the enemy.

7th. In a defensive war, all the supplies, forage, &c. that cannot be removed, must be destroyed ; " we will thus make a friend and ally of " Famine itself, and literally beat our enemy, by starving him into errors " or debility".

8th. The commissariat department must be characterised by vigour and economy ; and must be rigidly inspected. The slightest faults should be severely punished ; for upon its fidelity and capacity depends success.

The passage of Rivers.

The battle of Breslau (page 404) leads us to the following reflections : The success of an affair, especially of the passage of rivers, and such like operations, in which the troops can only come successively into action, depends generally upon the first attack. When the first columns debouching from a bridge or passage, are able to form and maintain themselves until the army is arrived and in a situation to support them, the success of the enterprise is secured. We may therefore conclude, that it is of vital importance to prevent this formation of the first columns; and that we must not hesitate a moment to precipitate our cavalry and infantry upon them. The least movement of doubt or uncertainty, loses all. And when this at-took is once resolved on, it should be made with fury; for if repulsed, nothing can be hoped from a second attempt. If General Lestewitz (commanding the Prussian centre) had observed these rules, it is probable that Prussia would not have lost the battle of Breslau.

The great error of the Duke of Bevern's dispositions was, that they were defensive; for if an army equal in number can only hope for success by anticipating its adversary, in order to overwhelm him on the principal point of attack; it is still more certain, that an inferior army, when it foresees a battle, should never await the enemy, but should imitate the fine example of Frederick at Rosbach and Leuthen.

The other measures for passing and defending rivers, are so fully explained in Chap. VI and VII, Vol. 1, that we think any further remarks unnecessary.

SECTION IV.

The Art of Combat, or Grand Tactics; Oblique and Perpendicular Orders of Battle; the Crotchet or Potence, retired or forward; Posts and Villages in Battle; Intervals in Lines; Attacks; Orders of Battle of Cavalry; &c.

THE third and last branch of the science is—the art of directing our forces, when brought together, to the greatest effect against the enemy's line of battle or position; in order that the whole force may make a *combined and simultaneous* effort against the *decisive point* of the position or line of battle.

Battles are only to be fought in the following cases:

1st. When some great advantage may be obtained;

2d. When the political or military circumstances of the army, render a battle indispensable;

3d. When the enemy are about receiving re-enforcements that will give them the superiority;

4th. When we are decidedly superior to the enemy, and when the chances and *advantages* of victory, are greater than the hazard and losses of a defeat;

5th. When the enemy's movements against our line of battle or operations, or communications, or magazines, render it necessary to attack and check them.

There are many precautions to be taken previous to a battle; such as providing ample supplies of infantry and artillery ammunition ; putting the fire arms in the best possible order ; arranging the hospital department, and providing it with dressings, nurses and attendants, wagons to carry the wounded, and all other accommodations.

The various signals will be determined ; and points of rendezvous for each corps, will be designated and communicated to their commanders, who must be made perfectly acquainted with the ground and roads, and provided with topographical maps.

If the army gain the victory, no respite must be given to the enemy ; the cavalry and reserves will be detached in pursuit of them, followed by the corps that are least fatigued, and then by the whole army. It is by vigorously pursuing a beaten, dispirited, and disorganised army, that we reap the advantages of victory ; the mere difference between the killed and wounded in the field of battle, is of no moment. It is by capturing whole regiments and divisions that we strike a balance in our favour. In the battles of Rosbach and Leuthen, the killed and wounded were trifling compared to the number of prisoners. The slaughter of 7,000 men, cannot be put in competition with 43,000 prisoners.

It is also a maxim in war—*never to postpone 'till to-morrow.* The non-observance of this, has lost many battles.

In the event of defeat, the army will retire in the best possible order ; in echellons of brigades or divisions, if the ground permit. The cavalry will cover the movements ; and all the advantages of ground, such as woods, defiles, villages, &c. will be taken advantage of to check the pursuing troops. The corps will take care to retreat upon the points designated *beforehand* by the General ; and they will not suffer themselves to be thrown off from their line or base of operations. To avoid this, they will march unceasingly. The retreat must be conducted with calmness and order ; and should the enemy, on the presumption of our fears or weakness, venture bold strokes, we must take care to punish his temerity, by facing about and retrieving the honour of our arms. No pains must be spared to keep up the spirits of the troops ; and even the motive of the retreat, may often be concealed, by giving out reports that the magazines are threatened by a corps in the rear which must be chastised. Every appearance tending to inspire confidence and courage in the troops, must be attended to ; and fresh dispositions for battle should be made, to convince both them and the enemy, that though we have been defeated, we are neither overpowered nor dismayed.

The demonstration contained in page 105 (vol. 1), proves that the best mode of bringing into action at the decisive point a superior mass, is to attack the extremity of the hostile line in an oblique or perpendicular order of battle. The only mode of effecting this, is to assume the initiative or become the assailant ; for we then know what must happen, and we make our arrangements accordingly ; whilst the enemy is compelled to think only of defending himself. If our stratagic movements to gain the threatened flank, be judicious, the enemy will be ignorant of our march until almost the moment of attack. The stratagic movements at Leuthen and Rosbach, are a proof of this.

There is in every camp or position, a point that may be justly called its *key* ; and upon the possession of which, the success of the battle almost always depends. So long as the enemy have not carried this point, their advantages are illusory ; but when once it is carried, all is lost. To discover this key, requires the greatest and rarest military talents ; the science of camps, and their attack and defence, are necessarily founded upon it.

But these decisive points are neither numerous, nor difficult to determine. In a scattered line, the centre is the key ; from which we may crush one of the isolated wings. In a continuous line, this point is the extremity that has the nearest relation to all the bases of operations. Prague, Marengo, Austerlitz and Ratisbon, prove this first rule ; and Leuthen, Castiglione, Ulm and Wagram, prove the latter.

There are also decisive moments in all battles. At Kollin, the decisive moment was when the refused wing came into action, and left Hulsen without support ; at Rosbach, it was when the Prussians enveloped with their infantry the heads and two flanks of the hostile columns, after beating their cavalry ; and at Leuthen, the decisive moment was when the Austrian potence (Nadasty's corps) was forced, and the Prussians reversed the hostile line.

Isolated divisions ; too extended movements which deprive an army of a portion of its force, and enable the enemy to overwhelm either part ; lines of battle weakened by too great extension ; and obstacles between wings or columns, which prevent their junction, and afford the means of separately vanquishing them—are in battles capital errors, and are violations of the fundamental principle. And it may be said of the finest combinations, that their advantages depend upon the very reverse of these errors.

The orders of battle of Frederick, were generally two lines of infantry, with cavalry on each flank, and a reserve of cavalry and infantry, or grenadiers. The van guard consisted generally of 30 to 50 squadrons, supported by 8 or 10 battalions of grenadiers, and one or two or three divisions of light artillery (mostly 12 pounders). The flanks were covered by the light troops. The van guard begun the action, and was supported by the army, which closely followed it.

As his orders of march were calculated to place his army at once in line obliquely or perpendicularly upon the extremity of the hostile line, the furious attack of the van guard was followed by that of the whole line in succession upon the enemy's flank. The success of the van guard, generally decided the affair ; for if it succeeded in breaking the extremity (or potence) of the line, it prolonged itself into the enemy's rear, whilst the army continued to advance against their flank and rear. In this manner the assailed extremity had to contend in succession with a whole army ; its destruction was therefore inevitable.

Frederick, like Napoleon, re-enforced the engaged flank, especially with a strong reserve of cavalry, and a corps of grenadiers. Even the *refused* wing was supported by a division of cavalry; for it is indisputable that there must be a division of cavalry on each flank, to profit of favourable moments for charging, until the reserve can arrive. The neglect of this rule at Kunnersdorf, lost that dreadful battle. The right, which was the engaged flank, had to operate perpendicularly against the hostile left on ground unfavourable for cavalry, because intrenched and of difficult access. The king had in consequence posted all his cavalry on his left; intending to bring it forward against the enemy's front and centre, when the right had taken these in reverse. The right succeeded in its attack; but the want of cavalry, and of a few divisions of light 6 pounders, to scour the length of the line and prevent the troops from rallying, lost Frederick the field and 20,000 of his best troops (one-half of his army).

The orders of battle of Frederick at *Kollin, Leuthen,* and *Zorndorf,* were the open oblique order against one extremity; and at *Prague, Rosbach,* and *Kunnersdorf,* he used the perpendicular order.

Guibert's definition of the oblique order, and which has been repeated by the author of the article in the *Memoriale du Depôt de la Guerre,* does not appear to be strictly correct, especially when applied to the battle of Leuthen. The following figures will demonstrate this :

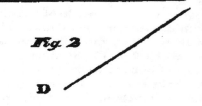

Fig. 1.

An army B, (fig. 1.) may be out of striking distance of the enemy, and consequently refused : and this army may be in parallel line with a wing very much re-enforced, without being oblique.

The army D, (fig. 2.) may be in line very inclined upon the front of the attack, and thus form a perfect diagonal, without being re-enforced.

An army may be perpendicular upon the flank, like the Prussian army at Kunnersdorff, with a wing re-enforced; and without being in a diagonal position (G, fig. 3).

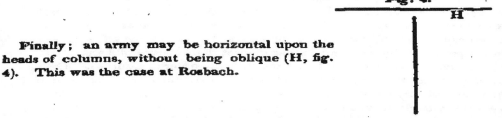

Fig. 4.

Finally; an army may be horizontal upon the heads of columns, without being oblique (H, fig. 4). This was the case at Rosbach.

There are many modifications of these different orders. Among others of the third, is the crotchet or potence thrown perpendicularly forward; such as was formed by the Austrian cavalry at Prague, and at Kollin.

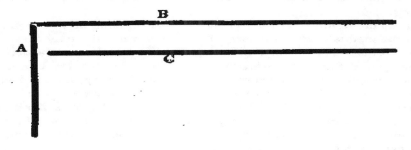

The crotchet A, being perpendicular to the enemy C, re-enforces the right wing of the line B, without being oblique. The same is the case with the crotchet thrown back, or retired.

The ancients more generally used the parallel order re-enforced, than the oblique order. Turenne used the first at Ensheim, and the second by his right at Sinzheim. But these manoeuvres, slowly executed in sight of the enemy by only one division of an army, afforded the latter time to establish a parallel line, and to re-enforce it at the same point. Tempelhoff might therefore say with reason, that Frederick had discovered all the advantages of an order similar to that of the battle of Leuthen; for till then, such an application had never been made of it. These advantages are superior to those of the other orders of battle that we have just referred to.

A parallel line greatly re-enforced at the most important point of the attacks, is doubtless a good disposition; and is conformable to the principle that we have established for the basis of all operations. It may therefore gain the victory; but it has many inconveniences. The weak part of the line being too near the enemy, may, notwithstanding its efforts to the contrary, be engaged and beaten. This would counterbalance and check any advantages gained at another point. The re-enforced wing may beat that which is opposed to it; but it cannot succeed in taking the hostile line in flank and reverse, without making a great movement that would separate it from its other divisions, in the event of these being engaged. If these divisions be not engaged, and can follow the movement of the re-enforced wing, this movement will be necessarily circular; whilst the counter-movement of the enemy, who will form the chord of the arc, will be much more rapid, and will afford them the means of assuming the offensive at the principal point, by carrying thither soonest their masses of force.

The case is very different with the Prussian order at Leuthen. The extremity of the attacked wing is not only overwhelmed by a whole line, but the flank of this wing, is constantly outflanked, and its line is taken in reverse without a manœuvre or prolongation of direction, by merely a simple front march of the oblique line. The divisions that are not destined for the principal attack, are, by their eloignement, out of reach of the possibility of being engaged with a superior enemy. So secure are they from this danger, that they are within reach of succouring successively the engaged wing.

These brilliant results of the *open oblique order*, cannot be too often the subject of the meditations of soldiers. But they are not the only ones, for this order affords another much more important and decisive advantage—the extremity of the attacked wing (we will suppose the two last brigades) receives successively the charge of half of the hostile army, without being able to check its march by a counter-manœuvre. What troops are capable of sustaining such a conflict, when they are besides taken in flank and reverse? Will not panic and confusion spread through the whole of a line thus overwhelmed on its flanks, and threatened with entire destruction by the direction of the enemy on its rear?

Such must be the inevitable results of an attack in oblique order, when we succeed in gaining the flank of our adversary in the manner laid down, and when we form our line by the simple and rapid method of Frederick.

The following figure exhibits this in a clearer manner; and shows the Prussian order at Leuthen.

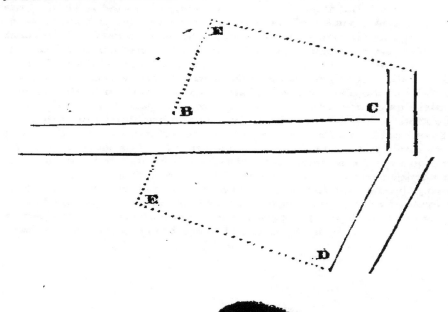

The left wing BC, will receive the fire of the 2d brigade of the army D; whilst the *first* brigade, formed into column of platoons, will outflank it, in order to quickly decide this first attack.

The 2d brigade, by following its oblique prolongation, will find itself immediately supported by the 3d, which will open its fire upon the extremity of the line, and continue to outflank it by marching straight forward. When it has passed the hostile extremity, the fourth brigade will have gained its place, and will do the same. If we suppose the army D, to have arrived on the dotted line EE, we see that its whole line will be engaged with the fourth, or at most the one third part, of the hostile army; whose battalions, successively destroyed, will be almost enveloped.

This demonstration will doubtless suffice to exhibit the advantages of the *open oblique order.* By this name we distinguish any disposition similar to that of Frederick at Leuthen, because it formed almost a rectangle with the Austrian line; and because it greatly differs from an acute angled order, which too much resembles a parallel disposition.

The peculiarity of the first, is, that the refused wing being nearer the hostile wing against which our efforts are to be directed, than to the rest of the line, it is able to sustain the principal point of attack; and the enemy cannot engage it in any affair, in which they will have great numerical superiority.

All these advantages of the oblique order, refer to the supposition of an army attacking in displayed line of battle. These same principles may be applied, and the same advantages may be obtained, by concentrating our masses a little more upon the extremity that we design to overwhelm; as is shown by the two lines in the following figure:

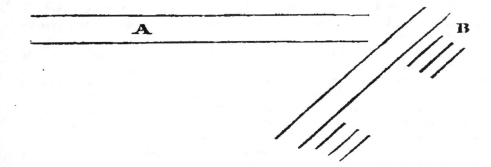

The army B, instead of forming two lines, like the army D, in the preceding figure, may make this disposition of only one half of its force; the residue should be disposed in close columns, at half distance, upon the two wings, in order to be able to manœuvre, or to strike when necessary decisive blows. This disposition in columns, will render much more moveable the portion of troops not destined for the first attack; and will prevent them from being engaged, in spite of themselves, by any movement of the enemy.

The battle of Leuthen furnishes this further important maxim—that an army whose flanks rest upon an obstacle, like the great pond of Gohlau, which supported the crotchet formed by Nadasty's corps, may be equally outflanked by an oblique attack. For this purpose, it will suffice to leave unengaged the hostile brigade that rests upon the obstacle, merely observing it with some troops; the line must then be disposed in such a manner, that the principal effort will be against the 2d brigade. It is easy to perceive that the line being broken, and having lost its point of support, the obstacles of ground will be of no avail; they may even contribute to the capture of the first brigade, if it attempt to maintain its position.

But the attack should never be directed against an extremity that is supported by an insurmountable obstacle, such as a great stream, or the sea.

This manœuvre is doubtless not so good as an attack upon a flank badly supported, or more easily outflanked; but it is nevertheless excellent. It proves that no position can secure an army against a skilful enemy; and that the only means of resisting him, is to manœuvre *in the same direction* that he does. It confirms all the maxims previously laid down.

Agreeably to all these considerations, it appears that the *writer* of the precedingly mentioned article, has unwarrantably disputed the glory obtained by Frederick by his oblique order—so different from any thing that had been written on this subject. This author attributes too much influence to the detailed and minute instruction of the troops; the vague expression of *manœuvring troops*, signifies nothing.

The secret of war is not in the legs; but is in the head that directs them. An army may make forced marches during a whole campaign; but its destruction will be no less certain, if the direction of these marches be erroneous.

The truth of this is proved by the late wars. The troops of Frederick did nothing under his successors; for the head that truly comprehended their use, died with Frederick. The French militia at the beginning of the revolution, were totally ignorant of the manœuvres of Potsdam; but led by Generals who knew how to direct them, they astonished Europe. The only advantage that the army of Frederick possessed, resulted from his order of march and formation, which we have already described. Its mechanism was the invention of this great man; but it would not have gained battles without the genius that applied its effects. If Napoleon had commanded the best disciplined troops, he could have achieved nothing more; nor could Frederick have done less, on the contrary hypothesis.

We are led by the description of the battle of Prague and its results, and by many similar events, to establish the following maxim:—

In general, it is very imprudent to attack an army encamped beneath a fortress; because, even in the event of victory, it is impossible to use our cavalry, which alone can complete the destruction of a vanquished army. For whatever advantages the infantry may obtain, they cannot pursue the enemy with sufficient vigour and speed to prevent their retreat and rallying. If Frederick had won such a victory as that of Prague, at 7 or 8 leagues from the fortress, the whole Austrian army would have been destroyed. Besides, the king need not have attacked the army under Prague. By directing his march upon Kollin and Kuttemberg, where the Austrian magazines were, Prince Charles would have been compelled to follow him, and to thus afford Frederick a more favourable opportunity of attacking him. Judging from events, the king would have met and overwhelmed the army from Moravia under Daun. The battles of Kollin, Rosbach, and Leuthen establish the following maxims :—

1st. If it be acknowledged that the most advantageous attacks, are those made by an united effort upon a single extreme of the enemy's line, it becomes indispensable to take measures to gain this extreme, by masking the movements for this purpose.

2d. Without this precaution, the enemy would be able to follow the march of the columns that are attempting to outflank them, and to always oppose to them their front, and to even take them in flank, in the same manner as the king did the combined army at Rosbach.

3d. It is therefore necessary to conceal the march of these columns by darkness, by favour of the ground, or by a false attack upon the enemy's front.

4th. These two *latter* means are preferable, especially when they can be united; because night movements are less certain and less orderly than day movements.

Lastly. In order to alarm a greater extent of front, we should make use of a body of sharp-shooters, formed into platoons; instead of menacing it by a corps united in a van guard. The number of these sharp-shooters may be as great as 6 or 8 battalions, according to circumstances; they should have a place of rendezvous, and be sustained by the cavalry and a few pieces of light artillery. This method is admirable either for deceiving the enemy as to the real value of these false attacks and the number of the troops that make them, or to occupy and keep in check almost his whole extent of front whilst the columns are marching to their destination. For if it be confessed that an army should oppose to an attack upon one of its extremities, counter-manœuvres having the same designs against one of the flanks of its enemy; it must be equally acknowledged that that mode of attack which will deprive it of this power, must be the most favourable; and it must be agreed, that a concealed movement is the only one to which an able enemy can oppose no counter-manœuvre.

The events at Rosbach and Leuthen, says Tempelhoff, lead us to establish the following maxims :

1st. When an army expects to be attacked by the enemy, it should never await the blow; but must ever advance and anticipate it, by attacking with impetuosity and without a moment's delay.

2d. If the enemy attempt to turn an army on the day of battle, the latter, if on the alert, may always prevent, and even outflank them.

To render this rule more intelligible, we will suppose two armies, A and B, (Fig. 6, Plate XIV.) marching in two lines that must meet at C, where they will form an angle.   It is evident that the army that first reaches this point C, will be established upon the flank of its adversary, and may envelop him.

The army A, marching to attack B, will probably move by lines and in columns of divisions or platoons; for this is the best order of march to attain the proposed object.   This army should push forward a strong body of cavalry, in order to gain more rapidly the flank that it intends to attack. If the army B have proper outposts and scouting parties, it can easily baffle this attempt; and it is quite certain that it can always reach the given point before its adversary; for having received in season intelligence of the march of the enemy, it will be able to arrive before them at their point of direction.   To do this, the army B will only have to *follow* the example of Frederick at Rosbach; he placed all his cavalry on the threatened flank, and instantly put it in motion.

When therefore the army B is formed at the point C before the army A, this latter will be taken in flank, and will be inevitably overthrown if the former take advantage of this circumstance with as much vigour and promptitude as Frederick did at Rosbach.

To convince ourselves of this, let us demonstrate the only counter-manœuvre that the army A can oppose to check the enemy.   When the cavalry have reached the height of C, (Fig. 7, Plate XIV.) the army A has no other means than to form a crotchet in D, at the point of contact with the enemy.   This manœuvre, which should be executed with great rapidity, will produce a little disorder.   The cavalry formed in C, by charging impetuously and all at once, and in a proper direction to outflank the enemy, will overthrow them even before they can display.

Tempelhoff also thinks, that the formation of this crotchet is subject to another inconvenience.   When an army marches by lines in columns, preserving their distances, these distances are still lost in some measure when a conversion is made that approximates the columns; and this is particularly the case, when the crotchet forms a right angle.

The lines in this case, become locked together in mass, and in inevitable confusion.   If the enemy charge at this moment, and the first line be repulsed, it will necessarily produce the rout of the second, and the disorder will be the greater.   The assailing cavalry can easily re-form, and renew their attack.   Meantime their infantry will begin to arrive; the battalions as fast as they form, will immediately advance to their support, because it is of great importance to act with vigour, without giving the enemy time to recover themselves; and this may be done without fear, for the army is all the while within supporting distance*.

* Jomini says, that Tempelhoff is here in a very great error, when he says that two columns in approaching each other a little at the moment of a change

To explain this still further, we will suppose the army B to be marching by the left by lines in platoons, and that its cavalry is 600 to 800 paces in advance; the left wing will arrive at the moment that this cavalry has charged, and is engaged in re-forming. The first battalions that arrive, will form line and cover this operation; and the two arms will then make a combined effort against the enemy. The army A, beholding its cavalry overthrown at the first shock, would doubtless attempt to form a crotchet with the infantry of the right wing; and to this effect, will retire the cavalry on the right, to prevent them from masking this manœuvre. But the infantry of B will not give them time to effect this; if they have continued to rapidly advance, they will arrive whilst this manœuvre is performing, and may easily put to the rout a corps thus surprised. Even if we suppose that the left wing of the army B, is more advanced than the other battalions by a few hundred paces; these will still arrive in sufficient season to support the attack and render it decisive. The result of this movement would be a species of order in echellon, in which each echellon would take its post when that which preceded it had gained a few hundred paces. By taking care to prolong them all upon the left, the enemy will find themselves completely outflanked and taken in reverse, before they can oppose any counter-measures. The crotchet that they may endeavour to form in D, would likewise be exposed to the whole effect of the artillery, which would scour it in every direction.

Cavalry may greatly contribute to the success of these kind of operations; and it must be said in praise of the Prussian cavalry at Rosbach, that they so prepared the road to victory, that the infantry easily completed it.

From the battle of Rosbach, we may draw this maxim:

That a general commanding an army skilful at manœuvring, should as often as possible attack his enemy in march; notwithstanding that the latter may be very superior in number.

The history of the seven years' war, proves that the king sought always to attack his enemies when they were in march. Daun knew this well; and he employed all his talents to avoid him, by choosing the most difficult positions, and preferring to make great detours rather than expose his army to be attacked in march.

Jomini lays down these further rules and principles on attacking an army in march; a subject that Tempelhoff has not sufficiently illustrated.

Attacking an army in march, is advantageous for the same reason that it is to attack the extremity of the enemy's line; for the army attacked on the heads of its columns, finds itself in the same position relatively to

of direction, would be thereby weakened, and more easily beaten. Besides, this change of direction, is not indispensable in the case here supposed: two brigades may be made to change front, and thus the throwing together of the two lines, will be prevented.

the enemy, as if it were assailed on one of its extremities. The following figure will prove this:

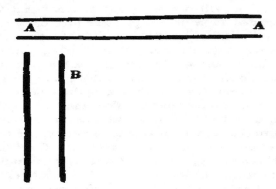

Here the army *A*, is in the same position as the Prussians at Rosbach; whilst *B* is in the same relative position as the combined army. By supposing them to be both in line, we see that *B* is attacked in the perpendicular order, and outflanked; and this would be the case with the head of the columns, if the army *B* were in march.

The advantage of this manœuvre, is in consequence of the army *B* being only able to bring its battalions into action in succession; whilst the enemy, by operating with vigour, crushes them successively in detail. To obtain this result, it is not sufficient to attack a column in march; the army *A* must take a proper direction; that is, it must prolong itself horizontally across the head of the columns, if the march of the columns be perpendicular; and perpendicularly, if the march of the columns be horizontal. The object of this, is to oppose the whole line to the head of a column, and consequently to a single extremity of the enemy's line.

We can readily conceive that if two heads of columns meet in the same direction and reciprocally display, the result will be a parallel order of battle—a shock of two fronts of equal strength—a total absence of all combination. The following figure explains this idea:

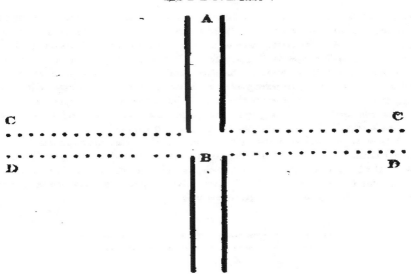

The army *A*, marching on two columns, meets the army B; both are moving in the same direction. The first, apprehending an attack, will undoubtedly display as fast as possible, and form on the dotted line *C C;* and if the latter did not do the same, it would be beaten, as is demonstrated in the preceding figure: *B* would therefore form on the dotted line *D D.*

This re-establishment of the parallel order—of one front against another—of battalion against battalion, is undoubtedly the result of ignorance and incapacity. The armies thus engaged, may destroy each other, but without any great advantage ; and if one of them should gain the victory, it will certainly not be in consequence of the good conduct of its General.

It may not be useless here to refer to our remarks upon Guibert's orders of march, and especially to that in his XVth Plate, which he has repeated in his Defence of the Modern System of War. It will be seen by examining that plate and our remarks, that this writer wishing the enemy to make a concealed march to gain the heads of the columns, brings the armies in contact, head of column against head of column, as in the above figure ; whilst by changing direction beyond the village, after the passage of the wood, and prolonging their movement horizontally with whole distances, the enemy would have been in battle array upon the heads of the columns by a mere conversion of platoons. They would thus have manœuvred in the manner of the first figure, and like the great Frederick at Rosbach.

This further application shows how much Guibert has mistaken the tactics of Frederick, notwithstanding their simplicity.

The position of the two armies at that battle, and these demonstrations, support our observations on the deployments described and advocated in *The General Essay on Tactics*. They may be indispensable for a part of an army surprised in march, and which is compelled to display to form the crotchet of which Tempelhoff speaks. But this deployment should only have relation to a van guard, or to the heads of columns suddenly attacked; the remainder of the army on learning this attack, may, without displaying, manœuvre in the direction that is most advantageous, either to protect the retreat of the engaged brigade that has formed the crotchet, or to act offensively upon the flanks of the enemy.

This latter supposition gives rise to an incidental discussion. Tempelhoff thinks that an army attacked in march, should first of all form the crotchet; that is, that the leading brigade should display. Its line of battle, formed on the right or left of the columns, will really form a crotchet or *potence;* as the following figure proves:

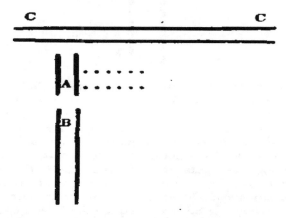

Here, *A* forms the van guard, or head of the columns *B*; if attacked by the enemy, it will display to the right or left, according to the direction of the attack, and will occupy the position of the dotted lines, which describe a crotchet or *potence* in relation to the column. This manœuvre is necessary, to resist the first efforts of the enemy *C*. The army being *thus shielded from the first danger*, the question occurs,

Should it follow the movement of this brigade, and establish the parallel order?

This question is connected with the following:

An army attacked on one of its flanks, and having made front or formed a crotchet with the brigade of the threatened flank; should this army continue its change of front in the same direction, and thus form parallel to the enemy?

These two very important questions appear inseparable; because the respective positions, imagined in order to their solution, present the same causes and results. We therefore unhesitatingly answer *No!* to both of them.

This manœuvre might at first appear most natural; and it is very commonly used by indifferent Generals; but is this proof of its wisdom? It is proved that the attack upon a flank is the most advantageous; why then should not an army *A A* (Fig. 8, Plate XIV.) whose van guard or extreme flank brigade *C*, is engaged in front with the enemy *B B*, endeavour in its turn to gain one of their flanks, and thus change the defence for the offence—a probable defeat, for an almost certain victory? What is to prevent a General attacked in this manner, from ordering the engaged brigade *C* to dispute the ground inch by inch, by retiring upon a brigade placed in intermediate echellon; whilst meantime the rest of the column or army *A A* changes direction by the flanks, by causing the platoons to march by their right or left flank, and thus throw itself in *D D* upon one extremity of the enemy's line?

The platoons of the menaced extremity, will continue or prolong their movement further than the others; the following ones will successively prolong their movement less; so that the last platoons will remain steady, or will advance in the primitive direction, in order to form the pivot. The result of this disposition will be an oblique order upon one flank of the enemy, who will not dare to engage in pursuit of the retiring brigades, and who may themselves be attacked with great advantage, if the General operate with vigour and ensemble. This manœuvre is a great deal more simple, and infinitely more rapid, than a change of front. It affords the inestimable advantage of establishing the whole army upon a single extremity of the enemy's line; whilst the change of front, which most probably could never be effected, only tends to the re-establishment of a parallel order. This manœuvre is something like the battalion *Prompt Manœuvre.*

If this manœuvre by the flanks appear complicated, others may be substituted for it; but always with this view—*to carry the mass of our forces against a single wing of the enemy.*

It is in circumstances like these, that a General will appreciate the advantages of a theory founded upon true principles. A common man, who has nothing but *his long experience,* will be always astonished, surprised, and embarrassed, when it is announced to him that the heads of his columns are attacked by a line, or that one of his flanks is overthrown. But if he have a just and accurate theory of his profession—if he know the real value of his position, and the counter manœuvres that he should oppose to the enemy; he will give his orders with that calmness and serenity of countenance, that inspires confidence; and he will transfuse into his army that feeling of security which will never abandon himself. Such were all the great Captains. In circumstances like these, a General can expect nothing more from his experience, than to be able to judge of distances, and to combine with a knowledge of the ground the ulterior movements that he should make to execute the manœuvres dictated by theory.

In contemplating the battle of Leuthen, we are astonished to find an army of 85.000 men putting itself with great gravity in line before 30,000; suffering these to manœuvre at pleasure, and waiting 'till they throw themselves in mass against their solitary left.

An army superior in numbers, should never display more men than the enemy has; it should even display less. The remainder should be disposed in columns ready to strike vigorous blows, or to manœuvre upon the extremity of the enemy and gain the decisive points. A grand army displayed, is no longer moveable like columns; and to render immoveable the forces not engaged, is to grossly violate the rules of the science.

The Austrians here committed another fault, that of marching their line by the flank, to sustain their left wing; their troops in consequence arrived one after another, and were beaten by a mass. The conduct of Frederick was, on the contrary, founded upon the most incontrovertible principles of the science. Although his army was far inferior to the enemy, nevertheless, by the superiority of his manœuvres he carried to the point of attack a greater number of men than the enemy brought thither; this must be always decisive, when the valour of the troops is nearly equal.

In time of peace, Generals should apply themselves to establish evolutions that facilitate the grand manœuvres of armies; and in time of war, they should choose fields of battle that will afford them the means of concealing part of their movements, and thus enable them to put in action more troops than their adversary. If in consequence of the nature of the ground, or vigilance of the enemy, they are unable to mask their movements; in this case, the object may be attained by greater facility of manœuvring, which will enable them to carry to the principal point of attack a greater number of troops than the enemy. The advantages of numerical superiority, result from being able to fight a greater number of troops; but this advantage not only disappears when the troops are not properly disposed and used, but numerical superiority then becomes an incumbrance, and only increases the disorder. Hence we may deduce the following maxim:

The General who, by the rapidity of his movements or skill of his manœuvres, puts in action at the same instant and at the principal point of attack, a greater number of men than the enemy, must necessarily be victorious, if the troops be equally valiant.

All manœuvres that do not tend to this end, should be proscribed.

The means of effecting this, are marches or stratagic movements, to take up lines of operation; and manœuvres, or the selection of orders of attack, to fight battles.

It is indisputable that all the rules of the art, as likewise all the faults that may be committed in war, depend upon this maxim. We shall be convinced of this by casting a glance over the most important of those rules and of these faults, and on their relation to the application of the system of masses against decisive points.

The oblique orders, attacks with a wing re-enforced without being oblique, attacks that outflank a flank, orders perpendicular to the extremity of a line of battle, and those against a scattered and isolated centre, are advantageous and almost always crowned with success; because they present a whole line to a single extremity or portion of a line, and consequently a mass superior to that of the enemy.

Men who would attribute every thing to natural genius, or to accident, may perhaps cite several events that are exceptions, and which succeeded by contrary principles. But they are mistaken—because they have confounded the *engaged masses* with the *masses present*. It is not the troops borne upon the rolls of an army, nor those that are ostentatiously displayed upon the ground, that decide the fate of battles; but it is those that are brought into action: the others serve only to embarrass. In testimony of these truths, we may cite the whole life of Napoleon, and of Frederick; and the exploits of all the great Captains.

Genius has undoubtedly a great share in victory, because it presides over the application of acknowledged rules, and seizes all the modifications of which this application is susceptible. But in no case will a man of genius act in violation of these rules; and *he* will never be acknowledged as a great Captain, who has won a battle by accident and against the rules of the science; for one of the party must win. Such a victory is only a proof of reciprocal incapacity; of a total absence of tactics. Such were the battles of the middle ages; the quality of the troops, and the valour of the chiefs, were the sole instruments of victory.

The idea of reducing the system of war to one primitive combination, upon which all others depend; and which should be the basis of a simple and accurate theory, presents innumerable advantages. It would render the study of the science much more easy, the judgment of operations always correct, and faults less frequent. Generals cannot sufficiently understand its advantages; it should regulate all their plans and actions.

The battles of Kollin, Leuthen, and Jagerndorf, as well as the principles herein laid down on the oblique order, prove that to secure the success of a well-combined and re-enforced attack upon the decisive point, it is essential to refuse the weakened wing. The battle of Neerwinden, in the last war, was lost by Dumourier in consequence of departing from this rule. This manœuvre is recommended by several writers, who have not however clearly explained its advantages, nor applied it to events. It is not only necessary, in order to keep out of reach of the enemy the weak part of the line; but it is also necessary and advantageous, to enable us to support the principal attack by the troops of this part. Accordingly, instead of bringing this part of the line into action against superior forces, and consequently exposing it to certain defeat; we have, by a disposition in echellon, the grand advantage of employing it to decide the victory.

The echellon order possesses very great advantages. In this disposition, the army is divided into several corps, each of which presents a sufficient mass of force.   These may manœuvre separately, and consequently with more ease; and their movements may also be combined towards a single object, and executed with all the necessary ensemble.   Each echellon covers the flanks of that preceding; the first only requires to be well flanked, unless it be already secured by the nature of the ground upon which it is supported.   The cavalry may be distributed in third line to each echellon; they will thus be always within reach to support the infantry, and even to charge the enemy and complete their rout.   This manœuvre offers also the advantage of not engaging the army.   If the first echellon be beaten, the second covers its retreat; and the General is free to choose between retiring the others in the best order, or directing them against any point that he may select.   The nature of this order of attack, shows that it is particularly advantageous when the success of the battle depends upon carrying a certain and principal position of the enemy; and as these main points are either in the centre, or on one of the flanks, it is easy to decide whether the head of the echellons should be formed upon the centre, or upon a wing.   The echellon that is destined for the first attack, must of course be greatly re-enforced.

The following figures show this disposition on the centre and on the flank. In its application in oblique, or perpendicular, or parallel order, against an extremity or centre, it is substantially the same as a continuous line, from the defects and accidents of which it is free.

            Fig. 1.   Fig. 2.

In describing and analysing the battle of Leuthen, Jomini represents the Prussian army as in open oblique continuous line; but the king (in his memoirs) describes the formation in echellon so minutely, and gives his reasons for using it, with such detail, that the former must be mistaken. Had this order been used at Kollin, instead of the open oblique continuous line, no subordinate could have violated the king's dispositions by imprudently engaging the refused wing, and thus reducing his admirable combinations to a murderous parallel order—to a mere contest of bone and muscle. Had Frederick's dispositions been executed, the army of Daun would have been destroyed, for the Prussian cavalry would have been in its rear and the infantry on its flank and rear.   Not a man would have escaped, for night was far off.

The capture of the grand army in Prague, would have been the consequence; and the war would at once have been transferred to the banks of the Danube, the Save, and the Rhine.

From the same cause *it is dangerous to attack a line by its two extremities, unless we are very superior in numbers;* because if one column be re-enforced, the enemy may overwhelm the other, and thus re-establish an equality of losses. Besides, we cannot outflank the two extremes of a line of equal strength, by adequate divisions, without extending them too far and isolating our attacks: this is proved both by the battle of Neerwinden in 1793, and by that of Stockback in 1799.

Finally; we may lay it down as a rule, *that a front attack is always useless when we can make an united effort against the extremity of a line;* we must, in this case, confine ourselves to the demonstrations already described.

A retired crotchet, or potence thrown back, like A, in the following figure, is only a proper defence when the enemy are already in march, and are obliged to divide their forces to outflank it. But if destined to cover a flank against an able and manœuvring enemy, it is a remedy worse than the evil that is to be averted. Indeed its own extremity must be as well secured, as that of a right line; for if it be possible to turn it, it can be of no utility. It possesses inherent defects. The troops next to the salient angle, cannot retrograde without reciprocally pressing upon each other, and falling into inevitable disorder. If, on the other hand, the troops in potence have to advance, they will form a great chasm or interval; or they will be obliged to oblique, and press to the right (or left); this will cause an undulation of the line that may produce the greatest disorder and most dreadful consequences, if the attack be made at the same moment. And a skilful General who is capable of seizing all favourable circumstances, will find means to establish cross-fire batteries on both sides of the salient angle, to scour in every direction the battalions adjacent to the angle.

At the battle of Prague, Prince Charles of Lorraine formed a retired potence on his right, covered by a *forward* potence of cavalry on its extremity. The Prussian cavalry charged the latter in flank, or upon its outer extremity, and overthrew it; and the king, by carrying a height that commanded the opening between the retired potence and the left wing, was able to establish a heavy battery that swept the length of the potence, against the front of which he made his principal effort. The same events and results took place at Leuthen.

These events prove, that nothing can prevent an able and manœuvring enemy from gaining the extremity of a crotchet, in the same manner that they would that of a right line. They will however be obliged to make a greater movement; and this will require considerable time, during which the army will be able to change its front, and to present its whole line where the enemy expected to find only a flank. This reasoning is unquestionable; for the army that attempts to turn another, moves upon an arc, of which its adversary forms the chord. The latter, therefore, by manœuvring on an interior right line, will move with more celerity and will be able to anticipate its adversary at the threatened point. The conduct of Frederick at Rosbach, demonstrates this. The combined army made a great circular movement to gain his rear ; the king on perceiving their manœuvre, marched perpendicularly to his rear, and threw his army across the heads of their columns which were badly enlightened, for they had no scouts, nor van guard. The king in this instance, moved upon the chord, whilst the combined army marched upon a great arc.

1st. When the two armies are equally skilful at manœuvring, the formation of a crotchet may be used with success against attacks upon a flank.

2d. To ensure its success, we must not content ourselves with the mere formation of the crotchet, which will only serve against the danger of the moment ; the army must change front in the same direction, in order to present its whole line to the enemy, and to repulse them.

3d. If the attacked army be sufficiently strong to act offensively against its adversary ; instead of effecting a change of front, which would be a movement purely defensive, it may, after rapidly forming the crotchet to hold the front of the enemy in check and secure its threatened flank, break the rest of the line into column of platoons or divisions, and prolong itself by the flank in the direction (or nearly so) of the position that it occupied; so as in turn to fall upon the extremity of the enemy who is attempting to assail its flank.

An enemy thus taken in front by the crotchet, and in flank and reverse by the remainder of the line, would be unable to resist : Fig. 9. Plate XIV. will render this manœuvre more intelligible. A is the army attempting to turn the right flank of B ; the latter forms the crotchet C, and the dotted column D, which prolongs its direction to EE, and thus forms on the flank of the line A. Perhaps it may be objected, that the latter would not permit this movement to be executed ; but to prevent, it must retire, or make face towards it by a change of front. This latter operation will not be easy in the presence of the crotchet, and of the line, which will be ready to form in a few minutes by a simple conversion of platoons.

4th. A crotchet *forward*, such as the Austrians formed with General Haddick's cavalry corps at Prague, and with Nadasty's cavalry at Kollin, does not cover the flank of an army so well as a crotchet in rear or retired. The reason of this is very simple ; because the enemy by a prolongation of the direction of their leading division, will take this crotchet C in flank, and will overwhelm it. To effect the same against the crotchet thrown back, the enemy is compelled to make the great movement that we have spoken of, and which will expose themselves to be taken in flank and rear. (Plate XIV. fig. 9.)

The battle of Malplaquet and the fate of Marshal Villars' left, or forward potence, shows how little is to be hoped from such a disposition even with the best troops. (p. 217, vol. i.)

5th. We may conclude from the preceding maxims, that an army by remaining stationary in a position, no matter how strong, may be always overpowered on an extremity, or turned; and that the only method of preventing this, is to manœuvre in the same direction as the enemy; that is, offensively, by menacing their own line.

The truth of this rule is proved by the battle of Austerlitz. The Emperor Napoleon remained in his position until the enemy had discovered their plans, and commenced their unconnected movements by their left; the French army then quitted its ground with the swiftness of an eagle, and assuming the initiative momentum of attack, separated and overwhelmed the enemy's left. Was it possible for victory not to crown such combinations?

Villages near a position, must be burnt in the following cases:—when they cover the approach of the enemy and are indefensible, or when we are too weak to occupy them—when it is dangerous to commit detachments in them, on account of being unable to support them, and when they favour the enemy—and when they are carried by the enemy, and are *decisive* points. For this purpose, a few batteries of howitzers are sufficient. The Duke of Marlborough acted in this manner at Hochstadt.

The accidental conflagration of the village of Hohenkirchen, forced the Prussians to retire from it, and enabled Marshal Daun to more completely turn and beat their right, and to connect with Laudon's corps in their rear.

When a village, or stone house, or such like obstacle in battle, cannot be forced without too great loss, choose another point of attack; for we are not compelled to run our heads against stone walls. In case of success, and of the enemy throwing into this obstacle a corps to check us and cover their retreat, pass it by unnoticed, or leave a corps to observe it, and push on after their main body. The neglect of these rules, has lost many battles; and among others, the battle of Germantown. Why should a regiment or two, under favour of ground or buildings, check a whole army, when by leaving two or three regiments we may secure them?

The following are the rules relating to posts and villages in lines of battle:

1st. An army posted behind villages, should cover its front with them.

2d. To this effect, they should be occupied by a few battalions and some artillery.

3d. The line should be near enough to support the villages, to be supported in its turn by them, and to withdraw the troops from them in the event of the enemy threatening to surround them by successes at another point.

4th. The practicability of turning these posts, and the nature of their defence, require that too much infantry be not placed in them; nor should too much importance be attached to their preservation.

These rules are justified by many battles. If the French Generals, on beholding their line menaced at another point, had withdrawn from Blenheim and from Oberklaw the greatest part of their infantry and directed it upon the flanks of the attack, they would very probably have gained the battle; for 20 additional battalions at the principal point, can effect great results. And if the French had lost the field, they would at least have preserved these 20 battalions, which were captured.

Tempelhoff lays it down as a rule—that no post which is too distant to be effectively supported, and which may be easily occupied by the enemy, ought to be occupied in defensive dispositions; unless it be unassailable on its whole front, and its flanks be well supported by the artillery of the line; and for this to be the case, it must not be distant more than one thousand paces. This rule is illustrated by the combat of *Kampen* (in the Duchy of Cleves) in 1758.

He also says, that if broken and woody ground afford great advantages for its defence, it also affords the assailants the means of concealing the point against which they intend making their greatest effort; and when they succeed in carrying against this point the greater part of their forces, the enemy are no longer able to resist. The truth of this was evident at the battle of Creveldt (1758). It is a maxim of great antiquity, in attacking and defending posts, that a man can pass where a goat can climb. The ground and environs of a position should therefore be most accurately reconnoitred; and small look-out posts should be kept at every practicable point.

The famous battle of Prague affords a fine subject of meditation on the influence that a small interval left in the line, had on the gain of the battle. This unfortunate fault came near costing the Austrians 70,000 men; it sheds great light on the inconveniences of isolated attacks, executed by divisions scattered along the front of the enemy—a system introduced by mediocrity of genius in the beginning of the wars of the French revolution.

This same fault happened by *accident* at Kollin, and was the cause of Frederick's losing that battle. Hulsen's corps being left without support, a great interval was consequently left between it and the rest of the army.

An accidental interval left by evacuating a redoubt (near Grabischen) which contained artillery and 100 men, was the main cause of the loss of the battle of Breslau; for from this redoubt, which they immediately seized, the Austrians cannonaded in enfilade the left of the Prussian centre. The redoubt was supported by troops outside who had advanced to defend the passage of the Lohe; the order to advance against the columns passing the bridges, was mistaken by the Major whose troops were supported upon this redoubt, for an order to evacuate it with his artillery, for he supposed that the garrison made part of his corps. The evacuation of the redoubt struck a panic into the raw troops near it, and they fled. The enemy immediately occupied it.

The Duke of Bevern, who wished to receive the Austrians under the cannon of Breslau, had his left uncovered. In order to support it, he was obliged to extend his line, and to leave a great interval between this wing and the rest of the army. This disposition formed a kind of order in *po-*

tence, similar to that of the Austrians at Prague; and it produced the same opening that was so fatal to them. The following figure exhibits this idea:

These intervals are always dangerous in a line, and are still more so in an angular line; because if the enemy succeed in establishing themselves at the point A, it is certain that the two wings will be enfiladed through their whole extent, and compelled to retire. Besides, one or other of these parts may be taken in flank and reverse  by the enemy; as was the case with the Austrians at Prague, and with the Prussians at Breslau.

The Duke of Bevern had no other mode of remedying this disposition, than to gain the flank of the enemy, either by cover of night or of the ground, and thus attack with his united force Nadasty's corps, which formed the Austrian extreme right. And this he might have done with the greater ease, as the fortress of Breslau would have protected his movements. He would thus have crushed a weak part, and have overwhelmed the line from one end to another, as the king did a few days after at Leuthen.

An enemy may be often drawn out of advantageous positions, by engaging them in a precipitate and disorderly pursuit. For this purpose, they must be attacked by a few battalions that will retire in disorder, but which will be supported by battalions suitably posted and in good order in the rear. This rule is proved by the battles of Prague, Zorndorff, and Kesseldorff.

All the rules precedingly established, are founded on the principle of a general attack upon a *single* extremity of a hostile line; and they appear wise and indispensable in the case of an army of inferior numbers.

If 50,000 men be divided into two corps of nearly equal force, to attack an army of 60,000 men; and if, in order to embrace the two extremes of the hostile line, they weaken and isolate their attacks; it is certain that the army of 60,000 men can move more rapidly in the interior of its line, than two isolated corps which have this mass between them. The following figure demonstrates this:

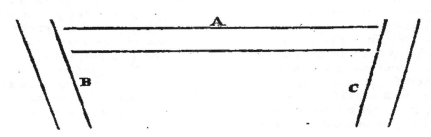

It is possible that the two corps B, and C, may gain some momentary advantages; but the army A, by leaving a division in observation before C, upon the ground most advantageous for the defensive, will be able to carry its mass upon the front, flanks, and rear of B, which will be undoubtedly destroyed.

If B and C made a third detachment against the centre, the result would be still more calamitous; for the attacks of these divisions would be every where without vigour and ensemble, and would be resisted by imposing masses that could not fail to overwhelm them. This was the fate of the Prussians at Kollin, because they did not execute the king's orders; and of the army of the Danube at Stockbach in 1799, because it attempted too much with inadequate forces.

The truth of this is so obvious, that it may be applied to even an army of superior numbers; as for instance, to an army of 50,000 men attacking another of 40,000 men upon both extremities.

If the attacked army be upon its guard, and occupy a military position, it will find ground in the extent of its position favourable to the defensive, and on which a few regiments will be able to check the march of the first hostile division. The army can then carry to the principal point, a force superior to the second division; and this force *by acting offensively and having the initiative of the movements*, may gain the flanks, and take in reverse and completely beat the second division. If the two hostile columns have between them insurmountable obstacles of ground, it would be practicable to destroy them both in succession. Napoleon has afforded memorable examples of this truth, in the battles of Lonado, Castigliona, Abensberg, Eckmuhl, and Ratisbon.

The observance of these rules is not strictly necessary when the attacking army is twice as numerous as its adversary, as in the case of Marshal Daun at Hohenkirchen; because in this case, it is able to engage a superior force at each point. There is reason to believe that it would even be against the interest of this army, to restrict itself to one point of attack; for as all its force could not there be employed at the same moment, the enemy might oppose an equal resistance at this point, and succeed in maintaining themselves. We must hence conclude, that it would be most advantageous in this circumstance, to manœuvre simultaneously against the centre and both extremities of the hostile army; because it would be overwhelmed at all these points by a twice superior force. But to lessen the inconveniences of dividing our forces, it is necessary that we have the initiative of the movements; that we be able to conceal them, so that the attacks will be begun at the same instant upon both extremities; and that the enemy shall be engaged without the power of carrying their forces from one point to another. To this end, we must avoid having insurmountable obstacles between the attacks, or separating them too far apart; for this would enable the enemy to manœuvre against one of the corps, before the other could simultaneously attack.

Accordingly, two maxims, apparently contradictory, result notwithstanding from the same principle; their application depends upon circumstances.

1st. An army attacking another that is superior or even equal in force, can only be certain of success by making an united effort against a single point of a weakened line, or against the extremity of a line that cannot be promptly supported, because its battalions will be engaged in succession.

2d. An army attacking another that is very inferior, should, on the contrary, form itself into two or three divisions, in order to put all its masses in action against inferior masses; for if it restrict its attack to one single principal point, the whole of its forces cannot there be brought into action, and the enemy by carrying thither all their forces may re-establish an equilibrium and maintain themselves. But it is indispensable that these movements, and the attacks of these divisions, be combined upon the same ground and at the same instant; in order to that unity of action, without which they would be exposed to be beaten in detail and successively, like the Austrians at Austerlitz, Abensberg, Eckmuhl, &c.

The attacks must be connected by a corps posted intermediately against the hostile centre, and which will also attack, or restrict itself to demonstrations, according to ground and circumstances. Perhaps it may be said, that the basis of this reasoning rests upon the local superiority of the physical forces; but by deeply studying the combination of their use, we shall be convinced that every thing is attributed to this combination. The preceding discussions and narrative sufficiently prove, that it is not enough to have 30,000 men to beat 15,000; and that the former may be beaten, if in the manner of using them, and in the choice of ground, there be a defect of disposition that deprives them of the advantage of numbers, and changes it into a real disadvantage by increasing the disorder and the trophies of the enemy. This was the case of the Austrians at Leuthen, and in the defiles of Hohenlinden, in 1800. These rules are still more applicable to grand armies that occupy very extended lines, and whose operations cannot be combined simultaneously upon a single point of these lines.

Next to the battle of Leuthen, that of Hohenkirchen most strikingly demonstrates the dreadful effects produced by an army establishing itself unperceived upon the extremity of a line. And the latter also shows the fatal results of the successive efforts of valiant regiments, which advanced *one after another* to be destroyed; for their valour ensured their destruction.

By perusing the interesting relation of Tempelhoff, we perceive how the Prussians were surprised in this battle on their extreme right, by an army that established itself almost perpendicularly upon their flank, and which threw a strong division into their rear—forming the following disposition:

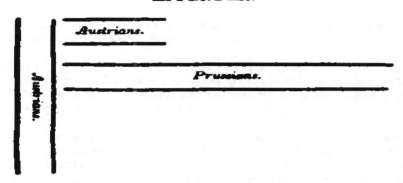

This relation shows that the Prussians were necessitated to support the first corps of the overwhelmed flank; and that for this purpose the troops marched thither as quickly as possible—that is, the nearest regiments were carried thither first, and were beaten by the time that the others arrived. It is to avoid these evils, that we have shown the necessity of not engaging all the troops at the enemy's point of attack, and that the corps engaged should be supported by only one brigade *in echellon;* and that the remainder of the army should manœuvre in such a manner, as to establish itself in its turn upon the extremity of the hostile line.

If we judge of the conduct of Frederick according to these rules, we will be convinced that he acted directly contrary to them; for he should not have directed all his troops towards Hohenkirchen, where they found the mass of the Austrian forces disposed in such a manner as to attack them on all sides and overwhelm them. He might have manœuvred with much greater advantage by carrying his mass to his left against the Duke of Ahremberg's attack, and by bringing to that point the corps under General Retzow; he would thus have balanced and checked the momentary successes of Daun. Besides, this plan perfectly coincided with that of Frederick—which was, to operate against the Austrian right, in order to communicate with Silesia.

But his measures cannot be reproached, for the fog and darkness disabled him from judging of the strength, position, and projects of the enemy. Frederick was not a man to combine the use of his forces in a manner so contrary to the great lessons that he had himself taught in his previous operations. Nor must he be reproached for having taken up a bad position, for he was aware of its defects. Two days before the battle, Marshal Keith said to him—*If the Austrians do not attack us in this camp, they deserve to be hanged!* Frederick replied laughingly—*We must hope that Daun stands in greater fear of us, than of the halter.* This anecdote marked the great man. Besides, it must be remembered that the Prussian army was in march in a fog, and that the enemy were supposed to be encamped at Lobau. Frederick. on finding them before him, thought it inconsistent with his dignity to retrograde. During the whole course of the war, the

Austrians had never attacked him once; and the recollection of this fact, justified his daring resolution, which showed what confidence he had in the resources of his genius to repulse Daun, if he dared to attack him openly. If this resolution be considered a fault, we must nevertheless confess that the motive was noble.

But if Frederick feared nothing from an attack by open force, he should have been the more guarded against a surprise, to which his position exposed him, because it facilitated it. It is astonishing that this great captain did not cause the wooded heights in advance of Hohenkirchen, to be watched. If he had placed upon them one free (light) battalion and one squadron of hussars, he would never have lost this battle. Instead of guarding them, he suffered the Croats to quietly occupy the reverse side of the mountain and all the villages that terminated at his camp; his right flank was thus already enveloped without fighting. Such an error of Frederick, is certainly inexcusable, and even incomprehensible. A similar fault greatly contributed to the defeat of the Austrians at the famous battle of Leuthen. By referring to this battle it will be seen, that Prince Charles and Marshal Daun did not scour and watch *the heights in front of those upon which their line rested ;* and that the king, under cover of these heights, concealed from them his manœuvres to overwhelm their left wing. It is true that the Austrians had pushed forward numerous corps upon Neumark; but these corps were beaten and repulsed back upon the right wing; and their strength was even in opposition to their use, for the service of guards and scouts is not performed with small armies. These two memorable battles authorise the following maxims:

1st. When an army occupies a camp upon heights or other ground that may become a field of battle, the heights or other accidents of ground in advance of its front and flanks, should be guarded; in order to prevent the enemy from gaining one extremity of its line by a concealed movement.

2d. It must not be hereby understood, that these heights should be guarded in strength; for this would only tend to prolong its line, to multiply dangerous detachments, and to weaken the forces by dividing them. Besides, numerous corps are not adapted to guard against a surprise and watch the enemy; they would only serve to awaken his attention by their presence.

3d. We must, on the contrary, post upon these heights or ground small independent posts, sufficiently numerous to communicate with each other, and with the army or intermediate posts.

It may be observed in general, that to observe or watch, is too often confounded with the idea of occupying in a military manner and in force. Armies have been beaten for having detached divisions to places where a corporal and four men only were necessary.

The conduct of Marshal Daun at Hohenkirchen, deserves unquestionable praise; it was his best. It seems however that he was wrong in not causing his right to attack before 8 o'clock, when his left was in the hottest of the battle from 5 o'clock, A. M. The attack of his right was to prevent the King from carrying succour from his left to the principal point; it should therefore have been simultaneous. He might have had weighty reasons for not seriously engaging this wing until after the success of the attack upon Hohenkirchen; but these should not have prevented it from making the necessary demonstrations to hold in check the forces of the Prussian left. But the greatest reproach that may with justice be alleged against him, is his not having pushed the Prussians more vigorously after their whole force was engaged and beaten, and when he had nothing to fear in marching against them.

A victory is gained to no purpose, if it be not taken advantage of. This is the greatest talent of a General; and it is in this respect that the Emperor Napoleon has surpassed all former ages, and transmitted to the Generals of posterity the greatest lessons.

The Marshal doubted his own victory, and thus lost all the advantages of it. Never did his genius sink so low as on this occasion. To vanquish the GREAT FREDERICK, seemed to have been beyond his hopes; and not being prepared for good fortune, he did not know how to seize it. The conduct of the Arch-Duke Charles after the victory of Essling, was precisely similar; had he crossed the Danube within 48 hours after the battle, Napoleon would have been a captive to the arms of Austria. When a General has not a just theory of the science, he imputes every thing to chance, *and becomes awe-stricken at a name.*

When an army occupies a position perpendicular to a stream which supports one of its wings, we must never attack this wing; because we would thereby expose ourselves to be thrown into the river, if the enemy changed front in mass with all their forces. But by attacking the opposite wing with almost our whole force, we have the *great chances* in our favour; for if this wing be impetuously attacked by a superior mass, it may be broken and driven back upon the rest of the hostile army, which will be thrown into disorder, forced back upon the river, and exposed to destruction.

This was the case at Wagram, where the Austrians imprudently advanced with their right along the Danube, whilst Napoleon judiciously carried the mass of his forces against their left. If General Hillers' corps had not quickly retreated, the Emperor Napoleon had only to abandon his communications by Vienna, destroy the bridges, and change front upon the Austrian extreme left, in order to drive them back into the Danube. The loss of a battle in such a position, would have terminated the war without risk on the part of Napoleon, who might have taken up his line of communication by Saxony, or re-established it by Passau.

Whenever an enemy makes extended movements to induce a General to divide his forces, instead of operating in the same direction, he should quickly unite all his divisions and make an impetuous attack upon the main body which was weakened in the expectation of inducing him to commit the same fault.

The battles of Zorndorff, and Marengo, prove that an army *may turn another, without being turned itself,* according to the direction of the secondary lines. At the former battle, the Russians (61,000 strong) were on the right of the Oder besieging Custrin. Frederick arrives with an army of 31,000 men, crosses the Oder by surprise below Custrin, and comes and places his army upon the Russian line of operations and upon the extreme right of the hollow square that they had formed. The misconduct of a few regiments, loses great advantages ; the King throws *forward* his right (that was refused) upon the left of the Russian square, and *refuses* his beaten left. *Thus taking up an entirely new order of battle in the midst of the action !* In case of defeat, the Prussians had Custrin to retreat upon ; whilst the defeat of the Russians, was probable destruction. The combinations of the battle of Kunnersdorf, or Frankfort, were precisely similar. In both instances he crossed the Oder, and chose such stratagic points as would secure the total destruction of the enemy, if his plans succeeded. The Russian loss at Zorndorff, was 18,600 killed and wounded, and 2,800 prisoners, and 103 cannon ; that of the Prussians was 10,000 killed and wounded, and 1,500 prisoners.

It may be said of the plans of battle of Frederick and Napoleon, that the stake to which they compelled their enemies, was out of all proportion to their own risk. If defeated, they would lose only a few thousand men ; but if they vanquished their enemies, they were sure to destroy them, by reason of their admirable stratagic points. They never fought for paltry towns or villages ; they fought to utterly destroy all means of further resistance.

The General who fights a battle with any other view, may win the field ; but he will never gain any advantage to his country. It is of defensive war, as of a fortress—its fall may be *delayed* by valour and skill— but unless succoured, it must at last capitulate.

We will conclude this subject with these maxims—

1st. It is indisputable that an army by assuming the initiative of a movement, may conceal it 'till it is in full execution. Accordingly, when the operations take place in the interior of his line, a General may gain several marches upon the enemy.

2d. It is therefore of the highest importance, in order to have just conceptions of the science and to a sound judgment of military operations, to banish from all combinations those narrow and idle calculations which suppose that the hostile General may be informed of the movement, and oppose to it the best counter-manœuvre at the very instant that it is begun.

3d. When two corps d'armée attempt to combine their operations so as to put the enemy *between two fires* at a distance of several marches, they form a double line of operations against a single one, and expose themselves to be beaten separately, if the enemy take advantage of their central position. This manœuvre is of the same kind as one made to a distance on the flanks ; both should be ranked in the class of *too extended move-*

ments ; as likewise should all those that do not produce a *simultaneous* effect at the instant of their execution.

4th. The maxims precedingly established, and the experience of many centuries, prove that whatever may be the circumstances in which a General is placed, he will obtain great advantages and have all the chances on his side by assuming the initiative of the movements, either in stratagic operations or dispositions for battle.

Let us suppose that an army of 40,000 men is charged with the defence of a country, against another of 60,000. If the former anticipate the enemy, it may, by stratagic movements, bring into action the greatest mass of its forces against a single point of the line of operations, where the enemy have not an equal force. The latter therefore will be compelled to fight to disadvantage, or to make counter-manœuvres that will retard their progress; whilst the former may oppose these counter-manœuvres, by again assuming the initiative.

By the application of this system, a General with inferior forces may bring into action in a decisive position, a greater number of divisions; and to this advantage he may still further add, by applying to dispositions for battle what we have just laid down in relation to stratagy; for he may so manœuvre as to have to fight only a part of the hostile corps that he finds upon the ground designated for the general effort. Accordingly, instead of having to contend against the whole hostile army, he may, by stratagy, have only to vanquish one of its corps; a great portion of which he may also paralyze, by directing his attacks upon the extremity of its line.

It was a saying of the Emperor Napoleon, *that the secret of successful war, consisted in operating against the enemy's communications;* and that he knew nothing more sublime *than to assemble an army, march* 12 *leagues a day, fight a battle, and sleep in safety.*

Let us conclude with a maxim which he ever observed:—We must give to our line of operations that advantageous direction which secures all the chances of the greatest success, and which places the enemy in a situation decisive of the fate of their army; we must then march rapidly upon them, to fight and destroy them; and if repulsed, we must profit of the superiority and grand advantages of the general direction of the operations, to attack them again, and again, and to fight until we have accomplished our object.

The Use of Cavalry.

In pages 66, 97, and 99 of Volume 1, we have presented some very important maxims on the use of cavalry.

Cavalry should be formed only two deep; for a greater depth produces disorder. And they should be drawn up in two lines; a third line is of no avail; for if the two first be routed, they will carry away the third in their flight. A third line should therefore never be used, except when we have not ground to display on.

Cavalry must be posted on *both* flanks, to profit of favourable moments. A strong reserve of cavalry will sustain the engaged wing, and will decide and follow up the success. It is the cavalry that must consummate the victory, by outstripping the enemy, seizing the passes and defiles before them, and leaving them no alternative but death or surrender.

Charges of cavalry will be begun at a distance of about 400 paces, and will be made on as great a front as the ground will permit—from that of a squadron, to the front of numerous reserves. They will take care to *instantly* re-form after a charge. When our cavalry are numerous, we must endeavour to fight upon ground where they can act to advantage—they will begin the attack, and will give the last touches to the victory. When we are weak in this species of force, and our enemy is strong in it, we must avoid ground favourable to its action.

Cavalry should never be placed in the centre of the first line of battle, as it is impossible for them to withstand the combined efforts of all the arms united. The battles of Blenheim, Minden, and Lobositz, are proofs of this rule, if indeed any proof were wanting. At Minden, and at Blenheim, the enemy (Marlborough and Duke Ferdinand of Brunswick) attacked the centre of cavalry with their infantry and artillery; and having thrown it back and into disorder, they charged with their cavalry and routed it, and thus isolated the wings of infantry, which fell in succession.

Turenne, and Condé, and other great Generals, used this mixture of cavalry and infantry; but *at that time* fire arms were very imperfect; only a few of the troops were armed with heavy and ill constructed matchlocks, and artillery was in its infancy. Since the substitution of the musket for the matchlock, and the great improvements of artillery, the nature of war has greatly changed; and any dispositions of troops that are not in conformity with these changes and improvements, must be vicious.

When the first line of cavalry is defeated, they should file through the squadron intervals and by the flanks of the second line, and immediately re-form in three divisions—one in rear of the centre of the second line of cavalry—and one forward on *each* of its flanks. The formations on the flanks must be thrown forward, in order that when the second line charges, these squadrons may take the enemy in flank. Care must however be taken, not to throw these squadrons too far forward; for then the enemy might take them in flank, as the Prussians did the forward cavalry potence at Prague. Fig. 10, Plate XIV, explains this manœuvre.

If in a charge of cavalry in two lines, it be desirable to gain the extremity of the enemy's line, a reserve formed into columns of squadrons behind the first line, might at the moment of the charge pass beyond the flanks of the enemy, and taking distances while advancing, form in order of battle by a mere conversion of squadrons to the right or left, and thus attack the enemy's line in reverse.

Cavalry when near the enemy, should keep their horses *saddled*; and all troops in the neighbourhood of an enemy, should sleep in their clothes, and with their arms beside them.   This precaution was observed by Zeithen's cavalry on the night preceding the battle of Hohenkirchen, and contributed greatly to save the Prussian army.

The charge of cavalry at Kollin, resembled very much that made at Reichemberg (1757), and many made in the late wars.   At Reichemberg, the Duke of Bevern's cavalry made a brilliant charge upon the Austrians, and overthrew them; but they were themselves driven back in disorder, because they exposed their flank to a wood that was filled with infantry and occupied by a few batteries.

A similar scene, but on a grander scale, and productive of more important results, was exhibited at Kollin.   The 55 squadrons of General Zeithen, intending to prolong themselves to the left to outflank the enemy's right wing and take their line in reverse, overthrew at the first charge the Austrian cavalry, and continued their movement between the wood of Radowesnitz and the Ravine; for the infantry that were in this wood, were to have been attacked by General Hulsen, and therefore to be *disabled* from annoying these squadrons.   Hulsen having been checked in his attack by the delay of the columns, could not effect it at the moment that the cavalry passed along the wood; the cavalry were in consequence exposed in flank to the infantry posted therein, who opened upon them a very hot fire, sustained by several discharges of grape.   It was natural for the cavalry to hasten to retrograde, and to retire from such an unfortunate situation.

At Reichemberg, the Duke of Bevern succeeded in getting possession of the wood, by causing it to be attacked higher up by the infantry of his right.   The charge, which was then renewed, was most successful; because the Austrian cavalry found themselves precisely in the same position that the Duke's had been before; that is, taken in flank by the troops posted in the wood.   Zeithen, however, could not renew his movement, because the wood was never carried.   But he ought not to have charged before the enemy were attacked or dislodged from the wood.

From these two events, we may deduce the following maxims:

1st. In making an important charge of cavalry along a wood or covered ground, it should be preceded a few minutes by a vigorous attack of infantry upon the wood or covered ground.

2d. If we have reason to suppose that the enemy have not occupied the wood or covered ground in force, we may content ourselves with scouring it with 2 or 3 battalions.

3d. When we have disposeable infantry, we should occupy the wood or covered ground, and post in it a few pieces of cannon, to second the charge of the cavalry, and secure their success or retreat.

4th. Another maxim also follows: If we post our cavalry near a wood, it is indispensable to strongly occupy it by infantry, to prevent the enemy from doing the same.

It must of course be understood, that we do not speak of a charge of van guard or light cavalry pursuing the enemy; nor of those decisive charges in battle, to check or suspend an adversary's movement. We speak of an offensive attack upon the enemy's line, for which we have time to combine the necessary measures.

The battle of Kollin proves that a General commanding an attack so important as that of Zeithen, should not be satisfied with seeing before him an adversary that he can easily beat; he should understand the relations between his movement and all the secondary attacks, in order to be able to subordinate his executive combinations to what is passing around him. The Prussians, by neglecting these principles, lost 1600 horses and 1400 troopers.

This murderous battle proves, that the valour, and even the devotion of an army, are useless, when the first dispositions, *or their execution*, are a violation of the rules of the science. Doubtless the courage of troops is one of the first instruments of victory; *but 'tis only so when well directed.*

SECTION V.

Compendious Summary of the Grand Principles of the Science.

FREDERICK wisely said, that the talent of a great Captain, consists in inducing the enemy to divide their forces. After a lapse of fifty years, many Generals have, notwithstanding, thought it *admirable* to divide *their own* forces as much as possible, and have inverted every principle of the science.

The fundamental principle is, *to operate a combined effort with the greatest possible mass of force upon the decisive point.* All combinations that have not for basis the application of this rule, *are vicious;* and all plans that are founded upon it, *are good.*

It is easy to conceive, that an able General may with 60,000 men beat 100,000, if he succeed in putting 50,000 men into action against a single extremity of the hostile line. The numerical superiority of the troops not engaged, becomes in this case rather an evil, than an advantage; for they only increase the disorder: this is proved by the battle of Leuthen. The means of applying this maxim, are not very numerous; we will endeavour to indicate them.

I. The first means is, to assume the initiative of the movements. The General who has this advantage on his side, is master of his own movements, and can select his point of attack; whilst he who, on the contrary, awaits the enemy, is unable to form any combinations, because he subordinates his movements to those of his adversary, which he has no longer time to check, when they are in full execution. The General who assumes the initiative, knows what he is about to do; he conceals his march, and surprises and overwhelms an extremity or weak part. Whilst he who awaits his enemy, is beaten in one of his parts, even before apprised of the attck.

II. The second means is, to direct our movements against the weak and most advantageous point. The choice of this point, depends upon the position of the enemy. The most important point, is always that whose possession will secure the most favourable chances and greatest results. Such are, for example, those positions that enable us to gain the enemy's communications with their base of operations, and to throw them back upon an insurmountable obstacle, like the sea, a great stream without a bridge, or a great neutral power.

In double and divided lines of operations, we must direct our attacks against the central points. By carrying against these the mass of our force, we will crush the isolated divisions that guard them. The corps scattered on the right and left, can then no longer operate in concert, and are forced to those eccentric and ruinous retreats whose disastrous consequences marked the fate of the armies of Mack, Wurmser, and the Duke of Brunswick.

In single lines of operations, and in contiguous lines of battle, the weak points are, on the contrary, the extremities of the line. The centre is more within reach of support from the right and left; but an attacked extremity is overwhelmed before sufficient forces can arrive to its support from the other wings; because these forces are more distant, and can only be brought up one after another.

A long or deep column attacked upon its head, is in the same situation as a line attacked upon its extremity; they are both engaged and beaten in succession;—this is proved by the battles of Rosbach and Auerstadt. It is however easier to make new dispositions with a deep column, than with a line assailed upon one of its extremities.

By executing, by stratagy, a general movement against the extremity of the hostile line of operations, we not only bring a mass into action against a weak part, but we may from *this extremity* easily gain the rear and the communications with the base or secondary lines. Thus, Napoleon, by gaining in 1805 Donauwerth and the line of the Lech, established his mass upon the communications of Mack with Vienna, which, with Bohemia, was this General's base; he thus rendered it impossible for him to unite with the Russian army, which was his most important secondary line. The same operation took place in 1806, against the extreme left of the Prussians, by Saalfeld and Gera. It was repeated in 1812 by the Russian army, in its movements upon Kaluga and Krasnoi; and again in 1813, by Bohemia upon Dresden and Leipsick, against Napoleon's right.

III. The result of the preceding truths prove, that if we must in preference attack the extremity of a line, we must also carefully avoid attacking both extremities at the same time, unless our forces are very superior. An army of 60,000 men that forms two corps of about 30.000 combatants, in order to attack the two extremities of an army of equal force, deprives itself of the means of striking a decisive blow, by uselessly multiplying the means of resistance that the enemy may oppose to both detachments. This army even exposes itself, by this extended and divided movement, to be overwhelmed by an enemy who may concentrate their mass against one of its corps, and annihilate it by a terrible effort of superiority. All multiplied attacks in a great number of columns, are still more dangerous, and are greater violations of the grand principles of the science; especially when these columns cannot be brought into action at the same instant and at the same point. It follows from this maxim, that when, on the contrary, our forces are greatly superior to those of the enemy, we should attack both their extremities; we thus succeed in bringing more men into action upon each of their wings, than they can; for if we keep very superior forces accumulated together upon one point, our adversary may perhaps display his forces, and bring into action an equal number. In this case, we must be careful to carry the main body of our forces against that wing where the attack promises the most decisive success; as we have already demonstrated in treating of the battle of Hohenkirchen.

IV. To make a combined effort with a great mass against a single point, it is necessary in our stratagic movements to keep our forces together on a space nearly square, in order that they may be more disposeable*. Great fronts are as contrary to sound principles, as scattered or divided lines, great detachments, and isolated divisions out of reach of support.

V. One of the most effectual means of applying the general principle that we have laid down, is to induce the enemy to commit faults that violate this principle. We may with a few corps of light troops, alarm them on several important points of their communications; and it is probable that the enemy, not knowing the strength of these corps, will oppose to them numerous divisions, and will divide their forces. These light troops answer at the same time the important purpose of enlightening our army.

VI. It is of the greatest importance when we assume the initiative of a decisive movement, to neglect no means of learning the positions of the enemy, and the movements that they may make. Secret intelligence (espionnage) is a great means of acquiring this information, and to the improvement of which, too much care cannot be devoted; but it is still more essential to thoroughly enlighten our army by partisans. The General should strew small parties in every direction; and their numbers must be multiplied with as much care, as we should avoid this system in grand operations. For this purpose, we must organize several divisions of

---

* We must not be understood as meaning a square solid column; but that the battalions shall be disposed in such a manner, as to be able to arrive from all points with equal promptitude upon the point of attack.

light cavalry, which will not be included in the fighting corps. If we operate without these precautions, we will be always in the dark, and exposed to those disastrous chances that may result from a secret movement of the enemy. We said above, that these partisans will at the same time contribute to alarm the enemy on important points, and will thus induce them to divide their forces*. These means are too much neglected; the department of secret intelligence is not organized sufficiently beforehand, and the officers of light troops have not always the information and experience necessary for conducting their detachments.

VII. To operate with success in war, it is not sufficient to skilfully carry our forces against the most important points; we must also know how to there engage them. When we establish ourselves upon these points, and there remain inactive, the great principle is forgotten; and the enemy may oppose counter-manœuvres. Therefore, in order to prevent them from doing this, we must, as soon as we have gained their communications, or one of their extremities, march against them, and attack them. This is the moment of all others that we must properly combine the simultaneous use of our forces. *It is not the forces present, but those engaged, that decide the fate of battles.* The former are decisive in the preparatory stratagic movements; but it is the latter that determine the success of the battle.

---

* The immense advantages that the Cossacks afford the Russian armies, are a proof of this. These light troops, though contemptible in the shock of a great battle, are dreadful pursuers. They are the most terrible enemy that a General has to contend against in all his combinations, for he is never sure of the arrival and execution of his orders, his convoys are in constant jeopardy, and his operations uncertain. Whilst an army had but a few regiments of these partisans, their full value was unknown; but since their numbers were increased to 15 or 20,000, we have been able to judge of their importance, especially in countries whose populations are not hostile to them.

To prevent their carrying off convoys, these must be escorted; and the escort must be numerous to secure its safety. The army is never sure of making a quiet march, for it does not know where are the enemy. These laborious services, require immense forces; and the regular cavalry is soon rendered unfit for service, by fatigues that they cannot sustain. The Turkish militia is just such a scourge to the Russian armies, as the Cossacks are to other European armies. Convoys are not more safe in Bulgaria, than they were in Spain, Poland and Russia. We believe that in other armies, a few thousand volunteer hussars or lancers raised at the moment of war, and directed by enterprising chiefs upon well selected stratagic points, would answer nearly the same purpose. But they must ever be considered as forlorn hopes; for if they are to receive orders from the General Staff, they will be no longer partisans. It is true that they will not possess the same qualities, nor be able to contend in the long run with *true Cossacks;* but to an inevitable evil, we must oppose every possible remedy.

To obtain this result, an able General should seize the moment that the decisive position of the field of battle should be carried; and he should combine the attack so as to bring into action all his forces at the same time, only excepting those destined for the reserve.

When an effort founded on these principles does not succeed, we cannot hope for victory from any combination; and the only measure that remains to be taken, is to strike a last blow with this reserve, in concert with the troops already engaged.

VIII. All the combinations for battle, may be reduced to three systems. The first is purely defensive, and consists in awaiting the enemy in a strong position, without any other object than to maintain ourselves in it. Such were the dispositions of Daun at Torgau, and of Marsin in the lines of Turin. These two events are sufficient to prove how vicious such dispositions are.

The second system is, on the contrary, entirely offensive; and consists in attacking the enemy wherever we can meet them—like Frederick at Leuthen and at Torgau, Napoleon at Jena and at Ratisbon, and the allies at Leipsick in 1813.

The third system is a kind of medium between the two others, and consists in selecting a field of battle possessing all the stratagic conveniences and advantages of ground; in order to there await the enemy, and to choose during the very battle the proper moment for assuming the initiative and falling upon the enemy with every chance of success. The combinations of Napoleon at Rivoli and at Austerlitz, of the Russians at Kunnersdorf, and of the Duke of Wellington at Waterloo and in most of his defensive battles in Spain, must be arranged under this class.

It would be difficult to give any fixed rules to determine the use of these two last systems, which are the only ones that are proper. The moral condition of the troops of each side, the greater or less fortitude or impetuosity of the national character, and the obstacles of the ground, must all be taken into consideration. Hence we see that these circumstances alone can guide the genius of the General, and that these truths should be reduced to the three following rules:

1st. With veteran troops, and on open ground, the positive offensive—the initiative of attack, is always best.

2d. In ground difficult of access by nature or *other causes*, and with disciplined and obedient troops, it is perhaps best to let the enemy arrive in a position that we have reconnoitred, in order to then assume the initiative against them, when they are already exhausted by their first efforts. The battles of Kunnersdorf and Waterloo were of this character.

3d. The stratagic situation of both parties, may nevertheless sometimes require one to attack the positions of the other by main force, without regard to any local consideration. Such, for instance, are the circumstances when it is necessary to prevent the junction of two hostile armies, to fall upon a detached portion of an army, or upon a corps isolated beyond a stream, &c. &c.

IX. The orders of battle or most suitable dispositions for bringing troops into action, should possess both solidity and mobility; for the troops must neither be too extended, nor too crowded together. A thin order, is weak; and troops crowded together in deep order, are in a great measure paralyzed, because only the heads of the columns fight, disorder is easily introduced, and the artillery makes dreadful havock. It seems to us that to fulfil these two conditions, the troops which remain on the defensive, should be in part displayed, and part in columns by battalions; like the Russian army at the battle of Eylau. But the troops destined for the attack of a decisive point, should be composed of two lines of battalions; and each battalion, instead of being displayed, should be formed in column of divisions, in the following manner:

6th.	5th.	4th.	3d.	2d.	1st battalion.

12th.	11th.	10th.	9th.	8th.	7 h.

A division consists of two platoons or companies; therefore if the battalion consist of six companies, it will form three divisions; this will in fact be a formation in three lines.

This order possesses infinitely more solidity than a displayed line, whose undulations deprive it of the impulsion so necessary in such an attack, and deny the officers the power of moving their men. But, to facilitate the march; to avoid too great depth of mass; and to, on the contrary, increase the front. without however diminishing its strength, we think it proper to form the infantry in two ranks. The battalions will thus be more moveable; for the march of the 2d rank, pressed between the 1st and 3d, is always fatiguing, wavering, and consequently less vigorous. They will besides possess all the strength desirable, because the three divisions formed upon each other, will present a depth of six ranks; this is more than sufficient. And the front, which will be thus increased by one third, will afford more fire, in the event of a combat of fire-arms; and whilst it imposes more upon the enemy by a greater show of troops, it will at the same time be less exposed to their artillery.

X. In grounds of difficult access, such as vineyards, enclosures and *fenced* countries, gardens, *woods*, and steep heights, the defensive order of battle should be composed of displayed battalions, covered by numerous platoons of sharp-shooters. But the troops destined for the attack, as well as the reserve, cannot be better disposed than in columns of attack formed upon the centre, as we have described in the preceding article; for as the reserve should be ready to fall upon the enemy at the decisive moment, it should do it with force and vigour, that is, in column*. This reserve may

* It has been said that the Duke of Wellington almost always fought in line. This may have been true in respect to the troops that were to remain

however be left in part displayed until the moment that it marches against the enemy, in order to impose upon them by its extent of front.

XI. In a defensive battle upon open ground, we may also substitute for these columns, squares of battalions, by doubling the lines of two ranks, so as to form four deep. Each battalion will thus afford a sufficient mass, for it will present a front of only 40 to 50 files.

This order seems very advantageous when we dread grand attacks of cavalry; for it affords both safety to the infantry, and a shelter to the artillerists and artillery train. Nevertheless, as it possesses less mobility and impulsion than that in columns of attack, this latter appears preferable; because with well drilled troops we may easily form the square with each battalion, by a simple conversion to the right and left of the central divisions. The General's plan of battle, the nature of the ground, and the species of troops, should decide which of these two orders of battle ought to be preferred. It is said that at Waterloo, the British troops were in squares of battalions, and their allies in columns of attack; this would be a mixture of the two orders proposed.

XII. If the science of war consist in combining a superior effort of a mass against weak points, it is indisputably necessary to vigorously pursue a beaten army.

The strength of an army consists in its organization—in the ensemble resulting from the connexion between all the parts, and the central point that puts them in motion. After a defeat, this ensemble no longer exists —the harmony between the head that combines, and the corps that should execute, is destroyed. Their relations are suspended, and almost always broken. The whole army is a weak part; and to attack it, is to march to certain victory. How many proofs of these truths do we not find in the march upon Roveredo and upon the gorges of the Brenta, to complete the ruin of Wurmser; in the march from Ulm upon Vienna, and in that from Jena upon Wittemberg, Custrin, and Stettin! This maxim is often neglected by indifferent Generals. It seems as if the whole effort of their genius, and the measure of their ambition, were merely to gain the field of battle. Such a victory, is no better than a loss of troops without any real benefit.

on the defensive; but we think that his offensive and manoeuvring wings must have been in columns. If this were not the case, those Generals would be greatly in fault who would suffer themselves to be beaten with equal forces by such a system; for a General could desire nothing more, than to have an adversary who constantly used it.

Besides, in laying down an order of battle as the best, it is not declaring that victory is impossible unless it be strictly applied. Localities, general causes, superior numbers, the moral of the troops and of the Generals,—all these are considerations that enter into the account. And to reason upon a general maxim, all these chances must be admitted to be equal.

XIII. To render decisive the superior shock of a mass, the General must pay the utmost attention to the moral of his army. Fifty thousand men are brought into battle against 20,000 for no purpose, if they be deficient of the impulsion necessary to break and crush the enemy. We do not refer to the soldiers alone; we allude particularly to the officers who should lead them. All troops are brave when their leaders set them the example of a noble emulation and patriotic devotion. A soldier should not stand fire from fear of a rigorous discipline; he should rush to meet danger from that self-love and respect that will determine him not to be surpassed by his officers in honour and in valour, and especially from that confidence in the wisdom and talents of his chiefs, and in the valour of his comrades, with which his leaders should know how to inspire him.

A General should in his plans be able to count upon the devotion of his Lieutenants to the honour of the national arms. He must be assured that a vigorous shock will take place wherever he orders one. The first means of attaining this, is to make himself loved, esteemed, and feared; the second, is to leave to this General the choice and the fortunes of his Lieutenants. If they have attained their rank by the sole right of seniority, we may decide beforehand that they will hardly ever possess the qualities necessary to fulfil their important functions. This circumstance alone, may be the cause of the failure of the best concerted enterprises.

National wars, in which we have to fight and conquer a whole people, are the only exceptions to the great rule of acting constantly in mass. In wars of this kind, it is difficult to enforce submission without dividing our forces; and when we attempt to concentrate to fight, we expose ourselves to the loss of the conquered provinces.

The means of guarding against these evils, is to have an army constantly in the field, and independent divisions to keep in subjection the country in the rear. In this case, these divisions should be commanded by enlightened Generals, who are good governors and men of justice and firmness; because their services may contribute as much as the force of arms, to produce the submission of the provinces confided to them.

FINIS.

TABLE OF CONTENTS.

VOLUME THE FIRST.

PAGE

INTRODUCTION. - - - - - - - - - - v

PART I. THE SCIENCE OF WAR IN GENERAL.

CHAP. I. On Military knowledge; the *Coup d'œil*; the state of war; an army in general; arms, material and mechanical, &c. - - - - - - - - - 9

CHAP. II. Military institutions and weapons previous to the discovery of gunpowder and fire arms - - - 14

CHAP. III. The discovery of gunpowder and invention of fire arms - - - - - - - - -

CHAP. IV. Military institutions and weapons since the invention of fire arms; modern ranks and grades; the composition and force of the French military power - - 24

CHAP. V. General principles of the orders of battle proper for the various arms, cavalry, infantry, and artillery; the orders of battle of the ancients, and of the moderns; field-artillery; grand and minute tactics - - - - 64

CHAP. VI. Calculation of the extent of front and depth of the habitual orders of battle of cavalry and infantry, in order to draw their ground plan; the formation of separate armies; the parks of artillery; service of the various arms in war; consideration of general and complex orders of battle - - - - - - - - - 90

CHAP. VII. The use of the arms of artillery and engineering; the service and material of artillery; description of cannon; their charge; their carriages; the theory and practice of gunnery; batteries, &c. - - - - 107

CHAP. VIII. On castrametation - - - - - 173

CHAP. IX. Military topography; general and particular maps; reconnaissances; the several kinds of war, offensive and defensive; the general disposition of an army upon a frontier; military positions; lines and bases of operations; the disposition of batteries; the principal operations that occur in the course of a campaign - - - - 185

TABLE OF CONTENTS.

PAGE

CHAP. X. Examples, and description, and investigation of several military operations and achievements, viz. the battle of Turckheim, by Turenne, in 1675 ; the battle of Malplaquet, by Marlborough and Eugene, in 1709 ; the battle of Denain, between Prince Eugene and Marshal Villars ; battles and operations of Dunkirk and Hondscoote, by General Houchard, in 1793 ; the celebrated and last campaign and operations of Turenne, in 1675, ending with his death   215

PART II.   FIELD AND TEMPORARY FORTIFICATION.

CHAP. I. The circumstances that give rise to fortification, and its importance and utility ; fortification, divided into temporary and permanent ; the duties and functions of the arm of engineering ; its service and material ; the education given to engineer officers ; general principles on the disposition and arrangement of works of fortification -   - 241

CHAP. II. Regular field fortification ; the principles by which the configuration of intrenchments is determined ; the profiles ; horizontal projection of the several systems of continuous lines, and of lines with intervals, &c. -   - 248

CHAP. III. The armament of intrenchments ; the batteries ; the construction of intrenchments ; the disposition of batteries -   -   -   -   -   -   -   - 273

CHAP. IV. The secondary means of strengthening intrenchments ; war pits, or *trous de loup ;* palisades ; fraises ; abattis ; chevaux-de-frise ; the closing of gates and passages ; the *cheval de frise ;* the barrier -   -   -   - 288

CHAP. V. Enclosed works, used separately to compose extended systems ; redans ; lunettes ; redoubts ; field forts, &c.   297

CHAP. VI. The use of waters for the defence of positions, and to increase the strength of intrenchments ; permanent field fortification, &c. -   -   -   - 319

CHAP. VII. Bridges, and the throwing of them across streams and rivers for the use of an army, and taking them up or in *replie ;* the works called tetes de pont ; the manœuvres of an army for the passage of a river in advance or retreat, and the passages of rivers ; passage of the Rhine at Tolhuys by *Turenne* and *Condé ;* passage of the Adda by *main*

TABLE OF CONTENTS.

force, at Lodi, by *Napoleon* ; passage of the Po below Placentia, by stratagem, by *Napoleon* ; passage of the Rhine in retreat, at Nordheim, by the *Prince of Conti*, in 1744   331

CHAP. VIII. On posts and intrenched camps : their site, constitution, elements and construction, &c.   -   -   -   353

CHAP. IX. The commandment of works ; irregular fortification ; the art of defilement ; caponnieres for the defence of ditches, &c.   -   -   -   -   -   -   -   366

CHAP. X. Description and investigation of several military operations in relation to the influence of temporary fortification ; the battle of Neerwinden in 1693, between the Prince of Orange and Marshal Luxembourg ; the battle of Fontenoy in 1745, by Marshal Saxe ; the battle of Fleurus in 1690, by Marshal Luxembourg ; the battle of Fleurus in 1794 ; the battles of Montenotte, Millesimo, and Dego, in 1796, by Napoleon   -   -   -   -   -   -   386

VOLUME THE SECOND.

PART III. PERMANENT FORTIFICATION, OR THE FORTIFICATION OF FORTRESSES.

CHAP. I. The circumstances that give rise to permanent fortification, and its use ; definition of a fortress ; the constructions suitable for the nature of the fortification of fortresses ; the properties of fortresses, and their influence on the operations of armies ; examples of the armies of Belgium and Italy, &c. ; the organization of frontiers by fortresses ; double and triple lines of fortresses   -   -   8

CHAP. II. Calculation of the strength of fortified towns ; regular fortification ; its tracé (ground plan), and primitive profile ; the origin and history of fortification, and its progress down from the remotest ages ; fortification at the epoch of the use of cannon ; the invention and tracé of the bastioned enceinte ; the bastioned front with *razant* lines of defence   -   -   -   -   -   -   -   16

CHAP. II. The theory of fortification ; the modern bastioned front ; the thickness and profiles of *revetements* ;

PAGE

description of the horizontal projection on the plane of site of all the elements of the bastioned front ; communications and passages of all kinds, &c. ; description of the relief of all the elements of the bastioned front ; the commandment of all the works ; planes of defilement ; the width and depth of ditches, &c. ; the buildings belonging to fortification ; the planning and construction of a fortress, &c   -   -   -   -   -   -   -   -   31

CHAP. IV.   General considerations on the attack and defence of a fortress ; the armament of a fortress : description of the operations of the attack and of the defence of a fortress, considered in their three principal periods—of investment—of the approaches to the foot of the glacis—and of the operations from the foot of the glacis to the reduction of the place ; conduct of the covering, or army of observation, and of the army of succour ; examples—of the allied armies in 1793 and 1794—of *Napoleon* at *Mantua*—of *Turenne* forcing the lines of *Condé* at *Arras*—of *Condé* forcing the lines of *Turenne* and *Ferté* at Valenciennes—of *Eugene* succouring *Turin* in 1706—of *Turenne* before Dunkirk, repulsing the army of succour under *Condé* —of the sieges and blockades of Philipsburg, Maubeuge, Charleroi, Mons, Landrecies, Tournai, &c.   -   -   73

CHAP. V.   The relation between the attack and defence, and general consideration of the subject ; general principles of the attack, and of the defence : analysis of the bastioned front described ; the theory of commandment ; determination of the relief of all the parts of the system ; the strength of assailable fronts, regard being paid to the collateral fronts; parallel of the attacks of the bastioned front in its various conditions ; principles on the general figure of an enceinte, &c &c.   -   -   -   -   -   -   -   -   160

CHAP. VI.   General reflections on the various systems of fortification ; description and investigation of the principal systems invented and used since the use of artillery and the discovery of the bastioned enceintes—*Errard's* system— Count *Pagan's*—*Vauban's*—*Coehorn's*—-*Cormontaigne's*— *Blondel's*—*Sturm's*—*Landsberg's*—*Glasser's*—*Rosard's*—*of*

TABLE OF CONTENTS.

PAGE

*Augustus II.—Belidor's—Filey's--Chiché's--Montalembert's
—Virgin's—Reveroni's—and Count Carnot's, &c.* - 189

CHAP. VII. The additional works for increasing the strength
of the fronts of a fortress ; inundations and manœuvres of
waters ; advanced ditches and advanced covert-ways ; tenaillons and counterguards ; horn and crownworks ; lunettes
considered under different points of view ; the defences obtained by casemates and crenated galleries ; general consideration of detached and advanced works - 226

CHAP. VIII. Illustration of the art of mining, and the principles and facts upon which it is founded : mining applied
to the attack and defence of fortresses ; subterranean war ;
the systems of defensive mines - - - - 262

CHAP. IX. The principles upon which all improvements of
fortification must be founded ; the proposed improvements
of Bousmard, Mouzè, Carnot, and others - - 303

CHAP. X. General consideration of irregular fortification,
and the causes of this irregularity ; the principles of defilement; application of the rules and principles of defilement
to a fortified front - - - - - - - 319

CHAP. XI. The supplies necessary for the defence of a fortress expected to be besieged ; the data from which to calculate the quantity of artillery, and the strength of the
troops and services of the garrison ; the quantities of weapons, munitions of war, and provisions, &c.; the situations
for the various depots and stores, and for quartering the
troops - - - - - - - - - - 349

CHAP. XII. The gates of fortified towns ; their situation and
architecture ; the drawbridges and fixed bridges, and their
profiles, &c. - - - - - - - - 373

APPENDIX.

Preliminary Notice - - - - - - - 385

SECTION I. The fundamental principles of military operations ; their division into three branches ; sketch of the two
campaigns of the Great Frederick in 1756 and 1757, to
serve as illustrations ; the battles of Kollin, Rosbach, and
Leuthen ; reflections on these campaigns ; maxims ; definitions of lines of operations and lines of manœuvre ; reflections on the lines of operations, offensive and defensive,

TABLE OF CONTENTS.

PAGE

taken by the Great Frederick, and by the French and Austrians, during the seven year's war ; on the lines of operations taken in several of the campaigns of the French Revolution——by Napoleon in Italy, in 1796—on the Rhine and Danube and in Italy, in 1799—by Napoleon in Italy, and by Moreau in Germany, in 1800—by Napoleon against Prussia in 1806 ; reflections and maxims ; configuration of frontiers ; retreats ; the retreat of the Great Frederick after the battle of Hohenkirchen, &c.   -   -   -   -   387

Section ii.   Orders of march ; detachments ; convoys -   441

Section iii.   Sieges ; the conduct of the army of observation ; subsistence and magazines ; the passage of rivers   448

Section iv.   The art of combat, or grand tactics ; oblique and perpendicular orders of battle ; the crotchet or potence retired or forward ; posts and villages in battle ; intervals in lines ; attacks ; orders of battle of cavalry ; &c.   -   451

Section v.   Compendious summary of the grand principles of the science   -   -   -   -   -   -   -   480

ERRATA.

In vol. 1, page 184, last line, instead of " Baron Allen," *read* " Baron *Alten.*"

In vol. 2, page 228, 23d line from top, instead of " slide horizontally," *read* " slide *vertically.*"   This is an error in the original : see the *Memorial de l'Officier de Genie.*

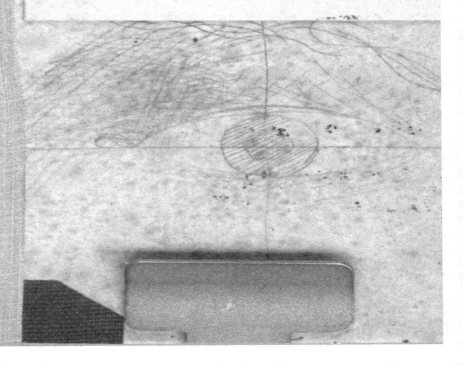

Check Out More Titles From HardPress Classics Series In this collection we are offering thousands of classic and hard to find books. This series spans a vast array of subjects – so you are bound to find something of interest to enjoy reading and learning about.

Subjects:
Architecture
Art
Biography & Autobiography
Body, Mind &Spirit
Children & Young Adult
Dramas
Education
Fiction
History
Language Arts & Disciplines
Law
Literary Collections
Music
Poetry
Psychology
Science
…and many more.

Visit us at www.hardpress.net

CPSIA information can be obtained
at www.ICGtesting.com
Printed in the USA
BVHW040248190819
556172BV00016B/1894/P

9 781406 989410